On the Move
Córas Iompair Éireann
1945–1995

ON THE MOVE
Córas Iompair Éireann
1945–1995

Mícheál Ó Riain

GILL & MACMILLAN

Gill & Macmillan Ltd
Goldenbridge
Dublin 8
with associated companies throughout the world
© Mícheál Ó Riain 1995
0 7171 2342 1
Index compiled by
Helen Litton
Design and print origination by
O'K Graphic Design, Dublin
Printed by
ColourBooks Ltd, Dublin

All rights reserved. No part of this publication may be copied, reproduced or transmitted in any form or by any means, without permission of the publishers.

A catalogue record is available for this book from the British Library.

1 3 5 4 2

The maps on pages 13 and 415 are reproduced by permission of The Irish Times. Photographs by The Irish Times, Bord Fáilte, J. G. Gilham, Tony O'Malley, Kevin Forde, Patrick Scally, Seán Kennedy, Glen Photography, from the Guinness Museum and from CIÉ sources.

Contents

Preface	ix
1. Early Diagnosis of Mania	1

Opening of Kingstown line 1834—Railway building mania—Drummond (Railways) Commission 1836—Determining the railway gauge—Westminster references to amalgamation or state ownership of Irish railways—Viceregal Commission proposes Irish authority to acquire railways.

2. Amalgamation: No Solution — 12

Government control of railways during World War and Civil War—26 railway companies merged into the Great Southern Railways—1927, 1932, 1933 legislation affecting road and rail—Tribunal of Inquiry 1938—The GSR stocks inquiry.

3. Born in Controversy — 28

Transport (No. 1) Bill 1944—Merger of GSR and DUTC proposed—Dáil debates—Dissolution of Dáil—Transport (No. 2) Bill 1944—Formation of CIÉ.

4. Trauma in Infancy — 38

First years of CIÉ—Coal crisis 1947—Financial crisis looms 1948—Inter-party government—Milne Report 1948.

5. Nationalisation: Another Beginning — 56

Controversy about Milne—Dismissal of Reynolds—CIÉ nationalised 1950—Store Street saga—Dáil debates.

6. Putting on the Pressure — 68

Breakeven clause of 1950 Transport Act—Capital expenditure begins to make up lost ground—Dieselisation approved—Scrapping of steam locomotives—The turf burner experiment—Closure of branch lines—Provincial bus services—Canals—Road freight—Dún Aengus—Shannon cruisers—Refurbishment of hotels.

7. A False Dawn — 89

Short-lived financial improvement—CIÉ asks for review of transport policy—GNR crisis—Formation of GNRB—Stormont prunes GNRB lines—Dissolution of GNRB — Appointment of Beddy Committee.

8. Beddy Report — 101

CIÉ submission to Beddy Committee—Focus on restoring traffic to railways—Beddy takes opposite approach—Smaller railway network proposed—Additional restrictions on road haulage rejected—Capital restructuring involves write-off of pre-1945 debt and all losses up to 1956.

9. Another Beginning — 126

Reactions to Beddy—1958 Transport Act—Dáil debate.

10. Railway Contraction 137
Appointment of Todd Andrews—Absorption of GNR—A new broom—Modernisation—Area management structure—Pricing package deals—Harcourt Street line—West Clare Railway closure—Controversies about Waterford, Tramore and west Cork closures—Closures in the midlands—Declining traffic on suburban lines.

11. Industrial Unrest 167
Road passenger services—Canal closures—Great Southern Hotels—Staff consultation—Conflict with union leadership—Lockouts—One-person operation of buses proposed.

12. Pacemaker 182
Financial review since the 1958 Act—Childers succeeds Lemass—Breakeven prospect recedes—CIÉ's Pacemaker study—Public debate—1964 Act concedes long-term subvention for CIÉ.

13. Principle of Subsidy Conceded 199
More industrial unrest—Emergence of NBU—New GM locomotives—1916 Rising marked—Renaming of rail termini—Dublin's traffic problems—Schaechterle studies—Expansion of Great Southern Hotels—School transport scheme initiated.

14. Inflation Takes Off 219
New subvention fixed in 1969—Childers moves on—Subvention level overtaken as inflation accelerates—Fresh crisis perceived—The first McKinsey Report—Government interventions with fare increases—Inter-party government allows increases.

15. Plans and Crises 242
Railplan 80—Higher rail frequencies attempted in 1973—New rail coaches arrive—Liam St J. Devlin appointed Chairman—Railway Development Plan—Dublin Transportation study—Dublin Rapid Rail Transport study—Reorganisation of rail freight—Fastrack established—Corporate and management objectives redefined—New GM locomotives (071's) arrive—Gormanston and Gorey accidents.

16. The Way Ahead 276
Limerick/Claremorris services withdrawn—Rosslare Harbour/Limerick closure controversy—The Way Ahead—Railway infrastructure developments—Linke, Hoffman and Busch coach-building project—Deterioration of rail rolling stock—State subvention escalating.

17. On the 'Periphery' 298
Great Southern Hotels run into difficulty—The Russell Court story—CIÉ withdraws from hotels—Rosslare Harbour—Road haulage difficulties and rationalisation.

18. Buses: Labour and Traffic Problems 311
Dublin buses—Industrial relations—Oireachtas Committee—Expressway network extends—Dublin's traffic—Bus control experiments—Automated vehicle monitoring—Decision to establish a Dublin Transport Authority—Bus priority measures—Van Hool and Bombardier buses.

Contents

19. SHORT-MEASURE SUBVENTIONS ... 333
Difficulties in the public finances—Inadequate subvention provisions for CIÉ —Expenditure cutbacks—NESC and Oireachtas Committee Reports— Second McKinsey study commissioned—The papal visit—Howth/Bray electrification proceeds—Buttevant rail disaster.

20. MCKINSEY AGAIN ... 346
The second McKinsey Report—New rail coaches approved—Maynooth commuter service announced—CIÉ faces widespread criticism.

21. PIT OF THE VALLEY ... 360
1983 subvention fixed £21.6 million below 1982 outcome—Jim Mitchell appointed Minister—Additional borrowing authorised—New subvention formula defined —Cherryville accident—Paul Conlon succeeds Liam St J. Devlin—Building on Reality modifies the new subvention formula.

22. DART AND GREEN PAPER ... 378
Opening of DART—Cost of DART—Halt in rise of CIÉ deficit—Green Paper on transport policy—Establishment of Dublin Transport Authority—Transfer of canals —Proposed reorganisation of CIÉ into three operating companies—OPO saga approaches a resolution.

23. THREE IN ONE: THE RAILWAY ... 400
New operating subsidiaries established—Iarnród Éireann—Submission to Oireachtas Committee—Modernisation—Market shares—Negative decision on further electrification—New commuter services planned—Upgrading Dublin/Belfast line —EU funding—New commuter rolling stock—New 3200 h.p. locomotives —Rosslare Harbour development.

24. THREE IN ONE: BUS COMPANIES AND GROUP ... 418
Bus Éireann's performance—Expressway—New buses acquired—Problems with payment for school transport —Bus Átha Cliath's initial near crisis—OPO implemented—Cost of redundancies—Minibuses—Quality bus corridors— Productivity gains—Financial results improve—Dermot O'Leary succeeds Paul Conlon as Chairman.

APPENDIXES ... 438
1. CIÉ 50-year overview
2. Ministers from the foundation of the state
3. Chairmen
4. Members of the CIÉ Board
5. Directors of Bus Éireann
6. Directors of Bus Átha Cliath
7. Directors of Iarnród Éireann
8. Members of Group Executive Board

BIBLIOGRAPHY ... 447

INDEX ... 450

The author humbly dedicates this book to the men and women of all ranks who have served in Córas Iompair Éireann since 1945.

Preface

A book about Córas Iompair Éireann can be written from several points of view: it could be a book about trains and buses, about services provided to the public, or a book about people, controversies and financial results. Alternatively, it could focus on public inquiries and consultants' reports on transport matters and on the action or inaction which followed therefrom.

My view is that all such matters must share the spotlight in the fifty-year review which G. T. Paul Conlon agreed I should undertake. To the extent that the book has a particular perspective it may be that of the boards and management who over the years were charged with operating CIÉ's mandate. Their attitudes and performance in handling the public transport brief, confronting, circumventing or capitulating as appropriate, to problems in the market or with government, are at the heart of the CIÉ story.

I have tried, within the space available, to sketch some political and economic changes as background to CIÉ's affairs. I have followed a broadly sequential or chronological approach, but sometimes I had recourse to fast-forward or flash-back techniques; it seemed more useful and considerate to the reader to stay for a while with railways, buses, hotels or such, bringing the story to a certain threshold before again submitting to the discipline of the calendar.

I am under a compliment to very many people for their help and I know that a mere acknowledgment will not discharge it. Former Chairmen of CIÉ, Liam St J. Devlin and G. T. Paul Conlon have been generous with their time, as was John F. Higgins, CIÉ's former General Manager. Thanks are due to Dermot O'Leary for his support. Among serving executives, Noel Kennedy, David Waters, Bob Montgomery (who has since left CIÉ), John Browne and Donal Mangan were especially obliging. I am also indebted to Group executives Joe Daly, Brian Dowling, Michael Grace and Colm Mac Giolla Rí. Oliver Doyle, Stephen Hirsch and Cyril McIntyre gave freely of their encyclopaedic knowledge in their own fields. Cyril Ferris, Tom Finn, Paddy Gallagher, Richard Grainger, Gerry Keane, Ray Kelly, Dymphna Kelledy, John McCarthy, John Markham, J. B. Martin, Seán Ó Brádaigh and John Sullivan each know how they helped me.

Retired staff Donal Stephens and Paddy Murphy were generous in their suggestions and assistance. Donal Stephens loaned valuable material to me and read much of the script, as did Cyril McIntyre. Stephen Hirsch read the script in its entirety, but my thanks to Paddy Murphy needs special emphasis. He gave time and patience to reading and commenting on repeated drafts.

Outside CIÉ I am grateful for insights received from former Secretaries of the Department of Transport, Communications and Energy, Noel McMahon and Donal O'Mahony and to John Lumsden currently Assistant Secretary, as well as to John Bristow of Trinity College, Dublin for his comments on an earlier draft. The staff of the Dáil library and the National Library of Ireland were always helpful as were staff of the Central Statistics Office, the Economic and Social Research Institute, and John O'Neill of the Central Bank. Dr Jim Crowley of University College Dublin and Antoin Daltún lent me papers from their respective collections, and Barbara Gilroy, formerly of the Chartered Institute of Transport in Ireland, also deserves my appreciation.

I acknowledge my considerable indebtedness to published material, particularly concerning the Irish railways; an amazing depth of interest in transport matters is evident from the amount of detailed recollections and research which continue to emerge from printing presses and especially from the quarterly journal of the Irish Railway Records Society.

Particularly grateful thanks are due to Celine Nolan for rendering into the decipherable some thoroughly indecipherable manuscripts, to Geraldine O'Brien for coping with seemingly endless corrections and revisions, and to Mícheál Ó Cíosóig for his constant and remarkably patient support.

I am happy also to express sincere thanks to Michael Gill for the very helpful and professional assistance provided by him and his team in Gill & Macmillan.

To all those who helped I say míle buíochas, but it is I who am responsible and who asks forgiveness for whatever errors or inaccuracies remain. The CIÉ story is an important one; I hope this is a worthy effort at its rendition.

Mícheál Ó Riain
1 April 1995

CHAPTER 1

EARLY DIAGNOSIS OF MANIA

Opening of Kingstown line 1834—Railway building mania—Drummond (Railways) Commission 1836—Determining the railway gauge—Westminster references to amalgamation or state ownership of Irish railways—Viceregal Commission proposes Irish authority to acquire railways.

CIÉ started life in the middle of the twentieth century, but to understand the vicissitudes of its birth and early years, one must look to some earlier people and events.

A portrait of William Dargan has pride of place in CIÉ's boardroom at its Heuston station headquarters. His statue stands outside the National Gallery in Merrion Square. A fine statue of another key figure, that of Thomas Drummond, is in the domed circular lobby of Dublin City Hall. We start our visit to the origins of CIÉ by recounting something of these two men.

William Dargan (1799–1876) was born in Carlow, trained as a surveyor and worked for Thomas Telford on the construction of the Holyhead road linking the port to Anglesey on the Welsh mainland. He returned to Ireland to set up his own construction business and after building the Belfast–Lough Erne Canal he was appointed contractor for Ireland's first railway from Dublin to Kingstown. The building of that railway, which was opened in 1834, had several features which it shared with later transport projects. Money—not less than £130,000—had to be raised by its sponsors, who negotiated a loan of £75,000 from the Board of Public Works. An Act of Parliament was required; permission had to be obtained for every yard of line and objections overcome from many quarters, with some odd results that still survive. The Grand Canal Company wanted none of these railways in Ireland and promoted the idea of a ship canal from the new Royal Port of Kingstown to Ringsend as an alternative to the railway.

The railway promoters had hoped that the line would run 'from at or near Trinity College to the pier at Kingstown', but the Dublin terminus was moved to Westland Row because of objections by the Board of Trinity College and by residents of Great Brunswick (Pearse) Street. At its other end the line was to have terminated at Old Dunleary Harbour, but the harbour commissioners changed their minds about the location of the new steam packet terminal, moving it to a site about half a mile to the east. In 1833 the Dublin and Kingstown Railway Company (D & KR) proposed to extend its line to Dalkey, serving the new terminal *en route*, but this was resisted by local interests led by Thomas M. Gresham—a noted landowner and hotelier —who received a silver salver from a group of Kingstown citizens 'as a mark of his spirited and successful efforts in opposing the extension of the Kingstown Railway'. The line opened on 17 December 1834 and despite opposition it was extended by half a mile to the present Dún Laoghaire station in May 1837, requiring a further Act of Parliament which was supported by Daniel O'Connell, MP.

William Dargan was involved in all phases of the development of the Kingstown Railway, but his construction activities ranged to much larger projects, including Ireland's second significant railway from Dublin to Drogheda which was formally inaugurated by the Lord Lieutenant in May 1844. Dargan also built the lines from Belfast to Armagh (Ulster Railway), from Dublin to Kilkenny, and to Cork (Great Southern & Western Railway), Belfast to Ballymena (Belfast & Ballymena Railway), Belfast to Bangor (Belfast & County Down Railway), Mullingar to Galway, Longford and Cavan (Midland Great Western Railway), and many others. He invested in railways and other businesses as well as being a builder, and became a director, and later Chairman, of the Dublin & Wicklow Railway Company.

By 1853, twenty years after he commenced work on the Dublin –Kingstown Railway, Dargan had built 600 miles of railway (Henry Boylan, *Dictionary of Irish Biography*, p. 83). That was the year of the Dublin International Exhibition which was promoted and substantially financed by William Dargan at a net personal cost of £20,000. The exhibition took place in five glass-domed buildings on Leinster Lawn, and such was its impact that a public meeting in the Round Room of the Rotunda on 14 July 1853 resolved that 'while we rejoice in being able to congratulate Mr Dargan . . . we are of the opinion that a great and combined exertion should be made throughout the country, to perpetuate in connection with his name, the remembrance of the good he has effected' (quoted by Raymond Keaveney in *National Gallery of Ireland*, p. 6). A committee of some fifty prominent citizens, variously known as the Dargan Committee and as the Testimonial

Committee, set about the establishment of the National Gallery of Ireland. Proposals to name the main gallery after Dargan were not successful, but the Dargan statue on the lawn of the gallery overlooking Merrion Square is a not unfitting memorial. Dargan's railway building reached its peak during what came to be known as the 'railway mania' of the 1850s. His eminence in the Ireland of his day may be judged by the visit to him of Queen Victoria in Dargan Villa (now Mount Anville secondary school) during her visit to Ireland in 1849. Reputedly he declined a baronetcy on that occasion.

In their authoritative *Railways in Ireland 1834–1984*, Oliver Doyle and Stephen Hirsch detail the frequently tortuous line-by-line story of railway development. They summarise the position in 1860:

> The Railway Mania was over, fewer small companies were being promoted, many of those already in existence were being absorbed by the larger companies . . . At the end of 1860 there were 30 companies operating 1,364 route miles with 324 locomotives, 867 carriages and 4,777 wagons. Passenger traffic was increasing despite a decreasing population, but goods traffic was declining.
> (*Railways in Ireland 1834 –1984*, p. 29)

Thomas Drummond was a key player in a creditable but vain effort which would have prevented this 'railway mania'. The Railways Commission, also known as the Drummond Commission, was appointed by royal warrant in 1836. Thomas Drummond (1797–1840), a Scot by birth, worked in the Irish Ordnance Survey from 1824 and became Under Secretary for Ireland from 1835 until his early death in 1840. He was the effective ruler of Ireland outside parliament (P. S. O'Hegarty, *History of Ireland Under the Union, 1801–1923*, p. 83), whose contributions included radical reform of the police force and of jury selection procedures. Roy Foster in *Modern Ireland 1600–1972*, p. 295, notes that the success of the government of Ireland during his era reflected much personal credit. Drummond, in a letter of 22 May 1838 refusing the appeal of thirty-two Tipperary magistrates for stiffer laws in relation to the possession of arms, coined the historic phrase 'property has its duties as well as its rights' which today is inscribed boldly on the plinth of his statue in Dublin's City Hall.

Drummond is said to have been the writer of the Railway Commission's reports published in 1838 which examined the possibilities for railway development against the background of an extraordinarily detailed survey, region by region, of the pre-famine condition of commerce and of the peasantry in Ireland. The population was over seven million, and the commissioners record in their first report that 'the first and most important conclusion at which we have arrived is that the intercourse in Ireland is not at present, nor is likely for many years to come, to be of that content and active kind which would justify the expectation that railways spread over the country in distinct lines from town to town could prove remunerative'.

Accordingly, in their second report they recommended a very limited network: basically two lines
- Dublin to Cork via Maryborough (Portlaoise) with offshoots to Kilkenny and to Limerick;
- Dublin to Navan, from which one line would proceed to Enniskillen and another to Armagh and Belfast.

The report recommended against a coastal route to Drogheda/Dundalk. In its view construction across several estuaries could be difficult and expensive; Drogheda could be served in due course by a branch line from the inland route. No railway was recommended for the west, which the commission noted as being served by the Grand and Royal Canals, the prosperity of which would be imperilled by building railways westwards to Athlone and beyond.

The commission proposed that the exchequer provide assistance for a considerable proportion of the costs at lowest rates of interest and on the easiest form of repayment. However, the commission went beyond the suggestion that government merely facilitate private construction: 'We would further venture to suggest that the government should undertake either or both of the principal lines, on the application of the counties interested; the outlay to be repaid by small instalments and at the lowest admissible rate of interest and under the provision that in the event of the returns not paying the stipulated rate of interest, the counties shall supply the deficit by presentments.' One year later, Lord Morpeth, Chief Secretary for Ireland, moved in the House of Commons that the Lords of the Treasury be authorised to issue Exchequer Bills to the amount of £2.5 million for railway construction in Ireland. The motion was narrowly carried by 104 votes to 100, but was subsequently defeated in the House of Lords.

The defeat of this proposed exchequer funding did not deter the promoters from developing plans far exceeding Drummond's proposals. In 1846 Acts of Parliament were in existence authorising the construction of 1,500 miles of railway in Ireland but, impeded by the Famine, only 123 miles had been completed and 164 miles were under construction, though hampered by financial difficulties. Around the same time about 26,000 miles of railway were carrying traffic in England and Scotland. Irish promoters recovered their confidence during the 1850s.

The map of the rail system in 1860 (page 5) shows that by that year only Counties Sligo, Leitrim, Mayo, Wexford and Donegal had not achieved railway service. Some parts were better favoured. There were two lines to Bray, Co. Wicklow, the result of competing interests to serve and develop

RAILWAY MAP OF IRELAND, 1860

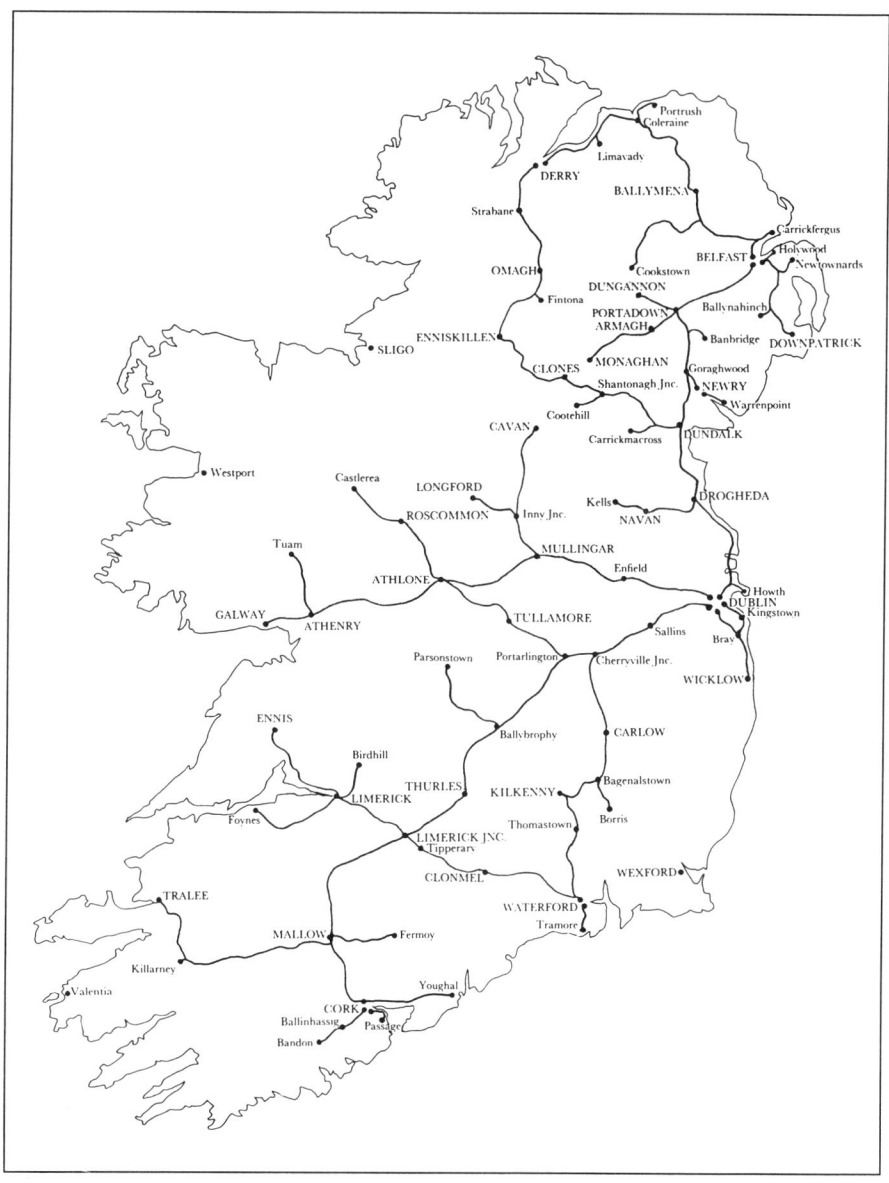

what was projected to be an Irish Brighton. Athlone was also connected to Dublin by two lines (via Mullingar and Portarlington) despite Drummond's reservations. The attraction of Athlone was that it was an important step on the way to Galway which, it was commonly believed, would become one of Europe's main transatlantic shipping ports. Nevertheless Lord George Bentinck, Secretary for Ireland, thought that more railways should be built, and in 1874 he moved that £16 million be advanced for the systematic construction of railways in Ireland. He noted that railways had been the chief factor in bringing England out of its depressed state in the 1840s. The Commons was not impressed; they rejected the motion by 332 votes to 119. The Irish railway promoters again seem not to have been seriously discouraged. Famine and depopulation notwithstanding, 100 miles a year were built over the next thirteen years.

IN DUE COURSE the railway system grew to the size and complexity displayed in the 1924 map (page 13) just before the bulk of Ireland's railway companies would be forced into amalgamation. By that time Ireland had over 3,000 miles of track, both standard gauge and narrow gauge.

The question of gauge is worth a moment. Ireland's standard gauge, or width between the rails, is 5' 3". This compares with 4' 8½" in Great Britain and most of western Europe. The 5' 3" came about as follows. The Kingstown line had been built to the British standard while the Railway Commission recommended that Ireland should have a 6' 2" standard. The Ulster Railway chose 6' 2" for its line from Belfast to Antrim. If a unified railway network were to be developed, an immediate decision would have to be made and adhered to. The Board of Trade requested their Inspector General of Railways to decide which gauge to adopt. Most engineers consulted on the issue thought the English gauge too narrow and the Royal Commission's recommended 6' 2" too wide. They recommended 5' or 5' 6", so the inspector split the difference; hence the 5' 3", formally confirmed in an 1846 Act, which is almost unique in the world and which has been applied to all normal rail lines in Ireland since that time.

While the standard gauge had been fixed at 5' 3", some of the country's most sparsely populated areas were spared the expense of constructing such lines by a number of Acts authorising lines with a 3' gauge. These narrow gauge lines built principally under three Acts—the 1883 Tramways (Ireland) Act and the 1889 and 1896 Light Railways (Ireland) Acts—were among the most colourful and interesting of Ireland's railway companies and especially loved by railway enthusiasts. Several of the narrow gauge companies had specific government support, i.e. state guarantees of interest on borrowed capital were allowed in partial relief of local authority guarantees.

The main narrow gauge and light railway sections were in Cork, Kerry, Clare, Cavan, Leitrim and Donegal. In Clare there were two separate companies initially (Ennis to Milltown Malbay and Milltown Malbay to Kilrush and Kilkee). There were at least three narrow gauge systems in Donegal, operated by at least six companies totalling 223.5 miles. Merely to illustrate how over 100 railway companies could exist in Ireland at various times, let us note the extraordinary network of companies in Donegal. The north of the county was served by the Londonderry & Lough Swilly Railway which also worked the lines of the Carndonagh Extension Railway and the Letterkenny & Burtonport Extension Railway. In the southern part of the county were the Finn Valley Railway and the West Donegal Railway, which amalgamated to form the Donegal Railway (DR), and the Strabane, Raphoe & Convoy Railway, which later became the Strabane & Letterkenny Railway (S & LR). The DR subsequently became the County Donegal Railways Joint Committee, following its takeover by the Great Northern Railway (Ireland) and the Midland Railway (Northern Counties Committee) in 1906, and absorbed the S & LR. The east of County Donegal was served by the Irish North Western Railway, which became part of the Great Northern Railway (Ireland).

The Light Railway Act of 1889 generated considerable controversy. *United Ireland* said 'this disreputable little bill is beggarly restitution out of a vast plunder'; and the *Freeman's Journal* commented that the Act 'was meant to be a bribe and the Irish members who voted against it were quite justified in so doing' (Sir James O'Connor, *History of Ireland 1878–1924*, Vol. 2, p. 137).

How successful were the over 3,000 miles of railway which were eventually built? The false hope that was placed in the railways as a cure for Ireland's national ailments can be seen in remarks of William Gladstone speaking in Westminster in 1844. 'If it should be desired by the Imperial Parliament to confer a pecuniary boon on Ireland there would be no mode in which that boon should be conferred so free from all taint of partiality and at the same time so comprehensive and effective in its application as some measure taken with a view to secure to it the benefit of cheap railway transit.' (Conroy, *History of Irish Railways*, p. 61). A hundred and fifty years later Joe Lee, in *Ireland 1912–1985*, remarks that 'the railway failed to fully realise the ambitious hope that it would act as an engine to pull the economy in its train'. Contemporary evidence from successive debates on the issue in Westminster is equally negative about their success and their general performance. On this topic John Conroy's *History of Irish Railways*, published in 1928, is especially useful. Despite the seemingly pessimistic views of the Drummond Commission, the railways, in modern parlance, were seen as a sort of panacea for economic ills. It was a popular and patriotic thing to promote railways; their boards were dominated by the titled and ascendancy classes throughout the nineteenth and well into the twentieth century, but nationalist figures such as Daniel O'Connell, Charles Stewart Parnell and Willie O'Shea, MP, one of the backers of the West Clare Railway, were happy to be associated with sod-turning ceremonies and inaugurations. Some railway companies foundered at birth; others merged into one another. Some owned track but did not operate, e.g. the City of Dublin Junction Railways Company which built the loop line linking the GNR terminal with the Dublin, Wicklow & Wexford terminal at Westland Row. Some went bankrupt, the earliest such failure being recorded as far back as 1865. The general view was that things would be much better if there were far fewer companies. In 1868 George McCarthy, MP would complain in the House of Commons that 'the number of railway companies [at that time] was 39, with 39 distinct policies, 39 solicitors, 39 engineers, 70 auditors and 333 directors; and the result seemed to serve the minimum of convenience with the maximum of charge'. Another member challenged the tot claiming that there were only nineteen rather than thirty-nine companies.

An argument for state ownership of the Irish railways appears as early as 1872 in the report of a Joint Select Committee of the House of Commons and Lords which noted reasons for government purchase of the Irish railways which did not apply in the case of England. There would be 'a greater proportion of saving in the management which would warrant a corresponding reduction in rates and fares', showing that the naive notion that management salaries have a significant leverage on transport operating costs is not merely a product of our own time. Sentiment in favour of closer state involvement in the railways grew rapidly, as revealed by Lord Claude Hamilton in 1873 when moving a motion in favour of state purchase of the Irish railways:

> All Ireland was unanimous on this question. Ninety per cent of Irish MPs were in favour of state purchase. The Grand Jury of every county in Ireland had signed a petition to this effect; so had the municipal corporations and the town commissioners of the smaller towns.
> (Conroy, op. cit., p. 64)

Lord Hamilton complained about the high level of rates and fares being charged: 'paralysing the fishing industry and seriously impeding development of Ireland's mineral wealth'. Mr Gladstone opposed the motion on 'grounds of practicality'; purchasing the railways would lead to working them and even if ownership could be separated from 'working' he would still be opposed to purchase. The motion was defeated.

A year later (1874) Mr Blennerhasset moved that 'it is expedient that measures should be taken to obtain possession of the Irish railways and place them under Government management'. A Select Committee in 1882 echoed the criticisms which individual MPs had been making and argued for amalgamation of the Irish railways: 'Such amalgamation should not only be urged on the companies concerned and aided with every facility which the Parliament can offer . . . but also if necessary be made the subject of direct Parliamentary action.'

A Royal Commission on Irish Public Works, known as the Allport Commission, picked up this theme in 1886. Allport recommended the establishment of an Irish Railway Commission composed of 'commercial men representing the various districts' who would be paid and be part-time. They would 'oversee, investigate, facilitating amalgamations while protecting the public interest'. Allport did not favour state purchase.

Parliament seemed to give the Irish railway question a rest for some years, but in February 1897 the pressure was resumed. Mr Farrell, MP asked for a royal commission to inquire into the feasibility and desirability of the state purchase of Irish railways. Mr Shee, MP raised the same question two months later, followed by Mr William Field, MP in February 1898. Twelve months later Mr Field returned to the issue moving an amendment to the Address to her Majesty. He asserted that railway rates and charges in Ireland constituted an 'intolerable grievance' and proposed the amalgamation or state purchase of the railway companies. He noted that the 'cost of construction of railways in England has been calculated from £47,000 to £50,000 per mile; in Scotland, £33,000 per mile, and in Ireland, £15,000 per mile. It is strange that we have higher rates than are charged in those countries. The railway administration in Ireland has been a powerful factor in . . . strangling the commerce of the country and preventing the development of industries.'

Mr Field's remarks were noted in *The Times* which said: 'There is much to be said for the contention that the system of competition and privately managed lines, though it produces on the whole admirable results in a country like Great Britain, is unsuitable for the economy and social conditions of Ireland . . . we are not opposed to any method of dealing with the Irish railways, whether state possession or state management if it can be proved to be practicable and advantageous.' (Mulligan, *One Hundred and Fifty Years of Irish Railways*, p. 168)

William Field, who was to lose his seat in the House of Commons to Countess Markievicz in 1918, was a tireless campaigner on the railway question and would appear as a witness in two separate capacities before a Free State Railway Commission in 1924. A butcher by trade, he was a radical on many issues and achieved the unexpected fame of being personally mentioned in the Nestor episode of Joyce's *Ulysses*. Field published his railway views in a paper entitled 'Irish Railways compared to state-owned lines' (1899). Barred by parliamentary procedures, he could not again move his amendment to the Queen's Speech in 1901, but the proposal was moved by Mr Hayden.

The parliamentary device of proposing an amendment to the Address to the King to resume the railway debate was again used in 1903 by O'Mara and Keogh. The views of the Catholic Archbishop of Dublin, Dr Walsh, were put on the Westminster record by Mr McVeagh. Dr Walsh had proposed that following the Canadian example the government should induce the railways to reduce the rates by 30 per cent to 40 per cent or even 50 per cent subject to a guarantee from the state to provide a dividend in case the experiment should not prove a financial success. Formal questions about the possibility of a viceregal commission to inquire into the position of the Irish railways were put by Archdale, Field and O'Brien in 1900, 1901 and 1904, and in the same year J. F. X. O'Brien moved that 'the railway rates and defective transit facilities generally constitute a serious bar to the rational advancement of Ireland and should receive immediate attention from the Government'.

The constant pressure was about to produce some results. In March 1905 a resolution from Mr O'Shaughnessy asking for a government inquiry into Irish rail charges was accepted without division, but the Viceregal Commission would not be named until July 1908. It was charged in its terms of reference:

> to inquire into present (railway) workings, to report on how far they afford adequate facilities for cheap and rapid transport of goods and passengers within the island and to Great Britain, what causes have retarded the expansion of traffic upon the Irish lines and their full utilisation for the development of the agricultural and industrial resources of the country and generally by what means the economical and efficient and harmonious working of the Irish Railways can be secured.

The main recommendation in the final majority report of the Viceregal Commission published in 1910 was the radical one, from a UK viewpoint, 'that an Irish authority be instituted to acquire the Irish railways and work them as a single unit'. Some continental railways were already state owned at that time.

The Viceregal Commission proposed terms for purchasing the railways similar to those envisaged in a Gladstone amendment to an 1844 Act which created an option for state purchase which was never exercised. Rather significantly the commission also proposed that an annual grant of £250,000 be paid from the exchequer to the new railway authority. The majority report had four signatories. Three signed a minority report which rejected state ownership, but which was very determined that amalgamation should take place and that it should not be frustrated by inter-railway rivalries; failing agreement within three years, the railway companies should be compelled to amalgamate within four years.

The Irish Times was appalled at the majority report. 'It is incredible that in the face of disapproval of such experts as . . . [those who signed the minority report] . . . the revolutionary proposals of the Majority Report should ever emerge from the stage of pious aspirations.' Fifteen years were to elapse before the railways in the Free State would be merged into a single unit, though it may be noted in passing that the unified system envisaged by the Viceregal Commission would have operated throughout the entire island of Ireland, rather than the Twenty-six Counties only. A further twenty years would pass before the state virtually acquired the railway system, and another five (forty years in all) before, for different reasons, a state takeover of the railways in the Twenty-six Counties would be consummated.

CHAPTER 2

AMALGAMATION: NO SOLUTION

Government control of railways during World War and Civil War—26 railway companies merged into the Great Southern Railways—1927, 1932, 1933 legislation affecting road and rail—Tribunal of Inquiry 1938—The GSR stocks inquiry.

A common thread through the minority and majority reports of the Viceregal Commission was that the economic backgrounds against which railways operated in Ireland and England were very different from one another. For example, minerals made up only 1.8 per cent of goods traffic in Ireland against 49 per cent in England. Both reports believed that amalgamation would result in better management, more efficient operations and a more economic service to the public.

Consensus having been achieved on the need for amalgamation, one may ask why did no action follow in the four years left before the 1914–1918 War? It is possible that the mere suggestion of state ownership was such a complication for government that it obscured the amalgamation thrust of both the majority and minority reports. Possibly the lack of action may be more simply explained by the lack of crisis. The student of government must surely observe that crisis begets action—and, conversely, lack of crisis perpetuates the status quo. Better that the crisis be serious, rather than merely chronic, if it is to be an effective spur to action.

In principle, the main railway companies were not hostile to the idea of a merger, but the practicalities of mergers were a different matter. They could not guarantee the perceived optimum interests of individual boards and their shareholders. Some companies were profitable and others very marginal. Some had seldom paid a dividend. Some were more efficient than others. Some were relatively well equipped, while others were already operating virtually obsolete equipment.

AMALGAMATION: NO SOLUTION

RAILWAYS IN IRELAND, 1924

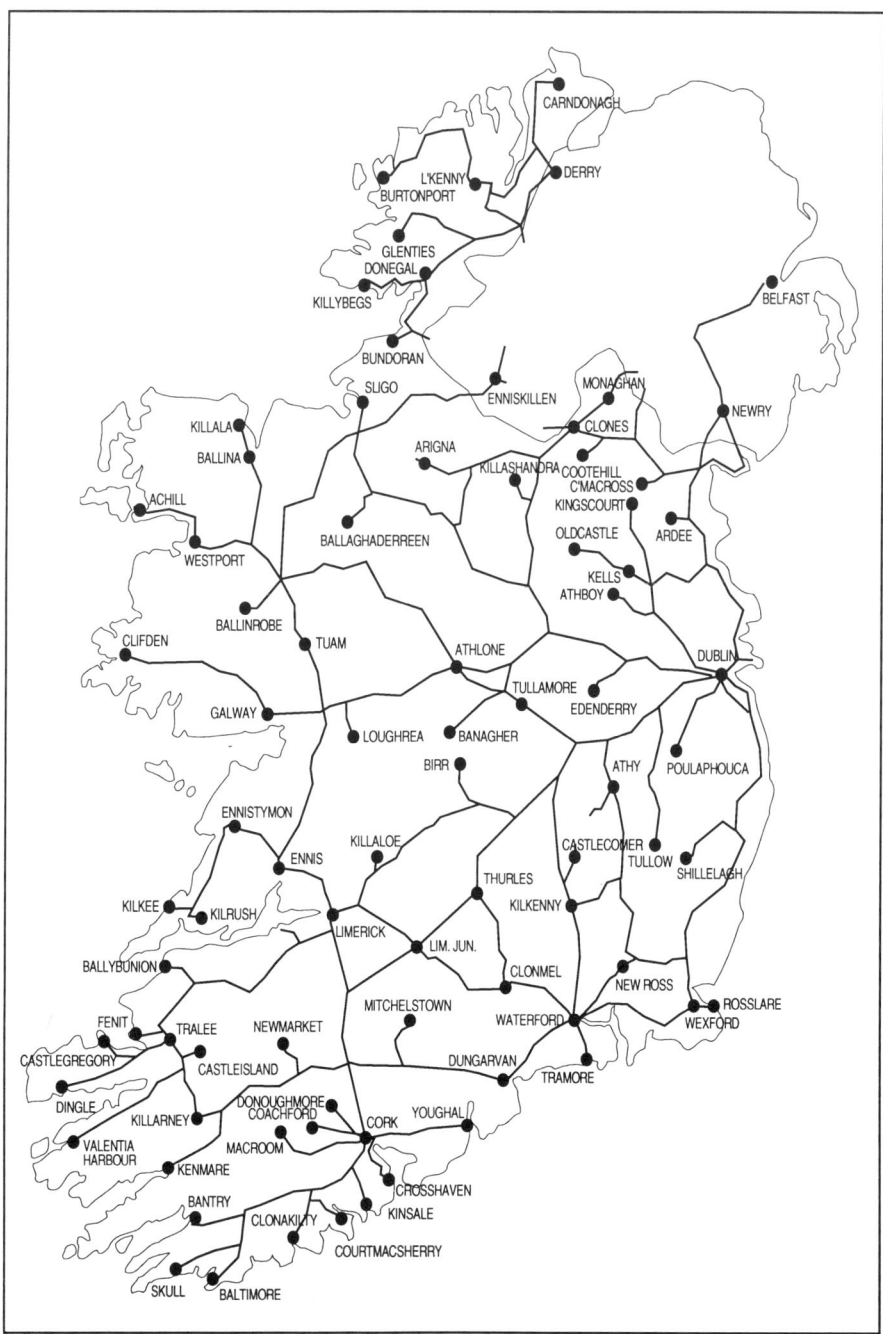

Even the pro-private ownership minority report suggested that if necessary compulsion be used to force through an amalgamation. In the absence of voluntary amalgamation, a national scheme should be proposed by some central authority which would then negotiate against a stiff deadline with individual companies. The majority, of course, thought that amalgamation would still be so complex that state purchase on a nationally promulgated formula basis would be the only practicable way of achieving the desired unified system. The debate went on, with each main railway company seeking ways to protect its own bargaining position. Then war broke out.

In Britain the railway system immediately came under government control. In Ireland an Irish Railways Executive Committee was set up in 1916 to manage all the Irish railway companies (North and South) and it continued to do so until August 1921. During this period, as reported by Meenan, *The Irish Economy since 1922*, railway wages rose by 300 per cent and other costs by an almost equal amount, while receipts were up by only 100 per cent. Financial disaster for the railways was already looming before the Treaty establishing the Irish Free State was signed on 6 December 1921.

During the Civil War the Dublin government continued effectively to control the railways but, as reported by Doyle and Hirsch, severe damage was suffered during this period, especially in Munster where several lines ceased operations.

> The Railway Protection, Repair & Maintenance Corps was formed late in 1922, with many unemployed railwaymen forming its backbone. Armour-plated motor cars, running on rail wheels, and armoured trains were used for transport and the Corp's first success was the reopening of the Thurles–Clonmel section. . . . By August 1923, the work of the Corps was largely completed. The Corps was much admired at home and abroad for its efforts.
> (*Railways in Ireland 1834–1984*, p. 31)

The Chairman of the Great Southern & Western Railway (GS & WR) in March 1923 stated *inter alia* that there had been 467 cases of damage to the permanent way, 291 cases of damage to bridges, 103 signal cabins damaged or destroyed and 468 locomotives, carriages or other rolling stock derailed or destroyed (*The Irish Economy since 1922*, p. 159).

Inaction such as Westminster had practised after the 1910 Viceregal Commission Report was an option not open to the new Dublin government. The largest railway, the GS & WR whose network included Dublin/Cork, Dublin/Carlow/Kilkenny/Waterford, Limerick/Waterford and branches in Kerry, Cork, the midlands and the west, gave notice that it would cease operations on 8 January 1923 due to acute financial difficulties. As an interim measure the government undertook to make up the deficiency between operating revenue and expenditure (interest excluded) so that the GS & WR could keep going. Other companies also faced problems and pent-up pay claims threatened to make such problems widespread.

Already in April 1922 the provisional government had appointed a Railways Commission, the first such Post-Treaty commission to deal with economic issues. The commission was required to 'inquire' into:
- the position of the Irish Railways;
- the best method of administration in the interests of the shareholders, the employees and the public; and
- the relations between the railway workers and the companies.

In its refreshingly brief and readable report published late in 1922 both in Irish and in English, the commission recommended state ownership of the railways with an independent railway board chaired by 'a railway expert with managerial experience'. The suggested composition of the remainder of the board was interesting: 'one from manufacturing industry, one from trade and commerce, two from agriculture, two from labour and a government official to represent the Irish Treasury'. Early commissions uniformly straddled the religious and class divide, but that point was not made explicit. The government would handle that matter if such a board was to be nominated, which it wasn't. A minority report took the anti-state ownership line similar to the minority report of the earlier Viceregal Commission, but in the prevailing circumstances it also suggested that the government should continue to control the railways for a period of three years through a railway board which, in addition to various interest groups suggested in the majority report, would also include four shareholder representatives.

The Free State Government acted more swiftly than its predecessors. In January 1923 it announced that if the railways did not amalgamate by July, legislation would be introduced to force them to do so. The stiff deadline did not produce the desired response. Thomas Johnston, TD, leader of the Labour Party, was to take the next initiative and introduced a Bill in November 1923 embodying the main principles of the majority report. President W. T. Cosgrave said that the government could not accept 'nationalisation' proposals for the railway, but he confirmed that it was strongly in favour of centralised management. The new situation affecting lines crossing the border also had to be recognised.

Mr Johnston's Bill was defeated, but within months of that debate a Railway Bill (1924) was introduced by Paddy McGilligan, Minister for Industry and Commerce. It provided for the merging of all railways in the Free State. Initially three railways listed on Schedule 1—the Great Southern & Western (GS & WR), the Midland Great Western (MGWR) and the Dublin & South Eastern (D & SER)—would form a new Great Southern Railway

(GSR) which would then absorb twenty-two other railway companies on terms to be agreed voluntarily between the parties or, failing agreement, on terms to be decided by the Transport Tribunal. However, complications arose: the Cork/Bandon & South Coast Railway (CB & SCR) had already agreed to merge with the GS & WR before the Bill was published, and the D & SER, in which English railway companies were prominent shareholders, did not like the proposal at all. A somewhat acrimonious correspondence with W. T. Cosgrave ensued. If the D & SER were to lose its identity, it wished to merge with the Great Northern Railway (formed from a number of mergers in 1876). Eventually the GS & WR, the CB & SCR and the MGWR formed the GSR. The D & SER appealed its position to the Transport Tribunal set up under the 1924 Act and it too went into the GSR.

On 30 January 1925 the tribunal published schemes for the absorption of the other companies listed on Schedule 2 of the Act, and in due course these were implemented. Only three rail companies were excluded from Schedule 2: the Dublin & Lucan, the Dublin & Blessington Steam Tramways and the Listowel & Ballybunion Railway. The latter line had a unique monorail system, but it had already ceased operations. Fergus Mulligan remarks that it 'expired in a fit of pique on discovering that it was not to be invited to the party'. The baronial guarantees through which various lines were subsidised by ratepayers ceased with the 1924 Act. Losses under these arrangements amounted to £107,000 in 1922. Compensation to the GSR for running services on these lines was fixed in 1924 at £48,688 for five years and £47,288 for the following five years up to 1934, after which no public support would be provided.

In its first year the GSR had 2,053 miles of railway and worked a further 128.5 miles—three colliery lines built by government (Wolfhill, Castlecomer and Arigna) and lines owned by the Fishguard & Rosslare Railways & Harbours Company. Receipts were £1,500,000 from passenger and £2,270,000 from goods traffic. The company had 623 steam locomotives, of which 42 were narrow gauge, all varying considerably in age and design, and 1,749 passenger rail vehicles.

In March 1927 the Chairman of the GSR reported that, compared to the pre-amalgamation year, a reduction in expenditure of £585,482 had been achieved and, allowing for the coal price increase, the imputed saving was £715,482. In a review of the GSR for the period 1924–1937, read to the Statistical and Social Inquiry Society of Ireland in 1938, Professor B. F. Shields confirmed that compensation for lost baronial guarantees was inadequate and that benefits accruing from the amalgamation included increased use of rolling stock, reductions in staff and lower inventory costs. Speaking in the Dáil in 1932 as Minister for Industry & Commerce, Paddy McGilligan, TD claimed *inter alia* that the 1924 Act had helped to keep several lines open which would otherwise have been closed. In addition, fares and rates had been reduced by between 10 per cent and 12.5 per cent. These assertions were undoubtedly true but they merit some comment.

Firstly, inasmuch as the overall finances of the railways were improved, some closures were averted which otherwise would probably have occurred. It was during the thirties that closures would begin. On the other hand, the reduced fares and rates appear to have been due more to the need to minimise loss of passengers and freight to road operators than to more economical operations. At the time of the 1924 amalgamation the increased popularity and convenience of the lorry, the 'omnibus' and the motor car was noted with some apprehension, but in today's parlance the threat was 'minimised'. Railway directors could sound their warnings, but there was a consensus view that once railways got themselves reorganised and efficient, they would survive and prosper in spite of the growth of road transport. The message, that if only the railways were efficient most of their problems would be solved, would echo and re-echo through two succeeding decades to 1945 when Córas Iompair Éireann was founded and re-echo in a slightly muted but persistent fashion for another twenty years after that date.

There was also a consensus that high transport costs were damaging to the economy. Prior to the 1924 Act the Fiscal Inquiry Commission had said:

> all the evidence points to the conclusions that transport costs in Ireland are excessive, and that Irish industry in nearly all its branches is hampered from this cause . . . The Committee is impressed by the serious nature of this disadvantage, and is led to the conclusion that the development of all means of transport, whether by land or water and its organisation upon economic lines is urgently required in the interest of industrial progress.

Various Westminster commissions had been saying this for perhaps fifty years and the same furrow would be ploughed repeatedly in our own time.

The Official Handbook of Saorstát Éireann (despite the 'Handbook' label it was a handsomely produced volume of 470 pages) commented in 1932 on the 1924 Act and the GSR's subsequent fortunes in an article by John Ingram who had been Secretary to the 1922 Railway Commission and who later would be Chairman of the 1939 Tribunal of Inquiry on Public Transport. He notes that 'it is customary to assert that the loss of traffic to the railways, especially to the Great Southern Company, has been caused by the advent of the omnibus and the motor lorry, and while to an extent this is true there are other factors which must not be overlooked'. The 'other factors' were 'the private motor car' which while probably accounting 'for a large proportion of the decrease in the number of passengers carried by rail has also developed a new business and has proved a boon to dwellers in out-of-the-way districts'. His rather dated language continues: 'The road motor lorry for the conveyance of goods and even livestock, is a serious competitor to the railway, and has advantages, when compared with the older means of transport which makes it a formidable rival to the permanent way.'

The serious competitive effect of road transport on railway tariffs was noted by John Ingram in 1932 to have caused passenger fares to be 'relatively lower' than 'pre-war', and while 'standard' rates for goods and livestock were higher than the maximum charges in force in 1913, the GSR had

> been compelled, by reason of road competition to grant such a large number of exceptional rates that a considerable volume of traffic is being carried by Railway at charges which compare favourably with those in operation in the year 1913. (*Saorstát Éireann Handbook*, p. 167)

Railway traffic and revenues were falling and their beleaguered spokesmen pleaded for permission to compete equitably with road operators. Bus and lorry owners could operate where they liked and charge what they liked. The railway companies, in contrast, were bound to operate the services for which they were licensed by the Railway Acts even when they were loss making; they were obliged to accept whatever business offered and to adhere to a non-discriminatory tariff which could not easily be varied.

The first attempt at levelling the playing field was an Act entitled Railways (Road Motor Services) Act in 1927 which gave railway companies the right to operate road services, subject to ministerial approval of proposed routes and charges. In Dublin the DUTC (Dublin United Tramways Company) was finding itself in competition with a raft of small bus operators, quite a number of whom were one-man outfits owned by ex-soldiers who had bought 14–20 seater buses with their army gratuities. The DUTC obtained its 'freedom' to operate buses under another Act—Dublin United Tramways (Omnibus Services) Act 1927—again subject to ministerial approval. In the Six Counties the GNR never got such freedom.

The 1927 Railways Act failed to achieve its purpose, either because of the formalities imposed on the railway companies, or because the traditions of a century of highly regulated rail operations sapped them of the initiative required to fight the road operators. However, GSR established a working agreement with the major bus operator, the Irish Omnibus Company, in 1927 and obtained effective control of that company in 1929. None the less its chairman felt it necessary in 1931 to call for fresh legislation, 'regulating transport and removing the disabilities at present imposed on the railways'. By that time licensed road vehicles of all classes had increased by 66 per cent to 49,000 compared to 29,000 in 1925, when the GSR was set up; over the same brief period goods vehicles had grown from 4,950 to 8,278.

Road transport was virtually unregulated. In an attempt to bring order to a situation approaching anarchy, the Cumann na nGaedheal government introduced the Road Transport Act 1932 prescribing that all scheduled passenger services be operated under licences issued by the Minister for Industry and Commerce. Such licences would require publication of timetables and charges. Contrary to the impression that some commentators have since given, the Act did not proscribe independent scheduled bus services—they could still operate and even open new services provided they fell in line with the licensing requirements. Another Act in the same year, the Railways (Miscellaneous) Act 1932, provided for the discontinuance or reduction of train services on lines constructed wholly or partly out of public monies, e.g. the baronial guarantee lines.

While these Acts may have seemed bold in the context of the times, they were merely tinkering with the problem. Within twelve months much more far-reaching legislation would be introduced by Seán Lemass as Minister in the new Fianna Fáil government. The first of two transport Acts addressed the struggle between rail and road (Road Transport Act 1933). It restricted the carriage of goods for reward to operators who had been operating at the time of the Act, and imposed restrictions on their area of operation. Furthermore, railways were given power compulsorily to acquire their road competitors—both passenger and road freight—on terms that if necessary would be determined by binding arbitration. The GSR would later have grounds to complain, reasonably so, that the terms determined by the arbitrator were frequently excessive.

Seán Lemass had no embarrassment about monopoly in the 1933 debates concerning this legislation. If at all possible he wanted to restore a 'monopoly' in each area where there would be one provider of transport services, well organised and efficient, rather than allow a major national asset—the railway—to be underutilised, while an 'excess of transport services' was being provided with harmful economic consequences. Objections to the legislation of 1932 and 1933 mainly came from those already involved in independent road operations, but as the terms unfolded they were assured that 'provided you were already at the party you would be looked after: you could continue to operate or be bought out'. Only those who hadn't joined the party could have cause for complaint. However, other objections were prompted by a profound distrust of the management of the railway companies.

From the viewpoint of the 1990s, the requirement that all passenger and freight transport providers be required to obtain operating licences and operate to certain standards seems eminently reasonable. The provision that a business could voluntarily acquire its competitors is also acceptable today, subject to stated considerations affecting the wider public interest. The power compulsorily to acquire your competitors is another matter. This provision and that which restricted participation in the road freight haulage industry only to the pre-1933 players, while perhaps reasonable in the eyes of the administrations of the 1930s and later, are seriously at odds with the fashion of the 1990s. A by-product of the legislation was that inadequate enforcement resulted in much illegal haulage taking place and in railway staff being diverted into policing their competitors so that it might be stopped.

If commentators complained that the railways were being unduly cosseted by the restrictions on road transport, Seán Lemass in the second of his 1933 Acts delivered very rough treatment to the shareholders of the GSR. The GSR stock which had been issued only eight years earlier was written down from £26 million to £12.4 million. Debentures were written down by 15 per cent, but ordinary shares were reduced by 90 per cent. One might say that if dividends were not being paid and the prospects for the company were poor, the ordinary shares were losing market value with or without legislation which merely changed their nominal value. On the other hand, shareholders complained vociferously that they were being deprived of the inherent 'break-up value' of the company which would be realised if it were allowed to go into voluntary liquidation. Neither the government nor the railway boards themselves would countenance liquidation.

Legislation aside, the transport scene was changing fast in the 1930s. Total freight movements were in decline due to the 1929 Depression and the Economic War, but road transport continued its rapid growth. The number of private motor cars rose from 9,246 in 1923 to 48,599 in 1938. The number of commercial vehicles, including agricultural tractors, increased from 3,507 in 1923 to 10,406 over the same period. In contrast to the increase in vehicle registration, passenger and freight 'operations for reward' by independent firms declined largely as a result of their acquisition by the GSR and DUTC. Independent bus companies fell in number from 107 to 48 between 1932 and 1938, mostly due to the acquisition of one-man companies by the DUTC, and the number of licences for goods transport also fell: from 1,356 in 1933 to 886 in 1938.

With the new flexibility granted by the Lemass legislation, railway closures began to take place. As reported by Doyle and Hirsch:

> In 1934 Bagenalstown/Palace East and the Edenderry, Castlecomer, Killala and Killaloe branches lost passenger services and the Kinsale branch closed completely. The first narrow gauge closure occurred in September 1932 when the Cork to Crosshaven line ceased to operate,

followed by Cork's other narrow gauge system, the Muskerry, in April 1934. In April 1939, the Tralee & Dingle section lost its passenger services while the Castlegregory branch was closed to all traffic. The Clifden branch, which had been open only for forty years, closed in April 1935, followed in September 1937 by the final closure of the Westport/Achill line. (*Railways in Ireland 1834–1984*, p. 95)

Despite the many changes, the main public transport companies, i.e. the GSR and GNR, did not prosper. Rail traffic continued to fall and railway finances to deteriorate. Concern about the adequacy of maintenance of the railway system was also being expressed. The seriousness of the situation caused government to appoint a Tribunal of Inquiry on Public Transport on 22 December 1938 which would submit its report only seven months later on 4 August 1939. Under the chairmanship of John Ingram, the four members included Dr J. P. Beddy, who would chair a similar investigation in 1956, and Dr Henry Kennedy, representing the agricultural industry. The tribunal studied traffic trends, service standards and levels of charges, and received detailed submissions particularly from the GSR. Describing the severe difficulties of the GSR, the tribunal noted:

> In 1938 the company reached a position in which there was insufficient net income to meet liabilities in respect of interest, rentals and other fixed charges and in order to avoid the possibility of the appointment of a receiver it was necessary to supplement net income by a transfer from reserves.

The GNR also resorted to the tactic of raiding reserves to pay its fixed charges. A majority report (Ingram and Beddy) recommended the establishment of a National Transport Council for the review of all forms of transport. In the interim the GSR should be controlled by a board of three including one government appointee. The report outlined the now very familiar list of the disabilities under which the railways operated *vis-à-vis* private transport. They included:

> Railways must accept all and any class of traffic, operate on the basis of public timetables, irrespective of the fluctuations in demand, provide a permanent way and maintain it, must provide for safety of passengers and goods by operation of their own signalling systems.

None the less a GSR proposal that it withdraw train services on about one-third of its system and develop bus services by building 126 new buses and building four new bus stations did not find favour with the tribunal. The report spoke of the 'fundamental importance' of public transport from the national point of view, of the railways' role in handling peak traffic and as a stand-by for privately owned transport. Accordingly, to obviate the very real risk of a receiver being appointed to the GSR, they recommended 'increased duties on motor vehicles operated by the "non-statutory companies" with the money being paid into a special fund and used to pay, if necessary, debt interest, rentals and other fixed charges'. In effect the 1939 report was proposing a cross subsidy between privately operated road and publicly operated rail services. Such payments would be repayable to the exchequer in circumstances that were not defined. With regard to the GSR's need for capital investment, the tribunal also recommended a government guaranteed issue of £1.25 million debenture stock.

However, the report was critical of the GSR in several respects, including the adequacy of its depreciation provisions, its failure to rationalise its services under the existing legislation, and rejected its proposal to impose a limit of a fifteen mile radius on the operation of commercial motor vehicles. The tribunal's minority report was written solely by Dr Kennedy, a mathematician turned economist who was chief executive of the Irish Agricultural Wholesale Society—a man who was generally disposed to challenge conventional wisdom. He argued that to regard motor vehicles primarily as competing with public transport was wrong—they were also replacing the horse, for centuries the privately owned transport mode for passengers and goods. Dr Kennedy was prepared to 'bite the bullet' of state ownership.

> There seems to be no prospect of the company being able to carry out its services without Government assistance of some sort. Of the forms which that assistance might take, I regard restriction of motor transport and especially of merchandise motor transport as being the most likely to impede economic development. The alternatives are subsidies and state ownership. I recommend state ownership as the less objectionable of the alternatives.

After considerable trauma in the industry the 1950 Transport Act would implement Dr Kennedy's preferred course. In the interim both the majority and minority reports were overtaken by World War II which began within weeks of their publication.

Due to the scarcity of fuel oils World War II provided a financial respite for both the GSR and the GNR. Severe petrol rationing drove passengers and freight back *en masse* to public transport. The extent of the improvement was remarked on by B. F. Shields in another paper to the Statistical and Social Inquiry Society of Ireland, which compared the 'exceptionally difficult' financial position of the GSR and GNR in 1938 when they had to raid reserves to pay interest charges, with their 1944 results when 'they could pay dividends on their guaranteed, preference and ordinary stocks after making large transfers to reserves'. Shields was very critical of the railways' accounting practices which were 'very old fashioned', made 'no allowance for depreciation or the removal of assets no longer used except where they are sold, nor is there any attempt at their periodical valuation . . . The Regulation of Railways Act stipulating this double accounting system was an invention, not of accountants but of legal draftsmen . . . It has no meaning and should be scrapped.' The relevance of these remarks becomes apparent later. They must cause serious doubts as to whether the railway companies' 'reserves' existed in any real sense.

The government had assumed control of the GSR in the meantime, on the lines of the Ingram Majority Report, not for financial reasons, but for strategic reasons of controlling the use of scarce supplies of coal and fuel oils. This was achieved by an Emergency Powers Order in February 1942 under which the Minister, Seán Lemass, appointed Augustine Percy Reynolds, Managing Director of the now renamed Dublin United Transport Company, as Chairman of the GSR. Percy Reynolds, an O'Connell Schools boy like the minister, was an accountant by profession, becoming senior partner in the firm, Reynolds McCarron & Co. He acquired a minority stake in the General Omnibus Company (GOC), the largest of Dublin's independent bus operators in 1929. With his partner E. T. McCarron he acquired total control of the GOC in 1932 of which he became Managing Director. The GOC was compulsorily absorbed by the DUTC in 1935, but in due course Reynolds became Managing Director of the survivor company. He would be a key and controversial figure in major transport matters for many further years. He resided in Abbeyville, the Kinsealy, Co. Dublin home which would later be better known when owned by C. J. Haughey. Racing was one of Reynolds's many interests and he was the owner of the Irish Derby winner in 1941.

The change of name from a 'Tramways' to a 'Transport' company reflected a major shift from the tram to the 'omnibus', a term (dative case for *omnes* —'all' in Latin) which quaintly would survive in many reports right into the 1960s. Trams were being withdrawn as the 1930s drew to a close. The last route to lose trams at the outset of World War II was the No. 18 from Ballsbridge to Harold's Cross in 1940, and by then trams had disappeared from the north city apart from O'Connell St where Nelson Pillar remained the terminus for the surviving Nos 14 and 15 trams to Dartry and Terenure, and for the Nos 6, 7 and 8 routes to Blackrock, Dún Laoghaire and Dalkey. These remaining trams helped to compensate for petrol shortages so that limited fuel supplies could be used elsewhere while the Emergency lasted.

On the railways where the GSR introduced some electric battery trains before the war a similar conservation of scarce coal supplies was possible. Professor James Drumm of UCD invented, and in 1929, patented an alkaline battery 'with a low internal resistance enabling a high rate of charge and discharge . . . particularly suited to rail traction' (*Railways in Ireland 1834–1984*, p. 136). After successful trials a two-coach articulated set powered by a 272 cell rechargeable Drumm battery weighing 15 tons entered service in 1932 on the Dublin–Bray line. The batteries were charged and recharged at specially designed substations located at Bray, Harcourt St and Amiens St stations. A total of four sets were built operating on both the Tara Street and Harcourt Street lines to Bray for almost seventeen years. Even the Drumm trains, and the DUTC trams, had to be withdrawn for a period in 1944 when the ESB's hydroelectric generating capacity was critically low in a dry summer and it was proscribed by government order from supplying electricity for traction purposes.

The Drumm trains were an interesting and useful innovation by the GSR, but the overall state of its locomotives and rolling stock at the outset of the war was recognised to be very serious. Seán Lemass would say in 1944 that the railway equipment which CIE would acquire from the GSR was 'very largely obsolete'. The railway companies had been starved of capital; funds could not be raised from commercial sources because of the financial predicament of the operators.

At the time of its formation in 1925 the GSR's stock of 623 locomotives of various vintages and design were already suffering from neglect; the best among them were 23 'fine machines' still being produced by the MGWR at its Broadstone works. At its Inchicore, Broadstone and Grand Canal St works the GSR laboured to maintain this assorted stock having little resources to build new locomotives, though three outstanding locomotives emerged from Inchicore in 1939, named Maedhbh, Macha and Tailte after legendary Irish female warriors. These 800 Class engines, collectively known as the Queens, were the most powerful express locomotives ever built in Ireland; they were the first engines capable of taking the heavier trains up the steep gradient out of Cork without support from a second engine pushing from the rear of the train. Rolling stock was similarly dated and about thirty passenger carriages built by the GSR during its existence counted for little. Electric colour signals instead of the traditional manually operated semaphore signals were installed on the Amiens St to Dún Laoghaire line. But there were very few such investments by the GSR.

More to minimise costs than for any operational reason, the GSR cannibalised part of the permanent way by singling some sections and using the released rails elsewhere on the network, mainly on the Dublin/Cork line. Thus from 1929 the former MGWR mainline to Galway was reduced to single track from Clonsilla westward to Mullingar, Athlone and Ballinasloe.

Some economies that followed the 1924 Act 'proved unwise', said Mr Lemass in 1944, and he instanced this singling of the Galway line. 'I think that those familiar with our transport problems will now admit that it was a mistake.' (*Dáil Debates*, Vol. 93, Col. 1791) In the event the singling was never reversed, and the main Galway services would eventually operate on the southern route to Athlone via Portarlington rather than on the old MGWR line to Athlone via Mullingar.

The GSR standardised its logo, tickets and colour schemes, leaving little evidence of the diverse crop of railways from which it had sprung. However, looking behind the public face, the Ingram Tribunal said that the GSR 'remained one of unequally developed, uncoordinated and sometimes antagonistic points'. In addition to its new logo the GSR, in accordance with the 1924 Act, had erected bilingual station identification boards, thus somehow suggesting that the GNR with English only notice boards, despite its headquarters in Dublin's Amiens Street, was a Northern Ireland company, not really part of the Free State.

With a new face, poor equipment and its management criticised by Ingram, the now 14-year-old GSR faced into the Emergency. Its services would be steadily reduced in frequency, speed and reliability. Coal shortages gradually became worse. In 1942 eleven branch lines were closed by government order. Many others were without services and mainline services operated only two days a week. In order to keep this skeleton service going, 'anything combustible ended up in the firebox: low grade coal, slack, turf, wood, cardboard and the odd bunkerload "acquired" from the GNR' (Mulligan, op. cit.). Mulligan claimed that 'Goods trains could take up to two weeks to get to Cork and passenger runs might well take a day and a half.' But this is the stuff of myth and legend. Delays did occur but in terms of hours, not days or weeks. Ironically, the difficulties of the railways led to a temporary revival in traffic on the canals which had been so undermined by their noisy competitors a hundred years earlier. Despite its operational problems the GSR's financial problems were less than pre-war. Its traffic increased due to the collapse of road competition, but its future was far from secure.

At the company's Annual General Meeting in March 1943, Percy Reynolds as the government-appointed Chairman of the GSR fired the first public salvo in a demand for government action to make the railways viable. He warned shareholders of the serious position which their company faced. *Inter alia* the railway was overmanned for the current wartime level of operations and the trade unions were 'pressing for too much'. His main point though was that it was not possible to raise the substantial capital without which the company could not survive as a significant or successful transport operator. A major capital reconstruction could not be postponed for much longer. For a brief period GSR shares languished still further on the Stock Exchange. However, on 16 June 1943 Seán Lemass as Minister for Industry and Commerce addressed the issue in an election speech at Inchicore and indicated that if returned to power the government would respond to the railway's need. Fianna Fáil was returned to office and a consensus developed that the government was prepared to intervene to place the company on a sounder footing. GSR stock began to increase in value resulting in a *cause célèbre* which interrupted the passing of transport legislation and toppled the government.

The facts were that Reynolds, the GSR's Chairman, was a government appointee who had called for a new deal for the company. From February to October 1943 discussions were indeed taking place between the GSR and the government. By September the bones of a new arrangement were agreed with Industry and Commerce. Government approval was given in October; GSR directors were advised on 19 October; shareholders were notified by post on Sunday, 24 October; and the press were advised of the proposal on 25 October. In retrospect there can be little surprise that the value of GSR stocks rose over this period. The wonder is that dealings in GSR stocks were not suspended once serious discussions about the GSR's capital requirements had begun to take place. But they were not suspended, and between March and November 1943 the value of GSR stock rose by £2.5 million. Ordinary stock worth £9 in March 1943 had jumped to £52 in March 1944, and debenture stock which was worth £56 in March 1943 was changing hands at £90 one year later (William Norton, *Dáil Debates*, Vol. 93, Col. 1863).

There was a public outcry. It was widely alleged that persons had misused information, which they had received in confidence in the course of their duties, to buy or to cause others to buy substantial amounts of GSR shares, secure in the expectation that they would realise a profit when eventually the government would announce its intentions.

In response to these allegations a Tribunal of Inquiry was appointed to establish if there had been any insider dealings or misuse of privileged information behind the stock market fluctuations between 1 January 1943 and 18 November 1943, the date on which the tribunal was set up. The tribunal met early in 1944 and produced a comprehensive report in September. Even at this stage the report makes an intriguing read as it details trading in GSR shares and the sequence of correspondence between the minister and the company. It referred to named civil servants, who had or who didn't have access to hard information concerning the government's intentions, and to the role of a certain stockbroker who had widely encouraged his clients, including several fellow members of Milltown Golf Club, to buy GSR shares. Had he obtained a tip-off from someone? The stockbroker was questioned by the tribunal, as were many others including two principal officers from the Department of Industry and Commerce. One was regarded as being indiscreet in comments to third parties, but had not himself purchased any shares. He resigned before the tribunal published its findings. The other principal officer had purchased shares but had not been officially aware of the minister's intentions. He was cleared of suspicion of malpractice and would subsequently serve as Ireland's Ambassador to the Hague and as Director General of Bord Fáilte. The tribunal concluded that in their opinion the stock market activity in GSR shares could be, and in fact was, prompted by intelligent anticipation of government action based on public pronouncements by the GSR's chairman and the minister.

During the time that elapsed between the start and the conclusion of the tribunal's investigations, the long-expected Bill was published. It proposed to wind up the GSR and establish Córas Iompair Éireann (1944 Transport No. 1 Bill). It was debated fiercely and at length. It was defeated on the grounds that such major legislation should not be enacted until the tribunal had completed its report on dealings in GSR stocks and shares. The Fianna Fáil government obtained a dissolution of the Dáil and was returned with a majority which allowed it to reintroduce the Bill and have it adopted as the 1944 Transport Act, changed only in regard to its effective date. Thus in a highly charged political atmosphere Córas Iompair Éireann was established, not in July 1944 as planned under the first Bill, but on 1 January 1945. The Transport Bill debates, described in the next chapter, give many signals of the problems which CIÉ would have to face in serving the transport demands of the twenty-six county state, which four years later would be retitled the Republic of Ireland.

CHAPTER 3

BORN IN
CONTROVERSY

Transport (No. 1) Bill 1944—Merger of GSR and DUTC proposed—Dáil debates —Dissolution of Dáil—Transport (No. 2) Bill 1944—Formation of CIÉ.

Pleading special circumstances related to the Emergency which the Dublin government had declared at the outset of the war, Éamon de Valera introduced a Bill early in 1943 seeking to extend the life of the Dáil. Faced by widespread opposition, the Bill was withdrawn and a general election ensued. In that 1943 election Fianna Fáil lost its majority, primarily because of the success of the new Clann na Talmhan who won 10 seats, but also because of increased support for Labour. Fianna Fáil continued in government, but de Valera warned that it could be pulled down at any time if all non-Fianna Fáil members (which included 12 Independent members as well as 10 Clann na Talmhan members) combined against it. Accordingly, Seán Lemass was Minister for Industry and Commerce in a minority Fianna Fáil government when he moved the second stage of the Transport (No. 1) Bill on 2 May 1944.

The possibility of defeat seemed to be far from Lemass's mind as he explained that the Bill was 'designed to facilitate a long term transport policy and has no special relationship to the transport difficulties which have been created for this country by the emergency' (*Dáil Debates*, Vol. 93, Col. 1785).

He subscribed to the view quoted by the Ingram Tribunal that the problems of public transport companies arose out of '. . . an uneconomic excess of transport facilities'.

> I think it will be generally agreed . . . that the pre-war position in respect of our public transport services was thoroughly unsatisfactory.

> Outside the municipal area of Dublin the public transport facilities were neither efficiently directed nor sufficiently extensive nor cheap enough to promote economic welfare. (ibid., Col. 1789)

Lemass said that the same state of affairs existed in Dublin up to 1935, about which time the DUTC began effectively to 'apply the policy of the Road Transport Acts and to become in a full sense a Transport Company'. Radical intervention by government was required.

> It may be contended that despite the disappointments of Government with the results of the 1932 and 1933 legislation, that . . . given better management the situation could be remedied without new legislation or without Government interference. The Government was unable to accept this view. (ibid.)

Accordingly, said Lemass, any scheme based on 'patching up the GSR Company' would not inspire public confidence and the

> situation was such that it could not be met merely by patching up the GSR Company, that it needed a new organisation, with a new legislative basis, a new financial structure, a new relationship with Government and the public, and even a new name to signal the break with the old traditions. (ibid., Col. 1790)

His solution, therefore, was to wind up and then merge the Great Southern Railways Company and the Dublin United Transport Company. Terms had already been agreed with the two boards, by which shareholders would convert their stock and shares into stock in a new company named Córas Iompair Éireann. In due course these terms were accepted by the shareholders though not without protest. In the case of the GSR debenture stock each £100 would be converted at par into 3% redeemable debentures. In the case of GSR guaranteed shares the shareholders would receive £50 of 3% debenture stock and £50 common stock for each £100 held. In the case of the DUTC their 6% preference and ordinary stock were converted into 3% redeemable debentures at £145 for every £100 held. The Bill provided that these redeemable debentures would be repaid between 1955 and 1960, with Lemass saying that this would be done 'out of surplus revenue which it is hoped will be earned by the reorganisation and by more efficient working in normal circumstances' (ibid.). The seemingly extraordinary optimism of this provision was commented on later by the young Deputy Jack Lynch among many others. Jack Lynch's speech showed that he had studied the Ingram Tribunal Report and B. F. Shields' papers to the Statistical and Social Inquiry Society of Ireland. He thought that if the redeemable debentures were to be redeemed at the allotted time, the company should at least be authorised to replace them with new borrowings. However, the idea that a state company could, and indeed should, repay its borrowings and apparently survive thereafter without significant debt was already established in government thinking (e.g. ESB). Presumably it was a Department of Finance-driven concept.

The stock conversions left CIÉ with a paid-up capital of £13.5 million, but the Bill authorised a total capital of £20 million, providing £6.5 million headroom for CIÉ to raise new capital by public issue of government guaranteed stock to renew the organisation's outdated and depleted equipment and facilities. In fact CIÉ's capital, both new and old, was to be guaranteed except only the £3.5 million common stock on which CIÉ was empowered by the Act to pay a maximum dividend of 6 per cent out of profits. Opposition speakers questioned why the state was providing for conversion of GSR stock at par if its assets were as obsolete as government maintained. Lemass reminded the Dáil of the major write-down of the GSR's capital which had already taken place under the Railways Act 1933. None the less William Norton was moved to say 'The shareholders of the DUTC and the GSR should erect a very lofty monument to the present minister as there is no doubt that he has been their fairy godmother.'

The Bill provided for a government-appointed chairman and for six directors to be elected by the common stockholders. Lemass opined the view that this would be a better sort of board than those where the entire membership was nominated by government. He instanced the ESB and Bord na Móna where members might be unduly influenced by government or by political considerations, rather than be concerned solely with the running of the company as a business, a remark, one would think, that might have been used to haunt him in later years. The 1945 recipe for the CIÉ Board would soon be regarded as a failure and would not be used for other commercial state companies. The government-appointed chairman would be the key figure in the new organisation. No meeting of the board might be held in the absence of the chairman; no decision might be reached without his approval, and by himself he would constitute a quorum at a meeting. No reference was made to Percy Reynolds during the debate, but everyone 'knew' that in due course he would become chairman. Critics said the new chairman would be a dictator in the affairs of the new company. In effect the minister would be able to run everything his own way through Reynolds.

The big issue was why government was not taking the logical step of nationalising the proposed concern. Deputy Maurice Dockrell put it succinctly: 'I think that there is a distinction without a difference between nationalisation and what is proposed in this Bill.' William Norton, leader of the Labour Party, berated Lemass for abandoning his previous position on public ownership. He quoted Seán Lemass's Dáil speeches as far back as 1931: 'We are strongly in favour of public ownership of transport services with unified control outside the municipalities. Inside the municipalities we are in favour of municipal ownership and control of these services.' Fine Gael speakers also favoured nationalisation, noting that President W. T. Cosgrave had said in 1925 that 'if the bill then being passed did not achieve its purpose nationalisation of the railways would be the next step'. There may have been no ideological enthusiasm for state ownership in Fine Gael, but speaker after speaker believed that it was the only realistic option and that the Bill before them was a 'cop-out'.

The GSR was repeatedly attacked. Paddy McGilligan was one of the many who said that the GSR shareholders had been 'getting their dividends out of money that should have gone to the replacement of assets'. Fitzgerald Kenny referred to debates in the Gladstone period and to the Viceregal Commission's recommendation that the railways be taken into public ownership. 'Nationalisation of the railways in this country cannot be regarded as a step towards socialism or anything of that kind. It is one of those exceptions to private enterprise that the nature of the thing demands, because private enterprise has not been successful and probably from the nature of things can never be successful in giving a cheap and adequate railway service here.' (ibid., Col. 1970)

Jim Larkin said that the minster had a right to change his mind but he should show why. After such reasonable enough statements Larkin digressed for a while with comments which merit quotation as a sign of the times in which he spoke: 'of course, unfortunately the women members of this house don't speak. Some day I hope to hear one of them utter a sentence.' He envisaged that women would promote honesty and probity in public life and, after being called to order for irrelevance, he concluded with a thundering denunciation of the Bill: 'This is a Bill born out of time; it is an abortion, born of mismanagement and fathered by cupidity.'

Lemass admitted that the government was once in favour of nationalisation, thinking there was no alternative, but now they saw an alternative and were against it, 'not because of any theoretical objections or stupid prejudices but because of practical consideration in the circumstances'. He said that 'Nationalised transport almost inevitably means subsidised transport' and in his view subsidies were not necessary: public transport could be financially viable. There was agreement on the great importance of transport to economic progress, but

> There may not be similar agreement concerning the Government's belief that a fully developed transport system operating on road and railway, extending to all parts of the country and providing in all parts of the country full transport facilities can be operated on a

remunerative basis. I mean by that earning from the sale of transport facilities [sic] sufficient revenue to cover all its operating costs and its overhead expenses, to meet the interest on its capital and to provide over and above, the reserves which are necessary to finance its further development . . . the Government does not believe in subsidised transport facilities . . . subsidised transport will inevitably mean inefficient transport and will ultimately result in an increase in the cost of transport to the community as a whole. (ibid., Col. 1795)

So, Seán Lemass rejected nationalisation because it would lead to subsidies, leading to taxation, leading to inefficiency and, at the end of the line, more costly transport would be the result. To these objections he added his concern that public representatives at every level would exercise undue pressures on a national transport company for equal services to every community and for favours for individual districts, businesses and industries. CIÉ should, in the interest of good management and efficiency, be protected from such representations. 'Why?' asked Deputy Dr Tom O'Higgins who rejected the minister's argument about a nationalised company having to yield to all pressures, mentioning that the Post Office didn't provide uniform service. Some places had post only twice weekly and no telegraph service.

At the time of the debate Dr Tom O'Higgins was Fine Gael leader in the Dáil. General Mulcahy, who had succeeded W. T. Cosgrave as President of the Party, had lost his Dublin seat in the 1943 election but would regain one in Tipperary at another general election which was not far away. O'Higgins's main attack on the Bill was connected with the tribunal on GSR share dealings. He moved that the Bill be refused until the tribunal reported its findings. None the less the Bill itself provided him with much to question. He focused in particular on the GSR/DUTC merger. 'Anybody leaning back and looking at the proposals would say amalgamation of the railway company is necessary because it was doing badly and amalgamation of the tramway company was necessary because it was doing well . . . Are we to understand that the tramway is merged with the railway company so that the tramway will act as a milch cow for the services over the remainder of Ireland?' (ibid., Col. 1833) Dr Tom O'Higgins mentioned that when the ESB was being formed and Dublin's electricity facilities were being taken over, specific legislation required that profits from the Dublin operations would not be used to finance developments elsewhere. The point concerning the treatment of the DUTC and its use to support the railways was taken up by other deputies and would echo down the years until 1972 when CIÉ's Dublin City Services ceased to return a profit. The minister's justification for the amalgamation did little to disarm his critics:

> Government considered that there would be substantial advantages to be served by combining the undertakings of the GSR and the DUTC ... the new company will be in a position to command the best administrative and technical abilities available to either company; it is anticipated that substantial economies can be effected by the standardisation and interchangeability of vehicles and planning and [that it] will permit full co-ordination of suburban transport facilities.
>
> (ibid., Col. 1811)

He added that if major population centres wanted their own companies, the sparsely populated areas would be left to their own devices, resulting in there being 'no national transport policy'. Dublin should recognise that most transport is to and from Dublin; therefore 'cheap and efficient transport from all points of the country will contribute to the prosperity of Dublin'. The *Irish Independent* was far from impressed with such arguments, saying that the proposal for 'the acquisition of the Dublin United Transport Company is audacious and unjust; it is a blow to private enterprise and is a dangerous precedent which may later on be cited in support of similar proposals to acquire industries, shops or farms as portion of some alleged scheme for "greater efficiency" or for "unification"'. The *Independent* perceived a sinister creep towards socialism in the proposal concerning the DUTC.

Seán Lemass's attitude to monopoly remained as it had been in 1933: his thesis was that there was always 'something like a monopoly' in public transport, e.g. up to 1920, before the days of the motor vehicle, railways had an effective monopoly in their own areas. No extension of monopoly was being proposed: the GSR and DUTC would merely retain what they had. 'Whatever theoretical case can be made for competition in encouraging efficiency or stimulating enterprise in other commercial spheres it can, in relation to transport, undermine the stability of services which are necessary to the national commercial life and it can in its effect do irreparable damage to the public interest.' (ibid., Col. 1796)

Redundancy provisions were renewed on the fairly generous basis provided for in the 1925 amalgamation legislation, as was the requirement that admission to CIÉ clerical grades be restricted to those who would succeed in an open competitive examination. This provision had more to it than the contemporary reader might suspect. In early railway days such highly valued positions tended to be filled on the 'say so' of individual directors who, accordingly, achieved extra influence and prestige in their own communities. In a more democratic society it was time to admit candidates 'on merit' and this had already changed with the 1925 amalgamation. Moreover, Lemass made it plain that he wanted to protect

CIÉ against TDs and county councillors becoming a new nominating coterie. The subject of Dublin Corporation's income from 'wayleaves' was a less sensitive matter, but it caused distress to several Dublin deputies. The DUTC paid annually for these wayleaves, i.e. for the right to operate trams and to maintain tramways on particular streets. Their rights and obligations were to operate 'in perpetuity' even it seems when trams ceased to operate. Mercifully, the opportunity was grasped in the 1944 Act to end these wayleaves arrangements, and it was provided that compensation to the corporation for their abolition would be decided by arbitration.

Seán Lemass's vision of a thriving, commercially profitable, well-managed transport company also envisaged that it would operate free of all unnecessary interference and restraint from government. Yet, in a long and important passage he showed how this freedom would be so heavily qualified that in reality it would mean little. Setting out the government's thinking on what were the essential 'features' of a satisfactory transport scheme he said:

> The first feature is adequate means of ensuring that the transport operating organisation will be able to get new capital in sufficient measure freely and cheaply. (Hence the provision where CIÉ would borrow under Government guarantee.)
>
> The second essential provision must be some effective means of ensuring that the management of the transport organisation will be conducted in accordance with the requirements of public policy; that the Government of the day will have power to insist that the transport organisation will be directed so as to facilitate the achievement of its economic aims.
>
> Thirdly, there must be provision to ensure that there will be adequate control by a public authority over the charges that are made for transport facilities of all kinds and in all circumstances. Fourthly there must be provision to ensure that the public will have ample powers to insist on the provision of adequate transport services in all parts of the country. Fifthly there must be ample safeguards to prevent discriminatory treatment of individuals using the transport facilities; safeguards to ensure that there can be no discrimination between one industry and another, as between one harbour authority and another; to ensure that all transport facilities will be equally available on certain equal conditions to all interests.
>
> Subject to these essential provisions and subject also to whatever legislation may be enacted to control conditions of employment in transport undertakings or relating to social services; it is the Government's view that the transport organisation, no matter how

constituted, no matter how directed, should be left free to run its business as it thinks best, that it should be relieved from the restrictions which were imposed by earlier legislation on transport undertakings, restrictions which were in the main designed to deal with conditions completely different from what now exist.

(ibid., Cols 1798/1799)

It all seemed to amount to a freedom 'to do as you like, provided you do as I want'; and Lemass showed no sign of being aware of the contradictions inherent in his statements. 'Removal of restrictions which were imposed by earlier legislation' was an intention which the Bill did not deliver in any significant way whatever. Special tariffs could be established for particular industries, but a later remark by Milne that such arrangements should be very limited shows that no real change was on its way. One of the key issues for railway managements was freedom to discontinue services on parts of an extraordinarily detailed network of branch lines built to satisfy economic ambitions which never materialised, or even in some cases, to satisfy the pride of local dignitaries. No change was made to the previous legislation regarding branch line closures, i.e. ministerial approval was required for any closure, thus ensuring that every such issue would be extremely political. One may say that Mr Lemass in the piece quoted above was being much more political than practical. The situation he described had something in it for everyone—the individual customer, transport workers, businessmen, local districts and local industries. He indicated how he expected that his 'essential provisions' would be achieved:

> As I have indicated the Chairman will be appointed by the Government. It is contemplated that the arrangement will ensure that the policy of the company will be related to national economic aims, that the company's finances will be well planned within the development period and that the issue of new capital will be limited as it is desirable that it should be limited, in view of the obligation the state is taking in relation to it, to sound projects. It will be the responsibility of the Chairman to ensure that the Government's liability under the guarantee is maintained at the minimum . . .
>
> (ibid., Col. 1810)

The shadow of the ongoing investigation into dealings in GSR shares overhung the debate and, unusually on a measure of this sort, the Taoiseach Éamon de Valera felt obliged to speak as the debate drew to a close. The government adopted the normal parliamentary procedure of moving an amendment to the O'Higgins resolution which had proposed that the second stage of the Bill should not be taken until the findings of the inquiry were available to the House. The government amendment was defeated by 64 votes to 63, with several Independents joining the opposition parties (Fine Gael, Labour and Clann na Talmhan). Later that night the President, Douglas Hyde, dissolved the Dáil on the advice of the Taoiseach.

When the Dáil convened the following morning to hear its fate there was uproar, and the story bears relating. A genuinely surprised Dr Tom O'Higgins said that all the opposition looked for was a postponement for two months; the decision to dissolve the Dáil was taken 'in pique and petulance'. William Norton developed this theme: 'We find the Taoiseach engaged in a night ride to the Park, arriving there about midnight as a political marauder beseeching the President to dissolve the Dáil, not because the Dáil wanted to be dissolved or because the people wanted a new election, but because the Taoiseach was in a temper, a temper no thermometer could measure.' The midnight ride to Áras an Uachtaráin became quite a celebrated event about which the *Dublin Opinion* would publish a collage of cartoons. But on that May morning Deputy James Dillon surpassed all in the rolling indignation and sarcasm of his contribution. To appreciate it the reader may note that Éamon de Valera had founded the Institute of Advanced Studies some years earlier and that President Douglas Hyde was 84 years old and not in good health at the time:

> The Fianna Fáil doctrine is that the Taoiseach hates politics, that he does not understand them, that he recoils from engaging them and loves to govern this country from the Olympian calm of the Institute for Higher Studies, his dearest pride and joy, with an Olympian patience that understands everything and understanding everything, forgives everything. Well it is a "quare" picture of the gentleman in the motor car blazing through the night up to the Viceregal Lodge to get poor President Hyde out of his bed to sign the dissolution: the Olympian calm, the Olympian patience, the Institute of Higher Studies and the President in his night-shirt tottering down the stairs to sign the dissolution. (ibid., Col. 2482)

De Valera's response was 'I warned you.' He had not wanted the 1943 General Election in which his party lost seats, but now his fortune was turning. In the 1944 contest the government party gained nine seats, partly due to a decline in Labour support caused by a split in the Labour Party and the creation of a new National Labour Party. In the new Dáil, Fianna Fáil had a majority of 14 in a total membership of 138, proportionally more than at any previous time. De Valera was elected Taoiseach by 81 votes to 37.

When the Transport (No. 2) Bill was moved in June the atmosphere was more subdued and the debate much shorter. Lemass returned to the monopoly issue: 'The essence of our transport problem is not the creation of a monopoly but the passing of a monopoly, i.e. railways once had a monopoly, but this was now undermined.'

He repeated his objection to 'state purchase of transport services' on the grounds that it would 'put transport in the front of party politics . . . the promotion or recruitment of every railway porter will be a matter about which political parties and political clubs will concern themselves', and matters of services or charges 'are things which will make or unmake deputies'. He persisted with the illusion that the Bill and its intentions were not restrictive: 'We propose that [CIÉ] be given maximum freedom in commercial operations.'

General Mulcahy, having regained a Dáil seat, led for the opposition and summed up their view of this 'non-nationalisation' Bill by quoting the description 'bastard socialism' used by Herbert Morrison, MP, 'a native speaker of the English language', of a similar measure by which private owners retained their property but were not allowed to run it (ibid., Vol. 94, Col. 855).

However, flawed or not, CIÉ was on its way. Commenting on the pessimism of some deputies about the ability of CIÉ to meet its obligations, in particular those related to the repayment of its authorised total of £16 million debenture stock, Seán Lemass said that he believed his critics were wrong, but admitted that they might be right. 'Probably, no Bill has come before the House since it was established that has been more fully debated than this one.' Its vital second stage, the hurdle at which it had previously fallen, was passed on 21 June 1944 with a comfortable majority of 69 (Tá) to 38 (Níl). The GSR stocks inquiry was still not published, but it would cause hardly a ripple when it did emerge.

CHAPTER 4

TRAUMA IN INFANCY

First years of CIÉ—Coal crisis 1947—Financial crisis looms 1948—Inter-party government—Milne Report 1948.

The first meeting of the Board of Córas Iompair Éireann was held on 2 January 1945 with Percy Reynolds in the chair, it being noted that 'Augustus Percy Reynolds [had been] appointed Chairman by Warrant under Section 39 of the Transport Act 1944 for five years from 1 January 1945.' E. C. Bredin, an engineer and formerly General Manager of the GSR, became General Manager, and Frank Lemass, an accountant, brother of Seán Lemass and formerly General Manager of the DUTC, became CIÉ's Assistant General Manager. Bredin would retire in 1946 to be succeeded by Lemass as General Manager.

CIÉ owned over 2,000 miles of railway, some 500 locomotives, 800 carriages and 1,300 wagons, i.e. over 2,500 rail vehicles in varying condition but mostly bordering on the antique. It also owned some 600 serviceable buses and 500 road freight vehicles, about 300 horses and perhaps 40 trams. It owned six Great Southern Hotels and, being the Irish shareholder in the Fishguard & Rosslare Railways & Harbours Company (F & RR & HC), it was the operator of Rosslare Harbour and leased 93 miles of line from that company connecting Rosslare to south Wexford, Waterford and Fermoy, Co. Cork. CIÉ also owned the Royal Canal, the property of the MGWR since 1845, when it was permitted by Act of Parliament to acquire the Canal Company provided it continued to operate the canal and charge approved tariffs to customers. The MGWR had bought the canal so that it could construct a railway along its banks to within 15 miles of Mullingar, thereby easing some engineering and land acquisition problems. Now of course the canal would be merely just one of many problems for CIÉ and would remain so for over forty years. CIÉ was Ireland's largest employer with a staff of over 21,000. It owned property in thousands of units throughout the Twenty-six Counties and based its headquarters in Kingsbridge station completed 100 years earlier for the GSWR, and commonly regarded as the finest piece of railway architecture in Ireland, ranking in the view of some commentators with the best in Europe.

The Milne Report would later estimate that CIÉ provided 80 per cent of the state's public transport services. The balance was provided by the Grand Canal Company and by railway companies whose lines crossed the border, i.e. the GNR and four small lines—Londonderry & Lough Swilly Railway; Co. Donegal Joint Railways Committee; the Sligo, Leitrim & Northern Counties Railway; and the Dundalk, Newry & Greenore Railway. The total rail mileage within the state of these separate companies amounted to 412, of which the GNR owned 225. In addition, 900 independent (mostly one-vehicle) concerns were licensed to provide transport 'for hire or reward'; of these only 28 were bus companies.

The early minutes of CIÉ's board meetings reveal little of the massive task of co-ordination with which the new company was faced. Some items though are worth quoting for the light they throw on the diversity of matters which the directors were required to approve. The first meeting authorised payment of special bonuses to staff for exceptional work following an accident at Straboe (near Portlaoise) on 14 December 1944 when the night mail from Dublin collided into the rear of a goods and livestock train. The goods train was stationary while its firebox was being cleared, the fourth such stoppage since it had left Dublin six hours earlier. References in reports of the accident to the total splintering of a 67-year-old, all-timber mail van and to the poor quality of fuel which caused the stoppage of the goods train, point up two of the problems which beset CIÉ in its early days. An employee of the Post Office died as a result of the accident. Another item at the first board meeting approved the leasing on a caretaker week-to-week basis of Eagle Lodge on the lands of Mullaranny (*sic*) Hotel to Dr Dyer, with the engineer's report being noted that the house was due for demolition. It was also decided 'in the national interest' to allow a 10 per cent rebate to the Royal Dublin Society for the carriage of bloodstock and livestock to its shows subject to the total of such rebates not exceeding £100. A contract with the Grand Canal Company to supply water to the Inchicore works was approved at a cost of 2*d*. per 1,000 gallons per day up to 150,000 gallons per day and 1.75*d*. thereafter, with a minimum charge of £600 per year. The new terms would increase the cost of water to the Inchicore works by £300 per annum. (After CIÉ's takeover of the Grand Canal in 1950, water would be supplied free to Inchicore; but when in 1986 the state assumed ownership of the canal the arrangement was terminated by the Board of Works.)

The minutes of the 21 February 1945 meeting reveal another quaint aspect of the early CIÉ:

> Horse Carters: proposed token scheme for efficiency. General Manager referred to a proposed token scheme for horse carters who had reached a certain standard of efficiency particularly in the care of their horses, harness and vehicles, the token to take the form of a button hole badge which would at the end of the year merit a cash prize relating to the particular token as under:
> 1st Class token £5; 2nd Class token £3;
> 3rd Class token £2; 4th Class token £1
> 57 carters qualified for tokens during the year ended 31 December 1944 which would entitle them to cash prizes to a total of £119.

Apparently the GSR had been operating this 'incentive scheme' (in today's parlance), but management deemed it necessary to have it revalidated by the CIÉ Board. On 20 June 1945 there was an item about a new bookstall contract for Eason's, while approval was given for the purchase from Eason's of their advertising hoardings at railway stations for £2,000. Apparently this was good value as management had a valuation 'based on recent estimates from builders' providers that they are worth £7607:8 shillings'.

The early minutes abound with such minutiae but more important business was also in hand. In December 1945 Mr Reynolds was reporting on discussions with AEC and Leyland's concerning a tie-up with either company supporting 'our proposed chassis building factory'. This proposal had its origins in the way in which the GSR's and the DUTC's orders for chassis had collapsed at the outbreak of the war, e.g. only 7 were delivered out of an order of 81 chassis placed by the DUTC in 1940. Reynolds was determined that this would not happen again. Discussions proceeded with Leyland's and in 1947 a contract was signed by which CIÉ undertook exclusively to buy Leyland chassis while Leyland undertook to assist CIÉ in establishing and operating a chassis building plant. Controversy about this arrangement with Leyland would break out in 1948 when it was criticised in the Milne Report.

On the broad front of public service the year 1945 saw improvement in both rail and road operations. Of course, after every merger, whether in the 1940s or the 1990s, one of the first tasks is to obliterate the names of the predecessors. CIÉ adopted a slightly altered version of the logo of the DUTC as its own symbol, substituting what became known as the 'flying snail' for the elaborate GSR logo incorporating the arms of Dublin, Cork, Limerick and Waterford. Of more importance, since the beginning of 1945 and particularly after the ending of the European War in May, the improvement in fuel supplies was such that in December 1945 CIÉ announced that it proposed to reopen all the branch lines that had been closed since 1942. There can be little doubt but that this decision emanated from government, or more precisely that the minister, abiding by his undertaking in 1942 that the closures would only last until times returned to normal, now decided that his orders suspending services on these lines would be withdrawn. In these circumstances CIÉ had no option but to resume service until it could succeed in obtaining formal agreement from the minister to closing the lines permanently. On the other hand, if they obtained such permission they would be required to operate replacement road services, and vehicles were not yet available for such substitute services. It is also probable that CIÉ may have felt that with its then tolerable financial results in 1945, including a surplus of £221,185 from the railway, it could afford for the moment to operate these lines. Work was required to restore the track, but in any event the planned reprieve would be very short term.

CIÉ was preparing other plans for radical improvement and modernisation of the ways in which it would respond to public demand for efficient transport services. These plans together with the financial report for the year to 31 December 1945 were announced at CIÉ's Annual General Meeting of Stockholders in Dublin's Gresham Hotel on 14 March 1946.

Preparation of the accounts for this CIÉ AGM was no easy matter. Craig Gardner, auditors to the DUTC since it was formed by the amalgamation of three tramway companies in 1875 and also auditors to the West Clare Railway, successfully won the CIÉ audit (Frank Lemass was an ex-Craig Gardner man) thereby displacing Price Waterhouse from the GSR audit. Tony Farmar in his *History of Craig Gardner & Co.* describes the challenge they faced:

> The new company was extremely extensive, with offices all over Dublin, thousands of employees all over the country, and a wide range of activities. Not least of the complications was the difficulty of consolidating the Great Southern Railway accounts, which were based on the old-fashioned double accounts system, as laid down in the Railway Companies (Accounts and Returns) Act, 1911, and the Tramway company's, which were based on normal commercial forms. The double accounts system had been invented originally by William Deloitte, and first enshrined in legislation in 1868. . . . Eventually the two forms of account were drawn together in a format recommended to the Minister by Craig Gardner's . . . The CIÉ audit structure soon settled down . . . Most of the physical auditing relied on certificates, and the meticulous internal audit staff. These station auditors were

responsible for checking the activity at the individual stations; their reports however were not confined to financial matters. In the old tradition of the railways they reported on whether the fires were lit in the waiting room, and how the station was kept in general, even down to whether the pennies were removed every day from the penny-in-the-slot locks on the lavatories.

(A History of Craig Gardner & Co., pp. 172/173)

The CIÉ Board on 6 March 1946 approved the text of the chairman's speech for the Annual General Meeting. The reported profits of £812,861, after payment of interest and dividend on debentures, were somewhat below the combined GSR and DUTC profit of the previous year. A tidy £324,000 was provided for tax and a 4% dividend was proposed to holders of the common stock. This, no doubt, was pleasant news to the shareholders, but the public at large would have been mainly interested in Reynolds's future policy proposals.

Rates and fares were to be reduced immediately by amounts of up to 20 per cent. No doubt this was seen to be commercially and politically wise at the time. It made commercial sense only to the extent that CIÉ's freight services could compete more successfully with the freshly burgeoning road competition, but in retrospect it contributed to the problems CIÉ would face in the next two years. Reynolds also announced that the board had decided that the railways would be progressively converted to diesel power. Five diesel shunters had already been ordered. Mainline stopping trains would be withdrawn; branch lines would be closed and replaced by road services. Another ten years at least would elapse before this heady cocktail of proposals would begin to be adopted in any serious way, and twenty-five years would elapse before they became the established pattern for CIÉ's railway operations.

During the rest of 1946 services generally were improved and, despite the policy announced at the AGM, several branch lines were reopened. A sign of easier times was that special trains were being operated to sporting events. But on the other hand the 1945 improvement in CIÉ's finances did not continue into 1946. According to the 1946 Annual Report published in March 1947, 'a disastrous strike of beet factory workers, the poor harvest and reduced production of turf due to bad weather conditions' caused a decline of 23 per cent in rail tonnage compared to 1945. Passengers were up on rail (+15%) and road (+14%), but receipts were virtually unchanged because of the March 1946 fare reductions. Livestock carryings which would be a major revenue source for many more years were down by 16 per cent. This was bad on the revenue side, and expenditure trends were also adverse: wages and salaries increased by £762,000 (+19%) while 'the quality of coal delivered to us in the last three months of the year had deteriorated' seriously. The directors' report presented these facts without comment as matters for the record. Presumably they believed that freight would recover, the rate of wage increases would slow down, and coal would get better. However, 'the reintroduction of Branch Line Services' was a different matter. 'Productive operating miles' had increased by 18 per cent, but passenger numbers had grown by only 16 per cent and the report said that reopened branch lines had been 'a large contributing factor to the loss on rail operation'. A railway deficit of £433,000 compared to the surplus of £221,000 in 1945. Other business sectors were profitable and CIÉ as a whole produced a net profit of £129,000—down £683,000 on its first year's results. The common stockholders were awarded a reduced (3%) dividend—one of the last dividends paid to private shareholders in an Irish railway company.

Much worse would happen in 1947. In January Europe became frozen over with the worst winter since records began. CIÉ's coal supplies had been causing problems in the final months of 1946, and in the New Year the freeze-up in Britain reached the point that coal could not be moved from the pitheads and exports of coal were prohibited. In January CIÉ's mainline passenger trains were reduced to four a week in each direction, while all services were withdrawn from several branch lines. In February services were reduced to three a week, livestock specials ceased and several fairs were abandoned. On 24 February all passenger services ceased with the exception of one passenger coach on night mails up and down to Cork and down to Athlone and Wexford. Goods trains continued on three days a week, but for all practical purposes passenger rail travel in the Twenty-six Counties had come to a standstill, except on the GNR and on Dublin suburban Drumm trains. At the same time travel by road had become perilous.

Michael H. C. Baker in *Irish Railways since 1916* recounts some of the travel stories of 1947 in graphic detail and describes the haul back to more normal service from this winter nadir of the railways. Having related how a railcar in County Donegal got stuck in a snowdrift 'to roof height' and a similar incident with a steam train in County Antrim, he continued:

> Travelling by bus was still more hazardous. The experiences of one particular CIÉ crew and their passengers amounting to an epic worthy of a Hollywood film script. The bus left Longford for Sligo, a 60 mile journey which normally took 6 hours, although the trains, when running, did it in two. Within a short while a blizzard descended and the bus found itself surrounded by drifts 10 to 16 ft high. As there was no chance of outside help the occupants set to work with shovels, an eventuality of this sort not having been entirely unforeseen, and began to dig. At more than one location they took 8 hours to progress one

mile ... Bit by bit they moved on, stayed when they could in hotels, although these were rapidly running out of food. The telephone wires were all down ... and three miles from their destination they were met by a party of 450 men, sent out by a councillor to clear the way. Six-and-a-half days after leaving Longford the bus entered Sligo in triumph, as the midday angelus was ringing, and at the head of a long convoy which had gathered behind.   (*Irish Railways since 1916*, p. 130)

Relief came to CIÉ on 12 March: American coal began to arrive and about the same time a thaw set in. However, lines which had previously been blocked by drifts were now inundated by floods and landslides caused by the melting snows. The coastal railway between Greystones and Dublin was cut in several places but was restored within a few days. Fuel supplies were still limited and normal services were not restored until June. In an impressively quick response to the coal crisis, some 97 coal-fired steam engines were converted to oil at a cost of £80,000. 'We propose to re-convert the oil burners to the use of solid fuel as soon as we are completely satisfied that the coal position has stabilised.' (Annual Report, 1947)

Passenger fares were increased in April 1947 up to just below the level from which they had been reduced twelve months earlier and rates for goods traffic were increased by 20 per cent. Traffic and revenue trends were confused both by the coal crisis and a two-month strike by bus workers. A further major wage award following intervention by the newly established Labour Court increased wage costs by £667,690 to the 'colossal figure' of £5,479,520, and wage costs had risen to 62 per cent of gross operating revenue. Despite massive changes in equipment, in standards and in working practices, that percentage would not change much throughout the ensuing half-century. Following this doleful tale of acts of God and man and after accounting for debenture dividends, interest and such charges, CIÉ incurred a loss of £912,000 for 1947 compared to its £129,000 profit in 1946.

The three-year-old CIÉ was already in crisis. In the first post-war flush of improving results it had placed orders for diesel electric locomotives, begun the construction of a Central Bus Terminal (Store Street, Dublin), and was making substantial investment in its workshops. Each of these initiatives would soon be deluged in controversy.

Meanwhile, Éamon de Valera's government had other matters on its mind. Seán MacBride's Clann na Poblachta was eroding Fianna Fáil's support and performed disturbingly well in a number of bye-elections. Despite his record Dáil majority, de Valera had the Dáil dissolved in midwinter before it had completed four years of its five-year term. The general election was held on 4 February 1948; Fianna Fáil lost heavily and was replaced in government by an 'Inter-party Government', so called because 'Coalition' was then perceived to be too derogatory a term. The new Cabinet was comprised of deputies from Fine Gael, Labour, National Labour, Clann na Poblachta and Clann na Talmhan, as well as James Dillon, still an irrepressible Independent.

Daniel Morrissey (FG) and principal of Morrissey's Auctioneers held the Industry and Commerce portfolio. Shortly after assuming office he received a most unsettling letter (13 March 1948) from the chairman of CIÉ, issued with the 'full concurrence of the Board'. He was told of the 1947 deficit of £900,000 and that still higher losses would occur in 1948. Reynolds asked for approval for increased charges and for staff reductions (2,500 staff reductions, plus perhaps another 1,000 due to branch line closures, were later mentioned by the minister in the Dáil). The letter continued by saying that the company 'considers the following measures necessary to permanently remedy the position of the railways':

(a) rehabilitation of the permanent way to enable increased speeds to be run with safety;
(b) replacement of carriages and wagons and the introduction of diesel electric locomotives;
(c) closing of branch lines;
(d) restriction of private road goods transport;
(e) contribution from the profits of the Omnibus Department.

It was only two years since the 1946 Annual General Meeting at which CIÉ had announced fare reductions and ambitious investment plans. The situation, or Reynolds's perception of it, had changed radically:

> given sufficient traffic the railway can operate cheaper than the road. The difficulty is to secure the traffic at rates high enough to meet present day expenditure. That it is losing high grade traffic to the road is borne out by the fact that the number of lorries taxed today is 18,750 compared with 10,400 in 1938 and that the railways are being used to transport low grade traffic is borne out by the fact that the tonnage carried in 1947 was as high as that carried in 1937.
>
> The Railway can be put in better circumstances but it cannot have the security necessary to its existence unless outside help is forthcoming . . . if then it is necessary for the country to have a railway it should be properly maintained and operated and to do this outside assistance is needed and a decision must now be taken as to the form this assistance should take.
>
> Outside assistance can be made available by
> (1) Nationalisation

(2) Subsidisation
(3) Restriction on other forms of transport.
(Chairman's letter to Minister, 13 March 1947)

An immediate response from the new minister was not forthcoming. Later on he would object to the fact that the letter had not been sent to Seán Lemass before he had left office, to which one might now say, in fairness, that the 1947 experience was so disastrous that it was reasonable to take two months to digest it and to test 1948's prospects before posing fundamental questions concerning CIÉ's long-term problems.

Three weeks later CIÉ's Deputy Chairman, Judge W. E. Wylie, formerly chairman of the GSR, wrote to Morrissey on behalf of the shareholder directors. Thirty years earlier in his professional capacity Evelyn Wylie had been prosecuting counsel at the trial of the 1916 leaders. To him much credit is given for strengthening the RDS during the 1930s and for gaining an international reputation for the Dublin Horse Show. Wylie's presentation of the facts was even blunter than Reynolds's and he challenged the whole rationale of the 'non-nationalised' CIÉ:

> If road freight, rail freight or even rail passenger services are involving the company in continued loss they must go, if the objective of the company is to produce dividends. If on the other hand the objective of the company is public service and the national good then private capital should not be employed.
>
> We are regretfully driven to the conclusion that there is no viable way and that the combination of public policy and private profit earning capital cannot succeed.

The minister replied on 5 June 1948. 'I have issued a request that there should be no increases either for omnibus, tram, railway or road freight services pending decisions by the government on future policy.' The deputy chairman protested immediately: 'Already this year we have lost £700,000 and that loss is continuing at a rate of £20,000 a week. . . . To alter that and to restore the possibility of a dividend we should immediately increase our income and drastically curtail our expenditure to neither of which essentials does public policy permit you to agree.'

The minister was not being idle, but his options were limited not merely by financial realities but by the political embarrassment that would be caused by acceding to the reality of CIÉ's needs. CIÉ was a 'hot potato'; it was regarded as a Lemass creation and had been criticised during the election campaign both for inefficiency and for the level of its charges. The minister desperately needed someone to solve this problem or at least to gain time before unpalatable but necessary decisions might have to be made. On 1 July 1948 he wrote to Sir James Milne, General Manager of the Great Western Railway until its recent absorption into the British Transport Commission. Sir James was requested

> to examine and review the position of rail, road and canal transport and to report to the Minister for Industry and Commerce thereon and on the steps it is necessary or desirable to take to secure:
> (a) the greatest measure of co-ordination of rail, road and canal transport;
> (b) the restoration of the financial position of the public transport companies; and
> (c) the most efficient and economical transport system.

Morrissey would later say in the Dáil: 'The Government came to the conclusion that the affairs of the company should be investigated by the most competent person available for the purpose. We were fortunate in securing the services of one of the greatest experts in road and rail transport administration. Sir James Milne is an Irishman who in a career of high achievement . . . has carried out many transport inquiries and has been consulted by Governments in other countries on transport problems.' (*Dáil Debates*, Vol. 118, Col. 45)

Sir James with the minister's concurrence co-opted three others who joined him as co-signatories of the report, while a further three were 'kindly placed at [his] disposal as technical assessors by the British Transport Commission and the Railway Executive'. The first three, like Sir James, were former officers of British railway companies and the second three were serving executives of the BTC. Mr Morrissey referred to them as 'a team of experts possessing experience and qualifications in transport so wide and varied that I doubt if such a concentration of knowledge and ability was ever before brought to bear on the transport problems of any country in the world'. Between them the members of the Milne team, during their careers, had acquired one knighthood, one CBE and one MBE. There seemed to be a naive confidence that these British experts would sort out the problems which were overwhelming our native talent.

The team was requested to submit its report before the end of the year and did so on 6 December 1948—five months after Milne's appointment. Critics of the report have said that an adequate review of the complex problems of the Irish transport industry was impossible in such a short time, and its conclusions therefore had to be suspect. Still, by the standards of 1948 it was a comprehensive document on the state of CIÉ and to a lesser extent on the state of other public transport companies, i.e. the GNR, the Grand Canal Company and the smaller independent railways. However, it entirely lacks any market analysis or consideration of alternative solutions such as would be regarded as essential elements in a modern investigation of its brief. The pros and cons of nationalisation which the majority or minority reports of so many previous investigations had proposed were not even considered by Milne, despite or because of his British experience. It has a patent bias in favour of the railways: there were no 'ifs or buts' about this question; branch lines should be maintained; the only difficulty it foresaw would be delays in bringing railway rolling stock up to a standard that would allow it to compete successfully with road services.

Milne did not recommend subsidies; it suggested that the government 'might however like to consider the possibility of assisting the company by affording some relief from the liability to repay sums advanced under the guarantee of debenture interest, and by meeting interest during construction on capital works undertaken in the national interest' (Milne Report, par. 4800). That was the extent of the direct financial assistance to CIÉ which Milne recommended. In the longer term the report envisaged that CIÉ would be able to pay the maximum dividend on the common stock, i.e. 6%, in addition to fully meeting interest on increased debenture capital. Coming from so eminent a group of transport professionals, this prospect must have been very welcome and encouraging. However, even on the face of it, many of the 122 'main conclusions and recommendations' necessary to achieve this happy state would involve considerable difficulty in implementation. Some years later Seán Lemass would correctly observe that none of its main recommendations had been implemented.

One Milne conclusion which CIÉ must have welcomed was that increased passenger fares on rail and buses were 'fully justified'. However, 'an increase in rail freight rates would not be advisable at present. . . . When the conditions under which the various forms of transport are allowed to operate have been equalised, better train services provided and transit times reduced', freight rates should be adjusted as necessary to cover costs. Better train services in the context of goods trains would have meant increasing speeds to pre-war levels. 'Equalisation' of the conditions under which the various forms of transport operated involved the novel and theoretically interesting concept of a central highways authority. It would take another fifty years for this concept to become fashionable internationally, though even today only one country in Europe (Sweden) has positively moved in this direction. Railways are at a major disadvantage, argued Milne, as have many others since that time because they have to carry the cost of building and maintaining the permanent way as well as its bridges, level crossings, signalling and safety systems, fences and ditches. In contrast, the users of the road system had their highways maintained at the expense of the public at large.

Milne recommended that the Central Highways Authority be charged with responsibility for building and maintaining all highways including the permanent way, major roads 'between towns' and the canals. The Central Highways Authority would be funded by increased duties from all commercial vehicles, privately owned or not, and by a levy on rail and canal revenues. Public transport would pay a levy determined by the relationship between road tax and petrol duties, which they paid, and gross revenues which they earned. The net effect on CIÉ of this proposal would be to relieve it of £400,000 of the cost of permanent way upkeep. The report estimated that the GNR would benefit by perhaps £100,000 and the Grand Canal Company by £3,000. This proposal evinced no interest from government or from the opposition and was hardly referred to in subsequent Dáil debates.

Another proposal which fell like the proverbial lead balloon was that CIÉ should reduce its accumulated depreciation provisions, thereby greatly improving its balance sheet by writing up the value of its assets and improving the profit and loss account carry forward. The accepted wisdom was entirely in the opposite direction. The GSR had not been making adequate depreciation provisions, but Milne was not concerned with the GSR record. His suggested retrospective adjustment of CIÉ accounts since 1945 would have had the result of converting the 1947 adverse balance of £811,901 into a credit balance of £75,000. Moreover, one of the reasons why the Milne investigation was launched was the CIÉ forecast of a 1948 loss of £1,300,000, unless urgent remedial action was taken. The new Milne depreciation formula would helpfully ease that problem also, by reducing the loss to £1,000,000. It reflects credit on the government of the day that this recommendation was ignored. Apart from the obvious point that CIÉ's critical cash position would not benefit from such an accounting change, there may have been a healthy fear of the scorn which would ensue if the suggestion was adopted.

A recommendation which did not attract immediate interest was that the Dublin government take an initiative with Stormont so that the Ulster Transport Authority and CIÉ jointly acquire the GNR in a two-tier arrangement whereby they would respectively assume ownership of the GNR track mileage, north and south, and become shareholders in the GNR which would continue as an operating company. As described later, Mr Morrissey began discussions with his Northern Ireland counterpart in August 1950, but it would take some time before joint cross-border action would result in the formation of the GNR Board in 1953. The report also suggested that a reorganised GNR takeoverthe other railways operating cross-border services. This would never happen; they would receive occasional transfusion but eventually they would wither and die. Milne recommended that the Grand Canal Company be acquired by CIÉ under section 31 of the 1944 Transport Act. Mr Lemass in 1944 had explained his hesitancy about involving the Grand Canal in CIÉ by distinguishing between its highway and its operating status. Such subtleties would now be less inhibiting. CIÉ and the Grand Canal Company would simply be merged under a new Transport Act.

Much of the interest in the Milne Report has been focused on its review of the state of CIÉ's equipment and its conclusion that diesel electric locomotives were not appropriate for Ireland. Milne also reviewed other capital expenditure projects planned by CIÉ in 1948; recommended that most of them be abandoned; and proposed a new capital expenditure programme. We will return to these later, but first the report's strong conviction of the importance and ultimate superiority of the railway mode for Ireland's transport needs merits more comment. As mentioned earlier, CIÉ's chairman in March 1946 had informed the shareholders that a programme of extensive branch line closures was planned. A copy of a now rare pamphlet published by CIÉ Public Relations Department in 1947 was shown to the author by Donal V. Stephens, a former CIÉ executive. Entitled 'Can we afford Branch Lines?: The essential facts on an important question', the small eight-page pamphlet is, despite its title, rather short on facts but presents the argument for branch line closures simply and starkly. After a brief summary it develops its argument before concluding with 'Questions and Answers', e.g. 'How can you hope to cater for fairs by lorries?' and 'Will not the closing of branch lines cause unemployment?' The summary reads:

> Operation of the C.I.E. railways has become more than three times as expensive as it was before the First World War. Here are the figures:
> 1912 £1,626,000
> 1946 £5,312,000
> Since 1912, too, door-to-door service by lorry and bus has been introduced—giving advantages to which the trading and travelling public is entitled, but which can never be given by railways.
> From the financial standpoint, therefore, it is far more difficult nowadays to justify railway operation than it was when labour and materials were cheaper, and when there was no competition from privately owned lorries.
> Yet there must be financial justification for running railways, because a railway system is essential to this State, it must be continued, and it should not require to be subsidised.
> What is the solution ?
> Our answer is that railways must be used for the work they do best —long-distance, heavy hauls, and mass movement of passengers—and

that where the work to be done is short-distance haulage of light trade and small numbers of people, it should be done by lorry and bus.

Our policy is to modernise our main-line railways, and provide road services to replace the branch lines which do not carry enough to earn their expensive keep.

The Milne Report's sympathies were entirely in the opposite direction. 'The closing of branch lines', it says, 'is one of the proposals put forward by the Company with a view to improving its financial position.' Forty-three such lines had been identified by CIÉ and Milne's hostility to CIÉ's proposals will be evident from the initial quibble that some of these lines 'cannot be properly termed branch lines as they provide connections between main and/or subsidiary lines'. It then contrasts estimated receipts and expenditures on lines which CIÉ proposed to close with 'estimated contributory value' to the rest of the rail system, and notes that the estimated losses on branch lines are 'open to a wide margin of error as they are necessarily compiled largely on arbitrary divisions of receipts and expenditure'. The Milne approach of course is the antithesis of cost-effective management: it does not consider whether better overall results could be achieved by new arrangements, and the same approach can appear today when vested interests argue for preservation of some activity or other which they claim can be justified by marginal costs. Meanwhile the overall viability of the concern in question can be ignored.

Milne's view was that

> The paramount consideration in investigating the question of closing branch lines should be whether their retention is necessary or desirable in the public interest. They are part of the national system of highways and if they provide convenient access to outlying districts their retention may well be justified even if the railway is unable to earn sufficient revenue to cover the full cost of providing and maintaining the rail tracks and service. There is no reason to suppose that branch lines in sparsely populated areas should cost more to maintain than ordinary roadways and, in determining their value to the community as part of the highway system they should receive equal consideration. (ibid., par. 226)

What if the population, sparse or not, prefers to use roads rather than the railway even if maintenance of the railway costs less than that of the roadway? What is the 'public interest'?—a chameleon-like concept which depends not merely on its physical surroundings but on the perspective of the observer. CIÉ were most unhappy with Milne's escaping from these questions.

> In all circumstances it is considered that any proposal to close branch lines solely on the grounds that they are at present unprofitable should be rejected. It is recommended that before any branch line is closed there should be a public enquiry and that the governing consideration should be whether the retention of the branch as part of the country's highways system is necessary or desirable in the public interest.
>
> (ibid., par. 231)

In conveying these views concerning the branch lines, the report reminded the reader that its recommendation concerning the central highway authority would reduce the cost to CIÉ of maintaining the permanent way, but it failed to note that the cost would remain the same even if placed on broader shoulders.

Milne's survey of CIÉ's locomotives was very revealing. The total stock of locomotives on 1 January 1948 was 491, with an average age of 51 years. A Table in the report shows that only 9 per cent (45) were less than 20 years old; almost 80 per cent dated from the 26 independent railway companies which were amalgamated into the GSR in 1925. Maintenance costs were excessive because of obsolescence, arrears of work caused by supply difficulties during the Emergency, and simply having too many engines for the work in hand. Milne contrasted the then current annual maintenance expenditure on all CIÉ's rolling stock, including engines, of 17.8*d*. (7.4p) per mile, with the 10*d*. (4p) per mile which should 'be possible in normal conditions'. Specifically, with regard to locomotives the report recommended that 100 be scrapped which would still leave a 10 per cent buffer for repairs and servicing over peak day requirements and a 27 per cent surplus over average day needs. The 491 engines comprised 65 classes of standard and 14 classes of narrow gauge units. A total of 79 classes, many of which comprised only one engine, seems barely credible even allowing for the fact that each of 26 companies was acquiring its own locomotives prior to 1925. Milne's suggested scrapping list would reduce the number of classes to 48. One must understand of course that CIÉ had inherited this stock only three years earlier; that new equipment was very difficult to obtain in the interim; and hence, that wholesale scrapping might have seemed imprudent. Moreover, as mentioned by Milne, CIÉ was without a chief mechanical engineer which might have been a contributory factory in the retention of such an excess of obsolete equipment.

CIÉ had announced its intention to convert to diesel electric traction in March 1947, but this policy found no favour with Sir James Milne and his team of committed steam railwaymen. Referring to four diesel electric shunters (500 h.p.) already acquired, Milne observed that British experience showed such engines to be 'economical only when rostered for shunting work for 18 hours daily'. By this measure Ireland would have a very limited demand for these engines. Two 900 h.p. diesel electric freight engines were due for delivery in November 1948 and Milne allowed that these be used experimentally. The big issue though was six 1800 h.p. express locomotives ordered from Metropolitan Vickers with Sulzer engines from Switzerland. Milne would not countenance this purchase. What Ireland needed was smaller more frequent trains and, in their view, diesel electric traction was an unproved technology.

> It is considered that the use of large main line diesel electric engines is unwarranted and in view of the high cost and untried performance of these engines, the design of which is still in process of development, it is recommended that endeavours be made to cancel the order placed for six large passenger engines which appear likely to cost about £80,000 each. (ibid., par. 105)

None the less, elsewhere and consistent with the idea of smaller trains they recommended purchase of diesel railcars:

> There seems to be considerable scope for the use of diesel rail cars in Ireland, and it is recommended that an order be placed for a limited number of cars, for experimental purposes, similar to those being acquired by the Great Northern Railway. (ibid., par. 189)

In addition Milne recommended that CIÉ build 50 new steam locomotives at Inchicore over the following six years. Other 'Principal Capital Schemes' were considered. Generally they received unsympathetic treatment and the most significant, those over £100,000, were dealt with as follows:

> Limerick Junction Reconstruction (£190,000): while a strong case could be made for an improved layout a modified and less costly scheme should be prepared.
> Store Street, Dublin, Omnibus Station and Central Offices (£500,000): 'It is considered doubtful whether the provision at Dublin's Store Street of a terminus for long distance omnibuses or the centralisation of headquarters' offices there can be regarded as sufficiently important to have justified the Company in embarking upon such an ambitious project, when capital resources are limited and large expenditure is required for the rehabilitation and improvement of railway facilities.'
> Broadstone—New Chassis Maintenance and Body–Building Shop

(£927,000): A modified scheme making use of existing buildings entailing an expenditure of not more than £100,000 was suggested.

Inchicore—New Chassis Production Factory (£500,000): 'The scheme to erect a new factory at Inchicore to manufacture motor chassis for the Company's use and for sale cannot be regarded as an essential adjunct to an efficient transport system. The agreement entered into with Leyland's in connection with this project, places onerous restrictions on the Company's powers to purchase, manufacture and market vehicles.'

To put it bluntly, Milne (pars 103–57) rubbished what CIÉ presented as necessary to renew its facilities and to move towards providing a more modern transport service. In retrospect the detached observer will conclude that Milne was wrong on many points and probably right on some others— for example, part of the economic justification offered for the proposed chassis-building factory was a 33.3 per cent import duty then operating, but output would apparently exceed CIÉ's requirements and the agreement would not have allowed export of the surplus. It would have to be sold to other Irish operators to maintain a viable throughput. Milne said that if a decision to manufacture vehicle chassis in Ireland was being made in the national interest, some concern other than CIÉ should be involved. In the seventies that approach would be adopted in relation to building buses and coaching stock.

Staff numbers in 1948 were compared with 1945 levels and the increase was regarded as unjustified. Milne believed that staff should be reduced by natural wastage and by a lesser amount than Reynolds had suggested to government. The Milne Report expressed satisfaction with CIÉ's road passenger operations 'which appear to be well and efficiently operated'. However the 'results of road freight operations are far from satisfactory. A large proportion of the fleet consists of obsolete vehicles unsuitable for the work on which they are engaged . . . the present stock of vehicles is excessive and should be reduced by some 100 to about 650 vehicles.'

Milne acknowledged that CIÉ, since its inception, had been confronted with very great difficulties and that 'the organisation was in a state of transition. It has had to deal with the dual problems of merging the managements and operations of two entirely dissimilar undertakings and of restoring the condition of the railway undertaking which had deteriorated seriously as the result of war conditions. These difficulties must, in fairness to the Company, be borne in mind when reviewing its activities.'

Milne was critical of the rather unique arrangement under which the Chairman Percy Reynolds had an extraordinary concentration of power in his own hands, independent of the other board members. The report remarks:

> It appears to be wrong in principle that the control of a large public undertaking should rest almost entirely upon the shoulders of a single individual. In our view, the Board should be strengthened and the Directors as a whole made responsible for the administration of the affairs of the Company. The duties of the Board in relation to the Government, and of the chief officers in relation to the Board, should be defined and the policy to be pursued in regard to the future should be clearly laid down for the guidance of staff.
> (General Review and Summary, par. 19)

The report also remarked:

> Large schemes for new works have been embarked upon without due regard to the effect they may have on the net revenue position of the Company or to the necessity for conserving capital resources for the renewal and rehabilitation of existing assets. (ibid., par. 18)

The final paragraph of the CIÉ section of the report records that 'No discussion of the changes in policy or organisation proposed in this report has taken place with the Board of Directors or officers of the Company.' (par. 497) Milne had explained while preparing the report that the tight schedule imposed on him by the minster would not allow him to have discussions with unions, board or with the stockholders. One must conclude that if normal discussions had taken place, some at least of the report's recommendations would have been modified.

Despite its fascinating insights into the transport industry of the 1940s, we must bypass much else that is in the report. As the Trojan horse of old was welcomed by the citizens of Troy, the Milne Report was initially welcomed in several quarters. It promised so many things: no branch line closures, abandonment of 'extravagant' schemes, a dilution of the power of Mr Lemass's rather unpopular transport 'dictator', no redundancies, no need for subsidies, and a transport system that would in due course be both efficient and profitable. But just as the citizens of Troy found that their horse contained unwelcome Greeks, the government found that the report contained much that was unacceptable or impractical.

CIÉ on the other hand had been under no illusions. From the outset they saw the Milne Report as a container of hallucinatory if not toxic gases.

CHAPTER 5

NATIONALISATION: ANOTHER BEGINNING

Controversy about Milne—Dismissal of Reynolds—CIÉ nationalised 1950—Store Street saga—Dáil debates.

Shortly after being submitted to the minister on 6 December 1948 the Milne Report was released to the public. Early in 1949 the nature and direction of the fall-out began to become clear. On 2 January the standing committee of Clann na Poblachta called for the resignation of 'those that have been responsible for the administration of CIÉ . . . pending investigation of the matters dealt with in the [Milne] Report'. The standing committee included two members of the inter-party government. Four days later W. E. Wylie, Deputy Chairman of CIÉ, wrote to the shareholders for whom he was the senior representative on CIÉ's Board. He circulated the 1948 correspondence between Percy Reynolds and the minister and between himself and the minister (see above) which immediately became part of public record (*Irish Independent*, 7 January 1949). In his own letter to shareholders Wylie was dismissive of the Milne Report:

> We would weary you by attempting in this memorandum to debate the relative merits of [diesel electric versus coal fired steam locomotives]. We only wish to say that possibly some of the stockholders may recall travelling during the years 1942–1946 in locomotives fired by coal when the fire box had to be raked out every 30 miles (and who can guarantee that such a position will not occur again).

Referring to the Milne position on branch lines (keep them open as long as they serve the public interest) Wylie said:

> Surely no clearer example of a clash between public policy and private enterprise could be found. 'You must keep the branch lines open—even if they are losing money' is a startling statement in an individualistic [sic] economy. Such lines are completely uneconomic and in our opinion can never be anything but a heavy loss maker whereas if replaced by road services they could be run on an economic basis.

Wylie made little comment on the capital expenditure projects criticised by Milne apart from his remarks in favour of diesel electric locomotives and rolling stock renewal before moving on 'to what is possibly the most important part of the report' (restrictions to be placed on private road goods transport).

> After many years experience in transport and with the knowledge we have of the country, we unhesitatingly state that there is not enough traffic to enable the railways to pay if unrestricted road transport is permitted. There is not sufficient traffic density . . . It is idle to think that management can make the Irish Railways pay if there is unlimited road competition.

This comment by Wylie implies that Milne was in favour of unrestricted road competition with rail. In fact Milne tried to have it both ways. On the one hand he said, 'Members of the public should be free to select the form of transport best suited to their requirements. Traders are the best judges of their own transport requirements, and freedom to operate their own vehicles is a safeguard against the danger of monopoly.' Elsewhere the report said that 'Retention of the right of traders to transport their own goods should be subject to such conditions as will prevent unfair competition. The interest of individual traders should be subordinated to the interest of the majority who have to rely on the services supplied by public undertakings.'(Milne Report, pars 35–48)

Those observations applied to what came to be called 'own account' haulage. Specifically in relation to commercial haulage, i.e. carriage of goods for 'hire or reward', Milne recommended two types of licence—local and long haul, with different levels of duty or licence fees. Local licences would limit their holders to 'the use of vehicles within a 15 mile radius from a point to be selected by the licensee and specified on the licence'. Another category, 'general licences', would be unrestricted with regard to distance but would involve double the standard rate of duty. Milne was not specific about amendments to the existing legislation which in effect since the 1933 Act involved quantity control of road haulage licences (ibid., pars 532–8). Fair competition, as envisaged by Milne, would involve private hauliers maintaining vehicles to an acceptable standard (enforced by regular examinations), and paying 'a minimum wage, which should not be less than that paid by public undertakings'.

For Milne to attach his colours to the masthead of freedom of choice and then to recommend such a variety of restrictions and controls on private operations might not have appeared as absurd in 1948 as it does today. Transport had been highly regulated for over a century. Wylie was dismissive of the entire package.

> To be quite frank, we do not know how to comment on these suggestions except to say that they show that the author cannot have paused for one moment to consider how such regulations should be made effective in this or any other country or whether double duty will stop anyone who can buy a lorry or get one on the hire purchase system from operating all over the country.

He notes that Milne accepted the case for increased charges which CIÉ had made in March 1948 but which the minster had rejected. Wylie continued:

> In the last three weeks we have lost almost £100,000 yet we are helpless to do anything. . . . We are the representatives of the shareholders who already have every £100 of their capital reduced to £10 and who are now faced with the loss of the remainder of their small savings without even being asked if they agree.

He quoted Milne's statement that 'taking the longer view the position should improve sufficiently to enable a dividend to be earned on the common stock . . .' and asked, 'What does taking the "longer view" mean?'

The government allowed another four weeks to elapse before declaring its hand. Its intentions were leaked to the *Irish Independent* on Wednesday, 2 February 1949, which reported that the paper's representative had been 'reliably informed' that the government has decided to 'implement substantially the Report of Sir James Milne and an instruction has been given to Mr Morrissey, Minister for Industry and Commerce to prepare a bill'. However, despite this 'reliable information', the headline indicated something quite different; it read, 'Transport System to be nationalised'.

The following day, Thursday, 3 February 1949, the minister sent for Reynolds to tell him that the government wished to replace him as Chairman, and on Friday evening the Government Information Bureau announced:

> The Government have under consideration the whole transport problem, particularly in the light of the recent report on transport in

Ireland submitted by Sir James Milne and having reviewed the position it . . . decided yesterday . . . [on] . . . the following proposals:

(1) The immediate acquisition of the transport systems (rail, road and canal) other than those of the GNR (Ireland) Company.

(2) The appointment by the Government of a transport board.

(3) Provision of compensation for stockholders and shareholders.

(4) Provision to ensure that dismissals on grounds of redundancy will not take place, and that such redundancy as may exist will be dealt with on the basis of allowing normal wastage . . .

The stock exchange was asked to suspend dealings in the 'stocks and shares of transport companies affected' including those of the GNR(I). Something had been learned from the 1944 share controversy, but there was no reference to Reynolds's position.

The Board of CIÉ met on Monday, 7 February, and its opening minute records:

The Chairman reported that the Minister for Industry and Commerce had sent for him on Thursday February 3, and indicated the Government decision to make changes in the direction of the company which would involve the present Board. The position of shareholders' directors could not be interfered with until legislation is introduced but he desired to replace him as Chairman as soon as possible.

At the conclusion of the Chairman's statement the remaining members of the Board expressed their regret and concern that such a decision should be come to without the Chairman having an opportunity to state his case either to the Government or before the Milne Tribunal.

That night Dr Tom O'Higgins, Minister for Defence, spoke to a meeting in Cork and his remarks indicated what would be the flavour of many subsequent statements about CIÉ. Transport management could be pilloried for the problems that existed and the previous government could be joined with them, making the attacks all the more rewarding. 'The Government', said Dr O'Higgins, 'found a situation where millions of Government credit had already been sucked up and absorbed following the mess and tangle which the late Government had caused regarding public transport. Last December they had reached the point where the company was completely bankrupt and where it could only be kept going by a subsidy or grant or credit of tens of thousands a week.'

On 18 February the newspapers reported that Reynolds had resigned and published a wordy statement to the effect that the minister made an order under section 39 of the Transport Act to give immediate effect to his resignation. The resignation and the ministerial order were fig-leaves, as we know from the CIÉ minutes: UK-based consultants had reported and Percy Reynolds was being dismissed. Thaddeus Cornelius Courtney was appointed in his place for an initial period of twelve months, but he would serve for nine years, until November 1958, during which period despite Milne, CIÉ railways would convert to diesel electric traction, losses would continue and another major government inquiry would be found to be necessary.

T. C. (Ted) Courtney was a 54-year-old civil engineering graduate of University College Cork and at the time of his appointment was Chief Engineering Adviser to the Department of Local Government. The press release on his appointment mentioned that his first post had been with the Cork, Bandon & South Coast Railway, but he had been with the CB & SCR for mere months before being involved in the construction of Ford's manufacturing plant at Cork and in Harland and Wolff at Belfast. He joined the National Army in 1922, moving to the Department of Local Government in 1925, then to Tipperary North Riding as County Surveyor and back to the Department of Local Government in 1934. While in Local Government he became involved in county council turf production schemes and in the Turf Development Board in 1941 where he worked closely with C. S. (Todd) Andrews, who would later succeed him as chairman of CIÉ. Together they co-ordinated a national turf-saving campaign which within a few months saw an impressive 34,000 people working on 946 bogs. Apart from his youthful spell with the CB & SCR, his railway experience included the more significant responsibility of being Railway Inspecting Officer for the Department of Industry and Commerce from 1939 to 1949 (*Custom House People*: Joseph Robins).

Percy Reynolds had a parting salvo to deliver. On the following Monday, 21 February 1949, the *Irish Independent* carried his statement, issued with the consent of the minister. It merits quotation for the light it throws on some realities of the transport situation as the forties ended, including the reluctance of governments to recognise such realities. Reynolds introduced his case with a bluntness that would attract little sympathy: 'The public will not travel by railway if there is any other transport available.' He instanced Curragh Derby Day in 1948: CIÉ had provided three special trains to the Curragh which carried 2,192 passengers, but there were 2,843 motors cars at the meeting. An excursion train from Waterford to another event carried less than travelled by hired buses.

He was scathing about the Central Highways Authority: 'an elaborate way of subsidising railways . . . would it not be much easier and cheaper (if subsidisation is to be the solution to the problem) to hand to the railways from the central fund the proposed new duty of 2½d. (1p) per gallon on petrol and oil?'

On diesel electric, Reynolds remarked that 'It is incorrect to say that diesel electric locomotives have a performance that is untried or that their design is in process of development. These locomotives have been in use in America and on the Continent for the past twenty years.' With regard to the Store St project Reynolds said that a central bus station was obviously required adding that 'centralisation of staff, now spread over six locations is essential for the proper administration of the company affairs'. One could say in defence of that project that transport managements had long been criticised for not bringing their act together, e.g. in the Ingram Inquiry Report (1939) and in the debates on the 1944 Act they were accused of still running the transport system as though it was owned by several competing companies.

Reynolds was very forthright with regard to the branch lines:

> The retention of branch lines is neither necessary nor desirable in the public interest. They do not provide convenient access to outlying districts and the permanent way on these lines was so neglected prior to the formation of the company as now to require too high a capital expenditure to put it in order. I am prepared to argue this case before any impartial tribunal you wish to set up.

The *Irish Press* on 22 February came to Reynolds's support in a lengthy editorial titled 'Reynolds v Milne'. After summarising the contrasting approaches of Reynolds and Milne to the railway problem the article concluded:

> The Milne report also made certain detailed criticism of the management and operation of CIÉ. But Reynolds exposes so many mistakes of fact in the report as to invalidate the recommendations that were based on it. . . .
>
> What is the position today? The Government have two reports, both of which make recommendations as to what should be done. Instead of adopting either of these views, all they have done is to decide to nationalise the railways. . . .
>
> Buying out the shareholders will not solve any of these problems. In short the Government are no further advanced than they were a year ago.

The *Irish Press* at the time was a strongly committed Fianna Fáil journal and the previous day it reported Seán MacEntee, TD (Fianna Fáil) rounding on the Milne Report in a speech delivered in Mullingar (*Irish Press*, 21 February 1949): the Milne Report, if given effect to, would throw the railways back to the days of the 'puffing billy'. The document could not stand examination or criticism. Sir James Milne had not the hardihood to recommend nationalisation of CIÉ, but it was being used by the government for that purpose. Criticism of Milne was not confined to Irish politicians: in England the journal, *Modern Transport*, published a leading article under the heading, 'Turning the clock back in Ireland'.

A special meeting of CIÉ's stockholders was held on 22 February when Wylie reported to them on the state of play. There was little else to do but wait on government's proposals concerning compensation. Wylie was reported as asking, 'Why was the Chairman, Reynolds not allowed to see Sir James Milne? Why had he no opportunity of putting before him his views and suggestions? There was such a thing as fair play!' This report must have upset government somewhat: they issued a formal statement that Sir James Milne had been given no instruction not to see Reynolds or the Board of CIÉ.

Within CIÉ some matters were moving fast. Inside a month of his appointment as Chairman, T. C. Courtney arranged to engage G. B. Howden, General Manager and formerly Chief Mechanical Engineer of the GNR, in a consultant capacity 'pending the enactment of legislation for nationalisation'. A year later Howden would become General Manager of CIÉ when Frank Lemass would be given the new title of Chief Officer. On the same day as Howden was engaged as a consultant, the board agreed that Dan Herlihy be seconded to CIÉ from the Department of Agriculture for a period of about four months to thoroughly investigate a proposal that CIÉ become the national operator of a new government scheme for transporting and spreading ground limestone. Herlihy would become CIÉ's Chief Engineer in 1950 (he was appointed General Manager in 1970) and the ground limestone scheme would be quite a significant CIÉ activity for several years. At the next board meeting O. V. S. Bulleid was appointed Consulting Mechanical Engineer and he would become Chief Mechanical Engineer a year later. Bulleid had been one of the technical assessors who worked with Sir James Milne on his report. Despite Bulleid's previous record as a steam engineer in the south of England, where he designed the Leader class of locomotive, he was to play a big role in CIÉ's later dieselisation programme. However, his interest in steam would be sustained in several years of experimentation with a turf-fired steam locomotive. Milne had criticised CIÉ for not having senior engineers in place. Courtney, an engineer himself, was quick to remedy this deficiency with these appointments of Howden, Herlihy and Bulleid.

Already, while the Milne Report was being written or considered, work had been stopped or virtually stopped on the Broadstone body-building shops, the Inchicore chassis-building factory (which would later be leased to the Board of Works) and the Store St Central Bus Terminal. The plans for reworking Limerick Junction were cancelled—reversing mainline trains would remain a feature of operations at Limerick Junction for another eighteen years. CIÉ also attempted to cancel the order already placed for six 1800 h.p. mainline diesel electric locomotives. Metropolitan Vickers agreed to terms for cancellation of the locomotive contract, but Sulzer, the engine supplier, had already built the engines and had them delivered to Inchicore, where they would lie in their crates for years until it was decided that, Milne or not, diesel electric traction was the way to go.

The Store Street story would become something of a saga. There was almost universal agreement that Dublin needed a central bus terminal for long-distance rural buses. At the time passengers travelling on these buses waited, boarded and dismounted on the footpaths at Aston Quay. Their plight had surfaced during the Dáil debates on the 1944 Transport Bill, with Alfie Byrne, TD appealing for less primitive facilities. The question was where to locate a bus terminus now that Store St had become a controversial issue. A body of opinion was in favour of Smithfield for the apparent reason that neighbouring buildings were derelict and that a large unbuilt-on space existed there. Some traffic experts also argued against the Store St site. Government decided that the newly created Department of Social Welfare would acquire the entire, uncompleted Store St building for its 900 staff, and in November the Taoiseach (John A. Costello) told Harry Colley, TD that 'CIÉ had indicated that they no longer required Store St for either bus station or offices'. Even the ground floor was to be adapted for offices. In fact CIÉ was considering the Smithfield site and a board minute in August recorded that the chairman reported 'on . . . acquisition of proposed site at Smithfield and mentioned that a draft contract had been received from solicitors re sale of Store St Bus Depot to Government'. It might seem that matters were moving fast, but three years would elapse, involving another change of government, before the matter would be finally resolved in a manner that would later become known as a win-win solution, with both CIÉ and Social Welfare in occupation.

Store St aside, in the ongoing affairs of CIÉ there was much excitement as Dublin marked the passing of its last trams. When the Terenure and Dartry lines had closed down in 1948 the authorities had a foretaste of what might happen on 3 July 1949 when the last, last Dalkey tram would run. On 19 July the Minister for Justice was required to comment in the Dáil on the disturbances that took place: 'A force of sixty guards including two superintendents, one inspector, eight sergeants and three motor cyclists were engaged in duty over the route. The crowds were so big however that even this force failed to prevent souvenir hunters from damaging the trams. No person is being charged in connection with the matter.'

In October 1949 the government published its Transport Bill which eventually would become law as the 1950 Transport Act. The debates and personalities that surrounded this measure might be controversial, but it was fairly simple in its effect. Government bought out the debenture stockholders at par by substituting 3% transport stock for their holdings. However, CIÉ would still be liable for interest on the new transport stock and were empowered to borrow from government if its funds were inadequate for that purpose. The common stock (or ordinary shares) were converted on the basis of £80 of 3% transport stock for each £100 held—not the complete write-off which Wylie had feared, but it should be noted that stock which had stood at £100 in 1925 was now written down to £8. In the case of the stockholders and shareholders of the Grand Canal Company, they received 3% transport stock on a £1 for £1 basis. The Grand Canal Company surprisingly enough had always managed to pay its debenture interest and its common stock also earned a dividend, averaging 'almost' 3% over the previous ten years. Profitable road freight operations and rents earned from canal property help explain this good performance.

With government now directly owning all CIÉ stocks they would appoint the entire board. CIÉ was released under the Act from all statutory controls over fares and rates. The minister explained that now that he would appoint the entire board he could rely on CIÉ to operate in the public interest and did not need therefore to retain the power to vet and approve all changes in fares. This would be 'the most direct and business like way' of dealing with a 'complex matter'. However, as events will show, the change was more apparent than real. As sole shareholder in CIÉ, government would still be able to say yea or nay to proposals to alter charges as circumstances, e.g. political considerations, would suggest.

Government also proposed to distance itself from the controversial issue of branch line closures. As circulated, the Bill proposed that final decisions covering lines already closed or suspended or only partially operated would be left to CIÉ, but any new proposals for reducing branch lines would have to be submitted for approval to a Transport Tribunal established under the Act. However, this was amended and, as ratified, the Act required that the Transport Tribunal would require to be involved in all decisions concerning branch lines, including the closure of lines already suspended. Authority to borrow an additional £7 million by way of new transport stock was also provided for in the Act, with the important qualification that such borrowing would require the approval of the Minister for Industry and Commerce and of the Minister for Finance. No changes were proposed in relation to private road haulage, i.e. the Milne licensing recommendations were not addressed. The Central Highways Authority—a major Milne proposal and the foundation for much of the report's strategy was also brushed aside by Daniel Morrissey. He explained to the Dáil that these matters could be considered by the new board which could make recommendations to government if appropriate. In other words the Central Highways Authority was dead. If government could not accept the concept from the highly rated consultants which it had itself engaged, it certainly would not accept it from the Board of CIÉ.

The common practice of finding a scapegoat for problems that might be due, in part at least, to government action or inaction was given a fine demonstration on 26 October 1949. The minister moving the second stage of the Bill described the situation as he found it—a loss of £900,000 in 1947 and a projected loss of £1,250,000 in 1948, which proved to be too low as the loss actually incurred amounted to £1,400,000. He summarised the 'drastic' measures which CIÉ had proposed to address this problem and explained his invitation to Sir James Milne to investigate and propose solutions. His review of Milne's findings began with the need to change the position of the chairman and with the report's criticism of financial control practices in CIÉ (*Dáil Debates*, Vol. 118, Col. 50). He then went through the various capital proposals criticised by Milne, but significantly perhaps in the light of subsequent decisions he made no reference to diesel electric locomotives. Then he revealed a 'further proposal of which Sir James Milne was not aware . . . a project for the construction of a six-storey luxury hotel at Glengariff. Land had been acquired and tenders for the building of the hotel invited. . . . It was estimated that the hotel, when completed, would cost approximately £1,000,000' (ibid., Col. 54). The CIÉ Board had abandoned the project before Milne was appointed and interestingly the old Roches Hotel in Glengariff, a property of high repute in the 1930s, had been acquired by the GSR in 1944, i.e. before the incorporation of CIÉ. The CIÉ decision not to proceed with the Glengariff hotel was made on 23 April 1947, some 2½ years before Morrissey's Dáil speech. This 'extravagant project' was now added to the armoury of brickbats which could be thrown at the deposed chairman.

Seán Lemass, the original sponsor of CIÉ and of Percy Reynolds, came to CIÉ's defence though in general terms rather than on specific points. Government, he said, was trying to rid itself of the transport problem by passing it to a board chosen by government and to a tribunal chosen by government. To which one might well say 'Good luck!' if the Bill could achieve that purpose. If, as Lemass argued, government was not taking enough firm action to produce a solution, it is probably not unfair to say that his proposed solution was simplistic if not disingenuous: the railways were the kernel of the problem; they were poorly equipped and therefore their costs were too high; they could not increase their rates to cover their costs or they would lose more traffic and make a bad situation worse. Having thus read the situation correctly, he evaded the unpopular questions of eliminating uneconomic lines and of restricting private transport, concluding as follows:

> If there is to be any solution to the CIÉ problem other than asking the taxpayers to subsidise its railway undertaking it has to be found in re-equipment and reorganisation of the railway undertaking in such a way as to secure a reduction in operating costs and thereby permit a reduction in freight charges which will ensure a larger volume of traffic. (ibid., Col. 1807)

At the committee stage of the debate, Deputy Peadar Cowan joined other north Dublin deputies to plead for the Store St project, unsuccessfully moving an amendment that 'notwithstanding' anything else in the Bill, CIÉ would operate a central bus station at Store Street. When wrapping up the discussion on this Transport Bill, Morrissey, in a subdued mood, was quite modest in his claims for its provisions.

> It does not in itself purport to provide an immediate solution for the transport difficulties by which we have been beset for so many years. I recommend it however as an appreciable advance on the road towards a final solution. The Bill establishes the machinery and the organisation which in capable hands and properly used should bring efficiency and prosperity to our transport system.
> (ibid., Vol. 119, Col. 1485)

The fireworks had exploded during an earlier debate on a supplementary estimate which Morrissey moved on 30 November 1949 to provide £4,091,000 for CIÉ to cover interest on debentures, working losses for different periods and about £2.5 million for capital purposes. Seán Lemass blamed the minister for the situation which had arisen. If he had accepted Milne's recommendations concerning depreciation and allowed the fare increases proposed by CIÉ in March 1948, he would not need the money now required.

The previous day a leading article in the *Irish Press* ridiculed the government's stance on CIÉ under the title, 'Muddling Along'. Lemass was known to be deeply involved in the *Irish Press* at the time and Daniel Morrissey was furious: 'Whatever tender spots the Deputy [Seán Lemass] has in his makeup none of them are located in his neck.' He protested at having to endure from Lemass 'a mixture of brazen impudence and frothy eloquence'. Thoroughly aroused, Morrissey decided to tell more about his frustrations with the Reynolds period in CIÉ:

> Remember further and do not forget it because it marks the mentality of the people who were in charge in CIÉ that as late as October 1948—four months after informing me that they had not the money to pay

interest on debentures that were due, and within three weeks of coming to inform me that they had not the wages to pay the wages of the men—they were embarking on a scheme at Broadstone at an estimated cost of £927,000.

Knowing . . . that they were going to lose between £4,000 and £5,000 per day for the whole of 1948, I as Minister for Industry and Commerce requested them to defer starting the work at Broadstone until such time, at least, as we got the report from Sir James Milne, and I was informed that they regretted that they could not accede to my request. They regretted! They were embarking on an expenditure of £1 million at a time when they didn't know where they were going to get the next week's wages. Then I am supposed to sit here and listen to Deputy Lemass, lecturing, denouncing and suggesting that nobody is right except himself. (ibid., Vol. 118, Col. 1622)

In conclusion, it may be noted that the decision to nationalise CIÉ was announced in February 1949; the relatively simple Bill to give effect to this decision was introduced in October, but did not complete its final stages until May 1950; the new board was appointed on 31 May 1950 and the following day the reorganised CIÉ succeeded to the business of its predecessor. There is little apparent reason for the fifteen months that elapsed between the February 1949 decision and its implementation in May 1950, though in the intervening period the External Relations Act had been repealed and the Republic of Ireland was declared. As we will see, delays between decision and implementation would be commonplace in relation to transport matters.

CHAPTER 6

PUTTING ON THE PRESSURE

Breakeven clause of 1950 Transport Act—Capital investment begins to make up lost ground—Dieselisation approved—Scrapping of steam locomotives—The turf burner experiment—Closure of branch lines—Provincial bus services—Canals—Road freight—Dún Aengus—Shannon cruisers—Refurbishment of hotels.

T. C. Courtney was confirmed as Chairman of the new CIÉ Board, appointed on 31 May 1950, which saw a clean sweep of the GSR shareholder directors who had survived through the period 1945–50. Indeed some controversy took place about the compensation they would receive for loss of office. The six new members included a Meath farmer and livestock exporter, who was also Chairman of the Dublin Port and Docks Board; a Cork-based company director; a former GSR Traffic Manager (1926–42); and two active trade unionists, one of whom, Senator J. T. O'Farrell, Irish Secretary of the Railway Clerks' Association (later renamed the Transport Salaried Staffs Association), was an old railwayman who had given evidence to the 1922 Irish Railway's Commission. These representatives of agriculture, industry and labour were charged with 'general duties' under clause 15(1) of the 1950 Act in language of which any draftsman or committee of draftsmen could have been proud. One can imagine it being reviewed in the minister's office—'Have we left anything out? Is there anything else we should add?' It is quoted in full for the more patient reader (author's italics).

> (1) It shall be the *general duty of the Board* so to exercise its powers under this Act as to provide or secure or *promote the provision of an efficient, economical, convenient and properly integrated system of public*

transport for passengers and merchandise by rail, road and water, with due regard to *safety* of operation, the *encouragement of national economic development* and the maintenance of *reasonable conditions of employment* for its employees and for that purpose it shall be the *duty of the Board to improve* in such manner as it considers necessary, *transport facilities* so as to provide for the needs of the public, agriculture, commerce and industry.

Once written and enshrined in law those 'general duties' may scarcely have been looked at again. Clause 15(2) was a different matter which would frequently be quoted, reviewed and tinkered with in succeeding years:

It shall be the duty of the Board so to conduct its undertaking as to secure, as soon as may be, that, taking one year with another, the revenue of the Board shall be not less than sufficient to meet the charges properly chargeable to revenue.

In striving to fulfil its all embracing 'general duties' the Board of CIÉ would fail to achieve the more specific 'financial duty'. Even if it were possible to breakeven, 'taking one year with another', one may doubt if government or the public would have allowed the new board to take the action deemed necessary. 'As soon as may be', of course, provided a sort of let-out for all parties. Perhaps 'as soon as may be' could mean 'never'? The realisation was growing among more serious commentators that public transport in many countries, better favoured than Ireland in terms of industry and population, had already become uneconomic in strict financial terms. However, no significant public voice was being raised in favour of the state providing regular financial support for CIÉ.

The conflict between 'improving transport facilities' and a good financial result emerges very early on in a sentence from the new CIÉ's first Annual Report for the period to 31 March 1951. 'A number of additional passenger trains was introduced with the object of improving the services to the public, although it was realised that the revenue they might earn would be unlikely to cover their cost of operation.' The range of innovations and investments made by the new board is impressive. In conjunction with the GNR (who provided the rolling stock) the first ever through service between Belfast and Cork was introduced on 2 October 1950. This 'Enterprise Express' was said to be well patronised. However, it would not last for more than a few years after which the 'Enterprise' reverted to Dublin/Belfast. 'Radio Trains', a form of excursion travel with music and comment broadcast through all carriages on a public address system, continued to be 'extremely popular and successful'.

The controversial years of 1948 and 1949, following the disastrous coal shortages of 1947, had seen very little investment in CIÉ's fleet. With the debate on nationalisation and related controversies behind them, the board, with government support, committed itself to major investment in new equipment. The most significant item was an order for 60 diesel railcars similar to those already acquired by the GNR. Milne had supported such an acquisition and GNR's Howden was now acting as consultant to CIÉ. When introduced in 1952 they would make possible the first major comfort improvement in railway travel for perhaps half a century. Showing a willingness to try to survive on the more significant branch lines, CIÉ also ordered 4 narrow gauge diesel railcars for the West Clare Railway. On 18 May 1949 the board had considered a report from Frank Lemass concerning the Drumm battery trains used on Dublin suburban lines for about seventeen years, and decided that they be abandoned forthwith. The total cost of the impressive new fleet of diesel railcars was estimated at £1,042,500. Apart from the railcars, 6 new passenger coaches were introduced in the new board's first ten months to 31 March 1951 and these were noted to be the first new coaches acquired since 1937. Another 116 were being built (mainly at Inchicore) costing £895,000. New goods vehicles totalling 1,057 were under construction (mainly at Limerick) at a cost of £506,000, of which 160 came into service within a year of the new CIÉ coming into being.

Thus in less than a year £2.4 million was committed to rolling stock renewal, which by general agreement was in an appalling state. Road freight vehicles costing £170,000 were also ordered, including 100 tipping lorries for the ground limestone scheme, and such assorted vehicles as horse boxes, furniture removal vans and road tankers. Fifty double deck buses, 159 new single deck buses, 20 tour buses and 2 ambulances were ordered at a total cost of £812,000 'to give additional services and to replace buses which are now obsolete'.

Accordingly, total new investment in the rail and road fleet in the ten months following the 1950 Transport Act amounted to £3.4 million, or just under half the additional £7 million capital authorised under the Act. Other capital schemes were very minor in comparison but give the impression of busy energy in action. 'A policy of providing improved electric lighting at the Board's principal stations and goods depots has been introduced and has been completed at North Wall (Midland), Waterford, and Kingsbridge Goods Depots'; new mobile cranes; modernisation of weighbridge facilities; extensive alterations for disembarking transatlantic passengers at Cóbh station; alterations and improvements in 'a number of the Board's station restaurants and refreshment rooms'; construction of 7 new restaurant cars (the first for twenty years); decoration and refurbishing of the 6 GSR hotels 'to maintain them in first class condition'.

There can be little doubt but that CIÉ was merely scratching at the surface of what was required after twenty-five to fifty years of neglect of its railway equipment and facilities, though ten to fifteen years would be closer to the mark for most road passenger services.

The expenditure on staff facilities deserves to be noted in the context of CIÉ being the country's biggest employer, having 22,100 staff represented by 29 unions. The 1950/51 Annual Report recorded that £13,800 was spent on extensions to the 'Staff Club' at Earl Place (Marlborough St, Dublin) and mess rooms, rest rooms, or dormitories at Cork, Broadstone, Limerick, Galway, Rosslare and Empress Terrace, Dublin, were repaired and decorated. The two trade unionists on the board must have welcomed such expenditure on primitive facilities, but they would have had mixed feelings about industrial relations matters. A six-week strike of 'certain operative grades' was claimed in the 1950–1951 Annual Report to have cost CIÉ £400,000—a very large sum relative to customer receipts of under £9 million. This six-week strike was then followed by an 'un-official' strike of railway employees at North Wall (Midland) goods depot: 'ninety five men were involved, all of whom were dismissed, subsequently eighty seven were re-employed, six did not apply and two were considered undesirable and not re-employed'.

This story is recorded not because of its intrinsic importance but rather to illustrate that labour relations caused difficult situations as far back as 1950. The ongoing problem principally arose from CIÉ being a large organisation, relative to the size of the community, in a very traditional and far from well-paid industry and represented by an excessively large number of sometimes competing unions. The industrial relations record would not all be bad. Relative to the national average and to the record of major transport concerns in other countries, it would prove to be not too bad at all, while some areas like rail operations would prove to be remarkably stable. None the less industrial relations was to be a perennial problem. Mostly well intentioned, patient and seemingly enlightened effort applied with varying degrees of energy from time to time, would often fail to avert conflicts, generating frustration for both management and unions, angering CIÉ's customers and hurting CIÉ in its image and in its pocket.

All told, CIÉ's first ten months of operation to 31 March 1951, under the new Act, resulted in a deficiency of £1.2 million, back to the crisis level of 1948. This was relieved by a non-repayable grant of £980,000 under the Transport and Marine Services vote by the Dáil on 15 March 1951. By the time CIÉ published these 1951 results, it was projecting a deficiency of £1,740,000 for the year to March 1952 (an increase of 40 per cent). By that time also Fianna Fáil was once again in government following the collapse of the inter-party government and the June 1951 General Election. Seán Lemass once again held the transport brief. In December 1951 it would fall to him to move another vote for CIÉ amounting to £1,817,000 which, he explained, was needed as a matter of urgency. Neither of these votes (March and December) included moneys for payment of interest on transport stocks which were loaned to CIÉ under existing legal provisions and were repayable out of some hoped-for future cash surplus.

Within weeks of his return to office Lemass had the more pleasant task of reversing the Store St decision. As heralded in the Dáil, CIÉ in November 1950 had sold its uncompleted Store St premises to the Department of Social Welfare—for £369,534, being the computed cost incurred to date. The board minutes on 21 June 1951, immediately after the change in government, record a letter received from the Secretary of the Department of Industry and Commerce stating that 'Government's policy was that the Store St premises or so much of it as may be necessary for the purpose should be used for a bus station and intimating that the Minister is most anxious that facilities for long-distance bus passengers should be provided at Store St at the earliest possible date and certainly before the coming Winter.' The board agreed that 'so much of the Store St building, as may be necessary . . . will be rented from the Department of Social Welfare . . . at the earliest possible date'. Another development that gave satisfaction to Seán Lemass and also to Daniel Morrissey was announced on 30 October 1951. The GNR was to be acquired jointly by the Dublin and Stormont governments for about £4 million, but the deal would not be consummated until 1953 (see below).

However, the more fundamental problems of public transport would not be amenable to quick solution by government decisions. T. C. Courtney's first report as Chairman of the reorganised CIÉ provides a competent thoughtful analysis of the public transport problem. Prepared out of the point-scoring limelight of public debate, it provides information on the investments already described and, even now, it is a useful data point for the changing situation in which CIÉ operated to its enormous and inherently conflicting brief. It is not appropriate to recount much of his analysis here, but clearly the advance of private motor transport was the kernel of the problem.

Year	*Motor Cars*	*Goods vehicles*		
		(1) CIÉ*	(2) Other hauliers	(3)Firms using own vehicles
1925	16,211	–	–	–
1938	48,599	647	1,300	8,400
1950	85,140	650	4,226	19,758

*GSR prior to 1945 (Annual Report, 1950/51)

Over the period covered by the Table, industrial output and the volume of imports had increased significantly. There was clear evidence too that people were travelling more. Tonnage carried by CIÉ on road and rail was being maintained at pre-war levels, but this concealed the fact that public transport was now catering for a declining and very price-sensitive market share. Passenger volumes on public transport were in decline. None the less costs were rising and, using the freedom conferred under the 1950 Act and presumably with the consent of Mr Lemass as Minister at the time, CIÉ had been forced to increase fares by 12.5 per cent on 10 September 1951 (previous increase, May 1949) and freight rates by 16.6 per cent on the same date (previous increase, April 1947).

In the new CIÉ's second year (to March 1952) the deficiency came to £2,092,000 compared to the projected £1,740,000 mentioned earlier. In the year to March 1953 the deficiency was held at £2,017,000. In recording these figures it is right to note that inflation which had averaged less than 1 per cent in 1949 and 1950 had soared to 8.1 per cent in 1950 and 8.6 per cent in 1951 (the Korean War years). Keeping up with inflation would never prove easy for public transport, but of course inflation was not the only factor involved in these sizeable losses. Results would be much better, with the deficiency almost halved to £1,021,000 in the year 1953/54 when inflation abated and another round of increased charges took their effect. The deficiency was reduced again in 1954/1955 to £867,000, at last falling below the pre-Milne level. The delight which this trend engendered was short lived. The deficit soared back to crisis levels (£1.6 million) in 1955/56, and continued deterioration was in prospect when government recognised in 1956 that the 1950 Act had not achieved a solution. The Beddy Committee of Inquiry into Public Transport was established as a result.

Such a financial overview only skims the surface of the 1951–57 period which involved an almost total conversion to diesel traction on the railways, cross-border co-operation to support the continuously ailing GNR, some branch line closures, development of road services, absorption of the Grand Canal and developing stresses between CIÉ and government. We will now explore such aspects of the pre-Beddy years.

An order for diesel railcars, as recommended by Milne, from AEC was authorised by the CIÉ Board on 14 September 1950, but in the protectionist circumstances of the time Seán Lemass wrote to the chairman 'regarding purchase in Britain of 60 complete diesel railcars instead of having the body work made in the Board's workshops or by firms within the country'. The minister suggested that 'if necessary the capacity of the Board's workshops be extended and staff trained with a view to executing all forms of work which may be involved in the provision of equipment for the operation of transport services'. The board considered and approved a draft reply to the minister explaining why the purchase of complete railcars was proposed (Board Minutes, 22 November 1951).

The problem for CIÉ was that rail services had to be improved urgently and the delay involved in tooling up and training for such a large production line would be considerable. Moreover, once initial requirements were met, how would the facility be justified? The Inchicore chassis-building proposal in 1949 had recognised this problem and envisaged selling surplus production. Later bus and carriage-building projects would encounter the same problem.

The minister accepted CIÉ's response and AEC proceeded to build and deliver. The 1951/52 Annual Report remarked on the first railcars being 'very popular with the travelling public who have commented favourably on their comfort and fine visibility'. Windows were larger than before and passengers also had forward views. However, the following year (1952/53) the report sadly observed that the 'continued strike of electricians in the Board's service considerably hampered the introduction of new rolling stock . . . Sympathetic action at the Port of Dublin prevented the unloading of a number of diesel railcars which were available in Great Britain for shipment to this Country.' The full 60 standard gauge railcars ordered were in service by the end of 1954 and a further 6 were built in Inchicore. For mainline use most of these railcars accommodated 44 passengers in mixed classes, but for suburban services they were fitted with up to 96 high density bus-type seats. In subsequent years as diesel locomotives came to be acquired the diesel railcars were demoted to secondary lines. Twenty years later they were withdrawn from service though a number, without their engines, would continue to carry passengers on the Dublin suburban lines.

Milne had recommended against diesel locomotives but the diesel question would not go away. Management submitted a report to the CIÉ Board on 8 January 1953 entitled the 'Resuscitation of CIÉ Public Transport Undertaking'. This report developed the view that:

> There is every possibility that if the Board was in a position to provide itself with modern equipment, particularly motive power on the railways, substantial reductions could be effected in . . . annual loss.
> (Annual Report, 1951/52)

Before the end of January the 'Resuscitation' document formed the basis for a memorandum to government which contained proposals affecting all the activities of CIÉ, but 'The most important changes visualised . . . were in railway working where it was proposed that steam locomotives should be substituted entirely by diesel traction.'(Annual Report, 1952/53) This memorandum was extremely bullish in tone: losses were falling in 1953 when it was submitted to the minister, but as we will see its optimism was extraordinarily ill founded.

> The Board, in its Memorandum to the Government, indicated that by changing over entirely to diesel traction and building new rolling stock, and improving facilities at various stations and goods depots, substantial economies could be achieved. These economies were of such magnitude as to give every hope of the Board being able to eliminate its losses on operation and enable the undertaking to be placed on a fully self-supporting basis, including remuneration of all existing and new capital required. (Annual Report, 1953/54)

Two months after this report went to government, Howden resigned as General Manager to take up an appointment as Chairman of the Ulster Transport Authority and Frank Lemass again became General Manager of CIÉ.

CIÉ WAS ALREADY operating six diesel electric shunting engines built in Inchicore, and two 'mixed traffic' diesel electric locomotives which had got through before the Milne barrier had fallen on diesel developments. In addition, CIÉ had decided to do something with those Sulzer engines which were lying in crates at Inchicore, casualties of the Milne Report and its fall-out. The original CIÉ proposal in 1948 was to build six 1800 h.p. diesel electric locomotives, each of which would be powered by two engines. It now decided on Bulleid's recommendation to manufacture twelve 960 h.p. locomotives using the Sulzer engines and electrical components from Metropolitan Vickers (Board Minutes, 20 March 1952). The mechanical elements, i.e. '12 bodies, 12 underframes and 24 bogies' were to be supplied by Birmingham Railway Carriage and Wagon Company at £12,977 per locomotive and the 'local cost' would come to £2,000 per locomotive (ibid., 12 June 1952).

Meanwhile the board regularly received applications from management for authority to scrap steam locomotives. A random example was the meeting of 28 May 1953 when the following locomotives received their death sentence:

Engine no.	Date built	Total miles run
7	1877	1,707,826
13	1880	1,654,155
31	1900	1,041,926
318	1901	948,407
459	1893	1,249,908
540	1909	1,195,104

The last named was a mere 44-year-old veteran compared to the venerable 76-year-old locomotive at the top of the list. On 30 June 1953 the scrapping list came to 29 steam locomotives, two of which were over 80 years old as they went to the breakers' yard.

The January 1953 memorandum to government on long-term prospects and investment needs received a favourable and early response (July 1953). The government welcomed the confidence expressed by the board and £5 million was approved for the acquisition of diesel locomotives. It was a momentous decision for CIÉ which a year later described the largest order ever placed for Irish railways.

> Tenders for the supply of a number of types of diesel electric locomotives were invited from manufacturers all over the world. Thirty-one tenders were received in reply, and, after detailed study it was finally decided to place an order for the supply of 94 diesel electric locomotives with Metropolitan Vickers Electrical Co. Ltd.
>
> This Company, in association with Messrs. Crossley Bros. Ltd., who will supply the engines, Metropolitan Cammell Carriage and Wagon Co. Ltd., who will supply the mechanical parts, and English Steel Corporation who will cast the bogie frames and bolsters, and motor cases, undertook to commence delivery of these locomotives one year from the date of completion of the contract, and to deliver at the rate of eight per month. The contract was signed on 5th May 1954.
>
> (Annual Report, 1954/55)

The order for 94 diesel electric locomotives was a record for British industry. Some small shunting locomotives were to be built at Inchicore. The ninety-four locomotives ordered from Metrovick, as they were commonly known, comprised sixty 1200 h.p. locomotives, and thirty-four 550 h.p. locomotives. Thirty-three of these locomotives were delivered by 31 March 1956. By that time also three diesel mechanical (214 h.p.) locomotives had been acquired to replace the remaining steam locomotives on the West Clare Railway, while nineteen (400 h.p.) shunting engines were being built or assembled at Inchicore. Deliveries from Metrovick would continue through 1957 and 1958.

The government approval in 1953 for the dieselisation programme also involved approval for expenditure of £250,000 for oil storage accommodation which compared to £5 million for the locomotives themselves. A major reworking of workshops and handling facilities, scrapping dedicated steam facilities throughout the network, and preparing facilities for the new era was also required.

However steam was not yet entirely written off. CIÉ also reported in 1954 that government had approved:

construction of 50 locomotives capable of burning either turf or oil, to be undertaken by the Board as soon as practicable after a suitable prototype has been developed, the financial arrangement in respect of this item to be separately considered when definite proposals are put forward to the Board. (Annual Report, 1953/54)

O. V. S. Bulleid, CIÉ's Chief Mechanical Engineer, was enthusiastically associated with this project of a turf-burning locomotive. Very considerable problems were involved but Bulleid was both innovative and persistent. Earlier experiments are on record: the Belfast and Northern Counties Railway (1862), the Great Southern and Western Railway about 1875, the Listowel and Ballybunion Railway in 1917 and a more serious investigation by the GNR in 1940. The revived interest in the early 1950s was prompted by strategic or political factors, i.e. the need for a reduced dependence on coal and other external energy sources, with their supply difficulties and price fluctuations. Public concern about this fuel dependency was reflected in Dáil exchanges when Seán MacBride asked Seán Lemass on 31 October 1951 for information 'as to the progress made by Córas Iompair Éireann in the development of turf-burning railway engines', and asked the minister to indicate to CIÉ 'that this matter should be treated as one of urgency'. The minister replied that 'The work is being pressed forward in an endeavour to get the engine ready by the end of this year.' CIÉ's Board minutes throughout 1951 and 1952 frequently record approval of expenditure on such items as a stoker engine, fans and macerators for the turf burner. Dáil interest continued and for several years CIÉ annual reports made brief references to ongoing experiments.

A monograph by J. W. P. Rowledge, published in 1972 by the Irish Railway Record Society and titled 'The Turf Burner—Ireland's last steam locomotive design', gives the whole story. Steaming trials began in August 1957 and before the end of September the turf burner was running with test trains at its maximum design speed of 70 mph. On 4 October 1957 it worked a five-coach test train to Cork and back as far as Portarlington using 'the equivalent of a single load of turf'. But difficulties were many and the turf burner never hauled a fare-paying passenger though it was used a few times between Kingsbridge and North Wall on goods trains. The turf burner was abandoned in 1958 after Bulleid's retirement. It was scrapped in 1965—'A pity', one retired executive remarked, 'such an oddity deserved preservation.'

The government response to the CIÉ memorandum of January 1953 also approved expenditure of £5,500,000 'spread over the next ten years on . . . the construction by CIÉ in their own works of carriages and wagons'. The average age of CIÉ's 1,300 'coaching vehicles' at the time of its nationalisation in 1950 was 49 years (Beddy Report). But already by March

1953 total 'coaching vehicles' were reduced in number to 1,152 comprising 673 passenger carriages and 15 restaurant cars, with the balance made up largely by horse boxes (174) and luggage, parcel and brake vans (154). It may say something about the significance of the horse in Irish life that horse boxes were included with passenger carriages among 'coaching vehicles', but cattle conveyance was handled by 'cattle wagons' in the goods vehicle category. As in the case of locomotives, board approval was required for the scrapping of carriages (road vehicles do not appear to have required similar authority). The minute of 28 May 1953 gives a sample of the scrapping decisions.

> General Manager submitted memorandum from Chief Mechanical Engineer seeking authority to scrap the following 28 railway passenger coaches comprising 6 first class, 8 third class, 5 third brakes, [combined third class carriage and luggage van] 8 composite coaches [combined first and third class] and 1 breakdown van, the age of which range from 46 to 75 years and the average age 65 years.

Thus, the youngest candidate for the scrap-yard, at that meeting, was built in 1907. The oldest had been built in 1878 while Charles Stewart Parnell was coming to the peak of his career.

New coach-building started slowly and it soon became clear that it would make little impact on the stock of over 600 passenger carriages. Accordingly, CIÉ sought and received permission in 1952 to import some 50 completed carriages in 'knocked-down' condition for assembly in Inchicore. These new coaches introduced in 1955/56 were known to railwaymen as the 'Park Royals', having been built by Park Royal Vehicles of Slough, Middlesex. Previous coaches were timber bodied mounted on steel underframes; the carriage body and underframe were built as two separate units. The new carriages were of lightweight construction, on Commonwealth bogies and the bodywork was integral with the frame. Richard Grainger, who later became Chief Mechanical Engineer of CIÉ, in a 1992 paper to the Institution of Engineers in Ireland, remarked on advantages of the new 'monocoque' design: 'Metal structures need minimal maintenance and repair compared to the traditional wooden body structure which despite using high quality hardwoods need regular and extensive replacement of body members.' The 'Park Royals' for most of their length were 10' 2" wide—the widest ever used in Ireland—though 8' 6" at each end was built to the standard 9' 6" width. The interior arrangement had three seats on one and two on the other side, with an off-centre corridor. Up to that time Irish railway carriages had largely been of the side corridor/seven compartment type. The 50 'Park Royals' were followed by another 55 similar vehicles over the next two years, with centre aisles and the larger 10' 2" width maintained through their entire length. *Irish Railways Today* by Pender and Richards provides an authoritative detailed listing of all rolling stock additions from 1950 to 1964.

The 11,700 wagons taken over by the new board in 1950 had an average age of 35 years, and the programme approved by government in July 1953 involved construction of 1,081 wagons. This approval largely overlapped a programme already adopted by the CIÉ Board in November 1952 for the construction of 1,000 twelve-ton covered goods wagons with underframes from Metropolitan Cammell Carriage and Wagon Company at a total cost of £640,000. At that time the board granted authority for the scrapping of 207 goods vehicles, all listed by type—covered, open, cattle and miscellaneous, including a solitary fish van. However, the board noted the traffic manager's comments to the effect that in view of the engineering report he had no option but to agree to the scrapping, but on the other hand wagon construction targets were not being achieved; 'since 1938 the number of wagons scrapped exceeded those built by 600 . . . progressive decrease in the number of wagons available can only result in a still further worsening of the Board's service to the public'. The relevant point of course is whether or not the number of serviceable wagons was appropriate to the traffic offering. The question of utilisation and average loads achieved would be given more attention in later years. The output of coaches and wagons was noted in 1954/55 to be the highest ever achieved at Inchicore works.

AS ALREADY NOTED, the original intention of government in the 1950 Transport Bill was that CIÉ have the discretion to reopen lines already closed or to close them permanently. The Transport Tribunal was to adjudicate on future closure proposals, but the Bill as amended required that all decisions concerning branch lines be referred to the Transport Tribunal. The board moved cautiously. In its first report it stated that it was 'examining carefully' the economics of branch line operation.

> An experiment on the Ballinrobe branch [i.e. Claremorris/Ballinrobe], under which similar services at equal charges on road and rail were available, was made for the purpose of testing public reactions and obtaining data which would assist in considering the problem of branch lines.   (Annual Report, 1950/51)

None the less CIÉ decided to submit some lines for consideration to the Transport Tribunal. On 30 August 1951 the board adopted a resolution 'To make appeal to the Transport Tribunal for exemption orders releasing the Board from the obligation to provide train services' on the following lines:

Woodenbridge–Shillelagh Birdhill–Killaloe
Skibbereen–Schull* Tralee–Dingle*
*Narrow Gauge Cork–Macroom

This resolution meant very little. Milne recorded in 1948 that the first three lines were already closed. Peter Jones in *Irish Railways Traction and Travel* dates the first two as having closed completely on 24 April 1944 and the third as having closed on 27 January 1947. The Tralee/Dingle line provided no services in 1948 other than a monthly livestock special. The last passenger train on the Cork–Macroom line had run in 1935 and it too was being used in 1948 only once each month for livestock. Even before the 1950 Act had come into effect, application had been made for permission to close some of these lines under the 1933 Act.

The new Transport Tribunal which was to adjudicate on these proposals had not yet been set up. In the Dáil on 29 November 1951 Liam Cosgrave asked the Minister for Industry and Commerce 'if Córas Iompair Éireann proposes to reopen the branch lines at present closed; and, if so, when?' Apparently not knowing of the CIÉ Board resolution of three months earlier, Seán Lemass replied:

> Steps are now being taken to set up the Transport Tribunal in accordance with Section 54 of the Transport Act, 1950, and the tribunal, when established, will be asked to expedite the consideration of any applications which the Board of Córas Iompair Éireann may decide to make to them in respect of branch lines. . . . it will be for the tribunal to decide, after inquiry, whether services will be restored either fully or to a modified extent, or will be permanently discontinued.
>
> I have already asked the Board of Córas Iompair Éireann to consider specially the position of all the branch lines on which services have been discontinued and to decide as soon as possible their future intentions with regard to these lines. (*Dáil Debates*, Vol. 128, Cols 91–3)

A fortnight later he assured Gerry Sweetman, who was concerned with canals in his Kildare constituency, that 'steps are at present being taken to set up the transport tribunal which will deal with questions relating to canals and branch railway lines'. When eventually established early in 1952, eighteen months after the Act came into force, the tribunal's chairman would be Dr J. P. Beddy, who would thereby acquire further familiarity with railway problems before leading the 1957 Committee of Inquiry which would focus further on the branch line question. CIÉ promptly submitted a second request for 'Exemption Orders', and in the following year it recorded that 'Exemption Orders' had been received in respect of eight branch lines out of a total of eleven applications then submitted. In 1954/55 the reference to branch lines in the Annual Report was more specific and provides further support for the view that, unlike the 1945–50 Board which wanted to close branch lines, the new board was trying to keep them alive— apart, that is, from those that were already dead.

The Transport Tribunal had made a 'modified Order' in respect of the Banteer to Newmarket branch line, authorising the discontinuance of all train services except special services for the carriage of livestock. However, CIÉ decided to experiment with a lightweight diesel unit so that it could continue to provide a service of goods trains, and to that end it ordered three small locomotives from the German firm of Deutz. The line was on record in 1948 as being used only for 17 livestock trains.

> This experiment is also intended to afford an opportunity to see whether or not the people in the area of the branch line are prepared to support these services to an extent that, coupled with the economies which are to be expected from the operation of a diesel unit, the branch will no longer remain a burden on the general finances of the Board.
>
> The future of certain other branches at present un-remunerative will depend on the information and experience gained from the new methods of operation. (Annual Report, 1954/55)

The experiment began on the Newmarket branch in June 1956 and was extended to the Gortalea/Castleisland and Clara/Banagher lines in early 1957 as the second and third units became available. As the time for a new major inquiry into public transport approached, it is appropriate to ask what in fact had happened to the branch line network since 1945 when CIÉ was first established: the answer simply is, very little. A number of lines had ceased to operate during the coal crisis of January 1947, but since then there had been no new closures. In effect, the 'Exemption Orders' issued between 1950 and 1958 only partly legitimised the status quo.

CIÉ'S BUS OPERATIONS during the fifties in contrast with rail operations were consistently profitable, returning a profit of £392,834 in 1951/52, the first full year of the new CIÉ Board, and £357,834 in 1957/58, the year during which the Beddy Committee was completing its work. The 1951/52 profit represented 9 per cent of receipts, while in 1957/58 the profit/revenue ratio had fallen to 6.5 per cent. CIÉ's total bus fleet numbered 1,014 vehicles in 1951/52 and grew to 1,153 by March 1958 (an increase of 14 per cent). Seating capacity grew more than these figures would indicate. Double deck buses increased from 507 to 674 (+ 32%), touring coaches grew from 52 to 60 while single-deckers were reduced from 452 to 415. Substantial building of buses took place especially in 1953/54, during which year 91 were put into service 'including 6 double-deck coaches for service between Collinstown [Dublin] Airport and the City, which are operated for Aer Lingus Teo'. The total number of new vehicles introduced between 1951 and 1958 was in the order of 250. In 1954 the last 'petrol engined and all four cylinder diesel engined buses were withdrawn from service' and resultant economies in operation helped to offset increased costs elsewhere.

An outstanding event in the fifties was the opening on 20 October 1953 of the Store St facility as the Dublin terminus for provincial buses and 'during the Christmas period no difficulties were experienced in dealing with the combined traffic of this Board and of the Great Northern Railways Board'. The opening was two years later than Seán Lemass had hoped would be possible (see above, page 72)—an extraordinary 'hope' in the circumstances of a building which had not yet had its shell complete when the Department wrote on his behalf in June 1951. The CIÉ facility was named Busáras with Áras Mhic Dhiarmada being used for the entire building. At the time the building was highly acclaimed both in Ireland and abroad and may be regarded as the single most outstanding achievement of its architect Michael Scott, whose firm also designed the Donnybrook Garage for CIÉ and would later design such other well-known buildings as the new Abbey Theatre.

An illustrated souvenir for Áras Mhic Dhiarmada, published by Basil Clancy at the time of its opening, had this to say:

> In Aras Mhic Dhiarmada, at once the headquarters of the Department of Social Welfare and the city's main bus terminal, Dublin boasts a masterpiece of contemporary architecture and construction which has already taken its place among the great buildings of our time. Work on it was begun in 1946 but changes in government policy prevented its completion until seven years later. Despite the delays and the sharply rising cost of materials, the building, one of the largest of its kind in the world, was completed at a cost of just over £1 million.

The Dublin public, with little else of twentieth-century architecture to behold, were not as fulsome in their praise. However, Busáras would wear well and would be compared favourably to most other public architecture of the sixties and seventies. Over forty years later it performs remarkably smoothly for Bus Éireann whose operations are now several times greater than those described in the design brief of 1946.

Dublin was growing fast during the 1950s and evidence of this expansion is apparent in the CIÉ reports of the period, e.g. in 1953 when 50 new double deck and 24 new single deck buses were put into service, the schedule of new and expanded services reads like a new residential property listing: Kilmacud, Mount Merrion, Walkinstown Cross, Ballyfermot Upper, Finglas, Coolock, Crumlin, Kimmage, Dundrum, Cabra West and Dún Laoghaire. The amount of detail in the reports of the fifties is constantly surprising, e.g. mention is made of the diversion of the City/East Wall route which arose because a severe storm and flooding of the Tolka River on 8 December 1954 caused the collapse of the bridge carrying the main GNR line to Belfast. New bus shelters and their specific locations are recorded. Just as the annual reports reflect changing standards for rail travel by drawing attention to such items as the installation of a public address system at Glanmire station, Cork, and replacement of gas lighting at certain other unnamed stations, in 1953 they recorded that 'a commencement was made on the installation of heaters in new buses for use on provincial services and it was decided as opportunity offered, similarly to equip the existing provincial bus fleet'. The reader who finds this surprising might need to be reminded that private cars were not supplied with heaters installed, except on the more advanced models, during the early fifties. Heaters were offered as optional extras on other models.

WITH THE MERGER of the Grand Canal Company into CIÉ, its working accounts disappeared from view. CIÉ's canal accounts henceforth covered both the Royal and Grand Canals. The road transport activities of the Grand Canal Company were merged into CIÉ's road freight department. Another effect of the merger was that the canal company staffs obtained improved pay and conditions as they came to be integrated with the CIÉ staff grades. The result was that the CIÉ 'Canal Working Account' showed a loss of £52,732 in its first full year after the disappearance of the previously profitable Grand Canal Company. CIÉ took pains to point out that the pre-1950 and post-1950 figures were not truly comparable.

The Grand Canal mileage was 361, which included the Shannon and River Barrow navigation system, compared to 95 miles for the Royal. The not inconsiderable work involved in the maintenance of this system is revealed year after year in the annual reports, e.g.

> Traffic on the Canal at Derrycarney, near Ferbane was interrupted from January to March 1954, due to a breach which occurred in the south bank of the canal. During the interval a substitute road service was operated between Tullamore and Shannon stations (1953/1954);
> Two pairs of lock gates for the Royal Canal and 6 pairs for the Grand Canal were constructed during the year and a new lockhouse was built at the 21st lock, Shannon Line (1954/1955).

In 1953 CIÉ took the initiative in asking the Minister for Industry and Commerce for approval of 'amendments to the Bye-laws of the Grand Canal to permit pleasure boats being used on that canal'. In the same year the Herbertstown branch of the Grand Canal (from Corbally to Naas) was closed, i.e. the Transport Tribunal 'released the Board from the obligation to keep the branch open to navigation'; it was retained as a water supply. Another branch in County Kildare, the Blackwood branch, a four mile stretch, primarily a feeder canal originating in the Prosperous area, had a different fate. The seldom used branch had been closed to navigation since 1952, and after an 'Abandonment Order' was made in 1955, it could be, and was, drained.

Freight was still moving on the Grand Canal as the following fairly typical extract from the 1955/56 report shows:

> There was no significant change in traffic on the canal.
> There was a decline of 1,300 tons in the carriage of artificial manures due mainly to the fact that sales were slow in the early part of the year. Cement traffic declined by 2,600 tons because of the slump in the building trade and the completion of the contract for building the ESB station at Lumcloon.
> Carriage of beet increased by 1,400 tons due to the increased acreage under cultivation and the higher yield per acre.
> There was an increase of 1,300 tons in the carriage of malt due to increased production of barley for malting.

At the time of that report CIÉ had approximately 50 barges in service and annual tonnages averaged 85,000 tons. In addition, a number of hauliers operated their own barges, though in 1955 these were noted to be in 'decline'.

CIÉ ROAD FREIGHT over the period 1952 to 1958 grew in terms of vehicle miles and tonnage carried. Vehicle miles grew by 12 per cent and tons carried grew by 27 per cent. If CIÉ was more than holding its road freight volumes, these volumes were a declining fraction of total freight moving by road. 'Own account' haulage was growing at a much faster rate, and the CIÉ figures conceal a reduction in 'scheduled services' which it had introduced during the wartime fuel shortages when private haulage was virtually non-existent. In contrast, CIÉ's 'direct services' had increased, e.g. contract arrangements with county councils for transport of road-building materials and carriage of ground limestone under the national scheme supervised by the Department of Agriculture.

The powered road fleet of CIÉ which appears to have been renewed on a fairly regular basis during the fifties changed little in total numbers (709 in

1952 versus 700 in 1958). However the increase in trailers (+14%) and containers (+ 74%) reflect the increasing power of the motor units and the increasing tendency towards bulk and specialised container traffic as against general merchandise. Livestock carried fell by about 15 per cent. Increasingly, smaller animals (sheep and pigs) were being moved by private hauliers and while fluctuating from year to year CIÉ carryings of cattle by road actually increased over the period.

Commercial goods vehicles operated by hauliers had actually declined, according to Beddy, in the five years to 1956, but the number of such vehicles operated on 'own account' had increased by 75 per cent over the same period and now amounted to 90 per cent of registered commercial goods vehicles. The use of private hauliers by CIÉ is another aspect of road freight activity which was not immediately apparent from the figures. For example, in the year to 31 March 1956 CIÉ carried 1.9 million tons of beet, road-making materials and ground limestone on its own road vehicles, and subcontracted 0.9 million tons to private hauliers from whom it collected a commission.

Meanwhile horses were still hauling loads but they were getting fewer. In 1958 horse-drawn vehicles numbered 300 compared to 396 in 1952. The animals dropped by a similar proportion: 218 in 1958 compared to 283 in 1952. Certain Dublin city mail services for the Post Office were operated by CIÉ horse-drawn vehicles until 1955, in which year they were replaced by 20 motor vehicles. Horses would survive for many more years and not be finally replaced until November 1968.

In terms of profit, road freight was not a specially good performer. Of course it performed very much better than the railway and never incurred a loss in the period we are covering. Nevertheless, in 1952 the profit reported for road freight was a mere one per cent of receipts, though in 1957/58 when receipts amounted to £1,741,000, profits came to £47,756—a 2.7 per cent profit ratio. The road freight profits throughout the period were declared after transferring £50,000 from the railway account as a contribution towards losses incurred on 'Railhead collection and Delivery Services'. Clearly that £50,000 figure must have been very arbitrary and could well have been inadequate. The point to note is that with or without that £50,000 the return from CIÉ's road freight activities was sufficiently poor to suggest that there were problems there somewhere which would emerge, as indeed they did, in later years.

THE STEAMER SERVICE to the Aran Islands came into CIÉ's remit in August 1951 when it was requested to take responsibility for the operation of the s.s. Dún Aengus by the Department of Industry and Commerce. The much storied Dún Aengus previously operated by the Galway Bay Steamship

Company was already a veteran with over fifty years sailing to its credit when it was taken over by CIÉ, and was noted to be the oldest vessel in regular operation by a European railway. It needed an immediate overhaul which was performed by the Cork Dockyard Company, and while CIÉ noted that it would have to be replaced, this took much longer than anticipated. The annual reports chronicle the vessel's performance: its serviceability, passenger and merchandise carryings, as is evident from this extract:

> The fine Summer and favourable sea-going conditions encouraged passenger travel to the Aran Islands. Merchandise traffic increased due to various works taking place on the Islands (such as road surfacing at Inishmore and installation of water works system), and to the demand for increased quantities of foodstuffs and other merchandise as a result of a greater number of visitors to the Islands. . . .
>
> The Dún Aengus was withdrawn from service for survey on the 3rd March, 1956, and at the close of the year was still absent, being replaced in the meantime by the vessel Nabro.
>
> Improvements to the bar of the s.s. Dún Aengus were effected and a refrigerator installed. (Annual Report, 1955/56)

The Dún Aengus continued to plough the waves of Galway Bay until it was almost 60 years old, being replaced by the Naomh Éanna which 'carries more passengers in greater comfort' on 7 May 1958. The balance sheets for 31 March 1958 and 1959 seem to indicate that the Naomh Éanna cost about £130,000.

CIÉ ALSO OPERATED cruisers on the Shannon. Board minutes (11 November 1954) record that the Minister for Industry and Commerce (William Norton) requested CIÉ 'to provide boats on the Shannon for conveyance of tourists and local residents'. The board's decision was succinct: 'Board to provide passenger service on River Shannon and its lakes. Service in first instance to consist of two suitable boats.' While the board made this decision only because of government pressure, the organisation set about the task with some enthusiasm, probably viewing the Shannon cruisers as nicely complementing its growing tourist activities. E. A. C. (Eddie) Kimpton, OBE, a former naval officer, was transferred from the road freight section to look after the business. The first cruiser purchased was the St Brendan, with a gross tonnage of 44.5 tons and 'covered accommodation for 150 passengers'. It had been built in 1937 and operated on the Seine under the name L'hombre during the Paris Exhibition of that year. At the time of its purchase it gloried under the name Cardinal Wolsey and was operating on

Cover of *Dublin Opinion* as general election campaign began, caused by defeat of Transport (No. 1) Bill 1944; from left: Dr Jim Ryan, Seán Lemass, Frank Aiken, Seán T. Ó Ceallaigh and Eamon de Valera (*Dublin Opinion*, June 1944)

THE HOLDING UP OF THE TRANSPORT BILL
" . . . . . and, to conclude,
The victory fell on us." (MACBETH.)

PHOENIX PARK MURDER.

Cartoons prompted by Eamon de Valera's late night visit to Áras an Uachtaráin to obtain dissolution of the Dáil following defeat of the Transport (No. 1) Bill 1944 (*Dublin Opinion*, June 1944)

Percy Reynolds, Chairman 1945–49

Seán Lemass, Minister for Industry and Commerce, for various periods 1932–54, and Taoiseach 1957–66 (G. A. Duncan)

T. C. Courtney, Chairman 1949–58

Frank Lemass, General Manager 1946–50, 1953–70

Dr C. S. Andrews, Chairman 1958–66

Erskine Childers, Minister for Transport and Power 1959–69 (Maxwell's Photo Agency)

T. P. Hogan, Chairman 1966–73

Dr Liam St John Devlin, Chairman 1974–83

No. 36, built by Bury Curtis & Kennedy of Liverpool in 1847 for the GS & WR; withdrawn in 1874; restored by CIÉ in 1950 and placed on permanent exhibition in Kent station, Cork

No. 184, built by the GS & WR at Inchicore works in 1880; withdrawn in 1964; preserved by CIÉ and now in the care of the Railway Preservation Society of Ireland

One of fifteen 60 class locomotives built by the GS & WR at Inchicore works between 1885 and 1895

Maedhbh—one of the three 800 class steam locomotives built by the GSR in Inchicore works in 1939; withdrawn in 1959; now on permanent display at the Ulster Folk and Transport Museum outside Belfast

Inchicore built 3rd class coach, dating from 1937; withdrawn in 1973

Drumm battery railcars, built in Inchicore works; entered service in 1939; converted to locomotive hauled coaches in 1950 and finally withdrawn in 1952

Cork to Belfast Enterprise service hauled by a 400 class locomotive leaving Cork tunnel

Belfast to Cork Enterprise service departing Amiens Street station, Dublin, hauled by one of the 800 class Queens

One of seven 160 h.p. diesel mechanical locomotives for branch line working; supplied in 1956 by Deutz of Germany, on display at Cahir station

One of five Mirrlees-engined diesel electric shunting locomotives built at Inchicore in 1947/48

the Thames. In 1956 the St Brendan was joined on the Shannon by the St Ciarán. This 20-year-old vessel had operated on the Norfolk Broads as the Wrexham Belle. The St Brendan seems to have cost about £21,000 and the St Ciarán about £38,000. Business on these Shannon cruisers never achieved CIÉ's expectations. Weather was blamed in some years for disappointing traffic—'river services of their nature are particularly dependent on good weather'—but in dry summers they would be unable to operate north of Athlone, thus cutting out Carrick-on-Shannon excursions. The traffic was mainly derived from charter parties (club, school or factory outings) and from CIÉ coach tours when a trip on the Shannon could be built into the travel programme. The operation of these Shannon cruisers never generated a profit but would continue for seventeen years.

Having taken the Dún Aengus and the Shannon cruisers on board, CIÉ would say 'enough is enough' when the next water-based service was offered to it. On 5 January 1956 it declined a 'request to Chairman from the Minister for Industry and Commerce suggesting that the ferry service to Cape Clear Island (Co. Cork) at present operated by the Minister for Lands be taken over and operated by the Board'.

IN THE CASE of CIÉ's hotels, the first report of the 1950 Board stated that they 'are operating successfully and money and care are being expended to ensure that they are maintained in a first class condition'. However, the 1951/52 accounts showed a loss of £25,000 for the combined hotels, refreshment rooms and dining cars and noted that the contract with Gordon Hotels Limited under which that company had been responsible for some years for the management of hotels and catering was not renewed. In the following year under CIÉ's own management 'economies were effected by the closing of Parknasilla and Mulrany during the off-season' and by the 'reduction in staff at other hotels to the minimum necessary to meet the amount of business offering during the Winter months'. A profit of £7,000 was achieved and each year thereafter profits improved until they reached £40,288 in 1957/58.

The reports on hotel operations throw a fascinating light on what we would regard as primitive hotel standards and facilities, even in first-class hotels, during the fifties. Progress which was deemed to merit comment in annual reports includes such items as:

> At Killarney Hotel a new souvenir sales shop was set up for dealing in hand-made products. This has proved very attractive and has been favourably commented on by visitors (1952/53).
> Telephones were installed in a number of bedrooms in each of the Board's six hotels and larger switchboards were installed at Killarney and Parknasilla (1953/54).

At Killarney Hotel five additional 'en suite' bathrooms were provided bringing the number of private bathrooms in this hotel to twenty-seven. Other improvements in the hotel included the ladies' powder room, staff quarters and kitchen service area and the provision of a mobile cocktail bar for use at functions, dances etc. (1955/56).

While such detailed comment gives the flavour of the times, it seems inappropriate in the published reports of a major transport concern. They would cease in 1958/59. It seems that the procedure required each hotel manager to report something every year and such minor items as improved lighting, redecoration of a number of bedrooms or the reconstruction of a dance floor could make it into the hotel and catering section of CIÉ's Annual Report alongside more substantial items such as the 'building of a new wing of thirty three en suite bedrooms' at Killarney (1957/58).

WE NOW RETURN to the broader picture of CIÉ's finances and its relationship with its political masters over the period 1953 to 1957 prior to the appointment of the Beddy Committee of Inquiry into Internal Transport.

CHAPTER 7

A FALSE DAWN

Short-lived financial improvement—CIÉ asks for review of transport policy—GNR crisis—Formation of GNRB—Stormont prunes GNRB lines—Dissolution of GNRB—Appointment of Beddy Committee.

In June 1953, with the 'consent of the Minister for Industry and Commerce and with the approval of the Minister for Finance', CIÉ issued £2,500,000 5% (guaranteed) transport stock. This issue would fund the initial investment converting the railways to diesel traction. Early in the following year CIÉ was able to accede to a government request to lend it £1 million of the receipts of the issue at a rate of 1.625% until certain payments became due. In April 1955 a further £4,500,000 transport stock was issued at a discount of 3.5% and an interest coupon of 4.25%. Meanwhile, as we have seen, CIÉ's operating results were improving: the 1953/54 losses at £1,021,069 were a full £1 million less than those incurred in the two previous years. Grants were received for the years to March 1954 to cover these losses, but CIÉ's improving cash and operating situation contrasted with that of the public finances which were getting into difficulty. Soon this would have repercussions on CIÉ.

At a general election in May 1954 after a number of deflationary budgets and with rising unemployment and emigration the minority Fianna Fáil government lost four seats and yielded power to a second inter-party government. Tim Pat Coogan in his *De Valera* observed that the new government's performance would call to mind not so much that of a 'phoenix rising from its ashes' but that of 'a raven flying over a stricken field'. It was the era of credit restrictions and of balance of payments crises aggravated by the Suez War. William Norton, leader of the Labour Party, became Tánaiste and Minister for Industry and Commerce, while Gerard Sweetman was installed as Minister for Finance. The Department of Finance seems to have decided that CIÉ was having it too easy and wrote to the Department of Industry and Commerce proposing a 'Statement of Principles' on the financing of CIÉ. This was discussed by the Tánaiste and his officials on the morning of 14 February 1955. There were three principal issues:

> (a) submission of an annual budget for consideration by the Department of Finance (and Industry and Commerce);
> (b) no further votes to meet operating losses which henceforth were to be financed by CIÉ's own bank borrowings—this had already been decided upon by the outgoing Fianna Fáil administration; and
> (c) clarification of sums which were to be repaid by CIÉ to the exchequer.

The Department's minute of that meeting in the National Archives reveals that there had been a dispute between CIÉ and the civil service as to what items were properly chargeable to revenue as against the capital account. In addition, both CIÉ and the Department of Industry and Commerce were concerned at the proposed closer involvement of the Department of Finance in CIÉ financing:

> The Tánaiste, [Mr Norton] said he could see no objection to the proposal that CIÉ should submit an annual budget with adequate explanations. CIÉ could not expect to quote their financial requirements and have them met without making some explanations. Having regard to previous episodes, viz. the charging to revenue expenditure of items on the approved Capital Programme of May, 1952 and to the attempted transfer of nearly £1 million capital expenditure to the revenue account in 1954/55, CIÉ could hardly expect that their claims would be accepted without examination. The Secretary [of Dept. of Industry and Commerce, Thekla Beere] explained that what CIÉ feared was an unduly detailed examination by the Department of Finance with consequent long delay. The Secretary said that . . . the application of the principle would depend on whether Finance would operate it in a reasonable manner and despite some previous experience to the contrary, he was not without hope they would do so.

While Ms Thekla Beere was the first woman to be appointed a departmental secretary, the practice continued of referring to the secretary as 'he'. She explained that CIÉ objected strongly to the proposal of 'no Vote payment towards operating losses and revenue charges'.

The Board were aiming at making good the negligence of many years . . . CIÉ regarded the necessary additional borrowing as a millstone round their necks which would defer further the date by which the Board might hope to become solvent. The Board felt that the Government should continue to assist them as hitherto in effecting the rehabilitation of the undertaking.

The Tánaiste said that what the Department of Finance proposed appeared to be, in effect, that CIÉ, in the expectation of being solvent within a few years, should telescope profits and losses over the next four or five years, borrowing to meet losses in the immediate future and repaying these borrowings from profits in subsequent years. As a surplus was in sight he thought it was reasonable to ask CIÉ to meet immediate losses from borrowing and he did not see how it would seriously affect the Board.

Thekla Beere pointed out that the Department of Finance claimed the right to exercise control over CIÉ's borrowings, and now that it would have to borrow to cover operating losses, CIÉ would be controlled by Finance.

The Tánaiste said that this difficulty would be met if Finance would give an assurance that temporary borrowing sufficient to sustain the activities of CIÉ and keep their workers in employment would be guaranteed and facilitated.

At this stage the Tánaiste spoke to the Minister for Finance on the telephone . . . following this conversation, the Tánaiste said that the Minister for Finance had accepted the proposal about CIÉ borrowing for renewals expenditure . . .

The Tánaiste asked the Secretary to arrange to inform Mr Courtney immediately of the agreed proposal for the financing of the Board's future operations.

There was no delay. T. C. Courtney, accompanied by Frank Lemass, the General Manager, and Archibald Malcolm, the Chief Accountant, travelled to the Kildare St Offices of the Department that afternoon. The Department's minute of the afternoon meeting records Mr Courtney saying that the decision showed that the arguments put forward by CIÉ had been given 'scant consideration', but the secretary assured him that the board's arguments had been fully considered. The minute concluded with CIÉ's chairman saying that

the Board's position would now be worse than had originally been thought because they would be faced with unexpected demands for interest on temporary borrowings which they had not envisaged. The

Board would, however, operate the Government's directions to the fullest extent possible but he wished to stress that the Board would have to get full co-operation in borrowing to meet their needs if the scheme was to be practicable.

The Board of CIÉ held a special meeting three days later to hear the chairman report on 'negotiations with the Departments of Industry and Commerce, and Finance in connection with the finances of the company'. It was formally resolved that:

> The Board views with alarm the decision that revenue losses should in future be met by borrowing by the Board and more so that the control of the Department of Finance should be extended as indicated in the memorandum.

Within three months, in June 1956, it was clear that the improvement in CIÉ's finances envisaged by the Department of Finance was not taking place. After the brief upswing of 1954 and 1955, CIÉ's operating results were deteriorating and instead of arguing about subventions it formally requested government for a review of public transport policy. In effect it told government that if it wished the railways to be maintained it would have to take steps to ensure that traffic be restored to rail from road. It restated its cash problems and its difficulties on that score are illustrated by the following extract from a later source—CIÉ's (September 1956) submission to the Beddy Committee:

> At the same time the Department of Finance insisted that the Board should pay £829,000 to the exchequer, which it claimed had been given by way of subsidy towards capital works. The Board is satisfied that this claim was unjust and indefensible and that even if the subsidy ... had to be refunded by the Board out of money raised by stock issue the amount of which could be so claimed would not exceed £249,000. The Board had to pay back the sum of £829,000.

As payments for diesel locomotives became due CIÉ proposed that there be another stock issue, but Finance could not agree with any new issue 'in current market conditions'. CIÉ found itself acutely short of funds. The papers in the National Archives note a conversation on 5 July 1956 between T. C. Courtney and Diarmuid Ó Riordáin, then Assistant Secretary of Industry and Commerce and later Secretary of the Department of Transport and Power. The note gives an interesting insight to the relationship between CIÉ and the Department, while also telling us that cash flow problems could be as real in the 1950s as in the 1990s.

Mr Courtney telephoned late last evening on the question of CIÉ's financial position. He said the Board was extremely short of cash. . . . It was estimated that payments due in the month of July would be nearly £300,000 short of revenue. Even if further temporary borrowing could be secured there was the statutory limit of £11.5 million, and CIÉ were only short by £300,000 of this permitted sum. The moneys which are required in the month of July are for capital purposes and it was quite wrong that capital expenditure should be met from temporary borrowing.

Mr Courtney went on to say that he had received no reply from us or from the Department of Finance as to whether Treasury approval could be secured to the raising of money by CIÉ in Britain. Their London bankers had anticipated an early reply in this matter from CIÉ. He wished to emphasise that the financial situation of CIÉ was becoming most dangerous and he urged that we should press the Department of Finance very hard. There was a payment of over £300,000 now due to Metro Vickers. CIÉ had held up payments for the diesels as long as possible but the position was now critical.

I told Mr Courtney I would make a report of what he had said, but that both this Department and the Department of Finance were already fully aware of the position.   (Initialled: D Ó R)

It would later be confirmed to Courtney that CIÉ was not to borrow abroad. In March, Frank Lemass had told Ó Riordáin of CIÉ's difficulties in raising extra cash from the Bank of Ireland. Ó Riordáin asked if other banks had been approached. Frank Lemass thought that this would be the equivalent of 'hawking about a government guarantee' and that CIÉ would not want to do this without the agreement of the Department of Finance. When consulted in the Department of Finance, Ken Whitaker told Ó Riordáin that there was no objection to CIÉ trying other banks. Both CIÉ and the government were under severe pressure as subsequent events revealed.

On the same day as the Courtney/Ó Riordáin phone conversation took place concerning CIÉ's impending cash crisis, the Minister for Finance circulated a confidential memorandum to his Cabinet colleagues entitled, 'Financial Position of Córas Iompair Éireann'. This cabinet paper projected CIÉ's total cash requirements up to 1960 at £25 million, including £9.89 million due in that year for refinancing pre-1950 borrowings. Working back to 1949/50 the memorandum quoted £44.07 million, including exchequer advances already made of £12.01 million, as the total sum required by CIÉ up to 1960. Most of this figure would of course be borrowed by CIÉ under government guarantee.

The Finance memorandum affords a rare opportunity of reading the official mind unscreened by considerations of public prudence and political effects. It concluded as follows:

> In the opinion of the Minister for Finance the continued investment of large sums in CIÉ can no longer be justified. Increases in wages and in the cost of materials and loss of revenue arising from the falling volume of traffic have swallowed up the economies expected to result from dieselisation and other re-equipment. Rising costs can no longer be offset by increases in rates and fares for such increases have reached the point of driving more traffic away from the public transport system. Competition from private mechanised transport in the form of lorries, vans, motor cars, motor cycles, etc. grows steadily year by year, large concerns, whether public bodies or private undertakings, and private individuals finding it cheaper and more convenient to provide their own transport. Even if further investment on the scale projected should be permitted, there would still be no prospect of solvency for CIÉ but, on the contrary, it is estimated that there would be a continuing operating loss of not less than £2.35 million yearly. The great bulk of this loss would be due to railway working despite the investment of the great bulk of all the new capital in this form of transport. The conclusion is thus inescapable that railways are outmoded as a form of transport, particularly in a small sparsely populated country such as Ireland, and that it would be highly improvident at a time when capital resources even for productive investment are limited to continue to invest huge sums in a form of transport that time and again has shown itself to be uneconomic.
> (Government memorandum, 5 July 1956: National Archives)

The very blunt and uncompromising tone of this 1956 memorandum from Gerard Sweetman was his response to the difficult questions put to government by CIÉ the previous month and his department's knowledge that CIÉ would shortly report a loss of £1,625,000 for 1954/55, up 60 per cent on 1953/54. It was only fifteen months since Finance and Industry and Commerce had been talking about CIÉ shortly becoming solvent. But now, after a surge of £800,000 in CIÉ's wages bill and £400,000 in its coal bill, they were overcorrecting in the opposite direction by projecting annual losses of £2.35 million. That estimate was near enough to what would emerge as the annual state subvention in the sixties. It might seem inspired for a 1956 paper to get so near to the future level of subvention, but so many other things would happen over the next few years affecting CIÉ's costs and changing its debt structure that the apparent accuracy of the 1956 estimate of future losses was quite fortuitous.

In any event, the Finance memorandum helped to provoke the Cabinet into realising that public transport was to be a perennial problem. Still, they could give it another little push off the immediate agenda. Within two weeks a Committee of Inquiry into Internal Transport (the Beddy Committee) was established.

IN ADDITION TO the CIÉ deficits and capital requirements, another public transport issue was exercising the minds of ministers. It concerned the GNR which continued to be the main public transport operator east of a line from Dublin to Sligo. In December 1948 the Milne Report had said that 'the time does not appear to be opportune for embarking on any drastic change in the constitution of the Great Northern Railway', but the possible 'solution' which it offered was close enough to that which Dáil Éireann and Stormont adopted in April 1953. In contrast to the GSR which had been created as recently as 1925, the GNR had existed as a unified company since 1876 and was publicly perceived to be an efficient well-managed organisation. It suffered, however, like its larger counterpart from the development of motor traffic through the thirties; had a brief respite during the war; benefited from reasonable coal supplies and strong cross-border shopping volumes in the immediate post-war years; but got into financial difficulties in 1949. The GNR operated both rail and road services in the Twenty-six Counties but was restricted to rail operations only in the Six Counties. Its rail network was approximately 30 per cent of CIÉ's, though it carried 87 per cent of CIÉ's passenger volumes principally because of much larger suburban traffic around Belfast. Like CIÉ much of its equipment was obsolete. The 1953 rescue action would prove to be short term. None the less it deserves to be recorded as a key part of the overall public transport story.

In August 1950 Mr McCleery, the Northern Ireland Minister of Commerce, began discussions with Mr Morrissey his Dublin counterpart about a crisis in the GNR. These discussions between Mr McCleery and Mr Morrissey 'were directed towards investigating the possibility of taking joint action' (*Dáil Debates*, Vol. 138, Col. 16). The GNR Board injected urgency into these contacts between Stormont and Dublin by giving notice to both governments on 20 December 1950 that they planned to announce withdrawal of railway services from 1 February 1951. This advice had an immediate effect. In January 1951 the two governments informed the GNR that they had decided jointly to acquire the company for £3.9 million and that pending acquisition the operating losses would be borne by the two administrations. This action averted the threatened close-down, but difficulties remained: the GNR Board pluckily rejected the £3.9 million purchase price, and the two administrations ran into problems as to how the GNR would be operated after acquisition.

After the June 1951 General Election Seán Lemass replaced Daniel Morrissey as the Dublin participant in these talks. Jointly with Mr McCleery he met the GNR Board and told them that the governments were prepared, if necessary, to acquire the company compulsorily for £3.9 million, but if 'a proposal were made on behalf of the stockholders for a voluntary sale on terms slightly more favourable they [the ministers] would be prepared to recommend acceptance to their respective Governments'. After a ballot of stockholders the board put a purchase figure of £4,500,000 to the governments, noting that neither the directors, the company nor the stockholders had the 'power to offer the undertaking for sale', but that the increased figure was 'tantamount to an offer for sale if the necessary statutory powers for that purpose existed'. On 30 October 1951 it was announced that the governments had agreed to purchase the GNR for this increased sum, but they had not yet agreed on how the railway would be operated. Negotiations continued throughout 1952. It is clear that Dublin had the future of the GNR's Dundalk engineering works, which employed 1,300 people, very high on its list of priorities. These were generously protected in the eventual legislation. It also seems from remarks made by Daniel Morrissey and William Norton in the Dáil (15 May 1953) that Dublin may have offered to integrate the GNR with CIÉ but that this was unacceptable to Stormont. The eventual settlement, following somewhat the lines of the Milne suggested formula, separated significant assets ('land', i.e. permanent way and stations) from the GNR for the reason, it would seem, that the Northern government did not want the Southern government to have any rights, even shared rights, to such assets within their jurisdiction. 'Land' within the Six and the Twenty-six Counties became the property of the two separate governments, though in the North it would be vested in the Ulster Transport Authority. The jointly owned GNR would then be granted the right to use this property for its railway operations. An exception to this condition about 'land' was the GNR engineering works in Dundalk which with all rolling stock and equipment would remain the property of the reorganised operating company.

The new organisation was established in October 1953 following adoption of parallel legislation, North and South. It was to be renamed the Great Northern Railway Board (GNRB) and have ten directors—five appointed by each government with one member on each side being nominated as a 'senior member' who year on year would alternate the chairmanship between them. Repaying an old debt, Seán Lemass's nominee as 'senior member' was A. P. Reynolds, the veteran GSR and DUTC supremo whom Morrissey had removed from CIÉ. The legislation provided for the two governments sharing the purchase price on a 50/50 basis, but operating losses incurred between January 1951 and the establishment of the GNRB were to be shared 60/40 between the Northern and the Southern governments, reflecting the different scale and profitability of the company's activities north and south. South of the border, in contrast to the north, it operated an extensive network of road passenger and freight services in north Dublin, Meath, Louth, Cavan, Leitrim, Sligo and Donegal. The new board was charged with reviewing the 60/40 formula and devising a new scheme for the apportionment of losses for submission to the two ministers on the 'general principle that each area will be responsible for the results of the operation of the undertaking in that area'. Moneys required for the Dundalk engineering works would be provided by Dublin. Money required for development of other property would be provided by each administration for its own area, while acquisition of rolling stock would be funded on a 50/50 basis. Closure of railway lines which provided cross-border service would be handled on the basis that the board could propose; the ministers could agree or disagree; but if one minister refused to accept his counterpart's position concerning a line in that minister's jurisdiction, he could insist on the line remaining open. However, in such a case he would be required to fund all losses which it incurred.

The GNRB Bill borrowed the optimistic language of the 1950 CIÉ Act in relation to breaking even, i.e. 'to secure as soon as may be, that taking one year with another, that the revenue of the Board shall not be less than sufficient to meet charges properly chargeable to revenue'. No doubt it was difficult to devise a better formula for ensuring that the GNRB would strive to be efficient, but in the light of experience in Ireland and abroad the legislators in 1953 must have known in their hearts that in prescribing breakeven results they were enshrining an impossible task into their new law. The GNRB was required by the Acts to pay interest on the £4,500,000 purchase price. It was not going to get an easy ride.

In the Dáil, government and opposition speakers were generous in their praise of the civil servants and of the several ministers (including Liam Cosgrave who had been Parliamentary Secretary to Daniel Morrissey) who had brought such a complex agreement to fruition and expressed the hope that such cross-border co-operation would continue. In answer to queries as to whether CIÉ board members would be involved in the GNRB or whether the old GNR's property in the Republic should be vested in CIÉ, Seán Lemass's polite response was that in his view the CIÉ Board already had enough problems of its own. Accordingly, CIÉ would not be involved in the GNRB though it accommodated the GNRB's long-distance buses at the Store St terminus.

The GNRB finally got under way on 1 October 1953 but was loss making from the outset. Its predecessor had lost £675,284 in 1951 and £945,000 in 1952. Over the next four years prior to the year of its demise the annual losses of the GNRB averaged £1 million. The Northern administration had nothing of the attachment to railways of its Southern counterpart. It placed its trust for an efficient public transport system on the successful road-based Ulster Transport Authority, successor to the Northern Ireland Road Transport Board established in 1935. The UTA was now being required to carry Northern Ireland's share of the GNRB's losses.

On 7 March 1956 *The Irish Times* reported that Mr Maginess, the Northern Ireland Minister of Finance, told the Stormont parliament that 'a great part of the railway system must be scrapped without delay'. The pruning of the system would be harsh and severe. The government, he declared, was prepared to act swiftly, strongly and ruthlessly.

> The alternative is bankruptcy of the UTA and the breakdown of public transport services. The Government is determined that transport after reorganisation must pay its way . . . The railway crisis is urgent and vital . . . We mean business . . . and not only mean it but are determined to see it through.

The UTA, mainly because of the GNRB's performance, was expected to have accumulated a deficiency of £4 million by 30 September 1956. Railway cutbacks were to be announced after the summer recess. Eventually in October 1955, just two years after the GNRB's establishment, Mr McCleery proposed the closure of three secondary lines: Portadown/Armagh/Tynan, Omagh/Enniskillen/Newtown Butler and Bundoran Junction/Beleek. The Northern minister also intimated that no long-term future was envisaged for the Portadown–Derry line.

This Northern initiative was taken despite the fact that a GNRB proposal of March 1954 to acquire 24 additional railcars at a cost of £528,000 had been accepted by both governments the previous December and that both governments were supposed to be evaluating a comprehensive programme, submitted in May 1955, for dieselisation of the GNRB at a cost of £5.5 million. William Norton who replaced Seán Lemass after the 1954 General Election met Mr McCleery to protest at these proposals.

In accordance with the GNRB Acts the proposed closures were referred to the Chairmen of the Transport Tribunals, North and South, for an opinion. After public hearings in Belfast and in Dublin the Southern Tribunal's Chairman, Dr J. P. Beddy, issued a reasoned opinion against the proposed closures, but the Northern Chairman, Sir Anthony Babington, took the opposite line. The Northern Minister refused to change his mind and rejected the GNRB view that the lines should be kept going until they could be operated with modern diesel equipment. Of course Dublin retained the right to insist on the lines remaining open, but if it did so insist, it would have to foot the bill for all their running losses despite the fact that the lines under threat ran mainly within the Six Counties. Eventually on 5

June 1957 the GNRB received formal notice from the new Northern Minister of Commerce, Lord Glentoran, that all train services were to be terminated from 30 September 1957 on Omagh/Enniskillen/Clones, Portadown/Armagh/Glaslough, and on the Bundoran, Fintona and Keady branches. Dublin assented to the closures, having little practical alternative but to do so, particularly as Lord Glentoran said he would exercise his option of terminating the GNRB agreement on 30 September 1958 when it would have completed its first five-year term.

The mileage affected was 115 miles—about 24 per cent of the GNRB's total system, but it would have a domino effect elsewhere. Connecting lines within the Republic—Clones/Castleblaney/Dundalk, Glaslough/Monaghan/Cavan and the Belturbet and Carrickmacross branches amounted to 84 miles, and the fourth Annual Report of the GNRB records that 'the Board decided to terminate on 30 September 1957 all rail passenger services on the aforesaid lines in the Republic and for an experimental period to operate freight traffic only'. The Southern Transport Tribunal consented to these withdrawals of passenger services. But that was not the limit of the fall-out from the Northern government's decision. The Sligo & Leitrim Railway Company, whose headquarters were in Enniskillen and which had been in receipt of subsidies from both the Dublin and Belfast governments, found that after the closure of the GNRB's lines through Enniskillen, it would have to cease operations. In effect, the consequences of the Northern decision was seriously to curtail railways in three northern counties and five southern counties, from Dundalk on the east coast to Bundoran on the west coast, and from Omagh in the north to Cavan town. Donegal and Fermanagh became the first counties for eighty years to have no rail connections whatsoever.

The town of Dundalk, so relieved by assurances about the future of its railway engineering works in the 1953 proposals, was now devastated. The euphoria experienced in County Louth as a whole by winning the 1957 All-Ireland Senior Football Championship—the first such victory since 1912—contrasted bitterly with Dundalk's mood of anger and betrayal at the axing of its railway hinterland to the west. An immediate agreement by Stormont to a Dublin proposal that the railway engineering works in Dundalk be separated from the GNR and spun off into a new Dundalk Engineering Company did little to abate the fear which descended on the town in 1957. It was agreed that the Dundalk Engineering Company would continue to provide engineering services to the dwindling GNRB system, while it would pursue a new brief to seek out new engineering projects. A. P. Reynolds, who clearly continued to retain the confidence of Seán Lemass, was appointed Chairman of the new company. Hope flickered, but only for a while as some of these new projects were announced, such as the manufacture of a Heinkel three-wheel bubble car and a foundry project to produce steel for razor blades.

The various GNRB developments were to have a profound effect on CIÉ. The Dublin–Belfast line was now the only railway linking North and South. A new arrangement would have to be made to ensure its survival. This would coincide with the post-Beddy transport legislation of 1958.

CHAPTER 8

BEDDY REPORT

CIÉ submission to Beddy Committee—Focus on restoring traffic to railways—Beddy takes opposite approach—Smaller railway network proposed—Additional restrictions on road haulage rejected—Capital restructuring involves write-off of pre-1945 debt and all losses up to 1956.

The inter-party government's response to the alarm bells loudly rung in Gerard Sweetman's cabinet memorandum was the appointment on 14 July 1956 of the Committee of Inquiry into Internal Transport under the chairmanship of Dr J. P. Beddy. Its terms of reference were:

> To inquire into and review the developments in internal transport in recent years as they affect public transport undertakings; to consider what measures are necessary, in the light of those developments, to ensure the provision of the transport requirements of the country on a basis which will best serve the public interests; and to report thereon to the Minister for Industry and Commerce on or before 1st November 1956.

Unlike Sir James Milne, whose experience was that of a UK railway executive and whose brief was to conduct the 1948 Inquiry himself with whatever assistance he might himself recruit, Dr Beddy was thoroughly experienced in Irish public affairs and was supported by committee members with experience in various fields of Irish life. A doctor of economic science, J. P. Beddy's formidable previous record included chairmanship of the Commission on Emigration (1948–1954), membership of the Ingram

Committee (1938) and chairmanship of the Transport Tribunal set up under the 1950 Transport Act. He had been first secretary and later Chairman and Managing Director of the Industrial Credit Corporation, had become first Chairman of the Industrial Development Authority when it was founded in 1950 and of its associate agency An Foras Tionscail. Other members of the Beddy Committee included J. F. Dempsey (later Dr Dempsey), General Manager of Aer Lingus, and Dr Juan N. Greene, a medical man who was President of the recently founded Irish Farmers Association. J. J. Stafford, a Director and General Manager of J. J. Stafford and Sons, Wexford, and Chairman of Irish Shipping, with S. F. Thompson, a prominent Cork-based businessman, made up the rest of the five-man committee. Tom Nally, then an Assistant Principal of Industry and Commerce, later an Assistant Secretary of the Department of Transport and Power, was secretary to the committee. It failed to complete its work in the extraordinarily brief allotted target of three and a half months, even shorter than the five months taken by Milne in 1948, but submitted an impressively detailed and thoughtful report after ten and a half months, on 4 May 1957. By that time the second inter-party government had fallen and Seán Lemass once again was Minister for Industry and Commerce. He would later describe it as 'the best of the very many reports upon our transport system which have appeared in the life time of this state' (*Dáil Debates*, Vol. 164, Col. 1053).

Unlike the Milne Inquiry, Beddy's consultations included extensive oral hearings with various groups including the management of CIÉ, other transport companies and trade unions. The report includes a substantial examination of traffic trends and fare levels for public transport (passenger and freight), comparing the latest (1956) data with 1951, 1947, 1938, even as far back as 1925. It examined the affairs of CIÉ (rail, road, canals, etc.), of the GNRB and of other public transport survivors, e.g. the Donegal veterans—Londonderry & Lough Swilly Railway Company which now provided only road services and the Co. Donegal Railways Joint Committee whose last line would close in December 1959. The Sligo, Leitrim & Northern Counties Railway Company was also reported on. It would expire even earlier, in October 1957, along with several GNRB lines on execution of the sentence pronounced by the Northern Ireland government.

Beddy also provides data on private transport, e.g. numbers of motor cars, commercial vehicles and buses. A particular phenomenon of the 1950s is revealed in the data: a surge in popularity of motorcycles, motor scooters and 'cycles with auxiliary engines' which grew six-fold from 4,645 in 1947 to 26,539 in 1956, a figure which compares with 22,709 in 1990. More importantly, it acknowledged that most freight movements were now carried by privately owned transport.

Two months after its appointment the Beddy Committee received a submission from the CIÉ Board (September 1956) which was subsequently printed and distributed to all CIÉ staff under a cover letter, dated July 1957, from Frank Lemass, General Manager: 'the Board wishes that each member of the staff be made aware of its views on public transport'—such public communication was rather unusual at that time, but its content was no less remarkable. It would be the last time that CIÉ asked for widespread restrictions of privately owned transport. The CIÉ Board posed four questions; these had previously been asked of government in its June memorandum.

> 1. Is a public transport system to be maintained for passengers and goods?
> 2. If a public transport service must be maintained, must railways form a part of it or can they be abandoned?
> 3. If railways are to be part of the public transport system, will the steps which are necessary to make them self-supporting be taken or will the State provide railway services and pay the necessary subsidy?
> 4. If it is decided that railways must remain and must pay their own way what steps must be taken now to restore sufficient traffic to enable them to do so?
> (CIÉ submission to Beddy Committee, September 1956)

Whether privately owned or not, CIÉ pointed out that public transport was an essential feature of all developed or developing economies. Public transport required some co-ordination, and the experience of cut-throat free-for-all competition in road transport in the period 1926/1932 was mentioned as justification for such control.

> During consideration of the various bills to deal with transport, no member of An Dáil suggested the abandonment of a public transport service—there may have been conflicting views as to the manner in which the service should be provided.
> In the light of these considerations, the Board of Córas Iompair Éireann are unanimously of opinion –
> (a) that public transport services are essential in this country
> (b) that public transport service should be nation-wide and under our control. (ibid.)

CIÉ's second question as to whether railways needed to be part of the public transport service or whether they could be abandoned was squarely answered, in the affirmative: 'The Board is unanimously of the opinion that railways should form a part of the public transport system.'

CIÉ reviewed its responsibility under the 1950 Transport Act: 'The decision that railway services should be provided was made by the Government and endorsed by the Oireachtas.' However, the submission politely conceded that 'if as a result of the present inquiry railways are abandoned in whole or in part, the function of the Board will still be to operate, as efficiently as possible, whatever transport services the government decides to utilise'. It was pointed out that the railways had been rehabilitated since the Ingram and Milne reports had been completed: from 1937 to 1950 an adequate renewal programme would have required 140 locomotives where only 8 were provided, 238 coaches where only 20 were built, and 4,200 wagons where only 1,400 were built. Since 1950 a big rehabilitation programme had been undertaken with government support. Progress on dieselisation and provision of new rolling stock had been substantial. 'Speeds have been increased throughout the system and frequent express trains have been provided on the main routes. The programme of work undertaken by the Board is not yet complete but Irish railways today compare favourably with most European railways . . . The railways are now in a position to give greater service to the community both for passengers and goods than ever in their history.' The problem which dominated CIÉ's submission and the remedies it proposed were summarised in the blunt sentence: 'They [the railways] are unable to pay their way only because the traffic which would enable them to do so is being withdrawn from them.'

CIÉ applied its entire argument against a total, i.e. 'all or nothing' abandonment of the railway emphasising the impact of abandonment on industry, agriculture (particularly livestock) and merchants. The cost of replacement services, resultant traffic congestion and the severe social consequences of reduced railways employment were dealt with, though in a somewhat summary and not totally convincing fashion. Even the residual value of the railways was mentioned. It would be low. 'The locomotives, rolling stock etc. could not be used because of the 5'-3" gauge, anywhere except in Victoria and South Australian Railways. At best such residual value as the railways possess would take considerable time to realise.' At no place in its 1956 submission to Beddy did the board address the possibility that the railway might simply have been too large, a position the GSR had taken in 1938, and the Reynolds board had taken in 1948. The furore that was taking place about curtailments in the GNRB's system may have encouraged discretion on that point. Let Beddy recommend closures if they wished, the CIÉ Board position was simply that it had a railway to run and the existing system would justify itself if only its rightful traffic were restored.

In discussing traffic loss CIÉ made comparisons with 1945, something for which they would be rebuked by Beddy in due course. The CIÉ perspective was that the 'increase in rail tonnage between 1938 and 1945 (+ 35%) despite a 46 per cent decline in the "volume of trade"' showed how the railway could prosper if commercial vehicles were removed from the equation. Similar figures were quoted for livestock. In contrast since 1945, when private commercial vehicles came back into use, the volume of freight traffic had fallen by 27 per cent despite a 165 per cent increase in the volume of production of transportable goods. CIÉ noted that the 1945 figures included 467,000 tons of turf and firewood 'not now available for transport', but its observation was not that this created a problem but that it created 'additional capacity' for other goods in the improved rolling stock of today. There was no suggestion that capacity should be reduced.

Beddy would brush aside these comparisons with 1945 and focus on the last pre-war year of 1938 in comparison with which freight tonnage on the railways was virtually unchanged, though livestock numbers had fallen by 53 per cent. Indeed freight ton miles showed an increase of 17 per cent between 1938 and 1956 proving that CIÉ was gaining long-distance traffic to compensate for loss of short-distance traffic to road transport. Beddy also challenged the long-standing CIÉ complaint that it was losing high-grade commodities and being forced to carry more low-grade goods, though in fairness that complaint was not advanced in the 1956 submission to the Beddy Committee. The CIÉ argument on this point had originated in the days of Percy Reynolds and had much currency since then. By analysing fluctuations in statistics of goods carried Beddy found that in 1956, compared both with 1938 and 1945, CIÉ was carrying very substantially less coal, turf, timber, flour, bran and other mill offal which paid low rates per ton, and gained traffic in groceries, drapery, chilled meat, ale and porter which paid rates higher up the freight tariff scale.

There was no difference of opinion between Beddy and CIÉ that railways were the main problem. CIÉ's losses were the result of its railway operations and the company as a whole could not prosper until radical change took place.

Passengers contributed £1,887,000 revenue to the railways in 1956 (71 per cent of total receipts) compared to £746,000 from freight. Taking 1945, the base year used by CIÉ in its comparisons, numbers had fallen by 8 per cent, but by analysing the figures Beddy noted that, excluding suburban routes, long-distance rail passengers were actually on the increase, and in 1956 were 4 per cent higher than in 1938 and a remarkable 26 per cent higher than in 1952. Suburban traffic was on the decline, down 39 per cent on 1938 and down 6 per cent on 1952. The fall in suburban traffic had entirely occurred on the Dublin/Greystones line; Cork/Cóbh had held its own. The decline in the Dublin suburban rail passengers was attributed to the private car by CIÉ, but Beddy also credited this loss to substitution of buses, faster and more comfortable than trams, on the Dalkey, Dún Laoghaire routes. CIÉ did not lose passengers; traffic merely transferred from one CIÉ service to another. Restriction of private transport was CIÉ's prescription for improving the finances of the railway, but these restrictions were intended for private freight movements rather than passengers.

> It must be accepted that the growth in the number of private cars indicates an improvement in the standard of living of the community. The Board does not ask therefore for any restriction on the use of private cars. It will continue its efforts, by the provision of faster and more comfortable trains to attract back to the railways the passenger traffic which it has lost. (ibid.)

Politically, of course, that was the only prudent position to adopt, and while it did not attempt to do so in its submissions, CIÉ could have boasted that its increasing long-distance passenger traffic, as distinct from declining and less remunerative suburban traffic, was being substantially helped by its initiatives in stimulating excursion traffic which by 1955 stood at 561,806 compared to 259,238 in 1938. The 1955 figures included 110,074 visitors to Knock Shrine compared to a mere 15,136 in 1938. The key problem therefore in the mind of the CIÉ Board, as they had signalled in several annual reports, was the private freight transport sector and the need to impose restrictions on that sector so as to restore freight traffic to the railway. Before tackling how that should be done, the CIÉ Board considered the distasteful possibility of subsidy and why it should be avoided. Their analysis of the dilemma ran as follows: the customer must pay the real cost of transport availed of if subsidy is to be avoided; theoretically, to balance revenue with expenditure, traffic can be increased or charges increased; but charges could not be increased without loss of traffic; accordingly traffic must be increased; but this was not possible because of road competition. By permitting this road/rail competition government was forcing itself into subsidy payments.

> Hence when the government decides to establish a public transport service and at the same time to permit manufacturers, merchants and semi-state bodies to set up private transport organisations to carry goods formerly carried by rail to an extent which creates difficulties for the public transport service, these difficulties can only be met by subsidy. (ibid.)

CIÉ was not going to allow itself to be tarred with asking for a subsidy.

On the contrary, CIÉ did not want subsidies which they considered undesirable for many reasons.

> (a) Payment of subsidy year after year must tend to destroy harmonious relations between the Government (i.e. Departments of Industry and Commerce and Finance) and the Board which is operating the public transport service for the Government.
> (b) It tends to destroy public confidence in the undertaking. The public who cannot be expected to know the true position must eventually tend to believe that it is those who operate the service who are responsible for deficits.
> (c) It has a bad effect on the morale of the whole undertaking. It is discouraging to all grades to find that no matter what effort is made the result is loss and subsidy—more grudgingly given as time goes on.
> (d) It has the effect of creating in the minds of Trade Unions the feeling that increases in wages and improved conditions can be readily provided— it only means an increase in the subsidy. (ibid.)

The Board of CIÉ suggested as a part alternative to radical restriction of privately owned commercial vehicles that the Milne recommendation for a Central Highways Authority be implemented. Such an authority as envisaged by Milne (see above, p. 48) would distribute the cost of highway upkeep on a fair and equitable basis between all forms of transport. The railway companies were bearing more highway costs per unit of traffic than road transport was bearing. The CIÉ submission estimated that application of the Milne formula to the 1956 situation would reduce the maintenance costs of the permanent way by £798,000 or 66 per cent of the railway operating deficiency. In due course Beddy examined and rejected this concept, which was more than had happened in 1949 when the Central Highways Authority proposal was simply ignored.

No doubt expecting that the Central Highways Authority would be a non-starter the CIÉ submission proceeded to discuss and propose restrictions on commercial vehicles. These proposals would today be greeted with disbelief and almost universal ridicule. They deserve to be viewed in the context of their time, though even in the 1950s support for restrictions of the type proposed had already become very thin. Seán Lemass in February 1956 had intimated that the public were getting uneasy with the present restrictions on the operation of private lorries (*The Irish Times*, 23 February 1956). The CIÉ submission made some general comments on the principle and practice of restriction:

> Restriction of any kind is objectionable to the section of the community

on which it is imposed, but the principle of restriction in the public interest is well established.

Railways have always been restricted in the matter of the choice of goods they will carry—the making of private settlements with customers which might not be made with others, the withdrawal of train services and up to the 1950 Act, the raising of rates and fares etc. There are at present restrictions on even the owners of private merchant lorries—they cannot haul for reward. The licensed haulier is restricted as to the goods he may carry and the area in which he may operate. Restrictions are also in force in industry. The Electricity Supply Acts prevent anybody other than the Electricity Supply Board from producing electricity for sale. In the case of cement, a licence would have to be obtained to permit the setting up of another cement producing organisation. Similarly, in the case of sugar production. Those three organisations have a monopoly in their business . . . (ibid.)

The CIÉ submission went on to compare prices for cement and sugar in the Republic, with lower prices available in the UK. 'These restrictions [on manufacture and importation of sugar and cement] and many others are imposed in the public interest. No one argues that they should be withdrawn . . . In the case of transport too some restrictions are necessary in the public interest.' Having thus set the scene the board's proposals followed.

The number of commercial motor vehicles registered in August, 1955, was about 40,175. The first step to be taken is to prevent any further addition to this number. New vehicles should require a special licence which should be granted only where the public transport undertaking was satisfied that the particular service for which the new vehicle was needed was one which could be better performed by a road vehicle in private hands, rather than by the public transport undertaking. Such services are milk deliveries, bread deliveries, sand, gravel and stone deliveries, etc. This restriction should apply to the replacement of existing vehicles in the hands of manufacturers and merchants as well as to new additional vehicles which they might be anxious to acquire.
(ibid.)

In effect the CIÉ Board of the time proposed a freeze on the existing volume of commercial vehicles and, when age overtook them, they should not be renewed unless some licensing authority were satisfied that public transport would be unable to provide a substitute transport service. CIÉ did not propose that this restriction on renewals would apply to licensed hauliers which were already restricted under the 1933 Road Transport Act and which were widely used by CIÉ as subcontractors. In addition the board was prepared to allow that 'in the case of the large number of light vans which are mostly replacing horse drawn vehicles and which work within a short radius, licences for replacements would be automatically granted'.

A still more severe restriction was then proposed in the CIÉ submission. Every merchant's (retailer or distributor in today's language) or manufacturer's commercial vehicle would be limited as to area of operation. It was suggested that the limit of operation for commercial vehicles should be fifty miles from the owner's principal place of business. This restriction should come into operation on an appointed day and should include provisions for such markings on vehicles as would make it possible for the Gardaí to decide whether or not a particular vehicle was engaged in the carriage of goods outside its limited radius. The limit of radius of working should apply to licensed hauliers as well as to 'own-account' vehicles and should remain in force for one year only. The limit should, if necessary, be reduced each succeeding year until the full traffic capacity of the railways is achieved.

> In this way, it is felt that it would be made quite clear to the public that the Government was serious in its efforts to prevent wasteful expenditure on transport, and to utilise to the full the transport equipment which the Board is operating for the State. The owners would be enabled to use all the vehicles they now operate until the vehicles reached the end of their useful life. They would not be allowed to replace their vehicles, except by special licence.   (ibid.)

The Board also argued that as the state in the long run had to foot the bill for any deficit in public transport, it should require that contracts granted by the state or local authorities should bind the beneficiaries to using public transport. This would not mean that building contractors could not use their own transport to move sand and gravel, but it would mean that major consignments over long distances would move by 'rail, as far as possible'. This would avoid, said the CIÉ submission, a recurrence of what happened under a contract awarded for an extension at Shannon Airport. A manufacturer of pipes used his own lorry and trailers day after day over a long period to transport 'a huge supply of pipes . . . the whole way from Dublin to Shannon'. The Department of Industry and Commerce was 'paying the manufacturer for carrying the pipes and, at the same time, paying Coras Iompair Éireann a subsidy for not carrying them'. Even today the logic of that argument at first glance seems attractive, though it ignores the cost of double handling and the involvement of two sets of road equipment, i.e. at Dublin and Limerick if the goods were to be moved by rail.

The CIÉ submission to the Beddy Committee ended by addressing the question of the canals. It described the types of traffic moving on the canals and said that privately owned barges had all been withdrawn, with the exception of two on the Barrow which were not expected to resume operations. CIÉ had proposed to the minister in January 1953 that it be allowed to withdraw its own barges from service with a consequent improvement of £80,000 in the board's finances. The minister had refused permission for this withdrawal of CIÉ's barges and did so in language which illustrates the enduring attachment of public administrations to the status quo, i.e. only in a situation of crisis should a possibly unpopular change be permitted. In the same year (1953) as the major dieselisation programme was approved with a view to eliminating CIÉ losses, the

> opinion was expressed [by the Minister] that the canal provides an alternative form of transport in times of emergency and if its use was to be reduced to the extent proposed, the condition of the waterway might be expected to deteriorate through misuse and to become unsightly. (ibid.)

Beddy made short shrift of this 1953 decision and recommended that 'CIE should be free to withdraw its barges from the canal but that the necessary care and maintenance of the [Grand] Canal, as well as that of the Royal Canal, should remain the responsibility of CIE' (Beddy Report, par. 450). That seemed to be the only CIÉ proposal which Beddy was prepared to accept.

BEDDY'S EXAMINATION OF the railways was exhaustive and authoritative. It found that the utilisation of CIÉ's permanent way, locomotives, coaches and wagons 'was extremely low by international comparison', but part of the quality of the report is that it was not satisfied merely to record such a fact: it sought out explanations as to why the situation was as they found it. A section of the report was titled, 'Circumstances which account for the present position of public transport organisations'. Its findings covered much that we have written about earlier, particularly the decline in population since the railways had been built—a decline which had no parallel in other countries with which the Republic's rail operations were compared. Geographic (e.g. no through traffic as in European mainland countries), demographic (low density of population and lack of sizeable cities), and economic (no heavy industries on the scale found in other countries) were other factors discussed.

Beddy also commented on the size of the Republic's road network and its low traffic density like that of the railways relative to other countries. The low level of utilisation of railway fixed assets in turn 'impacted on labour productivity'. Relative to thirteen European countries, CIÉ employees per million passengers carried was three times the average, per million passenger miles were more than twice the average, per tons carried twice the average, and per million ton miles almost three times the average.

There were wide discrepancies between the various countries with which Ireland was compared, depending on population densities and scale of economic activity, e.g. comparisons with Portugal and Spain were less unfavourable than with France or Germany. On one scale alone the Republic scored well with 6 railway employees per mile of line compared to 18 on average for all 13 countries reviewed, but such a low employee level reflected very low utilisation of large sections of the permanent way. With labour amounting to 56 per cent of CIÉ's railway operating costs in 1956 (64 per cent in the case of the GNRB), low labour utilisation was identified by Beddy as a major impediment to improved financial results. It was not suggested that the problem principally lay in overmanning but that the nature of the railway operation with infrequent services (6 trains or less per day in most stations) inevitably caused high numbers relative to traffic throughput.

Employee numbers had been reduced by 1,267 (10.4%) between 1950 and 1956 due in part to the dieselisation programme. Moreover, as 670 were employed in the construction of new rolling stock, the reduction in railway operating staff was not far off 2,000. Such a reduction without stoppages or threats of stoppages was a significant achievement of T. C. Courtney's period as Chairman. A main cause of the reduction was single manning of diesel locomotives. Firemen and certain ground staff involved in preparing steam engines for service and tending to them after work were no longer required. Courtney himself played a key role in negotiations to achieve reduced staffing with the ASLEF (Amalgamated Society of Locomotive Engineers and Firemen). The surplus staff were redeployed to non-ASLEF duties and CIÉ became one of the first national railway operators to have one-man operation of diesel trains; one-person bus operation would be a much more difficult nut to crack. Despite the reduction in railway operating numbers, the Beddy Report still observed that 'rail transport, even when operated on an irreducible minimum of staff and equipment . . . is a particularly uneconomic form of transport if the available volume of traffic is insufficient to secure a reasonable utilisation of the labour force and equipment employed'.

Some well-reasoned paragraphs on labour relations in the Beddy Report provide a background for matters we will meet in the next chapter. Observations on CIÉ's financial dilemma are followed by comments on shop-floor attitudes and conflicts which should surprise no observer of industrial relations, especially in so traditional and highly regulated an industry as the railways.

> Our railways have reached the stage at which . . . they have not earned any operating profit for many years—since 1945 in the case of CIÉ and since 1947 in the case of GNR. . . . Insufficient regard has been paid in wage negotiations to this background . . . there has been undue emphasis on the effects of the development of private road transport on railway operations; there is little evidence of a searching examination either by railway managements or by labour interests as to the real causes of the deficits and insufficient attention has been given to factors which clearly indicate that railway expenditure is at an unjustifiably high level.
>
> We have also received evidence of a regrettable absence of friendly co-operation between the railway managements and the trade unions. On the one hand, the trade unions have represented to us that the railway managements have displayed resistance to innovation and change and have made little effort, by joint consultation or otherwise, to secure the full co-operation of the staff with the result that 'inefficiency, waste and extravagance' evident to the employees have gone unchecked. Beyond statements to this effect the unions have produced little supporting evidence and certainly not enough to justify such serious charges. The Board of CIÉ has stated in evidence that the unions concern themselves only with wages and conditions of employment and have shown little knowledge of or interest in the wider aspects of the Board's operations. The Board has pointed out that a total of over 2,000 meetings between the management and union representatives at various levels . . . on only one occasion were matters raised other than those relating to wages and conditions of employment. The Board took strong exception to the allegation that it has displayed resistance to innovation or change and has, in turn, alleged that the trade unions themselves have been responsible for such resistance. As an illustration the Board mentioned a trade union requirement that a locomotive driver must be paid at the overtime rate after he has driven a distance of 140 miles in a day—a requirement which is, no doubt, reasonable in the case of a slow steam driven train. The application of the requirement in the case of a driver of a fast diesel locomotive means that on the Dublin to Cork express train he is paid the overtime rate after he has driven for a little over 2½ hours. As further examples, the Board has mentioned that the trade unions insist on conductors being employed on CIÉ omnibuses which are hired for

private use; that at Limerick, the rail and road parcels offices are adjacent but the unions would not agree to the amalgamation of the two offices; and that a traffic porter is not allowed by the unions to act as a lorry helper. Though restrictive practices of this kind were not relatively important, the Board considers that they are objectionable and militate against efficiency.

In the time available to us it has not been possible to enquire closely into labour relations. . . . We cannot do more than refer to the conflicting evidence and to the indications of relationships which are not conducive to harmonious or satisfactory operations or the welfare of the transport undertaking. (Beddy Report, pars 339/340)

On the major issue as to whether or not the state's railway system should be preserved, Beddy summarised arguments which could be advanced for the abandonment of railways as follows:

(a) The services given by railways could be provided almost as well, or better, by other means of public and private transport which would avoid the heavy railway losses now borne by the community.
(b) Railways are a necessarily expensive form of transport suited only to conditions of dense traffic since they involve heavy and relatively fixed expenditure on the maintenance of permanent way, signalling system, stations, amenities, level crossings, etc. as well as on the employment of a large staff, many of whom because of the nature of railway operations cannot be fully occupied, e.g. signal-men. Traffic density in Ireland is too low to permit of this expensive form of transport being operated economically.
(c) As compared with road transport, railways are at a disadvantage in serving our scattered population in the circumstances of the general geographic, demographic and economic background already outlined.
(d) It is no justification for the continuance of railways that (i) they represent an investment of large capital sums; (ii) railway transport is a feature in all countries; and (iii) the railways provide substantial employment. (ibid., par. 353)

As he read on, a reader of the report who had not previously seen or heard media summaries of its conclusions would have experienced a cold chill or a flush of delight depending on whether he loved or loathed railways. It would seem that the Beddy Committee agreed with all the arguments quoted in favour of abandonment of the railways. In particular, they endorsed (d) saying that much of the heavy capital invested in the railways had already been lost. The original capital had been substantially written down, but still the railways were unable to remunerate or even to preserve their reduced capital because of continued operating losses. The fact that other countries had railways was regarded as irrelevant; railways had to be looked at in the unique context of Ireland, and many parts of the country could be served only inconveniently by rail, instancing the area served by the Londonderry and Lough Swilly Railway Company which had closed its railways and replaced them by economically operated road services. With regard to the high level of railway employment, this was being maintained only through state subsidies which constituted a heavy drain on the resources of the community. Moreover, while CIÉ employed 11,000 railway workers, Beddy maintained that this number was about a fifth of total employment in road transport both public and private. The report disbelieved the scale of CIÉ's figures for the capital and operating costs of replacement road services and its estimates of the need for additional road investment.

In effect, Beddy quoted the arguments in favour of abandoning the railways and then undermined all the contrary arguments which favoured their retention. None the less in the following carefully phrased paragraph Beddy extricated itself from the conclusion which seemed to be emerging, that the railways should be abandoned.

> We would incline more readily towards the view that railways should be abandoned if we felt there was no possibility of radical changes being made to adapt them to the background against which they must operate and to the altered circumstances of the present time as compared with those prevailing when the railways were constructed. As now constituted and operated we see no reasonable justification for the continuance of the railway undertaking of CIE, but equally we consider it cannot be demonstrated clearly at present that under changed circumstances the railway undertaking would fail to justify its continued existence as part of an efficient and economically operated public transport system. We do not go so far as to say that the contrary can be demonstrated; rather is it our view that under conditions wholly different from those now prevailing, railways should be given a limited period of years in which to show that their continuance can be justified in the national interest. (ibid., par. 354)

In other words the railway system should not be abandoned but should be given a further opportunity to prove itself. Beddy said that if 'the length of line, number of stations, number and carrying capacity of carriages and wagons, number of employees etc. had been more closely related to the volume of suitable traffic available it might have been possible to demonstrate that it could operate economically in providing the safe, speedy, organised and disciplined method of transport for which the railways were designed'. One consideration in support of the proposed reprieve for the railways was the fact that the railway had retained its total volume of goods traffic (while livestock had declined and merchandise increased) in spite of the fact that 'until recently' locomotives, rolling stock, equipment and facilities were 'largely obsolete'.

It was also noted that the maintenance of its freight volumes had been achieved by CIÉ despite having its commercial 'adaptability' impeded by outdated 'common carrier obligations'. Tourism, balance of payments, national security, potential traffic problems and weather (fear of a possible recurrence of the 1947 freeze-up) were cautiously allowed to weigh in on the positive side for the railways, but not in a very decisive way (ibid., par. 355). While acknowledging the point that some traffic problems might arise, Beddy went on to argue against the view that widespread road congestion would follow from the transfer of rail traffic to Ireland's relatively uncongested roads.

The fundamental difference between Beddy's approach and that of the CIÉ Board revolved around questions of practicality and equity. Beddy saw that there was a certain volume of suitable traffic available for the railway, and believed that the railway should be reduced in size so as better to balance its capacity with this traffic. In contrast, CIÉ said that the railway was already there and government had given it the brief to operate it economically; adequate traffic should be forced off the roads and on to the railways so that it could be so operated.

Beddy could not countenance the CIÉ proposals to restrict private operators of commercial vehicles. It studied the genesis of this idea, noting that it was not part of the January 1953 dieselisation proposals which had been projected to eliminate losses and make it possible to 'remunerate all existing and future capital'. Those proposals had been based on three assumptions, viz.:

(1) that the volume of traffic carried by rail would be maintained;
(2) that substantial operating economies would be achieved by the change-over to diesel traction; and
(3) that any increased costs would be fully recovered by increased rates and fares.

There was no suggestion at the time that private transport would have to be restricted. What had happened since then to change the picture? No problem had been found with the first and second assumptions—traffic volumes had been held and substantial savings had been achieved. The third assumption was the one which had run into difficulty. CIÉ was finding itself unable to recover rising costs principally for labour and fuel which together had increased by £1.2 million per annum. A 10 per cent increase in rates and fares in 1955 had failed to produce the expected revenue increase due to market resistance.

To eliminate CIÉ's total loss of £1.6 m. in 1955/56 would require, said Beddy, securing 'by way of the proposed restrictions on road transport a diversion of sufficient traffic to the railway to bring in sufficient *net* receipts' of that amount. The required increase in gross income would have to be well above £1.6 m. so that *net* receipts would reach that figure. Beddy simply did not believe that the restrictions on private road traffic proposed by CIÉ could produce such a revenue switch. The tonnage gained, to a significant extent, would be short haul because that was the category of traffic where CIÉ was recording volume losses. Such short haul business would involve disproportionately heavy handling costs.

CIÉ had claimed to the committee that restrictions on private transport would result in a reduction in rail charges, but again Beddy was not impressed:

> Any such reduction would require a compensatory increase in the volume of traffic carried so that the total additional volume of freight train traffic required to eliminate the losses of the undertaking as at present organised would be of a magnitude which, we are satisfied, it would be impossible to realise. (ibid., par. 363)

However, the Beddy Committee said that even if they were wrong, and if the necessary traffic 'could be diverted to the railway, the imposition of restrictive measures to achieve that diversion could not be justified'. Some of their comments explain this attitude further:

> The freedom of the individual to transport his own goods existed long before the development of public transport. To restrict that freedom would cause widespread and justifiable resentment. (ibid., par. 364)
> There could be no justification for accepting restrictions of the kind recommended by CIÉ unless it could be shown clearly that the development of private transport has endangered the whole system of public transport and that there is a likelihood that those who cannot provide their own transport will be without transport of any kind. There are no reasonable grounds for such assumptions. (ibid., par. 365)
> Such a policy . . . would be designed not to prevent the collapse of public transport but to keep in existence a railway system clearly in excess of reasonable requirements. (ibid., par. 363)

RAILWAYS IN IRELAND, 1957

The report's debate on the low utilisation of CIÉ's railway assets, compared to that of other European countries, gave a sign of the direction in which they were travelling. The report then rejected abandonment of the railway system, rejected subsidisation and rejected the force-feeding of traffic on the railways. This left precious few more paths to explore. The report reviewed the change in circumstances that had occurred since the railways were built, notably depopulation and the development of another form of transport, and found that the remedy to the present problem had to lie in adaptation to those changed circumstances. This had not been happening at anything like the pace necessary:

> Some branch lines have been closed; a number of stations have been closed or reduced to halts and the number of railway staff has been reduced. Nevertheless, there is ample evidence that these and similar adjustments have not gone far enough. In the main, the structure of the railways has not altered in the same striking manner as the population has changed or as might be expected because of the rapid growth of motor transport. Hence, its structure is too large for the available volume of traffic. There is visible evidence of this delayed adjustment, under-utilisation and over-elaborate structure in the many small stations handling very little rail traffic; in the short distances between stations and halts (on average about 5 miles); in the relatively few services; in the large numbers employed in relation to the traffic handled; in the high ratio of numbers and capacity of carriages and wagons to the volume of passengers, merchandise and livestock and in the low average load per wagon. (ibid., par. 385)

The all important issue for Beddy was that the railways be operated under 'realistic conditions' which meant accepting the reality of Ireland's low density transport needs and the emergence of road transport as a more suitable mode for certain traffics. Public transport companies 'have not operated a public transport organisation in the fullest degree which implies carrying traffic in a manner which makes the maximum use of the special advantages of different types of transport. . . . Traffic which can be carried more economically, conveniently and quickly by one form of transport should not be carried by the other.' CIÉ was partly to blame for the loss of traffic to privately owned transport through not developing vigorous, enterprising, fully efficient road transport services. Beddy debated whether road services should be separated from CIÉ, and a new state-sponsored body established to provide nationwide road services, but decided against it.

When the Beddy Report was published in May 1957 the summarised message carried in the media was that it recommended closing down over 150 railway stations and over 1,000 miles of line. This was not far from the truth, but as one would expect from a committee composed of experienced public servants and businessmen, its recommendations were expressed in more circumspect language than the media and public commentators were prepared fully to allow them.

The report of the Committee of Inquiry contained no 'Executive Summary' or even a summary of recommendations, so that one had to wait until page 185 before at last finding its railway recommendations. This was deliberate. Beddy wanted the reader to understand the full analysis and background before coming to the recommendations which would, they knew, be enveloped in controversy:

> We recommend that the length of line and the number of stations should be reduced on the basis that as many as possible of the areas now served by CIÉ will be within convenient reach of a railway station by short distance motor transport, either private transport (i.e. not for reward) or public transport provided by the public transport undertaking and by licensed hauliers.
>
> We are unable to indicate in specific terms the altered pattern of lines and stations to which acceptance of this recommendation would give rise. (ibid., pars 389/390)

The committee sought detailed traffic statistics from CIÉ for mainlines and 'all or any' branch lines, but these could not be supplied in the time available.

> It is a reasonable assumption, however, that the mainlines offer the best operating prospects though the degree of difference between the various main lines cannot at present be stated. On this basis a general indication of the pattern we visualise may be seen from the Map on page 186. (ibid., par. 390)

That map is reproduced here (page 120) and reveals that Beddy 'visualised' a 65 per cent reduction in mileage of line from 1,918 to 850 and a reduction of 75 per cent in the number of stations (excluding 'halts'). The succeeding paragraph describes this pattern:

> Generally, we recommend that the lines from Dublin to Wexford (Rosslare Harbour), Waterford, Cork (Cóbh), Tralee, Limerick, Galway, Westport, Ballina and Sligo and from Limerick Junction, to Rosslare Harbour should be retained. At present Limerick can be

FUTURE RAIL SYSTEM ENVISAGED IN THE BEDDY REPORT, 1957

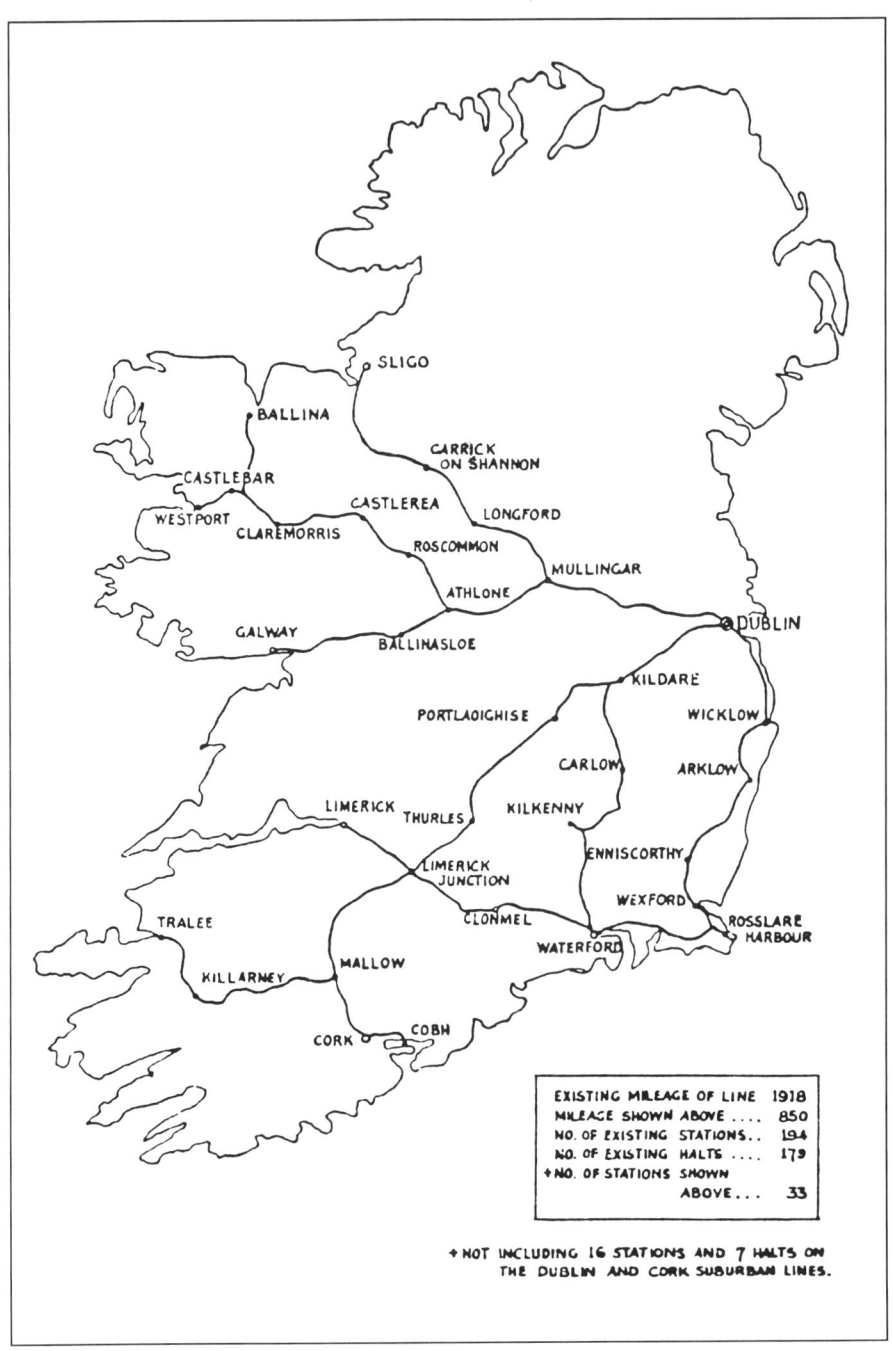

EXISTING MILEAGE OF LINE 1918
MILEAGE SHOWN ABOVE 850
NO. OF EXISTING STATIONS.. 194
NO. OF EXISTING HALTS 179
+NO. OF STATIONS SHOWN
 ABOVE... 33

+ NOT INCLUDING 16 STATIONS AND 7 HALTS ON
  THE DUBLIN AND CORK SUBURBAN LINES.

reached by rail from Dublin via Nenagh or via Limerick Junction and Waterford can be reached from Dublin via Carlow or via Portlaoighise; we have provided for the retention of one line in each case.

(ibid., par. 391)

The line from Limerick to Sligo via Tuam and Claremorris was not included in the preservation list but it 'should be examined specially in the light of its present and potential volume of traffic. It may well be that in the practical application of our recommendations a somewhat different pattern might emerge.'

The stations at the larger towns on these main lines should be retained but intermediate stations should be reduced to the status of halts or should be closed where circumstances permit. As an illustration, the only stations which, we visualise, would remain open between Dublin and Cork would be Kildare, Portlaoighise, Thurles, Limerick Junction and Mallow. Generally, there would be on average about 25 miles between stations and few areas would be more than 20 miles from the nearest railway station. The total length of line would be reduced to less than half of the present mileage, while the numbers of stations, excluding halts, would be reduced to about one-fourth of the existing number. (ibid., par. 391)

As can be seen from the language of paragraphs 389, 390 and 391 the report, while describing what it 'visualised' as remaining open, stopped short of definitively listing the lines on which the axe could fall. The question immediately arises as to how the contemplated closures might be authorised. Perhaps by Acts of the Oireachtas? Not likely! TDs would run scared from such a prospect. Continue the process of exemption orders being issued by the Transport Tribunal? Not practicable. The scale of closures envisaged could require a number of full-time tribunals sitting in permanent session. The main issue was how to get the recommended programme of railway rationalisation off first base. The committee's recommended solution was to abolish the tribunal (of which Dr Beddy was Chairman) and to grant CIÉ the power to close lines, while setting up a transport council which would be advisory and have no executive or judicial role.

Today's railway network closely resembles that visualised by Beddy, but the process by which this change occurred will have to await a later chapter. Thinking back to the 1950s and with the wisdom conferred by hindsight, it seems that the five-man Beddy Committee are due much credit for the manner in which they thought their way through a baggage of history, controversy and prejudice, and for the courage of their recommendations concerning the railway network. Their recommendations about severe pruning of the system were severely criticised by CIÉ, and generated what might be described as widespread pain and shock, especially in those communities that saw their deep and vital interests being savaged by 'unthinking and unsympathetic bureaucrats'. Today we can see that none of the alternatives which Beddy rejected could have been correct in the long term, i.e. abandonment of the entire system, payment of subsidies on a scale sufficient to maintain the existing system indefinitely or compulsory diversion of traffic from road to rail. Indeed one might speculate whether the scale of restrictions which it rejected would, if implemented, have survived a constitutional challenge. The advantages which Beddy claimed would follow from their proposals included:

> Traffic would be concentrated at fewer points; station staffs would be more fully employed; wagon-loading would improve and fewer wagons would be required; greater use could be made of containers and mechanical aids to handling so as to reduce the cost of double handling . . . Substantial economies in maintenance, in operating costs and in the staffing of the various departments of the railway undertaking should result and an opportunity would be provided to demonstrate how far the railway system can hold its place in an efficiently operated national transport system without incurring serious financial losses and thereby weakening the whole structure of public transport. (ibid., par. 392)

Only with regard to ending 'serious financial losses' would the committee's expectations prove in time to be quite wide of the mark. But before the community might set CIÉ another impossible target, Beddy recognised that even with the reduced rail network, major changes were needed to (a) relieve CIÉ of historically accumulated financial charges, and (b) to improve its business flexibility by removing nineteenth-century commercial restraints.

The key phrase in the terms of reference given to the Beddy Committee was to 'consider what measures are necessary . . . to ensure the provision of the transport requirements of the country on a basis which will best serve the public interests'. There is no reference to financial break-even for CIÉ or relieving the exchequer of any of its obligations. The only criterion which the committee should apply to its recommendations was that of best serving the 'public interests'. The committee concluded that these would best be served by a severe pruning of the railway system, but also, being mindful of CIÉ's financial problems, they had major proposals to make concerning CIÉ's capital structure, something which the Board of CIÉ had not discussed in its own submission to the committee. CIÉ's own reticence on this point might have been because they felt obliged to regard it as a 'no change' item. They were feeling bruised from various encounters with the Department of Finance mentioned in the previous chapter.

Beddy subjected CIÉ's financial records to a very professional type of examination, focusing in particular on the manner in which its balance sheet had developed through the initial GSR/DUTC merger of 1945, the reorganisation of 1950, and the subsequent issue of £7 million transport stock and payments (repayable and non-repayable) from the state since the 1950 Act. The report found that CIÉ was seriously 'over capitalised'. In other words, its assets were overvalued and it carried an unrealistically heavy debt burden. Consequently it developed a series of relevant recommendations, logically and piece by piece. It noted that the interest on government guaranteed transport stock which had been issued in 1945 to the amount of £12.5 m. to acquire the GSR and DUTC, and the additional sum of £1.25 m. in 1950 to acquire the Grand Canal Company had increased rather than reduced the undertaking's financial burden. Previously, interest on debentures or dividends on common stock could not be paid unless a profit was achieved. Now, the government paid interest on all of CIÉ's capital, but CIÉ ended up owing those payments back to the government, and year on year this debt grew as interest to government accrued.

> The likelihood that CIÉ will be in a position to repay the liability to the Central Fund in respect of these advances is remote and the interest on the accumulated liability is now a considerable annual burden which serves only to increase the accumulated deficits of the undertaking.
> (ibid., par. 412)

Beddy heavily criticised the 1950 Act, which nationalised CIÉ, for its failure to address the 'necessity for a radical reconstruction of its [CIÉ's] capital':

> Heavy losses had been incurred for some years [prior to 1950] in railway operation; locomotives, carriages and wagons were over-age and in a poor state of repair, and adequate renewals had not been carried out for many years. Indeed, owing to the worn-out condition of the railway assets and the very doubtful commercial future of the railway undertaking it is difficult to see that, apart from the Road Transport and Hotels Departments, the fixed assets had any real take-over value.
> (ibid., par. 406)

Some TDs had said as much twelve years earlier, when CIÉ was being set up, and again in 1950. Beddy's recommendations which followed these observations were:

(a) to eliminate the over-capitalisation present at 1st June, 1950, by writing down to nominal values or to values representing expenditure since 1st June, 1950, the Railway Lines and Works, the Railway Rolling Stock, and such items as the Canal, Canal Barges and Equipment, Docks, Harbours and Wharves, Fishguard and Rosslare Railways and Harbours co. and Barrow Navigation; and
(b) to eliminate losses accumulated up to 31 March 1956.

(ibid., par. 408)

The adjustments recommended by Beddy involved writing a total of £11,602,761 off the balance sheet. As a result of these write-offs, government should relieve CIÉ of the liability to pay interest on an equal amount of transport stock (saving CIÉ £340,000 per annum). In addition, CIÉ would be relieved of the need to charge depreciation on those written down assents with a consequent benefit of £350,000 per annum. Relief from the liability for interest on sums previously advanced by the state to pay interest on transport stock would amount to a further £140,000 per annum.

In summary, Beddy's financial recommendations would improve CIÉ's annual results by £830,000 per annum principally by removing some nonsense from the balance sheet and by recognising and eliminating more nonsense from the exchequer/CIÉ account. The Beddy motivation, expressed in much more polite language, was to introduce reality into financial statements which were burdened by unrealistic if not absurd valuations and provisions.

A similar impatience with restraints on CIÉ's flexibility in doing business with its customers is evident in Beddy's recommendations concerning 'common carrier' obligations. While these had been modified somewhat by the 1950 Transport Act, they remained largely intact as hangovers from nineteenth-century regulations imposed by the Railway Clauses Act 1845 and Railways and Canal Traffic Act 1851. Their continued existence inhibited CIÉ, perhaps to a greater extent than was strictly necessary, from aggressively confronting its competitors in the marketplace. Commenting on these restrictions and obligations, Beddy said that they had 'their origin in conditions which do not now exist. CIÉ must accept all traffic offered and must do so at rates not exceeding its published rates.'

> Our main railways have now been brought under State control and it is a primary duty of those who operate them to do so in the national interest and to avoid unfair discrimination. (ibid., par. 402)

The recommendation which followed was that

> beyond a general obligation to provide for the reasonable public

transport requirements of the community in a fair and satisfactory manner and to fix maximum rates and fares, CIÉ should be free from the special restrictions to which it is now subject. CIÉ should not be expected to meet unreasonable demands for transport facilities which could be provided only at a loss; neither should CIÉ be unable, because of fear of a charge of undue preference, to quote such rates and fares as it considers appropriate. (ibid., par. 403)

The Beddy Report dealt with the employment issue but did not quantify the job losses which would inevitably follow from the envisaged rationalisation of the railways. It suggested that the cost of redundancy payments, which should continue on the lines of the earlier Acts affecting CIÉ, should be paid out of a special fund which would be financed by a levy on road vehicle licences. That recommendation has the flavour of a temporary *ad hoc* fix and seems out of character with the generally strategic approach of the rest of the report.

As already mentioned, Beddy's terms of reference did not require the committee to prescribe a way for CIÉ to become solvent, financially self-supporting or suchlike. The drafters of those terms of reference sensibly set no such trap and the committee did not make the mistake of imagining it to exist. A gap would exist in the short term between the current (1956) loss of £1.6 million and the relief of £830,000 which would come from capital restructuring. Whether that gap could be closed in the medium term by reduced railway working, together with the benefits of greater commercial flexibility, is a question that was not put by Beddy as his report came to its end. A very thorough job had been done.

The report offered no promise of an easy tomorrow. There would still be problems. The ball was now back to government.

CHAPTER 9

ANOTHER BEGINNING

Reactions to Beddy—1958 Transport Act—Dáil debate.

The year 1957 would prove to be critical for public transport and would herald the greatest change in the Irish railway network since the nineteenth century. On 13 May the Beddy Report received main story treatment in all the Republic's papers. The headlines read '60% REDUCTION IN CIE RAIL MILEAGE URGED' (*The Irish Times*) and 'BIG RAIL CUTS PROPOSED; subsidies rejected; levy to compensate redundant workers; private transport encouraged' (*Irish Press*). The tone of leading articles in all the Republic's dailies was respectful of the apparent objectivity of the committee's findings. There was little suggestion of shock or horror. On the contrary, they accepted the inevitability of major reductions in the railway system and seemed to believe that complete closure might follow one day. Under the heading, 'Facing the Facts', *The Irish Times* leader summarised the report and its attitude thereto:

> The committee's main recommendation is that the railways should be 'cut down to size' by the drastic diminution of rather more than half the mileage with an even more drastic reduction in the number of stations. The case for such rationalisation is overwhelming. It has been made before—this newspaper has pressed it for very many years—and only one serious argument has ever been adduced against it: namely that the abandonment of branch lines and the smaller stations would entail heavy unemployment. On the other hand the curtailment of private transport which CIÉ has urged, could entail still higher unemployment . . . A nation as poor as ours cannot afford the luxury

of a public transport system which is both outmoded and extravagant. CIÉ is being offered the only practicable alternatives—either to make the most important part of the railway network pay, or to go out of business altogether....

This is a far more realistic 'blue print' for Irish transport than was Sir James Milne's Report of 1948. The five committee members have opened their eyes to the facts—which are that the railways if they are to remain at all, must be brought into conformation with the over-all pattern of transport, rather than that the pattern should be made to conform with the railways....

The *Irish Independent*'s leading article 'Abandonment of Railways?' was in a similar vein:

If the recommendations of the Committee of Inquiry are adopted the greater part of the railway lines operated by CIÉ will be abandoned... The problem must however be examined dispassionately. The horse has yielded on both road and farm to the motor vehicle. The waterways are almost abandoned as a means of transport. The stage coach gave way to the train. The tramway has been replaced by the motor omnibus. Has the time come when the railway must give way to motor services? The decision to be taken should not be influenced by sentiment, it must be dictated by cold facts of finance and economics...

The *Cork Examiner* was no less hardheaded in its remarks despite Beddy's proposals to deprive west Cork of its extensive rail network.

The Governments of the Twenty-Six Counties face the problem [of railway closures] less realistically than their opposite number of the Six Counties in the hope that conditions might be improved without too much upsetting of the employment pattern or of local social circumstances. We believe that the country will have to approach this problem on the basis that the committee has made a very strong case for its main recommendations.

There were no immediate comments from the Board and employees of CIÉ nor from the government, whose predecessors had commissioned the report in an atmosphere of crisis less than twelve months earlier. Brief comments welcoming the direction of the report were made by two road haulage associations, by the Livestock Exporters Association and by the Federation of Irish Manufacturers. Northern Ireland interests were quoted as saying that the committee's report had been expected to provide some support for the cross-border lines that were threatened with closure but the 'opposite' had happened.

CIÉ would convey its views in confidence to government concerning the Beddy Report, but also, in July, publication of the full text of its own (September 1956) submission to the Beddy Committee indicated that it still stood by that submission. While CIÉ could only be angry at the total rejection of its thesis, it could derive a grain of consolation from a comment in the *Irish Independent* leading article: 'We believe that the public is satisfied that in recent years the Board of CIÉ has done almost everything that could be expected in the way of modernising their services, making them more speedy and comfortable.' The *Irish Independent* published the full text of the report over three days—a far cry from what would be expected to happen similar reports in the 1990s!

With regard to the government's reaction to Beddy, the situation was read correctly, if inelegantly, by the *Cork Examiner*:

> Without waiting to consider the report the government through the Information Bureau issued it to the Press obviously with the purpose of observing the reactions of the public and a multitude of vested interests to the recommendations which are not a little drastic though necessary if the country is to get down to earth and eventually have an economic financially sound public transport service.

Dr Noel Browne, now an Independent TD, was clearly in touch with the feelings of the CIÉ Board and its employees and in sympathy with the logic of its thinking when he asked a question of the Minister for Industry and Commerce on 5 June 1957. Dr Browne asked the minister 'if in view of the obligations which the Transport Act 1950 imposes on the Board of CIÉ, to provide an efficient and economical transport system and their repeated inability to discharge their responsibility until private freight transport had been drastically restricted, he will now introduce the necessary legislation to help the company to achieve this end and to expand its haulage operations both by road and rail'. He asked another question on the same day concerning alterations to the law which would allow farmers to move their neighbours' goods within a two mile radius of their farms—a proposal which CIÉ favoured. Seán Lemass replied that government did not propose to decide on any such matters until it had the opportunity of considering views from various bodies on the committee's recommendations.

On the very day that Noel Browne's question was answered in the Dáil and three weeks after the publication of Beddy, Seán Lemass issued a separate statement accepting the Northern government's intention to close down 84 miles of line within the Six Counties: '. . . there is no practicable alternative to concurring in the closing of these lines'. Two weeks later, dealing with a question about Dublin's bus fares, Lemass reaffirmed that he was awaiting submissions on the Beddy Report before coming to his own decisions concerning its recommendations. Deputy Patrick Byrne (Ind.) had long been of the opinion that Dublin bus travellers were paying unnecessarily high fares so as to help carry railway losses. He quoted figures from the Beddy Report which showed that Dublin City Transport Services earned a profit of £335,000 for the year ended 31 March 1956, representing a return of 19.6 per cent on the capital investment in Dublin services and asked, 'Is it not the case that the Transport Report has revealed that the Dublin public are being grossly exploited by CIÉ in respect of transport service and as a matter of urgency will the Minister arrange to take steps to see that the public are charged less exorbitant fares for the inadequate services provided?' Seán Lemass's reply was peremptory: 'The answers to all parts of the Deputy's . . . question are in the negative.' The Ceann Comhairle called the next question while the frustrated Deputy exclaimed, 'it is highway robbery' (*Dáil Debates*, Vol. 162, Col. 847). Some years later when the same allegation that Dublin was subsidising rural services was again being argued in the Dáil, figures showing losses on Dublin suburban rail services would be brought into the equation and used by government to argue that the surplus on Dublin's total transport services was not what it seemed.

But meantime what was to be done about the wider question of public transport and the affairs of CIÉ? On 2 July 1957 Seán Lemass, when moving a vote for his Department, maintained his previous stance that views had been sought from interested organisations including the Board of CIÉ and that the 'Government do not intend to consider the recommendations [of the Beddy Report] until these observations and comments have been received', but still, he was prepared to shift slightly so as to show in which direction he was facing. Public transport operations on road and rail should be maintained, but

> The question which has to be decided is the part which the railways will play within that public transport organisation within the next ten years. . . . I do not think it is practicable to attempt to plan for more than ten years ahead. Secondly we have to consider the conditions which are required to enable these public transport services to be operated without loss, without subvention from the taxpayers.
> (ibid., Vol. 163, Col. 466)

He was setting a tough target—maintenance without subsidy of public transport on road and rail, a task that had eluded public transport since private motor transport had taken off thirty years earlier. While the decision-making process was under way, and civil servants in Industry and

Commerce and Finance parsed and analysed the Beddy document and submissions received, CIÉ's own situation was not improving. William Norton, a member of the government which commissioned Beddy, spoke about the report CIÉ had written to him twelve months earlier 'which indicated that they had rather lost faith in their ability to weather the storm financially in view of all the difficulties with which they were surrounded. They themselves saw nothing but bleakness in front of them.'

Hence their insistence that traffic be restored to the railway, if it was to survive. CIÉ's losses (£1.7 million reported in 1956/57) were still rising while consultations took place and decisions were being made. In the year to 31 March 1958 the deficit rose a further 31 per cent to £2,260,944. The CIÉ Board struggled to contain the situation. Fifty new diesel locomotives and 2 new railcars were put into service, resulting in the virtual completion of the order for 94 diesel locomotives which had been placed in May 1954. Another 1,156 new wagons were introduced. As dieselisation progressed operating economies were achieved. Even after an increased depreciation charge of £60,000, railway expenditure in 1957/58 had been reduced by £217,000, but railway receipts fell at the same time so that the overall improvement in railway results was a mere £43,000. This slippage in railway revenue was largely caused by a decline in first-class travel. Comfort standards improved with new locomotives and coaching stock but, unfortunately for CIÉ, passengers tended to trade downwards into second-class coaches, with loss of revenue to the railway. Road passenger results slipped by £242,000 largely due to a loss of one per cent, 2,500,000 passengers, on Dublin City Services.

1957 was a bleak year not merely for CIÉ but for the economy generally. Unemployment and emigration soared and Ireland was facing a crisis of self-doubt. It was the year of the First Programme for Economic Expansion which formally confronted the question as to how the state could be made economically viable. As CIÉ's results disimproved during the year, its board could at least have the comfort of knowing that it had formally and vigorously brought the nature of its problem to the attention of its reluctant shareholder. The choices had been spelt out and the decision as to where to go now rested with its government master.

Lemass held out until 27 November 1957 before announcing his intentions for CIÉ when introducing a supplementary transport and marine services vote. These included a major reduction in CIÉ's capital obligations, but the main interest of his remarks relates to the railways. He would remain vague about the future size of the railway network. That would have to be a matter for a new CIÉ board.

All the information available to me would make it quite clear that the elimination of branch lines would not make any appreciable difference to CIÉ's financial position. CIÉ tells me there are 22 branch lines which lose £100,000 per year. Relate that to losses of £2 million! The branch lines contribute traffic to the system worth over £800,000. This traffic might be held by road services but at a higher operating cost. In saying this I do not want to be taken as giving all the branch lines of the CIÉ system a reprieve. (ibid., Vol. 164, Col. 1051)

These remarks confirm that CIÉ was still arguing that paring the system was not the solution to the problem. The real solution in their view was to force traffic off the roads and on to the railways. Referring to the famous map on page 186 of the Beddy Report which visualised an 'appropriate' railway system, Lemass continued: 'It is the part of the committee's report which was perhaps most strongly criticised by the CIÉ Board having been based on insufficient operating experience and lack of appreciation of the value of contributory traffic.' In defence of the committee he added: 'They had not in mind making the attempt to specify the sections of line or the stations which should be closed down. They gave their views in that regard by way of illustration only and would I think agree with the view that the actual implementation of any such policy could only be undertaken by those who had day to day administrative responsibility and access to all the relevant facts.' In a telling final comment Lemass looked to the future which would prove Beddy to be not far off the mark (see maps on pages 117 and 120 to compare the Beddy projections with the actual railway system as it exists in 1995):

It may be that in the course of time some picture of the CIÉ rail system will eventually emerge which will have some resemblance to the proposal published in the report but I feel that nobody is at this time equipped to dogmatise on that point. (ibid., Col. 1054)

Lemass made it clear that unlike what was happening in the Six Counties, the final decision about the size of the railway system would not be made by government. The following quotation effectively summarises what he was about to propose:

The government's view is that the responsibility for taking decisions on the reduction of railway services, on the closing down of particular sections of line or on the shutting down of stations must rest upon the *Board* of CIÉ. It is proposed however to give the Board a statutory direction in a new bill which I shall be submitting to the Dáil early next year, a direction which will be subject to its existing statutory obligation to operate the whole undertaking entrusted to it without

> loss, a direction to keep open railway lines and railway stations unless they are satisfied that there is no prospect of economical operation within a reasonable time. Subject to that statutory obligation the Board will be empowered to close down any line or station or to withdraw any service for which they consider there is no future on their own decision and without having to seek the prior approval of the Transport Tribunal. (ibid., Col. 1054)

In the event the Transport Tribunal would be abolished. Lemass's November 1957 speech dealt with many other aspects of the Beddy Report, but the government's proposals did not take final shape until publication of the 1958 Transport Bill in May 1958 which indeed laid down that CIÉ would not need approval from any third party for future decisions affecting the railway network. It was going to be given freedom to make its decisions, but that freedom would be heavily qualified in the legislation itself, and even more so in its practical use.

CIÉ had come into being in 1945. The 1950 Transport Act which removed private shareholders from the company was described as a second start for a national public transport organisation. The 1958 Transport Act, learning something from the experience of the intervening years, attempted a third start. Whether the something learnt was sufficient or not will emerge as our story continues.

Before the government's definitive proposals were published, the Transport Bill was passed in draft to CIÉ for comment. A board minute of 19 February 1958 succinctly recorded that:

> Board approved of memorandum to be sent to Minister intimating that it was satisfied that proposed legislation would not succeed in bringing the undertaking to a self supporting position within 5 years as provided for in the draft bill.

The student of government will not be surprised that before long the membership of the board which took that position would be radically changed.

A few days short of the first anniversary of the publication of the Beddy Report, Dáil Éireann (8 May 1958) began its debate on the 1958 Transport Bill. Another Bill was to follow six weeks later (24 June 1958) dealing with the demise of the GNRB. The two Bills would take effect on the same date, 30 September 1958. To compress the story somewhat, the GNRB was to be merged with CIÉ, meaning that there would now be only one railway company within the state. Within the Republic the assets of the GNRB other than rolling stock were already vested in the state. These assets would now be transferred to CIÉ, with the exception of the Dundalk engineering works which were already managed by the Dundalk Engineering Company (see page 99) and would be vested in a renamed Industrial Engineering Company. The GNRB's railway rolling stock would be divided between CIÉ and the UTA, both of which would now operate services between Dublin and Belfast. GNRB's road vehicles would be transferred to CIÉ, as would the Great Northern Hotel, Bundoran.

The entire transfer of assets to CIÉ would involve no charge on its balance sheet. The fact that assets with a book value in excess of £3 million would not involve an increase in CIÉ's debt broke with the precedent of all previous transport legislation, i.e. CIÉ was required previously to remunerate the capital expended by the state on the purchase of the GSR, the DUTC and the Grand Canal Company. Indeed the GNRB had also been required to remunerate the capital paid by both governments in compensation to GNR stockholders.

The change in policy was not due to any generous impulse by the state but to a no doubt reluctant acceptance of some cold facts. Neither CIÉ nor the GNRB had been able to carry the cost of remunerating their original capital burdens without regular interest-bearing advances from the state. Transfer of the GNRB's operations in the Republic to CIÉ would impose operating costs on that company which would exceed likely additional revenue. Hence this free gift to CIÉ was no more than consistent with the Beddy finding that CIÉ was already overcapitalised in the sense that it bore capital liabilities well in excess of what it had been, or ever was likely to be, able to remunerate. Recognising this fact the 1958 Transport Bill also relieved CIÉ of £16.5 million of interest-bearing debt, principally comprising most of its pre-1950 debt. Also, in an attempt to improve the prospects of future viability, government accepted the Beddy recommendation that CIÉ be relieved of its 'common carrier' obligations which in effect required CIÉ to accept all traffic which might be offered to it and to charge for it in accordance with a detailed 'non discriminatory' published tariff. The rationale for this change from nineteenth-century thinking was that CIÉ, as a publicly accountable concern, could be relied on to give 'fair and satisfactory service' to all its customers. While doing so it should be able aggressively to compete with other transport operators, and to negotiate special deals with 'own account' operators so as to win traffic back or to obtain new traffic for its services.

In summary, the GNR merger with CIÉ, the capital restructuring and the removal of 'common carrier' restraints on trading flexibility were the main changes in the two 1958 Acts affecting CIÉ's operating and financial circumstances. As signalled in the previous November the Bill proposed no change in the railway network. This would be a matter for CIÉ itself, subject to an obligation to maintain railway services and to keep railway stations open, except where it would formally conclude that such services or stations had no economic future.

The vital question was whether this new package would enable CIÉ to breakeven and to avoid future losses. Beddy thought that even with its proposed major reorganisation of the railway system it would take time before CIÉ would prove itself to be viable. Seán Lemass was introducing his last major transport measure as Minister for Industry and Commerce. He was not yet prepared to change his position that public transport should be commercially self-sustaining, but he was prepared to provide CIÉ with some interim help.

> It cannot be expected that any reorganisation measures or release from financial obligations such as I have mentioned could enable the Board of CIÉ to achieve solvency immediately. Indeed the Bill envisages that the Board will not have achieved that situation for five years. I know that at the present time there are few railway systems in the world which are not losing money and that in expecting CIÉ to achieve solvency it may be said that we are asking them to do something that other railway executives are not able to do even under more favourable circumstances.
>
> That may be true but we must not allow the experience of other countries to lead us into slovenly thinking or relaxation of effort to improve the situation of CIÉ. (*Dáil Debates*, Vol. 167, Col. 1508)

The result of this thinking was that the 1958 Transport Bills provided that CIÉ would receive an annual grant of £1.175 million for five years. This uneven figure was made up of an initial £1 million for CIÉ's existing operations which was increased by £175,000 to help it absorb the GNRB's operations within the Republic. During the next five years it was envisaged, once again, that conditions would so change and the benefits of reorganisation would so accumulate that public transport would cease to require public subvention. The 1958 Transport Act laid down:

> It shall be the duty of the Board to conduct its undertaking so that as soon as may be and in any case not later than the 31st day of March 1964, its operating expenditure including all charges properly chargeable to revenue shall not be greater than the revenue of the Board.

The attentive reader will immediately spot the difference between this 1958 provision and the similar provision in the 1950 Act which read:

> It shall be the duty of the Board so to conduct its undertaking as to secure as soon as may be that taking one year with another, the revenue of the Board shall be not less than sufficient to meet the charges properly chargeable to revenue.

The new Act fixed 31 March 1964 as the date beyond which 'as soon as may be' could not be extended. Other than that, the draftsman of the 1958 Act, seemingly determined to make some change in the provision of the 1950 Act, merely managed to reverse the language of the earlier Act. The 1950 Act said that revenue should not fall short of expenditure, and now the 1958 Act laid down that expenditure should not exceed revenue! The new Act which eventually passed into law without a division provided that the state would fund redundancies arising within five years of the Act. This finding would not involve a special levy on road licences as suggested by Beddy—a 'startling proposal' in the language of the *Irish Independent*. Redundant employees (within the state) of the Sligo, Leitrim & Northern Counties Railway were similarly catered for. No new restrictions were placed on road haulage, which was relaxed for some commodities and for farmers carrying their neighbours' goods. The only other change affecting road haulage was that minimum fines were laid down for breaches of the Road Transport Acts and that the probation of offenders escape hatch could not be used for repeat offences.

During the debate on the 1958 Transport Bill, Michael O'Higgins, TD (Fine Gael) spoke of the 'hopes of more than one Minister for Industry and Commerce being dashed' by the transport problem. (If we go back to 1925, this would mean four ministers in all, i.e. McGilligan, Lemass, Morrissey and Norton.) Michael O'Higgins said: 'I do not intend to indulge in any taunting of the present occupant of that position because his hopes in the days of 1943 and 1944 have been dashed also.' Paddy McGilligan, TD was unable to show a similar restraint. He wanted to make a number of 'salient points', the first of which was: 'CIÉ is in its usual bankrupt position, a position in which it has been since the Minister put his hands to the amelioration of transport in this country.' (ibid., Vol. 164, Col. 1405)

Bringing the debate on the second stage to a close, Seán Lemass said:

> It is rather a large responsibility to have to carry, to have to produce proposals which will be regarded as workable by those who have to work them and which will achieve the purpose which Deputy Norton referred to, of keeping the issue of transport policy out of the area of party controversy. (ibid., Col. 1524)

He went on to thank the deputies for their constructive contributions, making an understandable exception for his old acerbic rival, Paddy McGilligan, who said Mr Lemass had followed 'his usual destructive line'. Noting Deputy Daniel Desmond's observation that he 'has some doubts as to whether this will be the last Transport Bill to come before the Dáil', Seán Lemass ended the debate with the words, 'We all have that doubt.' However, the 1958 Act would serve its purpose well enough for five controversial years before the ever changing economic and transport scene would force the government to act again.

Chapter 10

Railway Contraction

Appointment of Todd Andrews—Absorption of GNR—A new broom—Modernisation—Area management structure—Pricing package deals—Harcourt Street line—West Clare railway closure—Controversies about Waterford, Tramore and west Cork closures—Closures in the midlands—Declining traffic on suburban lines.

When the dynamic political or business leader decides that a fresh start needs to be made in some important sphere, more is looked for than a mere change in policy or a rewriting of the rule book. A change in management is sought which will bring new energy and new thinking to the activity required to be overhauled. In 1958 Seán Lemass looked for such a change.

T. C. Courtney had been Chairman of CIÉ since 1949, was 63 years old and his health was not good. His successor said that in his job Ted Courtney was not helped 'by the lack of firm direction by government nor . . . by the hostility of trade unions, his less than friendly relations with the civil servants and his inheritance from the war years of run-down equipment'.

Dr C. S. (Todd) Andrews was 57 years old and Managing Director of Bord na Móna. The programme of building turf-burning power stations was nearing completion and two briquette stations were under construction. Todd Andrews records that the organisation was soundly based:

> My function as Chief Executive was reduced to keeping up the momentum though much of my attention was also devoted to the promotion of good public relations. Such an administrative role did not suit my temperament . . . I was not by any means fully stretched.

He felt that it would suit him and Bord na Móna if he were taken out of the organisation and given some other task (C. S. Andrews, *Man of No Property*, p. 238). In 1956 at a government reception in Iveagh House he had confided these feelings to Seán Lemass in a casual conversation. Thinking little more about it he was surprised by a call two years later in summer 1958 from Seán Lemass and offered the full-time post of Chairman of CIÉ. Lemass also advised Andrews that he was considering the appointment of two other full-time directors which had been recommended in the Beddy Report. Andrews, in his autobiographies which concentrate more on his childhood and later republican activities than on his business career, records that he wanted to accept the CIÉ challenge but he had two reservations. He would not accept the job if there were to be two other full-time directors. 'I felt I could not do justice to the job unless I was the complete boss, subject of course, to the broad overall control of the Board of CIÉ.' Andrews' second reservation related to remuneration and is of interest mainly because of the attitude it reveals towards civil servants. 'I also asked him if I might assume that I would be employed on terms no less favourable than the incumbent Chairman both in respect of remuneration, pension rights and the considerable fringe benefits attached to the post. I did not trust the civil servants not to avail themselves of the chance to worsen the terms of the appointment; they were notoriously jealous of the higher salaries and perquisites of the heads of semi-state companies as compared with their own.' Lemass accepted both of Andrews' stipulations.

At a special meeting of the CIÉ Board on 28 August 1958 Courtney informed his colleagues that he had tendered his resignation as Chairman of CIÉ to the Minister for Industry and Commerce. The board's tribute to its outgoing chairman was something more than the formality which might be expected. It decided to place on record 'its appreciation of the immense services tendered to CIÉ by the chairman T. C. Courtney, including as it did the dieselisation of the rail services, modernisation of the rolling stock, the equipment and extension of hotels and retooling of workshops increasing thereby the earning capacity and general efficiency of the undertaking'. The meeting noted that consequent on the passage of the Transport Act the resignation of other directors was being sought by the minister.

On Monday, 1 September, the board met again, this time with Todd Andrews in the chair. It noted that his letter of appointment required 'Dr Andrews to devote the whole of his time to his duties as chairman of the Board and will act as Chief Executive Officer of the Board'. At this first meeting of the Andrews era the General Manager (Frank Lemass) submitted a proposal that CIÉ should cease trading on the Grand Canal. The withdrawal by CIÉ of its own barges from the canal had previously been proposed to government in 1953 and rejected. The Beddy Report supported

CIÉ's proposal to withdraw canal services. Seán Lemass, during the Dáil debate on the 1958 Transport Act, was not convinced that this should be done. With the new discretion conferred on CIÉ by the Act, management wanted action. The board decided that 'traders' on the canal should be consulted before a final decision was made. The withdrawal of CIÉ barges from the Grand Canal and its associated waterways (the Barrow and the Shannon) would not take place for another fifteen months (1 January 1960), and even then the Dublin–Limerick through traffic would be granted an extension. This hesitancy at Todd Andrews' first board meeting about making a firm decision concerning the Grand Canal gave, as we shall see, quite a false signal about future behaviour.

On Wednesday, 3 September 1958, Todd Andrews moved into his new office, an event which was recorded in *The Irish Times* on the following day:

> Dr C. S. Andrews former Managing Director of Bord na Móna yesterday took up occupancy for the first time of a quiet conservatively decorated office adorned with steel engravings of views of old Dublin and Kingstown Railway, the windows of which overlook the arrival and departure platforms of Kingsbridge Station. It was the first day in his new post as Chairman of the new Board of CIÉ.

In addition to Dr Andrews, two former GNRB directors joined the CIÉ Board, one of whom was W. McMullen, a former president of the ITGWU. To accommodate the three new appointees three others resigned. Mr Courtney remained on the board in a non-executive capacity. Absorption of the GNRB within the Republic was the first task to hand. That was to happen on 1 October.

Andrews used that occasion to issue his first public statement as Chairman. It was a 'call to the colours', welcoming new staff and appealing to all staff for loyalty and co-operation in facing the challenge of giving the Irish public an efficient and successful transport organisation:

> Today the part of the GNRB Board within the state rests in CIÉ. This creates a new situation in public transport in Ireland. I feel honoured at being given the task of heading this great concern...
>
> The Board feels sure that the highest traditions of the two undertakings will be fused in the new organisation and will help to create an efficient and economic public transport system of which Ireland will be proud. Such a system can be created only by a belief in success and high endeavour on the part of all employees.
>
> It will be the aim of the Board to promote conditions in the organisation where initiative will be encouraged, and where merit will

be recognised and rewarded . . . We start our task with great goodwill from the public. It is only by serving the public successfully that we can retain and increase that goodwill.

But in many areas his message may have been crowded out by the excitement accompanying the GNRB's last rites. In Dublin there was a strong party atmosphere, but Belfast was more sombre in mood. *The Irish Times* reported from both locations in its issue of 1 October 1958.

TRAIN'S RUN TO HOWTH MARKS END OF G.N.R.

There was 'rock 'n roll' on the departure platform at Amiens Street station last night before the last train left for Howth. Several hundred people were present to bid it a noisy farewell which reached its crescendo as the train drew slowly out of the station over scores of signal detonators which had been placed on the line.

At one minute past midnight the Great Northern Railway ceased to exist and the trains become the property of Córas Iompair Éireann. Just before the train was due to leave, the platform gates were flung open and the crowd surged towards the carriages. From that stage onwards, the discord mounted as the groups in the individual compartments roared out their own particular musical selections, but most of the songs they sang had one thing in common— they were of the sentimental type.

RAIN SET MOOD FOR LAST G.N.R. TRAIN OUT OF BELFAST

It rained all day in Belfast yesterday, a steady, drenching, persistent downpour.

'You could say that the weather matched the prevailing mood', said Mr G. B. Howden, who was deeply involved, in his time, with both the G.N.R. and C.I.E., and is now chairman of the Ulster Transport Authority. . . . 'This is a sad moment for us all', Mr Howden had said, his mind slipping back over the years to 1930, when he was brought across from England to relay the track across the Boyne Bridge for a virile, expanding young railway company (then 50-odd years young, and in the very prime of life).

No pomp attended its departure. It pulled out of platform 4 dead on time, past a couple of blue and cream diesel cars—all earmarked for the wearing of the green, whether it happens to be the familiar green of the C.I.E. coaches or the surprisingly similar shade favoured by the U.T.A. . . .

The journey to Dublin was uneventful. As the train left Dundalk,

half a dozen dull explosions—fog signals, an old railwayman said—
and a half-hearted cheer sent it on its way.

A final word on the GNR may be allowed from C. L. Fry, the man whose name should be associated with that of Tommy Tighe of CIÉ, who restored, indeed rebuilt, Fry's model railway before it was put on permanent display in Malahide Castle, Co. Dublin. Fry had this to say about the GNR:

> The Great Northern Railway and Tramway has always been the pride of its operator and its well kept station and premises with its immaculately kept blue engines picked out in black and white linings and with bright red underframes, its polished teak coaches and its handsome cream and blue diesel railcars and trams all enhanced with the company's coat of arms. This surely must have been the most handsome livery of any railway anywhere. What a pity that soon it will be seen no more. (*Irish Independent*, 24 September 1958)

With the expiry of the GNR, CIÉ acquired 2,500 additional employees, 120 miles of permanent way, 160 buses, 300 road goods vehicles and 11 Howth trams. Since 1901 these trams plied up and down from Sutton to the summit of Howth Head, but since January 1954 when their abandonment had been announced, they continued to run only because suitable roads for buses had not yet been completed. The CIÉ take-over granted them no reprieve. Within another eight months they would be gone, and *The Irish Times* noted that despite their possible interest as a tourist attraction, Bord Fáilte had made no representations about keeping them in operation.

The allocation of GNRB's rolling stock and locomotives between CIÉ and the UTA would be more complex. The GNRB had 168 steam locomotives of various vintages, of which almost 50 per cent (83) moved to CIÉ. A smaller proportion of GNRB's other rolling stock became CIÉ's property. Of 60 diesel railcars owned by GNRB, 24 transferred to CIÉ. Of GNRB's 442 passenger coaches, CIÉ took only 119, and of 850 other rail vehicles owned by the GNRB, 247 seem to have moved to CIÉ (GNRB and CIÉ Annual Reports). In spite of CIÉ's previous efforts it would have more steam-powered operations in the early sixties than it had previously intended.

The GNRB's headquarters had been in Amiens Street, in the 1880s' red sandstone building beside the granite railway station which had been opened by the Lord Lieutenant in 1846. Amiens Street station and its red sandstone annex joined Kingsbridge, Busáras and Broadstone as one of CIÉ's major architectural landmarks in the capital.

The brusqueness, directness and go-go energy of Todd Andrews was well known even before he moved into his Kingsbridge office. He quickly set out to try to reshape CIÉ. He described this process in *Man Of No Property* and few would now disagree with the story as he began to tell it:

> Experience soon confirmed my belief that the re-organisation of CIÉ was a crash operation which . . . required the virtually complete authority of one man. The board was, of course, entitled to be kept informed on what the chairman was doing; . . . but the board was not in a strong position to oppose whatever line of action he adopted. In the event of serious fundamental disagreement between the board and the chief executive, I suppose either they or he would have to resign. In my term in CIÉ there were no such disagreements.
>
> Seán Lemass's brother, Frank, was the general manager of CIÉ when I was appointed. . . . Frank Lemass and I established a close rapport from the beginning. . . .
>
> I approached the task of managing CIÉ with great confidence, and with a lot of goodwill from the public, the civil servants and the trade unions. The Irish Transport and General Workers' Union wrote to welcome me and wish me well. Jim Larkin junior, of the Workers' Union of Ireland, whom I knew slightly, called on me. He was far and away the most competent, best trained and most intelligent of the trade union leaders with whom I came in contact. He was a very tough negotiator but deals made with him stuck. Unfortunately his union had very few members in CIÉ.
>
> There were 20,000 employees in CIÉ [22,109 according to the 1958/59 Report]. The company's operations extended into the remote reaches of the country. Every skill and trade was represented in its work force. My first act was to visit all the major railway and road transport centres and as many of the small installations as time permitted. I saw and spoke to as many of the staff as possible. . . . The exterior of the buildings bore evidence of decay, office equipment was mostly obsolete and in some cases the premises appeared not to have been cleaned for years . . . At Inchicore we had the largest engineering workshop in Ireland. It was just like a scrap yard. Even the latrines were open-ended which meant that the backsides of the men at stool were visible to everyone. The stores had stocks of materials which had not moved for generations . . .
>
> It was clear to me that, as a priority, the appearance of the company premises required improvement if for no other reason than to indicate to the public and to the staff, whose morale was not of the highest, that a change was on the way. We had the buildings painted outside and inside. Station masters were encouraged to cultivate their gardens and good housekeeping was insisted on. It took a long time to get rid of the

obsolete engines, miscellaneous scrap, useless stores and accumulated apparatus. The task was finally accomplished by detaching an engineer and giving him carte blanche to dispose of the junk in any way he judged fit and at any price he could get. Much of it was a hangover from the major railway companies amalgamation of 1924 and the change-over from steam to diesel locomotion.

(Man of No Property, pp. 245, 246)

The Andrews broom swept thoroughly. To his mind smartness in appearance was an essential counterpart of efficiency and courtesy in service. Without smart looking facilities, staff would not be motivated to appear smart and to be efficient. His concern with smartness and cleanliness was also based on a progressive concept of the dignity and value of each employee. Staff deserved better facilities than those which the tall, angular and distinctive looking Todd Andrews observed in the extensive initial tour he made of CIÉ's various premises. In addition, the clean-up and facelift which he ordered had a marketing aspect and it would take years to complete. Refurbishment of the Amiens Street buildings was tackled at an early stage.

The granite facade of the station was cleaned of grime accumulated over the previous hundred years. The station concourse was redecorated and given improved lighting 'aimed at giving a gay and bright appearance to the terminus'. An acceptably proportioned neon sign proclaimed 'CIE' from the central station tower and could be seen from the still standing Nelson Pillar in O'Connell Street. The red sandstone offices nearby housed the newly centralised traffic department and were 'entirely re-equipped, renovated and redecorated'. *The Irish Times* reported that an innovation in office equipment—a Telecord Dictaphone—was installed, whereby 'substantial savings have been made . . . The latest remote controlled speech recording installation . . . enables members of the staff in various offices to dictate their letters by speaking into it. Forty five of these dictating telephones have been installed. The staff in the typewriting bureau embraces 13 Dictaphone transcribing typists, seven copy typists and a supervisor. Previously this work was handled by 38 shorthand typists. About 850 letters are transcribed daily in the bureau.' (17 March 1959) Strange how such a loudly trumpeted innovation, 'the first of its kind in the country', now seems to be incredibly dated. In CIÉ and elsewhere this 'Telecord' system would fail to deliver satisfactory results as much because of human as of technical problems. M. J. Hilliard, Parliamentary Secretary to the Minister for Industry and Commerce, was invited along to review the facilities where he made a suitable speech:

the centralisation of the traffic department at Amiens Street, should prove to be a most valuable reform. It was the bread winner of the undertaking and it was right that it should be housed in up-to-date surroundings and equipped with modern aids and conveniences.

(ibid.)

The visiting dignitary also inspected the first of a number of 'holiday camping coaches'—retired railway coaches converted into holiday caravans which were to be located at various CIÉ stations around the country as part of CIÉ's tourism promotion efforts. Whatever about the suitability of the coaches themselves, their location in the surroundings of CIÉ railway yards would make them spectacularly unsuccessful. The scheme would be abandoned even sooner than the Telecord equipment. Mr Hilliard ended his visit to Amiens Street by recording a message to staff on the new system.

A more enduring innovation was the substitution of telephones for telegraphs in the important railway communications system, with 'a network of selective ringing telephones radiating from the principal centres' (Annual Report, 1958/59). Todd Andrews' tour of CIÉ facilities had more purpose to it than a mere inspection of physical appearances. He wanted to get to know and to be known by members of staff. Andrews was a Dubliner with a lower middle-class background. With family connections in the Dublin inner city area of Summerhill, he had been brought up in Terenure—a salubrious enough suburb—but the Andrews lived 'over the shop' across the road from Terenure's tramway terminus. He mentioned in *Man of No Property* that he had known the tram workers well and had grown up with those now operating buses. His sympathies lay with their social class rather than with the traditional railway managerial class, the members of which he treated with, at best, polite disdain. Andrews recognised that CIÉ had an unsettled labour record, but he imagined that with the positive progressive attitude he brought to his job and the respect he believed he had already earned from trade unions, he would be able to achieve a sea change in CIÉ's industrial relations. One of his first initiatives on the labour side of CIÉ was a radical reorganisation of communications procedures. As we proceed through the Andrews period we will discover how he felt himself unfortunate, indeed unfairly thwarted, by what would transpire between the Board of CIÉ and the trade unions, between the trade union leaders and their members.

Todd Andrews had thirty years' experience, firstly in the Irish Tourist Association, then in the ESB and eventually fifteen years at the head of Bord na Móna as it grew from infancy to success, when he toured CIÉ. Initially a UCD commerce graduate, by training and experience he had by then become a professional manager, though in temperament and language he was somewhat unique. He knew he was taking over a company in difficulty. It was natural that he would think in management terms about the people he met.

> The second fact that I observed in the course of my initial tour [in addition to the condition of the facilities] was that there was in CIÉ a reservoir of unused talent with no outlet. There was no shortage of ideas and honest effort but it lacked direction and co-ordination. In management terms it did not make sense that the four main branches of the organisation—the rail and road passenger and freight services—should be working in the same territory but without any real local liaison. In addition there was virtually no devolved responsibility; if a clerk was wanted at an office in Tralee or Galway, permission for the appointment had to be obtained from headquarters in Dublin. I also noticed that for an organisation involving so much engineering work few professional engineers were employed. Clearly a fundamental reorganisation of the management system was called for.
>
> (*Man of No Property*, p. 246)

The result of this analysis was the introduction of area management by which Todd Andrews gave CIÉ a severe internal shake-up, the like of which would not be repeated until 1986, when the state with the encouragement of outside consultants would require CIÉ to be reorganised into three separate operating companies. Todd Andrews also used consultants and he did so in many areas, such as organisation and methods—work study as applied to the office, extension of existing work study in manufacturing and operational areas, and also in the area of human relations. One of their first main tasks was to design and implement the area management concept. Consultants (Production Engineering) were used to set up the area offices with new management accounting and control procedures. Through this approach, decision-making would be delegated down from headquarters to the operating regions, where it was centralised in the sense that the area manager had authority over all appropriate local rail passenger, rail freight, road passenger and road freight operations. The areas were in turn broken down into a number of sub-areas to be run by district managers who were also given a large degree of local autonomy.

Bus operations in Dublin had always had a fair degree of autonomy as Dublin City Services. This arrangement would continue, but now other CIÉ operations, including rail, road freight, rural and provincial city buses were to be managed on an area basis. The five 'Areas' were Dublin, Cork, Limerick, Galway and Waterford. The area managers were young, an enthusiastic group, who succeeded in making their enthusiasm felt throughout the organisation. . . . Three were mechanical engineers by profession and one a chartered accountant; all of these were recruited outside the organisation. The fifth was a member of the existing staff who had exceptional qualifications in the theory and practice of transport. (ibid., p. 247)

They underwent a tightly organised six-month training course which involved visits to Holland and to Swiss transport companies. Of course the area management approach had the all important support of a vigorous and committed chairman/chief executive and anyone with experience of organisational change knows that such support is half the battle. Area management was an undoubted success. Inevitably some matters could not be delegated: tariff policies and pay scales had to be co-ordinated at a central level, but within their areas and within their budgets the new breed of managers had discretion which enabled quick resolution of local problems, be they of an operational, industrial relations or marketing nature. Public relations also benefited as local representatives, i.e. TDs, county managers and county councillors had easy access to the local man as did editors of regional papers, and vice versa.

At headquarters two positions of deputy general manager were created, one to co-ordinate the work of the areas and another to deal with central services, accounts, personnel and commercial. A central Transport Control and Planning office was established to control 'the integration of road and rail services and a research and development unit to investigate the introduction of more efficient handling and transport technology'. A £35,000 grant was received from the US-financed Counterpart Fund for the research and development activity. Before Andrews' time training had been referred to occasionally in CIÉ literature as an important activity, for instance in relation to hotels, but it was given a major boost by his leadership. Áras Éanna, a training centre in Gardiner Street, Dublin, became a catalyst for change in attitudes as it provided 'state of the art' training courses in supervisory skills, work study, cost control, marketing, public relations and languages, as well as in the more specific areas of transport operations. Andrews, a committed Irish language advocate, was delighted that the training centre came to be staffed largely by Irish-speakers giving a fillip to the use of Irish in CIÉ's affairs.

Four months after his appointment Andrews was able to promulgate the board's strategy for tackling its myriad responsibilities. The objective of breakeven in 1964 seemed achievable. On 14 January 1959 he addressed the Dublin Chamber of Commerce. The address was significant in a number of ways. It showed that CIÉ was changing gear, and it wanted everyone to know what it was about, and why. The *Irish Press*, 14 January 1959, gave the story under a six-column headline, 'CIÉ TO MEET THE CHALLENGE'.

> Bidding for a ten per cent increase in rail and road traffic revenue, CIÉ was now going over to the attack, its chairman, Dr C. S. Andrews, stated in Dublin yesterday.
>
> They intended to meet the challenge that they must pay their way within five years, he said, and they had developed a line of action which they thought offered good hope for success.
>
> Dr Andrews gave some clues to this five-year plan. More and cheaper traffic. A fight to save the railways and a change-over to diesels on the old GNR section. Package deals with firms to carry their traffic on an annual basis. More cross-Channel container traffic. A possible vehicle ferry service on the lines of the Larne–Preston route. Economic running. And full joint consultation with the trade unions.
>
> 'We intend to deserve success' Dr Andrews told the businessmen. And, he said, CIÉ realised that their success would depend on their ability to sell themselves.
>
> The response that CIÉ will make to the challenge will be a threefold one:
>
> 1. By making use of its new found freedom of commercial action to seek for more traffic;
> 2. By the application of the most up to date methods of management;
> 3. By more efficient and more economic operation of the system including the elimination of patently uneconomic services.

Today's reader of company policy statements will discern nothing that is revolutionary in this three-pronged approach. What was new about it at the time was CIÉ signalling that it was going on the attack and its belief that it could achieve the financial objectives which had been laid down for it. CIÉ was setting out 'not merely to prevent a decline of traffic on the railways', but was setting a target of increasing the board's revenue by 10 per cent.

> We have already initiated what will become a progressively intensive campaign to sell more business. We intend to offer package deals to firms to carry all their traffic on an annual contract basis. This is made possible by the flexibility which the Board enjoys now in quoting rates. Andrews said that with the 'increasing interest in scientific management it is becoming more clearly apparent that firms should concentrate on the work for which they have special skills'.
>
> (*Irish Press*, 14 January 1959)

The implication was that CIÉ had the transport skills which others lacked. You do your job, whatever it is: CIÉ will handle your transport problems and would establish a section 'freely advising on transport problems' without obligation. This unit would be charged with 'adapting public transport to the use of containers and other modern equipment and techniques'. The movement towards containerisation was still in its infancy and many years of industrial relations conflict would frustrate significant containerisation at Dublin Port. CIÉ's own Rosslare Harbour would be more fortunate. Already CIÉ had been asked by the National Farmers' Association (the precursors of the IFA) to examine the possibility of a CIÉ-sponsored vehicle ferry service. Andrews told his audience that this was being done.

In due course CIÉ would participte in Irish Ferryways, a joint operation with Containerway, which had an important pioneering role in the development of containerised exports and imports. Andrews announced that more flexible pricing was to be an inherent part of the new business approach.

> One of the predicaments facing us is that the old scheme of railway charges was related to factors which are no longer valid since road vehicles destroyed the railway's monopoly. The change to a new basis of charging is a delicate task which cannot be done overnight: it involves the acceptance of calculated risks. (ibid.)

CIÉ would face this delicate task and take risks if necessary in the realisation that in the end the customer was boss and had to be wooed rather than forced to use public transport.

> I think it is quite unrealistic to appeal to firms to support public transport in the public interest for patriotic or sentimental motives unless we who are responsible for public transport take vigorous steps to make the public interest and the interests of the individual firm coincide . . .
>
> It is necessary not merely that total transport costs should be low but that the costs of each firm should be kept as low as possible. This is the objective of the new rates policy . . . in many cases where firms have left us in the past, the convenience of a public service was outweighed by the basis of charging. With the new basis of charging by contract for a firm's entire transport service, we are confident of regaining these traffics. (ibid.)

Andrews would be associated in the public mind with widespread railway closures, and by the time he spoke to the Dublin businessmen the Harcourt Street–Shanganagh line had already been closed. Some people may believe that Andrews was far from enthusiastic about the railways, that he might even have been hostile to them, but in public he was positive enough though realistic.

> We intend to fight and fight hard to save the railways. We are convinced that for any foreseeable time they are an essential factor in the development of the national economy. We must not waver in our resolution to remove lines which cannot be made viable. To try to maintain patently uneconomic lines solely for reason of sentiment would involve not merely waste of effort but would imperil the network as a whole. We are not going to close any line where there is any hope that our best efforts can save it. [In effect the 1958 Act gave him little choice on that score.] (ibid.)

Dr Andrews had a keen sense of the importance of public relations and he gave it substantial attention. To him, if you had a policy or even an aspiration towards improvement, you had a duty to staff and to the community to articulate it. In due course you should tell them what you had achieved. At a minimum it was a matter of 'not hiding your light under a bushel'. Through a series of speeches to various groups he communicated with politicians and civil servants, with CIÉ's customers, with staff and with the public as a whole. The week after his Dublin speech he made a similar address to a group in Galway, where he opined that the Naomh Éanna service to the Aran Islands might be better handled by a competent local group, if such a body were sufficiently interested.

Many years later, reflecting on his early days in CIÉ, he said:

> We received a good press. The newspapers gave full recognition to the success of our efforts. The approbation of the newspapers added greatly to the internal morale and self-confidence of the staff; they felt that they formed part of an organisation which was publicly respected. We never, to the extent I could prevent it, used the work 'image' in CIÉ. In my opinion the creation of 'images' in business and in public life is too often what the dictionary defines it—an artificial representation of the object. There is a suggestion of fraudulence about the process. (*Man of No Property*, p. 248)

In the 1960s he was not alone in this objection to the use of the word 'image', but since that time constant usage makes his own reservation seem pedantic and idiosyncratic. *Nuacht CIÉ* was the name of the relaunched staff journal. Associated with the training section, it was another weapon in the struggle to shift the CIÉ culture from one focusing on internal operational problems to one where the paramount consideration would be competitiveness based on improved standards in efficiency, cleanliness and service. There was another purpose to *Nuacht CIÉ* as Andrews confided to its editor: CIÉ would always have some tension in relationships with politicians whose main concern would be with responding to public demand, irrespective of the reasonableness of such demand. CIÉ could not afford to confront or to criticise politicians: however, by constantly telling CIÉ's own story, *Nuacht CIÉ* would help somewhat to disarm potential adversaries.

SIX WEEKS AFTER taking up his appointment in CIÉ, Andrews presided at a board meeting which received two recommendations from the general manager concerning branch lines. The first was that the Sallins–Tullow branch line be finally closed. This was a 30 mile line running from Sallins, Co. Kildare, on the Dublin–Cork line through Dunlavin and Baltinglass in west Wicklow to Tullow, which was little more than 10 miles from Carlow town. The line was mainly used for a monthly cattle fair and its demise was barely noticed. The second recommendation was similarly uncontroversial at the time, involving the closure of the line from Harcourt Street, Dublin, to Shanganagh Junction, the last stop short of Bray, leaving untouched the coastal route to Bray from Westland Row. The line had a chequered start. A Dublin, Dundrum & Rathfarnham Railway Company, renamed the Dublin & Bray Railway in 1851, had been granted the rights by Act of Parliament to build the Dublin/Dundrum part of this line. Another company, the Dublin & Wicklow Railway (DWR) had the authority to build the Dundrum–Bray section. However the former company failed and the DWR opened the line on 10 July 1854. The handsomely designed Harcourt Street terminus was opened on 7 February 1859. The CIÉ decision to close the line took effect from 1 January 1959—just a few weeks short of the centenary of the terminus. Andrews, in his Chamber of Commerce speech, said that the annual direct cost of operating the line was £77,000 and the receipts were only £21,000 per annum.

The story was first reported on 29 October 1958, and the speed with which this announcement was made two months after the appointment of the new board is one of the few surprising aspects of the decision. The *Irish Independent* carried the story under a single column headline. On the same page a four-column headline was given to the conferring of the freedom of the city of Dublin on the Bishop of Bathurst, New South Wales. An article by Fr Luke M. O'Reilly, entitled 'Prisoners of Chinese Reds', got six columns, but the story which dominated page after page, including one full-page

One of two Sulzer-engined diesel electric mainline locomotives built at Inchicore works; entered service in 1950; withdrawn in 1975

Experimental turf-burning locomotive designed by OVS Bulleid and built at Inchicore works during the 1950s

One of sixty A class mainline diesel electric locomotives built by Metropolitan Vickers for CIÉ in 1955/56

One of thirty-four C class diesel electric locomotives for operations on secondary lines, built by Metropolitan Vickers for CIÉ in 1956/57

Park Royal: An eighty-two seat standard class coach assembled by CIÉ at Inchicore works from parts supplied by Park Royal Vehicles of London and introduced in 1955

Craven: A sixty-four seat standard class coach jointly built by Cravens Ltd of Sheffield and CIÉ at Inchicore works and introduced in 1964

One of fourteen Maybach-engined shunting locomotives built by CIÉ at Inchicore works; introduced in 1961

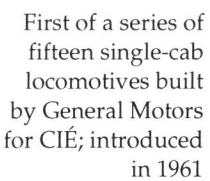

First of a series of fifteen single-cab locomotives built by General Motors for CIÉ; introduced in 1961

Suburban push/pull train formed of converted 1951 built AEC railcars, powered by a B201 class locomotive at the rear, approaches Howth Junction, mid-1970s.

Busáras and the Custom House seen from across the Liffey
(W. H. Conn, *Dublin Opinion*, 1953)

Gandon: 'Pon my word, taking it all in all, that young man didn't do so badly by my Custom House.'

One of the first GM locomotives acquired by CIÉ (950 h.p.), January 1961, contrasted with an old steam engine. The light grey colour scheme was soon abandoned.

The *Naomh Éanna* on the Galway–Aran Islands service was given a new colour scheme in 1960.

Heuston station, CIÉ group headquarters, built for Great Southern & Western Railway, 1845; architect: Sancton Wood.

Connolly station, headquarters of Iarnród Éireann, built for the Dublin and Drogheda Railway, 1844; architect: William Deane Butler

Broadstone, headquarters of Bus Éireann, built for the Midland Great Western Railway, 1850; architect: John Skipton Mulvany

Portarlington: a fine example of rural station buildings; architect: Sancton Wood

photograph, was the consecration of Cardinal Roncalli as Pope John XXIII. The single-column Harcourt Street story ran as follows:

> Rail services on the Harcourt Street (Dublin–Bray) line will be withdrawn from January 1. Dr C. S. Andrews Chairman of CIÉ said in a statement, the line had been operating at a loss for many years and its continuance [sic] had been decided on in pursuance of the directive that CIÉ must be self supporting within five years . . . Dr Andrews said that 74 people would be redundant as a result of the decision. The redundancies would be a matter for negotiation with the trade unions for transference or for compensation for the workers concerned. The passenger traffic on the line totals about 1,000 a day. There is very little freight traffic. An additional bus service will be introduced between Bray and Dublin via Dundrum.

On 10 November, Dublin County Council debated the closure, but its members were principally concerned with the proposed replacement bus service. They refused to accept a motion requesting that the decision be reversed but agreed to ask that it be deferred until alternative road transport could be provided. On 18 November the *Irish Independent* returned to the story but still without a note of controversy:

> Harcourt Street Station which will be closed by CIÉ on December 31 and auctioned in the New Year. It may be acquired as a site not only for a concert hall as already reported but for a great all purpose hall run on a commercial basis. Fears have been expressed that great as is the need for a concert hall in Dublin, it would not be a paying proposition and the Government and Dublin Corporation have shown no inclination to finance such a project. The proposed all purpose hall could be used as a banqueting hall with seating for over 1,000 people.

The report mentioned the question of matching the acoustic requirements of a concert hall with the space requirements of a banqueting hall but believed they could be solved. The hall, the readers were assured, would not be in competition with hotels or catering establishments. A committee to develop the project included some interesting names: Joe Groome (Groome's Hotel and Vice President of the Irish Tourist Association), Capt. Peter Jury (Shelbourne Hotel), Michael Scott (architect) and the inimitable A. P. Reynolds. The same report observed that a 'proposal to convert the railway line to a motor road' had been described by engineers as 'impracticable and too costly'.

On 22 November the CIÉ Report for the year to 31 March 1958 became public and this gave an *Irish Independent* leader writer an opportunity to refer critically to the Harcourt Street line decision:

> To judge from the decision to close the Harcourt Street–Bray railway line at the end of this year, the order of the recently passed Transport Act to get rid of losses within the next five years is being interpreted in a very simple fashion—to cure the malady by killing the patient.

The leader writer who claimed in the previous July that the *Independent* had long been advocating a radical reduction in the railway network may have had a night off when that piece was penned. The same theme was picked up by a letter writer on 27 November: 'The proposed closing of the Harcourt Street line is just another nail in the CIÉ coffin. The constructive thing to do is to build up publicity for all such stations instead of closing them down.'

When the day came and the last train ran, an unsigned nostalgic piece appeared in the *Evening Press*.

> When the last train from Harcourt Street whistled its way through the wooden station at Ranelagh yesterday afternoon, it must have disturbed the memories of many who lived along the line. As youngsters our whole world revolved around the station . . . How often the guard or engine driver held the train as we rushed panting with breakfast filled mouths up those long stairs of the station.

They loved to skate on the station's wooden platform during freezing winter days and so on. An earlier piece in the *Evening Press* (4 November 1958) spoke about the half-dozen or so individual passengers who boarded and unboarded at Leopardstown, all known by name to the station master. 'A large slice of railway history will have to go. It's a great pity but a necessity.' The commentator who today deplores the 1958 decision as shortsighted has the benefit of thirty years' hindsight. Over that period the population of the catchment area of the old line, which had been built rather optimistically to exploit Bray's potential for being an Irish Brighton, has increased twenty or thirty times over. At the time, commuter traffic on the main coastal line to Bray via Sandymount, Merrion, Blackrock and Dún Laoghaire was also in decline. It would continue to falter for a further ten years until growing traffic congestion would reverse the downward trend in rail commuting.

The legal processes involved in closing rail services on particular lines had been greatly simplified under the Transport Act 1958 (section 19), but what should happen to the railway lines when closed, as well as to railway stations, bridges and signal boxes? CIÉ could be involved in third party liability claims if persons suffered injury to themselves or their property which could be linked in some way to CIÉ's continued ownership of the line. The solution lay in the making of an abandonment order followed by the sale or transference of ownership and ownership obligations to other parties. Frequently a considerable period could elapse between the formal closing of a line, the making of an abandonment order and eventual disposal of the property. For example, the Tralee/Dingle line, closed under a Transport Tribunal exemption order on 16 June 1953, was the subject of abandonment orders on 13 September 1956 in respect of property within the Tralee urban area, and on 9 January 1958 in respect of the rest of the line. The abandonment orders did not complete the process; they merely signalled that the property could now be disposed of. On 19 October 1961 the board finally disposed of the Tralee/Dingle line and the minute is typical of what would happen the several hundred miles of unused line which then existed or would be created by future closures.

> Authority sought to settle with the undermentioned adjoining owners on the basis that they accept a conveyance of the site of the line adjoining their premises for the sum stated below [ranging from fifteen shillings to five pounds ten shillings per plot of land] and at the same time release the Board from its fencing and other obligations ... CIÉ will make a contribution of five pounds five shillings towards each of the adjoining owners' legal costs.

At the same meeting the board authorised the making of a whole raft of abandonment orders, mostly affecting GNR 'stump' lines in Counties Cavan and Monaghan, on which passenger operations had already ceased, although two virtually inactive lines in Kerry (Headford Junction/Kenmare and Farranfore/Valentia Harbour) and the Claremorris/Ballinrobe line in Mayo were also listed.

The pace of the abandonment process for the Harcourt Street/Shanganagh line was much swifter. On 8 January 1959, a week after closure, the board resolved that the abandonment process for the Harcourt Street/Shanganagh Junction railway line be set in motion. The abandonment order for the Harcourt Street station was made within three months—on 19 March 1959—and the premises were sold on 23 March to the Agricultural Credit Corporation. The section from the terminus to the Grand Canal obtained its abandonment order on 29 October 1959, with the balance of the line being the subject of four more abandonment orders, the final one of which involved the Grand Canal/Dundrum section on 27 September 1962. Abandonment orders were very precisely expressed, e.g. the abandonment order for the Dundrum/Shanganagh section of line, authorised on 10 October 1961, applied to the property 'from and including overbridge No. 15 adjacent to Garda Barracks, Eglinton Terrace situated in the townland of Dundrum, Parish of Taney and County of Dublin to and including the accommodation level crossing situated on the said railway line in the townland of Shanganagh, parish of Rathmichael'.

Such carefully, perhaps lovingly, drafted resolutions applied not merely to the busy townlands of south Dublin, identified always by the legally defined Church of Ireland parishes, but over the next few years by rod and perch they snaked their way deep into the remote drumlin country of Paddy Kavanagh, the west Cork of Frank O'Connor, the midlands of Maria Edgeworth and Oliver Goldsmith, and the Atlantic coast of Percy French's famous song.

The CIÉ legal office at St Johns, Islandbridge, had to be increased in size. It was also charged with the legal disposal of many hundreds of CIÉ-owned railway and canal workers' dwellings, e.g. some 300 residences at the Inchicore engineering works, station masters' houses, or keepers' cottages at level crossings and canal locks. Some such tenancies still survive for operational reasons. The story has a fascination of its own as CIÉ tried to rid itself of its role as Ireland's largest landlord outside of the major local authorities. The exercise was mostly, but not always, painless as not every tenant would move or pay rents due or otherwise co-operate with what was required to complete the process.

To return to railway closures, Todd Andrews says:

> The 1958 Act gave CIÉ a free hand to close down lines and stations for which it saw no prospect of economic operation . . . An investigation of uneconomic routes and services was begun in 1959. The investigation followed a set procedure. Before any proposal to close down a line or station was submitted to the board a study in depth was made of its current performance together with an appraisal of its future prospects in traffic and financial terms. Enquiries were addressed to government departments and local bodies seeking information about any future developments which might affect its potential. CIÉ had to give an assurance that there would be sufficient road transport facilities to ensure a satisfactory substitute service.   (*Man of No Property*, p. 251)

The last sentence in that quotation is misleading. CIÉ was not required by the 1958 Act to give such an assurance to anybody. It was not even required by that Act to provide substitute services. Instead, it had been explained in the Dáil that licences would be issued to other parties to supply services if CIÉ were to decide that it could not or would not operate replacement services. The reality of course was that CIÉ believed that as the national transport company it should operate substitute services; not to do so could generate unmanageable adverse reactions and create the risk of a private operator gaining status and kudos with potentially harmful consequences for CIÉ.

In any event the 1958 Act's requirement that railway services be maintained except only where it was established that they were and would continue to be uneconomic, imposed a responsibility on the board which resulted in a practice of formally adopting a resolution on the following lines:

> That having considered the General Manager's (or Traffic Manager's) report and being satisfied that the operation on the railway line between 'X' and 'Y' of every service of trains both ways, whether for passengers or merchandise and whether serving or not serving any of intermediate stations, is uneconomic and that there is no prospect of the continued operation of any of the said services being economic within a reasonable period, the Board hereby directs that the said service shall be terminated and all the said intermediate stations shall be closed as early as is possible after publication of the notice required by Section 19 of the Transport Act 1958. The Board directs that the said notice shall be published in (named newspapers, local and national).

If the initial closures decided on by the Andrews board provoked virtually no controversy—they were long anticipated and accepted as inevitable—there was an entirely different reaction when the board at its meeting on 13 June 1960 decided on its next list of condemned lines. The first line identified for closure at that meeting would principally affect the south-east, i.e. the line from Macmine Junction on the Dublin–Wexford line running westwards for some 12 miles or so before splitting into two lines—north to Muine Bheag (Bagenalstown) and south to Waterford City (a total of 55 miles of line). For some reason this decision was put on ice and would not be implemented for three years. In due course it would not cause a major problem: Wexford, Waterford, Rosslare, Carlow and Kilkenny retained rail services, and the main loss in the south-east would be the rail connections between Wexford and Carlow. The next three lines on the June 1960 condemned list caused enormous controversy:

> Waterford/Tramore: 8 miles linking the city of Waterford to the nearby dormitory town and holiday resort of Tramore.
> West Clare Railway: 53 miles of narrow gauge line linking Ennis westwards to Ennistymon and thereafter running south to Moyasta where it divided into two lines—one to Kilrush on the Shannon

Estuary and the other to the seaside resort of Kilkee.

Cork/Bandon and South Coast Section: 93 miles linking Cork City with Bantry, Co. Cork, and connecting branch lines to Baltimore, Clonakilty and Courtmacsherry.

The case for retaining the Waterford/Tramore line rested on the significance of Tramore as a summer holiday resort and excursion centre. Its fame as a seaside resort, its importance to the national tourist industry and to the economy of the area was trumpeted. The death of Tramore was prophesied from platform and pulpit. 'The agitation, though noisy, was not taken up seriously by the general public who were well aware that the line no longer served any valid purpose.' (ibid., p. 251) The line closed on 31 December 1960.

In a similar dismissive comment Andrews said that 'in the case of West Clare the campaign was relatively light hearted. It amounted to an appeal that the line be retained as a memorial to Percy French who had immortalised it in a ballad.' The chorus of that ballad may be worth repeating:

> Are you right there Michael, are you right,
> Do you think that we'll be there before the night,
> We've been so long in startin', that you couldn't say for certain,
> But we might now Michael, so we might.

The line managed to survive the affectionate ridicule of Percy French and had been converted to diesel operation in 1952 with Walker diesel railcars, and in 1955 with 210 h.p. diesel locomotives also from Walker. None the less CIÉ claimed in 1960 that the line was losing £23,000 a year and that a replacement bus service would lose no more than £4,000. With not a little hyperbole one deputy complained in the Dáil that closing the line would make west Clare as remote as the Aran Islands. During these and subsequent closures the ministerial reply to Dáil questions on branch lines would run on the following lines:

> Under the Transport Act 1958, CIÉ is empowered to terminate any particular train service provided the Board is satisfied that its operation is uneconomic and that there is no prospect of its continued operation becoming economic within a reasonable period. The Act also imposed on the Board of CIÉ the general obligation to conduct the undertaking so as to eliminate losses within a five year period.
>
> Under the legislation I have no function in the matter which is entirely for CIÉ. It is of course open to the Deputy to address his inquiries to the Board.

Todd Andrews claimed that, if retained, the West Clare 'would probably be the most expensive monument ever erected to a poet', but Michael H. C. Baker (*Irish Railways Since 1916*, p. 167) says:

> Percy French had the last laugh, for a permanent reminder of the gentle fun he poked at the West Clare now stands in the yard of Ennis station in the form of a statue of him, a few yards in front of one of the unpredictable engines which 'Michael' used to drive. This is an 0-6-2T . . . She is more cosseted now than she ever was in the days when she was active, receiving fresh coats of red, white and green paint whenever her gloss begins to fade, and probably also earning more money from the tourists who come to Ennis to have a look at her and the Percy French memorial.

The West Clare line closed on 31 January 1961. But such was the appeal of the line that a large handsome volume, *The West Clare Railway*, was published in 1994 (Plateway Press, UK). The protests concerning the Cork, Bandon and South Coast line were much more organised, bitter and persistent, though in the end that line too would close—on 31 March 1961. On 26 October 1960 Michael Pat Murphy (Labour), the most vociferous of the Cork deputies in the campaign against the proposed west Cork closure, put a question to Seán Lemass as Taoiseach. He had attained that office in June 1960 following Éamon de Valera's election as President of the Republic. Deputy Murphy's question was not about intervening as such, otherwise it would have been ruled out of order. It was about the Taoiseach's refusal to meet a 'representative delegation' to discuss the planned closure. Mr Lemass would not budge. On the same order paper Deputy Murphy was joined by Seán Casey and Florence Wycherley, also from Cork, in a question to Erskine Childers, Minister of the newly created Department of Transport and Power. On becoming Taoiseach Sean Lemass had split the massive Department of Industry and Commerce which had been his own portfolio for most of the previous twenty-seven years. The Department of Transport and Power took responsibility for CIÉ, Aer Lingus, Aer Rianta, Irish Shipping, B + I, ESB and Bord na Móna away from Industry and Commerce. All but the ESB had come into being as government concerns during Lemass's long though broken tenure in Industry and Commerce since 1932. The new minister who always liked to be forthcoming with information answered the Cork deputies:

> CIÉ have indicated that the out of pocket expenditure on the West Cork railway exceeds the revenue by £56,000 per annum: this figure is arrived at before charging fixed expenses e.g. contribution to

workshop, administration and head office expenses which are estimated to amount to £22,000 per annum.

(*Dáil debates*, Vol. 184, Col. 40)

Deputy Murphy in supplementaries invited the minister to note that this amounted to only 13 per cent of the total railway losses. What about the other 87 per cent? The deputies alleged that the CIÉ Board was divided on the issue. What was the basis for the minister's statement that only fifteen extra vehicles were required to replace the railways?

On 2 November Michael Pat Murphy returned to the fray, asking Erskine Childers to require CIÉ to meet a delegation from west Cork. He quoted an undertaking given by Seán Lemass as the responsible minister in May 1958 that 'where a proposal to close a branch line was made, the Board of CIÉ would receive a deputation from local interested parties'. Would the minister now state 'what change of policy has resulted in the Board's refusal to receive such deputation?' The minister replied that there had been no change of policy. CIÉ had informed him that the board had never refused to receive any deputation from local interested parties in connection with a proposal to close a branch line.

The Cork deputies wanted to raise the matter on the adjournment of the day's sitting but they were refused. Had CIÉ refused to meet a deputation or not? Had or had not a meeting been formally requested? Todd Andrews later commented on the protest generally, revealing something about his capacity to handle himself in a 'scrap' and also about the deputation issue:

> Local politicians, traders and professional people launched an organised attack on the competence and motivation of CIÉ. The campaign had the blessing of the Church. Protest meetings were held and CIÉ was bombarded with demands for a stay of execution. Political pressure was brought to bear on members of the government to support the retention of the line. My telephone brought endless calls from interested parties to receive deputations. One TD was particularly offensive. I heard him out politely until I thought he had outstepped the bounds of toleration at which point I replied in kind. I made an exact note of the dialogue including my own scatological advice to the man concerned and sent it to our minister, Erskine Childers, with a protest that I was not paid to take abuse from Dáil deputies.
>
> Our refusal to receive deputations from members of the Oireachtas and local councils was represented as 'an attack on the democratic process'. That phrase was to me a very weary cliché in the vocabulary of agitation. Two other popular clichés of abuse 'dictator' and 'fascist'

> were freely used. At this stage the campaign changed its character and became something of a contest of wills. Some people seemed more concerned with overcoming the refusal of CIÉ to receive deputations than with the actual preservation of the line. I was well aware that a number of ministers and their official advisers considered our attitude to be unduly stiff necked. One of the top civil servants went out of his way to remind me of the appropriateness of the Latin proverb *Suaviter in modo, fortiter in re*. (*Man of No Property*, p. 257)

The truth of the matter about deputations is that when Todd Andrews was eventually formally requested to meet a deputation from the Cork area, he responded by saying that he would not meet a group to discuss keeping the line open; however he was prepared to meet a group to discuss the organisation of substitute services. However that agenda issue was resolved, a deputation did come to Kingsbridge and the story goes that Todd Andrews greeted them pleasantly, asking for their train tickets so that he could make some special arrangements concerning their return journeys. Nobody had a train ticket! The entire group had travelled by car—so exchange number one was won by Todd Andrews. It's a good story. Whether it is true or not, there is no doubt that passions in west Cork ran extraordinarily high during 1960/61. As recently as March 1991, thirty years after the closure, a book appeared entitled *The Cork, Bandon and South Coast Railway —The Final Farewell*. It was written by Colm Creedon who had been secretary of the Save our Railway Association from 1957, when it made a submission to the Beddy Committee, until 1963 when it was dissolved both in sadness and in bitterness. Creedon gives a still interesting account of the campaign to keep the line open. It confirms that feelings ran extremely high, and seemingly still do, as the following extracts demonstrate:

> From October 1960 onwards the campaign to save the Bandon section gathered momentum. Practically every organisation in West Cork met specially to protest and several public meetings were held . . . This ground swell of opposition to the closure was well publicised by the newspapers with almost daily front-page reports of developments. The *Cork Examiner*, in particular, was very vocal, publishing several scathing editorials on the dire effects of the close down plan . . . Dublin papers also carried the latest protest news . . . Despite mounting anger the response from both CIÉ and the Government was negative and unbending. . . . Their only 'concession' was their willingness to discuss the alternative road services. It was like telling a condemned prisoner that there could be no discussion about an appeal or commuting the sentence but only concerning the type of headstone over his grave.

This was dictatorship at its worst. Matters came to a head shortly afterwards when the Taoiseach, Seán Lemass TD, refused to receive a representative deputation headed by Cork County Council and including both Catholic and Church of Ireland Bishops of Cork and Ross, and all the West Cork local councils and commissioners. This was a total negation of democracy. The views of 100,000 people in the affected area were ignored. There is nothing irrevocable in this life. There is no humiliation in admitting an error when unforeseen consequences become apparent. Yet CIÉ and the Government continued to collaborate in their pig-headed determination to steamroll the West Cork railway into oblivion . . .

The Clonakilty *Save the Railway* Committee decided that a direct approach to President de Valera was now the only hope of averting closure. Over three Sundays in January and early February, 30,000 people throughout West Cork signed petition forms outside Church gates, demanding a reprieve for the rail services in the area. Regrettably, on February 23rd, the President, no doubt under pressure from the Government, let it be known that he could not receive a deputation carrying the petition, which now had risen to 37,000 signatures.

The deputation was once again to have included Church leaders, including Cork's outspoken Bishop Lucey, who had made the sensible point, at a recent Confirmation ceremony in the area that even if the railway closed, taxpayers in West Cork would still have to subsidise CIÉ losses without getting any benefits in return.

(Creedon, *The Cork, Bandon and South Coast Railway*
—*The Final Farewell* , pp. 119/120/121)

James P. O'Regan, a Clonalkilty businessman, described by Colm Creedon as one of CIÉ's biggest customers, initiated legal action. An application to prevent the closing of the line before the hearing of his action was withdrawn when the Attorney General requested that the plaintiff pay £4,500 to keep the line open for the two months in question. The line was closed on 31 March 1961, but the legal action against CIÉ, based on the assertion that the prospects for the line were sound and improving and therefore could not legally be closed, was set to continue. Creedon's narrative continues:

The Minister for Local Government had refused to sanction any road improvement grants for West Cork until the outcome of the legal proceedings became known. Since the closure, CIÉ lorries and trailers were causing massive congestion in Bandon, Clonakilty and Skibbereen, and were a danger to other vehicles on the narrow twisty main roads linking these towns. The transfer of traffic from rail to road was not the success that the Minister for Transport and Power had hoped for. (ibid. p. 130)

A general election took place in October 1961, which resulted in a fall in seats for Fianna Fáil. However, Seán Lemass remained Taoiseach in a minority government. The High Court action by Mr O'Regan came up for hearing on 6 March 1962, almost a year after the line had closed, but no hearing took place. Pleading inability to bear inevitably heavy legal costs including possible appeal costs in the Supreme Court even if he won in the High Court, Mr O'Regan withdrew his action.

After the closure of the west Cork lines in 1961 the CIÉ Board took a breather. Perhaps waiting for resolution of the legal action which was being taken against them for the west Cork closure, or wearied by the onslaught which they had suffered in the south-west, no further reductions in the network were announced for a while. Indeed in August 1961 CIÉ stated that no further closures were planned within the five-year period governed by the provisions of the 1958 Act. That should have meant no change before early 1964. Things did not work out quite like that.

THE MID-CENTURY PRUNING of Ireland's railways took place in three main stages. The first as we have seen was in the North, when in 1958 the GNRB slashed its secondary lines leading to the closures in the Republic of the Sligo, Leitrim & Northern Counties Railway and related CIÉ closures in the north midlands. The second tranche in 1961 affected three coastal counties, i.e. Clare, Cork and Waterford. The third purging of the hangover from the railway-building mania of the nineteenth century was carried out in January and March 1963. The focus this time was on the central midlands and the south-east, i.e. Portlaoise/Kilkenny, Castlecomer Junction/Deerpark, Portlaoise/Mountmellick, Kilfree/Ballaghaderreen, New Ross/Macmine Junction, Muine Bheag/Palace East, Clonsilla/Navan, Navan/Oldcastle, Athy/Ballylinan, and Enfield/Edenderry.

These closures had taken place by the time the 1962/63 Annual Report was published. In addition, regular passenger services ceased on the Cóbh Junction/Youghal, Limerick/Tralee, Ballingrane/Foynes, and Waterford/New Ross sectors. Oliver Flanagan, TD protested in the Dáil about the Portlaoise/Mountmellick line, but generally the 1963 closures did not provoke much passion. Perhaps the relative prosperity of the affected areas and their ease of access to the main trunk railway routes explains the comparative lack of clamour.

Railway station closures were also taking place, and the smallness of the towns on the 1962/63 casualty list says something about the world that was passing. It included Kildangan, Mageney, Milford, Gowran, Bennett's Bridge, Ballyhale, Mulinavat, Kilmacow, Kilmorna, Devon Road, Barnagh, Ardagh, Kilgobbin, Duleek, Beauparc, Gibbstown, Wilkinstown, Nobber and Kilmainham Wood. Only the most dedicated traveller of Ireland's byways would easily pinpoint the location of all these placenames, unless he cheated by referring to an old railway map! Another 68 stations were closed during 1963/64 and regular passenger services were withdrawn from the Claremorris/Collooney line.

Three years would elapse before any more closures took place and this time (27 March 1967) they all took place in Munster: Thurles/Clonmel (25 miles) Rath Luirc/Patrickswell (17 miles) and Mallow/Grace Dieu near Waterford (75 miles)—subsequently a two-mile section was built to Ballinacourty to cater for magnesite traffic to Dungarvan. With these last three closures the cumulative reduction in the rail network of CIÉ was 785 miles relative to the 1958 level of 2,700 miles after absorbing the Dublin–Belfast line as far as the border (Source: Annual Reports). It is interesting to compare the reduced figures with the network 'envisaged' in the Beddy Report of ten years earlier. The total CIÉ rail track in 1968 (first track, other track and sidings) amounted to 1,915 miles or 29 per cent less than 1958. Using the mileage for 'first track' rather than total track the reduction was 33 per cent. Adjusting the 33 per cent to exclude the Dublin/Belfast element, the reduction was 35 per cent over the ten years. The Beddy Committee's estimate of the 'probably justifiable' track length posited an eventual 60 per cent cut rather than a 35 per cent cut which occurred. After 1967 the main survivors of the list pencilled in for amputation by Beddy were Limerick/Claremorris/Collooney up through the province of Connaught, Limerick/Tralee, and that extra line to Limerick particularly commented on by Beddy—Ballybrophy/Roscrea/Nenagh/Limerick which parallels the line from Limerick Junction to Limerick City.

Rail closures during the Andrews years were not the only significant developments in the period's railway story. On the locomotive side, the Bulleid turf burner was an early casualty. On 23 December 1958, three months after Andrews' arrival, the board decided that experiments with the Bulleid turf burner should be abandoned. Enquiries were to be made about the possibility of converting other steam engines to turf burning, but the much more important dieselisation programme was not 'to be held up pending these enquiries'. The turf burner project was dead. Dieselisation proceeded rapidly. In January 1961 the first American-built locomotives were delivered—fifteen 960 h.p. diesel electric locomotives by General Motors. An order was placed with Maybach Motorenbau for fourteen sets of power equipment for 400 h.p. diesel hydraulic locomotives to be manufactured at Inchicore. Seven 160 h.p. diesel hydraulic locomotives were accepted from Klockner Humboldt Deutz in January 1962, and during 1961 and 1962, 37 additional diesel electric locomotives were ordered from General Motors. In the following year, 1962/63, a total of 56 diesel locomotives were brought into service.

The abandonment of steam was only a matter of time. It was announced that from 1 April 1963 steam locomotives would not operate, except 'for short periods during which steam would be used for beet traffic'. To have completed the conversion to diesel traction within ten years from the 1953 submissions to government on railway equipment was a considerable achievement in the circumstances. A serious crisis in public finances had occurred in the intervening period: the Beddy Committee had sat and reported; CIÉ was under strong pressure from government to seek extra credit from locomotive suppliers (1957) and later to reschedule its capital programme (1959); the GNR equipment had been absorbed and the CIÉ mandate had been revised by the 1958 Transport Act.

In addition to the conversion to diesel traction, rolling stock renewal had continued, running times had been reduced, equipment utilisation had been increased, appearances and decor had been improved, and the checker board black and white tiling at the main railway termini had been introduced. Catering standards had also been given a lift. Rail hostesses were introduced on mainline trains—Sláinte and Fáilte to Cork and the Cú na Mara to Galway. Passenger marketing initiatives increased options for excursion tickets and off-season travel including school tours, bringing business, popularity and renewed respect to the rail system. In addition to being the first all-diesel year, 1963/64 is also a useful benchmark for assessing progress in that the five-year 'reorganisation' period provided for in the 1958 Act expired in March 1964. By that time total rail passengers numbered 9.8 million, down 16 per cent on the 11.7 million carried in 1958/59. The decline in passengers may in part be attributed to the reduction in the network of over 30 per cent. However the simple change in numbers carried does not give the full story.

Railway passenger miles in 1963/64 were virtually the same (+1%) as in 1959, indicating that long haul passengers were continuing to grow as in the fifties, and in terms of passenger miles compensated for declining numbers on the short haul suburban services. Indeed falling numbers on Dublin suburban rail services had generated controversy in 1960 when CIÉ responded by closing a number of halts on the Dublin/Greystones line and reducing the number of midday and late evening trains. In the Dáil, Liam Cosgrave and Richie Ryan of Fine Gael raised the matter with Erskine Childers, suggesting *inter alia* that the reduction in services was not legal because the notice provided by CIÉ did not fully comply with the requirements of the 1958 Act. Mr Childers was not impressed.

Lionel Booth who, like Liam Cosgrave, represented the Dún Laoghaire/Rathdown constituency, had a somewhat different attitude to CIÉ's cutbacks on the suburban line to Bray (9 June 1960):

> I have always felt that some very drastic move would have to be made. I know it is unpopular to say so but I think that CIÉ has done a very good job in their proposals for economic working . . . yesterday 15 passengers in six coaches passed Merrion Gates . . . the train had left the city at a quarter past one.

He was speaking in a 1960 debate on the estimate for the Department of Transport and Power, the first to be introduced by Mr Childers, who was generous in his praise for CIÉ and who in turn received compliments from the deputies for the progress that was being made. The West Cork confrontation had not yet occurred.

ON THE FREIGHT side, from 1960/61 onwards, slow, cumbersome and labour-intensive handling systems were being replaced. Generally the reorganisation of goods depots paralleled the changes that were being made in passenger facilities, as evidenced by the 1961/62 Annual Report:

> New and economical methods of working with the aid of mechanical equipment were adopted in the goods stores at Limerick, Waterford, Kilkenny, Dundalk, Wexford and Clonmel. Extensive improvements in ground installation and traffic facilities were completed. New wagon loading and unloading facilities for beet were constructed at nine stations and successful experiments in the mechanical loading of beet at farms were carried out. Equipment for the handling of grain in bulk was erected at Boyle and Longford.

In 1962/63 it was stated that 'palletisation of freight for transport by rail and road was extended. Mechanical handling giving better customer service and more economical handling was introduced at Sligo, Athlone, Thurles, Drogheda, Mullingar, Ennis, Nenagh, Roscrea, Galway, Tralee, Cork, Mallow, Limerick and North Wall.' The same report recorded that the first automatic barriers were installed at Grange level crossing, Co. Tipperary. The following year a similar reference was made to the level crossing at Commons, near Castlebellingham, Co. Louth. There is no particularly obvious explanation for the selection of these two sites for CIÉ's first automatic level crossing installations.

The two main thrusts of CIÉ's plan to increase its rail freight were improved service and negotiation of 'package deals' with significant customers. To achieve self-sufficiency by 1964, real progress had to be made on the freight side. In the early 1960s freight contributed 35 per cent of CIÉ's total revenue and 55 per cent of rail revenue. The area management structure became fully operational in 1961, supporting a strengthened central commercial department in exploiting the commercial freedom granted by the 1958 Act. The Assistant General Manager (Operations), Ned O'Flaherty, defined the 'package deal' as a flexible arrangement to cater for almost any sizeable transport operation, e.g. the distribution on a national scale of a firm's products by CIÉ's network of rail and road services, or the transport of 'traffic streams', such as fertiliser, butter, grain, on a continuous or a seasonal basis (*Administration*, Winter 1968).

As promised, charging had become more flexible. The intention was that charges should realistically relate to the true cost to CIÉ of the movement involved. They also had to have regard to competitors' charges and to the shipper's costs for providing his own transport. A difficulty in the 1960s which continues to this day is that of satisfactorily computing in-house transport charges. Merely asserting that CIÉ could do it more cheaply would gain few customers. That claim had to be proven.

In 1962 it was said that 400 package deals had been completed and a figure of 1,200 such deals was mentioned in 1964. Rail freight did move upwards and by substantially greater amounts than the 10 per cent target mentioned by Andrews in his January 1959 speech. By 1963/64 rail freight tons were 16 per cent above 1958/59 levels and freight in ton miles were up 17 per cent. However, livestock carried by rail continued to decline and in 1963/64 numbered 11 per cent less than in 1958/59. The downward movement in livestock numbers must have been due as much, or more, to changes in the cattle and meat trade as to incursions by privately owned transport on traditional rail movements.

ROAD FREIGHT GREW much faster than rail freight growing by 115 per cent over the five years from 1958/59 to 1963/64 and passing out rail tonnage in volume terms. It stood at 7 per cent less than rail freight in 1958/59, and 71 per cent higher in 1963/64. Nevertheless, in revenue terms rail freight remained well ahead of its road competitor because of distances carried. It had always been claimed that the railway was best suited to long haul traffic and market performance proved this to be true. A major contract for carriage of fertiliser from the new Nitrigin Éireann plant in Wicklow required construction of 700 yards of new railway line which was catered for by one of the provisions of the 1963 Transport Act (see below). Both the NÉT contract and another for the conveyance of mineral ore from

Silvermines, Co. Tipperary, to Foynes, Co. Limerick, did not come on stream until after 1963/64 and so is not included in the above tonnage figures.

It is time to move from railways to road passenger, canals and labour aspects of CIÉ in what came to be called its five-year 'reorganisation' period following the 1958 Act.

CHAPTER 11

INDUSTRIAL UNREST

Road passenger services—Canal closures—Great Southern Hotels—Staff consultation—Conflict with union leadership—Lockouts—One-person operation of buses proposed.

Road passenger operations experienced much less revolutionary and controversial change in the Andrews years than had been the case with railways. Still, they were frequently a matter of public unease because of industrial relations confrontations. These will be a main concern of this chapter. The buses themselves continued to be built by CIÉ at Spa Road, Inchicore, on Leyland chassis. Since the Leyland contract had been signed in 1948, Leyland, up to 1964, supplied 1,350 chassis to CIÉ (600 single deck and 750 double deck). A new fleet of 60 double deck buses, increasing the capacity to 74 seats per bus, and manufactured by CIÉ, was introduced in 1960/61. The following year the Annual Report records that 'fifty eight single deck buses were manufactured at the Board's works during the year and fifty three buses were adapted for one-man operation'. As we will see later, both the larger buses and one-man buses became industrial relations issues. Heaters were being installed in double deck buses and in the year to March 1963, 400 out of 755 buses had the job completed.

A new 'golden brown and black' colour scheme for railway carriages and engines had its counterpart in 'monastral blue and cream' for double-deckers and 'rose pink and cream' for single-deckers. 'Monastral blue' was a very dark, almost navy blue, while 'rose pink and cream' became 'broken white and cherry red' after initial trials. This aspect of the CIÉ facelift proved a shock to some of the public. Irish buses were green; London buses were red; but now 'our' buses were being painted like any provincial UK bus company!

A new bus terminal at Parnell Place, Cork, on the River Lee, a fair example of the period's architectural taste, was opened in May 1960. A passenger sales bureau was opened in May 1961 in O'Connell Street, Dublin, with somewhat more restrained external finishes as befitted its location. A 'travel kiosk' in the centre of O'Connell Street was removed at the same time.

Comparing bus passenger carryings in the first and last years of the five-year period shows a 5 per cent fall, but the year ended March 1964 was affected by strikes. When this factor is excluded, it emerges that Dublin city and provincial city bus passengers were increasing at a rate of about one per cent per annum. Rural bus services on the other hand increased carryings by 55 per cent in the five-year period.

IF DEAD OR rotting wood was being trimmed off the railway system, harsher treatment was needed for the canal network. As mentioned earlier the board, in October 1959, postponed a final decision about the Grand Canal, but not for long. On 26 November a press advertisement announced that all trading on the Grand Canal and its associated waterways, the Barrow and the Shannon, would cease from 1 January 1960, with the exception of through traffic from Dublin to Limerick. At the time 'trading' by CIÉ on the Grand Canal meant the operation of about forty barges and 29 freight depots. A large weather-beaten black timber notice board across the whole width of Portobello Bridge in Rathmines, Dublin, had listed such depots to which you could deliver or from which you could collect your goods before and after they were carried on the canal. The irrelevance of the canal to Ireland's commercial life in 1960 will be evident from the full list of depots closed: Ringsend, 12th lock, 13th lock, Sallins, Robertstown, Lowtown, Rathangan, Monasterevan, Courtwood, Vicarstown, Athy, Ardreigh, Levitstown, Mageney, Carlow, Rhode, Daingean, Tullamore, Rahan, Belmont, Shannon Harbour, Banagher, Portumna, Kilgarvan, Luska, Dromineer, Mountshannon, Scariff and Killaloe. The exclusion of the Dublin/Limerick through traffic from the January 1960 close-down was for the convenience of Guinness who for well over a hundred years had been moving their porter and stout to Limerick by canal. In Limerick, indeed the four-day canal trip was deemed by local connoisseurs to add to the quality of the pint. Guinness had also travelled on the canal system to Waterford, Ballinasloe and Carrick-on-Shannon. In the reverse direction, empties had to return to Dublin and malt was an important traffic on the Barrow from the barley-growing regions of Kilkenny and Carlow. Movement of sugar from the Carlow factory of Comhlucht Siúicre Éireann to Dublin had also provided significant traffic to the canal in its final years, as had fertilisers, tar and pitch, though at the time of closure this traffic was already lost to road and rail tankers. The need to complete construction of a new Guinness store in Limerick was all that kept the Dublin–Limerick through traffic alive, and that was to be for a few months only. It too ceased in May 1960. The barges were auctioned off in St James's Street Harbour. A proposal that they be rented out by CIÉ to individuals who would convert them to houseboats attracted little interest and was abandoned.

The Royal Canal had long ceased to carry any traffic at all. In 1946, as recorded by Peter Clarke (*The Royal Canal—the complete story*), only two boats, privately owned, were operating, one based in Killucan, Co. Westmeath, and the other based in Dublin, near Croke Park. By July 1951 these last survivors had ceased to operate. In ownership of the canal CIÉ was the successor of the GSR, and before that, of the Midland Great Western which had acquired the Royal Canal in 1845. Legislation as far back as 1817 restricted CIÉ's options with this unused waterway, which it was still required to keep open for navigation. A special Transport Act was passed by the Oireachtas unanimously, if somewhat sadly, in December 1960, giving CIÉ authority to close the Royal Canal to navigation. The closure formally took place on 6 April 1961, ten years after the last barge had operated. The board then authorised the building of a dam across the canal at Ballinea, three miles west of Mullingar, and 'most of the western section dried out and soon it was impossible to distinguish points of the canal from the surrounding landscape'. Local authorities, which for some years had wanted to build low bridges across the canal at various points, were given that permission.

Back to the Grand Canal. In the same year as the Royal Canal was closed to navigation, the Naas, Kilbeggan and Ballinasloe branches of the Grand Canal were similarly closed. CIÉ's finances were improving as a whole and Todd Andrews felt that some money could be 'devoted to the development of the canals for amenity purposes at least in Dublin'. He had no doubts about any other use:

> All commercial traffic had ceased and it was clear that as a means of transport of commodities the canals were obsolete. Their enforced acquisition was nothing but an economic burden which should never have been inflicted on CIÉ . . . I saw the city manager and proposed that CIÉ would landscape the canal banks from Ringsend to Inchicore if the corporation would agree to maintain them. We would also undertake to keep the canal channel clean. My proposal, which I recall was made over lunch in the old Red Bank restaurant, [later converted into the Blessed Sacrament Chapel in Dublin's D'Olier Street] was drowned in a deluge of official verbosity. Any further interest I had in the matter was directed to getting responsibility for maintaining the canals transferred to the Office of Public Works. I did not succeed.
>
> (*Man Of No Property*, p. 251)

The Todd Andrews reaction to the verbose caution of his Dublin Corporation lunch guests was typical of the man. If he had been of a different temperament he would not have achieved the shake-up which he pushed through in CIÉ during his term of office. The aversion of Dublin Corporation to getting involved in the canals would ease somewhat in the following years in the sense that they would assist in the care of its banks, but CIÉ, government, the corporation and the local authorities knew from 1960 onwards that it was inappropriate and unfair to CIÉ that it should have responsibility for the maintenance of the canals. In 1964 Erskine Childers would say that he was considering the position of the canals with CIÉ now that they had no transport function. Several years would elapse before government confirmed that they were considering transferring the canals to the Board of Works. A government decision that this was to happen was put on record by Minister Pádraig Faulkner on 30 November 1978. His successors over several more years, including Peter Barry, Albert Reynolds and P. J. Fitzpatrick, would explain how 'the matter was still under consideration' and that the issue was a complex one. The ball would be kicked to touch year after year until CIÉ, in July 1986, was eventually relieved of its legal responsibilities for the canals, a full quarter of a century after commercial trading had ceased on the Grand Canal and the Royal Canal had been closed to navigation. The delay was symptomatic of a 'do nothing until you have to' phenomenon which should not surprise the student of public administration. The minister who eventually grasped the rushes, thistles and docks of this question was Jim Mitchell as part of the 1986 reorganisation of CIÉ.

TODD ANDREWS WAS also frustrated in an initiative he took in relation to the Great Southern Hotels. In his autobiography he said he recognised that the functional relationship between the railway and the hotels ceased once the bus and motor car replaced the railway for those whom the hotels were designed to serve.

> However they were still valuable assets . . . and we decided to enlarge and modernise them in order to cater for the increased traffic which the tourist industry was endeavouring to develop. For decoration purposes we were able to avail ourselves of the Arts Council scheme under which modern Irish paintings were supplied at [a fair] price for display in public buildings. The scheme gave a considerable boost to Irish artists and we were proud to be associated on a large scale with it. (ibid., p. 265)

It was one of Todd Andrews' enthusiasms to be a patron of the arts. Under this Arts Council scheme CIÉ obtained Evie Hone's famous window 'The Four Green Fields' for display in the new Passenger Sales Bureau in O'Connell Street, Dublin. The window was eventually transferred to the new and extended Government Buildings in Merrion Street when the former College of Science was adapted for that purpose.

CIÉ had seven hotels, Galway, Killarney, Kenmare, Parknasilla, Mulrany, Sligo and Bundoran (inherited from the GNR). It used them to support its own tourist promotions and CIÉ became the largest retailer abroad of Irish holiday packages. Whether the existence of the hotels was a main catalyst for CIÉ's high profile in tourist development or whether the stimulus came from the natural role of a transport company in developing new traffic may be a matter for debate. CIÉ was proud of its hotels and they consistently returned a modest profit which, in view of their age and the location of some of them, was a creditable achievement. It is fair to say that outside Dublin and Cork in the early sixties they were the only significant hotels in Ireland which were being adequately modernised and aggressively promoted. In a logical move, foreshadowed by Ken Whitaker's *Economic Development* published in 1956 and recognising that the hotels were a very different business to the running of trains, trucks and buses, CIÉ created a subsidiary, Ostlanna Iompair Éireann (OIE), in which the Great Southern Hotels with their management, group marketing and accounting would be centralised. The decision to establish OIE was made in July 1959, but the new company was not incorporated until 1961 and began trading on 1 April 1962. In the North, the UTA had inherited four former railway hotels but had failed to modernise them. Todd Andrews' account of what happened throws an interesting light on his own attitudes and contacts at the time.

> I had established close personal links with Sir Arthur Algeo, the chairman of the UTA, and we often discussed areas of mutual co-operation which might be of advantage to our two companies. It occurred to me that one obvious method was to amalgamate the two hotel groups.
>
> I raised the matter with the Taoiseach, Seán Lemass, and with our minister, Erskine Childers, and both felt that the project was worth pursuing. I was authorised to approach the UTA with two options; we would buy their hotels for £1 million (a figure rather above their market value) or we would set up a joint company with equal shares to operate the hotels, north and south, as an integrated group. Algeo strongly supported the idea of amalgamation and he personally favoured the second of the two proposals but the deal was, of course, subject to the agreement of his political superiors. The minister responsible for UTA affairs in the Six County government was William

> Craig who indicated privately to Algeo that he would not be wholly opposed to the idea of the joint venture.
>
> As a next step Mary and I were invited, not for the first time, to spend a fishing weekend at Algeo's home in Ballymoney and it was arranged that Craig and his wife would meet us for Sunday lunch. In the course of the afternoon drive around the countryside the minister, Algeo and myself had a further discussion on the hotel project.
>
> Craig's view was that this was the kind of co-operation between north and south which should be encouraged. He did not think there was any political principle involved and undertook to put the proposal before his government colleagues at Stormont. Unfortunately they were not equally open-minded. Approval could not be obtained for either of our proposals and the idea was summarily dropped. The UTA hotels were subsequently sold to an English hotel group for £600,000.
>
> (ibid., p. 265)

If the deal had gone through, CIÉ might not have made its own later move with the Russell Court Hotel in Belfast, a project that would prove disastrous for OIE, as will emerge in a later chapter.

TODD ANDREWS' DISAPPOINTMENT with the Dublin reaction to his canals proposals and with the Belfast rejection of his hotels idea is peripheral to the main story. A much more serious and abiding disappointment occurred in the field of labour relations:

> I went into CIÉ with a determination that, whatever else worked, good labour relations practice would prevail. I knew the unions were satisfied with my appointment as chairman. But I had the naive belief that the unions' attitude towards the great semi-state bodies like the ESB, Bord na Móna, Aer Lingus and CIÉ corresponded with my own. To me these were nationally owned and community based enterprises. I thought that the unions accepted these organisations as being in a different category from private businesses or public companies.
>
> (ibid., p. 254)

Andrews described himself as a 'Jeffersonian democrat' and a socialist who regarded state companies as 'socialism in the practical form'. Before his arrival in Kingsbridge industrial relations had been quiet for a few years. Average days lost in the three years 1956 to 1958 for the entire staff of over 20,000 came to no more than 75 per annum. Nevertheless, the public and Andrews' own perception was that CIÉ's industrial relations were poor.

They would remember earlier not so good years such as 1955, when 2,188 staff had been involved in disputes, and total days lost amounted to 10,785. In fairness to CIÉ 1955 had also been an exceptionally bad year nationally for man-days lost in industry.

In his initial reorganisation of CIÉ, Andrews changed the people in charge of personnel. In his first year he also launched a formal scheme of joint consultation. Rates of pay and conditions of employment were excluded from this scheme. Such matters should remain for direct negotiation between trade unions and management. A total of 32 (subsequently 37) Joint Consultative Councils were set up at various centres throughout the country. (CIÉ staff were based at 300 different locations.) The local councils comprising elected staff representatives and members of management met at least twice yearly, normally for a full day each. In addition, a Top Consultative Council was set up involving CIÉ's senior managers and union officials nominated by the Irish Congress of Trade Unions. The top consultative group met quarterly. Paddy Murphy, the Assistant General Manager (Personnel), said in 1968 that 'before each meeting a statement was issued by the Company which covers all the company's activities and deals with the revenue position; new business secured; plans for improvements in rolling stock, buildings, equipment and staff facilities and amenities; and external developments affecting the Company' (*Administration*, Winter 1968).

CIÉ was the biggest employer in the state, apart from the state itself, and formal consultation machinery on CIÉ's scale had never before been attempted. Some people in CIÉ felt that the consultative councils were excessively influenced by trade union officials and that, despite circulation of minutes and coverage provided in CIÉ's staff journal *Nuacht CIÉ*, a weakness in the system was that such officials did not relate adequately to the shop floor. Such reactions are predictable and understandable. The source for these comments thought that the situation was much improved by the later development of works councils, e.g. at Dublin city garages. This should not detract from the credit due for the 1959 joint consultation initiative. Andrews observed that these consultative councils were not an original concept of CIÉ's: they derived from a movement (the Whitley Councils) started in England after World War I. 'But whether because of the scale on which they were established or the vigour and effort with which they operated I know of no organisation which used them more advantageously than did CIE.' (*Man of No Property*, p. 261)

There were thirty-two or thirty-four unions in CIÉ, depending on by whom or when they were counted, and individual grades were represented by up to four unions, e.g. by both Irish and British-based general unions and craft unions. Twenty-one unions had less than 100 members in CIÉ and constant difficulty was experienced by the serving of competing, unrelated and sometimes conflicting claims. The Irish Trade Union Congress had split itself in two during the forties, one each for Irish and British-based unions. It had reunited in the late fifties as the Irish Congress of Trade Unions (ICTU) and now in 1961 it agreed with CIÉ that the thirty odd unions co-operate in a CIÉ group of unions, with six subgroups, one for each major employee category—clerical and supervisory, road passenger, road freight, rail operative, shop workers and building trades. Unfortunately this less than perfect effort at co-ordination—it excluded the non-congress Electrical Trades Union—would be further weakened in 1964 when the National Busmen's Union was formed outside congress and would not be admitted to the CIÉ group.

The establishment of a group structure for CIÉ's unions was followed by efforts to set up an agreed scheme for the resolution of disputes with the company and, if necessary, for arbitration. Discussions continued for two years with succeeding annual reports recording that agreement had not yet been reached. Eventually the 1963/64 Annual Report noted that: 'After lengthy consideration, new machinery was established in consultation with the Irish Congress of Trade Unions for the negotiation and settlement of trade disputes within the Company.' This machinery would be short-lived. In June 1965, following a Labour Court decision to involve itself in resolving a bus dispute, CIÉ told the court that it was undermining CIÉ's established negotiating machinery. On 29 June 1965 the board decided to withdraw from the painfully negotiated machinery. Thus serious attempts to improve institutional arrangements between CIÉ and its labour force ran into early and terminal difficulty.

The story of Andrews' industrial relations travail is primarily focused on the busmen, but it is worth retelling in some detail because of the permanence of the issues and because of the personalities involved. Industrial relations on the railway had been, and would continue to be, relatively stable; when they did occur, upsets were more likely to be connected with maintenance trades rather than with railway operatives. Dieselisation of the railways and pruning of the network had reduced the number of railwaymen without incurring industrial strife. In contrast, road passenger services were increasing their staff numbers, but their industrial relations would prove to be chronically unstable.

Early in 1960 the new 74 seater double-deckers came on stream. The ITGWU served a claim for additional pay. Andrews would not agree that increased seating capacity on a bus was an adequate reason for a pay claim. His experience in Bord na Móna had not prepared him for a prevalent mood in labour relations, that change of any sort would be used to advance a claim for a compensation increase. The matter was resolved without a dispute, but what is significant was Todd Andrews' surprise at the process. The initial claim was served, negotiations took place, and an agreement was reached with the negotiating officials. Unfortunately the men would not accept the settlement.

> I could not understand this change of front. I thought that once agreement had been reached with their representatives the deal was final. It was explained to me that the negotiators were not the union; the last word lay with the union membership and the settlement terms had been rejected after a ballot of the men concerned. It followed that the negotiations did not resume at the point in the wage structure from which they originally started but rather from the point where they left off. With that sort of negotiation CIÉ had no chance. The management were on a hiding to nothing. The amount involved in this instance was relatively trivial and was not worthwhile bringing to an issue. The effect the incident had on me was to diminish my trust and sympathy with the unions or rather with the ITGWU. (ibid., pp. 254/255)

It would be remarkable if Andrews was really as surprised as he claims he was at these events. His argument was that trade unions needed strong, 'pyramidal' leadership and contrasted his contemporary, John Conroy, President of the ITGWU, with such figures from 'the great union traditions' as 'Big Jim Larkin, O'Brien, Foran and Tom Kennedy'. Andrews' disdain for Conroy is remarkable: 'He had become a Buggin's turn president of the ITGWU moving up the ranks.' 'He was a man of narrow integrity.' 'Conroy's frame of mind exasperated me.' Conroy was also compared disparagingly with Jim Larkin, Jun., to whom Andrews suggested that the WUI should make a bid for CIÉ's busmen. In retrospect, the antipathy to John Conroy may in part be explained by Andrews' own sense of failure with CIÉ's industrial relations and his need to find a scapegoat for that failure.

The next dispute after that relating to the new 74 seater double-deckers was much more serious. Following a fashion of the period the ITGWU served a claim for busmen for extra compensation for weekend working. In CIÉ and other employments such claims enabled the claimants to gain bigger increases than were indicated by whatever 'wage round' was current. The claims were expressed in terms of compensation for 'unsocial hours'. The increasing popularity of the five-day week gave some weight to the feeling that extra pay was indeed justified. The claim was for 'double time on Sunday' instead of 'time and a half' and 'time and a half' instead of 'normal time' for Saturday working after 12.00 hrs. The Labour Court hearing resulted in a recommendation for 'time and a half' for Saturdays and no change for Sundays. The Labour Court recommendation was accepted by CIÉ and rejected by the unions who said that it would benefit their members by a maximum of seven shillings and sixpence (37.5p) a week. The unions announced that there would be no weekend working until their claim was settled. CIÉ responded: 'If you stay out on Saturday and Sunday we will not let you back on Monday.'

Andrews recalled: 'We could not accept that it was reasonable for the employees of an essential public service to choose when they would or would not work.' The scene was set for a bitter struggle. The first weekend strike took place on Saturday and Sunday, 18 and 19 February 1961, but due to the intervention of Jack Lynch, Minister for Industry and Commerce, direct negotiations did resume and on the Monday the men were allowed to return to work. The direct negotiations did not find a solution. ICTU became involved unsuccessfully as a mediator; another weekend strike occurred in March, and a lockout ensued.

Todd Andrews takes up the story:

> The unions had good reason to think that we would not enforce the threatened lock-out. 'Lock-out' was a dirty word in Dublin since the days of William Martin Murphy before the First World War and not merely in the ranks of the trade unionists but among the public at large. For someone like me whose normal sympathies would be with the bus workers . . . to take such a decision produced a severe cauterising of conscience. The fact is that we in CIÉ thought the union leaders did not seriously believe in the merits of their case and were giving no guidance to their members. We believed too that the proposed weekend strike was an easy way for the union to have its meat and its manners. It could stage a cheap strike, showing militant leadership, without dipping into its very substantial fund for strike pay . . . The lock-out started and gave the political opposition and all the loud-mouths in the country an opportunity to draw analogies between 1913 and 1961, between the Dublin United Tramway Company of that day and the new CIÉ. This analogy was particularly distressing for me. (ibid., p. 256)

Jack Lynch again intervened and the dispute was eventually resolved with the appointment of a special committee to investigate the claim. The committee consisted of An Breitheamh Cearbhall Ó Dálaigh, of the Supreme Court; Leo Crawford, Joint General Secretary of the ICTU, and Frank Lemass, General Manager, CIÉ. The committee recommended 'double time' for Sundays and 'time and a half' for Saturdays, providing a maximum increase per busman of fifteen shillings and ninepence (79p). The dispute left a bad taste all round. Instead of improving, industrial relations in CIÉ were deteriorating, and worse was to come.

Some have alleged that CIÉ management, specifically Frank Lemass, fought this and other disputes 'to the last drop of Andrews' blood'. The personal feelings of Todd Andrews revealed in his memoirs show that he was very much in charge. It seems likely indeed that operational management would have yielded before Andrews did. Later in 1961 (November) a strike of footplate staff in Cork was caused by a disciplinary matter and disturbed train services for a month. In total 42,545 man-days were lost in 1961, more than in the previous seven years combined.

The following year saw a 50 per cent reduction in man-days lost but it involved the first strike related to one-man bus operation. This had been first proposed for single-deckers in 1959. The objective was to start with private hire and day-tour coaches. Increased driver pay and no redundancies or loss of earnings were part of the package. The unions did not formally consent, so to bring matters to a head, the board decided on 10 April 1962 that conductors would be dispensed with on private hire and tour buses with effect from 1 May. On 2 May board had a special meeting to discuss the resulting unofficial strike which had taken place at Dublin City and Broadstone depots. The strike paralysed Dublin City Services and also stopped many provincial services. After some days the unions made the strike official—a regular enough ploy so that union officials and the Labour Court could become involved in trying to find a settlement. Andrews records that 'In the Labour Court hearings that followed the unions not only accepted the principle of one-man bus operation but also the terms under which it would be applied.' (ibid., p. 259)

A year later CIÉ moved to the next stage of one-person operation (OPO) —as it would become known in gender neutral language. This involved introducing OPO to 100 provincial scheduled routes operated by single deck buses. The ITGWU refused to allow this extension of OPO, using it to lodge a claim for substantial improvements in a wide range of fringe benefits, e.g. holidays, sickness benefits, pensions and travel facilities which would apply to all bus crews, whether or not they were affected by the OPO. CIÉ 'refused to give in to this arbitrary demand'. It proceeded to insist on provincial single deck OPO and the unions withdrew their labour. Again this was seen, not as a 'strike' but as another 'lockout' which lasted a month until the government intervened, in effect telling CIÉ to defer OPO. Andrews' reaction was to insist that this instruction by government should be given in public. The story gives a rare insight into what can happen when a strong personality is sure of his ground and takes a firm stand with his political master.

> Jack Lynch phoned me to say that 'the Boss' (i.e. Lemass) wanted me to take the men back. I told him I would refuse to do so unless I got a directive either from the Taoiseach or from himself as Minister for Industry and Commerce to end the lock-out and that the terms of the directive be published. At Lynch's suggestion I decided to discuss the position personally with the Taoiseach and reiterated my demand for a formal public directive. I said to Lemass that in every man's life there comes a time when he must make a stand. There would be no compromise on the question of the lock-out unless it was made clear that the decision had been taken out of the hands of CIÉ. (ibid., p. 257)

It should be explained that the Department of Labour had not yet been set up, and Jack Lynch was involved because the Department of Industry and Commerce still had responsibility for labour matters. Of Jack Lynch, Andrews had the impression that 'my abrasive manner was offensive to his nice personality'. In his discussion with government he was also 'playing from strength'. He would resign if he had to and Seán Lemass, realising that CIÉ was being revived from its 'moribund condition', would be 'hesitant' to dismiss its chairman:

> With typical decision, without discussion, he [Seán Lemass] said, 'All right. I'll tell the minister to issue the directive.' When I got back to my office there was a message from Jack Lynch asking me to come to see him. We agreed on the form of the directive and he promised to send it to the press. Later he phoned to say that he had read over the directive to 'the Boss' who agreed with the wording but did not think it was necessary to publish it. I replied that unless it was published the lock-out would not be lifted by me. He phoned me back again in due course to say that publication had been arranged. (ibid.)

Andrews had lost the battle with the unions, but had shown, at some cost, that he could not easily be 'pushed around' by unions, by the 'loud mouths' or even by ministers.

The correspondence between Jack Lynch and CIÉ was duly published in the newspapers on 2 April 1963 and later reprinted in Basil Chubb's *Source Book of Irish Government*. Chubb's interest in the affair concerned whether the minister was entitled to issue a 'directive' to CIÉ. In fact, the minister's letter 'strongly requested' CIÉ to defer the operation of one-man buses, advising that he had told the unions that he would give CIÉ a 'directive' to accept the recommendations of the commission he was setting up. Deputies Noel Browne and Jack McQuillan raised the question in the Dáil: 'Under what powers vested in him by the Oireachtas can the Minister direct CIÉ to accept his proposals?'

Andrews saw it in simpler terms: he would do what he was told to do, or resign. He wanted the instruction to be given in public and in this he was successful. On the specific issue which caused the dispute, Andrews summarised the outcome: 'In effect it took four years of continuous effort including every known form of negotiation, conciliation and Labour court mediation, as well as two strikes, before CIÉ succeeded in implementing the one-man bus programme on a limited scale [i.e. on provincial single deck scheduled services and on a staggered basis].' (ibid.)

The final resolution of the campaign by CIÉ for OPO would not be achieved for another twenty years. We will return to it as the story unfolds, particularly in relation to double deck buses. Meanwhile, a tactical breakthrough was achieved in Busáras resulting in CIÉ's new express services taking off on a driver-only basis. Dublin area management decided in February 1961 that they would not wait on a national accord on OPO. They wanted to launch an express bus service to Cavan—one of the areas which had previously been within the remit of GNR's rail and bus services:

> The idea was to set up a new type of bus service, a non-stop express service between Cavan and Dublin. Passengers would buy their tickets before boarding at each end. Various sections would be timed by agreement with the union's representatives the aim being to achieve the fastest possible run consistent with safety. A coach not a standard bus would be used. And the service would be driver only.
> (Kerry Brady: *Nuacht CIÉ*, Nollaig 1991)

Discussions took place, informally at first and then formally, with representatives of No. 9 Branch of the ITGWU. Kerry Brady describes in *Nuacht CIÉ* how he struck a deal for driver-only buses by persuading people that in this case they were dealing with a new type of service which could expand bus operations if it was successful. He held out the prospect, depending on results, that the service could be extended to Enniskillen and Donegal. By September local agreement had been reached; the central personnel department was informed and a detailed agreement was drawn up for the operation. On 27 November 1961 the Cú Uladh, the name given to the first express bus, took off from Busáras without a conductor. Quickly, it was a success. It took an hour off the stage carriage service time. Within a couple of years driver-only express services were operating through to Enniskillen, Derry and Letterkenny. The seeds of the Expressway division of today's Bus Éireann had been sown and were thriving, while the painful saga for other OPO services had many more years to run.

CIÉ's conviction that outdated or wasteful practices had to be eliminated had given rise to another problem in connection with 'helpers' on road freight vehicles. After the usual meetings between management and unions the issue was referred to the Labour Court which proposed that CIÉ dispense with helpers on 'Doubles' equipped with servo brakes. CIÉ, fortified with the Labour Court opinion, announced that this would be done on 8 October 1961. The ITGWU gave notice that if this happened all road freight workers would cease work on the same date. Interestingly, though, on 27 September CIÉ temporarily backed off from implementing the Labour Court recommendation. The board minute records that 'in face of the exceptionally difficult harvest conditions it was decided to postpone the introduction of one man operation [of road freight 'doubles'] until 31 December next. ITGWU to be so informed.' It would be tedious to recount the detail of subsequent negotiations, but CIÉ was increasingly unhappy with the Labour Court and a board resolution of 14 February 1963 deserves quotation:

> That the Board records its dissatisfaction with the manner in which the Labour Court has dealt with the cases of (a) the manning of road freight doubles and (b) the one man driving of omnibuses as a result of which its confidence in the Court is seriously impaired and further requests the Chairman to convey the terms of this resolution to the Minister for Transport and Power and to protest to him in the strongest possible terms.

Reading between the lines, what was happening was that CIÉ would make a proposal which the Labour Court would modify or agree with; CIÉ would accept the Labour Court recommendation; the unions would not; a dispute would develop; the Labour Court would again become involved through its conciliation service though a formal court hearing would not take place. Nevertheless, in the opinion of Todd Andrews the court would compromise itself by this procedure. The CIÉ Board found this practice intolerable. It had a stiff economic mandate from government and it saw one-person operation of certain services as an important step towards reducing costs. The Labour Court did not disagree with CIÉ but, on the other hand, saw its ultimate role, perhaps correctly, as that of resolving disputes. CIÉ claimed that the Labour Court was lacking in firmness and consistency and denied CIÉ the support to which it believed it was entitled. Andrews and his board felt frustrated and betrayed.

However, there was no gainsaying the fact that CIÉ had a serious labour problem with its bus operations, especially in Dublin. The trade unions too had a problem and CIÉ proposed to the unions involved that they jointly commission a report on Dublin's busmen from the highly respected Tavistock Institute of Human Relations. The institute began its survey of busmen's attitudes to their job, pay, supervisors, working conditions and unions during 1963. It was an interesting and enlightened initiative which in due course would help both sides better to understand the causes of tension which seemed to affect relationships within the workforce, and between them, their employers and their unions. However, it was too late for the ITGWU, which lost a large number of its bus operatives to the newly formed NBU while the Tavistock survey was in progress.

In a later chapter we will come to other disputes, especially in 1965, which sadly would shatter all previous records for days lost due to industrial unrest. However, the five-year reorganisation period for CIÉ to become self-sustaining was to expire in 1964. It is time to review how CIÉ performed relative to its breakeven targets and to describe the Pacemaker initiative taken by CIÉ to help government rethink the mandate conferred in 1958.

CHAPTER 12

PACEMAKER

Financial review since the 1958 Act—Childers succeeds Lemass—Breakeven prospect recedes—CIÉ's Pacemaker study—Public debate—1964 Act concedes long-term subvention for CIÉ.

The alarm with CIÉ's difficulties in 1957, which prompted the establishment of the Beddy Committee, the passing of the 1958 Transport Act and the appointment of Andrews as Chairman, was fully justified by the financial results for the year to 31 March 1958. A net loss of £2,588,000 was incurred.

The impact of the new Act, reducing CIÉ's interest liabilities, and writing down assets, which in turn reduced CIÉ's depreciation charges, took effect at varying times during 1958/59. Consequently the 1958/59 loss of £1,949,864 did not have the full benefits of a year's experience with the new financial structure. The first full year under the new Act, 1959/60, showed a big improvement—an end of year deficit of £709,006 which was almost £1.9 million less than in the last year before the Act was introduced. Probably half of the improvement is attributable to the benefits of the financial restructuring and the balance can be credited to a general improvement in CIÉ's performance. This was indeed a promising start towards achieving a breakeven result. Another four years remained to eliminate CIÉ's losses, and in the meantime CIÉ would receive an annual non-repayable grant of £1,175,000. The 1959/60 net deficit of £709,000 was £466,000 less than the government grant, so that the balance, together with substantial sums generated by disposal of surplus assets and equipment, could be used for capital purposes. In addition, funds were raised for CIÉ's capital programme by the issue of £3 million 5% transport stock at 96.

An indication that government departments would not change as readily as railway colour schemes was provided by an exchange with the CIÉ Board about the sinking fund for this issue. The prospectus for the new 5% stock provided for the creation of a sinking fund at a rate of 1.5 per cent per annum. But the Department of Finance later advised the board that the minister believed that the sinking fund should be accumulated at a rate of 2 per cent per annum. CIÉ protested at this changing of the rules after the event, and in due course the minister backed down.

Erskine Childers was a happy man when he moved the vote for his new Department of Transport and Power on 9 June 1960. Financial results for the first year of CIÉ's five-year reorganisation programme were encouraging.

> The most important improvement was on the railways where the company reduced the loss from £1,200,000 to £500,000 by a combination of increased revenue and reduced expenditure, a most remarkable result and with possibly no parallel in railway history...
>
> I have confidence that the policy which the Board of CIÉ are pursuing with lead to the realisation of the objectives of the Transport Act 1958—a self supporting transport system free from the demoralising effect of subsidisation by the state.
>
> (*Dáil Debates*, Vol. 182, Col. 825)

Childers went on to claim, as he would do again on a number of occasions, that 'proposals for reorganisation of the British Transport Commission are similar in many respects to those adopted here and tends to confirm the wisdom of the policy for the reorganisation of CIÉ'. The BTC was being reconstructed as British Rail, and its new Chairman, Dr Beeching, would be identified as the man who closed secondary railways throughout Britain just as Todd Andrews was about to do in Ireland. Childers became quite fulsome about CIÉ in the light of its improved results:

> If ever we needed an example of how desperately this country requires modern, searching, unsentimental twentieth century dynamic thinking and action through the application of modern, fast moving techniques, CIÉ can be that supreme example. (ibid., Col. 826)

Paddy McGilligan described these remarks as 'another rhetorical outburst' from the minister, but he too was generous to CIÉ though his comment was touched with sarcasm: 'the electrifying process of examining costs, reducing waste, stepping up output so well demonstrated by CIÉ is required in almost every part of our national economy'. Major Vivion de Valera reflected the views of many deputies: 'The Minister can claim to be the first who has come into this house and been able to report a real progress in the almost intractable problem of land transport in this country. (ibid., Col. 995)

CIÉ continued its progress towards break-even in 1961 to the delight of virtually everyone and in the year ending 31 March 1961 the deficit came to £246,000, a full £929,000 less than the £1,175,000 annual subvention. There has been a suggestion that the sale of assets was used to make the year 1960/61 look so spectacularly successful, but this is not borne out by examination of the accounts. The dissenters to the general euphoria were those who were deprived of railways even if replacement buses and road freight services were acknowledged, by the public who used them, to result in an improved service. In the view of its critics, CIÉ's rush towards break-even forced it to make anti-social decisions forced by the arbitrary deadline specified in the 1958 Act. The remarkably low deficit of £246,000 was down 90 per cent on the loss incurred in the last year before the 1958 Act was introduced. The railways contributed the lion's share of the improvement since 1958/59. No wonder Erskine Childers preened himself on these results, but he would not do so for long. The downward slope of CIÉ's deficits took a sudden lurch upward in the following year. The deficit of £246,000 jumped to £1,696,000 in 1961/62. The main cause of the deterioration was the eighth pay round. The background and causes of this pay round are not for us to consider here. Suffice to say that in CIÉ the difficulties arising from the pay round were compounded by a raft of what today would be known as 'special claims' which were settled on the terms of Labour Court recommendations. They related to 'amelioration of working conditions' and to 'status increases'. The result was a 20 per cent increase in the CIÉ wage bill and the net deficit leaping ahead of the fixed subvention. In July 1962 Todd Andrews reviewed the situation in an address to the Institute of Public Administration in Dublin's Custom House:

> The financial progress which the board has made since it took office has until recently been quite remarkable . . . the deficit was brought down to a figure of £246,000 and at the beginning of the past year we had hoped to maintain this progress. Our prospects of continuing such financial progress were completely upset, mainly by the impact of the eighth round of salary and wage increases and concurrently improved conditions of employment, in which our employees at all levels quite reasonably participated . . . Wages and salaries account for 60 per cent of our total expenditure and over a wide sector of operations the percentage is as high as 75 per cent. It is for this reason that these rounds impinge on CIÉ more heavily than on most other industries. An increase in expenditure of this magnitude is extremely difficult to offset by a corresponding increase in revenue, and the public could not be expected to accept, nor indeed would it be practicable to attempt to

enforce, an increase in rates and fares of such order as to offset the round. *(Modern Transport*, 14 July 1962)

Andrews explained that the 'temporary annual subvention' of £1,175,000 would minimise the effect of the £1.7 million deficit, 'but it is no consolation to the taxpayer that the subvention has to be used for this purpose'. Government was committed to achieving a self-sustaining public transport system (not merely a railway system, as Andrews repeatedly pointed out— to him whatever mode was most appropriate and economical to the business offering was the correct one). Government had nailed its colours to the mast of self-sufficiency by 1964. Andrews had saluted those colours. He showed no sign of wanting to draw them down:

> This deficit represents, fortunately, an acute rather than a chronic state of affairs; it is high but it is not disastrous and provided we are not discouraged by such a setback (and there is no reason for discouragement) and provided we apply ourselves with vigour and determination to our task . . . there does not seem to us any reason why at the expiry of the 1958 Act we should not be able to face the future without a subsidy. (ibid.)

Todd Andrews' formal measured language in this address to the IPA contrasts with the more pungent style of his autobiography published in 1982. His optimism about eliminating the deficit by 1964 was qualified by stated assumptions that future wage rounds would bear a 'direct relation to productivity' and that remaining 'wasteful and obsolete methods of working would be finally eliminated from the organisation'. Even with these qualifications there has to be some doubt as to whether Todd Andrews really believed in July 1962 that the 1964 breakeven target was still attainable. However, it would have been too early for him publicly to express such doubts, if he had them.

In the event, the £1.696 million deficit of 1961/62 would almost be a floor for subsequent deficits. A bus strike cost £342,000 in May 1962 and despite increased fares the 1962/63 deficit rose to £1,760,000. The notorious ninth round, which occurred at the beginning of 1964 costing £1.7 million in a full year, provided a 12 per cent pay rise across the community after the intervention of the Taoiseach, Seán Lemass, who took the politically helpful position that as national wealth was increasing everyone was entitled to take a share. The calculation which produced the 12 per cent figure was based on compensation for the previous year's inflation, plus an increase equal to the growth in national income, plus compensation for projected inflation. The indisputable consequences of this pay round were highly inflationary and were widely regarded as having been very harmful to the economy as a whole. In 1963/64, the last year of the 1958 temporary annual subvention of £1,175,000, the CIÉ deficit came to £1,606,000.

Pulling the five years together: CIÉ lost £1 million approximately in the first two of the five-year period, but when the slide started it lost another £5 million—a total of £6,029,000 against the aggregate subvention of £5,875,000. We have already reviewed traffic trends and noted growth other than on Dublin suburban rail. There are a few other points worth recording. Before the 1958 Act CIÉ had a total of 486 locomotives in use (347 steam and 139 diesel). By 1964 the total was down to 210 diesels (- 67%); coaching stock had also been reduced (- 27%); and freight rail vehicles had been reduced by 16 per cent. The reduction in railway lines, amounting to 29 per cent in total, affected only 5 per cent of revenue. Two hundred and eighteen stations and halts had been closed down (compared to 317 envisaged by Beddy). The total effect of the reduction in rolling stock, lines and stations was significantly to improve the utilisation of the remaining network of lines and equipment. Utilisation was still low by international standards because of the size and spread of the Irish market, but the gap noted by Beddy was closing.

Prior to the end of the five-year 'reorganisation period', Mr Childers introduced a rather minor Transport Bill in May 1963. The main purpose was to tidy up some points concerning construction of railways (for the NET plant in Wicklow), arranging that the redundancy rules would apply to workers transferred from the GNRB, safeguards for workers transferred to OIE, and similar matters. In addition, rules and limits relating to temporary borrowings were modified largely because with CIÉ's deteriorating results a cash shortage was imminent. The debate on this 1963 Bill gave a foretaste of what would take place a year later when the more substantive 1964 Bill would mark the end of the period covered by the 1958 legislation. Matters had changed greatly since the heady days of 1960. Childers now recognised that 'the Board seems to be without prospect of overtaking the effects of the eighth round'. A new policy would have to be developed, but 'whatever [this] may be the main arterial railway system of the country will be maintained'. On the other hand, he said that 'in the long term the tax payer will not be asked to pay subsidies in order to maintain any type of public transport if another less costly and more efficient type, either publicly or privately owned, can be provided'. There was no suggestion that the minister thought that there could be any conflict between those two statements.

The 1963 Bill would be passed without a division, but still the opposition had to have its innings. The somewhat donnish and lecturing style of Erskine Childers irritated some, and amused others. Gerard Sweetman, protesting that he sympathised with the minister in his predicament, managed to do so in terms calculated to embarrass Childers while having a long side swipe at Seán Lemass about the twenty years that had passed since CIÉ was established.

> The Minister has my sympathy in having to stand up and admit to the House on this Transport Bill that the position in relation to transport is hopeless, that he cannot solve it and that he does not know where it is to end. . . . It was rather interesting, as one listened, to compare the speech he made now with the thundering, bragging bravado of the present Taoiseach . . .
>
> When he came to the House in 1944, he said he had produced a scheme to reorganise the transport company as a result of which the Government and the people as a whole could look forward to a transport system that would operate successfully for 50 years at least . . . Fourteen years went by and the Taoiseach came back to the House in 1958 and again he said there was to be a rejuvenated railway . . . Nobody need ever again worry about transport because of . . . the Transport Act of 1958. There is this much to be said for it—it has lasted half as long as the one before it. (*Dáil Debates*, Vol. 203, Col. 332)

No reading of Mr Lemass's speeches would justify the 'thundering, bragging bravado' allegation that he claimed his 1944 plan would last for fifty years or that he thought the 1958 Bill would solve Ireland's transport problems. However political licence seems to excuse it. Mr Sweetman could safely indulge himself. His own comments about the railway system in the 1957 memorandum to government (see page 94) were not on the public record.

More than twelve months before this debate took place, in March 1962, the management of CIÉ had begun a ground-breaking study of the options for Ireland's public transport. The story would eventually emerge in October 1963 under the title, 'CIÉ Report on Internal Public Transport', but it would be more widely known by its original CIÉ code name of 'Pacemaker'. In February 1963 Donal Stephens, Development Manager of CIÉ, in a paper called 'The Transport Dilemma', which like Andrews' paper was one of a series read to the IPA, gave an advance warning of the Pacemaker approach. Extracts from two prominent economics columns of the day provide us with a foretaste of what was to come. Hugh Munro in *Hibernia* (April 1963) said:

> Since the large-scale development of motor transport in the 'twenties, the problems of public transport have bedevilled the Irish economic scene. Repeated solutions for these problems have been tried and have failed, and vast amounts of ink and breath have been expended in discussing the problem. Donal Stephens of CIÉ is . . . continuously

> interesting ... He is scrupulously fair-minded as between public and private enterprise. It is a measure of his objectivity that one tends not to dispute his conclusions, but to ponder on them and develop them.
>
> The paper hinges upon the distinction which he makes between economic *demands*, *needs*, and *wishes* in the transport field. *Demands* are things you need and are willing to pay for. A *need* is a thing people need but which cannot be sold on a commercial basis. ... Lastly, a *wish* is a thing you would like, but don't need, and are not willing to pay for ... a system such as CIÉ has [requires it] to meet not only the demands but also the needs of the public, and may even fulfil some of its wishes, in the matter of transport; ... in other words, CIÉ is obliged to provide transport over and above what the public is willing to pay for by way of passenger tickets or freight invoice ...

In *The Irish Times*, Garret FitzGerald wrote a weekly 'Economic Comment'. He quoted a speech by the Minister for Transport and Power about the need for a further review of transport policy. He had much to say about that subject and about its handling by elected public representatives whose ranks he had not yet joined. The minister had announced, 'that an impartial pilot study covering a complex field of enquiry' was to be undertaken, 'to reach a clear understanding of whether public transport can operate efficiently or economically enough to meet the needs of trade and industry'. Contemporaries would have regarded those remarks as mere well-intentioned 'Erskine speech'. There is no record of such an 'impartial pilot' study ever being completed or how a 'pilot' study in the transport field could have achieved much that was useful. However, the minister had also referred to the Board of CIÉ making its own assessment. Garret FitzGerald commented that the first fruits of this assessment were revealed in Donal Stephens's paper on 'The Transport Dilemma'.

> This paper sought rather to analyse the basic transport problem, and to pose the questions that will need to be answered ... This new and radical approach by CIÉ to the problem of Irish transport policy is a most welcome development, for our transport policy has grown up under pressure of circumstances over a period of just forty years. The Transport Act, 1958, was an immense improvement on its predecessors, but it nevertheless represented a compromise to gain time for a thorough factual review without which a fundamental revision of policy could not seriously be attempted. The intentions of this Act were—perhaps deliberately—obscure, requiring as it does, that the Board of CIÉ should provide 'reasonable' transport services. ... Moreover, the Act leaves to the discretion of CIÉ far more than it is

fair or reasonable to leave to such a body. CIÉ has, in fact, been asked to be judge and jury in its own case—to decide what are 'reasonable transport services', and how national economic development is to be encouraged within the transport sector, while at the same time being required to balance its accounts. When it has attempted to balance its accounts by closing branch lines it has exposed itself to violent criticism from the Dáil—in many cases from the very same people who gave this direction to CIÉ by voting for the Transport Act when it was passing through the Dáil. (*The Irish Times*, 27 February 1963)

CIÉ in its 1962/63 Annual Report had stated that on occasions, when faced with a conflict between making operations economic and providing service, they concluded that the requirement to provide service held precedence over the financial obligation. In strictly legal terms this may not have been correct, but there was no reason why any group other than a competing transport operator would have wished to test the issue in court. The upcoming 1964 legislation would not resolve that issue and later annual reports would continue to reflect the view that in certain circumstances (never defined) service would be given precedence over economy. FitzGerald made his own summary of the 'Transport Dilemma'.

> Our cities are congested because we have failed to devise and implement a system of charging car users the cost of the space they are using in driving through and parking in the city streets. Our public transport is perpetually in deficit because it is required to operate services for which the public are unwilling to pay the full cost. The country is full of people who cherish the irrational belief that the rest of the community owes a duty to them to subsidise their travel to and from work, or their travel at busy peak periods, or, indeed, their travel in comfort by rail instead of road . . . the recent Dáil debates on inland transport must have shattered the delusions of many who believed that we were evolving towards a mature democracy. (ibid.)

The 'recent Dáil debates' which dismayed Garret FitzGerald were on a Private Members Bill to delete the 'breakeven by 1964' clause from the 1958 Act. That clause was held to be the cause of the many controversial decisions which had been made by CIÉ. The Private Members Bill was proposed by Deputies Noel Browne and Jack McQuillan, now members of the National Progressive Democrat Party, and debated during November/December 1962. The proposers maintained reasonably enough that public transport could not be self-sustaining, but they developed that argument through abuse of Todd Andrews and the minister. In this they were joined by Deputies Thaddeus Lynch (FG) and Martin Corry (FF), who were smarting over the axing of the Waterford/Tramore and West Cork lines in their respective counties. Seán Dunne, the Dublin Labour TD, and Oliver Flanagan (FG) of Laois/Offaly were equally derogatory about CIÉ and the minister. To quote from Oliver Flanagan:

> Viewing the general standard of conduct of the Board of CIÉ in recent years, one is inclined to wonder whether they are operating from Kingsbridge or Grangegorman [mental asylum] because of the very high incidence of lunacy associated with the general management of CIÉ. . . .
> (*Dáil Debates*, Vol. 198, Col. 101)

Dinosaurs did not exercise the fascination at the time which would later accrue to them, but Childers was likened to one 'not because of any physical resemblance, but because of the structure of his thinking'. The debate was left almost entirely to what may be described as 'rogue deputies'. The Bill was defeated by 63 votes to 12. Fine Gael abstained from the vote which caused Noel Lemass (son of Seán) to ask where were the 'scurrilous tongues, Thaddeus Lynch and Oliver Flanagan' who so denounced CIÉ's management but did not enter the division lobbies. On the whole the debate makes distasteful reading. It certainly revealed a high degree of antipathy to CIÉ, but because of limited participation by front bench deputies, it could hardly be judged as representative of Dáil opinion of the period. A motion, about the same time, proposed by Deputy Kyne (Labour, Waterford), that Erskine Childers' salary be reduced because of his failures with regard to transport policy, was supported by Fine Gael as well as by Labour. By the time he wrote in early 1963 there was a growing consensus that breakeven would not be achieved by March 1964 and Garret FitzGerald's column continued:

> An effort must be made to break out of the straitjacket into which Irish transport policy has been forced through the weakness of successive Governments, and the irresponsibility of successive Parliaments . . . If the Government and the Dáil feel that it is desirable that a railway system should be maintained even at the cost of heavy subsidies, they must be prepared to vote these subsidies openly . . . A case can certainly be made for special subsidies of these kinds, where they are designed to secure valid social ends, but there is no case for taxing other forms of transport, or restraining the growth of alternative services in order merely to obscure the issue and to evade responsibility for the consequences of decisions.
> (*The Irish Times*, 27 February 1963)

The following 2 September, when the Annual Report confirmed the CIÉ loss of £1,696,000 for 1962/63, press comments revealed that in two respects public attitudes had changed radically since the 1950s: CIÉ was now regarded as a well-run organisation and the target of breakeven was seen as 'well nigh impossible' (*Irish Independent*). Prompted by the Annual Report, all four of the Republic's dailies published lengthy leading articles on these lines. Inter alia *The Irish Times* (3 September 1963) said:

> Under the Act, the board was required to be solvent by March of next year. On the present figures, it has not got a chance. But that is not to say that CIÉ, stimulated on the one hand by new powers enjoyed by no comparable organisation in these islands, and hamstrung on the other by the deadline of March 31st, 1964, has not done a good job in the four years in which it has had an opportunity of revolutionising Irish transport. Over three years ago, a spokesman of the company was able to express his confidence that . . . the apparently conflicting targets of solvency—imposed by the Oireachtas—and service—imposed by the basic concept of a State enterprise—would be reconciled without difficulty. Now we must think again. . . . it is time to take into account not only the remarkable success of CIÉ in surmounting unforeseeable difficulties such as strikes and major wage increases to give the nation the results published to-day; but also the shape that the coming legislation ought to take . . . New ideas, radical pruning and equally impressive expansion have marked the board's recent history . . .

The *Cork Examiner* had supported the campaign against closing the Cork, Bandon and South Coast lines, but now it was generally complimentary about CIÉ and its criticism was focused on the five-year breakeven target of the 1958 Act.

> The solvency target, laudable in itself, was vitiated by the arbitrary time limit which imposed on the administration a course of ruthless action directed against rail branches. It was a classical example of the end being made to justify the means . . . If any lesson is to be learned from the effects of the 1958 Act it is the futility of laying down rigid targets without regard for the consequences of possible economic upheaval, and the danger of setting up one criterion of value namely profitability, against another, namely service which the public expects to continue and is prepared to pay for.
>
> (*Cork Examiner*, 4 September 1963)

The Annual Report (1962/63) which prompted these editorials mentioned that 'Pacemaker' was being prepared: 'It will provide, it is intended, data to assist government in formulating its public transport policy and in framing the new legislation which must be enacted early in 1964.' (Annual Report, 1962/63)

Thirty years after its completion and submission to government in October 1963 the Pacemaker project still impresses. Only seven years had passed since the previous Board of CIÉ had told the Beddy Committee that since the Oireachtas had decided that the railways should be retained, and as CIÉ had been charged to operate them without subsidy, the only practicable course open to government was severely to restrict private transport. Sensibly the new board and management realised that however logical it might have seemed in 1958, such thinking was now thoroughly out of date. The total change in approach is so obvious that a remark by Seán D. Barrett, 'Pacemaker retreats a little from the 1957 proposals' (*Transport Policy in Ireland*, p. 14) is much less than fair.

The two-volume Pacemaker Report was remarkable for its time in the extent of the data compiled and in the analysis attempted of the existing inland transport systems, rail and road, passenger and freight, public and private. It then defined, costed and evaluated 'alternatives to the existing public transport system'. Perhaps more remarkable was Pacemaker's lack of recommendations. This is explained by its terms of reference, which in summary were to examine factors that determine public transport policy and its implementation, to review 'salient features' of CIÉ—operational, commercial, traffics, industrial relations and finance—and to examine the costs and consequences of alternative forms of public transport rail and road systems. Finally the authors of the report were required to review alternative public transport *policies* as distinct from transport *systems*. There the terms of reference ended. The authors were not required to recommend any particular policy or course of action. They had been 'required only to reach conclusions, to give reasons for them, and to point out the consequences' (Pacemaker I, p. 3). CIÉ's deliberate intention was to present the report to government, more or less saying, 'previous policy has been determined on the basis of inadequate data, projections and understanding of possible alternatives, e.g. abandonment of the railways was not really considered. To the best of our ability we have now studied that possibility among others. Now it is up to you as legislators to make up your mind as to what is to be done. In other words, "Over to you" or in tennis parlance, "It's your serve."' Pacemaker is so detailed in its analysis and so carefully phrased in its findings that it would do a disservice to the report and to the reader of this book to attempt to summarise it. However, we are concerned with the consequences of Pacemaker and some main findings must be noted before moving on to the ensuing legislation.

Firstly, Pacemaker concluded that none of the alternative public transport systems identified was so manifestly superior to others that 'it could lead to immediate action with short-term favourable results'. (If the case were otherwise, CIÉ might have made less of a virtue of Pacemaker's reticence about making recommendations.)

Secondly, 'due to the environment in which public transport now operates it may face the dilemma of either providing service at the expense of solvency or of being solvent by refusing to provide service'.

Thirdly, 'private transport in urban areas . . . is self strangulating'.

Fourthly, 'public transport policies of necessity are a compromise' between what is theoretically satisfactory and what is acceptable in practice. 'It rests with the national transport policy-makers to investigate and state the degrees of compromise which are the practical alternatives to the degeneration of transport.'

Pacemaker's analysis of the profitability of CIÉ's transport network—section by section—can be summarised as follows:

Rail:	410 miles of track are wholly profitable, 300 miles are marginally profitable and 750 miles are unprofitable.
Dublin City Bus:	Of 79 bus routes, 35 operate at a loss and 8 are only marginally profitable. Considerable cross-subsidisation is taking place. Overall the Dublin bus services are profitable.
Provincial Bus:	Only 72 of 234 services are wholly profitable. Overall contributions of 1% being achieved against a required 4%.
Road freight:	Contribution of 11% being achieved against a required 26%. Therefore they are 'marginally' rather than 'wholly' profitable.

Rail traffic was unevenly distributed:
>25% of the network generated 52% of the total ton miles.
>Five large stations forwarded 71% of all traffic.
>Ten large customers accounted for 70% of freight traffic.

Pacemaker identified and evaluated two main alternative systems: an all-road system and a combined system where mainline rail would carry freight only and passenger operations would be by road.

An all-road system 'would have the advantage of a flexible relationship between expenditure and revenue so that deficits when they occurred could be kept within reasonable limits'. However, an all-road system would involve capital expenditure on additional road vehicles, additional costs of road construction and maintenance, redundancy costs and heavy deficits during a transition period while the railways were being wound down and road services were being developed. The costs of transition should not be borne by CIÉ if the new public transport system was to have a reasonable chance of being viable. With regard to the combined system of rail freight and passenger by road, the Pacemaker view was that 'The all freight rail system would be subject to the risk of unacceptably heavy deficits in the absence of restrictions on road freight trunk haulage . . . It cannot, therefore, be seen except as an interim stage on the way to an all-road system.'

Erskine Childers was the sort of man who must have relished Pacemaker. Other ministers might have said, 'Don't give me all this.' 'What are you saying?' 'Tell me what you want.' Childers himself liked to get into the innards of a problem. In addition to giving its report to government, CIÉ made formal presentations to officials of the Department of Transport and Power taking them through Pacemaker's conclusions, section by section. Diarmuid Ó Riordáin was now Secretary of the Department. He was not a man to be confused by the detail of what he heard. To him, whether right or wrong, abandonment of the railways was politically unthinkable. He would tell the minister that if he took such a proposition to Cabinet it would be thrown out in summary fashion. At any rate Childers had already stated in the Dáil that a new transport policy would involve the preservation of the newly called 'arterial' rail links. Ó Riordáin quickly summarised what he was hearing and, spotted by a CIÉ person attending the presentation, he simply wrote on his note pad, '£2 million per annum'. Many months would pass before that figure became known to the public.

On 17 December 1962 Childers delivered a lengthy address (short addresses were never his style) to a packed meeting of the Institute of Transport in the Dawson St, Dublin, premises of the Institution of Engineers. The occasion was heralded as one where the minister would reveal his thinking on future transport policy. He dealt at length with Pacemaker, whose authors must have been gratified at the exposure it would receive in the following day's papers, though Childers added much material of his own including statistics about European transport trends. *The Irish Times* carried the story under the headline, 'Railways' Arterial Structure To Stay'.

Childers went back to the basic question: why should government be involved at all in transport matters? He had come to the conclusion that public transport could not be governed by the simple rules of supply and demand. 'The Government', he said, 'must reserve the right to determine by appropriate legislation the overall direction of transport policy.' Having said that and having described Pacemaker's findings, the minister revealed little about the government's intention other than that the 'arterial structure' of the railways would stay. He also added that 'the commuter rail system in

Dublin was likely to remain essential even though it would be operated at a loss'. This endorsement of Dublin suburban rail services was a sign that, at the time he spoke, in the early sixties, Dublin's traffic was a cause of increasing public annoyance. All the minister offered was 'A serious problem of traffic congestion in Dublin was a separate problem [from CIÉ's] and must not be left without a solution.'

The 1964 Transport Bill was published on 31 April. For all the debate that had taken place over the previous two years about transport policies and priorities, the Bill was a simple measure which proposed that CIÉ receive an annual £2 million non-repayable grant for the next five years, at which time the grant could be revised for a further five years. A £1 million repayable grant made in 1964 became non-repayable, and redundancy compensation provisions were to continue as before, but in future they would be funded by CIÉ rather than directly by the exchequer. Redundancy settlements for 1,768 employees had cost the exchequer £1.8 million in the previous five years. Allowing for the fact that wages had increased by perhaps 35 per cent over that period, it was clear that with current losses of £1.7 million CIÉ would have little spare cash to pay redundancy costs or major cost increases of any kind out of the proposed £2 million annual grant. In the context of redundancies, Childers noted that 'no further major reduction in the railway system is now foreseen', but 'redundancy arising out of the automation of level crossings which is analogous to the closing of railway services' would continue.

Raising the annual subvention from £1,175,000 to £2 million and shifting responsibility for redundancy payments back to CIÉ were the only significant features of the Bill. The famous financial obligations placed on CIÉ were changed to the extent that the board would take the state grant into account before ensuring that 'expenditure shall not be greater taking one year with another than the revenue of the Board'. Another provision changed the requirements for entry to clerical grades in CIÉ. At the time an open competitive exam was necessary for clerical entry, something that had been inherited from the 1924 GSR legislation. This was increasingly cumbersome in the 1960s, though CIÉ had for years been interpreting the three words—open, competitive and examination—in a somewhat different form than had been intended by the 1924 Act.

The un-named political correspondent of *The Irish Times* (before the days of newspaper bye-lines) was disappointed: '[The Bill's] limits seem to imply that the 1958 Transport Act is still the transport charter and nothing more is required at this stage.' He went on to ask about

> Dr Andrews' 'Pacemaker Project' which examined all the future problems of transport including the hypotheses of abandoning the railways . . . and the role of transport in the Second National

Programme. The least that was expected by experts last night was that a White Paper on Transport would have been produced showing what the discussions had been like, what Dr Andrews' report consisted of and how such a tremendous inquiry added so little to knowledge of future problems and their estimated solution.

The Pacemaker report itself was distributed to trade unions, business organisations and 'other parties on request'. It was also placed in the Dáil library on 9 March. On 20 May Erskine Childers introduced the 1964 Transport Bill in the Dáil. He delivered a typical speech until after repeated mentions of the Pacemaker Report he was interrupted by Paddy McGilligan. 'When was that published? When was it given to deputies?' The minister answered, 'I could not say, some weeks ago.' McGilligan: 'Weeks? Nobody has seen it that I know of. It was rather a secret document.' The minister replied that there was no secrecy, but McGilligan, terrier-like, harassed the minister in the fashion of a lawyer trying to break a witness. In quick succession he asked sixteen questions about this Pacemaker Report and concluded: 'He [the Minister] does not know when the report was published. Is that clear?' (*Dáil Debates*, Vol. 209, Col. 1744) McGilligan would lead for the opposition in the ensuing debate, and despite the many public references to Pacemaker over the previous six months, it seems that he genuinely did not know anything about it. While he was speaking, a party colleague got him a copy from the Dáil library. Later Childers was able to confirm that, as promised in the Dáil, Pacemaker had been in the library for over two months.

That detail from the debate brings us back to the reality of many Dáil discussions on transport—frequently misinformed, prejudiced and adversarial. Paddy McGilligan, an outstanding Minister for Industry and Commerce in the 1930s, a UCD law professor and subsequently a Minister for Finance and Attorney General, had not studied his brief or, as is more likely, he didn't have one. He just freewheeled: '[The Minister's speech] is a most shameful oration to the Dáil delivered by a shameless person.' A short while later in the debate a misunderstanding arose between him and Childers. It would be tedious to give the details. It concerned whether the surplus from Dublin city buses was exceeded by, or was in excess of, the losses incurred on Dublin suburban rail services and on what basis these rail losses were calculated. McGilligan initially didn't understand what the minister had said, but he would not allow the minister to clarify the point and persisted in his misunderstanding. Another unseemly row developed, which gives the impression that deliberately harassing Childers was a tactic used to see if he could be made to lose a sometimes overbearing composure.

One of McGilligan's points was, now that all agreed that CIÉ would not be profitable, it was time to make it fully accountable to the Dáil. Ministers should not be able to resort to the standard reply—'The Minister has no function in the matter.' McGilligan said that the house should 'be able to have an examination of even the day to day administration that is required after the fiasco that has been made by those to whom the minister gave unfettered control'. Childers countered that claim by quoting McGilligan's remarks of fourteen years earlier: 'I think we should get very definite agreement here that if these concerns [state companies] are to be allowed to run with any pretence of efficiency you cannot have day to day interference by parliamentary questions with day to day activity.' (*Senate Debates*, Vol. 37, Col. 718)

The main theme running through the debate was the government's volte-face on subsidy. Deputy Seán Casey listed five separate speeches by the minister, between 1960 and 1963, when he spoke against subsidy. Childers was unapologetic about his previous stance

> If I had hinted at any time during this period of ... reorganisation, that a subsidy would be inevitable, all the people would ... howling like wolves at CIÉ's feet and it would have been impossible to carry out the reorganisation that was so essential. ... There are railways in Europe that are subsidised and that are efficient. I hope CIÉ will join with them ... I have every hope that CIÉ can avoid all the temptations that a subsidy offers. (*Dáil Debates*, Vol. 210, Col. 607)

Nothing daunted by the criticisms he had been subjected to for previous 'rhetorical outbursts', he referred to a 'reorganisation statement of CIÉ' which had been sent to every deputy:

> I defy anyone to say that it was not a magnificent piece of work, that it was not a splendid piece of reorganisation once the immense complexity of a transport system ... are recognised. (ibid.)

The doggedness of Childers since his appointment in 1959 in explaining and lecturing on the transport scene; his patent enthusiasm for his brief; his persistent defence, even stonewalling, in the Dáil about a whole variety of controversial issues, particularly the closing of branch lines; and the amount of abuse he had to withstand, caused partly perhaps by his 'upper class' style and demeanour, earned him regard and praise from Todd Andrews in his autobiography, *A Man of No Property*.

Childers' shortcomings were such that once, in a meeting with his minister, Andrews was provoked to mutter 'magarlaí' a number of times. Ó Riordáin recalled that when he had gone, Childers wanted to know what was that word which Dr Andrews used. Ó Riordáin hesitated, Thekla Beere gave him no support. Childers insisted that he be informed. 'Minister', said

Ó Riordáin, 'Dr Andrews was saying balls in Irish.' (Source: conversation with author)

The 1964 Transport Act was duly passed in July after a relatively easy passage. We return to the ongoing activities of CIÉ which were little affected by this legislation. Its task was unchanged and unclarified. It had no new guidance in making the difficult decisions between providing and not providing services in the many grey areas where social rather than commercial criteria dominated.

CHAPTER 13

PRINCIPLE OF SUBSIDY CONCEDED

More industrial unrest—Emergence of NBU—New GM locomotives—1916 Rising marked—Renaming of rail termini—Dublin's traffic problems—Schaechterle studies—Expansion of Great Southern Hotels—School transport scheme initiated.

CIÉ entered a new phase with the passing of the 1964 Transport Act. The state wanted the existing rail network to be substantially maintained but now it accepted that the railways could not be operated without incurring losses. The new consensus also recognised that profits from road services would compensate for only a part of the railway losses. The £2 million subvention for five years to enable CIÉ to break even, after interest charges and sinking fund provisions, emerged with time to be reasonably well judged. For CIÉ management a psychological burden of 'achieving the impossible' had been lifted. The Pacemaker Report had forced government to face up to reality which it had previously denied. At the same time the new arrangement avoided giving CIÉ a blank cheque, and maintained pressure on CIÉ to improve its economic performance. The only false note was the cautious hope expressed by Childers that it would emerge towards the end of the five years that the subvention for the following five years would be at a lower level.

In the first year (1964/65) covered by the 1964 Act, CIÉ's net deficit fell slightly to £1,475,319 from the previous year's £1,605,881. As a result over £500,000 out of the £2 million subvention was available for capital purposes. The fall in deficit was almost entirely due to the bounce back of road passenger profits to £660,000 from the £273,000 to which they had fallen in 1963/64 as a result of that year's bus strikes. However, that improvement in bus operations was substantially offset by an increase in the deficit on railway working.

Overall, it was a good result and in the sixth year of Todd Andrews' leadership there seemed to be no change in the momentum of aggressive marketing and renewal. The 1964/65 Annual Report claimed that the commercial sales campaign enabled CIÉ to maintain its share of the transport market. New 'Package Deals' listed in the report related to cross-channel bacon traffic, steel traffic from Cóbh and fertilisers from the new nitrogenous factory at Arklow. A revised system of charging 'for rail merchandise traffic of 1 ton and less was, in general, well received'. Aerlód Teoranta, a new subsidiary company to handle air freight, was incorporated in July and unit-load traffic 'involving the shipment of freight in containers to Britain and direct door-to-door collection and delivery, continued to expand . . .' CIÉ's increasing involvement in tourism merited several mentions.

> A comprehensive programme of expansion, renovation and redecoration was carried out in the seven Great Southern Hotels, the station buffets and railway dining cars . . .
>
> Increased promotional work was undertaken abroad. Returns from coach tours reached a record level, with a notable increase from the American market. 'Golden Holiday' tours were vigorously promoted on the British market: a 104-seater aircraft was chartered each week during the summer to bring tourists from Manchester, via Shannon Airport, to various centres where hotel accommodation and day tours were provided. With the co-operation of other tourist interests, two world-master coaches were brought on a tour of Great Britain in February and a one-day promotional tour to Northern Ireland was also undertaken. A special promotional campaign, aimed at the American wholesale tour operators, was carried out in August.
>
> (Annual Report, 1964/65)

The year 1964/65 may not have been exceptional in the amount of work involved in modernising CIÉ's operations, but the range and geographical spread of the items reported is impressive enough. It runs from improvements to railway stations, pre-heating of trains, installation of automatic level crossings, new sidings for freight handling, extended use of mechanical handling, commencing construction of 260 new single deck buses, radio control of buses, and computerisation of payroll, through to the continued run-down of horse transport at Dundalk, Mallow, Sligo, Mullingar, Youghal and Athlone.

In Northern Ireland the UTA terminated all its rail freight services and this presented CIÉ with a problem. Rail freight originating in the Republic for Six County destinations and for Donegal could not, sensibly, be transferred to road on reaching the border. Accordingly, CIÉ began by arrangement with the UTA to operate rail freight services on the UTA's network which it continues to do today.

In 1964/65 the 'Flying Snail' emblem adapted from the old DUTC logo in 1945 was put to bed. The new logo incorporated the still used 'broken circle' within which the letters 'CIÉ' simply stand. An interim logo using the corporate initials 'C.I.E.' (with full stops) in a rectangular block of black was used on some road freight vehicles for a while, but was abandoned in favour of the 'broken circle'. More remarkable than the new logo and the continued drive towards modernisation was CIÉ's entire absence of industrial disputes in 1964/65. In contrast, for the country as a whole 1964 saw well over three times the ten-year average of days lost due to strikes (545,000 days lost in 1964 versus an average of 148,304 1954/63). This better than national performance by CIÉ was short-lived. In 1965 the CIÉ situation deteriorated sharply while the national figures were unchanged. Indeed, CIÉ's 20,000 approx. employees contributed a very disproportionate 24 per cent share of the national days lost in 1965.

In 1964 the NBU was given formal recognition by CIÉ, to the dismay of some of its executives, who thought that recognition was not necessary and would prove to be very unwise. The immediate outcome was that the NBU consolidated its position by attracting additional members from other unions. It served a large claim but was to bide its time before taking industrial action. Meanwhile the 'ninth round' was mostly compensated for by an increase in charges, but in addition to the substantial basic increases of that pay round, 'major claims were made on the company for increased wages and reduced working hours for road passenger grades; for reduced working hours for road freight operative grades; for service pay for electricians; for a transport differential for skilled shop workers and a further salary status claim for clerical staffs' (ibid.). In the light of this raft of special claims, labour unrest was inevitable. In 1965 the NBU took action. It announced that to advance its claim for a general improvement in pay and conditions it would force a series of one-day stoppages. A special meeting of the board was held on 25 May 1965 to consider the situation. The minutes record the GM's (Frank Lemass) report that the

> NBU in support of its claim for a status increase and a 40 hr 5 day week had served notice of a one day strike by its members on Friday, June 4 which would be followed by a series of such strikes of which seven days notice would be given. He also reported that the group of unions [i.e. unions other than the NBU whose separate] claim for service pay and an extra week's annual leave had been rejected by the Mediation Board which met on the 19th May, were arranging to hold ballots of their members to decide whether strike notice should be served on the company or not in support of their claims.

It was decided that employees in the NBU who took part in the strike action on Fri. 4th June be permitted to resume duty on Sat. 5th June. This decision was made to alleviate inconvenience to the public which would occur at the Whit weekend. It was also decided to inform the NBU that should its members propose taking one day strike action in the following week they would not be permitted to resume duty.

The first such stoppage occurred on 4 June, and as other union members refused to pass the NBU pickets a widespread suspension of services took place. Another one-day strike occurred on 12 June and CIÉ implemented its warning to the unions: it refused to allow workers to resume duties unless each man gave an undertaking that there be no more one-day stoppages. The stoppages were front-page news; once again CIÉ was accused of having engineered a lockout and repeated attempts were made to debate the situation in the Dáil.

The board met again in special session on 23 June to hear Frank Lemass report on a meeting with the Labour Court which on its own initiative had decided to investigate the dispute. It was at this meeting that CIÉ decided, as mentioned earlier, to abandon the internal negotiating machinery.

> At its invitation the Court indicated that it proposed to investigate the claim of the NBU and those of the group of unions. He [the General Manager] impressed on the Court that its decision to investigate the claim of the group of Unions which had been processed through the CIÉ negotiating machinery, would result in a breakdown of the established negotiating machinery. Notwithstanding his strong protest the Court adhered to its decision. In these circumstances it was decided to withdraw from the negotiating machinery and give notice accordingly to the ICTU and the Trade Unions concerned.
> (Bord Minutes, 23 June 1965)

Services were restored by the Labour Court recommending and CIÉ accepting a 'no victimisation—no undertaking about future one day stoppages' formula for return to work. The complete shut-down of bus services had lasted twelve days. The CIÉ attitude with regard to internal mediation, paralleled in other major employments at the time such as the ESB, was that if internal mediation boards or tribunals were to be used as mere stepping stones to the Labour Court, they served little purpose and merely prolonged the negotiation process. If trade unions were not prepared to look positively on the recommendation of these bodies, on which they were themselves represented, they should be abandoned. Predictably, of course, fault would be found with this position. In 1966, when a major strike by 1,600 CIÉ craftsmen seemed imminent, *The Irish*

Times reported the remarks of a union spokesman that blame for 'the situation should rest with the Minister for the course taken by CIÉ in withdrawing from the [Mediation] Council'. It is highly unlikely that Mr Childers or any official of his Department was consulted on the CIÉ decision.

Countrywide, the year 1966 was the worst to date for days lost by industrial disputes. The newspapers carried banner headlines about strikes, threatened, actual and averted, day after day, e.g. 'Childers makes dramatic appeal to the ESB', 'Banks closed from today'. New proposals for reforming the Labour Court were reported periodically. Nationally, days lost in 1966 were up 50 per cent on 1965, while days lost in CIÉ moved in the opposite direction and fell by 50 per cent. None the less CIÉ contributed 9 per cent of the country's man-days lost in 1966, which showed that despite the fall in disputes CIÉ's staff in 1966 were three to four times more prone to strike than the labour force as a whole. To recap the scene on Dublin's buses in the 1963–1966 period: the ITGWU had its strike in 1963, related to OPO introduction; 1964 was a quiet year while the ninth round ran its course through the system; 1965 was the year in which the NBU set out to prove its mettle and stoppages occurred; in 1966 the WUI had to have its turn.

The WUI strike was by road workshop staff and was supported by all busmen. In those days everybody respected everybody else's picket. Congress had not yet devised the distinction between a 'members only' and an 'all out picket'. As a consequence of CIÉ refusing to move from a Labour Court recommendation, bus services were suspended for over a fortnight in high summer (from 8 August to 24 August) and the dispute was eventually settled at a conciliation conference under the auspices of the Labour Court. That WUI led stoppage in 1966 meant that in the four years since 1963, Dublin's buses had experienced three serious interruptions in service. Todd Andrews was serving out his last few months as Chairman, his hopes of achieving good industrial relations in CIÉ littered around him. But there are a few other matters to cover before recording the end of his chairmanship.

CIÉ HAD A generally very positive experience with diesel traction, but after fifteen years in operation a problem was developing with the original diesel electric locomotives built by Metropolitan Vickers. They had been equipped with Crossley 1100 h.p. engines (001 Class A Co-Co) delivered in 1955 and 1956, and Crossley 550 h.p. engines (201 Class C Bo-Bo) delivered in 1957 and January 1958. In simple terms, the Crossley engines were derived from British marine diesel installations and were found to be not suitable for the vibration levels involved in high-speed rail operation. In contrast, US manufacturers had been designing purpose-built diesel engines for railway operation from before World War II, at which time Britain was still an unquestioning believer in the superiority of steam traction. Then, as we have recorded already, in January 1961 CIÉ received its first US locomotives, built by General Motors and with GM 950 h.p. diesel electric engines. The success of these 15 'B Class' locomotives convinced CIÉ that its earlier 'C Class' locomotives should have their Crossley engines replaced. In June 1963 AEI were engaged as consultants for re-engining the 20 'C Class' locomotives and initially 2 of them were converted to operate with Maybach MD650 980 h.p. diesel electric engines. Continued satisfactory experience with the GM equipment resulted in the later decision to re-equip the rest of the Crossley engined locomotives with GM power units—1325 h.p. for the 60 A Class locomotives and 1100 h.p. for the 34 C Class locomotives.

Meanwhile CIÉ received 12 additional General Motors 1100 h.p. locomotives (181 Class B Bo-Bo) in two batches on vessels of the then thriving Irish Shipping Ltd—*Irish Alder* (9 November 1966) and *Irish Oak* (10 November 1966). *The Irish Times*, which reported these arrivals, recorded that the locomotives cost £800,000 and were 'needed to meet demands for motive power caused by a sharp increase in wagon load traffic'. As we have seen rail freight was indeed increasing. After these 1966 arrivals there would be no additions to the fleet of diesel locomotives for another ten years, when again they would come from General Motors and be far more powerful than any of their predecessors.

A word is due here on CIÉ's acquisition of coaching stock during the sixties. The 'Park Royals', mentioned earlier, were the coaches built by CIÉ at Inchicore from parts supplied by Park Royal Vehicles, London. They were introduced into service mainly in 1955 and 1956 and accommodated 82 passengers. In 1963 and 1964 some 38 new coaches were introduced, built from parts supplied by Cravens Ltd of Sheffield. The 'Cravens' were 14 inches longer than the Park Royals and slightly narrower (9' 6" compared to 10' 3" for the Park Royals). They provided 64 seats each compared to the 82-seat Park Royals, indicating that with 18 seats less per coach passenger comfort was being improved. In 1967 a further 14 Cravens were built bringing the total of this type to 52.

The next batch of coaches in the early 1970s would be built in the UK and by another supplier/manufacturer—BREL, a division of British Rail. The output of the Cravens in the 1960s marked the beginning of the end of the 100-year-old Inchicore facility as a coach-building plant, though it would resume briefly in the 1980s. Locomotive construction in Inchicore had already ceased. Henceforth, Inchicore would mainly be a maintenance, overhaul and conversion facility.

THE YEAR 1966, noteworthy for CIÉ in the receipt of its second batch of GM locomotives and for its industrial disputes, was also the fiftieth anniversary of the 1916 Rising. The generation of 1916 and of the War of Independence was alive, active and respected. It was well positioned in places of power and influence. The population of the Republic accepted that the independent status of their state derived wholly and solely from the 1916 Rising and its aftermath. The jubilee of the Rising would have to be celebrated in a proud and fitting manner. A government established committee chaired by the Taoiseach, Seán Lemass, sat in 1965 to plan the fiftieth anniversary celebrations. Among many other proposals, mostly short term in nature, the committee adopted a proposal originating within CIÉ that the Republic's main railway stations be renamed to commemorate the sixteen who were executed after the Rising. Todd Andrews informed the CIÉ Board of this 'proposal from government' on 16 December 1965 and the minutes recorded that it was agreed to do as suggested. Ireland's rail termini had hitherto been known only by their location, i.e. street, city or town—thus Amiens St, Westland Row, Galway, Limerick and so on. Even Kingsbridge was named after the nearby bridge and continued to use that name when the bridge itself had its name changed to Seán Heuston in 1956. The new names, with the old names in parentheses, were Heuston (Kingsbridge), Connolly (Amiens St), Pearse (Westland Row), Ceannt (Galway), Kent (Cork), Colbert (Limerick), Casement (Tralee), Clarke (Dundalk), MacBride (Drogheda), Mac Diarmada (Sligo), MacDonagh (Kilkenny), Plunkett (Waterford), O'Hanrahan (Wexford), Daly (Bray), and Malin (Dún Laoghaire).

The selection of Connolly for Amiens Street station arose from the nearness of that station to James Connolly's 1916 headquarters in Liberty Hall. The Pearse brothers had been born adjacent to Westland Row. Kingsbridge was renamed after Seán Heuston, who had been a railway clerk in that building when as a commandant in the Volunteers he took control of the nearby Mendicity Institute on the quays during the Rising. CIÉ intended that for general operational and public use only Heuston, Connolly and Pearse would be used, and that the other stations would continue to be known simply by their city or town name. Heuston, Connolly and Pearse achieved acceptability soon enough, though in due course Pearse would cease to be a mainline terminus and as a station on CIÉ's DART system it would be less significant than nearby Tara Street, which in 1966 was not considered worthy of having anybody's name attached to it. Another change in 1966, on the recommendation of a joint trade union/CIÉ management committee, was the introduction of bilingual bus destination scrolls. CIÉ had been required by various Acts to have all permanent public notices in Irish, but this had not been done for bus destinations up to that date. A minor controversy arose over a newly devised phrase, 'An Lár', for town and city centres but it rapidly achieved acceptance. Another controversy arose about the scrolls having been manufactured in England, due it emerged to the sole Irish supplier being unable to cater for the scale of the order in replacing all CIÉ's destination scrolls over the period required.

At the time of the main celebrations of the Rising in April 1966, a foretaste of future disturbances to Dublin–Belfast rail services occurred on 17 April. 'Six concrete posts and bolt nuts had been laid across the line at Killester' and *The Irish Times* reported that 'CIÉ are imposing a strict security alert following an attempt to derail a passenger train'. The report went on:

> A statement from the Republican Publicity Bureau in Dublin said yesterday: The Republican movement had no connection with the blocking of the railway line at Killester this morning and with any other incidents which have occurred in the last week. Such actions are contrary to Republican practice.   Signed J. McGarrity, Sec.

Two days later a telephone pole was felled across the Dublin/Cork line at Clondalkin. These incidents were never explained. In some way they may have been stimulated by the 1916 celebration fervour which north of the border had caused particular unease and a major security clamp-down on 15 April.

If 1966 was a year of celebrations as well as strikes, it was also a year of resignations. Eamonn Andrews, the famous Irish star of BBC television, resigned from the chairmanship of Radio Éireann-Television, stating disagreement with government over matters of policy. His resignation was announced on 26 April 1966. A successor was not appointed immediately, but within a few weeks Todd Andrews was being mentioned as likely to be appointed to the chairmanship of RTE, as it would later be called, and *The Irish Times* mentioned that Todd Andrews was expected to retire from CIÉ in the autumn. In June, Todd Andrews was indeed appointed Chairman of RTE but he continued to be Chairman of CIÉ through the summer of 1966.

A board decision in August of that summer proved that the pace of change in CIÉ was not sufficient to clear out all the relics of earlier days. At that meeting approval was given for the purchase of 'seven three ton mechanical units and twelve trailers at a cost of £21,500 in connection with a pilot scheme to mechanise goods collection and delivery from North Wall Point Depot'. Horses were still being used when Andrews left CIÉ. Their final exit would occur in November 1968.

Todd Andrews retired from CIÉ on his 65th birthday—16 September 1966 after being Chairman for seven years. Unlike the situation that existed when T. C. Courtney replaced A. P. Reynolds, and when Todd Andrews replaced T. C. Courtney, there was no sense of CIÉ being in crisis or needing to take a radical change of direction when Todd Andrews stepped down. He was leaving what in effect were the combined offices of chairman and chief executive. The succession underlined the situation of normality which was perceived to exist. T. P. Hogan, who had been a non-executive member of the board since 13 August 1957, that is, since the days of T. C. Courtney, became Chairman on 7 October 1966 on a part-time basis for an initial period of less than two years (until 3 August 1968). However, his term of office would later be extended so that he would serve as Chairman until 1973.

Being a part-time Chairman with extensive other business interests Hogan, unlike his three predecessors, would not be chief executive. That role would now be filled by Frank Lemass who had carried the title of General Manager of CIÉ for twenty years (apart from a brief period when he was redesignated 'Chief Officer'). For all that time he was the 'number two' full-time executive. Now, however, with Hogan becoming a non-executive Chairman, Frank Lemass joined the board to fill the slot left vacant by the resignation of Todd Andrews. Henceforth he would be the 'number one' executive and would use the title 'Director and General Manager'. While only a coincidence, it may be noted in passing that within a month of Frank Lemass being confirmed as the senior executive in CIÉ, another significant figure in the CIÉ story—his older brother Seán—resigned as Taoiseach (9 November 1966). With the movement of Todd Andrews and Seán Lemass the generation of the War of Independence was stepping aside. Jack Lynch was elected Taoiseach; his cabinet appointments left Erskine Childers as Minister for Transport and Power, who now would also be responsible for Posts and Telegraphs—quite a large additional responsibility as An Post and Telecom Éireann were not yet established as autonomous state companies.

CIÉ at the end of 1966 was half-way through the five-year £2 million per annum subvention period laid down in the 1964 Transport Act. In the remaining period there were no industrial relations problems comparable to those which occurred in 1963–1966, no major re-equipment programme, apart from the re-engining of the earlier diesel locomotives already referred to. However, other problems began to acquire a new significance—Dublin traffic and government interference with CIÉ exercising its statutory freedom to fix transport charges. These two issues would cast their shadows over public transport throughout the following decade. Another development which would adversely affect CIÉ in the more hostile circumstances of the next decade was the expansion of the Great Southern Hotels. Finally, in this preview of the rest of the period to 1969, an important development was the introduction of free school transport. It would have enormous social consequences and be a positive influence on CIÉ. We will now discuss these items in turn.

DUBLIN TRAFFIC DID not suddenly become a problem in the late sixties.

Indeed, a member of the CIÉ Board (J. T. O'Farrell) had spoken publicly about it in the early 1950s. Later when tram tracks were being lifted CIÉ complained that the problem of keeping its schedules running was seriously aggravated by 'indiscriminate parking'. Between 1954 and 1957 the second inter-party government charged the Secretary to the Government, Dr John O'Donovan, TD with looking into the Dublin traffic problem and proposing a solution. No discernible action followed from that decision. A minor aggravation to the whole traffic problem was that CIÉ buses still operated with 'semaphore' indicators at the front of the bus so that following traffic would not know how or when a bus was changing direction. Following a confrontation by the Gardaí in August 1958, buses quickly had front and rear indicator flashing lights installed. Something more fundamental than that overdue bus modification was required, and in 1961 a German planning consultant, Professor K. Schaechterle, was engaged by Dublin Corporation to study the city's traffic. A major traffic survey covering all major routes into and out of the inner city was conducted in 1961. However, the subsequent first report from Schaechterle, titled 'Dublin General Traffic Plan (Part 1)', was not received until 1965, and then in 1968 Part 2 of his report was published under the title 'Dublin General Traffic Plan—Parking Study and Recommendations'. Meanwhile attempts to achieve some easement of congestion in the city centre were made by the gradual introduction of one-way traffic flows, e.g. on Westmoreland St and D'Olier St, on Capel St and on parts of the Liffey quays. Right-hand turns were also being eliminated at major intersections and a second batch of one-way traffic flows was introduced for Stephen's Green, Dawson St and Kildare St. The situation was deteriorating all the time, and the Annual Report in 1965/66 illustrates how serious the problem was perceived to be.

> Traffic congestion continued to worsen during the year and on a number of occasions during the months before Christmas traffic almost came to a standstill in Dublin City, during peak hours. Bus schedules were completely distorted and there were delays of up to three-quarters of an hour for passengers. The basic cause of the problem is that the street network in the city is not capable of dealing with the traffic during peak hours. The position is aggravated by illegal parking of motor cars.   (Annual Report, 1965/66)

In that extract CIÉ seemed to be placing blame for the traffic mess on the inadequate street network. In practice, CIÉ recognised that traffic management and bus control measures could play an important part in easing a situation which was rapidly becoming impossible. In May 1966 one-way traffic rules were applied to a further south city area affecting Harcourt St, Harcourt Rd, Leeson St, Earlsfort Terrace and Adelaide Rd.

However, illegal parking of cars was still subject to direct control by the Garda on the beat and one-way streets, while of considerable help to traffic flows, achieved only half their potential if lanes on both sides were being blocked by parked cars. It is not enough for a problem to be bad before legislators and the community are prepared to accept inconvenient change. The problem must first be allowed to get very bad indeed. Slowly reacting to the publicly acknowledged parking problem, legislation was eventually introduced to permit the appointment of traffic wardens and the first twenty took up duty in 1968. Clearways were then introduced in certain areas, and in January 1970 Dublin saw its first parking meters. Maybe some order was emerging from the chaos described in the 1965/66 Annual Report, but Dublin had more than doubled in population since the 1930s. Its car population had trebled since 1950 while the number of Liffey bridges was still the same as it had been a hundred years earlier.

CIÉ's problem in providing a reasonable service to the bus traveller in the developing traffic chaos evoked a number of responses. Radio control of buses was being introduced from the mid-sixties so that drivers could report their position to a control centre, following which they could be advised to vary their routings or the control centre could reschedule other buses where available and contactable. One of the problems for the bus traveller and for CIÉ was 'bunching' of buses caused by traffic hold-ups. Commuters would be driven to fury by excessive waiting only to find that when a bus arrived, it arrived not singly but in a 'convoy' with one or two others. In the 1940s and early 1950s nearly all services ran to Nelson Pillar. As traffic grew and one-way streets were introduced, bus termini were moved out of O'Connell St to the quays, to D'Olier St, to Abbey St, to Talbot St, College Green and so on. As one-way streets were introduced bus routings had to be changed, though CIÉ would argue the case for some 'contra flow' exceptions for buses. It would plead for many years before even one was permitted.

In 1966 CIÉ undertook an 'origin and destination' survey of its own passengers and itself engaged the corporation's consultant, Professor K. Schaechterle, to prepare a bus plan. From the perspective of the 1990s one can comment that the time which elapsed between the commissioning of studies from this consultant and the submission of his completed reports is somewhat surprising. No doubt enormous volumes of data required processing with fairly primitive machinery and periodic reports and discussions would take place with 'steering committees'. In any event Schaechterle's 'A Plan for Dublin Bus Services' was submitted to CIÉ in 1969; one of its conclusions was that Dublin needed a central bus terminal for its city routes. However, before the Schaechterle Report was finally received, some conclusions were drawn from CIÉ's own survey. Erskine

Childers, introducing the vote for the Department of Transport and Power on 9 November 1967, was able to comment as follows:

> The Origin and Destination Survey conducted by CIÉ in which the travel patterns of 227,000 Dublin citizens were recorded has now been analysed. The preliminary report will disappoint those people who very humanly may have believed that the CIÉ bus services must be outdated and distorted. . . .
>
> The remorseless facts obtained by data processing prove that taken at large and wide, the services are in the main rightly directed. One single fact will be of interest. Only 11 per cent of the Dublin bus travellers change buses to reach their destination and the figure is about 7.5 per cent at the peak period of travel.
>
> Any dramatic change will not take place. To a certain extent the pattern of services is dictated by the present road structure. Should Dublin Corporation adopt any striking proposals for circular roads, through roads and new bridges, then there might be some changes.
>
> (*Dáil Debates*, Vol. 230, Col. 2196)

In his usual manner he had many comments to make about CIÉ's efforts to deal with Dublin's traffic problems—redesign of schedules, use of radio, changes in organisation and so on. He concluded:

> Although the one way streets and clearways have been contributing to more rapid traffic flows the growth of private car transport inevitably will increase the gravity of the bunching problem during peak hours and no scientific estimates of bus routing can prevent disruption of time schedules at peak periods. This problem of bus bunching is receiving and should continue to receive priority attention. (ibid.)

New buses were being introduced from November 1966. The 78-seat Atlantean double-deckers were claimed to be of 'a radically improved design incorporating many new features including a driver controlled front entrance—which by itself has virtually eliminated platform accidents. Some teething troubles with this new design were experienced, the most serious of which was concerned with ventilation, and steps were taken to put the matters right.' (Annual Report, 1966/67)

These references to the Atlanteans prompt two comments. The first is that a major cause of stress among bus crews identified in the Tavistock Institute Report arose from driver/conductor relationships. Conductors blamed drivers for their manner of stopping and starting vehicles and the priority which they seemed to place on making up time so as to maintain the timetable. Drivers, on the other hand, were critical of the manner in which they received signals from their conductors. The driver controlled doors greatly eased that particular problem. The second comment is that the technical problems experienced in the early days of the Atlanteans would not be solved. CIÉ, however, had made a major commitment to the Atlanteans and by 1969 a total of 217, almost a third of the fleet, would be of this type. In retrospect CIÉ would recognise that the design was fundamentally flawed—breakdowns and maintenance costs were excessive; reliability was low. Fleet problems would combine with traffic problems to cause major traffic headaches for Dublin City Services during the 1970s.

The second problem in the late 1960s, identified above as one which would affect CIÉ throughout the 1970s, was government intervention in the fixing of transport charges. The 1967/68 Annual Report stated the issue succinctly:

> In order to meet increasing costs the Board had intended to raise charges in 1967 but deferred doing so at the request of the Government until 1st January, 1968. The result for the year would have been better by an estimated £900,000 had the increase in charges been introduced as originally planned.

Inflation was on the rise—1967 + 3.1 per cent, 1968 + 4.8 per cent; the Suez crisis was increasing fuel costs; projected inflation for 1969 was over 7 per cent. The government and its advisers believed that while imported inflation was unavoidable, much of the inflation was due to domestic pressures. The solution was to moderate wage demands, and to achieve this end prices should be controlled. Accordingly, the government persuaded CIÉ to defer its planned increase in charges. In the year affected by the postponement of increased charges the CIÉ deficit exceeded the £2 million subvention by £480,000, i.e. by 25 per cent—not a disastrous result in one year, but recurrent freezes on CIÉ's charges in the 1970s were to have very serious consequences for CIÉ and, in turn, for the size of the state subvention.

THE THIRD FACTOR we've headlined as one whose influence would run through the 1970s was the development of the Great Southern Hotels. Through the 1960s OIE, which included CIÉ catering services as well as the seven Great Southern Hotels, was consistently profitable, and in the year to March 1969 a profit, after financial charges, of £186,000 was earned on a turnover of £2,041,000. OIE with the wholehearted support of its CIÉ parent had been consistently upgrading its premises. In 1962 only 26 per cent of the hotel bedrooms had private bathrooms. By 1969, 80 per cent of rooms had private bathrooms installed. This extensive conversion to rooms with bath inevitably meant the loss of some bedrooms, but additional building including the construction of the Torc, Killarney, and the Rosslare Inns (subsequently renamed the Torc Great Southern and the Rosslare Great Southern) increased the total number of bedrooms in OIE's hotels by 37 per cent. CIÉ was increasingly active in attracting foreign tourists; it was doing so profitably. The OIE expansion seemed logical and was widely commended. In addition to the new Killarney and Rosslare Inns, construction of the Corrib Inn in Galway (later the Corrib Great Southern) was under way. OIE sought to acquire or build a hotel in the Dublin area; a Dún Laoghaire site was proposd at one stage. Experiencing several difficulties in Dublin, the search would shift to Belfast. The ambitious OIE investment programme in existing and new hotels was being done without an equity base. The reliance on loan capital, the seventies recession in tourism and extraordinary bad luck with its Belfast venture due to the 'troubles' in Northern Ireland, would combine to make OIE a serious problem for CIÉ during the next decade.

IN 1967 DONOGH O'MALLEY was Minister for Education, having succeeded the already reforming George Colley and Patrick Hillery in that post. 'All were young, and anxious to make their mark by injecting some life into a traditionally moribund department.' (J. J. Lee, *Ireland 1912–1985*, p. 361) Decisions in Marlborough Street were going to have an important impact on CIÉ and on its community role. 'Investment in Education' the report of an OECD survey team under the chairmanship of Patrick Lynch, had been published in 1965 and 1966 (two volumes). It highlighted inequities and inadequacies in the existing system. A series of changes were made by Colley and Hillery, but the lion's share of the favourable public notice was won by Donogh O'Malley when he announced that free secondary education was to be made available to all, by September 1967. It was also proposed to increase the school-leaving age from 14 to 15 years. The objective was to provide three years of post primary education to every pupil. 'Investment in Education' had shown that 10,000 pupils aged 11 in national schools lived more than five miles from a secondary school and of these, 2,000 lived more than ten miles from such a school. These children in remote areas suffered a serious disadvantage in access to post primary education. A genuine reforming zeal rather than political opportunism was the motivation behind free secondary education and the raising of the school-leaving age. But neither initiative could achieve its purpose outside the main centres of population unless it were accompanied by a school transport scheme financed by the exchequer. That is where CIÉ came into the picture with a thoroughly remarkable achievement.

Beginning from zero, and within a period of twelve months, CIÉ implemented a scheme providing free transport daily to secondary schools for 56,500 individual children who lived three miles or more from such schools. Over the same period (May 1967 to March 1968) CIÉ took over an existing scheme providing transport for 2,000 children to primary schools and expanded it to accommodate 13,000 pupils. Seán Mac Gearailt, Secretary of the Department of Education, described the achievement in *Administration*, Winter 1968.

> In the normal way, the provision of service for some 50,000 children might have been expected to take upwards of three years, having regard to the transport resources available and the amount of organisation required. So that no child would be denied the benefits of free education, however, it was decided to make an all-out drive to have the scheme functioning to the greatest possible extent inside twelve months: this to be followed by a long-term programme which would involve the manufacture of a large number of new school buses.
>
> The basic task was to identify the children eligible for transport (including the large number entering post-primary schools for the first time in September, 1967, under the free education scheme) and to provide transport to bring each pupil to the nearest post-primary centre . . .
>
> Identification of the eligible pupils necessitated the cooperation of all the school authorities and this was given without reserve. Information about pupils commencing school in September, 1967, was obtained through an advertising campaign in the provincial press. Armed with the information thus collected and with their expert local knowledge on road conditions, CIÉ commenced to plan routes, draw up timetables, arrange pick-up points etc. in consultation with the school authorities and the liaison officers.

The secretaries of the vocational education committees acted as 'Transport Liaison Officers' and central administration was confined to a 'small section in the Department of Education'. The hard slog of getting the scheme going was carried by CIÉ. Use was made of every available passenger vehicle. Some 100 older buses were renovated and retained in service. Buses normally engaged on tourist and holiday traffic during the summer months were diverted to school services at the end of the holiday season. Fifty used buses were hired from Ulsterbus and reconditioned. School services were also subcontracted to any private operator who could provide suitable vehicles. By March 1968, 795 vehicles were employed in transport to post primary schools, of which 300 were provided by CIÉ, and the balance were privately owned buses and minibuses.

Because school buses operate only about three hours per day—the aim was to ensure that no journey should exceed 45 minutes—CIÉ, with union agreement, recruited part-time drivers for the school buses. Some driving experience was required, but farmers, agricultural workers, shopkeepers, garage proprietors and housewives (the first CIÉ female bus drivers) all featured in the occupations of the part-time recruits. Arrangements had also to be made for the repair and maintenance of the old and generally odd assortment of vehicles. Mechanics working from their home base were equipped with tool kits and were 'on call' for immediate action for bus breakdowns no matter how remote the location. Because of the spread of the operation the possibility of the school buses being maintained at CIÉ garages could not even be considered. A special colour scheme and logo (yellow and white) was adopted for the school buses—not for any commercial reason, but so that the Bus Scoile could be easily identified by pupils and by other traffic. Safety had to be a high priority: driver training, vehicle licensing and driver-controlled doors were all part of the vast logistical and administrative exercise.

Lily Buckley was one of the first school bus drivers and she told her fascinating story in *Nuacht CIÉ*, Nollaig 1993. She describes her background, working on the family farm, no prospect of a paid job, getting married to Dan, working on his farm and conditions becoming more difficult as the 1960s progressed:

> Then one day Dan and I were walking in from the fields and a school bus pulled up beside us and the driver asked for directions. Dan turned to me and said: 'Now there's something that you could do. You could drive a school bus.' I trembled at the thought, but as the day wore on I began to think about it seriously and by the next day, I was searching the telephone book for the number of CIÉ. John Whelan, a man of about six feet and about twenty stone weight arrived the following week with a 45 seater yellow bus to see if I was 'bus-driving material'. I had to take the wheel right away and drive the bus through the town, turn it a few times and bring it back to where we started from. The following week I had to do another test. My training was done in Mallow. The strain was terrible and every time the instructor was due to arrive, I'd get physically sick. But after three weeks training, I passed my test on the first attempt. Over the weekend, a bus was delivered to me for work on Monday morning. I'll never forget it . . . I was given one long route serving the Post Primary school in Millstreet, and it took me around the most mountainous districts in the area. I had steep hills and deep inclines to encounter . . . everybody had a bag of books, a bag of sports gear and some had musical instruments as well . . .

Barge on the Grand Canal, 1959 (Guinness Museum)

Last delivery by CIÉ horse leaving Transport House, Bachelors Walk, November 1968 (*The Irish Times*)

Cattle wagons—two weeks' output—built at Inchicore, 1948

Standard twelve ton unbraked open wagon of the 1950s, designed for carrying loose material; built at Limerick and Inchicore

Standard ten ton unbraked wagon for transporting various bagged and boxed commodities, dating from the 1950s; built at Limerick and Inchicore

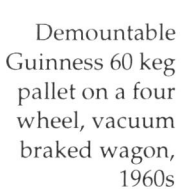

Demountable Guinness 60 keg pallet on a four wheel, vacuum braked wagon, 1960s

St James's Street Harbour on the Grand Canal prior to the closure of the canal to commercial traffic, 1959 (Guinness Museum)

Fifty-four ton, vacuum braked bogie ore wagon, designed and built by CIÉ at Inchicore works in 1976/77 for Tara Mines Ltd. The lid is removed and the wagon is discharged in a rotary tippler.

Twenty ton vacuum braked barytes ore wagon, with fold-down sides for removal of load by bulldozer blade, designed and built in Inchicore, 1970s

Train of fifty ton, air braked bogie bulk cement wagons headed by a GM 181 class locomotive crossing Malahide viaduct in 1979

Demountable 20 ft ISO Acrylonitrile tank, used for deliveries to the Asahi Plant in Ballina, Co. Mayo, on a specially modified, vacuum braked wagon, 1980

Furniture removals van, 1960s

Three ton Scannell tractor and covered trailer for delivery of freight packages in the Dublin area during the 1960s

Containers manufactured by CIÉ, mounted on AEC Mercury lorry and trailer, 1961

Irish Ferry Containers, with CIÉ's co-operation, commenced a ferry service between Greenore and Preston in 1960.

Interior of Royal Saloon, built in Inchicore *c.*1885, and used as late as 1952 by Archbishop Cushing of Boston, leading a Marian pilgrimage

Interior of the Presidential coach, 1980s

Mac Gearailt recorded in 1968 that 'the long term implementation programme involves the manufacture of 240 special new school buses, for which the government has allocated the necessary capital. One hundred of these vehicles are being built by three firms in Dundalk. The remaining 140 are being built by CIÉ.' But Lily Buckley would have to wait many years for her own 'luxury of luxuries', a good engine, a good heater, and a pleasure to drive.

The reduction in the number of one and two-teacher primary schools increased the requirements for transport for younger children. This concentration of schools into larger units enabled standards in most schools to rise and provided economies in buildings and facilities. However, other benefits recorded by Mac Gearailt were more personal to the pupils:

> In our uncertain climate, generations of children have had to face heavy wettings on the long journey to school and in many instances remain in the wet clothes through the day. There is also the fact that children are saved the hazard of walking or cycling to school on roads which have become very dangerous because of the increased volume of motor traffic. (*Administration*, Winter 1968)

Others would bemoan the passing of the small schools, and even the loss of the learning opportunity of the long walk home, but in time the community jury would return a very positive verdict.

One overview comment from Mac Gearailt was that 'It can be truly said that the new transport scheme has brought something of a revolution to rural Ireland.' Of course there were other factors contributing to the revolution, but Mac Gearailt was unstinting in his admiration of CIÉ's role and acknowledged 'the debt of gratitude we all owe to CIÉ for the manner and the expedition with which they organised the nation-wide scheme of school transport'. CIÉ was paid for the school transport schemes by direct payment from the Department of Education on a negotiated basis covering a direct cost plus a contribution towards overheads. By the end of 1969 the total number of children covered by the school transport scheme had risen to 90,500 and a total of 1,580 additional passenger vehicles (including subcontractors') were involved. Twenty years on, we will reach a period of disagreement about this annual payment. In the meantime there would be controversy about the three-mile cut-off point for eligible pupils, but CIÉ would find and propose a solution to that problem. Other problems would be in the nature of 'Why doesn't the school bus stop at *my* gate?' and questions about school bus pick-up points were even allowed in the Dáil, but such controversies only reflect how the school bus had become an essential though taken for granted service in the Ireland of the 1970s and since. At the time of which we are writing, another important transport change with social consequences was the introduction of free transport for old-age and blind pensioners—180,000 were eligible. In addition, free transport was also authorised for War of Independence veterans—another 7,500 qualified under that heading which was also financed by a direct payment (from the Department of Social Welfare). Free transport for pensioners was to become a permanent and much cherished privilege of the senior members of Irish society.

APPROACHING 1969 AND the end of the five-year period of the £2 million subventions, CIÉ did a public stocktaking of its performance. The Winter 1968 issue of *Administration*, already referred to, was solely devoted to CIÉ and contained several articles by senior CIÉ executives reporting on their spheres of responsibility. It paralleled the series of Custom House addresses given to the IPA by Todd Andrews and his management in 1963. CIÉ also produced a pocket-sized booklet of statistics and graphs covering the 1964–1969 period. Frank Lemass, in a foreword to the booklet, said that in addition to recording recent performance it provided 'an indication of the magnitude of the work still to be done to maintain a fully integrated and modern transport system suitable to our national needs'. One looks critically for such an 'indication' in the booklet but it doesn't seem to be there. The story told was quite creditable in itself. On the financial side the total deficits for the five years exceeded the £10 million subvention by only 5 per cent (£543,000), but this meant that none of the £10 million could be used for capital purposes. All capital expenditure had to be financed from borrowings, apart from what was generated by depreciation or sale of assets. The traffic performance is summarised in the following table:

% Variation 1968/69 versus 1963/64

Rail passenger miles	+ 7
Rail freight tons	+ 27.6
Rail freight ton miles	+ 53.5
Rail livestock numbers	– 17.4
Road freight tons	– 6.8
Dublin city bus passengers	+ 3.7
Other bus passengers	+ 50.3

Some comments can be made on these figures. Slightly over two-thirds of the increase in DCS passengers came from children covered by the school transport scheme. Leaving these passengers aside, Dublin bus traffic was virtually static. Slightly over half the increased carryings on 'other bus services' could be attributed to the school transport scheme, meaning that they were growing at about 5 per cent per annum. One other figure is very relevant to these passenger numbers—a 36 per cent increase took place in the number of private car registrations over the same period. Private travel was growing faster than CIÉ's passenger traffic.

The exact nature of the decline in road freight is not easy to pinpoint. The British seamen's strike in 1967 and contraction in the ground limestone scheme affected carryings, but there are inconsistencies in the statistics between one year and another which make analysis difficult. It is noteworthy though that a publication intended to present a positive picture of CIÉ's performance clearly shows a decline in road freight. In contrast to that fall in tonnage, the road freight profit moved upwards from £36,864 in 1964/65 to £123,000 in 1968/69 including CIÉ's profit shares from Irish Ferryways and Horse Ferries International, a joint operation with Lambourne Racehorse Transport Limited of England. Impressive gains had been recorded in rail freight (+ 27.6%) over the five years. The much smaller growth in rail passenger miles (+ 7%) conceals a continued loss in passengers on the suburban lines which was more than offset by the extra passenger miles generated by increased numbers of long-distance passengers. Total rail passenger numbers had in fact fallen by 15 per cent over the five-year period. Apart from rail, all businesses other than the Galway/Aran service were showing a profit.

One of the most remarkable comparisons to be made between 1969 and 1964 relates to wages and working conditions. Annual labour costs had increased on foot of the national wage rounds by £4,230,000, but the costs of other changes in conditions of employment added another 67 per cent (£2,820,000) to the increase caused by the wage rounds. The most significant of these changes was a reduction of 2½ hours without loss of pay in the working week of virtually all CIÉ's operative staff. As a result Dublin City Services operative grades now had a 40-hour week with other operative grades having a 42½-hour week. Social welfare contributions and contributions to admittedly inadequate pension schemes had also risen steeply. Staff numbers on the other hand had fallen by only 312 on a base of 20,148—a mere 1.5 per cent decline. CIÉ had to make up ground on pay and conditions of service and claimed to have made a 13 per cent increase in labour productivity. That increase would be seen in the 1970s to be far short of what business reality now required.

A further 135 miles of railway had been closed to services between 1963/64 and 1968/69. Utilisation of locomotives and rolling stock were shown to have improved, but we will return to this topic in a later chapter. CIÉ's charges had increased a number of times, but charts were produced to compare the growth of charges with the increase in labour costs. e.g.

> – Over ten years since 1959 railway fares had increased by 58 per cent and labour costs by 88 per cent.

– City bus fares had increased by 64 per cent and bus labour costs by 95 per cent.
– Freight charges had increased by 40 per cent and freight labour costs by 88 per cent.
– CIÉ could also show that its fares and rates had increased less than the average national earnings index: CIÉ passenger fares + 34 per cent and freight rates + 25 per cent, while average national earnings had risen by 46 per cent over the five years to March 1959.

Whilst these comparisons reflect credit on CIÉ a less positive picture would be revealed if increases in rates and fares had been compared with movements in the consumer price index which had risen by 27 per cent compared to 34 per cent for CIÉ fares and rates. It can fairly be said of course that if 66 per cent of your costs are labour related, then labour costs must impact your charges more than any indicator of general inflation. Compared to other countries, CIÉ noted that 'recent statistics published by the European Conference of Ministers of Transport show that CIÉ is favourably placed in the top bracket of eighteen European countries in relation to the growth rate of passengers and freight carried by rail and in relation to the low level of government payments to the railways as a percentage of operating receipts' (*Córas Iompair Éireann 1964–69*).

CIÉ could fairly present a favourable picture of itself in 1969 as its £2 million annual subvention came up for review, but you had to be quick to catch it. Another oil crisis occurred, inflation rates began to soar, and tourism suffered as the 50-year-old stalemate in Northern Ireland began to crack.

Chapter 14

Inflation Takes Off

New subvention fixed in 1969—Childers moves on—Subvention level overtaken as inflation accelerates—Fresh crisis perceived—The first McKinsey Report—Government interventions with fare increases—Inter-party government allows increases.

The ever conscientious Erskine Childers faced the Dáil with a fifty-page speech on 27 March 1969. It was to be his last time as Minister for Transport and Power to move the vote for that Department. The substantive vote had been passed some months earlier and he was moving a token £10 supplementary estimate so that deputies could debate their choice of issues in the Transport and Power field. Having reviewed various changes by head and subhead in his department's expenditure, Childers began to talk about CIÉ. He referred to the deficit of £2,480,000 incurred in the year 1967/68 which was £480,000 more than the subvention; and explained the deficit from the aspect of labour costs, industrial disputes, fuel costs, financial charges, new business gained, and productivity increases. He addressed the railway losses, increased depreciation charges due to the 12 new locomotives, new freight traffic gained and reduced passenger traffic which he attributed to restrictions on travel connected with the foot and mouth disease outbreak in Britain. He spoke at length on various railway fare initiatives, describing the conditions on which they were available. The possibility of expanding Dublin commuter rail traffic then got his attention. A new station was being built at Kilbarrack, cross-city through services were being introduced, the feasibility of extending commuter rail services to Cabra, Glasnevin, Clondalkin, Ballyfermot and Drumcondra was being examined.

The deputies had been fidgeting as the speech went on—perhaps another thirty pages remained to be read. Could the minister not get his speech on the record without reading it all out? 'It must be very boring for the minister to have to read all his statement and we have copies of it here!' But nothing could be done about it. The minister ploughed on with his script, probably relishing this annual exercise rather than being bored by it. As a result few deputies were able to speak before the allotted time for the debate ran out. The speech and the debate showed no sign that the national transport company might be entering a problem period. Indeed, as a result of fare increases allowed in January 1968 (after a deferment) and further increases in December/January 1968/69 the deficit was declining in the year to March 1969 towards the close of which Childers was speaking. That was the last year covered by the £2 million subvention, fixed by the 1964 Act, and the deficit fell just below the £2 million subvention—£1,861,000 compared to £2,438,000 recorded in 1967/68.

Four months later (July 1969) Erskine Childers moved to the Department of Health after ten years in Transport and Power. His successor was Brian Lenihan, described by Joe Lee as 'an amiable virtuoso of shadow language' (*Ireland 1912–1985*, p. 480). There was a difference of style and commitment. Childers had been in Kildare Street for the long term. Ministers would now change regularly, after and sometimes between general elections, for the next twenty years.

In his first months as Minister in charge of transport, Brian Lenihan would deal with Dáil questions concerning a proposed rail link to Dublin Airport and replacement of existing jointed rails with long-welded rail track (Deputy Richie Ryan), and with the format of accounts (Deputy Garret FitzGerald), but he would be absent due to illness in December 1969 when a motion was moved to set a new level of subvention for the five years to March 1974. Simultaneously, a new Bill was debated providing for further capital advances.

Erskine Childers, Minister for Health, must have been slightly chuffed when, in Brian Lenihan's absence, it fell to him to move these important measures. Sector by sector he gave a favourable review of progress over the five years since 1964. He then came to the proposed increase in annual subvention from £2 million to £2,650,000 per annum for the five years to April 1974, on which date it could be altered for the ensuing period.

> As in 1964, the annual grant has been fixed at a level which should provide the board, management and staff of CIÉ with a difficult but realistic target, the achievement of which will call for continued effort and initiative. I have every confidence that these will be provided.
> (*Dáil Debates*, Vol. 243, Col. 978)

The ensuing debate included a serious constructive contribution from Tom

O'Donnell, the new Fine Gael spokesman on Transport and Power. Patrick McGilligan had retired from politics and his replacement as Fine Gael spokesman on transport matters had studied Pacemaker and CIÉ's review of progress since 1964. His focus was forward rather than backward looking. Dr John O'Donovan, who had left Fine Gael to join Labour, spoke for that party. He made the surprising observation that the main importance of the railways lay not in the carrying of freight but in the carriage of livestock over long distances to the main ports. He was clearly drawing on research which had been published in his *Economic History of Livestock in Ireland* (1940) and showed no awareness of the change in the cattle and meat trade since the days when cattle were mostly exported 'on the hoof'. The only discordant note in the debate came from Michael Pat Murphy, the veteran of the west Cork rail closure saga. He regretted the absence of Paddy McGilligan from the Dáil, but he himself had gone to the Dáil library, as he said McGilligan would have done, where he found ample quotations from earlier Childers speeches about the evil of subsidies. His bitter protest was why, if subsidies could now be tolerated, had they not been provided before west Cork was raped of its railways?

The new five-year subvention (£2.65 million per annum) would prove to be disastrously wide of the mark. This was the period when the smooth economic trends established since World War II were upset by worldwide recession and inflation. A symptom of this new experience was that the expression 'discontinuity' became popular in management jargon. In the very year in which it was proposed (1969/70) the figure of £2.65 million was £584,000 short of the figure required. It was over £3 million short of the deficit in the following year (1970/71). The extent to which the £2.65 figure was wrong over the five-year period is evident from the following table.

£ m.	69/70	70/71	71/72	72/73	73/4
Proposed subvention	2.650	2.650	2.650	2.650	2.650
Actual deficit	3.234	6.171	6.493	8.476	11.666
Actual subvention provided	2.650	5.630	6.000	8.300	10.750

The total subventions paid (£33.33 million) were £20 million higher than the £13.25 million figure proposed in December 1969, while the actual deficits came to the still higher figure of £36.04 million. The three factors primarily responsible for this enormous discrepancy between intention and result were unprecedented levels of inflation, even higher levels of labour cost increases, and inability to recover costs by increased charges, caused in part by direct government restraint on CIÉ's pricing proposals. In the view of Donal O'Mahony, Secretary in the 1980s of the Department of Transport and Communications, the result of government price restraint was that by the mid-1970s CIÉ was on such a slide that the task of stabilising its finances became virtually hopeless. To understand what was about to happen it may be helpful to note the year-on-year inflation rates from 1970 through to 1985 and the twin 20 per cent peaks which occurred in 1975 and 1981.

Annual Increases in Consumer Price Index

	%		%		%		%
1970	8.2	1974	17.0	1978	7.6	1982	17.1
1971	9.0	1975	20.9	1979	13.2	1983	10.4
1972	8.6	1976	18.0	1980	18.2	1984	8.6
1973	11.4	1977	13.6	1981	20.4	1985	5.4

(Source: Central Bank of Ireland)

As we shall see later, the state subvention increased each year through this entire period. It would be wrong to infer that inflation was the only factor of importance in the deterioration of the finances of public transport, but it does provide a relevant backdrop to the story which unfolds. Increased investment in the railways, effectiveness or ineffectiveness of labour management, chronic slippage in the profitability of Dublin's transport services, the effect on business of the ever upward trend in fares, and changes in competition are other elements in the mosaic of the CIÉ story in the 1970s and beyond. That mosaic would attract experts of varied backgrounds to conduct several minute examinations as the years passed by. We will report on some of their findings.

Three months after the £2.65 million annual subvention was adopted in December 1969, it fell to Brian Lenihan to move a token £10 vote for his department. Some extracts from his upbeat response to the debate show that nothing untoward was perceived to be on the horizon.

> CIÉ alone employs in the region of 20,000 people. Every party in the House now subscribes to the necessity, from the social and community point of view, of preserving the nucleus of a rail service and we intend to maintain it. Recently we passed a Transport Act designed to ensure its maintenance. However, apart from the rail service, every other major aspect of CIÉ and Ostlanna Iompair Éireann, the hotel subsidiary, is showing a profit... (*Dáil Debates*, Vol. 244, Col. 467)

He reviewed each activity and demonstrated that not merely were they in surplus but the surplus was growing, using such expressions as 'fantastic increase' and 'four fold jump in four years' in describing the performance of provincial bus services (tours included). Apart from the operation of the railways and canals, which he omitted to mention, CIÉ was charged 'to make money and to operate in a businesslike and commercial way and I am glad to be able to tell the House, and it can be seen from the figures, that this has been done in a proper spirit and a proper way'. He was especially enthusiastic about the hotel group which had 'shown itself to be outstandingly viable and outstandingly commercially minded . . . I have said to the managing director of CIÉ and Ostlanna Iompair Éireann that I would welcome public participation in Ostlanna Iompair Éireann by way of investment in the hotel group and that I anticipate developments in this direction inside the next few months.' (ibid., Cols 467–70)

The profit of £354,000 on Dublin City Services mentioned by Lenihan in December 1969 was past history. It was plummeting while he spoke to £61,000 in 1969/70 and would turn into a loss of £285,000 in 1970/71. The OIE results with which he was so satisfied were also on the slide and 1970/71 would be the last year of profit before the hotels went into terminal financial decline.

In 1969/70 wage rounds and Labour Court recommendations increased CIÉ's labour costs by 10.6 per cent. In 1970/71 the increase was 18.5 per cent, and a further 16 per cent was incurred in 1971/72—a cumulative increase of 52 per cent over three years. The annual reports somewhat plaintively drew attention to the inescapable impact on a labour-intensive industry of such levels of increase. Another fare increase was proposed in May 1970 and CIÉ called a press conference for 10 June 1970 to announce its new charges. The press conference was cancelled; the board had notified the minister of its proposals and at his 'request had deferred action pending consideration of the matter' (ibid., Vol. 247, Cols 640, 641). CIÉ modified its proposals on lines which he suggested and reconvened its press conference a week later. The minister explained that CIÉ 'had agreed to limit the increases so that they do not go beyond the Government's price control policy whereby increases in labour costs in 1970 in excess of 30s. a week per worker are disregarded'. However, Frank Lemass made no secret of the fact that the problem which had prompted the initial fares proposals was one which would not go away.

Tom O'Donnell raised the question two weeks later, on 23 June 1970; he asked the minister 'whether in view of the recent statement by the general manager of CIÉ that the financial situation of the company was very serious, he proposes to increase the annual subvention to CIÉ and thus prevent any further increase in fares during the current year' (ibid., Col. 1606). Lenihan's reply was that he was considering the matter, but in answer to a specific suggestion he assured the deputy that 'I see no necessity to set up a select committee of the Oireachtas to examine the entire operations of the national transport organisation.'

In retrospect, it seems odd that legislation passed only six months earlier had firmly nailed down the £2.65 million subvention in a situation that was clearly a volatile one. Tom O'Donnell had a similar thought. He asked the Minister to come clean on this and cut out the bluff. Is it not a fact that when he introduced the Transport Bill here last December making financial provision for the next five years for CIÉ he was then in possession of the facts revealed by Mr Lemass last week?

(ibid., Col. 1608)

The minister assured the deputy that he was not aware of CIÉ's deteriorating situation when the legislation had been introduced. The deterioration was continuing fast and only four months after his June intervention to scale back proposed fare increases, Brian Lenihan sanctioned further increases. His reply to several questions about this second batch of increases revealed the serious situation of which he claimed to have been previously unaware.

> Without a further increase in fares and rates, CIÉ's deficit for the year to 31st March, 1971 would reach an estimated £7.56 million before taking account of the statutory subvention of £2.65 million per annum. The estimated net deficit of approximately £5 million is accounted for almost entirely by increased labour costs, which for the current financial year are expected to amount to £4.5 million.
>
> The Government consider that an additional burden of this magnitude cannot be placed entirely on the shoulders of the taxpayer but should be borne, as far as possible, by the users of public transport.
>
> (ibid., Vol. 249, Cols 285, 286)

However, 'In order to alleviate hardships for parents', fares for schoolchildren should be maintained at the existing level for twelve months for which a special subsidy of £228,000 would be paid by the Department of Education. The minister said that even with the increased charges the deficit for the year to March 1971 would still exceed the subvention by almost £3 million. He was 'gravely disturbed by the progressively deteriorating financial position of CIÉ' and announced that 'The position is at present being investigated by a joint committee of my Department, the Department of Finance and CIÉ with a view to identifying possible corrective measures.'

The annual report published in due course claimed that the postponement of CIÉ fare increases during 1970/71 lost it £2 million revenue. As the Dáil extracts show, the minister had changed his position both on the level of fare increases and on the matter of an investigation. The joint committee, of which he spoke, was established in October 1970 and chaired by Diarmuid Ó Riordáin. The committee in turn commissioned the highly reputed international management consultants, McKinsey & Co., to 'help them analyse the problem' and to propose 'ways in which the adverse trend in CIÉ's finances could be arrested'. The McKinsey study team worked with the interdepartmental committee and the resultant report titled 'Defining the role of public transport in a changing environment' was completed in July 1971. There is a sameness in the analysis of the problem by McKinsey with that made by Pacemaker seven years earlier, but unlike Pacemaker, McKinsey moved beyond analysis to the making of recommendations. McKinsey found that

> current problems—like those of public transport companies in other countries—result largely from two factors. First, costs were rising rapidly at a time when many opportunities to improve productivity have already been exploited. Second, growing private transport competition—from both motor cars and lorries—is limiting the possibility of increasing rates in line with costs.

The second of those two factors was identified as far back as the thirties by Ingram, by Milne in 1949 and by Beddy in 1956. Again, as had been observed so often, the railway was the main problem.

> 40% of the route mileage has been closed since 1944 [but] in the last 2 years railway losses have increased rapidly and are now of sufficient magnitude to cast doubts on the long-term viability of the railway in a country of low population density and limited industrial capacity.

Like Pacemaker, McKinsey compared the railway deficit with the cost of replacement road services, and it also calculated the transitional costs of moving to an all road system. It attempted a cost-benefit analysis of the railways and found that:

> After analysis of social costs and benefits . . . many railway services make a major contribution to the community. It has been concluded that these services should be retained and developed further to play an important continuing role in the future national transport system. [However] even after the effects of social costs and benefits are included the continuation of some railway services cannot be justified. Restructuring of the railway is necessary, therefore, to eliminate these services and improve the railway financial results by about £1 million annually. (McKinsey Report, 1971, p. iv)

Despite increased freight and passenger carryings, McKinsey found that the 'operating ratio', i.e. the ratio of total revenues to total costs in the freight sector, was deteriorating.

> Analysis of individual traffics showed that, for freight, part of the reason for the decline in revenues in relation to costs was the increasing proportion of such low revenue traffic as mineral ores, cement and fertiliser. The most important reason, however, has been the increasing competition from road transport for higher valued freight traffic, which was the staple railway traffic in the past. Between 1960 and 1970 road transport increased its share (in ton miles) of the total freight market from 79 per cent to 83 per cent . . . During this period the average revenue per ton-mile earned by the railway for merchandise traffic actually fell. (ibid., p. vi)

With regard to passenger traffic McKinsey found that mainline services were turning in a positive performance, but the Dublin commuter rail system was incurring a serious deficit. In summary, operating profits from the passenger business (apart from commuters) were 'making a major contribution . . . towards the fixed costs of the railway'; operating profits were also being earned by bulk freight trains and container trains, but commuter services and wagonload services were both 'making negative contributions'.

> Further analysis showed that while wagonload services are generating positive cash flow and can be treated as a wasting asset to be run down over time, commuter services are completely unviable financially and on a commercial basis should be terminated immediately. (ibid.)

The restructuring which McKinsey recommended involved major changes in rail freight handling systems which were reflected in 'Railplan 80'—a CIÉ study with which we shall deal later in the next chapter. It recommended further closing of many small freight and passenger stations. Certain 'all freight lines' and 'lightly loaded stopping passenger services' could also be dropped. 'Bus services could be substituted—for example on the Limerick–Claremorris line.' Like Beddy, McKinsey questioned the second line to Limerick and proposed that all Limerick traffic be carried via Limerick Junction. No action followed on this proposal and a limited service still operates on the second line (from Ballybrophy).

As we have seen above, McKinsey's recommended restructuring was expected by them to improve financial results by 'about £1 million annually'; they envisaged no way by which the rail deficit could be eliminated or even substantially reduced. Accordingly, it proceeded to find serious fault with the manner in which the state subvention was administered.

> Two drawbacks exist in the current system of providing financial support to CIÉ. First, little guidance is given on how the annual subvention is to be applied, which has led to irreconcilable objectives for CIÉ management and board. Since CIÉ has to manage its affairs within a fixed grant, it must periodically curtail activities that it can no longer afford to continue. In such circumstances, any management would normally curtail the most unprofitable activities. However, some of CIÉ's most unprofitable activities are also those of greatest social value, and in eliminating them CIÉ would be violating the spirit of its mandate in response to financial pressures. . . .
>
> Second, current losses on the railway are so large that even substantial improvements in operating performance have little impact on the deficit. This has a damaging effect on management morale.
>
> (ibid., p. vii)

To ease this 'management morale' problem McKinsey suggested that loss making services, which were regarded as being socially necessary, should be identified and specific grants paid by the state for the maintenance of those services.

> To avoid the conflict that exists for management between the financial and social objectives of CIÉ we concluded that it is necessary to make explicit the relationship between the social value of a service and the price to be paid for it. To permit this, the current financing system should be replaced by a system in which above-the-line grants —related to social benefits and operating costs—are paid to those socially desirable, but financially uneconomic, services that it is in the community's interest to support. These services include much of the rail network, many commuter services, and many bus services.
>
> (ibid., p. x)

However, McKinsey fell a good deal short of proposing such a system in its specific recommendations. It must be assumed that the interdepartmental committee which was advising McKinsey, if not McKinsey themselves, thought that the change involved in analysing services and fixing subventions, piece by piece, could be excessively cumbrous, controversial and expensive in administration. However, the idea was intellectually appealing and, as we shall see, would surface time and again in other consultants' reports.

McKinsey's own proposal was a compromise between the existing blanket subvention and a detailed service-by-service subvention system. This involved a special payment for maintenance of the permanent way and a single specific subvention for Dublin rail commuter services. The language used echoes the conviction that 'subsidies are demoralising'—a view which we have seen expressed so many times before.

> The current loss on the railway is an intolerable burden on the whole of CIÉ. It is also of such proportions as to weaken management morale and the will to seek effective improvements. To lessen this load, and to set the railway the challenging but not insuperable task of making a nominal return on its capital investment, we recommend that the railway should be given an annual grant to cover the costs of track maintenance and renewal, signalling staff and gatekeepers, subject to the reduction in route mileage discussed in the report. This grant, worth about £4.3 million per annum at current cost levels, would recognise the economic and social contribution that the railway can make to the total economy, particularly by linking the south and west of Ireland to Dublin and the East coast. (ibid.)

In other words, McKinsey recommended an 'infrastructure grant' but the idea of a general scheme of specific subventions for individual services was not abandoned. They left it on the record for possible future implementation but initially believed that a

> payment [for a socially desirable service] would be confined to the Dublin commuter services, and would cost around £400,000 per annum . . . Given these payments, the managers concerned will be responsible for running these services in an efficient, commercial manner, making a nominal return on capital after payment of interest charges. (ibid.)

McKinsey also recommended that current capital investment in the railways be increased by between £7 million and £10 million over the next five years 'to allow the remaining rail services to play the most effective role possible'. Part of this would be spent on the Dublin commuter services which should be 'upgraded through the provision of new rolling stock so that their contribution towards solving Dublin's traffic problem can be increased'. Secondly, capital would be needed for the rationalisation and development of freight services; new rolling stock and mechanised handling equipment was required. McKinsey also proposed some changes in the area management structures so as to give overall financial responsibility for rail operations to a single executive.

When the McKinsey Report was published (1 October 1971) it was specifically welcomed by CIÉ which

> was gratified by the emphasis which the McKinsey report placed on

the social role of certain of its services and by the recognition that certain CIÉ transport services should be paid for from public funds because they are socially desirable.

Like other social services such as the public water supply, the health services and education, public transport in many cases confers social benefits on the community which are not measured automatically in terms of commercial profit alone . . . CIÉ are already operating a number of services such as the school transport and the free transport for pensioners and veterans in which the social content is formally recognised by direct Government support.

(*The Irish Times*, 1 October 1971)

Commenting on the specific recommendation that an annual grant be given towards covering the cost of the rail infrastructure, CIÉ said: 'This grant recognises the fact that the railway network serves the same national purpose as our national primary roads system.' The recommendations 'on replacing subventions by financing through operating and infrastructure grants, taken with the proposals on modifying the CIÉ management structure', would give a new and clearer profit focus to various divisions. CIÉ also thought McKinsey's recommendations would remove 'any conflict between CIÉ's commercial and social objectives' (ibid.).

Already the 1969 transport legislation was an embarrassment; the state subvention had been increased from £2.65 million to £5.63 million by a 1970 Transport Act, which provided that in future the subvention could be supplemented annually by Dáil vote rather than be limited for five years, as had been the intention in the 1964 and 1969 legislation. The subvention was again increased to £6 million for 1971/72. On 24 June 1971, while McKinsey was conducting its investigation, government announced that a White Paper would be published on transport policy but just twelve months later, on 21 June 1972, it was announced that this White Paper was postponed indefinitely. In the meantime McKinsey had reported; its recommendations would have to be accepted or rejected if a White Paper was to be published; that might cause problems, so why bother? Let's pretend there was no crisis and carry on as before.

The government had other things on its mind—raging inflation, Northern Ireland, joining the EEC and a general election around the corner. When the Republic did gain accession to the EEC, as it was then called, Brian Lenihan left Transport and Power to succeed P. J. Hillery as Minister for Foreign Affairs. Lenihan had been in Transport and Power for three and a half years. Michael O'Kennedy succeeded him but would hold office for a mere two and a half months, much of which was dominated by the general election campaign. Fourteen years would elapse before a new generation minister had a Green Paper published on transport policy. In turn, the

Green Paper (1985) promised a White Paper, but that too would never emerge.

CIÉ was developing its own railway rationalisation plans, but it also attached an importance to the McKinsey Report which was not conceded by those who had commissioned it. In its 1971/72 Annual Report, published almost twelve months after McKinsey, CIÉ commented that implementation of McKinsey's recommendations would 'mean the ending of blanket subventions for CIÉ in favour of a system of grants based on the value of particular services to the community. *These grants would be paid by way of revenue* (author's emphasis) towards the cost of providing the services. The Board favours the adoption of these recommendations as subvention policy.' For all their attractiveness to CIÉ, it was to government that the McKinsey recommendations on the subvention policy were addressed and they were simply filed away. Even when the overall subvention later came to be broken down into different elements for nominated purposes, as required by EEC legislation, the change would not vary the public perception of a blanket subvention to cover annual 'losses'. For another twelve years subventions to CIÉ would continue on the instructions of successive governments to be presented as 'below the line' payments to offset operating deficits rather than as 'above the line' payments which could be credited to revenue. That issue will surface a number of times in later chapters.

Before passing from the McKinsey Report, it should be noted that it received some public criticism. John Carroll, Vice President of the ITGWU, was cautious, saying that 'the government must be held responsible for the situation in which CIÉ found itself', and he warned against 'any hasty decisions' which might result in redundancies. Dr Seán Barrett, who had previously received a postgraduate transport research scholarship sponsored by CIÉ, was a Trinity College lecturer in economics. A week after the publication of the McKinsey Report he wrote two articles in *The Irish Times* (7 and 8 October 1971) titled 'How McKinsey missed the bus' and 'The Cost benefit analysis—a unique McKinsey stew'. Barrett's opening statement about McKinsey was that 'it is bad value for the £61,000 of public money it cost' and he continued: 'The report fails to recognise the high cost of public transport in Ireland.' Barrett criticised the report for making assertions which were not supported by analysis, but that remark could be applied to assertions of his own, e.g. that 'public transport in the Republic is twice as expensive as in Northern Ireland and Canada, 50% more expensive than in France, 40% more expensive than in the United Kingdom and 35% more expensive than in the United States'. The support offered for this dramatic assertion was a six-line table showing 'transport costs per mile' based on dividing fares between two points in each of six countries by the mileage involved. There was no indication whether the fares were excursion or normal, whether they were typical or not, or whether they were rail or road, though two of them, Paris/Cherbourg and London/Glasgow, were identified as return fares, while the Irish fare selected, Dublin/Monaghan, was a single bus fare. McKinsey was described as being 'ignorant', 'unsure' and 'uncertain' of 'some transport legislation'. This serious charge was based on a couple of McKinsey's observations. One was that if CIÉ withdrew from its most unprofitable services 'it would be violating the spirit of its mandate'. This, said Barrett, ignored the commercial freedom granted under the 1958 Act. Of course he was right: it was perfectly possible under the 1958 Act to close down Dublin rail commuter services or anything else—there wasn't even the requirement to replace the service by buses. McKinsey was also held to task for saying that certain things would happen 'provided CIÉ has freedom to set its own rates and fares'. Barrett knew the law: CIÉ already had the legal freedom to set its own charges. McKinsey's fault was that it recognised the political environment affecting services and charges in which CIÉ operated. Barrett found a number of interesting and amusing inconsistencies in McKinsey and criticised the basis of McKinsey's cost-benefit analysis, but his general thesis was that the national transport company was inefficient, and his fault with McKinsey was that they had not proved this to be so. The two *Irish Times* articles were picked up by the London press and McKinsey promptly issued a long reply, calling Dr Barrett's criticisms 'trivial, misleading, or just downright wrong'. McKinsey also said: 'It is not our normal practice to make public comment about reports submitted to our clients.' Their reply was intended to 'restore a correct perspective to the public discussion now taking place', but they would 'take no further part' in that discussion (ibid., 27 July 1973). Barrett would be a fluent and controversial critic of CIÉ for years to come. Regard for balance and even accuracy in his analyses would sometimes seem to be subservient to a concern for achieving impact with well-timed comment.

Since Frank Lemass had become Chief Executive after the departure of Todd Andrews in October 1966, efforts to improve rail services had continued, but because of the changes that had already taken place the additional improvements did not seem to be dramatic. Limerick Junction had been reorganised so that trains would no longer have to reverse into the station—a reorganisation originally planned twenty years earlier but abandoned in the wake of the Milne Report. The re-equipment of rolling stock, bus fleets and road freight vehicles proceeded at a normal pace; hotels continued to be improved and expanded; substantial progress was made in the international tourism sector; and, while labour relations were no cakewalk, strikes had declined to a fraction of their former level. Significant improvements were made to staff amenities during Frank Lemass's period at the top, including the provision of a new sports and social complex for Dublin's busmen at Coldcut, Co. Dublin. While these improvements in staff amenities continued a trend from the Andrews period, the climate of the Frank Lemass years was such that further investment in social facilities was both expected in large employments (including the ESB and Aer Lingus) and was seen to be genuinely appreciated by employees. Inflation, a rising deficit and approaching paralysis of Dublin's traffic were the toughest problems Frank Lemass had to grapple with during the four years he was chief executive. He retired from being General Manager in 1970 at the age of 60, though he remained on the board until his death four years later.

IT IS TIME to note some consequences for CIÉ of the growing Dublin traffic problem of the period. One result was a deterioration in the financial results of Dublin City Services, but the incidence of strikes, inflation and deferred fare increases makes it impossible to apportion a proper share of the blame for this deterioration to the traffic problem. Dublin bus passenger numbers started to fall in the late sixties, and here again industrial disputes must bear some blame for the decline. However, bus service was deteriorating due to the traffic situation which demanded more attention than it had been receiving.

Two months after Frank Lemass retired, the Minister for Local Government authorised a few short-lived traffic experiments designed to make traffic, and especially public transport, flow more easily. The 1970/71 CIÉ Annual Report recorded that the Board co-operated with the Dublin Corporation Traffic and Parking Committee in two significant experiments:

> During Traffic Improvement Week in February [1971] special measures were taken to improve vehicle movement in Dublin. Fifty extra buses were put on at peak periods and twenty nine additional suburban railway services were scheduled daily. Enforcement of parking regulations improved traffic flow and buses moved with greater regularity.
>
> In the first week of March an experimental bus lane was introduced in the North-Eastern section of the city [at Fairview and a short section of Malahide Road]. Thirty additional buses were used and the public were given the inducement of 11p fare reduction on these routes. Additional suburban trains were introduced. Overall travel time for persons using the corridor was reduced by 10.6% and there was a substantial transfer of car users to public transport.
>
> (Annual Report, 1970/71)

The Gardaí concluded, it was confirmed later, that the inconvenience caused to other road users more than outweighed the advantages gained from these experiments. No doubt they were influenced by the media concentration on the 'awful' chaos caused by the bus lane experiment, which was demonstrated by newspaper and television pictures of long lines of stationary cars side by side with a virtually empty bus lane. CIÉ officials took representatives of the Gardaí and of the corporation to Paris, Lille and to west London to show them 200 examples of successfully operating bus lanes. However, the travellers were not sufficiently impressed by what they saw. Bus lanes giving priority to public transport would not be introduced on a permanent basis for another ten years. The Gardaí, Dublin Corporation, the Department of Local Government (later renamed the Department of the Environment) and CIÉ were all required to be involved in these experiments, while the government department with nominal responsibility for transport had no clear role in the matter. Concern was beginning to be voiced with this anomalous situation and with the indecision in traffic management matters which resulted from the involvement of so many disparate interests. However, like other policy issues such as the basis and the treatment of the subvention, it would hollowly echo and re-echo through the years—sometimes partially but never wholly addressed.

Meanwhile Dublin suburban rail traffic was growing. Published statistics did not distinguish commuter rail passengers from mainline passengers, but the 1969/70 Annual Report notes that 'there was a significant increase in commuter traffic using suburban rail services in Dublin. Track and signalling alterations were carried out at Connolly and Pearse Stations to permit major extensions in through working on these services.' A census taken in December 1970 on Dublin suburban rail services showed a daily increase of 14 per cent on the corresponding period in the previous year. Commuter rail services were increasingly recognised as important. Erskine Childers in 1964 had described them as 'essential'. Dáil questions were now being asked about their possible expansion. McKinsey claimed that these commuter services generated social benefits which exceeded their operating losses. Barrett challenged that conclusion and he would be supported by a group of British economists in a report discussed below. An indication of the recognition of deteriorating traffic conditions was that a Dublin Transportation Study Group had been set up in 1970—a joint exercise between a United Nations team and An Foras Forbartha, a physical planning agency attached to the Department of Local Government. As will be seen, long delays would affect decisions indicated by that report.

Daniel Herlihy succeeded Frank Lemass on 2 November 1970. Herlihy had joined CIÉ from the civil service as far back as 1950. Shortly afterwards, he was appointed Chief Engineer and subsequently became Deputy General Manager. His experience was wide, his intelligence acute, but he was already over 60 and in declining health. In the phrase sometimes used to describe appointments of senior established figures to top jobs in politics or the church, he might have been considered a 'holding appointment'. A much younger man, still in his thirties, John J. Byrne, was appointed Deputy General Manager. Byrne, an engineer, had been recruited into the railway side, had been promoted to the position of General Manager of OIE in its period of expansion, and now became the number two man in CIÉ as a whole. Dan Herlihy remained as General Manager for only two years, retiring in August 1972 before reaching retirement age due to his health problem. John J. Byrne was selected to succeed him. Probably the major achievement at top level of the brief Herlihy period was an impetus given to planning the use of new technology to adapt services, especially railways, to the ever growing and increasingly competitive transport market. In that market, public transport held a fairly constant volume of business but a declining market share. Railplan 80 was the outcome of these studies and would be announced by John Byrne in November 1972, three months after Herlihy's retirement. Before dealing with Railplan 80, we must return to the very sensitive issue of charges and to further consultants' reports generated by this issue.

AFTER THE JUNE 1970 increase in charges involving cancellation of a CIÉ press conference, and a further increase in October 1970, more increases took place in August 1971. If this were to continue, political problems were bound to arise; the government called 'halt' when increases were again proposed in May 1972. CIÉ's objective was to keep its subvention within tolerable limits and it saw no alternative but to raise charges to compensate for continuous inflation in labour costs. Following the earlier price rises, CIÉ experimented with strongly marketed discount fares to stimulate new demand. A 'Spring Double' was launched in 1972 and in December a 'Christmas Fares' promotion resulted in an increase of about 30 per cent in mainline passengers for an increase in revenue of 18 per cent. The most famous of these promotions was 'The Great Train Robbery' from 1 January to 11 March 1973, which produced a 12 per cent increase in revenue for a much larger increase in passengers. In a severely inflationary period, the falling margins which resulted from these promotions and their successors—another 'Great Spring Double', 'Get Out and About', and 'Crazy Sam'—were not producing the necessary bottom line results. By the time of the May 1972 decision, once again to seek higher fares, price control had become a major element in government economic policy in the hope of reducing upward wage pressures.

As measured by the Consumer Price Index, prices had increased by 18 per cent between mid-August 1970 and mid-August 1972. Brian Lenihan was still Minister for Transport and Power, but P. J. (Paddy) Lalor was briefly holding the Industry and Commerce portfolio with responsibility for price control. When informed of the intention to increase rates, Transport and Power in turn advised Industry and Commerce and asked for an urgent decision; they saw no alternative but to increase fares unless the state subvention was to grow by another substantial block. P. J. Lalor in turn submitted the proposed fare increases to the National Prices Commission (NPC) for evaluation. This body had been set up in October 1971 and all significant price increases throughout the economy were capable of being referred to the commission by the minister for investigation. The commission operated within guidelines set by government such as that pay increases 'incurred in 1970 in excess of 30 shillings per week or 7% whichever is the greater would be disregarded' when a case for increased prices was being examined. In 1971, to be considered relevant for price increase approval, pay increases should be in accordance with the Employer Labour Conference National Agreement which came into force in December 1970, i.e. £2 per week for adult male workers with pro rata increases for adult female workers. (Equal pay for equal work was not yet an approved concept with trade unions or employers.)

These guidelines underline the deliberate and determined nature of the arrangements which were deemed necessary to control prices. At a later stage pay increases above national agreement norms could be taken into account provided they had been approved formally by the Employer Labour Conference. The objective was to discourage employers from paying increases above national guidelines and forcing them to achieve productivity increases so that any above the norm increases could not be passed on to the consumer. Each month the NPC would issue its bulletin to the minister, listing hundreds of recommended price increases. The noted economist, Professor W. J. L. (Louden) Ryan, later governor of the Bank of Ireland, was chairman of the commission, and its members comprised one representative each of the Confederation of Irish Industries, the Federation of Trade Associations and the Irish Housewives' Association, together with two representatives of ICTU.

The NPC received CIÉ's submission from the minister on 21 July 1972 for 'urgent consideration', but because of other work and August holidays it was not considered until the meeting on 4 September. In that month CIÉ had hoped to introduce some of its proposed new charges, with others scheduled for introduction in January 1973. At any rate the manifestly overworked commission thought that the issue was so complex that they engaged a consultant to review the whole question of CIÉ's charges. The first commission statement emerged in early December (NPC: Occasional Paper No. 4), and it included a preliminary report from the as yet unnamed consultant. Subsequent papers from the commission reveal that the consultant was the Economists' Advisory Group—a London-based group of seven academic and one business economists. On 15 December *The Irish Times* carried the story of the commission's first report on CIÉ under the heading, 'Prices body indicts company, but backs toned-down increases', and continued

> that the NPC turned down increases proposed by CIÉ of up to 3p in Dublin bus fares and of 12.5% on provincial bus fares. The report and the paper . . . is highly scathing about CIÉ's efficiency.

As an interim measure the NPC recommended significantly lower increases than had been sought, except in the case of bus passengers' fares where they recommended that there be no increase at all.

The NPC explained that neither it nor its consultant had sufficient time to complete its investigation of the case for increased charges. It was seeking a further report from its consultants, but the recommended increases should be approved until it would be able to submit a final recommendation. However, trouble for CIÉ was implicit in the observation that the application for price increases was caused not merely by the impact of labour costs, but by a 'fall in capacity utilisation' and 'what appears to be a relatively poor performance in terms of other changes in economic efficiency'. The commission's strictures and the interim nature of its price increase proposals enabled P. J. Lalor to take the politically easy step of refusing approval of the recommended increases. CIÉ, it seems, did not protest at the minister's refusal to apply the interim increases. In their view they were seriously inadequate. The consultants claimed that previous price increases were excessive and that charges other than for mainline rail were higher than UK charges. Their report bears the marks of a hasty job by academics who failed to consult with people in the field. They highlighted some apparently unjustifiable aspects of performance, but they made enough errors for CIÉ to be able to protest strongly. An article by Dr Con Power, subsequently economics director of the Confederation of Irish Industry, reported the CIÉ view in the same issue of *The Irish Times*.

> The findings of the National Prices Commission on the State transport body are utterly refuted by CIÉ in a hard-hitting document . . .
>
> A spokesman stressed that CIÉ was not challenging the idea of a prices commission generally—its complaint was, he said the 'inadequate research methods' and 'partial analysis' of this particular paper. He added that the NPC paper was 'a lightweight' in comparison with the surveys of the U.K. National Prices and Incomes Board, which he admired greatly. 'Even on the most general reading,

there are major errors in the NPC paper which could have been avoided had there been any form of preliminary contact with CIÉ'. . . . 'The inference that CIÉ prices have risen considerably faster than prices of transport in Britain is not substantiated at all in respect of freight rates', CIÉ says. 'For passengers the conclusion is subject to the serious shortcoming that the CIÉ figures used are standard prices whereas significant numbers of CIÉ mainline passengers travel at less than these rates.'

In the case of mainline rail services, it was asserted, the proportion of all passengers who travelled at less than the standard rate has increased from 43% in 1966–67 to 59% in 1972; similarly, the proportion of gross rail freight revenue obtained at lower than standard rates rose from 8% in 1965–66 to 69.7% in 1971–72. Another major CIÉ grievance is the fact that the NPC report makes no mention of the 'Great Train Robbery' promotion and its results.

(*The Irish Times*, 15 December 1972)

The CIÉ response supports the argument that actual revenue earned per passenger mile or per freight ton mile is the only reliable way of making inter-company, inter-country and inter-period comparisons of transport charges. Transport professionals hold that view, but critics with axes to grind tend to argue from different bases. One significant NPC criticism was, that notwithstanding there being 'no increase in the real volume of business, employment in CIÉ rose by 6% between 1965/66 and 1971/72'. The CIÉ explanation was that the increased numbers were caused by the shorter week which was conceded to CIÉ operatives after Labour Court hearings. However, the number of jobs provided in state companies was a very high government priority at the time and that may have been another factor in the upward creep in employment. Brian Lenihan's speeches seemed almost to boast of the 20,000 employees. Frank Lemass in *Business and Finance* (13 March 1970) was reported as saying that while jobs would be lost in some sectors, 'new employment opportunities' would arise elsewhere. 'I would not be at all upset at the idea of numbers increasing.' Trade unions welcomed the NPC's broadside at CIÉ, protesting that its management was 'top heavy and remote' and that there was a 'tradition of smothering initiative, critical comment and imagination', but they added that 'it is essential that there be no absolute loss of job units in CIÉ as a result of rationalisation programmes'.

In its case for price increases, CIÉ claimed that even with the increases sought, the deficit for the year to March 1973 would exceed the budgeted subvention of £6.15 million by £470,000, making a total deficit of £6.62 million. In due course the 1972/73 results revealed the still greater deficit of £8.24 million, three times the level provided for in the 1969 Act. The second report by the NPC and its consultants was published in June 1973 and dealt with Dublin city buses and suburban railways. *The Irish Times* carried this story under the headline, 'Major distortions alleged in £61,000 report on CIÉ—criticism by English Consultants firm'. The £61,000 report was the McKinsey document discussed above, the price of which Seán Barrett had drawn to public attention. *The Irish Times* report states:

> Today's report, by the English based consultants, the Economists' Advisory Group (EAG) . . . takes McKinsey to task for the way they assessed the social benefits of maintaining the Dublin suburban trains, compared with the alternative use of buses and cars.
>
> 'We believe that there are some fundamental objections and many questionable points of details in this [McKinsey] analysis', says EAG.
>
> (ibid., 21 June 1973)

The reader can be spared the details of the faults which the EAG found with McKinsey's cost-benefit analysis. While the consultants differed with McKinsey about how to do the sums, the real issue was whether the Dublin suburban rail system should be maintained, severely pruned, or abandoned. A public which was increasingly critical of the earlier decision to close the Harcourt Street line was not impressed by the dispute about cost-benefit analysis techniques. It had made up its mind that the Dublin suburban line was necessary. The EAG criticised cross-subsidisation between various Dublin bus routes. Cross-subsidisation can be anathema to professional economists because it 'distorts true market costs'. The EAG argued that there should be no cross-subsidies and that such loss making services as were required for social reasons should be supported by specific government subventions. The general thrust of this second NPC paper on fare increases (Occasional Paper No. 8) was about CIÉ's pricing philosophy, which seemed to be based on considerations of 'what the traffic could bear'. Such an unsophisticated, if practical approach was not acceptable to the EAG's team of academic economists, and *The Irish Times* reported the NPC as claiming

> that CIÉ regards the relationship between prices and costs as of minor importance and it says the CIÉ's application for fares increases last year were not explicitly related to any objectives of pricing policy.
>
> (ibid.)

The NPC signalled that still more work was in progress and their third report on CIÉ's affairs was published a month later as Occasional Paper No. 10. In this paper the consultant dealt with more specific pricing issues. The paper proposed that rail fares should be higher than bus fares for similar distances, rather than lower, as was the practice. It argued that short-distance bus fares should not be increased to the extent proposed, but longer-distance fares should bear a higher increase. There was a simple problem: CIÉ was trying to reduce a clearly excessive number of stages on their bus routes and the smallest coin it had in use was the new penny. It did not want to re-introduce the halfpenny which had disappeared from fares before decimalisation of the coinage on 15 January 1971. With a minimum 1p increase on the new decimal fares, proportionally greater increases on lower fares were inevitable. Stages were being lengthened as part compensation for the effects of decimalisation. Finally, the NPC recommended that price increases be implemented in a manner that would ensure that no increases would exceed 12.5 per cent. It seemed to be getting tired of the whole issue and complained a number of times in its three papers that it looked for, but could not find, 'any statement of national policy for transport' against which they could properly assess transport charges.

> It is not the business of the National Prices Commission to try to formulate such a policy or even to take a view on what transport policy ought to be. . . . Our recommendations merely help to maintain the existing national policy for transport, whatever it is. We hope nevertheless that the formulation of a rational, national transport policy will not as a consequence be regarded as a matter of any less urgency. (Occasional Paper No. 10, p. 13)

The three papers of the commission and their consultants' reports are logically constructed. They clearly reflect the economic discipline of the EAG and of the commission's chairman, Louden Ryan. For all these merits they have a very academic flavour, detached from the world of political, social and business realities so evident in the earlier McKinsey study. Commenting that it believed that the reports of its consultants 'provide a sound starting point for the formulation of a national transport policy', the NPC concluded with words which in effect said, 'Don't bother us again, unless you sort yourselves out first.'

> If the transport policy lacks a clear economic rationale, there is little point in referring applications for increases in rates and fares to the Commission, because we can deal only with economic considerations or those social costs and benefits which can be quantified in money terms. (ibid.)

They could protest if they wished. Within a week of the NPC's report a new government announced that it had approved fare increases, which were well above those which the commission had laboured to produce. A general election had been held in February 1973. After sixteen years in power, Fianna Fáil was defeated; Brian Lenihan lost his Dáil seat, and Erskine Childers was on his way to Áras an Uachtaráin. In the new Fine Gael/Labour coalition, Justin Keating replaced P. J. Lalor as Minister for Industry and Commerce or 'Minister for Higher Prices' as he would be called by some in the circumstances of the time. Peter Barry was the new Minister for Transport and Power and Richie Ryan became Minister for Finance. The new team of ministers was prepared to bite the fares bullet. Concerned with the size of the rapidly growing state subvention and the possibility that it would rise to £19 million in 1974/75, they were prepared to allow more of the spiralling costs to be recovered from the consumer. The alternative was substantially to increase the state subvention. This they were not prepared to do, but no individual minister allowed himself to be identified with the decision. A government statement on 26 July 1973 ended the twelve-month stalemate on CIÉ's fares and rates.

> CIÉ has been operating on a substantial subvention from the government. . . . If the Government is to finance its social programme and plans for economic development the increases in CIÉ losses cannot be allowed to continue unchecked. The Government has, therefore, decided that the losses on CIÉ must in the current year be contained within the very substantial figure of £12.5 already provided for and as a consequence they are unable to accept in this instance the recommendation of the National Prices Commission in their reports for April and June. These recommendations on the most up-to-date estimates would require an increase in total Government subvention to CIÉ to a figure of £13.5 m. in the current financial year and, in the absence of a further increase in fares and rates, a total of £19 m. in 1974/75. (*The Irish Times*, 27 July 1973)

The specific fare increases 'sanctioned by government' were detailed in the announcement. Not merely were they higher than those painfully argued for by the NPC, suggestions about reversing the 'tapering' involved in CIÉ's proposals, so that proportionally greater increases would apply to longer journeys, were simply rejected; 4p bus fares increased to 5p, while 10p fares increased to 12p and 14p fares rose to 15p. Similarly, the consultants' view that passenger rail charges should be increased more than bus fares was ignored: many 4p suburban rail fares were unaltered, as were all 20p fares. Several intermediate fares bore large increases as stage lengths were changed. The NPC must have felt pretty aggrieved that their labours were so summarily treated. In retrospect, the fault lay in the issue having been referred to them in the first place or else they should have been advised not to take it on themselves to try and rework the entire system of charges and also not to attempt to redesign the system of government subventions which they did in their remarks about paying subsidies for specific services. Their comments on this point were on the same lines as McKinsey's and similarly they were ignored.

A statement from CIÉ said that they were pleased at the fares decision by government which they put into a political and financial context.

> . . . we were naturally concerned at the mounting level of deficit arising from the provision of services at a fixed price while costs were rising. As public transport is essentially a social service all fundamental decisions on prices must naturally be made by the Government in the context of taxation generally. CIÉ last increased its rates and fares in August, 1971, i.e. two years ago since when its labour costs had increased by £33 million. (ibid.)

No trade union spokesman commented on the government decision, so the final word on this phase of postponements, studies and eventual decision on fares can be left to the spokesman of the Consumers' Association, the name adopted by the reorganised Irish Housewives' Association, an articulate lobbying group of the period. Their message hardly gave clear advice to government as to what was desired of them:

> The Consumers' Association object very strongly to the price increases announced this morning, no matter how well justified. These increases, coupled with the Government rise in the cost of social services put an unfair burden on the middle income group; therefore some form of alleviation is necessary and we press for a Government total anti-inflationary policy involving the whole community. (ibid.)

It would be wrong to assume from the outcome of this price saga that the national transport company could now complacently carry on as before. A major rethinking of railway operations was under way; new coaching stock was being acquired and a greatly changed rail timetable had been introduced in March 1973. A new minister had moved in and he had to agree to major price increases soon after taking office. He would appoint a new chairman before the year ended.

CHAPTER 15

PLANS AND CRISES

Railplan 80—Higher rail frequencies attempted in 1973—New rail coaches arrive — Liam St J. Devlin appointed Chairman—Railway Development Plan—Dublin Transportation study—Dublin Rapid Rail Transport study—Reorganisation of rail freight—Fastrack established—Corporate and management objectives redefined— New GM locomotives (071's) arrive—Gormanston and Gorey accidents.

'Railplan 80' was the neat title applied to the outcome of a special CIÉ task force charged with examining 'ways and means of halting and, if possible, reversing the deteriorating financial position of the railway'. Completed in October 1972, work had commenced some six months after publication of the McKinsey Report which had the more grandiose title of 'Defining the Role of Public Transport in a Changing Environment'. In his foreword to Railplan 80, John Byrne, CIÉ's General Manager, stressed that the document was 'prepared independently of McKinsey'. There is a touch of 'one didn't need McKinsey—this is all our own work and better' about John Byrne's remarks.

Railplan 80 set its focus on the year 1980 and attempted to lay out the steps necessary to deliver a modern, efficient and more economic railway system by that date. Some of these steps were already in hand and others would begin to be taken within a few months of the document's completion, thus revealing that Railplan 80 was a compilation of immediate plans together with long-term strategy. The plan was serious and ambitious in tone. 'Capital limitations and the effects of inflation have in recent years prevented the railways from assuming market leadership in the field of transport. The reversal of this situation is essential for the success of Railplan 80. All available skills, technical, commercial and financial must be co-ordinated and directed to the task of preparing the railway for the challenge of the 1980s.'

By the standards of internal planning documents Railplan 80 was impressive enough. It comprised four substantial volumes, which were not formally published, but inevitably some of it appeared in the newspapers. It was 'adopted' as a draft plan by the CIÉ Board on 30 November 1972 and became the basis for submissions to government in 1973 which were accepted in principle in March 1974. CIÉ would then announce its 'Railway Development Plan' in July 1974, by which time some aspects of Railplan 80 were already being implemented, while others would be changed as experience required. The author found it interesting that some persons directly involved in the preparation of Railplan 80 regard it as historically the most significant planning document ever prepared in CIÉ. Others had a much more modest view of the document, regarding it as no more than a useful benchmark as to where the rail system stood in 1972 and of the way in which it should be going.

In Railplan 80, CIÉ for the first time formally accepted that it could and should work towards a major reduction in railway staff numbers—a reduction of 1,800 was targeted by 1980 which could, it was believed, be achieved by natural wastage and redeployment. The number of passenger and freight handling stations should be severely pruned. Freight handling at the remaining locations should be mechanised to a much greater extent than achieved by previous efforts in the 1960s. These now seemed to be primitive relative to what was required in a more competitive and sophisticated era. The most significant change presented in Railplan 80 was the concept of the block train—standard size trains whether for passengers or freight which would travel unchanged from origin to destination. Adding and removing carriages or, more especially, wagons *en route* was to be avoided. The fascinating routines of shunting and of coupling and uncoupling which attracted generations of children to spending hours with their train sets were to be removed from the real railway world. Faster and more frequent trains would result and utilisation of rolling stock would increase substantially. Push/pull configurations would eliminate shunting at suburban rail termini. These features of Railplan 80 would come to be realised through the next decade, but Railplan 80, despite or because of the detail of its proposals, would prove not to be the definitive blueprint which it claimed to be.

New coaches were being acquired when Railplan 80 emerged. The Dublin rail termini were being reorganised and a much changed timetable was being planned for 1973. A complete reworking of railway signalling, essential to improving utilisation of track and rolling stock, was not part of Railplan 80 as it was already being reviewed by another group, and electrification or other modernisation of the Dublin suburban rail system was under separate study. Track improvements achieved a somewhat greater significance in subsequent years than Railplan 80 seemed to envisage. New and more powerful locomotives (the 071's) not referred to in Railplan 80 would soon be ordered and the plan's proposals for handling 'less than wagon load traffics' would be greatly modified. We shall return to many of these matters as the story continues, but we begin with the first three months of 1973 and with three significant changes which would have an immediate and permanent impact on rail passenger services.

Heuston station in 1972 had only two platforms under cover and one other platform outside the railshed, which was still known as the 'Military Platform'. Between the two undercover platforms, one of which was used as an arrival and the other as a departure platform, lay four carriage sidings. A new island platform was built on these centre sidings, thus doubling the number of undercover platforms. A section of the existing track on the eastern end of the railshed was removed so that, as the Irish Railway Record Society (IRRS) recorded in its *Journal*:

> At the upper end of the station there is now a good-sized concourse, extending the whole width of the roofed part, and covering much of what was track. The new concourse is tiled in black and white, as are the former platforms, and railings and barriers have been erected for better control of the passengers and guidance of them to their trains.
>
> Already the new provisions have served well, and during the rush-period at the end of the year the advantage was felt of having four covered platforms available—especially in the evening time when, for instance, there are eight departures between 18.00 and 19.05.
>
> The alteration for the better in the general interior aspect of the station is remarkable. The occupying of the centre of the covered area by a wide new platform, instead of by four rows of carriages, lends a new look of spaciousness to the whole and with the repainting of the roof in a light shade, a rather gloomy and dingy station has become quite attractive and fit for the heavier traffic it is now handling.
>
> (*IRRS Journal*, February 1973)

These modifications to a layout which had existed for 130 years indicated the way the railway planned to move—more frequent, faster and shorter trains, rather than the long and slow trains which had sufficed in the past. The changes were also very much connected with the move of western (Galway, Westport and Ballina) trains to the southern line to Athlone via Portarlington, rather than via Mullingar on the midlands line. These services would now operate from Heuston, relieving Pearse to specialise in rapidly growing commuter services. Traders in Mullingar protested at the downgrading of their station and the availability of less passenger accommodation to Dublin and the west, about which the IRRS commented that the Mullingar public had been poor supporters of the railway. Traders in the Westland Row area of Pearse station were equally upset at the removal of traffic which had frequented their premises since the western rail services had moved there from Broadstone in 1937. It was alleged in the Dáil (3 December 1974) that the decision not to use Westland Row as the departure point to the west had the effect of closing a number of businesses in that depressed area. The newspapers, dutiful as ever in reporting grievances, also carried complaints about the difficulty, due to traffic problems, which passengers experienced in making trains on time at Heuston. Signalling at Heuston and Pearse was modified and modernised to enable the new arrangements to work efficiently. Belfast, Sligo and south-eastern services would operate from Connolly.

New coaches were arriving from British Rail Engineering Ltd (BREL). The two previous major coach investments by CIÉ were the Cravens over the period 1963–1967 and the Park Royals of 1953–1956 which were now in service for twenty years. The BREL coaches were variously known as Mark 2's and as ACs. The Mark 2 appellation arose from the fact that within the British Rail system they conformed to the Mark 2D design. Explanation of AC as a description was more straightforward: the new stock was air conditioned. The Mark 2's, as we will call them, marked a really major shift in passenger comfort. Unlike the previous fleets of Park Royals and Cravens they were imported wholly built from the UK, though the authoritative *Irish Railways Traction and Travel*, published in the UK, records 'final minor finishing work by CIÉ at Inchicore Works, Dublin'. The new stock, some 71 coaches in all including restaurant cars, a new presidential coach and brake generator vans, were delivered between late 1972 and early 1973. The generally matter of fact reporting of rail events in the *IRRS Journal* edged towards the euphoric in its somewhat quaint descriptions and comment on aspects of the new stock which would now be considered commonplace.

> As the months pass, our members will have opportunities of sampling the up-to-date brand of travel which the new carriages will be providing . . . The Board's literature properly placed passenger comfort in the forefront of what was to be said. From the well-printed 'hand-outs' we find that one of the chief features of the carriages is the air-conditioning. Air within the vehicles is maintained fresh and controlled to the temperature of around 70 °F, and this in both winter and summer; the air is, of course, filtered constantly, and circulated on a 4 minute circuit. Seating is 'ergonomically' designed (whatever that may mean) in order that the traveller may rest while seated and not suffer the fatigue induced by ill-shaped seating. Lighting is fluorescent throughout, the lamps being set at a level and intensity to allow

> comfort in reading. Insulation against sound is a part of the construction, and travel in the new carriages is certainly remarkably quiet. A point worth mention is that the windows are comparatively shallow in depth, and this, while it may be objected to from the point of view of outside appearance, has the virtue of keeping the seated passenger's eyes from 'following' the rapidly passing track and ground, and thus saves that eye strain which too often besets us as we sit and gaze outwards. (ibid.)

The journal's report continues in language and detail similar to that of motoring correspondents describing new car models.

> In each train set is included an Electric Generator Van, containing two Diesel engines which drive generators to give power for lighting, heating, cooking and air-conditioning: the current is a.c. at 380–220 volts, and goes direct to the heating units in the train. The kitchen facilities in the kitchen vehicles are all-electric, and the equipment includes practically all that is usual in, say, a hotel kitchen: there are a refrigerator, toasters, grillers, fryers, and a cooker of large size, with power-points for use with extra items as required. The kitchens of all the cars were fitted out at Inchicore, and stainless steel is used freely in the interior fitment. The trains are designed for at-your-seat service of meals; the passenger will order, and have his order brought to him where he sits. There is also bar service. Much of the comfort of the new trains is derived from use of bogies of the well-tested B4 type in the passenger-carrying vehicles. For the generator vans the B5 is fitted, this having heavier springing. Friction dampers are installed, and the control of rolling tendencies at speed seems to be good. (ibid.)

The new coaches were 9 feet wide compared to 10 feet 6 inches previously in use by CIÉ. They accommodated 64 passengers in standard class or 42 in first class which for a while was renamed 'super standard'. The *IRRS Journal* had much more to say before concluding:

> The placing of these vehicles in service by CIÉ is a tremendous advance . . . This improved stock should do a lot to dispel that strangely-persistent notion that rail travel is slow, uncomfortable, and unkempt, not to say old-fashioned in its general aspect. In another matter, too, the fresh introductions will release very serviceable coaches for the increasing suburban traffic, which is at present forced to supply its customers with carriages which have, in many cases, outstayed their welcome. (ibid.)

The arrival of the new coaches enabled CIÉ to begin its Supertrain promotion in December 1972 which was then boosted by implementing the Railplan 80 concept of faster and more frequent trains in its Summer 1973 timetable. The proposal to increase speeds of necessity involved shorter and hence lighter configurations so that the power to weight ratio of trains could be substantially improved. At that time mainline passenger services were operated by heavy train sets, which resulted in a 'present maximum power to weight ratio of 4.5 h.p./ton'. Consequently the highest average speeds on mainline passenger trains were as low as 31 mph. on Dublin/Rosslare and 58 mph. on Dublin/Cork. The Railplan 80 proposal was to increase the maximum power to weight ratio to 6.8, giving improved running times 'within the present constraints of track and signalling'. These 'present constraints' would prove to be very restrictive and it would be well into the 1980s before they could be adequately resolved. Railplan 80 also envisaged that a major reduction could be achieved in turnround time of train sets at rail termini due to adoption of the push/pull principle.

> Push/pull can be operated with a single locomotive at one end of the train and a driving compartment at the other end, remotely controlling the vehicle. However in order to achieve the required performance, sufficient horsepower for traction purposes must be provided and this necessitates the use of two locomotives of the type in our existing fleet. The use of locomotives in multiple working (two locomotives) at the leading end of the train while providing the required traction performance will not permit of fast turnround. (Railplan 80)

Accordingly, the CIÉ proposal was to operate its mainline passenger services with two locomotives, one at each end of the train set, until new locomotives could be acquired. Surprisingly, as we have said, Railplan 80 makes no mention of new locomotives. In the event, within two years of the document's completion the board authorised the purchase of new locomotives, more powerful than any in the existing fleet.

The Summer 1973 timetable took a substantial step towards the introduction of uniform size passenger trains and higher daily frequencies. Railplan 80 had proposed increasing Cork/Dublin services from 6 to 7, Belfast/Dublin from 4 to 6, while Limerick, Galway and Rosslare services to Dublin could move up from 3 to 5 per day. The *IRRS Journal* (June 1973), in an article by D. Murray and B. Carse, was most impressed.

> From 2 April the system is able to boast of a most remarkable service on all the main lines, there being a frequency of trains hitherto unknown on all the routes from the capital. It is now possible to travel between Dublin and Rosslare, Waterford, Cork, Tralee, Limerick, Galway, Westport, Sligo, and Belfast and return, in a single day. The

evening services to most provincial centres outside Dublin are now duplicated, and it would even seem to be approaching a time when there will be an every-hour service available between Dublin and Cork.

The same issue of the *Journal* carried another article in which D. Murray comprehensively reviewed CIÉ's services on its mainline routes over the entire twenty years since 1953, noting all significant variations in frequencies and in *en route* stops. That article is a rich lode for the railway enthusiast to mine, but we can afford only to note that 1973 was a benchmark year for modernisation of coaching stock and for an attempt to improve rail frequencies and running times all under the Supertrain promotion.

The other important development on the rail side of CIÉ's operations in 1973 was concerned with planning for commuter services. With some exceptions, a consensus had developed that suburban rail services needed development if Dublin's traffic problems were to be kept within tolerable bounds. McKinsey said no more than that additional investment was required to upgrade the service. Remarks in the *IRRS Journal* about carriages on these services having 'outstayed their welcome' made the point that such investment was overdue. The introduction of the new Mark 2 coaches to mainline service enabled CIÉ to move some stock to the commuter services, but these were the already 20-year-old Park Royals. In addition, some early 1950s railcars had their engines removed and were adapted for use on the suburban push/pull train sets. The Foras Forbartha Dublin Transportation Study (DTS) had been completed and published in early 1973. Government announced early in 1974 that the recommendations of this report were 'accepted in principle' whatever that would prove to mean. With regard to the railways, the DTS recommended that services on the existing suburban rail links should be improved by increasing peak hour capacity and proposed such other measures as the provision of parking at stations and of feeder buses. It also recommended that suburban passenger services should be provided on the Galway and Cork lines 'as far as Blanchardstown and Clondalkin to provide several stops at each of these major development centres'. This latter possibility and a preliminary study on electrification of commuter services had already been researched for CIÉ by the Dublin-based consultants, De Leuw, Chadwick and Ó hEocha, in a report completed in February 1971.

As a follow through to the DTS and to focus public thinking on possibilities for commuter rail, CIÉ commissioned a new study in October 1973 to determine the feasibility of a Rapid Rail Transport System for Dublin which could include some underground sections. This was announced at a 'breakfast news conference' (an interesting innovation) on

12 December 1973. In no way was it a solo run by CIÉ. A technical consultative committee, drawn from the Department of Local Government, Dublin Corporation, An Foras Forbartha, and CIÉ, was constituted to advise on technical aspects of the work. John Byrne announced the names of the high-powered consultants who were to complete their work within twelve months. The main consultants were Alan M. Voorhees and Associates, London, whose proposed rapid transit system for Newcastle upon Tyne was under construction at the time. Messrs Mott, Hay & Anderson, who were advising on the Channel Tunnel project, would assist Voorhees. The Irish firm of De Leuw, Chadwick & Ó hEocha would act as advisory consultants (*Nuacht CIÉ*, Nollaig 1973).

The last annual report of T. P. Hogan's period published in late 1973 would record that CIÉ carried more passengers than in any previous year. 'On the railways it carried 12 million passengers an increase of 8% over last year (1971/72) which itself was 6.5% more than in the previous year.' The report also recorded the continuing recovery of Dublin suburban train services '. . . showing a growth of 7.5% on the previous year. New push/pull type trains were introduced more suitable for suburban working although still far from ideal.' Sidney Parade station had been reopened in the Sandymount area, after many years of closure, and on the northern side a new station was being built at Bayside, near Sutton. Bayside was opened in 1974 and in 1975 Booterstown was reopened after being closed for fifteen years. The number of cross-city train services 'introduced for the morning and evening commuter peaks in the Dublin area' were increased from 43 to 74 per day according to the 1973/74 Report and a further 8 push/pull train sets were added to the service. Automatic ticket checking was introduced at a number of commuter stations.

Some pointers as to the future problems can be noted in the 1973/74 Report:

> Dublin bus services in spite of deteriorating traffic conditions, had an increase in passenger carryings [+ 4.5%]. The [traffic] position was further aggravated this year by the exceptional incidence of bomb scares and the growth in the number of major road works. Vandalism on late night buses assumed serious proportions. Police protection in patrolling 'black spots' had to be sought on a number of occasions.
> . . . The Northern Ireland political situation affected CIÉ's tour operations as it did Irish tourism in general. A cutback in operation costs enabled the deficit [tours and private hire] to be held at £185,000 —marginally lower than the previous year's deficit . . .
> (Annual Report, 1973/74)

The report noted the delay in getting approval for fare increases—the May

1972 application still rested with the NPC—but made no argument or complaint about the delay or about the various NPC papers which we have already discussed. These papers had been published well before the CIÉ report itself was circulated, but T. P. Hogan did not think it appropriate to make public comment on such an issue in his final annual report.

In December 1973 the term of office of T. P. Hogan expired and Minister Peter Barry appointed his fellow Corkman, Liam St John Devlin (later Dr St J. Devlin) to be the new Chairman of CIÉ. Devlin would have a rather different approach to the use of annual reports as a vehicle for putting his point of view on the record. Before his time the annual report contained no chairman's statement and little overall review of transport policy issues. St J. Devlin's reports would have much to say about these matters.

It was rather unusual to move a person from the chairmanship of one state company to a similar appointment in another state company. But that is what happened in the case of Liam St J. Devlin who had been Chairman of the B + I Board since 1965. He had also been a director of Irish Shipping since 1959. A chemistry and physics graduate of University College Cork, his involvement with transport really began when as managing director of Melina Ltd, an industrial chemicals firm specialising in perfumes, he became a member of the Cork Harbour Board. While Chairman of the B + I Line, he was appointed Chairman of the Public Services Organisation Review Group whose report on the structure of the whole range of public administration came later to be known as the Devlin Report. Then when a Review Body on Higher Remuneration in the Public Sector was set up, Devlin also chaired that body which caused considerable controversy with its recommended rating of various public sector jobs on a remuneration scale based on various criteria of significance and overall responsibility.

He had also been involved in Cork regional tourism. Thus when appointed at the age of 49 to the chairmanship of CIÉ he had considerable experience at senior level in the apparatus of state administration, public and private enterprise. He assumed office on 1 January 1974 as a part-time Chairman, who was expected to apply 50 per cent of his time to his responsibilities in CIÉ. At the same stage Devlin relinquished his other public service appointments apart from the Pay Review Group and a Top Appointments Committee. However, chairmanship at various times of the publicly quoted Jones Group and of the Rohan Group in the engineering and construction sector as well as membership of the Board of Allied Irish Banks (later called the AIB Group) and membership of the Governing Body of UCC, meant that he had considerable responsibilities outside CIÉ. He would prove to be a very active chairman of CIÉ and *inter alia* he made a point of visiting every significant staff location at least once a year, with the schedule for these visits occasionally published in *Nuacht CIÉ*. When his first five-year term of office expired on 31 December 1978, his contract for a second five-year term was on the basis of his spending 75 per cent of his time with the organisation.

When he became Chairman in 1974 he believed that CIÉ needed to rethink its role as the national transport operator and, more importantly, that an entirely new sense of urgency was needed in tackling its operational problems. His style was one of straight talking and quickly moving to whatever point he considered important. A result was that some people sensed that their own hard work and experience was being treated with less consideration than they themselves thought it merited. Devlin saw a company whose deficit would reach £11.6 million (before state subvention) in the year of his appointment—virtually four times the figure laid down five years earlier. In the following year (1975) it would increase to over £28 million compared to the prospect of a £19 million deficit which had so shocked the new government in February 1973 (see page 240). No matter how strongly and logically one might argue that identifiable external factors had caused this deterioration, no incoming chairman with a dynamic reputation to uphold could buy into such arguments. None the less, he would soon remark on 'the effect of rapid inflation on an activity which is highly labour intensive as well as being highly capital intensive. In such a predicament money values appear to ridicule annual comparison.' (Annual Report, 1973/74) Certain points struck him forcibly, especially that CIÉ was overmanned. While the twelve-month-old Railplan 80 envisaged a reduction of 1,800 in railway staff over seven years, Devlin's view was that much more severe and faster reductions should and could be achieved. He publicly committed himself to a total system of one-person bus operation, but while this goal would not be realised during Devlin's tenure of office, the staff reduction achieved by the organisation during that ten-year period would reach an impressive total of 5,000.

Two incidents relating to his initial experiences in CIÉ may be told before returning to the main transport story. John Byrne, General Manager, called his new chairman even before the date on which Devlin would formally take up his appointment, to warn him that a serious situation was developing with the OIÉ hotels. This related principally to the Russell Court Hotel in Belfast, to which we will return later. Byrne invited Devlin to appraise himself of the background. 'No', said the new chairman, in words which in effect said that 'There are many more vital matters to look at first. I will come to the hotels in due course.' The second incident also had a hotel aspect to it. St J. Devlin, in a note to the author clarifying a reported attitude of his, recorded that

> CIÉ had a practice of holding an internal management conference each year in one of the OIE Hotels. When I attended the first of these conferences, I was disconcerted by the time wasted discussing

unrealistic goals, when the problem of fundamental operations needed to be addressed. In my frustration I expressed strong views on the lack of urgency in tackling the real issues which appeared to me to be accountable management, re-organisation of operational processes and over manning. I was informed subsequently by the General Manager that I was insensitive and that the other managers were upset. I was neither contrite nor displeased. That was the last of these 'club' weekends. (Letter to author, 31 March 1994)

The 'unrealistic goals' concerned medium and long-term strategies with which the new chairman felt very uncomfortable when, as emerges later, he found that CIÉ would formally set itself budgets which month after month were seldom achieved.

The government had been considering CIÉ's plans to modernise the railway, in the light of McKinsey's (1971) recommendations and its own Railplan 80 (1972). On 14 March 1974 Peter Barry, Minister for Transport and Power, announced the government's decision which amounted to 'approval in principle for a £23 million programme'. The *Irish Press* commented that this approval was based on the evidence of various reports that the 'deficits which the network has incurred could only be cut down by major changes in operational methods and technology'. *The Irish Times* reported Mr Barry as saying that government had decided that the railway system should be preserved 'subject to further concentration and reorganisation' in accordance with the general concepts outlined in the McKinsey Report as developed by the further studies by CIÉ. The approval in principle applied to capital investment projects without which CIÉ's deficits would actually deteriorate.

> If the present system remains unchanged, the railways deficit would amount to over £30 m. in 1981 compared with the estimated £19.2 m. in 1972/74 ... The McKinsey Report and the CIÉ studies show that the present rail freight network is too comprehensive serving a large number of small under-utilised stations. The need for rationalisation and modernisation of rail freight traffic is therefore acute in order to avoid a continual erosion of freight traffic, with consequential deterioration in financial results and employment prospects. CIÉ proposes the replacement of the traditional slow mixed goods trains by fast block trains which would serve a smaller number of more highly productive locations equipped with modern handling facilities. CIÉ also propose using fast specialised trains operating on fixed schedules for sundries traffic. (*The Irish Times*, 15 March 1974)

The Irish Times report commented that 'At the time of its publication the

McKinsey report was criticised by people living in areas where it recommended that either stations or branch lines be closed or downgraded.' However, 'no mention is made either in the Minister's statement, or in an accompanying CIÉ statement of possible closures under the modernisation plan'. Both the minister and CIÉ were being coy about closures. Clearly the intention of this March 1974 announcement was to be positive and to avoid protests from threatened interests. The 'bad news' could be put on hold for a later occasion.

The Irish Times leader was enthusiastic. Titled 'On The Rails', it reflected a popular view.

> It is good to learn that the Government has decided to embark on a major modernisation of the railway system. They should have decided to do as much a long time ago, thus saving a considerable wastage of time, money and environmental amenities. (ibid.)

The *Irish Press* leader was somewhat ambivalent. Under the heading, 'Modernising CIÉ', it began:

> It would be nearly impossible to visualise this country without Córas Iompair Éireann. In itself this might not be a very good reason for the investment of a further £23 million in the national transport company.

It then reviewed McKinsey, acknowledged the problems of inflation, private transport and restrictions on fare increases as causes of CIÉ deficits and expressed dislike for the 'image of the company as simply a kind of social service'. The article ended in the upbeat admonitory style easily adopted by leader writers.

> We need an efficient and economic public transport service and this has as much to do with the attitude of management and staff as with ton mileage or passenger mileage. The tons of freight and the hundreds of thousands of passengers make up a huge market at the door of Heuston Station, and the new investment of £23 million should be directed towards at least achieving a break-even position in that market. (*Irish Press*, 15 March 1974)

So much publicity was given to the £23 million that a comment is required to put it into context. CIÉ revealed that the normal capital investment programme over the years 1973 to 1978 would amount to £3.8 million per annum. Accordingly, over a five-year period the £23 million plan represented a mere £4 million addition to normal capital expenditure. An extraordinarily good return seemed to be in prospect for this extra investment, i.e. a fall of over £10 million per annum in the projected deficit. Of course, reorganisation of services and labour savings were essential parts of the proposed plan, and to them most of any improvement in performance deserved to be attributed.

Armed by government 'approval in principle', CIÉ became more specific about its intentions. On 10 June 1974 two 'major changes in the handling of parcels traffic' came into effect.

> These were the introduction of Fastrack—an express parcels service channelled mainly through Heuston Station, Dublin—and the centralisation of the standard rail parcels service in a new depot at Connolly Station, Dublin . . . linked by an automated conveyor belt with the Central Sorting Office [Post Office] at Sheriff Street . . .
> (*Nuacht CIÉ*, 14 Meitheamh 1974)

The idea behind Fastrack was that only special parcels paying a premium rate would move on mainline passenger trains. The 'standard' rail parcels service would operate only on dedicated parcels or mail trains from the new depot at Connolly station. In other words, CIÉ was segregating the parcels business into two classes, with a higher standard of service and higher charges being applied to the Fastrack element. It was explained that 'removal of normal parcels traffic from passenger trains facilitates the fast turnover at terminals which is a requirement of the frequent train service offered since April 1973. It also ensures VIP treatment for Fastrack parcels.' (ibid.) A new treatment for standard parcel traffic, also known as 'sundries', in cage pallets was also envisaged and is described later.

In contrast to the agony and furore which occurred with the previous attempts to increase fares, relatively little protest attended further widespread fare increases which were approved by the Fine Gael/Labour coalition in 1974, just twelve months after the previous increase. This time they had received rapid investigation by the NPC which desisted from appealing for a national transport policy or attempting to analyse CIÉ's pricing philosophy. The increases were implemented on Dublin City Services on 15 July and on mainline rail on 22 July. The passenger rail increases approved were approximately 20 per cent.

It was a sign of a change towards public acceptance of the need for higher fares that St J. Devlin would select the period of these increases to present CIÉ's Railway Development Plan to the national and provincial press. This was done in the week ending 10 July 1974 and somehow the capital expenditure of £23 million mentioned by Peter Barry in March had become £27.5 million in July. Once again *The Irish Times* was very positive but under the heading, 'The Right Lines', its leading article warned that 'any enthusiasm or euphoria about the new deal should be tempered by a contemplative look at the essential facts and figures of railway finance' (*The Irish Times*, 11 July 1974). Looking at some facts and figures, it recognised that the railways would always be in deficit.

The Railway Development Plan was communicated to staff at over 300 meetings in the same week as the press conferences were held. The presentations continued to be sensitive on two issues—staff reductions and station closures. Staff would have to be reduced, but the target used by St J. Devlin for railway job losses was the still 1,800 figure first mentioned in Railplan 80. Devlin tread carefully; jobs in CIÉ were highly valued; union co-operation was essential; and he would emphasise a point, less commonplace then than now, that job reductions would increase the security of the remaining jobs. A headline in *The Irish Times* story read, 'All jobs will be safe under new scheme, says chairman', but no doubt *Nuacht CIÉ* reflected the position more accurately.

> The planned reduction will take place over a period of five years. Normal staff turnover will account for most of the job reductions and the major changes will occur in the large centres where the opportunity for staff development is greatest. Special re-training and re-settlement programmes designed for the placement of railway staff in other CIÉ activities and in local industries will cater for any balance. There will be full and continuing consultation with the Trade Unions concerned. (*Nuacht CIÉ*, 26 Iúil 1974)

Devlin drew attention to the current success of the railways in attracting passengers—the loss of 21 million passenger journeys between 1960 and 1970 had been more than recovered by the increases achieved between 1971 and 1973. On the matter of station closures CIÉ was still unspecific. It was pointed out that 45 out of 118 stations generated approximately 3 per cent of passenger train revenue, while 82 of 142 freight depots handled only 10 per cent of freight tonnage. Some 22 'freight locations' were nominated for 'reconstruction and development' and 29 others were nominated for 'major alterations and development'. Clearly a major objective of the steady communications effort in the month of July 1974 was to condition the public to the fact that extensive station closures were in the offing and that in future CIÉ would do much more to improve its finances than simply increase its charges when allowed to do so. Those locations not listed for development could fear the worst, but consultation was promised before final decisions would be made.

Nuacht CIÉ carried a lengthy article by P. J. Darmody, Dublin Area

Manager, explaining the proposals and their background. Initially, Darmody was assigned overall responsibility for implementation of the plan. Earlier comments on Railplan 80 and the Summer 1973 timetable covered much of the Development Plan's proposals for passenger trains. However, specific speed targets were announced in Darmody's article, e.g. on the Dublin/Cork line with the higher power/weight ratio, a maximum running speed of 78 mph. should be achieved, reducing the journey time to 2 hours 30 minutes with two intermediate stops and 7 minutes recovery time. Many years later the two and a half hour Dublin/Cork service would still be in the 'target category'.

With regard to freight, statements by St J. Devlin and Peter Barry had outlined the new thinking, but Darmody's article in *Nuacht CIÉ* deserves quotation for its factual treatment. It shows just how dated the existing practice was.

> The traditional slow mixed goods train, of loose coupled rolling stock, still caters for 75% of the freight business. The maximum permitted speed for these trains is 35 m.p.h.; the average speed is about 27 m.p.h. This factor, combined with frequent stops made by most freight trains at wayside stations to detach and attach wagons, causes under-utilisation of locomotive power, wagons, and track capacity. Shunting and the marshalling of wagons, which are inherent features in traditional freight train operations, increase their running times and give rise to considerable costs.
>
> It is proposed to replace slow mixed goods trains with special block trains made up exclusively of one type of traffic i.e. bulk cement, palletised cement, palletised fertiliser, bulk oil, general containers etc. These trains will consist of special vacuum-braked wagons and will be capable of speeds over 50 m.p.h. Shunting and detaching of wagons en route will be eliminated.
>
> The vast majority of vehicles in the present wagon fleet are general purpose wagons (covered, open or flat wagons), but there are about 600 special vacuum-braked wagons designed to carry particular traffics. . . . The average special wagon carried eight times more tonnage than the average traditional wagon. The proposed wagon fleet which will consist entirely of special wagons purpose-built for each type of traffic . . . will be approximately one-third of its present size and will be more fully utilised.
>
> The present freight network is too unwieldy, both in number of routes and the number of locations served. It is proposed that activities and investment will be concentrated into a smaller number of more highly productive locations, which will be equipped with modern mechanical handling facilities.   (ibid., 12 Iúil 1974)

The proposal which emerged was that the number of stations catering for wagonload traffic would be reduced from 139 to a possible 56 and the number of wagons was to be reduced by two-thirds. The ending of loose coupling would remove a traditional sound from the railways—the cacophony of wagons clashing into one another when goods trains slowly decelerated at station after station as they wound their way across the country.

The rail freight traffic which caused most problems was 'sundries', i.e. a conglomeration of packages varying in size, shape, weight and destination. Grouping these 'sundries' by destination, and loading/unloading to and from rail and road vehicles, had made the handling of this traffic the most labour intensive of all CIÉ's activities. The Rail Development Plan proposal was that this 'smalls' freight traffic 'be grouped into cage pallets and transported in fast specialised trains operating on fixed schedules' (ibid.). The cage pallets would be loaded into 60 ft wagons.

Consultation with unions and with commercial interests proceeded apace. John Byrne was reported in *Nuacht CIÉ* on 27 September that 'CIÉ had almost 400 meetings with staff since its plans were announced in July.' The issue of closures or changes in station status was being handled with apparent delicacy.

> We have been handling queries from TD's and local representatives as well as from industry and individuals.
>
> Understandably there has been unease in towns where the local station was not earmarked for development . . . In all cases where we are asked if stations are to be downgraded or closed, we explain that decisions will only be taken after exhaustive investigation and that prior notice will be given to people to enable them to submit any information which they believe may not be in our possession. We also explain that no changes will be made which will prevent the status of a location being upgraded should potential support justify it . . . I should say that no significant changes are proposed in the passenger network at present. However, the freight business must be judged by substantially commercial standards and consequently the proposed freight changes are more fundamental.

The timing of these assurances of consultation with affected interests was somewhat unfortunate. On the day these comments were published in *Nuacht CIÉ*, M. J. Hayes, the Secretary of CIÉ, attached his signature to a long notice for publication in the national press. Headed 'Córas Iompair Éireann, Transport Act 1958', it was one of a series of such legal notices, and to give the flavour of the radical cutback that was planned, it merits quotation. It began as follows:

> Pursuant to Section 19 of the Transport Act, 1958, the Board of Córas Iompair Éireann hereby gives notice as follows:
>
> On and from the 2nd December, 1974
> (i) The railway stations at
>
> | | | | |
> |---|---|---|---|
> | Abbeydorney | Carrigaloe | Dunleer | Malahide |
> | Adare | Carrigtwohill | Gormanston | Patrickswell |
> | Ardfert | Castlebellingham | Howth | Rush and Lusk |
> | Balbriggan | Cóbh Junction | Killeagh | Rushbrooke |
> | Baldoyle and Sutton | Donabate | Laytown | Skerries |
> | Bray | Dun Laoghaire | Lixnaw | Thomastown |
>
> will be closed to sundries and wagon-load traffic;
>
> (ii) the railway stations at Balla, Buttevant, Clara and Fota will be closed to wagon-load traffic;
>
> (iii) the railway stations at Abbeyfeale, Ballingrane, Foynes, Limerick Junction, Newcastle West, will be closed to sundries traffic;
>
> (iv) the railway station at Rathkeale will be closed to sundries traffic and to cattle, sheep and pigs traffic;
>
> (v) the railway stations at Askeaton, Glenmore and Rosslare Strand will be closed to sundries, wagon-load and beet traffic;
>
> (vi) the railway station at Grange will be closed to wagon-load traffic and to cattle, sheep and pigs traffic;
>
> (vii) the railway stations at Collooney and Moate will be closed to sundries and wagon-load traffic and to cattle, sheet and pigs traffic.

The announcement then detailed the substitute arrangements that were being made for the services that were being withdrawn. The list of stations affected may seem to be almost random, but in the east ten stations were affected between Bray and Castlebellingham, and on the north Kerry line, Listowel was the only station left to handle wagonload and sundries traffic. It was the first of six phases of withdrawal of freight facilities from a total of over eighty stations.

At the board meeting (September 1974) where these freight closures were decided on, Devlin took one of his occasional organisational initiatives. Already in the previous March the area management structure had been modified to place 'greater emphasis on planning at central level and on the management of profit and business centres in the areas'. Each area would now have three managers, each responsible for one of the three principal businesses: rail, road passenger and road freight, reporting to the area manager. The September management change was at a much more senior level and involved the creation of an Executive Board:

> consisting of the General Manager and the Heads of Function [which] should be responsible for the formulation, co-ordination and review of policy in the areas of organisation, personnel, development and finance. While the determination of overall company policy would naturally continue to be a matter for the Main Board, the Executive Board would be responsible for monitoring the effectiveness of settled policy for the main functional areas. (Board Minutes, September 1974)

St J. Devlin himself would not be a member of the Executive Board. As emerges later, in fairly quick succession a number of other developments at board provide evidence of a new hand at the tiller.

CIÉ's financial year was changing from April/March to the calendar year, consistent with the change made at that time by the exchequer. The figure of £2.65 million still existed on the statute book as the fixed subvention; each year since 1969 additional moneys had been voted for CIÉ on the Transport and Power estimate and the Public Accounts Committee criticised that practice. Hence in December 1974 the Minister, Peter Barry, introduced the 1974 Transport (No. 2) Bill, the main purpose of which was

> to provide statutory authority for subvention payments to CIÉ amounting to £11.3 million in the nine-month period ending on 31 December, 1974, which are additional to the annual grant of £2.65 million payable to the Board under the Transport Act, 1964 (Section 6) Order, 1969. (*Dáil Debates*, Vol. 276, Col. 664)

During the debate the minister reviewed CIÉ's recent performance and difficulties. The main problems were inflation and government restrictions on CIÉ's proposals for increased fares, even when approved by the NCP; the restriction on fare increases were responsible for the £4.7 million of the additional £11.3 million which was now being sought. The 1973 energy crisis had also contributed to CIÉ's problem through increasing its fuel costs, but incidentally the importance of public transport to the community had been underlined by that crisis which caused serious problems for the private motorist. Peter Barry reviewed the Railway Development Plan and then outlined how 'Under EEC regulations governing State aid to transport undertakings the existing blanket subvention arrangements for CIÉ are no longer appropriate.' Accordingly, the 1974 Bill repealed section 6 of the Transport Act 1964,

> which provided for a fixed annual grant for CIÉ, subject to review at

> five-yearly intervals. Henceforth grants to CIÉ will be paid in accordance with the relevant EEC regulations and provision for these payments will be made in the Estimates for my Department.
>
> (ibid., Col. 667)

He detailed the specific EEC regulations, which since that time have been quoted each year in CIÉ's Annual Reports, as the basis for its annual state subventions. He then enunciated the detailed policy which the Irish Government was proposing to the Commission in relation to future subventions so that they would accord with those regulations (ibid., Cols 668, 669).

The ensuing debate travelled around the normal circuit including labour relations, efficiency, traffic congestion, the railplan, fare levels, and a call from Deputy Fergus O'Brien for a public inquiry into CIÉ. A new suggestion was that CIÉ be split up into separate rail and road companies (Deputy Sylvester Barrett). The minister, responding to the debate, expressed himself as very pleased with the attitude of many deputies towards CIÉ and summarised his own attitude to the organisation.

> It was not a question of just criticising CIÉ and everything they do and of suggesting that they should be made to balance their books and be more efficient. In this debate I detected an appreciation of the value of CIÉ . . . their employees number 20,000. They provide rail, bus and freight services, they are involved in the tourist and in the hotel trades and they have many other activities. When I was in Opposition I said that because the organisation is continually exposed to the public too many people criticise CIÉ. There was an attitude towards the employees that they were putting their hands into our pockets and taking their wages. I never agreed with this view and, since I have come into much closer contact with the company, I disagree even more with it. We should be proud of the fact that CIÉ provide so many services in such an efficient way. (ibid., Cols 1663, 1664)

In summary, Peter Barry in 1974 had approved 'in principle' the Railway Development Plan, authorised additional fare increases, initiated a new subvention system for CIÉ, and expressed a positive public attitude to the organisation. On 9 January 1975 the minister met the board at Heuston. In welcoming the minister, St J. Devlin said that 'they were a relatively new Board'. Four of the seven-member board had been appointed during the previous year. Even in 1958, when Todd Andrews took up office and the GNRB was assimilated into CIÉ, only three board changes occurred.

While many of them were still learning the business, they had given

> thought to what the role of CIÉ should be. They were glad to have this opportunity of hearing the Minister's views. Their problem was one of numbers and, as already outlined in the Rail Development Plan, it was hoped to reduce the number of employees on the railway by wastage. However, it was quite clear that if the deficit was to be contained, it would be necessary to reduce numbers elsewhere as well and this was best achieved by improving the earnings of the main body of staff through the negotiation of productivity deals based on reduced numbers. (Board Minutes, 9 January 1975)

Thus did Devlin signal that the 1,800 staff reduction target mentioned in Railplan 80 might be only the tip of the iceberg of job reductions. Another aspect of Devlin's approach which would re-emerge in annual reports is then minuted as he continued his welcoming of the minister:

> The Chairman said that there appeared to be a role for private bus operators and that the provincial road passenger services of CIÉ should be designed to complement the services provided by these operators rather than to eliminate the private sector by aiming for a monopoly ... (ibid.)

That was a brave sounding comment whatever it would mean in practice. And as we see below, it would be reflected in the 'corporate aim' set for the road passenger division. Continuing, St J. Devlin said

> ... that there did not seem to be any obligation on CIÉ to operate road freight services and under EEC Regulations these could not be supported by subvention unless the Minister adopted a deliberate policy of imposing public service obligations. (ibid.)

In effect, the view which later would be generally accepted was now emerging that road freight operations by CIÉ had to be profitable if they were to continue. The minister's comments made a number of significant points.

> Two years ago when he first became Minister he had the impression that CIÉ was losing sight of its main task which was to run trains and buses. It had been his opinion that CIÉ should concentrate on these operations and cut back on peripheral activities. Now after two years he had not changed his views significantly. He still felt that it was the responsibility of CIÉ to carry people and goods within the State at the lowest possible cost. In fact, he had wondered whether the Department should be costing practically every journey to isolate and identify the social, environmental and commercial aspect of each

service. Obviously this was not possible with the present staff of the Department but it was an exercise on which CIÉ itself should have information.

In regard to the railway, it was his intention that the railway network should not be cut back further. The present network will be retained and should be run as efficiently and as effectively as possible. In the new Rail Plan which they had submitted to his Department, there was a commitment to improved services and to accelerate transport for the convenience of customers. This was an aspect of operations which he would like to stress . . . (ibid.)

The minister's impression that CIÉ was losing sight of its main task of running trains and buses would have provided wonderful news copy if it got out. The fact of course was that CIÉ activities in tour promotions, possible property development, technical innovations to ease urban traffic congestion, hotel developments, Aerlód, Irish Ferryways and Continental Freight Services (including capital participation in Irish Continental Line) all generated media interest which was disproportionate to the coverage given to the hundreds of train departures and thousands of bus schedules every day. Trains and buses attracted media interest only in times of difficulty. However, Devlin thought that the minister could well be right and he would press for divestment of several 'peripheral activities'. The first to go were the Shannon cruisers which had already sailed for the last time under the CIÉ flag at the time of the minister's visit. The 1973/74 Report recording the decision to withdraw from the cruiser service on the Shannon which had been operating for almost twenty years noted that 'The pioneering role of the Board on this waterway has led to extensive development by private operators.' (Annual Report, 1973/74) It may be noticed in passing that the canals—'a non-trading activity'—still hung out of CIÉ's coat tails and the cost of maintaining them in 1973/74 was £206,000, an increase of £47,000 on 1972/73.

A month after the minister's visit the board adopted a formal statement of personnel policy. It also agreed on a statement of CIÉ's 'corporate aims' —the first time, it appears, such aims were discussed and formally adopted by board. This defining of 'corporate aims' followed a new fashion in management practice, but it was genuinely appropriate that such a new board strive to establish and then to articulate a common view as to what the organisation was attempting to do. The 'aims' had been discussed in draft before the meeting with the minister and at the subsequent meeting they were formally adopted.

Corporate Aims as set out hereunder were confirmed by the Board.
(1) to provide reasonable, efficient and economical transport

services within the capacity of the undertaking's financial and human resources, with a commitment to the railway and road passenger modes;

(2) to develop these modes in accordance with a long-term strategy and to initiate new concepts in the organisation and operation of urban transport services;

(3) in acknowledging the development of private sector public transport services, it is the aim of the Board to co-operate, where feasible, with these services with a view to establishing a transport infrastructure which will facilitate the economic development of Ireland;

(4) to contain the operating deficit on CIÉ transport services within a specified limit;

(5) to secure a progressive improvement in wages and living standards of staff through improved productivity.

(Board Minutes, 6 February 1975)

It is to be expected that the statement of 'corporate aims' for a statutory publicly owned service organisation would contain little that would be revolutionary and it is the change in emphasis relative to previous practice that is of most interest. Thus in the first 'aim' it is said that CIÉ shall provide services *'within the capacity of the undertaking's financial and human resources'* (author's emphasis). This was an attempt to correct a previous view quoted earlier that if in certain circumstances, which were never explained, a choice had to be made between 'service' and 'economic operation', service would win out. A letter from the Department of Transport and Power (27 November 1970 to T. P. Hogan) had challenged the basis of the earlier view. The reference in (3) to private sector public transport was also new and, as we have seen, it had been signalled a month earlier in Devlin's remarks to the minister. In practice, private hauliers and private bus operators (particularly in connection with school transport) had been used more commonly by CIÉ to supplement its own transport capacity than was sometimes appreciated. The emphasis on labour productivity—related to improved conditions for staff (5) —was to be a cornerstone of the era's personnel policy and be important in CIÉ's successful attempts to reduce 'overmanning'. Having recorded its corporate aims, the board attempted to reflect those aims in 'current targets' for business managers. The language of these 'targets' is a good deal less precise than management theorists might desire. They read more like guidelines than targets, but that arises from the nature of the exercise. Targets arise in a specific way mainly in relation to annual budget setting and the language of the minute shifts from the word 'targets' to the more appropriate word 'policies'. Being a serious attempt to define parameters for CIÉ's businesses, they merit quotation.

Specific management policies will vary from time to time to meet the above objectives and the following are recommended strategies:

1. MAINLINE RAILWAY

(a) to maintain a reasonable network which would allow for the present and future movement of people between centres of population and which would provide for the efficient distribution of goods whose transport is suitable to rail;

(b) to aim at a position where the shortfall on railway operation does not exceed the deficit for the year ended 31 March 1974, or some fixed sum at 1975 values, provided that a reasonable rates and fares policy is permitted.

2. URBAN PASSENGER TRANSPORT

(a) to provide comprehensive public transport services for passengers—particularly commuters—in the urban areas;

(b to provide these services in co-operation with the local authorities and in accordance with an agreed subvention if required.

3. PROVINCIAL ROAD PASSENGER

(a) to operate a comprehensive network of road passenger services in co-operation with the railway and other road passenger operators;

(b) to operate provincial road passenger services at a profit.

4. ROAD FREIGHT, TOURS AND INTERNATIONAL FREIGHT

To participate in other businesses if they are cognate with the main business of CIÉ and only to the extent –

(a) that they do not duplicate the activities of other State-sponsored bodies;

(b) that they do not conflict in a major way with the private sector;

(c) that they make profit.   (ibid.)

The financial results criteria in 1 (b) and 2 (b) are worth noting, as is the emphasis on profit—4(c)— in relation to road freight and to 'other business'. In succeeding years road freight would sometimes incur losses, but the profitability target was not one which would be abandoned. The reference to 'other businesses' being required to be profitable again flashed a warning light at what Peter Barry had called 'peripheral activities'.

In what was a remarkable board meeting, Devlin as Chairman then put forward proposals for the reorganisation of management. The ensuing minute is lengthy and discursive about the responsibilities of many management positions. A new position created was that of Director of Transportation 'to co-ordinate the Railway and Area operations'. The appointee would be John F. (Jack) Higgins who would play a vital role in CIÉ's affairs for many years ahead. Another new post created was Assistant General Manager (Railways), Matt Devereux, under whom responsibility for railway maintenance and operations would be integrated. A serious problem of locomotive reliability was arising, the 1973 passenger timetable was causing great difficulties, and the appointment of Devereux to this important post was intended to address these problems. In all, six AGM positions and two positions of Director (Transportation and Administration) were authorised.

Thus the new board at its February 1975 meeting had debated and articulated its corporate aims, its 'targets' for the various functional managers, and had created new management posts. Two short months later the tone of the board meetings changed dramatically to one of crisis containment. Devlin insisted that because of new circumstances, of which he had become aware, the whole focus of the organisation had to shift to improving the immediate cash position. Again the minute is lengthy but some extracts will quickly indicate the Devlin emphasis.

> The Chairman said that he and the General Manager was [sic] concerned that the forecast deficit for the year 1975 was now of the order of £25 m. and it is likely that this sum will be increased. He said that the size of this deficit was a serious matter, as it exceeds the agreed subvention by £8 m. and it was quite clear that the survival of the undertaking in it present form is at risk . . .
>
> What worried him was that there appeared to be no sense of crisis among middle and lower management. In fact, there may be a feeling that these losses are inevitable and that at the end of the day the Government will pay up.
>
> He said that a decision had been taken to suspend recruitment for a period of three months and, if this is to be seen as a credible effort to cope with our problems, then other economies must also be seen to be taking place. If necessary, we have got to start by saving peanuts because we have got to demonstrate an attitude of mind. In addition all levels of management have got to be seen to be devoting their entire attention to day-to-day operations. There is no point, at the present time, in devoting time and energy to medium and long-term planning when the medium and long-term are themselves in doubt.
>
> The new organisation structure which was introduced in February of this year is, he said, a good structure, but like all structures it cannot work without the commitment of the individuals concerned. It was necessary, therefore, for the Board to be seen to demand this commitment. After all, it was their structure—there had been a full discussion on it before it was formally approved.
>
> Continuing, he said that there was no doubt about the present crisis. Month after month the Board met to review the accounts and it had been very frustrating to see the forecast deficit escalating time and again and the Board were unable to do anything to control the matter.
>
> (ibid., 7 April 1975)

There followed a list of specific recommendations, e.g. 'that the management will present to the Board, for consideration at its next meeting, their recommendations on major savings on services and deferred capital expenditure . . . recommendations on a list of executive posts which can be eliminated . . . list of housekeeping savings which can be achieved by tighter supervision, for example heating, lighting, stationery, telephones etc.'. The chairman's proposals also included a virtual embargo on foreign travel. The board endorsed these proposals which did not, as might have been expected, come from the general manager. However the chairman assured the board that the proposals had the general manager's support. Still, strain was inevitable between a new very active part-time chairman and a youngish general manager who had taken up his position only three years earlier under a rather different regime. When appointed, he would have seen himself as chief executive, reporting to a non-executive chairman. While engaged on a part-time basis, Devlin was adopting a more executive role than his predecessor.

Following the meeting the chairman communicated widely to staff on the recruitment embargo and on the other cost-saving measures which had been discussed by the board. Somehow the phrase 'we have got to start by saving peanuts' got into the communications to staff so that this call for immediate belt-tightening came to be known, remembered and sometimes disparaged as the 'peanuts speech'.

If CIÉ felt it was in crisis, the government seemed to feel that the national situation was little better. The January budget had been cast against an expected 20 per cent annual inflation rate, but the mid-February and mid-May figures revealed 23 per cent and 24 per cent inflation. The social partners were renegotiating a national pay agreement. As a result, on 26 June the government introduced a raft of measures to discourage further increases in public service pay and to reduce the Consumer Price Index as a deliberate 'braking tactic' on national pay escalation. Richie Ryan's speech, as Minister for Finance, explained the government's tactics and how they would affect CIÉ among others.

> If inflation is to be defeated, any attack on it must comprise two related elements: first, steps to break the 'inflationary mentality'—in other words, measures to convince people that there is nothing inevitable about the continued rise in prices—and second, the more specific measures which will ensure a gradual winding-down of the inflationary spiral.
>
> The Government have therefore decided to increase the subsidy to CIÉ in order to reduce fares to their level before 12th May last; this will mean that fares can be reduced by an average of 25 per cent. The

> amount of the reduction in any particular fare will, of course, depend on the amount by which it was increased in May.
>
> (*Dáil Debates*, Vol. 282, Col. 1954)

The Fine Gael/Labour government, which had approved CIÉ price increases in 1973 shortly after coming into office and then delayed but approved further increases in 1974 and in 1975, now did a perfect U-turn, at least with regard to the suburban rail and bus fare increases which had come into effect in May 1975. The circumstances and the action were both without precedent and thankfully would not be used as a precedent for the future. Other measures introduced on the same day included subsidies to reduce the price of bread, flour, milk, butter and town gas. VAT was removed from electricity, gas, heating fuels, clothing and footwear. CIÉ was assured that it would receive a subsidy to compensate for its loss of revenue and that the subsidy would be paid by way of increased subvention. Therein lay a problem because the size of the subvention was the measure by which CIÉ's efficiency was commonly judged.

CIÉ was struggling with its retrenchment measures, but at its 3 July meeting something unexpected occurred.

> Before proceeding to the proposed economy measures which was the next item on the agenda, the General Manager submitted a statement incorporating his resignation. In the statement reference was made to the low morale of officers and managers and there was criticism of a dictatorial style of management which was seen as arbitrary.
>
> (Board Minutes, 3 July 1975)

The chairman was recorded as disagreeing with Mr Byrne's view on these matters. It is not the purpose of this book to explore the stresses and strains, or what would sometimes be called the 'internal politics' of the CIÉ organisation. The reader knows that few human organisations, business, educational, political or religious, are exempt from internal rivalry, power play and clashes about role and style. Evidence exists that there was some such friction earlier in the CIÉ story, for example, between railwaymen of the traditional school and newer management brought in by Todd Andrews. In the early fifties *The Irish Times* had even published a leading article about the appointment of Dan Herlihy over the long-established railwayman, P. T. Sommerville-Large. Similarly, there was conflict connected with some of Frank Lemass's moves in the late sixties and his handling of an A. D. Little report on management organisation—a report which was jointly commissioned by CIÉ and the then Minister, Erskine Childers. Such matters are not explored in our story; it is the progress of the organisation as a whole rather than the fortunes of individual members of management that concern us.

John Byrne's resignation at the early age of 39, after being in CIÉ for fourteen years including three years as General Manager, was a rather more public matter. The board at its meeting on 3 July 1975 asked Mr Byrne to 'reconsider his decision' which he 'was not prepared to do'. They discussed the situation, adjourned the meeting, and resumed some days later when it was 'agreed to accept the resignation'. The board and John Byrne issued a 'joint statement' which said:

> The Board while regretting Mr Byrne's decision, appreciates the personal reasons involved and thanks Mr Byrne for his enthusiastic management and his large contribution to CIÉ.

An 'explanation' for his decision was given by John Byrne to *Nuacht CIÉ* and is interesting, not for any credible gloss it throws on the real reasons for his resignation, but as an indicator of the bullish tone about Ireland's economic progress which was acceptable in the mid-seventies. Seriously inflationary though the period was, Ireland had joined the EEC and Byrne referred 'to our newly discovered body of oil and mineral resources with their attendant industries, and an accelerating agricultural expansion' as the background to his reasons for leaving CIÉ. For whatever reason, Byrne was turning his back on the Rail Development Plan, the Dublin Rapid Rail studies, the Transportation Centre, and on a bus-building project which will be discussed in a later chapter, where the principal focus shifts off the railway story on to urban transport. John Byrne's involvement in that bus story (Van Hool McArdle) would continue after his resignation.

John F. Higgins, who had held the title of Director of Transportation since March 1975, was appointed General Manager on 5 December. The position had been publicly advertised in Ireland and abroad. Regarding that public advertisement, at least some things had changed since CIÉ under Todd Andrews in the late fifties had advertised abroad as well as at home for a chief financial officer. That advertisement had been regarded as casting a slur on the accountancy profession in Ireland. An *Irish Independent* leading article described the advertisement as an inexplicable mistake and asked that it be withdrawn. Jack Higgins, a graduate engineer (UCD), had done postgraduate training with Metropolitan Vickers and had been with CIÉ for twenty-one years. He had been one of the first Area Managers (Limerick) and Manager of Dublin City Services for eight years (1964–1972) before becoming Director of Operations, the post he held before his appointment as Director of Transportation. He would prove to be a forceful long-term General Manager with a leaning towards technical and engineering innovation.

Looking back on the 'crisis year' of 1975, Devlin in a closely written Chairman's review (Annual Report, 1975) summarised many of the events we have noted. Some extracts may be quoted.

> It was a difficult year; the deficit amounted to £28.1 m., there was an embargo on recruitment, a definitive retrenchment programme was adopted and implemented, some services were attenuated and others were withdrawn. But notwithstanding the forces of recession and inflation, a new dynamism emerged . . . There is an overmanning situation in CIÉ but this arises from the structure of the services, the working methods and systems employed rather than from exceptionally low individual productivity . . . To resolve this problem of rising costs and falling revenue it is necessary to design services, which will stimulate growth in the volume of freight and in passenger numbers, which will reduce manning and costs, and which will increase basic wages and stabilise employment. These aims are not incompatible but they call for new ways of doing things, more enthusiasm and commitment from the staff and better management . . . The Rail Development Plan was reviewed and subsequently modified.

Passing from the Chairman's review, the 1975 Annual Report gave some indication of the results of the cost-cutting campaigns launched mid-year. Staff numbers were reduced by 1,171—an achievement without precedent in the history of CIÉ. As well as the reduced timetables, four more branch lines were closed.

Ardee–Dromin	Loughrea–Attymon Junction
Collooney–Claremorris	Listowel–Ballingrane

All four branch lines had carried freight, but Loughrea had also carried passengers, and an interesting aspect of the decision concerning a 'substitute' bus service will receive comment when we turn to road passenger matters. During 1975 freight services had been withdrawn from '39 smaller stations in accordance with the Rail Development Plan'. More significantly, in terms of the overall history of the railway in Ireland, 'the conveyance of livestock by rail was discontinued'—the carriage of livestock had been decontrolled by the 1972 Road Transport Act. The disappearance of livestock from the railways had been coming for a long time. Livestock movements by rail had fallen from 700,000 in 1957 to 350,000 in 1967 and to 116,000 in 1972/73, after which figures were not separately published. Clearly this traffic was quite inconsistent with the new thinking on rail operations, i.e. block trains, regular schedules and specialised containers. Protests were few and two references in the Dáil were 'matter of fact' and uncontentious.

The high frequency rail timetable introduced with much fanfare in April 1973 proved to be too ambitious. 'After a year's operation it was difficult to maintain schedules and punctuality . . . because of poor punctuality and unreliability of stock the timetable was revised in December 1974.' (St J. Devlin to press conference, 31 January 1977) It would be further revised in April 1975 and 'attenuated' in November 1975. The explanation offered by Devlin included 'operational difficulties . . . because too much was expected of non-AC equipment [i.e. the older passenger coaches] and organisationally there were separate management structures for maintenance and for operation'. As shown above, the board's management reorganisation in February 1975 sought to resolve the second of those two problems and as a result, claimed Devlin in January 1977, 'the conflict between maintenance capacity and operational demand has since been more easily resolved'. The IRRS was more specific in its explanations for the hauling back of the 1973 timetable.

> Between the summer of 1973 and January 1975, however, there occurred a series of mishaps—accidents, fires, and malicious damage —resulting in the loss to service of some 16 locomotives. In addition, there was a period of industrial action by the maintenance staff at Inchicore Works, in the form of a 'work to rule', which had the effect of severely restricting the overhauls of rolling stock in the latter half of 1974. Thus, the management of CIÉ was faced with the alternatives, of endeavouring to maintain the existing timetable, although the trains therein had become unpunctual and unreliable; or of introducing a new timetable which, while not as restrictive as was that of pre-1973, would involve a considerable reduction in services from those available in 1973–4. (*IRRS Journal*, June 1975)

The *Journal* (article by D. Murray) was positive in its comments on the new timetable despite the cutbacks. 'The service which has now been introduced, while the trains are less frequent, and not so fast, does make an adequate provision of trains to and from all main centres.' (ibid.) An interesting detail was that an additional Limerick–Ennis service was introduced. In effect, a commuter service was beginning to be developed between Limerick and Ennis while the rest of the line from Ennis north through Connacht to Claremorris on the Dublin/Sligo line was destined for closure.

Adverse public reactions to the poor punctuality and to low capacity trains in the high frequency 1973 timetable was another reason for pulling back in December 1974. The public did not easily adjust to the fact that if shorter trains were operating more frequently they might not be able to get a seat on a train at 1800 hours and have to travel at 1700 hours or at 1930, say. The reservations system that can precisely tailor demand to available capacity in the airline industry was a sophistication that the railways could not afford, nor would its public tolerate. The CIÉ statement about revising the 1973 timetable did not say that insufficient serviceable locomotives were causing a problem, but there was a strong public impression that this was the case. The *Sunday World* suggested that cracked wheels on locomotives was the cause of CIÉ's reliability problems more so than damage caused by the Northern Ireland 'Troubles'. As noted already, new locomotives had not been part of Railplan 80 or of the Railway Development Plan, but they were on their way. The public presentation on the latter plan focused mostly on freight handling and freight system rationalisation, but the acute reader might have noted a single reference in the final sentence of *The Irish Times* report on the July 1974 press conference which quoted John Byrne as saying that new more powerful locomotives were going to be acquired.

The £23 million capital programme 'approved in principle' by Peter Barry was not broken down in detail, but it does not appear to have included a specific provision for new locomotives. For apparently 'political' reasons *vis-à-vis* the Departments of Transport and Power and of Finance, purchase of the locomotives was being pursued on a separate track. In any event CIÉ had come to recognise that it was short of adequately powered reliable locomotives and in September 1974 the board received a formal review of the organisation's locomotive stock in relation to its requirements. This submission traced various developments—reduced availability and increased demand for reliable locomotives—since the last purchase in 1966. The most powerful locomotives in the CIÉ stock were 1325 h.p. 'transplants', i.e. 1955/57 Metropolitan Vickers locomotives re-engined with General Motors 1325 h.p. power plants. The 'transplants' still relied substantially on their 20-year-old electrics and transmissions and did not match the 1960–1966 General Motors locomotives in terms of reliability. The submission concluded that CIÉ's needs could best be met by the acquisition of 18 diesel electric engines of 2250 h.p. each. The board gave authority to management to negotiate with General Motors for the acquisition of such diesel electric locomotives.

The question of approval by or agreement with the Department of Finance about these engines costing £3.6 million was not resolved at the time they were ordered in January 1976. As a result, board agreed that the arrival of the new 2450 h.p. locomotives in September 1976 should be given a 'low profile'. However, on the morning of their arrival, the board noted that this intention was being frustrated by stevedores in Dublin Port attracting publicity to the arrival of such a large cargo and its method of handling. The new locomotives (O71's) arrived on 2 September 1976. Their arrival created a transportation story of its own.

> For shipping to Ireland the locomotives were loaded on barges in Chicago, and towed for 800 miles down the Illinois and Mississippi rivers to New Orleans. The barges were then loaded aboard the 39,000-ton *Tillie Lykes* which brought them to Dublin.
>
> (*Nuacht CIÉ*, D. Fómhair 1976)

The *Tillie Lykes* was the largest ship by that time to discharge its cargo at Dublin and exceeded the capacity of any existing berth in the port. Scotsman's Bay, off Dún Laoghaire, provided an adequate anchorage for the unloading of the barges which were then towed into Dublin Port where the locomotives were hoisted from barge to quay at North Wall extension. The unloading at Scotsman's Bay was delayed by bad weather and *The Irish Times* and *Irish Press* carried overhead photographs of the *Tillie Lykes* as it lay at anchor. The *IRRS Journal* had an intriguing information snippet on the *Tillie Lykes*, reflecting cold war attitudes of the period.

> As the *Tillie Lykes* came to Dublin Bay, she was watched closely by a Romanian trawler, one of a number of which have been operating in the Atlantic near the Irish coast, and there were many speculations about this. Some thought that the trawler's crew feared that some form of up-to-date weapons were finding their way to Europe in the disguise of locomotives for CIÉ; the trawler, when the transfer of the locomotives had begun, went off to the fishing grounds, apparently satisfied that no ulterior practices were in hand by CIÉ or by the USA.
>
> (*IRRS Journal*, October 1976)

The curious way the 071's arrived was sufficient for it to be mentioned in *Ireland—The past twenty years, an illustrated chronology*, published by the IPA in 1986. In addition, two passengers on the Dublin/Malahide commuter train in 1976 recalled to the author in 1994 that they were holding their umbrellas to protect themselves from the leaking roof when they read about the 071's in their morning newspaper. 'At last,' one remarked to the other, 'something is about to happen to the railways.' However, rail commuters would have to wait several more years before services would improve significantly. Devlin's rather low key remarks (below) on the arrival of the powerful new 071's must have had mind, one suspects, of unapproving civil servants in the Department of Finance as much as of staff or the general public.

> The purchase of these new locomotives at this time is in accordance with our normal practice of renewing and updating the fleet. We are replacing locomotives which have been damaged and others which will be retired and, in addition, we are providing for an increase in

services. . . . It should be evident to all that the acquisition of these locomotives reflects the commitment of the Board to the railway operation and its development. (*Nuacht CIÉ*, D. Fómhair 1976)

A digression from railways to a spectacular collapse of a canal may be allowed for a moment. The issue of *Nuacht CIÉ* which reported Devlin's low key comments on the new GM locomotives also reported that

> The Grand Canal, closed to navigation between the eighth and ninth locks at Clondalkin for part of August and September, was reopened to navigation towards the end of last month. The section was closed following the collapse of the canal bed into a Dublin County Council sewer tunnel which was being excavated under the canal.
>
> The collapse occurred on 1 August as workmen were jacking pipes under the canal bank. Within a few hours the level between the two locks had completely drained into the sewer tunnel and the nearby Camac river. Several million gallons of water escaped into the tunnel before the level was completely reduced. As a result, the supply of water to the Dublin Corporation filterbeds at Gallinstown was interrupted. Water from the canal at this point is supplied to the nearby industrial estate and to the Guinness brewery. (ibid.)

The 071's did not immediately enter service. Sadly it was to take eight months to reach agreement with the trade unions for their operation. Eventually they played an important role in the Summer 1977 timetable. 'The enhanced power to weight ratio . . . will enable us to operate faster journey times on all of the radial routes', promised St J. Devlin in January 1977 when he announced

> increased frequencies on certain lines, earlier arrivals at principal termini, earlier departures and a more reliable service. The accelerated services and earlier arrivals will be of benefit for business travel and day trip travel. For example the first train from Cork will arrive in Dublin at 10:30 hours. There will be reductions of 15 to 30 minutes in journey times on other services, for example Heuston–Tralee, 30 minutes saving; Heuston–Galway, 20 minutes saving; Heuston–Westport, 20–25 minutes saving.
> (Press statement, 31 January 1977)

The intention was largely to reintroduce the benefits, though modified, of the 1973 timetable. However, the fastest Dublin/Cork trains in the 1977 timetable would have a scheduled running time of 2 hrs 45 m—not the 2 hrs 30 m targeted since 1972. The new locomotives were only one of the changes to rolling stock since 1973. The older coaches bought by CIÉ (Park Royals and Cravens) used to have internal power supplied by generators located under floor which were belt driven off the axles of the coaches in motion. These individual generators, expensive and difficult to maintain, were abandoned and now train sets had full electric requirements supplied from a central generator van in each train. More importantly, major railway improvements in infrastructure were under way. The permanent way itself, signalling and related communications systems were about to be transformed.

THE DECEMBER 1975 issue of *Nuacht CIÉ* carried suitable Christmas messages to staff from St J. Devlin and the new general manager. No one was to know that on New Year's Eve CIÉ would suffer the second fatal rail accident of its thirty-year existence. The first of these accidents had occurred a year earlier in October 1974 and the *IRRS Journal* in February 1975 described that extraordinary event in which a runaway train and two other trains were involved.

> A serious and unfortunate accident occurred on the morning of Monday 21 October 1974, with two fatalities, the first instance of fatal accident to fare paying passengers since the formation of CIÉ—and, in fact, since before the amalgamation of 1925 which formed the GSR . . . The push-pull train from Pearse to Howth Junction stopped on its way at East Wall Junction, and the driver and guard alighted to investigate a suspected mechanical trouble. The matter seen to, the guard rejoined his train and gave the bell-signal for a re-start; but although the driver had not got back into his cab, the train moved off and was soon making high speed. (*IRRS Journal*, February 1975)

A railcar set was operating empty to Skerries on the same line and it was decided that it should not halt at Skerries, but continue to Drogheda, near where it was hoped to derail the runaway train. However, the runaway train was travelling so fast that it overtook the railcar set near Gormanston. The relative speeds of the two trains were such that the collision was severe, causing some derailment. At the time, the 06.50 Dundalk–Bray train was standing at Gormanston station. As the collided trains entered Gormanston station, a derailed car struck the platform edge and rebounded into the side of the stationary train, heavily damaging almost all of its vehicles. The passengers killed were in the stationary Dundalk–Bray train. No passengers were aboard either of the other trains.

The second accident, at the end of 1975, was caused by another unusual event, damage by road traffic to a railway bridge as a passenger train approached.

Five people lost their lives and 22 were injured on New Year's Eve when the 08.05 Rosslare/Dublin train was derailed at Clough Bridge between Ferns and Gorey. The derailment was caused when a hydraulic excavator on a low loader struck the bridge and dislodged the girders and sleepers some minutes before the train was due. The engine passed over the gap, derailed and capsized. The first two coaches were completely demolished. The Board wishes to extend again its sympathy to the relatives of those who lost their lives as well as those who were injured in this accident. (Annual Report, 1975)

Chapter 16

The Way Ahead

Limerick/Claremorris service withdrawn—Rosslare Harbour/Limerick closure controversy—The Way Ahead—Rail infrastructure developments—Linke, Hoffman and Busch coach-building project—Deterioration of rail rolling stock—State subvention escalating.

Inherent in an emphasis on a radial network in the Railway Development Plan was a suggestion that tangential lines would have to go. On 8 January 1976 the Limerick/Claremorris line was the subject of the following board resolution.

> That having considered the data placed before it by its officers, and being satisfied that the operation on the railway line between Limerick and Claremorris of the service of trains for the carriage of passengers is uneconomic and that there is no prospect of the continued operation of such service becoming economic within a reasonable period, the Board hereby resolves
> (1) to terminate on and from 5th April, 1976 the said service of trains;
> (2) to provide as an alternative for passengers in the affected area (as well as the existing road passenger services) new road passenger services . . . (Board Minutes, 8 January 1976)

Despite a vigorous protest campaign and a Dáil motion proposed by thirteen opposition members, regular passenger rail services ceased on the appointed date. However, regular goods services continued to operate while the seasonal traffic of pilgrims to Knock and beet to Tuam also moved on the line for several years. Board resolutions in similar terms affecting two connecting services in the south of Ireland, which were passed on 2

December 1976, attracted louder and more sustained protests than had happened in the west. The first resolution concerned services between Rosslare Harbour and Waterford for 'the carriage of passengers, of merchandise customarily carried by passenger train, and of beet'. The second resolution similarly concerned passenger trains between Waterford and Limerick, but freight trains between Limerick and Waterford were not affected. No implementation date was fixed in either resolution, both of which included the clause that the 'Board resolves . . . to have regard to those local authorities and other organisations who wish to make submissions in connection with the said services by deferring to its January Meeting the fixing of a date for the termination of the said services.' This unusual clause deferring a decision recognised that closure was not practicable without arrangements being made with other parties.

Within a month, on 10 January 1977, J. A. O'Connor, CIÉ Area Manager, Waterford, was assuring local representatives that 'the Board had decided to defer for a reasonable period of time the fixing of a date for the closure while the conversion of the viaduct [across the River Barrow] to a road toll bridge and the implications of the proposed road network on both sides of the bridge were being considered' (quoted in *Dáil Debates*, 22 February 1977, Vol. 297, Col. 124).

The main thrust of the protests concerned the beet growing industry in south Wexford which produced 40 per cent of the beet processed in Thurles. Figures were produced claiming that the extra cost of moving this traffic by road to Thurles was very substantial. Objectors pointed to the inadequacy of the local road system and the danger to agricultural employment and prosperity if beet growing in Wexford were to cease. Rosslare Harbour interests also added their weight to the protests and expressed fears that despite CIÉ's involvement in the harbour, the removal of the railway link to Waterford and Limerick imperilled its future. Evidence that traffic to and from the harbour was almost exclusively by road would not stifle these concerns. In contrast to the outcry about the Rosslare Harbour/Waterford links, the proposal to cease passenger train services from Waterford to Limerick generated little passion. The *Limerick Leader* seemed to be relatively unconcerned. The *Tipperary Star* and *The People* (Wexford) viewed the situation entirely differently. An article in *The People*—'Has CIÉ gone off the rails?'—conveys the outrage felt in the Wexford area at the threat to 'their' railway and to the beet industry.

> There are times when the national policy adopted by CIÉ would make a normal man break down and weep. Take the railways for example. Never a day passes but some plan is put forward not for encouraging people to make more use of the rail network but rather for some of their stretches to be closed down . . . Sometimes it seems that CIÉ is

trying to commit suicide the slow way—a careful sawing at the veins of the wrist and a complete disregard for the warnings of the general public using it. (*The People*, January 1974)

Comhlucht Siúicre Éireann Teoranta (CSET) associated itself with criticism of CIÉ's proposals and St J. Devlin felt called upon to protest to its chairman about the embarrassment which it was causing to another state company. CSET responded that if CIÉ were losing money on the transport of beet to Thurles, that matter should have been discussed in the first place between the two companies.

Peter Barry was no longer Minister for Transport and Power. After three and a half difficult if productive years in Kildare Street he had moved to the Department of Education in a cabinet reshuffle. His successor in Transport and Power, T. J. Fitzpatrick from Cavan, had just moved into office when the Rosslare Harbour/Waterford row broke. He chose a Fine Gael meeting in Thurles on 19 January 1977 to speak on the matter and, recognising where the real pressure lay, his script, as reported in *The Irish Times*, referred only to the Rosslare Harbour/Waterford line rather than to Limerick/Waterford passenger services.

> The Minister for Transport and Power, Tom Fitzpatrick, last night emphasised that there was no question of closing the rail link between Waterford and Rosslare in the immediate future. Mr Fitzpatrick referred to the concern which he understood was widespread in the areas affected, that CIÉ had taken a decision to close the line and that in fact the closure was imminent and that once and for all he wanted to put the record right. (*The Irish Times*, 19 January)

He explained the 'unusual and indeed exceptional circumstances which must be considered and resolved'. He recognised the importance of the sugar beet industry to Wexford and to Thurles, where he was speaking. His script ended: 'No decision has been taken to close down the Rosslare Harbour/Waterford line and no such decision will be taken until the problems which I have mentioned have been fully considered and a satisfactory alternative method of transport in this case has been provided... Indeed it is obvious that it cannot and will not be closed down for a considerable time if at all.' However, when a public outcry is in full flight, it needs more than such an apparently categorical assurance from the minister to bring it down. Sylvester Barrett, the Fianna Fáil spokesman on Transport and Power, put down a motion concerning the 'Rosslare/Limerick Junction service' which the Dáil debated on 22 February 1977, a month after the minister's Thurles speech.

Sylvester Barrett contrasted the position of the people of 'east Galway,

Three single-deckers (ex GSR) at Cork's Parnell Place bus station in July 1946 (J. G. Gillham)

Standard R Leyland double-decker of the DUTC in 1939

Four generations of CIÉ double deck buses in line-up of preserved vehicles (from left): Leyland RA37, built in 1959; Leyland R788, built in 1957; Leyland R389, built in 1949; and AEC Regent AR438, built in 1948, restored to its original Great Northern Railway livery

Busáras on opening day, 20 October 1953; standard country buses await departure to Ballina, Limerick and Sligo. Three hundred and sixty-one of these Leyland Tiger buses, with bodywork built at Spa Road workshops, entered service between 1949 and 1954. (*The Irish Times*)

Three luxury coaches for CIÉ's coach touring holidays at Busáras in the 1950s (Bord Fáilte)

The new fleet of Leyland RA double-deckers at Donnybrook garage in 1958; bodies built at Spa Road works, Inchicore

Leyland Leopard Expressway coach at Cahir; similar to standard single deck buses of the period but with coach seating; two hundred and thirteen of these vehicles entered service between 1971 and 1974.

Leyland Atlantean buses were bodied by CIÉ at Spa Road, first rear-engined buses in the fleet; six hundred and two were built between 1966 and 1974.

Two hundred and thirty-eight Leyland Atlantean AN68 type double-deckers were bodied by Van Hool McArdle at Spa Road between 1974 and 1979. This example is painted as an advertising bus for Shell oils. A number of these vehicles later had their original Leyland engines replaced by DAF units.

School bus: one of two hundred and thirty specially built Bedford buses for the school transport scheme, introduced in 1967. The school bus fleet eventually grew to over eight hundred vehicles.

Bombardier single-decker: prototype inter-urban single-decker, built in 1979 by FFG of Hamburg, outside the Bombardier factory at Shannon in 1981

Bombardier Expressway: one of twenty single-deckers for Expressway services built by Bombardier at Shannon in 1981 with Detroit diesel engines and Allison transmissions

Bombardier tours coach: one of thirty coaches for CIÉ Tours International built in 1981 at Shannon, similar to the Bombardier Expressway buses in mechanical specification

Bombardier KR rural bus of which two hundred and twenty-four were built at Shannon, first by Bombardier and later by GAC, between 1985 and 1987; powered by DAF engines with Allison transmission

Bombardier double-decker in two-tone green livery which became the standard Dublin city bus of the 1980s; three hundred and sixty-six were built at Shannon.

Expressway/Supabus: the first of fifteen Van Hool integral coaches with Cummins engines purchased in 1986 for the expanding Supabus cross-channel coach services

At Broadstone for the Irish soccer team homecoming in 1990, Plaxton Expressway coach and Leyland Atlantean open top double-decker of Bus Éireann

Plaxton Expressway coach (1990): striking new livery on two hundred coaches of DAF, Leyland, Van Hool and Volvo manufacture, with bodywork by Alexander, Caetano, Plaxton and Van Hool

Leyland Olympians: all double-deckers placed in service by Bus Átha Cliath since 1987 have been Leyland Olympians with bodywork by Alexander of Belfast. This example was painted in EC colours to mark the Irish presidency of the EC from January to June 1990

A Leyland Olympian of Bus Átha Cliath being used as an advertising bus for Iarnród Éireann

Mayo and parts of Clare' affected by the closure of the Limerick/ Claremorris line with those in the affected areas of Leinster and Munster, where there was a prospect that they could retain their railway because T. J. Fitzpatrick, unlike his predecessor Peter Barry, was prepared to intervene. The debate in some ways resembled those of the fifties and sixties. While Tom Fitzpatrick did not claim to have intervened to keep the line from being closed and pointed out that it was a matter for the board, on the other hand if people were prepared to believe he had intervened he would take the credit. He simply repeated what he had said in Thurles about the need for new road arrangements and that the line would not be closed until these were made. However, he would not let the opposition away with their indignant protesting and added that '700 miles of line were closed by Fianna Fáil at a time when the social need for public transport was definitely greater than it is now and when the losses being incurred by CIÉ were only a fraction of present day losses' (*Dáil Debates*, Vol. 297, Col. 113).

Michael O'Kennedy (FF), showing appropriate concern for his North Tipperary constituents' interest in the Thurles sugar factory, played the barrister's part in the debate arguing points of fact and interpretation, but solicitor Tom Fitzpatrick was also a lawyer and did likewise.

What was CIÉ's attitude to what was going on? It accepted that closure of the Rosslare Harbour/Waterford permanent way could only be accomplished if the Barrow viaduct were taken over by another party who would convert it into a road bridge. Kilkenny County Council held the ace in the pack; the Barrow viaduct lay between Kilkenny and Wexford. There would be no change in the rail link unless they granted planning permission for the conversion of the Barrow viaduct. This they were not prepared to grant. In the case of the Waterford/Limerick line, it would remain in existence as CIÉ intended that it continue to be used for freight trains.

A government amendment to the Fianna Fáil motion was carried, but the issue was not closed. Fully five years later (February 1983) another Dáil debate would take place on a similar motion concerning the Rosslare Harbour to Limerick line, this time a private member's motion from Deputy Hugh Byrne of Fianna Fáil. Despite expenditure of £1 million in 1978 on the development of a beet-handling facility at Wellington Bridge in south Wexford, Devlin, on 4 December 1981, had indicated that the Rosslare Harbour/Waterford line could not be justified indefinitely. Local interests also smelt trouble in a second McKinsey study of CIÉ which, to say the least, was ambivalent about the railway system. The 1983 motion was passed with a government amendment noting that CIÉ had the authority to make its own decisions, but simultaneously and very pointedly asking CIÉ to note the size of its annual subvention from the state. The minister in 1983 was Fine Gael's Jim Mitchell. He publicly claimed to have intervened with CIÉ and made no apology about doing so. In due course a major road would be built from Wexford to Waterford via New Ross and another road would link Wexford to a vehicle ferry at Passage East. Despite the road improvements the Barrow viaduct would never become a road bridge and the rail link would survive.

It is time to return to the implementation of other aspects of CIÉ's Railway Development Plan. St J. Devlin held a press conference on 31 January 1977 at which he released the delayed accounts for 1975, reviewed progress and policy across the whole range of CIÉ's activities, and charted 'The Way Ahead' under which title his presentation was subsequently published in pamphlet form. Under the headline, 'Devlin's Epic', *Business and Finance* noted the background of rising deficits, rising fares, industrial unrest, the Rosslare Harbour rail link controversy, and difficulties with maintaining bus and train schedules.

> The previous week, the *Evening Press* newspaper was entertaining its readers with a series on 'Why CIÉ Should be Scrapped'. Sylvester Barrett of Fianna Fáil is urging a Major Inquiry into how the company is run, the implication being that if Devlin and his top managers left CIÉ the world would be a happier place.
>
> Last week's news conference was very much a full-dress affair. Most newspapers had not one but two reporters. RTE was there with its arc lights. On the stroke of 12, the journalists were presented with the 1975 annual report, a 73 page script by Devlin, and sundry other bits and pieces. The mass of words fell some way short of War and Peace, but it was still indigestible. Devlin strode in and made us an offer we could not refuse. He proposed to read the script, he said we might ask questions if we liked but he would prefer to leave them till after lunch. Was this agreeable to us? This approach left the journalists a little cynical. Such a wealth of information was too good to be true. What, behind it all, was the story?
>
> As things turned out, the Dublin dailies agreed on the story. It was not in the Chairman's 73 page script at all. CIÉ is seeking a 25% increase in bus fares. That fact is undoubtedly interesting, but Devlin had a more intricate message to put across.
>
> (*Business & Finance*, 10 February 1977)

The failure of the press conference to gain favourable headlines for CIÉ on the following day may not have upset St J. Devlin unduly. He had lectured rather than briefed the media. He wanted to impart a message of long-term significance which was comprehensive as well as intricate. It ranged over corporate aims, public transport policy, the need to reduce costs so as to improve margins and so hold the state subvention to 1976 levels in real terms. It discussed personnel policy, problems and achievements for each of the rail, road, passenger and freight, hotels and other businesses. For the moment our narrative will stay with the mid-1970s attempt to renew the railway. While the other CIÉ businesses had an interesting and compelling story to relate, they must wait a while. Devlin summarised CIÉ's three-pronged approach to the 'upgrading of the radial lines' as depending on

> – A substantial improvement in the quality of the permanent way i.e. the track. Only in this way can we raise speeds.
> – The automation of signalling throughout the system to eliminate delays and increase the capacity of the track so that more trains can be operated.
> – The provision of air-conditioned modern carriages on all routes to make railway travel more comfortable and more enticing.
> (The Way Ahead, January 1977)

These three factors applied to the entire railway system, including the Dublin suburban rail system for which electrification proposals were being developed. There had been persistent underinvestment in the track and it had virtually come to a halt during the 1930s. By the mid-1970s much of CIÉ's rails had been 'life expired' for up to thirty years. So a major renewal job had to be done. From Erskine Childers to Peter Barry, assurances had been given that the railway was to be preserved. Uncertainty about the railway's future should no longer excuse starvation of the system. Accordingly CIÉ, backed by government's 'approval in principle', seriously began to tackle the railway infrastructure.

Three important innovations came into play: continuous welded rail (CWR), concrete sleepers, and new techniques and equipment for track laying, inspection and maintenance. Previously rails had been laid in seven to eight metre lengths so that expansion and contraction of the rails due to temperature changes could be accommodated by the opening and closing of the joint gaps between the rails. The CWR track was designed to limit these contractions and expansions by the generation of 'internal stresses, resulting in what are known as Thermal Forces in the rail' (P. O. Jennings, 'Engineering in CIÉ', Supplement to the *Engineer's Journal*, January 1984). The CWR was purchased in 36 m lengths, welded in CIÉ's Portlaoise depot into 108 m lengths and transferred to the site where they were welded into 432 m to 540 m lengths before laying. The role of sleepers was summarised by Jennings as distributing the wheel load from the rails to the ballast, i.e. the stone chip track bed, and forming the tie between the rails so as to maintain the gauge. In the 1950s imported sleepers had become very expensive for the requisite quality; Irish timber used during the war years had proved to be short lived and unsuitable. Reinforced concrete sleepers had been experimented with, giving service of up to twenty years before failure.

However, with later pre-stressing and post-tensioning techniques superior concrete sleepers were now possible. Concrete sleepers could be home produced from native materials and allow for new fastening materials for the CWR rail. In 1974, the year the Railway Development Plan was announced, CIÉ established a plant at its Portlaoise works to build sleepers. In due course it could manufacture up to 80,000 sleepers per year under licence from a specialist rail engineering concern in Munich. The laying of sleepers and CWR together with renewing or deepening of the ballast was a major engineering undertaking even if the total track length now stood at 1,900 miles compared to the over 3,000 miles which had once existed. Articles in the *IRRS Journal* and in the *Engineers Journal* describe the progress of the work and the special equipment designed to carry it out with minimum 'possession of the track', the phrase used to describe the suspension of rail operations while the track was being modified or repaired. The methods used for track relaying were described as a breakthrough from the 'ingenious' methods first developed by the Belfast-born MGWR engineer, Arthur White Bretland, in the 1920s though, ironically, the Bretland track layer had principally been used to remove rather than to lay track. His invention had been used to single the old MGWR line from Mullingar to Athlone in the 1930s.

While new materials and techniques were available, for reasons of cost, progress was slow with the renewal of the track. The target set in 1976 was to complete 30 miles a year—a rate which had achieved 200 miles of CWR rail on the Dublin/Cork line by late 1983. To support normal maintenance and to ensure high rail reliability, CIÉ in 1976 acquired a Theurer EM50 Track Recording Car, 'the first of its kind to be placed in service on a European Rail System' (*Nuacht*, Eanáir 1976). The EM50 was a diesel railcar which measured the geometry of the track whilst travelling at up to 30 mph. In those pre-microchip days its readings were recorded by pens on pre-printed paper rolls. Deviations from prescribed standards would then be attended to by specialist maintenance machinery. P. O. Jennings was able to record later that 'the track maintenance system is now totally mechanised'. Important passenger lines were being tamped and aligned at least once a year by eight tamping/lining machines. Ballast measuring and topping up was also being handled mechanically. These improvements to the permanent way, i.e. installation of CWR, with concrete sleepers, mechanical inspection, tamping and ballast restoration, resulted in major savings in a very labour-intensive aspect of the railway. No longer did most of the work have to be done by the muscle power of labour gangs equipped with crowbars. Still, Jennings in the *IRRS Journal* would note that some physical human inspection was still required. The track is patrolled two to three times weekly by a track patrol ranger who provides 'continuity of presence on the railway, notes track defects and reports them to his inspector, and carries out minor track adjustments, clears drains, cuts brushwood, attends to fencing etc.'. Separately, a revolution was taking place in railway signalling which also had a big impact on the staffing levels. The continued increase in automatic level crossings was another factor with manpower implications.

Labour savings were not the main reason for the changes made to CIÉ's signalling. The existing equipment was outdated and limited the use which could be made of the track. This became especially apparent with the 1973 high frequency timetable and the routing of trains to the west via Portarlington rather than Mullingar. Jack Higgins in a later paper to the Institute of Transport (16 October 1979) stated the alternatives as either new signalling to improve track utilisation or laying additional track. The first phase of the new system, known as CTC (Centralised Traffic Control), was contracted to Westinghouse in 1973 and financed by funds drawn down from the European Investment Bank. Work began in February 1974, laying 350 miles of underground cable from Inchicore to Ballybrophy on the Cork line with a specially designed mechanical plough operating at 4 miles per hour. Two branches, Cherryville to Athy on the Dublin/Waterford route and Portarlington to Tullamore on the Athlone line, were also joined into the CTC system which came into operation on 26 January 1975. The system was controlled from a newly built control centre at Connolly station. *Nuacht CIÉ* summarised that

> The new signalling system will provide increased track capacity and is designed to allow the running of more frequent trains at higher speeds to the south and west. The old style semaphore signals are being replaced with three-aspect electric colour light signals located at 1,000 yard intervals. (*Nuacht CIÉ*, Bealtaine 1975)

Devlin's marathon presentation to the January 1977 press conference explained the workings of the system in surprising detail and announced that CIÉ was planning to implement an automatic signalling system throughout the whole network which would be controlled from Connolly station. CIÉ also envisaged a national communications network which would incorporate its internal countrywide telephone system, its data transmission system and the signalling system. Canadian consultants had been engaged to study the feasibility of the concept. Devlin in 'The Way Ahead', and Higgins, in 1978, envisaged that in the next stage signalling would be controlled by a VHF system linked to a 'back-bone micro wave system'. As the years passed CIÉ would progress its communications and signalling systems, but the structure described in 1977 and in 1978 would prove to be too sophisticated and expensive for it ever to materialise. Further development of CIÉ's signalling and communications systems followed in the 1980s.

The third prong in the three-pronged approach to the 'upgrading of radial lines', announced in 'The Way Ahead', was the introduction of 'air conditioned coaches to all mainline services'. Such a plan (or ambition) was announced initially in 1974 as part of the Railway Development Plan, but CIÉ was to experience enormous problems and delays in getting new mainline rolling stock. The story of these delays ranks as one of the more depressing aspects of CIÉ's affairs during Devlin's tenure of the chairmanship. Much else was achieved in terms of railway renewal during his period in office, but mainline coach renewal did not take place. In 1976 CIÉ initiated discussions with a German company, Linke, Hoffman and Busch (LHB), regarding its estimated requirements for 200 railway coaches over the following five to six years. The proposition put to LHB was that they take over a substantial part of CIÉ's railway engineering works at Inchicore and set up a coach-building plant. In 'The Way Ahead' Devlin presented the proposition in very positive terms.

> Linke, Hoffman and Busch is a public sector company with considerable experience in the manufacture of railway rolling stock. They export to countries all over the world and we believe that, if they do come to Ireland, they will not alone produce quality stock for CIÉ but will also be able to sell more competitively on export markets. We have negotiated a satisfactory fixed price with the necessary escalation clauses. Preliminary discussions have taken place with the Trade Unions concerned and we believe that this venture offers tremendous opportunities not only for CIÉ and the staff in Inchicore but also for Ireland. We hope that operations will commence before the end of this year. In the meantime we have submitted our proposals to the Department of Transport and Power.   (The Way Ahead, January 1977)

The Industrial Development Authority was described as having taken an interest in the project. The CIÉ rationale for the LHB proposal was based on the conviction that manufacture of sophisticated modern coaches demanded a major investment in design skills and in manufacturing plant, as distinct from that required for a repair and maintenance facility which is what Inchicore had largely become by the early 1970s. Manufacture should be for the long term. It was not a start/stop activity and the manufacturing specialist needed to have a reasonable prospect of continuing demand which CIÉ itself could not provide. An important additional argument was that successful manufacturing required a different type of organisation and work ethos from repair and overhaul. This could best be achieved if manufacturing were carried out by a separate commercial entity. The LHB proposal would have met all these points. LHB was a dedicated manufacturing organisation with advanced design skills; it would largely recruit from CIÉ's own staff who would then be employed in a new industry released from the traditional working practices of a century-old establishment; LHB was serving a world market and having met CIÉ's requirements there was the prospect that they would serve some of that market from its Irish base.

Far from operations beginning before the end of 1977, as envisaged by Devlin, government never approved the proposed LHB coach-building plant in Inchicore. Cost appeared to be the main impediment to a decision but other issues also arose. For one thing, consideration of the LHB proposition was complicated by difficulties that had already arisen in the case of the Van Hool McArdle bus-building project at CIÉ's road transport works at Spa Road, Inchicore. The Van Hool proposal (see page 326) had been based on the same rationale as was now advanced for the LHB concept. The fact that the railway engineering works and the bus works were both in Inchicore in west Dublin was a coincidence that did not help acceptance of the LHB project. The railway facility had been inherited by CIÉ from the GSWR via GSR, while the bus-building facility at a separate location in Inchicore had once been the DUTC's tram-building factory. CIÉ needed new coaches firstly for its mainline services, but new coaches would also be needed for an electrified Howth/Bray line if it were approved. The possible expansion of suburban rail services to Blanchardstown and Maynooth could further increase the demand for coaches. One way or another CIÉ's need for coaching stock was real, and urgent.

The LHB coach-building project was submitted to the Department of Transport and Power before the January 1977 press conference. Three months later CIÉ followed with its detailed proposals for electrification of the Dublin suburban Howth/Bray line as a first step in a proposed comprehensive rapid rail system for Dublin, which concept government had welcomed when first proposed by the Dublin Rapid Rail Transport Study (DRRTS), which itself followed from the Dublin Transportation Study (DTS) conducted by An Foras Forbartha and published in 1972. A decision on the electrification of the suburban line would be announced in May 1979, but a decision on coaches would be delayed until 1981 both for mainline services and for the electrified suburban line.

In the intervening years, evidence accumulated that mainline coaching stock was seriously inadequate. In March 1978 the board was beginning to be very concerned. It decided that its chairman should seek a meeting with the minister as soon as possible to discuss

1. Renewal and electrification of the suburban line;
2. Acquisition of mainline passenger coaches;

3. An indication of the Government's future policy for the railways; and
4. The future role of public transport in the conurbations.
(Board Minutes, 16 March 1978)

During the board discussion on this proposed meeting, Jack Higgins warned that with increasing passengers the total mainline coach fleet was in constant demand and the frequency of the mainline services might have to be curtailed unless there was an early assurance that new mainline coaches could be obtained.

In the restrained language of annual reports, the 1978 Report noted that 'During 1978 the number of passenger journeys increased on both the main and suburban lines. At the same time passenger rolling stock continued to deteriorate. At weekends we have to withdraw suburban stock to supplement mainline services.' The following year (1979) the Annual Report said that '. . . the quality of our rolling stock is deteriorating. We will have to retire coaches from the suburban and mainline services in the near future. The maintenance of service standards has become progressively more difficult because of the deficiencies of the rolling stock.' The *IRRS Journal* made several references to the condition and to the scarcity of the stock over this period, and Dáil debates provided additional evidence of how the situation was becoming intolerable. In March 1980 Deputy Austin Deasy (FG) asked four questions covering government proposals for CIÉ's rolling stock, safety aspects of the existing stock, and its attitude to the LHB proposal of CIÉ. By that time the minister was Albert Reynolds, who was absent on the day Austin Deasy's questions came up for reply. His place was taken by Mark Killilea as Minister of State. Deasy's question about safety referred to 'comments made by the Chairman of CIÉ that Dublin suburban railway services may have to be cut by 50% due to the poor condition of the existing stock'. The Minister of State gave the predictable assurance that

> Railway rolling stock is inspected regularly . . . and that vehicles found to require attention for safety reasons are immediately withdrawn from service for repair. I have been assured by the board that in no circumstances are unsafe carriages allowed to operate.
> (*Dáil Debates*, Vol. 319, Col. 306)

He did not discuss whether sufficient safe coaches were available for use. Labour's Barry Desmond was not impressed by the simple statement about safety which evaded the question of coach numbers, and asked

> Is the Minister aware that his immediate predecessor was . . . brought through the CIÉ rolling stock repair shed and that this stock was

> shown to the Minister as being in a highly dangerous and disastrous state and that the Minister's predecessor freely acknowledged that the rolling stock was in a highly dangerous condition? There are photographs available which I can produce to the Minister if he wants them. (ibid.)

The Minister repeated that CIÉ would not compromise on safety, but Barry Desmond would not be put off.

> Is the Minister not aware that the Chairman of the CIÉ board and his senior engineering rail operatives and rolling stock staff showed the Minister the rolling stock and bogeys underneath and said that if it was required to run this stock at more than 30 mile an hour it was liable to go in one direction and the passengers to go in another. (ibid.)

That is but part of the several angry columns about rolling stock which were prompted by Austin Deasy's four questions. Mark Killilea stubbornly kept quoting capital approved for the electrification of Dublin suburban lines twelve months earlier, but would not be specific about coaching stock for any of CIÉ's needs.

Deputies Deasy and Jim Mitchell focused several supplementary questions on the rationale for the LHB proposal, on trade union objections to that proposal, and asked why CIÉ with its fine traditions in Inchicore could not build the required coaches themselves. They were not satisfied with Killilea's replies and the Ceann Comhairle threatened to suspend the House. On the adjournment, Jim Mitchell returned to the LHB angle of the question and the threat to CIÉ workers which this seemed to involve. He was assured that the Cabinet had made no decision on that proposal. The variety of themes in this Dáil fracas on 20 March 1980, e.g. rail safety and preservation of jobs, were distracting from the main point that no decisions were being made on the manifest need to replace seriously deteriorating rolling stock on mainline services. The number of rail passengers had increased by 87 per cent between 1969 and 1979 and by 40 per cent between 1974 and 1979. However, the number of passenger coaches had fallen from 418 in 1969 to 382 in 1974 and to 349 in 1979. Obviously coach utilisation was improving but at the same time all but 72 of CIÉ's 349 coaches were over 10 years old. The Cravens were over 12 years old and the Park Royals were approaching their twenty-fifth anniversary despite having had an initial planned life of fifteen years. Both Cravens and Park Royals were young compared to some other coaching stock.

The railway deficit was growing fast and despite the increase in rail passengers it appeared that government enthusiasm for the railways, which had blossomed at the time of the 1974 Railway Development Plan, was now evaporating. On the freight side there had been considerable investment in facilities, in rolling stock and in rationalisation of services. Some freight traffics had developed successfully, especially bulk movements (mineral ores, cement, chemicals, oil and fertilisers), palletised movements (cement and fertilisers) and company trains, e.g. unitised load or container trains for the Bell Line to Waterford and for the B + I. On the other hand 'sundries' continued to be in serious difficulty. The Railplan 80 (1972) proposal which survived into the Railway Development Plan (1974) of carrying sundries in 60 ft vans was abandoned in 1976. Instead, after an experiment on the Sligo line, sundries came to be carried in 10 ft containers using 'caged wheeled pallets'. A considerable reduction had been achieved in pilferage and in damage to goods which had increased as the use of light packaging had become commonplace. A complicating factor was that CIÉ experienced much labour unrest in introducing the new sundries system, one example of which was related to the use of articulated tailgates on new road vehicles for carrying the caged pallets. Such labour difficulties were mentioned a number of times as the reason why the sundries business was failing to grow as expected. Instead, it fluctuated between 1972 and 1976 but held fairly steady in total volume, after which it started into an apparently inexorable decline. Trade union problems could not provide sufficient explanation for the fall. 'Own account' transport and private haulage were eating their way into the business. The question came to be asked whether the effort to develop or even to maintain sundries traffic was worth it, given its disproportionally high handling cost.

CIÉ could claim in 1979 that it had cut railway staff numbers by 23 per cent from 10,400 in 1975 to 8,000 in 1978 (submission to Joint Oireachtas Committee, April 1979)—compared to the much smaller reduction projected in the Railway Development Plan (1974)—and that rail passengers were up 14 per cent over the same period. But the failure of government to make a positive decision about coaching stock caused the board to question whether its masters really had a long-term commitment to the railway. Even after the 1979 announcement of support for the electrification of the Bray/Howth line, there was a view in CIÉ that while government accepted that Dublin's traffic problems required a modernised suburban railway system, it had become deeply sceptical about the mainline system.

On foot of the earlier (1974) government statement of support for renewing and developing the railway system, CIÉ itself decided in 1976 to commission a major study of long-term possibilities for the railway. Martin and Voorhees Associates and Henderson, Hughes and Busby were jointly commissioned to study the south-west rail corridor. In December 1976 this was extended to cover the entire mainline network. The objective was to assess the best long-term investment policy, taking account of policies for national and regional development. This ambitious study was to examine such issues as electrification, train frequency, speed, phasing of improvement, the future role of the railway and the impact of rail investment on other transport modes. On completion, an outline of the type of rail service to be provided over the following twenty-five years would be available. Clearly, by 1979 the railway's financial results were such that this idea of a long-term plan for the railways was a dead duck and was shelved. Whether scepticism about the mainline railway was merely at civil servant level or whether it had taken over at cabinet level, people in CIÉ were unsure. There was a fear that at some level it had been decided to kill off most of the mainline railway system and that a policy of attrition was being used to achieve this end.

GOVERNMENT DELAYS REGARDING the building of coaches was but one of several causes for CIÉ developing what the record shows was a simmering frustration with the Department of Transport in the late 1970s. Of course, stresses are bound to arise between a state corporation like CIÉ and the government department to which it is responsible. Commentators from Seán Lemass to the present day accept that a 'cosy relationship' should not be allowed to develop. It has been said that the right balance is achieved in the relationship when a situation of 'constructive tension' has been created. Among their various priorities civil servants give a high ranking to protecting the minister from problems with the public and other politicians and to protecting the public purse. Sometimes these aims can be in conflict with one another. For example, if the minister is protected from the odium of allowing CIÉ to increase fares to compensate for cost increases, then extra pressure inevitably falls on the exchequer. The Department of Finance then comes into play, righteously refusing pressures from other departments. The preferred course, if possible, is both to protect the minister and to protect the exchequer at one and the same time. Prima facie, this could be done simply by concentrating all the pressure on CIÉ to reduce its costs. However, the Devlin Board had resolved to take a more radical approach than previously to cost reduction, as evidenced in 'The Way Ahead' and in various annual reports. Considerable progress had been achieved in reducing staff numbers and in increasing utilisation of rolling stock, but because of continuing inflation, national pay rounds, Labour Court recommendations and persistent government interference with fare increases, the deficit was rising. CIÉ could claim repeatedly that it was not master of the size of its deficit which was largely decided by outside forces, but like it or not, the deficit was the measure by which CIÉ was commonly judged.

The board minutes include unusually frank reports of discussions with the minister and with officials of the Department in 1978 and 1979. They give an insight into the frustrations which CIÉ was experiencing. The period was one when Pádraig Faulkner was Minister and Noel MacMahon was Secretary of the Department. Lest our extracts give the impression that the period was entirely negative, one should note that Faulkner was Minister when electrification of the Howth/Bray line was approved in 1979; it was he who announced the less significant though long overdue intention to transfer the canals to the Board of Works, and he also sponsored the 1978 Road Transport Bill which reformed road haulage legislation. The reader may form his own opinion from the following extracts from the board minutes as to whether the relationship between CIÉ and the department during this period had or had not achieved the 'constructive tension' which commentators think desirable.

> The Chairman reported on a meeting which he had with the Minister for Tourism and Transport [January 1978]. He had sought this meeting with a view to discussing CIÉ policy with the Minister. . . . The performance of CIÉ was measured as that of a State-sponsored body, very often it was looked upon as the most expensive State-sponsored body and there were allegations from time to time about the apparent inefficiency of the management. Public transport was a public service and the Chairman urged the Minister to emphasise this fact in public and in his discussions with his Cabinet colleagues. He said that the cost of Health Services or the cost of Posts & Telegraphs or the cost of Social Welfare was never held up to ridicule. These were looked upon as necessary public services for the community. The same applied to public transport but . . . CIÉ was constantly being pilloried and indeed pressured to reduce its deficit whilst at the same time they were expected to expand public transport particularly in areas where there was a social need. The Minister accepted the proposition and said that it would be a mistake for CIÉ to believe that the Cabinet did not appreciate the good job they were doing. His colleagues knew that CIÉ were doing the best they could within the resources which were available. It was natural that other politicians would appear to be more demanding and perhaps more critical because they had to deal with complaints. (Board Minutes, 19 January 1978)

The foregoing might be summarised as follows: Devlin complained to the minister at the way CIÉ was being treated by politicians and the media, to which Faulkner more or less replied that 'Sure, we all know you are doing your best', but gave no assurance that the treatment would change. It was an exchange that must have given little satisfaction to either party. Devlin's report to his board continues:

> The Minister then raised the matter of the suburban electrification and he questioned the large investment. The Secretary of the Department, Mr Noel MacMahon, commented that in recent weeks the Department had approved the building of two car ferries, the total cost of which approximated to the cost of the electrification of the suburban system. He also made the point that once every two years it was necessary to expend £70 m. on the building of a power station and that the Government were at present considering the building of a nuclear power station which would cost approximately £300 m. These were decisions which had to be taken and the money had to be raised. In this context, the expenditure of £38 m. on the electrification of the suburban line was not excessive and it had to be seen as a necessary public service. The Minister promised that he would do all he could to promote Government acceptance of the scheme. (ibid.)

Thus Noel MacMahon was siding with the suburban rail electrification project and helping to put it into a wider context for the benefit of his minister, but sixteen months elapsed before a decision. At the same meeting Devlin told his minister about a problem CIÉ had with the then Minister for Labour who had alleged in a letter that £11 million was being 'paid as overtime by CIÉ when proper management would provide 3,500 more jobs. This was unfair to CIÉ.' Devlin said that the figures which had come from the NBU were incorrect. He complained at the Department passing on these allegations to CIÉ instead of investigating and rejecting them (ibid.).

This minute ended with references to fares increases which provided another example of how CIÉ's statutory freedom to fix its rates and charges was allowed or not allowed to operate. CIÉ sought to do what it thought was practical, but politicians and civil servants would rather do what they thought was politic. CIÉ management had several battles on its hands as it was told, 'Don't do it that way, do it this way and at any rate get more out of the increases than you say is possible.' At the subsequent January 1978 Board meeting the chairman reported

> that the Minister had written to say that an increase in the minimum fare for Dublin City Services was not politically acceptable. The letter also indicated that the new fares increase could not be introduced until the 1st April and that the percentage of increases should be recast to generate £1½ m. more revenue. The management would be writing to the Minister to point out that the only alternative would be a general increase of 33⅓%, which would not be acceptable to those who lived furthest from the City centre, it would prove a particular hardship to the working classes in the Ballyfermot and Ballymun areas and it would ultimately lead to a reduction in passenger numbers. (ibid.)

This to and fro about fare increases was not, as we've seen in the last chapter, an isolated incident. St J. Devlin in 'The Way Ahead' referred to deferral of fares and fares and rates increases in 1972/73, 1973/74, 1974 and 1975, and a government subsidy for road passenger services in 1975 and 1976 (in lieu of fares increases). Disagreements were happening again in 1978 and not for the last time. The point is important enough to illustrate by another minute—from the February 1978 meeting.

> The Chairman reported that a letter had been received from the Department concerning the Board's application to the National Prices Commission for an increase in rates and fares. The Government had discussed the Board's submission and were not in favour of a 50% increase on the minimum fare with no increase in the 15p fare and the 25p fare. The Government directed that CIÉ should arrange an across-the-board increase on rates and fares which would bring in an additional £9 m. in the current year. . . . It was pointed out by the General Manager that the increases which were being directed by the Government could mean a reduction in numbers travelling and it might not be possible to achieve the revenue target. It was agreed that this point should be made in the General Manager's reply to the Secretary of the Department of Tourism and Transport.
> (ibid., 16 February 1978)

The delay in deciding on the electrification of the Dublin suburban line was a topic which concerned Devlin at the next meeting of the CIÉ Board. He said that

> The Secretary of the Department indicated to the General Manager last November that he was prepared to recommend the electrification programme, subject to further clarification of a number of points which he listed. Subsequently these points were clarified and the Chairman said that even now as we approached the anniversary of the submission, the Department of Tourism and Transport had not yet submitted a preliminary memorandum to other departments and to the Department of Finance. This meant that there could be further delays of up to six months or more before the Government would give a decision. In the meanwhile, the coaching stock on the suburban line was deteriorating and another set had to be withdrawn in recent weeks. . . . a complete collapse of the service could be foreseen over the next three to four years. (ibid., 16 March 1978)

One should say that the government had many problems of its own. The easy budget which followed Jack Lynch's record victory for Fianna Fáil in 1977 was not producing the hoped-for economic recovery. Instead matters were deteriorating. Wage inflation persisted despite a slow-down in the growth of the CPI index in 1978; unemployment remained high; an international recession was not abating. The public deficit on current account was causing growing concern. Political struggles were engaging the attention of many ministers and Pádraig Faulkner was not regarded as being able to command much authority in Cabinet. CIÉ was being pushed into a very uncomfortable financial situation with government instructions on fares, labour policy and on subvention limits.

In November 1978 management told the board that the original subvention figure of £30 million for CIÉ was likely to be £7 million short of what was required. Jack Higgins pointed out that the £30 million had been decided on 'unilaterally by the Department' on the basis that

> the Board should be capable of working to this figure by reducing costs and increasing fares. Notwithstanding, the Department would not approve of the mix of fares increases proposed by the Board and furthermore the implementation of the National Prices Commission approval was delayed. In preparing the budget, provision was made for a 5% increase in wages and salaries as a result of the National Wage Agreement. In practice, the increase was of the order of 8%.
>
> (ibid., 23 November 1978)

In the following month the Dáil increased the CIÉ subvention to the required £37.7 million and the 1978 Annual Report later attempted to put this subvention in context:

> In 1975 the Board of CIÉ commenced the implementation of a definitive retrenchment programme with a view to containing the deficit in real terms. Because a reduction of almost 20 per cent in total employment was achieved during the period 1975/78 it was possible to effect this containment, as the following figures illustrate:
>
> | | *Subvention* | *% of total expenditure* |
> |------|--------------|--------------------------|
> | 1975 | 26.5 m. | 27.96 |
> | 1976 | 31.9 m. | 28.94 |
> | 1977 | 33.2 m. | 27.12 |
> | 1978 | 37.7 m. | 26.93 |
>
> . . . if, in 1978 CIÉ employed the same number of people as were employed in 1974, then the additional cost in wages and salaries would have been £12.1 m. The reduction in numbers was compensated for by an increase in productivity.

Early in January 1979 Mr Faulkner had another discussion with St J. Devlin who, in spite of the apparent stresses between CIÉ and the Department, had recently been reappointed as Chairman. The subvention had grown from £13.9 million in his first year as Chairman (1974) to £37.7 million in 1978 when his initial contract expired, but Devlin's active and aggressive style was clearly appreciated by government. Contrary to impressions within the organisation, Devlin's reappointment was not a last minute cliff hanger affair. The decision to renew his contract was made well in advance of New Year's Day 1979, when it came into effect, but Devlin for reasons of his own did not reveal that decision within CIÉ until it was announced in late December. The new contract would require him to increase rather than to decrease his involvement with the organisation.

Despite this apparent vote of confidence in Devlin's chairmanship, the pattern of criticism of CIÉ from cabinet continued. Two points had been raised at a cabinet meeting which the minister wanted to discuss with the chairman when they met in January 1979. They indicated serious scepticism at cabinet about the effectiveness of CIÉ's board and management, especially in the context of government's preoccupation at the time with wage increases throughout the public service. The two points were 'a suggestion that CIÉ had negotiated concessions with the Labour Court which might undermine the Government's pay policy' and 'a suggestion that the reduction in numbers employed in CIÉ over the past three years was not reflected in the accounts of CIÉ due to the high cost of overtime and redundancy payments'. The minister also told the chairman of cabinet views concerning media treatment of the then current NBU dispute. They wanted CIÉ to advertise its own position. The board minutes (18 January 1979) indicate that the chairman satisfied the minister on all these points and that the minister would communicate with his colleagues.

However, a critical observer might take the view that a forceful, well-briefed minister could have been able to handle such issues on the spot with his cabinet colleagues rather than have to relay their comments to CIÉ's chairman and then revert back to them with CIÉ's responses. In the subsequent discussion at the CIÉ Board one member protested at suggestions from the minister that CIÉ was breaching National Wage Agreements.

> He pointed out that the recent decision of the Department of Posts & Telegraphs to allocate 80% of productivity savings to their employees would raise serious issues for CIÉ. CIÉ had negotiated on the basis of 50% which was the limit imposed by the Department of the Public Service and they would now find that further claims may be made as a result of the higher share out by the Department of Posts & Telegraphs. (ibid., 18 January 1979)

A serious industrial relations situation existed in the Post Office and within a month the first national postal strike in fifty years would start and last seventeen weeks. The point about the terms made to postal workers was more apt than the reader might first think. Mr Faulkner, the Minister who was conveying his colleague's concern to CIÉ about the level of its labour settlements, was also responsible for the Department of Posts and Telegraphs which was being accused of having broken government guidelines on productivity agreements.

At the time CIÉ was briefing another important audience—the Oireachtas Committee on State Sponsored Bodies—whose report on CIÉ would be published at the end of 1979. This body, comprising TDs and Senators from the government and opposition parties, heard CIÉ's case and the Department's views. As we shall see, CIÉ emerged well out of these hearings and government's handling of the annual subvention, of investment decisions and of various other transport issues came in for serious if only implicit criticism from the committee composed of government supporters and critics alike.

Jack Higgins reported to the same meeting that the Transport Salaried Staff Association (TSSA) 'were contemplating industrial action as a protest against Government's lack of support for public transport and in particular the failure of the government to authorise the electrification of the suburban line'. He had requested them 'to delay any action for the time being'. He advised them of something which had already been noticed by board. The previous year a Green Paper had been published on National Development. CIÉ protested to government about its critical reference to the 'loss' incurred by CIÉ without adverting to the social and economic implications of public transport. CIÉ might also have noted that the Green Paper made no mention of government restrictions on fare increases which contributed to the size of CIÉ's 'loss'. The subsequent White Paper—Programme for National Development 1978–1981—was much more acceptable to board which expressed the hope that as a result of the 'change in emphasis concerning the importance of public transport', a favourable decision would soon be made with regard to electrification of the suburban line (ibid.).

THE BOARD OF CIÉ was not alone in hoping for an early decision in favour of electrification of the Howth/Bray line. The matter was frequently raised in the Dáil. In the background, however, there was the complication that in its 1977 General Election manifesto, Fianna Fáil had promised that if elected to government it would appoint a national transport council. The Confederation of Irish Industry (CII) had been recommending the creation of such a body since 1973. Eventually a Transport Consultative Commission was set up in September 1978 and charged initially with giving priority to the question of Dublin's traffic problems. On 7 February 1979 Labour's

Deputy Ruairí Quinn asked six separate Dáil questions concerning the 'improvement and development of public transport' in urban areas. Ruairí Quinn then a newcomer to the Dáil hoped, no doubt, that this volley of questions would provoke the minister into giving a positive answer about suburban line electrification or that the minister would at least give an undertaking to make an early decision. Answering for Pádraig Faulkner, T. J. Fitzpatrick from Dublin South Central (not the T. J. Fitzpatrick from Cavan who had been Faulkner's predecessor as minister) handled Ruairí Quinn's questions. However, his formal replies did not give Ruairí Quinn the information or undertaking sought. Quinn remarked that 'this is the fourth time that I have formally asked the question [about the electrification proposal] since coming into this House'. Try as he might, with a total of eighteen supplementaries he got no further than learning that the Department had 'recommendations ready to submit to Government'. 'That', conceded Ruairí Quinn, 'is progress of a kind.' Three weeks later, on 14 March 1979, the issue was ventilated again in the Dáil when Richie Ryan moved a motion:

> That Dáil Éireann, noting the increasing inadequacy of the road network and the steady deterioration of rail rolling stock, calls on the Government to implement the CIÉ proposals for the Dublin Rapid Busway and rail system as a matter of urgency, thereby providing an effective commuter service whilst also creating much needed employment. (*Dáil Debates*, Vol. 312, Col. 1543)

He noted that in 1970 the existing rail system was transporting 14,000 commuters every day. 'Eight years later the same system . . . with depleted services . . . was transporting 33,000 people on the antiquated rolling stock that was breaking down frequently.' In the usual fashion of ministers, Pádraig Faulkner moved an amendment which was duly carried, deleting all the words after 'Dáil Éireann' and substituting words more to his government's liking.

However, a decision on the Howth/Bray line was imminent. On 31 May, in the middle of the Republic's first election campaign for members of the European Parliament, in which the government appeared not to be doing well, it terminated its evaluation of the proposal and announced that the electrification of the Howth/Bray line was approved. *The Irish Times* reported

> The Government's decision which was widely welcomed, was announced by the Minister for Tourism and Transport, Mr Faulkner, and a statement later from the board of CIÉ said that work on the £46 million project would begin immediately. Electric trains could be

providing a day-long service on the line in three years from now . . .

The decision was a momentous one. Chapter 22 will describe the implementation of that decision after a review in some intervening chapters of various traffic management and bus control efforts to ease Dublin's growing problem of traffic congestion. With the electrification decision made, one might expect that relations between CIÉ and the Department would change for the better. However, problems relating to continually increasing fares and the size of the subvention would grow rather than diminish as 1979 progressed. Before continuing with this story (see Chapter 19), we will turn to some other areas of CIÉ's operations. As only 35 per cent of CIÉ's revenue (70 per cent of its deficit) derived from the railways, other aspects of its story merit attention.

CHAPTER 17

ON THE 'PERIPHERY'

Great Southern Hotels run into difficulty—The Russell Court story—CIÉ withdraws from hotels—Rosslare Harbour—Road haulage difficulties and rationalisation.

CIÉ had always felt comfortable with its Great Southern Hotels. They had a quality image and were successful financially. The hotels integrated well with CIÉ's successful tour promotions which attracted significant extra travellers to CIÉ's rail and road services. Governments could only approve of CIÉ's hotel and tour promotions and their manifest contribution to Irish tourism. Earlier chapters have told how the hotels were modified through the years to meet the needs of the modern tourist, how a separate subsidiary, OIÉ, had been incorporated to look after them and how their number was increased with the addition of new hotels at Rosslare, Galway (Corrib) and Killarney (Torc) in the late 1960s. CIÉ abandoned a plan to build a hotel in Dublin. They looked at Belfast and there, in 1968/69, they found and acquired an old but well-positioned hotel, the Russell Court. The old Russell Court was demolished, and a first-class modern 200-bedroom hotel was built on the same site. At the same time, OIÉ opened its very successful Restaurant na Mara as a premier seafood restaurant in the Dún Laoghaire station building.

The new Russell Court was opened for trading on 11 August 1972. A mere six weeks later on 25 September it was bombed, presumably by the Provisional IRA; extensive damage was caused and the hotel had to be closed. Substantial damages were sought and collected from Belfast Corporation, though CIÉ believed them to be inadequate. The hotel was repaired and partially reopened as a 70-bedroom hotel in May 1973. It was again damaged by a bomb attack on 17 March 1975 and was not reopened. The unfortunate saga of the Russell Court did serious damage to the OIÉ company. The Great Southern Hotels in the Republic, while never physically damaged, were not immune to the effects of the Northern troubles. The worldwide publicity given to rioting in Belfast, to the People's Democracy marches in January 1969, and to the battle of the Bogside in August of that year, started a decline in the number of foreign tourists visiting Ireland. The international tourist industry as a whole went into recession in the wake of the oil crisis. This confluence of events weakened the Great Southern Hotels themselves as well as CIÉ tour operations. However, the Great Southern chain might well have weathered the storm without serious difficulty were it not for the tragedy of the Russell Court.

One must look back to 1965 and the symbolic importance of meetings in January and February of that year between the Northern Premier Terence O'Neill and Seán Lemass to understand why OIÉ should have considered Belfast as a possible site for expansion. In November 1966 Lemass had resigned but the friendly cross-border contacts continued. In October 1967 Erskine Childers as Minister for Transport and Power and Brian Faulkner as Northern Ireland's Minister for Commerce signed an agreement to link their cross-border electricity systems. The cross-border thaw continued and in January 1968 Taoiseach Jack Lynch welcomed Captain Terence O'Neill to talks in Dublin. That was the year in which the Russell Court was acquired, but it was not long before the attempt to achieve a peaceful normalisation of the relationships between the two communities failed. In November, as loyalist protests gathered strength, Terence O'Neill was moved to make his famous 'Ulster at the Cross Roads' speech, and the following April he was forced from office. The timing of the Russell Court project, while understandable in the context of the late 1960s, could not have been worse.

OIÉ was already haemorrhaging when St J. Devlin became Chairman of CIÉ in January 1974. The Annual Report for the year to March 1974 was published in the normal way. The next set of accounts, with the change in accounting to the calendar year, were for the nine months to 31 December 1974, but accounting problems with OIÉ and its Russell Court subsidiary, called Great Southern Hotels (NI), delayed their publication until January 1977. In fact, because of the state of the Russell Court's affairs, CIÉ's auditors were not prepared to give Great Southern Hotels (NI) a 'clean certificate' as a going concern. As GSH (NI) was a subsidiary of OIÉ, the directors of that company would not sign the heavily qualified accounts. Without completed accounts for OIÉ a consolidated set of CIÉ accounts could not be produced, hence the delay. A simple decision, i.e. a guarantee from the Board of CIÉ to GSH (NI) would have cleared the accounting log jam. CIÉ could not or would not give such a guarantee to GSH (NI) without the approval of its shareholder, the government, or more particularly, the Department of Finance. The Department of Finance could not easily be persuaded that the necessary guarantee be given. At a later stage they would be equally difficult about agreeing to OIÉ selling the Russell Court and to liquidating the GSH (NI). The student of accounts who wants to explore the Russell Court story will find much interesting material in Note 12 in CIÉ's own financial statements in the years from 1969/70 to 1972/73, in Note 7 of the 1973/74 accounts, and mainly in Note 18 of subsequent accounts up to 1983.

The general reader may note that the 1974 accounts recorded a nine-month loss for the hotel group of £604,000. As development during and since the 1960s was financed entirely by loan capital the interest burden on the hotels over the same nine-month period was £489,000. A report in 1973 by the international firm of consultants, Arthur D. Little, concluded that an equity investment of £1.5 million was required. In 'The Way Ahead' (January 1977) St J. Devlin said:

> Since then further losses sustained in 1974 and 1975 have escalated the financial crisis. . . . The point of 'no-return' was reached when it became clear that the Group could not continue on a 'going basis'. Old and new strategies were then reviewed and the following decisions were taken by the Board:
> - CIÉ would increase its equity holding in OIÉ.
> - CIÉ would convert its loan of £440,000 to OIÉ into equity capital.
> - The resort type hotels (Bundoran, Sligo, Mulrany and Kenmare) and the Belfast Hotel (the Russell Court) would be sold.
> - All surplus lands associated with the hotels would be sold.

One might ask, if Mulrany and Kenmare were chosen for disposal as 'resort type hotels', was Parknasilla not also a resort property? In addition, 'an aggressive marketing strategy was formulated and profits were projected for a period of five years'. CIÉ envisaged that 'as a result of these steps it would be possible to operate the remainder of the Group on a "going concern" basis, meeting annual interest charges and ultimately reducing capital loans'. The sought-for change in OIÉ's capital structure took place on 11 March 1977 when the equity was increased by £1,839,795 through £1,400,000 being contributed by way of cash from the parent and the balance by converting a CIÉ loan into equity. In 1978 CIÉ was optimistic enough to say the 'strategy adopted in 1976 to sell four hotels and re-invest the proceeds in refurbishing the remaining six hotels has been successful. The outlook for 1978 is for a significant increase in profits.' (Annual Report, 1977) However, the Russell Court remained unsold and for another five years it continued to impose heavy carrying costs on OIÉ.

It is appropriate here to bring the story forward to its conclusion. In 1978 a small profit of £22,000 was recorded for 'hotels and catering' services and in 1979 it might have seemed that the problem was over when profits rose to £254,000. However in 1980, with a new recession in tourism, this result collapsed dramatically into a loss of £260,000. The loss rose to £539,000 in 1981 and to £885,000 in 1982. The 1982 result signalled another financial crisis in OIÉ. CIÉ's accounts were again delayed and this time Devlin in his Chairman's review was more explicit about the cause of the delay than he had been in 1974. In succinct and forthright fashion he explained CIÉ's hotel dilemma.

> It is unusual that I should be writing this review when the one which I wrote last year for the 1980 accounts has not yet been published. In the circumstances an explanation is due and I will summarise, briefly, the reason why the accounts for year ending 31 December 1980 have not yet been printed or distributed. . . .
>
> The financing of the Hotels subsidiary has been the subject of negotiation and discussion with the Department of Transport for a number of years. In 1973 a firm of business consultants was employed to undertake an examination of the OIÉ hotels and to make recommendations regarding their future and the financing of that future. In 1981, at the request of the Minister for Transport, there was an examination of the financial state of the hotels by a firm of Merchant Bankers and they made certain recommendations. Numerous submissions have been made to the Department of Transport and these have been revised at regular intervals.
>
> The hotels have been under-capitalised because the development which took place prior to 1972 was financed by loan capital. Apart from an equity injection of £1.4 m. in 1977, the company has had to pay substantial interest in the years 1974 to 1982. During this period four hotels were sold and an effort was made to dispose of the bomb-damaged hotel in Belfast. When, in the view of the Board, a satisfactory tender was obtained for the Belfast premises, the Government of the day directed that the asset should not be disposed of.
>
> Unfortunately no Government has indicated a policy for the hotels nor has any Government responded to the Company's request for adequate equity finance. Because of the absence of a decision, the insolvency of OIÉ and the Board's reservation concerning the continued operation of OIÉ as a going concern, the accounts of the subsidiary cannot be consolidated with the accounts of CIÉ and this has been the reason for the delay in the publication of the annual reports.   (Annual Report, 1982)

As we've seen, criticism by Devlin of government decision-making at this time was not confined to hotels. A partial explanation for what was happening was that there had been six separate ministers in charge of CIÉ since Devlin's appointment eight years earlier. Such a turnover is bound to inhibit the positive guidance from government which should follow from periods of sustained analysis, reflection and the making of sound decisions, which confront rather than attempt to evade reality.

In the following year, 1982, the loss on CIÉ hotels suffered a further sharp rise but progress of a sort was being made. Devlin reported:

> Since my last report permission has been granted for the sale of the Russell Court Hotel in Belfast. The sale was completed early this year for £1.1 m. sterling. Also this year the government provided an equity injection of £3.4 m. and both of these amounts were used to repay one of the major bank loans. The Annual Accounts for the OIÉ hotels have now been signed by the Directors and consolidation with the CIÉ accounts has been possible.
>
> In January 1983 a programme for re-organisation of [hotel] services and a reduction in the number of permanent staff was drafted. This programme was agreed with the trade unions in February and submitted to the Minister for Transport for approval. No decision has yet been given because the Government is considering a future policy for the hotels. It is not yet known whether CIÉ will be required to dispose of some or all of the present chain.   (Annual Report, 1983)

A new minister, Jim Mitchell, was in charge of CIÉ. When he reported in 1983 that the Russell Court had been sold, his predecessor, John Wilson, who earlier had refused permission to dispose of the property, challenged him as to whether a fair price had been received. The story of CIÉ's ownership of the Great Southern Hotels ended rather dismally with note 6 to the accounts for the year 1984 recording that

> The share capital held by Córas Iompair Éireann in the subsidiary company, Ostlanna Iompair Éireann Teoranta was disposed of on 9th March, 1984 for £1.

The same note recorded that the accumulated loss of the hotels group up to 31 March 1984 amounted to £9.853 million which was discharged by a special and cumbrously named payment from the exchequer of 'non-repayable non-interest bearing advances'—in normal language, a grant or transfer.

The hotels by government decision were transferred to CERT, the state tourism training agency, but CIÉ asked and was allowed to retain

Restaurant na Mara, operating in the original Dún Laoghaire terminal of the D & SER as a 'flagship' for its catering division. Thus ended the involvement of Ireland's surface transport companies with hotel operation. In the nineteenth century various railway companies had built hotels for their customers. Even before the railways, the canal companies had built and operated hotels, e.g. Portobello, Dublin; Robertstown, Co. Kildare; and Shannon Harbour, Co. Offaly. Ironically, now that the problems caused by the Russell Court disasters and by the tourism recession of the 1970s had been overcome by government permission to sell the Russell Court and by a capital injection to make them viable, the Great Southern Hotels would come to be operated by a late twentieth-century phenomenon of the transport industry—the financially strong airport authority, Aer Rianta, which prospers on revenues largely derived from financially weaker airlines.

PETER BARRY IN 1976 had questioned some of CIÉ's 'peripheral activities'. Devlin, while still new in the job, was of like mind and listed such activities as 'maintenance of canals, the operation of cross-channel freight movements, financial participation in ferry operations, the management of a harbour and the operation of a chain of hotels'. Inadvertently, no doubt, this list omitted Aerlód, the air freight subsidiary.

> It is difficult to explain the compatibility of these activities with the Board's main task of providing reasonable, efficient and economical transport services within the capacity of the resources available. Effective management at all levels is essential to our future. We have the right people and we must not encumber them with activities which are superficial to our main goals. (The Way Ahead, 1977)

Rosslare Harbour and the Great Southern Hotels were big operations from which CIÉ could not withdraw without government decisions, even if it chose to do so. As time passed, Devlin seemed to accept both of these enterprises as presenting an appropriate challenge to CIÉ. The canals were solely a matter for government. The 1950 legislation required CIÉ to maintain the canals and only an amendment to the law could release CIÉ from that chore. Accordingly, the activities which, realistically, were within CIÉ's discretion to withdraw from, were its involvement in cross-channel freight movements (Irish Ferryways), its financial involvement in the Irish Continental Line, its continental freight operations, and Aerlód. All of these activities ceased by the end of 1977. First, in 1975 CIÉ withdrew from operating vehicles on the continent in exercise of three multilateral licences which it held from the EEC. The operation lost £106,000 in its final year. Aerlód was also incurring losses and in April 1976 it was disposed of to a 'management buyout'. In the case of Irish Ferryways, including the Irish Continental Line involvement, the 1976 report recorded that while it was profitable, CIÉ had decided to 'terminate this activity as projected profits would not justify the capital investment required over the next 2/3 years'. As a result by the end of 1977, apart from the hotels and maintenance of the canals, the only CIÉ business which did not involve internal transport was Rosslare Harbour. The hotel story has been briefly told; the passing of the canals from CIÉ care will be told later.

As in the case of the hotels CIÉ's involvement in Rosslare Harbour had its origins in the nineteenth century and in some intricate historical obligations undertaken by its predecessors. As Devlin indicated, the board in early 1977 saw no prima facie justification for CIÉ's operation of Rosslare Harbour. The legal situation, as summarised in the 1957 Beddy Report, was that Rosslare Harbour, the railway between Fermoy and Rosslare, Fishguard Harbour, and the railway between Fishguard and Goodwich in south Wales were the property of the Fishguard & Rosslare Railways & Harbours Company (F & RR & HC). However, an agreement dated 27 May 1896 had assigned management and control of the undertaking in Britain, as well as the steamer service between Rosslare and Fishguard, to the (British) Great Western Railway Company. In due course British Rail succeeded to these rights and obligations, eventually selling the shipping service to Stena Sealink. The 1896 agreement ceded responsibility for Rosslare Harbour and the railway from Rosslare to Fermoy to Irish interests which in due course passed from the GSR to CIÉ. None the less the F & RR & HC survived and its board comprised representatives of British Rail and of CIÉ.

Naturally enough, seeing the F & RR & HC as an anachronism, St J. Devlin observed a number of times during his early years in office that he thought that it should be dissolved. Seemingly lawyers in Britain and in Ireland considered that this would be an excessively complicated exercise. Several nineteenth-century railway Acts and questions of property rights would have to be explored and amended. Both Westminster and Leinster House would need to be involved. Why bother dissolving the F & RR & HC? The 1896 agreement was operating satisfactorily. If they addressed the proposal at all, the two administrations rejected it, accepting the handyman's counsel 'If it works don't fix it.' In 1995 the F & RR & HC still exists, its directors meeting with whatever minimum frequency is required by law, while the business of the two harbours at Rosslare and Fishguard and of the shipping and railway lines continue to be operated under the 1896 agreement, the centenary of which will occur when this book has reached its readers' hands.

In the 1950s CIÉ was operating three canal docks or wharves (Spencer, Ringsend and St James's Street Harbour) as well as Rosslare Harbour and the North Wharf at Waterford. The others fell into disuse or into other hands, but Rosslare had survived and would become an important national asset and a source of pride to CIÉ. Well before Devlin, in the early 1960s, CIÉ declared an intention to develop Rosslare Harbour into a major modern port. As drive on/drive off ferries for commercial transport and private cars became popular on European sea crossings, facilities in the Republic of Ireland lagged behind those available abroad. Even as late as 1964, visitor cars out of Rosslare and Dún Laoghaire were hoisted by crane from the quay and lowered into ships' holds for transportation. In Rosslare there was the added complication that cars had to be transferred between the pier and the mainland on rail wagons before being slung aboard ship.

In 1963 British Rail constructed a side-loading facility at Fishguard for roll-on/roll-off cars. CIÉ provided matching facilities at Rosslare Harbour. Then in the autumn of 1967 Irish Shipping Ltd announced an intention to use stern loading vessels at Rosslare for a continental service to be operated by Normandy Ferries. CIÉ provided the necessary facilities, catering for roll-on/roll-off freight units in addition to motor cars and passengers. A new stern loading ramp was constructed, customs and immigration facilities were provided, and with the arrival of the *Leopard* from Le Havre on Sunday, 19 May 1968, Rosslare became the first Irish port to have a direct passenger car ferry with roll-on/roll-off freight service to the continent.

The GSR Hotel in Rosslare was also completed in 1968 and Michael Viney, then economic development correspondent of *The Irish Times*, could write of Rosslare Harbour, 'controlled and operated by CIÉ . . . as a premier port of thoroughly modern equipment and organisation' (*Administration*, Winter 1968). The Rosslare operation was continuously profitable and once other 'international activities' were terminated, the board renewed its commitment to Rosslare. In 1978 the CIÉ Annual Report noted that 'inadequate facilities continued to cause congestion problems at the port'. Circumstances could arise during the holiday season where one vessel had to wait at anchor while another occupied the single Ro/Ro berth which had been built almost ten years earlier. 'As a consequence the government has now approved the building of an additional pier.' (Annual Report, 1977) A profit of £558,000 for Rosslare Harbour was recorded in 1978. During 1979 'Design work on a new jetty, berths and other facilities was completed. Dredging commenced in October and it is hoped to have the entire scheme completed early in 1980.' The second pier came into service on 25 May 1980, in which year in addition to Sealink and Irish Continental Line, B + I began Rosslare operations with a service to Pembroke. Rosslare Harbour, despite earlier doubts, would stay a prosperous activity within the CIÉ fold, with further major developments in the late 1980s and the early 1990s.

ROAD FREIGHT WAS not a 'peripheral' CIÉ activity. It was a core activity, but was seen by the Devlin Board as less fundamental to CIÉ than its railway and its nationwide bus services. Both in the 1971 McKinsey study 'Defining the Role of Public Transportation in a Changing Environment', and in CIÉ's 1979 submission to the Oireachtas Committee on State Sponsored Bodies it was classified under 'other transport activities'. The difference of attitude to road freight, as against rail and road passenger activities, mainly arose from the fact that CIÉ was very much a minority provider of road freight services. As McKinsey observed, 'much of CIÉ's road freight business could be undertaken by the private sector both by own account operations and by hauliers without additional costs to the community. Therefore there is no justification for giving financial support to CIÉ for those services.' Explaining CIÉ's approach to road freight, Devlin, in a paper, 'CIÉ and the Future', read to the Chartered Institute of Transport in Limerick on 20 February 1975, noted that

> There is no provision for Government subvention in regard to this business. . . . We are in road freight for profit and the measure of that profit will determine the strength of the activity . . . financial constraints will apply more stringently in this area than in any other . . . The Board has agreed to make a substantial capital investment over the next four years on new vehicles . . . it is anticipated that the implementation of this plan will enable CIÉ Road Freight services make an annual profit of about £150,000 after allowing for overheads by 1977.

In 'The Way Ahead' the intention with regard to road freight services was made more precise. In future 'the goal for road freight is to concentrate available resources on the development of railhead road freight and other road services which complement the railway operation' (The Way Ahead, January 1977). Already £750,000 had been spent on road freight vehicles, including units fitted with tail-lifts and specially modified vehicles for the carriage of Asahi traffic between Ballina and Killala. Surprisingly, the dramatic conversion of a £740,000 road freight deficit in 1975 into a £3,000 profit in 1976 was modestly described only as 'a considerable improvement' in the 1976 Annual Report. Further remarks elaborated on CIÉ's road freight business and some of its problems.

> The policy of retrenchment and reorganisation . . . coupled with a buoyancy in revenue, were the main factors in the improvement. The increase in revenue derived principally from increased carryings of limestone, beet, imported motor vehicles, steel, cement and fertiliser. This improvement was partly offset by decreases in meat, materials for County Councils and certain other traffics.

The retention of over-age units in the operating fleet was reflected in high maintenance costs and unsatisfactory utilisation, and the replacement of these vehicles is an urgent requirement. Negotiations continued during the year on a productivity scheme for road freight operatives and, while agreement was not reached, progress was achieved in reducing staff numbers and in converting two-man services to one-man operations. (Annual Report, 1976)

The next two years' profits of £7,000 (1977) and £8,000 (1978) meant that road freight continued to break even on annual revenues of over £11 million. Reorganisation and re-equipment resulted in vehicle and labour productivity being increased. The three years 1976–1978 seemed to show that CIÉ had got the balance right in the road freight division, but there was a severe turn for the worse in 1979 when a loss of £688,000 was incurred. The tonnage of goods carried (including hired hauliers) slipped 14.5 per cent on 1978 levels and CIÉ claimed that 'this was due substantially to the loss of ground limestone traffic following the partial withdrawal of the government subsidy' (Annual Report, 1979). The slippage in loads continued and over the next three years the deficit steadily rose: £1.105 million (1980), £1.47 million (1981), and £1.625 million (1982). This trend was arrested in 1983 when a loss of £670,000 represented an improvement of almost £1 million in one year. By that time the tonnage carried on CIÉ's road freight was down almost 50 per cent on the 1976 figure. Much of the tonnage lost was ground limestone (the government limestone subsidy scheme had ceased entirely) and contract work for local authorities. However, a substantial decline also took place in general freight carried by CIÉ road transport, paralleling the railway decline in this traffic.

Better to understand what was happening, it is necessary to look at national developments in the road haulage sector. Compilation of national statistics for road ton miles is not a simple exercise and one cannot pinpoint when road passed out rail as the dominant mode for the transport of goods. At any rate, by the late 1950s it was overwhelmingly evident that the existing legislation controlling commercial road transport was seriously outdated. The controlling legislation was the 1933 Road Transport Act which had frozen licensed hauliers at the level which then obtained—though permitting licences to be bought or sold between hauliers including the national transport company. However, since its establishment in 1945 CIÉ itself had not acquired any private haulage firm. While it was clear to all that the situation had changed radically since 1933 and especially since the end of World War II, it was still possible for government to postpone a reform of the industry by claiming that insufficient statistical information was available to show what was really happening in the marketplace. That gap in information was addressed in 1964 by a special survey of the road haulage industry carried out by the Central Statistics Office. However, governments had many other things on their minds and little account was taken of these findings.

The first modest amendment of the 1933 Act was introduced by Brian Lenihan in 1971, decontrolling the carriage of livestock and some other commodities, as well as removing the weight restrictions imposed on licensed hauliers under the 1933 Act. The Confederation of Irish Industries (CII) continued to be concerned at what it regarded as a very anomalous situation and undertook a survey of its own in 1974. It concluded that expenditure of transport users was broken down between the different categories of road transport providers as follows:

'Own Account', i.e. companies' own transport	62%
Private licensed hauliers	16%
CIÉ road freight	13%
'Hackers' within port areas where licences were not required	9%

The complaint of the CII and others was that firms were being forced to operate their own vehicles because of the limited services available from public road transport companies (both private hauliers and CIÉ). These 'own account' vehicles were not being used economically. In particular, 'own account' vehicles typically carried only one-way loads because they were unable legally to sell empty return capacity to another party. A senior representative of CIÉ sat on the CII committee which reported on to the industry, and Devlin made it clear that CIÉ was not contesting the facts.

> The Minister for Transport and Power has indicated that it is his intention to liberalise road freight at the end of this year. CIÉ are not in disagreement with this policy, but they are concerned that if there is liberalisation, then equal competition must be established through the regular policing of the qualitative and personnel controls imposed by EEC directives. ('CIÉ and the Future', 20 February 1975)

CIÉ's continuing strategy was to make its road transport more complementary than it had been to its railway operations, but if the playing field was to be levelled, they wanted it to be levelled properly. It withdrew from the carriage of bloodstock and other specialist traffics by road. The next attempt at legislative reform was a Bill circulated by Peter Barry in 1976 which proposed to liberalise the road haulage industry from most of its 40-year-old shackles. Fianna Fáil in opposition took the view that this 1976 Bill went too far, too fast, and they adopted an unusual Dáil tactic. Instead of awaiting the second stage of the Bill and then attempting to amend it in the committee stage, they put down what was called a 'reasoned amendment', totally rejecting the entire 1976 Bill 'because the provisions in the Bill would cause heavy unemployment in the rail and road freight sections of CIÉ and among the employees of licensed hauliers at a time of high unemployment. They said that the Bill contained no provisions to control the standards of road transport and heavy road vehicles and that the provisions of the Bill would cause further heavy congestion on an inadequate road system and put the continuation of the railways in jeopardy.' (*Dáil Debates*, March 1978, Vol. 304, Col. 1468)

Again the Dáil had other matters on its mind, including the annulment of the 1945 'Emergency', the declaration of a new national emergency, and the passing of an Emergency Powers Bill following the assassination of the British Ambassador, Christopher Ewart Biggs, by the Provisional IRA in July 1976. An unfortunate fall-out of that Bill was the resignation of Cearbhall Ó Dálaigh as President, in protest at an insult 'to the dignity and independence of the Presidency as an institution'. Ó Dálaigh's action followed on the Taoiseach, Liam Cosgrave, refusing to accept the resignation of his Minister for Defence, Paddy Donegan, who had described Ó Dálaigh as a 'thundering disgrace' for having referred the Emergency Powers Bill to the Supreme Court for a ruling on its constitutionality. We mention that incident only to indicate again how badly outdated legislation could survive, when more controversial matters emerged to engage the attention of its legislators. The Peter Barry Road Transport Bill was a casualty in these affairs. Its second stage never reached the floor of the Dáil and it lapsed with the General Election of June 1977.

His successor, Pádraig Faulkner, in the new Fianna Fáil government moved a fresh Road Transport Bill in March 1978. He believed a more 'phased' approach to liberalising the road haulage business was appropriate. The 1978 Bill proposed that each existing haulage licence would allow its owner to operate six vehicles rather than one, subject to a maximum of eighty vehicles for any one operator. Another provision extended the 'exempted areas' around the main ports, e.g. operations within 15 miles of Dublin's GPO had previously been exempt from the need to hold a licence to carry freight for reward. This limit was now increased to 20 miles. In other port areas such as Cork, Limerick, Galway and Waterford, the limit of the exempted areas was increased from 10 miles to 15 miles. In addition, vehicles under 2.5 tonnes unladen weight (maximum fully laden weight 6 tonnes) were exempted from all licensing controls. Another provision eased the prohibition on operators leasing rather than owning vehicles. This provision merits comment because the background tells much of changing public attitudes. Faulkner recognised that manufacturers could lease premises, manufacturing and office equipment; accordingly, it was anomalous that they could not lease vehicles. Still, he only modified rather than repealed the provisions of a 1956 Act prohibiting the leasing of vehicles. In retrospect, the 1956 Act was a panic measure introduced by William Norton and welcomed by the entire Dáil following a Supreme Court decision that the lessor of a vehicle was not an operator and hence did not require a haulier's licence. The Dáil unanimously agreed that this finding threatened to destabilise the entire transport industry and so rushed through Norton's Bill.

Introducing his own Road Transport Bill, Pádraig Faulkner quoted figures showing that 80 per cent of the total road freight movement outside the exempted areas was moved by 'own account' operators. The size of this own account share was a distortion caused by outmoded legislation. The Bill would facilitate the growth of a much stronger licensed haulier sector. The ghosts of Seán Lemass and Erskine Childers must have been shocked by the almost casual way in which their successor Pádraig Faulkner referred to the carriage of freight on the railways; they were no longer regarded as fundamental to the movement of goods.

> That finding, [concerning own account operators] taken with the fact that the railway share of freight transport was virtually frozen to a few traffics especially suited to rail, demonstrated that the restrictive legislation maintained for over 30 years with the objective of securing freight traffic for the railways, or, road services operated by the railways, had totally failed in its purpose.   (ibid., Vol. 304, Col. 1452)

Deputy Tom O'Donnell for Fine Gael once again delivered a well-researched and comprehensive speech on the road transport scene—a comment that is prompted by the relative rarity of such qualities in Dáil contributions on transport matters other than in the briefs of the ever changing minister himself. The opposition did not oppose the Bill. Road haulage generated only 11 per cent of CIÉ's revenues in 1978 and had never generated more than 15 per cent of the total. The change that had occurred in the internal transport of freight of all kinds was so enormous that there was no argument about it. Slowly the legislation was being adapted to accommodate this change. It is time to move on to a faster-growing and more critical sector of CIÉ's public transport services—the movement of people by road.

Chapter 18

BUSES: LABOUR AND TRAFFIC PROBLEMS

Dublin buses—Industrial relations—Oireachtas Committee—Expressway network extends—Dublin's traffic—Bus control experiments—Automated vehicle monitoring—Decision to establish a Dublin Transport Authority—Bus priority measures—Van Hool and Bombardier buses.

Sometimes it is useful to state the obvious. To the average citizen 'going by CIÉ' means taking a bus. The wait at the bus stop, getting a seat, conditions on the bus, traffic *en route* and arrival at one's destination are ingredients of the normal customer's exposure to CIÉ. In the year 1975 almost 14 million passengers travelled by train, but 307 million travelled by bus. Thus 22 people boarded a bus for every passenger who boarded a train. In 1979, with train travel growing and Dublin bus passenger numbers on a downward slope, the ratio of total train to total bus passengers improved. But still bus journeys outnumbered train journeys by almost 14 to 1. The experiences in the 1970s of operating a fleet of 2,600 buses of assorted types over about 67 million miles a year and carrying up to 300 million passengers, in environments as diverse as congested cities and underpopulated mountain districts, is the subject of this chapter. Reliability is a *sine qua non* of scheduled transport. Properly to fulfil its function, public transport must be regular and dependable. When one applies the old adage that 'the exception proves the rule' to public transport, it emerges that regularity and dependability is indeed the public transport rule. So it was, and is, with the daily operation of CIÉ buses, and when they occur, exceptions are front-page news.

As we have seen earlier, bus operations had problems with inflation and, consequently, with profitability and with achieving necessary fare increases, especially in urban areas. But in this chapter the focus is firstly on labour relations, especially in relation to Dublin buses. It then turns to the rural bus scene before returning to urban areas and to attempts by CIÉ and others to grapple with the strangulating tentacles of the traffic octopus. Decisions and problems about renewing the bus fleet will finally engage our attention.

THE BULK OF CIÉ's employees, 70 per cent, are engaged in operating and supporting bus services; accordingly, industrial relations upsets can have widespread service effects. Through the 1970s such upsets among bus workers presented a major challenge to the expertise of CIÉ, of its unions and of the state's labour relations institutions. Bus workers expected pay to rise not merely to keep up with inflation, but also to provide them with the improved living standards being achieved generally in the community. This was not easy to arrange in a major employment —Ireland's largest—which was beset by pay relativities and which, because of its subvention status, was always in the eye of government. Successive governments deplored industrial disputes while simultaneously subjecting CIÉ to restraints which deprived its management of that room for flexibility which can be at the heart of successful industrial relations practice. Resolution of recurring problems among bus workers were all that more difficult because of trade union structures and trade union rivalries, especially in the case of Dublin's bus operations.

A repeated Devlin message to CIÉ employees was that board aimed to increase workers' living standards through pay increases which could be made possible by higher productivity. However, bus workers in Dublin would not accept that single change in working conditions, i.e. one-person operation of double deck buses, which would deliver a major productivity boost. Problems simmered because of the tension generated on the job by traffic congestion, by irregular working hours and by equipment faults. In addition bus workers, like others in the transport industry, have special communications problems with colleagues, supervisors and trade unions, because of their varying duty rosters, dispersed locations and being 'out on the job' for almost all of their working day.

In 'The Way Ahead' St J. Devlin confronted the public perception about industrial relations in CIÉ.

> It has been suggested that industrial relations are bad in CIÉ, that there are frequent strikes, that staff morale is low and that the management is responsible for this state of affairs. An analysis of the stoppages over the past three years does not support these allegations . . . It is important that these allegations of industrial unrest and management incompetence be shown to be false and without any basis in fact.
> (The Way Ahead, January 1977)

The incidence of strikes in CIÉ, as a whole, relative to the national data show that days lost per 1,000 workers were substantially (about 70 per cent) lower than the national figures in 1967, 1968, 1969 and in 1970. In 1971 CIÉ's strike performance was worse than the national average when an NBU-led dispute relating to a transfer to a new garage in Phibsboro caused a complete, though brief, suspension of Dublin's bus services. The following year, 1972, was virtually strike free, while in 1973 CIÉ's record was about average. However, 1974, Devlin's first year as Chairman, was a disaster in terms of CIÉ strikes—the worst ever year for days lost—99 per cent of which were lost on Dublin buses. He explained what had happened.

> Road passenger staffs are represented by the National Busmen's Union (NBU), which is not affiliated to the Irish Congress of Trade Unions (ICTU), and by the Irish Transport and General Workers' Union and the Workers' Union of Ireland, both of which are affiliated to Congress. There is often a conflict of ideas and aspirations between the NBU and the Congress unions. Such a conflict gave rise to a major strike in Dublin City Services (DCS) in 1974. In this case, a claim by all the unions for a five-day week had been conceded and had been accepted by a ballot of all the busmen, but a few days before the five-day week was due to come in, the ICTU unions changed their minds. CIÉ was then faced with a strike whether or not the five-day week was implemented. The eventual resolution of this strike was agreement on a 5.4 day week and a special compensatory allowance to existing staff in respect of Sunday duty. The result of this dispute was a loss of 168,263 man days. (ibid.)

A few important details may be added to illustrate that the stoppage was one of classic complexity. It was unofficial to begin with, and lasted for nine weeks from 5 May to 8 July. On average 2,500 men per day were affected and for long periods Dublin traffic came to a virtual standstill. Twelve days into the strike, the Republic suffered its worst ever overspill of 'Northern violence'. Three car bombs exploded in Dublin's city centre and another in Monaghan, killing 31 people and injuring 150. The strike ran on and in mid-June the government decided to call on the army to provide relief transport, particularly for the old and the young. The weekend of that decision, damage was caused by fire to six double-decker buses in Donnybrook garage. The decision to use army lorries was suspended but implemented later as the stoppage continued. Many Labour Court conciliation conferences took place and the Chairman of the Labour Court took the very unusual step of writing to the newspapers to explain the problem, saying that 'In spite of the best efforts of the public agencies concerned with industrial relations neither group of men is prepared to change its attitude.'

Eventually work was resumed on the basis of the original 6-day week with the promise of further negotiations. After several more conciliation conferences and formal court hearings, a 'two tier' roster which had the effect of a 5.4-day week was agreed on 8 September—four months after the most serious ever Dublin bus dispute had begun. There was no change in the length of the working week which at 40 hours per week was not at issue. It was the kind of dispute where neither reason nor concession appeared capable of achieving a solution. The previous major Dublin bus strike of 1966 looked simple in comparison. Questions concerning the dispute were raised in the Dáil. Michael O'Leary, as Minister for Labour, was under pressure to achieve a settlement. He explained his and CIÉ's dilemma during an adjournment debate on 5 June 1974.

> I have been concerned from the start about the effects of the strike on employment and about the hardship it has imposed on the general public, particularly the old and those attending hospitals and clinics. A great strain has been placed on the Garda at a time when they are already heavily committed on the security front. As I said here on 16th May . . . It should be possible, given a willingness, to isolate the agreement reached in principle on the introduction of the five-day week from the practical difficulties of operating schedules in the context of the five-day week . . . I met the unions this evening to see if the present deadlock situation could be reversed and I shall resume these discussions at 11 o'clock tonight. I shall continue, as I am continuing tonight to maintain a strong and determined attempt to bring the parties to a frame of mind which will allow a settlement to emerge. It will not be a simple task to reverse this deadlock situation, as the course of the dispute clearly shows.
>
> (*Dáil Debates*, Vol. 273, Cols 599, 601)

O'Leary, himself an experienced trade unionist, read the situation correctly. The 'frame of mind' for a resumption of work was not achieved for another five weeks. Fatigue and public pressure on the strikers were major factors in the decision to resume work. After that 1974 trauma CIÉ's record of days lost per employee was again below the national average until 1979. In January of that year there was a nationwide bus stoppage, but it lasted for only four days and caused only 10 per cent of the man-days CIÉ had lost in 1974. In contrast, for the country as a whole, 1979 was the worst ever for industrial disputes. Nurses, guards, postal and airline workers all took action over special claims and Dublin had no garbage collection for an extended period. It was also the year of the papal visit in October, during which there was a national industrial relations truce. The papal visit provided CIÉ with a major transport challenge to which it responded superbly, as we shall see in the next chapter.

1979 was also the year of the first Joint Oireachtas Committee investigation of CIÉ. After five decades of Dáil argument about the need for more information concerning the operations and policies of state-sponsored bodies, it was the Fine Gael/Labour coalition in 1976 which introduced legislation under which the Oireachtas could set up a committee to have hearings on the affairs of such bodies—they could question management, civil servants, trade union officials and others, employ consultants and issue reports. Away from the adversarial games of Dáil debates, the members of these committees could achieve an understanding of the real problems of state companies which all too frequently were understated, concealed, if not misrepresented in brief, sometimes loaded, references to such companies in ministerial speeches or in media comments. The Joint Oireachtas Committees lapsed each time the Dáil was dissolved, so that it was not until 1979 that a re-established committee came to review CIÉ. In its comprehensive examination of public transport services, consideration was given to the state of the organisation's industrial relations. The committee's report recorded several positive views on industrial relations in CIÉ from those immediately concerned:

> The Chairman of CIÉ stated that 'industrial relations in the whole of CIÉ have been remarkably good'. The representative of the National Association of Transport Employees said that industrial relations on the rail side were excellent. A representative of the Irish Transport and General Workers' Union stated that 'The public image of industrial relations in CIÉ is based primarily, if not exclusively, on what happens in the bus sector . . . The difficulty the busmen experienced was their inability to have their skill and expertise recognised simply and solely because they worked for an industry which required a subvention.' A representative of the National Busmen's Union stated that 'We have not had many disputes but when they arise they always made the headlines.' Apart from stoppages in Dublin City Services over the last few years, the number of man-days lost as a percentage of man-days worked in CIÉ is quite small. But stoppages in Dublin City Bus Services have led, according to an ITGWU representative to 'the image the public have of CIÉ: because busmen stop, CIÉ is riddled with industrial relations problems; it has an incompetent management and it has an equally incompetent trade union structure'.
> (Joint Committee on State Sponsored Bodies, October 1979)

Having heard these views and having received a blow-by-blow account of all the minor, mostly unofficial, stoppages which had occurred in the three previous years, the Joint Committee's own view was cautiously expressed: 'the overall industrial relations record of CIÉ is not as bad as it is popularly believed to be'. The deputies and senators noted a 'number of constructive aspects of the industrial relations scene', including the 'considerable responsibility' shown by trade unions 'when through negotiation, agreement was reached to reduce, through voluntary redundancies the staff of CIÉ by over 18 per cent over the last five years', and the appointment of a full-time secretary based in ICTU's headquarters to 'service the various trade union groups and to strengthen and improve the working arrangements and communications'. The creation of this ICTU Secretariat meant a breakthrough with the Congress Unions, of which St J. Devlin personally was quite proud, and this appointment of a full-time congress officer was prominently noted later in CIÉ's Annual Report (1979). Other initiatives in the industrial relations area during this period included the decentralisation of decision-making on certain personnel matters and the formation of additional consultation machinery, particularly within Dublin City Services.

Meanwhile at government level a decision had been made to appoint 'Worker Directors' to several named state boards, including CIÉ, by the passing of the Worker Directors (State Enterprises) Act 1977. For reasons unconnected with CIÉ the Act did not take effect until 1980. The worker director legislation prompted the ICTU to organise a series of seminars for shop stewards in the several organisations affected. Devlin spoke on the 'Role of the Board' to eight of these seminars organised specifically for CIÉ shop stewards. Subsequent comments prompted by these seminars throw an interesting light on his board's recognition of the need for sustained effort in the sensitive area of internal communications.

> Staff in CIÉ have an interest in Worker Participation, they have a greater interest in trying to understand the corporate strategy and policy decisions of the Board and the executive decisions of management.
>
> This need for understanding and the desire for information underlines the problem of communication. The effective exchange of information depends on dialogue. In a very large undertaking this dialogue is not easy and it becomes more difficult if there is a multiplicity of businesses as in the case of CIÉ. It is the Board's wish that the undertaking should move towards an open form of management. Frank and generous exchange of information and reaction is encouraged. Managers are endeavouring to bring about more effective communication at every level. . . .
>
> We are simultaneously engaged in radical change affecting both methods of operation and personal attitudes. The dilemma of establishing effective communication in an atmosphere of major change is one which can only be resolved by patience, perseverance and person to person dialogue. (Annual Report, 1977)

Provincial Bus Services suffered less than Dublin City Services from traffic congestion and labour questions. If success is measured solely in terms of growth and profit consistency, then the provincial bus services of CIÉ were an unqualified success. In 1974 passengers numbered 46.7 million, more than double the 19.9 million carried ten years earlier. Over the same period, Ireland's car population had grown by 70 per cent from 281,000 to 488,000, while rail passengers had grown by 37 per cent from 9.3 million to 12.7 million. The demand for travel was constantly increasing and in relative terms traffic growth on CIÉ's provincial buses was outstripping the other sectors. Provincial bus services comprised city services in Cork, Waterford, Limerick and Galway, rural stage carriage services and long haul intercity services. The city services experienced problems in profitability, passenger decline and traffic similar to those of Dublin—especially in the case of Cork which was sometimes said to have problems more intense than those of Dublin. The rural stage carriage services consistently grew in volume through the 1970s, but by 1979, with increased use of private transport, they too began to decline in growth and ceased to be profitable. The longer haul services had no such setback.

The introduction of the first express buses to Cavan, Monaghan, Enniskillen and Derry in 1961 (page 179) had been followed by similar express buses throughout the state, so that by 1971 the map of CIÉ's express bus network covered Dublin to Wexford, Waterford, Cork, Tralee, Limerick, Ennis, Galway, Westport, Ballina, Sligo, Strabane and Letterkenny via major intermediate centres with populations in excess of 10,000. The manifest success of the one-person operated express buses was enhanced by the brand name of Expressway, launched in June 1975 with substantial press, radio and television advertising. The subsequent growth was remarkable. CIÉ's published statistics tended to combine Expressway data with rural stage carriage services, but when identified on its own, percentage annual increases of 25 per cent to 35 per cent were reported.

Express and limited stop bus services were now operated on a wide scale to centres which were also being served by rail. A contributory factor was that as mainline rail services increasingly operated with less *en route* stops, train frequencies to some significant inland centres were falling. Another change was the recognition that important discrete groups could now be targeted by the express buses, in particular the youth market, with its particular price and timing requirements and its easier acceptance of bus standards of comfort. Overall, the long haul buses complemented railway capacity, especially at weekends. The social phenomenon of the student or young working adult from the country, living in Dublin but returning home for the weekend, both helped and was helped by the development of Expressway. It was a market in which private bus operators were also very active, cleverly using a charter stratagem to compensate for their generally not having scheduled service licences.

The realisation that long haul bus traffic was a market that could be profitably catered for, and did not need to be looked at purely from the angle of the railway, was rather slow in coming. Indeed, some say that elements of the old attitude survived well up to the launch of Bus Éireann as an independent operating company in 1987. For example, when the Limerick/Claremorris rail line was closed to passenger traffic in 1976, some area management people immediately thought that express buses should be operated from Tuam and Gort to Dublin. However, the CIÉ decision was that long-distance passengers to and from Tuam and Gort should be funnelled by feeder buses on to the Dublin/Galway railway line at Athenry. As a result, private bus operators stepped in, taking much of the traffic to Dublin from these points with scheduled services which they still operate.

In May 1975 a Galway/London bus service was launched and run in conjunction with the National Bus Company in Britain serving Athlone, Dublin, Birmingham, Coventry and Watford at weekends from May to September. The UK sector was initially served by British-owned buses as CIÉ's own coaches were mechanically restricted to speed levels which were unsuitable for Britain's motorways. Another important development was Interlink, whereby express services were linked at various transfer points so that convenient 'cross radial services' such as from Sligo to Cork or Dundalk to Limerick became available. The 1978 Annual Report noted that the Interlink concept 'proved very successful and contributed to the increase in numbers and in revenue' (25 per cent). Cross-channel services were developed in parallel with Interlink so that in 1980 a new service operated from 'Limerick and Tralee to Bristol and London via Rosslare Harbour' (Annual Report, 1980). Of course these cross-channel services, marketed as Supabus, were but a small part of Expressway's total activity. The Expressway story strongly makes the point that when a good transport product could be offered to a growing market, without the infrastructure problems and social service considerations which affected railway and urban bus transport, CIÉ management and staff are more than able to make a very successful business out of it.

THE STORY OF CIÉ's urban bus services might fittingly be told under such a title as 'The Struggle with Traffic'. The several Schaechterle studies of the 1960s, commissioned by Dublin Corporation in relation to traffic in general and by CIÉ in relation to its bus schedules and routings, have been mentioned in Chapter 15. Traffic problems are the result of a street network becoming incapable of allowing a smooth flow of the vehicles which seek to use it. The simple choices for dealing with such problems include increasing road space, i.e. the width and the number of streets and/or reducing the number of vehicles using them and/or regulating the way in which vehicles travel on the given street network. The Schaechterle reports might be said to have had their principal effect in gradual attempts to regulate the behaviour of vehicle users—introduction of one-way streets, reduction in right-hand turns, and control of parking through the introduction of parking meters, clearways and traffic wardens. Such measures can be grouped together as traffic management devices. They were capable of ameliorating a situation with a given level of road space and vehicle numbers. The option of increasing road space in Dublin had been used only to a limited extent and then, apart from new suburban road networks, it had been used mainly in the more dilapidated areas of the city. The option of freezing, restricting or forcing a reduction in vehicle numbers was not, and never would be, applied except to the extent that this might be a by-product of more rigid parking restrictions. Leaving aside questions of road space and the number and behaviour of vehicles using it, a fundamental long-term factor in traffic generation is the cumulative effect of decisions about the arrangement of residential areas, shopping and employment centres in the context of the city's overall population and economic growth.

In Dublin a number of reports had a critical impact on such decisions. Professor Myles Wright, under contract to the Department of Local Government in 1967, submitted a report 'The Dublin Region—An Advisory Regional Plan'. Many of the recommendations of this and previous reports (e.g. Buchanan) were incorporated in statutory development plans for the Dublin region drafted by the area's local authorities (1968) and later adopted (1972). An important feature of these plans was the development of three satellite towns to the west of the city—Tallaght, Clondalkin and Blanchardstown. CIÉ's role in this process of studying, proposing and planning varied from that of active participant to very interested spectator. When it came to the Myles Wright proposal for three satellite towns and its inclusion in the draft regional development plan of 1976, CIÉ adopted a very critical stance. New towns should be provided with well-planned adequate traffic systems internally and for access. In CIÉ's view, this argued strongly for public rather than for private transport, which in turn argued for their location around transport centres based on the available and underutilised railway infrastructure. However, this argument made no headway with Dublin Corporation. The corporation, in the person of Matthew Macken, City Manager, was adamant in its attitude to the representations of CIÉ. The new towns would be served by roads, not by railways. However, the possible importance of public transport was recognised by the inclusion in the final draft development plan of protection for a dedicated busway route from Tallaght to the city via Crumlin. On the other hand it was a proposal and no more. Though land was set aside for the busway, the project did not move from concept to construction.

These development reports, plans and debates were prompted by growth in the population of Dublin County, including Dublin City and Dún Laoghaire, of 32 per cent between 1955 and 1971 and to a projected 1,150,000 by 1991. The population of the Dublin region as defined by the Dublin Transportation Study had been 470,000 at the turn of the century and was projected to reach 1,300,000 by 1991. In fact the 1991 census eventually recorded a population of 1,350,000 for the eastern region which was somewhat greater than the Dublin region defined by the DTS. In addition, the number of private cars registered in Dublin had increased six-fold since 1951 to a figure of 187,000 in June 1979. The TCC report (March 1980) estimated that the figure could rise to 300,000 by 1991, but subsequent growth was slower than anticipated.

As far back as the 1950s bus speeds had been falling, and bunching of buses was occurring as a result of traffic hold-ups, generating popular ridicule of CIÉ and of its staff. The earliest attempts to improve the situation involved the use of telephones linking 'area inspectors' at bus termini with 'stance inspectors' at key city locations. The theory was that once they knew what was happening along the route, the inspectors would be able to take corrective action, turning buses at strategic points on a route, or introducing another bus if available, or directing that a particular bus proceed to point X before taking on passengers, and so on. Waiting passengers frequently found such interventions to be neither beneficial nor intelligible and the credibility of CIÉ as a serious operator continued to suffer. The inadequacy of such a system will be apparent from some numbers. In 1970 CIÉ was operating about 13,000 bus trips every day, with an average of 40 stops per trip—about half a million opportunities for passengers to board a bus over a 400 mile network.

Jack Higgins was still Manager Dublin City Services (DCS) in October 1970 when he wrote a comprehensive article in *Forum*—a short-lived CIÉ journal —about urban bus control. He described the advantages and limitations of using on-board mobile radios.

> They allow continuous two-way contact with the driver so that bus positions can be recorded and corrective action implemented within a very short period of time. However . . . mobile radios were relatively expensive, bulky, very demanding on vehicle batteries and to some extent unreliable. Trade Unions and staff were not well disposed towards them. In the past decade . . . size, weight and power requirements have been substantially reduced. Integrated circuits and solid state components have become standard and contribute to better reliability. Increasing lawlessness and acts of violence on buses have

made busmen more conscious of the benefits of quick communications. (John F. Higgins, *Forum*, October 1970)

As a result it became possible in summer 1969 to experiment with radio telephones in DCS. On a cross-city route, one of those which suffered most from traffic congestion, thirty-five buses were equipped with open call radio telephones and controlled by one inspector at the Central Control Office in O'Connell Street. Closed-circuit television was used to cover the two major queuing points on the route. The experiment proved very successful. Passenger waiting time on the route was 25 per cent less than on comparable cross-city routes, and passenger complaints were reduced by 33 per cent.

However, CIÉ quickly exhausted the number of radio channels available to it under the technological constraints of the time. The solution was to design, develop and implement an Automatic Vehicle Monitoring system (AVM) using less radio space while covering the entire fleet and giving more punctual and comprehensive information than previously. All buses could be interrogated automatically by a computer based in the O'Connell St headquarters of DCS and their location displayed on visual display units (VDUs), corrective action decided on and then communicated to the bus driver. The new system was very sophisticated by 1970 standards and Jack Higgins's article must have dazzled the probably computer-illiterate readers of *Forum*. A CIÉ pamphlet, 'The Dublin Transport System' published in 1975, further described the AVM approach updating Jack Higgins's 1970 article in *Forum*.

During 1976, CIÉ reported that with 'traffic speeds in Dublin amongst the lowest in Europe, as low as six miles per hour in the peak, the AVM system went on operational trial at Phibsboro Garage for a ninety day period from November 1975 to February 1976'. The test was described as 'very successful and by effecting a more even flow of buses . . . the level of service for passengers . . . was greatly improved'. The 'bus convoy' problem was solved. However, inventing, developing and testing the AVM system was only part of the task. It had yet to be accepted by bus crews.

Fifteen months (April 1977) after the initial test, AVM's introduction on four routes was 'being monitored by a special management/worker committee with assistance by the Labour Court'. By the end of 1979, 400 buses (almost half the Dublin fleet) had AVM units and the Annual Report (1979) said that 'it is planned to extend this system to the full fleet by the end of 1980'. Things did not run quite so speedily and it was 1983 before the entire DCS system was AVM controlled. However, CIÉ's technical team had developed a system that found widespread recognition abroad and an international symposium on the AVM system was held in Dublin during May 1979, attended by public transport operators and planners, as well as equipment specialists from many countries (Annual Report, 1979).

The Toronto transport authorities later acquired CIÉ's AVM system for operation in their city. The delay caused by industrial relations in bringing the system up to full steam was symptomatic of a contemporary malaise that affected many employments which attempted radical innovation. Less radical change could also generate resistance. One such was the withdrawal of thirty-three buses from routes where travel was falling so that they could be redeployed as appropriate to serve developing areas. Such a proposal in 1976 was frustrated by industrial action which resulted in a loss of £280,000 in revenue. The Minister for Labour became involved and an implementation date in January 1977 was finally agreed (Annual Report, 1976). More positively, a productivity agreement involving semi-skilled and unskilled garage and workshop staff was fully implemented in three of six Dublin garages (1977).

The proposal to introduce one-person operation of double deck buses in Dublin continued to be resisted. In 1977 it was referred to the Employer/Labour Conference which set up a special committee to examine the problem. This initiative also failed and in 1979 the stalemate was reported to the Joint Oireachtas Committee investigating CIÉ: the NBU's executive was mandated by its members to negotiate on the proposal, but the two ICTU unions, the ITGWU and the WUI (later merged into SIPTU) refused even to discuss the proposal. The Oireachtas Committee noted the many advantages which CIÉ said would follow from one-person operation including, from the bus worker's viewpoint, substantially higher pay and improved job satisfaction. Appreciating that these advantages were challenged by the workers, the committee proposed that a closely monitored twelve-month experiment be conducted on four (preferably dissimilar) routes so that these advantages, as well as financial benefits to CIÉ, could be proved or disproved. No trial followed. Also, during 1979 the Labour Court in a recommendation referred to the 'need for serious discussions' on one-person bus operation of double deck buses. 'It was eventually arranged by the Labour Court to hold separate consultations with CIÉ and the individual trade unions during 1980.' (Annual Report, 1979) No agreement emerged from these talks. Several more years would pass before harsh confrontation would produce a resolution.

ABOUT 400 NEW bus shelters were erected during the 1970s, with an advertising firm bearing the cost of their erection. Audio advertising was also introduced on double deck buses (1976), but the 'musak' interspersed with commercial plugs was not a success and mercifully, in the view of many, the experiment was soon abandoned.

On the traffic front some change was also taking place, but the slowness with which Dublin's matrix of traffic authorities arrived at their conclusions would be noted with only slightly concealed irritation by the Oireachtas Committee. One of their thirty-three conclusions was that 'a new authority must be established with full powers to develop and implement a traffic management policy for Dublin as a whole if there is to be any hope of stopping continuous deterioration in traffic conditions'. They were beating a well-worn path. The Dublin Transportation Study (1971) had noted that 'five road authorities, one "semi-state body" and three government departments have responsibilities for transportation in the Dublin region. The activities of these bodies will have to be co-ordinated . . .'

It will be recalled that Dublin's single bus lane experiment in 1971 had so upset the Gardaí and the corporation that it had been abandoned after one week. As a result, measures to give public transport some priority over private cars were stymied until 1977, when 'the process of defining bylaws and regulations for the introduction of bus priority schemes was begun' (John F. Higgins, 'Public Transport in the Dublin Conurbation', paper to Chartered Institute of Transport, Edinburgh, October 1984). At least the problem was now being addressed. A Technical Traffic Unit representing Dublin Corporation, Gardaí, Department of the Environment and CIÉ undertook specific studies on possible bus priority schemes and a proposal for a contra-flow bus lane in Parliament Street was recommended to Dublin Corporation.

So the issue of priority for public transport was under 'active consideration', but it was not until 1980 that the 'short but effective contra flow lane for buses was introduced in Dublin's Parliament St'. Remarks by Deputy Ruairí Quinn in the Dáil on 25 March 1980, the day that lane was opened, throw light on the tortuous process that preceded that decision. He was arguing for a Dublin Transport Authority.

> It is quite clear from my experience on the city council and on the traffic subcommittee that the kind of nonsense in terms of duplication which exists between the Garda authorities, the Department of Justice, the Department of the Environment, CIÉ and the local authority is getting in the way of an effective decision. One has only to look at the file in relation to bus lanes to see that clearly identified. The city council for at least four years have been in favour of bus lanes. A superintendent, having regard to his own function as a law enforcement officer and taking account of his [legal] job first and his traffic management job second, effectively stymied a democratic request, obtaining virtually all-party support in the city council, on the grounds that he does not have adequate staff resources.
>
> The request which went to the traffic group, a consultative body of various interests, for bus lanes as far back as 1974–75 always met this

problem. I am glad to see that the Department has agreed to the bus lanes and that the first one has been opened today.

(*Dáil Debates*, Vol. 324 , Col. 650)

The unambiguous support for public transport priorities in the almost 10-year-old Dublin Transportation Study (1971), fortified by the Oireachtas Committee Report (1979), got fresh impetus from the Transport Consultative Commission (TCC) Report on Passenger Transport Services in the Dublin area (1980). Within a week of the publication of the TCC Report, the Minister, Albert Reynolds, announced that he accepted the recommendation that a Dublin Transport Authority be established. Mr Reynolds had been Minister since January. It was his first ministerial office following appointment by Charles Haughey who had succeeded Jack Lynch as Taoiseach. As we will see, Reynolds was Minister for Transport for only eighteen months.

Implementation of the Dublin Transport Authority decision would take another six years, but in the meantime a Dublin traffic task force comprising representatives of the Department of the Environment, the Department of Transport, Dublin Corporation and the Gardaí was set up, though a protesting CIÉ was not included among its members.

Already the Matt Talbot Bridge, the first city bridge across the Liffey for almost one hundred years, was opened in February 1978. It lay down river from Butt Bridge. In 1979 clearway hours were extended. In 1980 the CIÉ Annual Report noted 'a belated acknowledgement of the need for bus priorities'. By December 1981, 37 bus priority measures were implemented and a further 23 were introduced in 1982, during which year a second new Liffey bridge was opened near Seán Heuston Bridge and was named after a long-serving Dublin City Councillor, IRA veteran and sometime TD, Frank Sherwin. Traffic flows on the Liffey quays were reversed, easing traffic movements in several central city areas. By October 1984 Jack Higgins reported to the Edinburgh Conference that a total of 67 bus priority schemes had been introduced involving a total length of 15 km.

IT IS TIME to consider the buses themselves against this background of the personnel problems of DCS, bus control initiatives taken by CIÉ, the limited road and bridge building undertaken by the local authority, and the gradual introduction of bus priority schemes. In the early 1970s CIÉ had a major problem with its bus equipment, but to understand how it occurred we must briefly backtrack in time. In the days of Percy Reynolds (January 1947), an agreement had been concluded with Leyland Motors Ltd, then a world leader in bus and truck manufacture. This agreement bound CIÉ to Leyland for a period of seven years for all passenger service vehicles which fell within the Leyland range, and for all goods carrying vehicles of 5 ton capacity or over. In return, Leyland agreed to supply spare parts for all CIÉ Leyland vehicles at their original cost price and to co-operate in the establishment of the proposed chassis-building project. When the chassis project failed, the rest of the provisions continued.

The wisdom of this agreement was questioned in the Milne Report of 1948 which thought that the then independent Bedford Company might be a more suitable supplier for some needs. However, and particularly because of inflation, the benefits were significant; the agreement was renewed several times until 1974 and discounts on spares in the range of 31 per cent to 80 per cent were availed of. Up to 1964, 1,350 chassis (600 single deck and 750 double deck) of various designs were purchased and 'proved to be very reliable'.

After 1964 'a marked deterioration in the performance of Leyland equipment' was noted (Internal CIÉ Report, 1977). There were three different types, each with its own set of problems. The first group was 270 single decks (C type) which were built between 1965 and 1968 from Leyland parts at Spa Road, Inchicore, on Leopard chassis with air suspensions which gave an uncomfortable ride and were unreliable. They had to be modified at some expense to CIÉ.

The second group comprising 213 single decks (M type) were regarded as 'very unsatisfactory'. German-made springs had to be substituted for the Leyland springs. Rear axles were noisy, failed prematurely and had to be replaced, but the engines presented the most serious problem. Their initial life and life between overhauls was 'approximately half that of previous Leyland engines' and they were replaced by Cummins or GM engines.

The third group of faulty buses was 600 rear engined double deck buses built on Leyland Atlantean chassis. The fault list with these buses is barely credible. 'The main problems were premature failure of the fluid clutch, gear box, alternators, starters, hydraulic accelerator control, fuel pump, power steering rams, engine overheating and oil carry over from the compressor to the brake system . . . Again alternative engines, transmissions and power steering equipment is being tested.' They had a most damaging effect on the whole DCS operation in terms of cost and reliability for over a decade.

In quick succession, two important decisions were made. Firstly, it was arranged that a Belgian company should take over the bus-building works at Spa Road, Inchicore (April 1973), and the original Leyland contract was terminated (July 1974). A new seven-year contract (covering only the supply of spares) was negotiated with Leyland though CIÉ suffered a penalty in that, by 1977, the discount on spares fell to 27 per cent. In the case of its Spa Road works the view in the 1970s, as in the case of railway coach manufacture (see page 284), was that manufacture of buses was no longer a necessary or appropriate activity for a transport operator. CIÉ's demand for buses was not sufficient for economic production in a modern manufacturing facility. Van Hool was a well-established specialist manufacturer, based near Antwerp, and had the prospect of developing its own export demand from its Dublin plant. Van Hool formed an association with the small Dundalk firm of Thomas McArdle Limited and set up Van Hool McArdle which leased the Inchicore body-building workshops and took over 248 CIÉ staff in April 1973.

The first buses built to the design of Van Hool McArdle, based on a Leyland AN68 chassis, were accepted in June 1974. This chassis was a 'considerable improvement' over the Atlantean. 'After 18 months there have been little or no problems with these buses.' The bodies of the Van Hool buses 'were the first all-welded tubular steel framed double deckers ever. That construction technique had previously only been used for single deckers.' A report in *Nuacht CIÉ* described the 'clean square lines' of the bus, resulting from less use of glass fibre, and the good visibility arising from deeper windows possible with the 'strong rigid framing'. The intention was that Van Hool McArdle was to build all CIÉ's double-deckers, single-deckers and school buses for a period of five years. However that was not to be.

CIÉ was dissatisfied with the Leyland chassis and power units. In co-operation with Van Hool McArdle it set about finding more reliable equipment. Following a study in 1973 of the power units available worldwide, CIÉ decided on GM engines and Allison transmissions or Cummins engines and Voith transmissions as an alternative, resulting in cancellation of the Leyland contract for power units. There was no indication of problems with the Van Hool contract when St J. Devlin during 1976 reviewed the overall state of the bus fleet and CIÉ's proposals for new buses.

> There have been times when only 75% of the Dublin City fleet has been available for service. These difficulties forced a re-examination of the bus programme. As a result of an extensive survey and discussions with other fleet owners, three new bus types are being developed in conjunction with Van Hool/McArdle. . . . They will be constructed in Dublin and the first of the single-decker fleet will be available by the beginning of 1978. (Annual Report, 1975)

When Van Hool came to Inchicore, it planned to build luxury coaches and service buses for export in addition to building for CIÉ. It soon found its costs too high and capacity inadequate in the Spa Road facility. As a result, it decided to build an entirely new facility with a capacity to build 600 buses per annum, and to double its staff to 600. CIÉ welcomed this proposal, wanting Van Hool to move away from 'the present unreliable Leyland design' as quickly as possible so that new types could be manufactured. Accordingly, 'it was decided to reduce the total number of buses required on the initial contract and, as a result, CIE agreed with Van Hool McArdle for the payment of a cancellation fee of £685,716' (Annual Report, 1976). This arrangement was acceptable to Van Hool which believed that a new bus design would give it an advantage in its export sales.

The CIÉ concept was a 'family' of buses—double deck, city single deck and intercity single deck—which would be specially designed to meet all of its major fleet needs. CIÉ prepared preliminary designs and specifications, but the arrangement with Van Hool ran into serious difficulties. In the 1976 Annual Report, Devlin reported that difficulties with Van Hool were more fundamental than the quite serious matter of the power equipment and bus design. The stumbling block was the cost plus basis of the initial contract. In the following annual report Devlin explained the problem encountered in agreeing a contract for the proposed new bus family.

> We negotiated with Van Hool McArdle for a fixed price contract with escalation clauses to provide for cost increases in material, labour, etc. Unfortunately, this contract has not been signed by Van Hool McArdle and we have had to review our arrangements for bus building as it would not be in the interest of CIÉ to continue to have buses manufactured on a cost plus basis. This arrangement has proved to be very expensive, it has not been possible to forecast the real cost of the buses and there was no incentive for productivity or cost saving by the manufacturer.

The following year Devlin referred to the 'suspension of our arrangements with Van Hool McArdle for the construction of buses'. A long battle had begun between Van Hool and CIÉ. The Belgian Ambassador became involved, making representations to the Irish Government at ministerial level to try to have the commitment to Van Hool re-established. John Byrne, now an independent consultant, who had negotiated the original 1973 arrangements with Van Hool, was engaged by Van Hool to support their case against CIÉ. The Irish Government did not intervene to restore the contract as Van Hool believed was likely to happen. CIÉ did not yield ground and the protracted legal processes ran their course until 1992 with CIÉ not having to bear any penalty beyond the original 1976 cancellation fee.

The real issue of getting a mechanically reliable, robust and cost-effective fleet of buses had still to be resolved. The Van Hool initiative had failed; time was lost; but following the TCC report on Dublin's traffic which proposed a 'new deal' for buses the government authorised expenditure of £40 million on renewing CIÉ's buses. The company had to look elsewhere for its needs. In 1977 CIÉ asked Otto Schultz of Hamburg Consult, the renowned bus designer, to design its bus family. The contract included designing and supplying three prototypes based on GM engines, Allison transmissions and Rockwell axles. With its experience on the rail side, CIÉ had acquired great confidence in General Motors and in its products.

CIÉ negotiated with American Motors General (AMG) Corporation, a subsidiary of American Motors, to manufacture the buses designed by Hamburg Consult. It leased a factory (formally the Rippon Piano factory) at Shannon for this purpose. However, AMG pulled out at the last moment. CIÉ reapproached General Motors who in 1973 had not wanted to become involved in building buses other than to their own design. After a number of meetings they again declined the invitation to manage the Shannon facility. However, a solution soon emerged: Cruse Moss, an executive of AMG, the company which had jilted CIÉ on the eve of a press conference at Shannon, suggested that a joint venture be formed between Bombardier of Canada, an experienced bus builder, and a private company, General Automotive Corporation (GAC), in which he had a substantial interest. The result was the creation of Bombardier (Ireland) with which CIÉ did a deal.

Devlin explained CIÉ's objectives, and the arrangements made with Bombardier in the 1978 Annual Report.

> We have negotiated with American Motors Corporation, General Motors Corporation and Bombardier Ltd, of Canada. Our aim has been to find a partner who will provide us with the necessary bus-building techniques, a partner who has experience of the General Motors power package and a partner who will exploit export markets for buses built in Ireland to CIÉ designs. It has not been easy to achieve all of these objectives but arrangements have been completed with Bombardier Ltd to manage a new bus-building facility in the Shannon Industrial Estate. The main features of the arrangement are that CIÉ will own all the assets, including the jigs for the manufacture of the buses and all other ancillary tools and machinery . . . Bombardier Ltd will have the responsibility for the employment of the labour, the management of that labour and the construction of buses in accordance with CIÉ's requirements. . . . Bombardier will have the right to use CIÉ designs and facilities to build buses for customers other than CIÉ, and will pay a royalty to CIÉ for each bus . . . Production is expected to commence towards the end of 1979 and first buses should be available by August, 1980.
>
> There is a view that our Dublin City services fleet of buses is aged. In fact, the average age of the fleet is only eight years. The major

problem with our buses is that the basic design and the engine are unsatisfactory.

A continuous supply of satisfactory buses now seemed to be assured. In early May 1981, some months behind the target date, the first buses emerged from the new Shannon factory. Much official embarrassment and media amusement occurred at the formal opening ceremony when a distinguished visitor was injured by glass flying from the ceremonially broken champagne bottle and when an electrical snag affected the first vehicle as it was being driven off by Albert Reynolds. CIÉ's ambitious 'family of buses' concept, which it brought to Shannon, involved intercity buses (KEs) and double deck buses (KDs) fitted with General Motors 6V71 6.9 litre engines with Allison fully automatic transmission and Rockwell axles. The city single deck buses (KCs) were powered by a new Cummins engine in the development of which CIÉ had participated prior to its production. This engine, the turbo-charged L10 10 litre in the city single deck buses, was used with a Voith automatic transmission and Kirkstall axles. The KCs were larger vehicles than their rural cousins, with 35 seated and 39 standing, though the standing capacity was later reduced to 30. The fourth type built at Shannon was the rural single-decker (KRs) for stage carriage services. These buses, powered by DAF engines and Allison transmissions, had a seating capacity of 47.

The first buses to come from the Shannon plant were the intercity single-deckers or express buses (KEs) of which 52 were built in total. The next buses produced were the double-deckers which began to be produced in volume in 1981 and 1982. By December of that year, there were 276 Bombardier double-deckers in operation and the total output eventually came to 365. The large capacity city single-deckers were built between 1983 and 1985, coming to 202 units. Finally, 227 rural single-deckers were produced between 1983 and 1987.

As major bus priority measures were introduced and bus passenger numbers were again increasing in Dublin, Jack Higgins could boast in 1984 that the average mileage per new double-decker bus was 42,300, 50 per cent higher than the older fleet and the average mileage between failure was 11,433 compared to 2,167 for the older vehicles. The maintenance costs per mile were down more than 50 per cent at 24p instead of 57p. J. B. Martin, later Bus Éireann's chief mechanical engineer, would report in *Transport* (March/April 1985) that maintenance staff was being reduced by almost 50 per cent as the Bombardiers replaced their predecessors, some of which were an incredible 45 years old. The major reduction in maintenance costs between the Bombardiers and their predecessors was expected to continue as they advanced in age. However, this expectation would prove to be seriously wrong. Major problems began to emerge with the integral structure of Bombardier vehicles and other problems would arise with the Bombardier company itself.

The structural problem principally affected the double deck buses and became manifest within eighteen months to two years after they had entered service. Under Irish road conditions, which were demonstrably more damaging to the bodies than those experienced in several other countries, faults developed in frame members and extensive modifications were required. Similar problems developed progressively with the intercity or express buses, and to a lesser extent with the city single-deckers. In the case of the last of the Bombardier buses, the rural single-deckers, the design defect was remedied in production and subsequent structural problems were avoided.

While the production of buses was taking place, a major row broke out involving CIÉ, the government and Bombardier Ireland. The question was a matter of production levels.

The initial CIÉ plan was that it would accept 150 buses per year from Shannon, based on an average 16-year life for each of its 2,600 fleet (including school buses). The economic throughput of the plant was 250 per annum or 5 per week. The challenge to Bombardier Ireland was to find foreign markets for the units produced surplus to CIÉ's requirement. Production was slow initially, and such was the backlog at the beginning of 1982 that CIÉ decided for that year to accept buses at a faster rate than 150. They took confidence from such earlier statements as that of Albert Reynolds to the Fianna Fáil Ard Fheis in April 1981, that 'between now and 1983, 500 new buses will be delivered from the new bus building factory at Shannon', and from a statement in the Dáil in July 1981 by his successor as Minister, Patrick Cooney of Fine Gael, that 'because of a backlog in the company's bus replacement programme the requirement for new buses would be unusually high'. The Bombardier understanding was that CIÉ would accept 250 buses in 1982 to make up the backlog in the deliveries.

In August 1981, the month after Minister Cooney's Dáil statement, CIÉ advised the Department of Transport of its capital expenditure plans for bus-building for 1982. The Department responded in January 1982, authorising a capital expenditure of £20 million which was quite inadequate for an accelerated acquisition programme. In February, CIÉ told the Department that this limit on its capital expenditure for new buses would force an employment cut of 100 at the Shannon factory. Discussion between CIÉ and the Department continued until at the end of August 1982 when the company was finally given a £25 million limit. The phrase used was 'capital allocation' for the building of buses, but the moneys were not being provided by the Department—instead they set a limit to what CIÉ could borrow for its new buses.

The Department of Finance concern at that time was to control total borrowing by the public sector as a whole. By August 1982, when the Department said its final word on how much could be spent on buses, Bombardier had produced so many vehicles that CIÉ's capital authority for buses was exhausted. Accordingly, it advised the Department that the factory would have to cease production. In October the issue became a national one. The failure of government to authorise sufficient capital expenditure in 1982 to clear the backlog in a planned acquisition programme was the immediate cause of the fracas. The secondary cause was that Bombardier had not found an external market for its Shannon-built products. If foreign sales could have been obtained—two sample buses went to Iran and to England—the October 1982 crisis about the future of the plant might have been averted. A later effort to supply buses to the 1984 Olympic Games in Los Angeles also collapsed in failure.

After the 1982 blow-up, staffing was indeed reduced at the Shannon factory; in that year 218 buses were produced (217 double-deckers and one single-decker). In the following year a new capital expenditure limit imposed by government reduced CIÉ's purchases from Shannon by 45 per cent to 120 buses (77 double-deckers and 43 single-deckers). Output fell again to a total of 95 single-deckers in 1984 but rose in 1985 to 246 single-deckers, of which 182 were the new rural or stage carriage single-deckers.

The story of Bombardier in Ireland largely revolved around the American entrepreneur, Cruse Moss, who had introduced CIÉ to Bombardier of Montreal and designed the joint venture between that company and GAC. However, in 1983 the Canadian company elected to sell its entire stake in Bombardier Ireland to GAC leaving Cruse Moss in sole control. CIÉ's arrangement with Bombardier Ireland was primarily a management contract for the Shannon plant and it was concerned at this change in the make-up of its contract partner. Under the terms of the agreement CIÉ was entitled to withdraw from the contract on certain conditions by giving due notice. Such notice was given in August 1983. The Shannon company changed its name from Bombardier Ireland to GAC Ireland Ltd. Production continued for CIÉ, but GAC itself withdrew from the Shannon operation in 1985.

After GAC's departure, CIÉ operated the plant, to complete 24 more rural single-deckers, until it closed down in 1986. During the six years of the Shannon bus-building project a total of 847 buses were produced for CIÉ, in effect replacing half its fleet other than school buses. In the changed situation after 1986, CIÉ would adopt a radically new practice for its bus acquisition—inviting tenders and buying off the shelf on the basis of price and quality. For a variety of reasons the great experiment of building buses in Ireland for CIÉ and for export petered out, sadly, but inevitably, in a much changed world of competitive international trading.

IN THIS CHAPTER we surveyed the road passenger services and recorded improvement in the Dublin bus situation. In earlier chapters we referred to the proposed electrification of the Dublin suburban railway, but this was only phase 1 of a larger rapid rail system proposed by the Dublin Transportation Study in 1972 and developed in the Dublin Rapid Rail Transit Study (DRRTS) for CIÉ at the request of the Department of Transport and Power. Phases 2 and 3 of the DRRTS proposals would extend the electrified system to the new western towns of Tallaght, Blanchardstown and Clondalkin, provide a northern spur to Finglas and Ballymun, include busways to Dundrum and Tallaght, and have all these services connecting to a Dublin Transportation Centre west of O'Connell Bridge, which itself would have underground rail links to Connolly and Heuston termini. Like mainline coaching stock, the rapid rail system was still an unsettled question. Our narrative must revert to these questions and to the uneasy situation with government, in the context of a rapidly rising subvention, and disarray in public finances, which we left in January 1979 while Pádraig Faulkner was still Minister.

CHAPTER 19

SHORT-MEASURE SUBVENTIONS

Difficulties in the public finances—Inadequate subvention provisions for CIÉ—Expenditure cutbacks—NESC and Oireachtas Committee Reports—Second McKinsey study commissioned—The papal visit—Howth/Bray electrification proceeds—Buttevant rail disaster.

From 1975 to 1978 cumulative inflation as measured by movements in the Consumer Price Index amounted to 44 per cent. Over the same period the increase in the CIÉ subvention was 42 per cent—£37.7 million in 1978, compared to £26.5 million in 1975. Thus in real money terms the subvention was being kept at a constant or slightly reduced level —meeting the target that CIÉ had publicly committed itself to achieve. This was a substantially better performance than was generally allowed, but it was not going to continue. The government's ambition for CIÉ, to the extent that it was formally articulated, was the more severe one of freezing the subvention in current terms. Of course government knew that in inflationary circumstances such a target would not be realistic for services like health, education or social welfare, which were under its direct control. Public transport was an activity delegated to a state company and the bulk of its revenue still came from its customers. Accordingly, it could be subjected to much rougher treatment. In the 1979 budget the CIÉ subvention was fixed at the previous year's level, actually somewhat below that level, and the consequences are revealing. They set a pattern that would be repeated again and again for several years.

Many years earlier CIÉ had demonstrated from simple arithmetic that in an inflationary period and a given level of activity, its revenue from traffic carried would have to grow much faster than its costs if the subvention were to be held at the previous year's level. Even when revenue grew faster than costs, the deficit might grow still faster. In 1978 CIÉ's traffic revenue covered 73.1 per cent of its expenditure, with the balance made up by government subvention. In 1979 the inflation rate almost doubled, to 13.2 per cent from 7.6 per cent in the previous year. If CIÉ's costs in 1979 were to grow by the inflation rate and its revenue also rose by 13.2 per cent, the inexorable arithmetic of its accounts would increase the deficit by 55 per cent. The reader who doubts this conclusion is invited to test the arithmetic. What actually happened was that CIÉ's costs rose faster than the Consumer Price Index principally due to wage inflation and the four-fold increase in fuel costs. Revenue also rose slightly more than the CPI increase, but the rise in the deficit was almost 55 per cent, up from £37.5 million to £57.5 million.

Quite early during the year the embarrassing truth emerged that the budget provision for the subvention was going to be grossly inadequate. CIÉ so advised the minister. St J. Devlin was summoned to meet him (Pádraig Faulkner) on 2 July 1979 and he reported on that meeting to the CIÉ Board on 12 July:

> the Minister said he and his colleagues, particularly the Taoiseach [Jack Lynch] and the Tánaiste [George Colley, also Minister for Finance] were concerned about the escalating deficit on CIÉ's operations. It would appear that the subvention required for the current year would be £50 m., if not more. The Minister said that it was very embarrassing for him because he had agreed when the estimates for the year were being discussed that the subvention for CIÉ would be of the order of £37 m. It was very difficult at this late stage to seek a further £13 m.

For the record, the figure in the Annual Estimates was £35 million rather than £37 million. The reader might be tempted to ask why the minister had agreed to such a figure in the first place. It can hardly have been a realistic estimate. However, Devlin's position would not have been helped by such an impertinence. The minute continues:

> The Chairman pointed out to the Minister that the budget for 1979 was based on guidelines which were pre-set by the Government. CIÉ was instructed to abide strictly to these guidelines which, among other things, provided for a wages increase of 6%. There was no provision for an increase in oil costs nor was there an anticipation of the present oil crisis. Since the beginning of the year both the wages content and the expenditure on oil in the CIÉ budget had escalated at an astonishing rate. The increase in wages and salaries in the current year would amount to £16 m. and this arises because the current National Understanding if accepted provides for increases far in excess of the

6% guideline. Furthermore, the Labour Court award to the busmen was a substantial one and it will in all probability affect claims from all other groups in the organisation. . . . It is now estimated that the increase in diesel oil costs for CIÉ will amount to £5½ m. during 1979. . . .

The Minister said that while the reasons might seem to be outside the control of CIÉ, nevertheless a new plateau in subventions had been established and the Government might not find it possible to pay £50 m. on a recurring basis for the provision of public transport. The Minister also commented on the difficulty which CIÉ had in controlling the Trade Unions. The Chairman replied that, in fact, industrial relations in CIÉ were excellent if one took into consideration the total number of man-hours worked and the fact that most stoppages were brief and unofficial. (ibid.)

The figure of 6 per cent provided for in the government pay guidelines for 1979 compared to an eventual 11 per cent (approx.) for the calendar year, based on 9 per cent for nine months followed by 7 per cent plus £2.40 per week for the following six months in a fifteen-month national agreement. As the year unfolded and various additional wage settlements were painfully arrived at after Labour Court investigations, the year end deficit exceeded £57 million and the government subvention after two supplementary estimates came to a total of £56 million. Several Dáil members were strongly critical of this 'behaviour of CIÉ coming with their hands out for more money'. They might not have known the background to the original budget subvention for CIÉ, nor have fully understood that the CIÉ result was but a small aspect of the disarray in public finances as a whole. The national budget had estimated exchequer borrowings at £779 million, but the eventual out-turn would prove to be £1,218 million (16 per cent of GNP compared to a projected 10 per cent).

In the less public atmosphere of the Joint Oireachtas Committee, deputies and senators recognised that the procedure for setting the annual subvention and for making adjustments thereto was 'deeply unsatisfactory' and harmful to CIÉ's internal morale and to its public relations. Sometimes increases in subventions were the result of governments refusing permission for fares to be increased to the levels assumed when the original subvention level was set. The October 1979 report of the Oireachtas Committee said that the state and CIÉ should submit themselves to a new discipline in fixing future subventions. Their proposal can be summarised as follows.

(a) The initial level of subvention set in the annual estimates should continue to be based on estimates of labour costs, bearing in mind 'the exigencies of negotiation'.
(b) Any excess of labour costs over this level should be met by

increased productivity or by increased fares and rates.

(c) Any cost to CIÉ of delays in granting rate and fare increases which resulted in lower revenues than those planned in the annual estimates should be recouped in supplementary estimates which would identify the cause of the lower revenues.

(d) Unanticipated material costs, such as fuel, should also be compensated for, at least partially, by a supplementary estimate.

The Oireachtas Committee did not rule out the possibility of other factors such as 'an unexpected shortfall in revenue' justifying an additional subvention, but believed that 'it should be the exception, not the rule'. The committee also took a strong position in favour of the subvention being paid 'above the line' as revenue, in accordance with EEC's recommendations, rather than as an after-the-event compensation for 'losses'. Eight years earlier McKinsey had urged a similar change and before that the National Prices Commission and its consultants had taken the same approach. The committee's report was never debated in the Dáil and government made no decision on any of its recommendations. However, pressure of events resulted eventually in some decisions along the lines recommended by the committee.

Professor Christopher D. Foster of the London School of Economics and Political Science and of Coopers and Lybrand Associates acted as a consultant to the Joint Committee, but the views published were those of the committee—practical and pragmatic. At about the same time Professor Foster also prepared a report on Ireland's Transport Policy for the National Economic and Social Council (NESC) which was more controversial in its approach and conclusions. The NESC Chairman was the Secretary of the Department of Economic Planning and Development and included among its high-powered membership was the Secretary of the Department of Finance and two of his predecessors in that key office. Accordingly, the decision of the NESC on 16 February 1978 to undertake a study on the 'principles which should underline transport policy in Ireland' can be taken as indicating serious high-level concern about the transport situation. The NESC commissioned Professor Foster 'to examine these principles'. His report was completed in May 1979, but its text, amounting to 148 pages, was not published until early in 1980. In a mere three and a half pages the NESC expressed its own views, posing questions that they thought should be answered, but offering no suggestions as to what those answers should be. An addendum by Patrick Murphy of the Irish Employers' Confederation and of CIÉ seriously challenged a number of Foster's conclusions, particularly those concerning the railways.

As might be expected, the Foster/NESC Report took a position similar to that of the Oireachtas Committee concerning the existing subvention arrangements and their being paid 'below the line'. However, in the NESC document, where Foster had a free hand to express his own views, he was critical of cross-subsidisation and very sceptical of the value and the future of the railways. The Oireachtas Committee would not have shared these attitudes. The Foster/NESC Report was especially critical of the organisational arrangements where internal transport policy as a whole was no particular department's responsibility falling as it were between the Department of Transport, which was concerned with rail infrastructure and public transport operations, and the Department of the Environment, which jealously retained responsibility for roads on which the overwhelming proportion of the nation's transport services were operated. Like the Oireachtas Committee and other earlier reports, Foster urged that a Dublin Transport Authority be established. As we know already, a decision to create such an authority would follow the next report in line (TCC).

Little imagination or understanding of public bureaucracy is needed to believe that when Minister Faulkner and his Departmental Secretary, Noel McMahon, met St J. Devlin on 2 July 1979 to discuss the likely shortfall in the subvention, he and/or his officials knew pretty well what was in the already completed Foster (NESC) Report. They would also have known or been able to guess how the TCC and the Oireachtas Committee investigations were progressing. A thoroughly unpalatable situation was on their hands. Electrification of the Bray/Howth line had been announced in March at a cost of £46 million in the middle of the European election campaign. The Minister for Economic Planning and Development was believed to be hostile to that project. At any rate the decision was made and it provided for the entire capital cost being borne by the exchequer, i.e. CIÉ was not to be liable for interest charges on the £46 million. Within six weeks of that decision being promulgated, the Department of Finance persuaded the cabinet to reverse the decision on interest charges. Noel McMahon would have known that this change made nonsense of the financial basis of the electrification proposals and that it would simply increase the annual subvention which his minister would have to find for CIÉ. In addition, CIÉ was still pressing for a decision on the larger rapid rail proposals for Dublin; its mainline rolling stock was deteriorating all the time and, despite growing traffic, carriages were being withdrawn from service; the bus fleet was also unsatisfactory. Three reports (Oireachtas Committee, NESC and TCC) were to hand or well advanced and they would give no comfort to the hard-pressed minister.

The dilemma was: how to sort out this appalling accumulation of financial pressures against a background of heavy criticism of CIÉ, a public that was demanding solutions to its transport problems, accelerating inflation and deteriorating public finances. Sadly, the minister seemed to think he needed more time and still more advice. He could appoint another strong and authoritative consultant whose concentration would be focused on the specific problem of CIÉ rather than on transport principles or policy. Devlin got the impression that this was what would happen and he so informed the board on 12 July. A beleaguered board, faced with the possibility of new management consultants, naturally decided that it should get in first with its own proposals.

> In the circumstances, he [CIÉ's Chairman] felt it was necessary that a response should be made as soon as possible and, accordingly, he and the General Manager met the 40 top managers of CIÉ and directed that studies be commenced immediately to identify areas where substantial savings in expenditure could be achieved.
> (Board Minutes, 12 July 1979)

Devlin told CIÉ's managers that their approach should be radical and 'political considerations should not be taken into account'. He advised the board that suggestions being examined included selling the entire hotel group to private interests, and that if this were done the international tours business and the operation of tour buses might also be terminated. A loss was being incurred on the carriage of sundries and withdrawal of this service should be considered. The effect of eliminating major loss making road passenger services needed to be examined. The chairman had advised the minister that such studies were under way. Normally the minutes did not record individual contributions to a board discussion, but this was an exceptional occasion and the record is extensive. Some extracts give the crisis flavour of the meeting.

> One member said that management and staff had been very successful in negotiating and implementing productivity during the previous 4 years. 4,000 people lost their employment in the interests of securing the jobs of the remainder . . . Trade Unions and the staff accepted these proposals . . . and in doing so they demonstrated a commitment which was significant and unique. (ibid.)

A colleague put forward a less labour-focused viewpoint.

> CIÉ must manage and . . . In view of the possible appointment of management consultants, he was in full agreement that management should investigate all the options in regard to the reduction of costs and, if necessary, the elimination of activities. Final recommendations should, however, emanate from the Board. (ibid.)

Another contribution was minuted as follows:

it was quite clear that the Board could not be held responsible for the escalation in the deficit. It was clear to the Board at the beginning of the year when the budget was being prepared on the guidelines advanced by the Government that it would not be possible to contain the deficit. . . . He supported the view that we should carry out our own investigations in advance of consultants and that we should at all costs ensure that we continue to manage. (ibid.)

St J. Devlin had one other proposal for his board: that the government consider signing a concordat with CIÉ and the trade unions in regard to CIÉ's operations for the next three years.

> The concordat would commit the Government to a specified ceiling of subvention which would be indexed. The concordat would require CIÉ to increase the volume of traffic—continue to improve productivity and take the necessary decisions to ensure that the organisation would operate within the subvention . . . the trade unions would be asked to co-operate with CIÉ in achieving the aims agreed.
> (ibid.)

The board agreed with the chairman's approach. Studies should be undertaken and the board would consider their outcome before communicating further with the minister. The concept of a concordat should be promoted further. If management consultants were appointed, CIÉ, through its officers, should be involved and should have the opportunity to comment on their proposals.

The chairman's review in the following two Annual Reports (1979 and 1980) mentioned that the board had proposed a 'Concordat' embracing government, trade unions and CIÉ. The concordat concept might have seemed attractive to the board, but government was exceedingly busy on other fronts and would have known, firstly, that a concordat would tie its hands in a rapidly changing period and, secondly, that such an initiative could have awkward and unforeseen implications across the uneasy public sector as a whole.

Devlin had surmised correctly. Two months later, in September 1979, Pádraig Faulkner announced that McKinsey International Inc. had been commissioned 'to examine the reasons for the deterioration in the financial position of CIÉ and recommend such corrective measures as may be possible to bring about an improvement in the position'. In the Annual Report for 1979, Devlin mentioned the NESC, the Oireachtas Committee, TCC and McKinsey, and commented on this

> preoccupation with examining, investigating, surveying and reporting

on public transport . . . not many organisations have been examined and investigated as often as CIÉ and, notwithstanding the plethora of reports, government have neither interpreted or modified the statutory duty imposed on CIÉ by the Transport Act of 1958.

As McKinsey's team of sharp, dark-suited, mostly American consultants planned their assault on CIÉ, they faced resistance from the TSSA whose members controlled the company's information system and refused for a while to give their co-operation.

AMID ALL ITS troubles in 1979 the company faced, and rose to, a different and exciting challenge which provided a case study in effective public transport. Pope John XXIII had broken a centuries old tradition, that the Pope become a virtual prisoner within the Vatican, when he visited Lourdes in 1954. His successor, Pope Paul VI, made a small number of foreign journeys to the Holy Land and to the United Nations General Assembly. A younger and more extrovert Pope, John Paul II, seemed to throw caution to the winds and decided to travel widely. In the third year of his papacy he chose to visit Ireland. As the twentieth century draws to its conclusion, the excitement generated by John Paul's visit to Ireland in 1979 may be difficult to understand. The Irish people felt proud that this new, brave and charismatic figure from Communist Poland, had elected to visit Ireland ahead of so many other possible and internationally more prestigious destinations. Vast crowds were expected to attend the several public papal ceremonies—in Dublin, Limerick, Knock, Drogheda and Galway. How could they travel? With minimum hesitation the Gardaí, prompted by CIÉ and others, recognised that Ireland was assured of a series of gigantic traffic seize-ups unless some radical and courageous initiative was taken. The solution was daringly simple—virtually to ban the use of private cars and to place the onus on public transport for the great mass movement of people that was bound to arise. In Dublin a five-mile traffic cordon was placed around the Phoenix Park and all private traffic was banned from main roads over much longer distances. *Nuacht CIÉ* published a special issue to record the events of the four-day visit, 29 September to 1 October 1979, when '1,400,000 came to see Pope John Paul in the biggest single transport opportunity of its kind in history'.

> DUBLIN'S BUSES TRIUMPH IN TRAFFIC-FREE STREETS
> It was an incredible task by any standards—Dublin's buses had to carry most of the population of the city and tens of thousands of people from Leinster to a 15 acre site in the Phoenix Park . . . over the space of six hours in the biggest park and ride operation in history.
> (*Nuacht CIÉ*, October 1979)

Use was made of every possible privately owned bus and of CIÉ's part-time school bus drivers. In subsequent days, the Dublin arrangements were duplicated on a smaller scale by rail and road at the other locations where John Paul appeared. The *IRRS Journal* duly published its reports detailing the number, the timing and the make-up of the 350 trains involved. The *Journal* was perceptibly exhilarated by CIÉ's success and proudly it quoted *The Irish Times* of 8 October 1979.

> The paper said: 'Over the three days of the Visit, CIÉ supplied the public with 1,400,000 return journeys—400,000 by rail, 250,000 by provincial bus, and 750,000 by Dublin city buses. Its completion demonstrated that CIÉ has the organisational ability to handle mass transport provided that it is given reasonable conditions under which to operate.' The same journal [*The Irish Times*] added: 'By rail CIÉ, despite having to use obsolescent suburban equipment and an insufficiency of main line rolling stock, succeeded by switching and shuttling and contriving, in bringing 400,000 people to and from the five centres.' In an even later paragraph, *The Irish Times* remarked: 'One obvious conclusion to be drawn from the experience is the absolute necessity for an adequate system of clearways for buses in Dublin', and ended with a well-earned tribute in these words: 'It is but just to say that all CIÉ's workers, especially those who laboured unnoticed behind the scenes, deserve the utmost credit for the success of the largest transport operation in the country's history.'
> (*IRRS Journal*, October 1979)

In the same issue the *IRRS Journal* carried a report on a speech by Jack Higgins in which he called for a 'Reassessment of the financial state of the rail system' and for 'early investment if services were to be maintained'. He pointed out that 'completion to target of the Howth–Bray electrification project would not be possible unless clearance is received for the purchase of the rolling stock involved'. The *IRRS Journal* added a comment of its own:

> We may hope that the excellent performance of the railway staff and management in meeting the challenge of the Papal visit, despite so many problems—especially the shortage of coaching stock—will emphasise the recent call by the General Manager for a reasonable long-term investment policy for the railway. (ibid.)

However, the McKinsey consultants were now *in situ* and on 12 December 1979 Pádraig Faulkner moved to the Department of Defence. He had been Minister for Tourism and Transport for almost two and a half troubled years for CIÉ since his appointment by Jack Lynch after the 1977 General

Election. When C. J. Haughey became Taoiseach in December 1979, George Colley held the transport portfolio for a five-week interim period before being appointed to the new post of Minister for Energy. The new Minister, Albert Reynolds, presented a thrusting and decisive image. Early in 1980 his audience at the Chartered Institute of Transport's annual dinner listened to a minister who seemed to understand that transport, public and private, had suffered from previous indecision. He gave the message that he believed that public transport deserved a new deal from government. However, decisions would not be made until he received the reports of the Transport Consultative Council on Dublin's transport problems and of McKinsey concerning CIÉ. Then, he assured his audience, decisions would flow fast. Understandably, he was playing for time while he read himself into his responsibilities, which included the Department of Posts and Telegraphs. Something else would happen as he warmed to his brief: two serious rail accidents were about to occur.

The first took place on 15 November 1979 when the '08.27 passenger train from Bray to Connolly collided with the rear of the 08.17 Bray–Howth train which had been standing at Dalkey outer home signal which was at Stop because of a broken signal wire' (*IRRS Journal*, February 1980). *The Irish Times* reported that 'about 100 passengers, including many school children were on each train when they collided . . . at a deep railway cutting where the line emerged from the Vico tunnel at Sorrento Road'. Happily there was no fatality and but one serious casualty, that of the driver of the oncoming train who was trapped in his cabin for two hours before being airlifted to hospital. The detailed engineering planning involved in the major modernisation of the suburban railway—its electrification, with new signalling technology and control systems, was already under way and the Dalkey crash must have increased the consensus that the existing system was dangerously obsolescent even if some debate persisted on whether electrification was really necessary.

Some months later a private member's motion, noting the NESC Report —Transport Policy—was debated in the Dáil. Such a motion was a relatively rare occurrence and was in the name of Deputy Ruairí Quinn who called upon 'the Government to ensure that it will not authorise the reduction of the public transport services, as provided by CIÉ, and requests the Government as a matter of urgency to reform the present duplication of transportation administration and to establish without delay a Transport Authority for the Dublin Region' (*Dáil Debates*, Vol. 319, Col. 606). A main argument of Quinn's tightly argued presentation was that the existing administrative machinery for transport both nationally and in the Dublin area was inefficient and badly organised, mentioning the 'political weight of the Custom House [Department of the Environment] in relation to roads' in contrast to indecisiveness elsewhere in relation to public transport. 'Until

Great Southern Hotel, Galway

The Parknasilla Great Southern Hotel

The Corrib Great Southern Hotel, Galway, opened 1971

New roof-top Claddagh Grill in the Great Southern Hotel, Galway, 1962

Rail hostesses were first introduced in 1961; the picture dates from 1968.

Railway dining car interior, 1990s

Bloodstock transporter with side and rear access, 1949

Matador lorries; a major part of the road transport fleet in the early 1950s

CIÉ logo adapted from the DUTC logo in 1944; frequently called the 'flying snail', it was replaced by the 'broken circle' logo in 1964.

Laying of slab track between Dún Laoghaire and Sandycove, 1981

Track laying at Barrow Street, near Pearse station, 1982

Interior of Pearse station signal cabin showing electromechanical lever frame manufactured by GSR in 1936; it remained in use until construction of DART in 1982.

Signalmen J. P. Byrne and Dennis Wildes at the computerised CTC (Centralised Traffic Control) at Connolly station

Demountable 20 ft ISO tank for transporting Harp lager, Dundalk, 1993

Thirty ton rail mounted gantry, suitable for all types of ISO containers; capable of stacking units 3 high, Limerick, 1993

No. 8 (Dalkey) tram being carried on an Iarnród Éireann trailer to St Patrick's Day parade, Dublin, 1994

Delivery of tanks *en route* from Holland to the Harp lager brewery in Dundalk, 1992 (Glen Photography)

Arrival of first of nine BREL-built intercity carriages at North Wall, Dublin, 1994

Road Liner ERF heavy transport trucks acquired 1993

Rail Link Mitsubishi trucks acquired 1994

such time as roads and transport are under the same political umbrella we are not going to get the sort of transport policy that we need.' (ibid., Vol. 319, Col. 828)

Ruairí Quinn criticised Foster's anti-rail and right-wing bias and his sceptical approach to rapid rail proposals. He welcomed Albert Reynolds's appointment. He applauded the earlier decision to electrify the Bray/Howth line and said that his party was proposing that the DRRTS be encouraged and that the second and third stages of that proposal be given the go-ahead.

Albert Reynolds was addressing the Dáil for the first time as Minister for Transport and he gave the same positive message as he had given to the Institute of Transport dinner. He said he had identified the problems which

> are there for everybody who wants to see them, out in the streets of Dublin, Cork and in many other aspects of transport throughout the country . . . when I take on a job I like to see it through. I am not under any illusions about the complexity of the task facing me in this area. When I have all the information that I need the House can be assured that I will put my proposals before the Government.
> (ibid., Vol. 319, Col. 850)

Within a month the very comprehensive first report of the TCC, under the chairmanship of Professor Michael MacCormac, was published and Albert Reynolds announced that the Dublin Transportation Authority proposal was accepted. There was no dissenting voice to that decision, but the electrification project for the Dublin suburban railway was not without Dáil critics. The TCC itself said that the case for the rapid rail transit system, including phase 2 and 3, was 10 years old and needed to be reviewed. It asked that this be done 'within six months'. No such review was undertaken, but the TCC comment together with a Voorhees Report gave Austin Deasy (Fine Gael Transport spokesman) the opportunity to ask Albert Reynolds 'if he will re-examine the decision to electrify the Howth–Bray railway line at a cost of £46 million' (ibid., Vol. 320, Col. 1815). The point at issue was electrification versus diesel operation, and the minister explained that this had already been thoroughly studied. 'There was no question of the government re-examining the decision which is now in the course of being implemented.' Answering supplementaries, Albert Reynolds summarised the case for electrification:

> The marginal cost [of electrification over dieselisation] . . . is less than £1 million. In my view that is far outweighed by the benefits that would accrue from it. As we know, electric traction has considerable advantages in the movement of urban passengers and demands high

acceleration and deceleration with light, fast trains. These trains are more acceptable from an environmental point of view. In an electrified system there will be a certain security of supply because the electricity will be coming from a national grid. There is over-dependence on diesel oil in the present situation. The electrification of the Howth–Bray line means that it could be directly linked in to other parts of the city.

(ibid., Vol. 320, Col. 1816)

The linkage 'to other parts of the city' mentioned by the minister was a reference to the suitability of electric traction for the underground links proposed by the DRRTS.

While electrification of the Howth/Bray line was going ahead, the problem of inadequate and outdated mainline coaching stock remained. When CIÉ published its 1980 Summer timetable, the *IRRS Journal* commented on the extreme shortage of passenger rolling stock, a situation accentuated by 'the loss in sundry mishaps [principally due to terrorist and vandal attack] of no fewer than eleven coaches—the equivalent of an entire train. . . . The Summer of 1980 was going to cause great strain on CIÉ's resources in carriages.' Passenger accommodation was withdrawn from day mails and no radio trains were to be operated. After thirty years they had probably run their course in more ways than one. The railway division of CIÉ was grappling with its equipment problems, planning electrification and contemplating newspaper reports and government denials that a major close-down of the railways was being plotted by McKinsey when, on Friday, 1 August 1980, nine months after the Dalkey accident, another and much more tragic rail accident occurred.

'Rail disaster worst in Ireland this century' was one of several *Irish Times* headings in the dramatically illustrated three pages given to the fatal crash at Buttevant, Co. Cork. Others read: '17 killed in Cork train crash—CIÉ'; '42 detained in two Cork hospitals'; and 'Crash scene resembled battlefield'. The main story was as follows:

> At least 17 people were killed in yesterday's rail disaster in Buttevant, Co. Cork the worst in Ireland this century. The 10 a.m. Dublin to Cork train with about 230 passengers aboard was passing through Buttevant station when it left the rails and careered into an embankment, causing the leading coaches to jack-knife across the line. A Garda spokesman at Mallow Hospital said early today that 17 bodies had been brought there, ten males and seven females. It was feared that more bodies were still in the crashed carriages. The Minister for Transport, Mr Reynolds has ordered a full public enquiry into the tragedy. Most of the dead and injured were in the first three carriages which became a mangled and grotesque looking wreckage. The first carriage was

actually compressed and flattened with gaping holes visible in the roof and floor areas. A number of bodies were thrown through the floor on impact and these were the last of the dead to be recovered late last evening as huge cranes gently prised the coaches upwards allowing doctors and ambulance workers access . . . Cork County Disaster Plan last activated for the Whiddy Island explosion went into operation.

The report in *Nuacht CIÉ* (September 1980) on the 'worst rail tragedy in CIÉ's history' confirmed the final death toll as 18 and that over 40 were injured. The *IRRS Journal* recorded graphic detail of the damaged rolling stock. It said that the first three coaches 'were totally demolished' and then noted that a 'striking feature' of the accident was that damage suffered by the demolished coaches was in 'marked contrast' to the damage done to the Craven coaches.

> The demolished coaches had been built between 1953 and 1964, and their design lacked some points which are now considered as standard on modern designs of passenger train equipment. There can be little doubt that if sufficient up-to-date rolling stock of integral body construction, equipped with the 'Buck-eye' type of couplings, and with anti-collision gangways, had been included in the assembly of the train the consequences would have been much less severe.
>
> (*IRRS Journal*, October 1980)

The 1980 Buttevant disaster should not have occurred for various reasons identified in the subsequent government investigation. However, its tragic consequences gave chilling support to the case for renewal of CIÉ's mainline coaching stock which several years earlier had been submitted for government approval.

Meanwhile in October, four worker directors had joined the CIÉ Board and at the same time Jack Higgins, CIÉ's General Manager, was appointed to full board membership. The deficit was growing inexorably and by the end of 1980 it would have grown to £76 million, a further 27 per cent above the figure which had so shocked Pádraig Faulkner a year earlier. The situation of the public finances was even more serious. The parity of the Irish pound with sterling had been ended in March 1979. Such was Ireland's economic performance and inflation rate that the punt had since devalued by 20 per cent *vis-à-vis* sterling. The 1980 Budget had set a borrowing requirement of £896 million, 10 per cent of GNP, but at year end, borrowing would total £1,721 million or 19 per cent of GNP. The McKinsey Report was nearing completion. 1981 would be another interesting year.

CHAPTER 20

MCKINSEY AGAIN

The second McKinsey Report—New rail coaches approved—Maynooth commuter service announced—CIÉ faces widespread criticism.

McKinsey dispatched their report to Minister Albert Reynolds on 15 December 1980. It was released in February 1981 with a statement saying that

> At this juncture the Government considers that because of the fundamental importance and significance of the matters dealt with in the Report it should be the subject of public debate and consultation with interested parties, before decisions are taken.

The following day's editorial in *The Irish Times* summarised what it saw as the key recommendations.

> Abolish CIÉ and put in its place three CIÉ's. That is the short message of the McKinsey Report to the Government, which is given the fancy title, 'The Transport Challenge'. The three new companies are to be a national railway company, a Dublin bus company and a national bus company for all outside Dublin. The report examines the transport system in general, casting a consistently weary look at the railway system. It does not think much of its future—if it has one at all. The Government is handling all this in a wary fashion. And well they might.

The paper criticised how the government 'solemnly' asks for a public debate on 'this report—a massive, thick, tightly packed book . . . by landing [it] on the desks of newspapermen at 5 o'clock in the afternoon before publication', and commented that

> CIÉ has got something of a bad name. Much of this may be a consequence of the shilly-shallying of various Governments, which could never consistently fix in their minds just how much of the service should be frankly subsidised as a social necessity.

McKinsey's brief had been to 'examine the reasons for the deterioration in the financial position of CIÉ and recommend such corrective measures as may be possible to bring about an improvement in the position'. It had been 'guided' in its work by an Interdepartmental Steering Committee. The electrification of the Howth/Bray line had been decided on before the McKinsey study began, so this was 'excluded from the study'. The decision to set up a Dublin Transportation Authority had been made during the course of the study and McKinsey were 'asked by the Steering Committee to take account of this development'. The DTA decision can now be seen to have had a major influence on McKinsey. This body, so McKinsey believed, would 'manage the infrastructure of Dublin's urban transport in its entirety, including the planning and development of Public Transport Services' (McKinsey, letter to Minister, 15 December 1980). Thus DCS was going to have a new 'boss' other than the Department of Transport. Therefore it could be separated from CIÉ. Why then leave the rest of the company intact? It too could be split up. With regard to the main question put to McKinsey, i.e. 'the reasons for the deterioration in the financial position of CIÉ', the consultants rediscovered the unpalatable truth that they were mainly outside the control of the board.

Substantial improvements had been achieved in productivity—of labour and equipment—as a result of which, just as in 1971, McKinsey could find no dramatic opportunities for improving financial performance. The main trouble with CIÉ, or so it seemed to McKinsey, was that it had been created around the railway and hence had no choice but to support the railway. As a result, the railway was not adapted as radically as the market required. In the future it would be better for the railway to stand alone for all to see as separate from road services. Hence the three-company concept emerged—Dublin city bus, the railway, and a company to operate the provincial city, intercity and rural bus services. The case for the break-up of the company was also supported by the argument that public transport was really a government concern and should receive more direct attention from government. Public transport requirements should be defined, not by CIÉ, but by government. The civil service should acquire more 'skills in analysis and planning' so as to be able to specify government's wishes for the operator. DTA would do that for Dublin; the Department of Transport should do it for the railway and for provincial bus services. McKinsey considered whether CIÉ should continue as a 'holding' entity, and decided 'no'.

It is interesting to reflect on the possible origin of this argument for disestablishing CIÉ. Did the idea originate with the Interdepartmental Steering Committee or with McKinsey or just 'emerge' between them? Within CIÉ there was a strong view that the main mover of the break-up proposal was the Steering Committee. McKinsey concluded its argument for the break-up by such remarks as that it was the 'only possible option for the future of CIÉ . . . as an institution, CIÉ has outlived its usefulness'. However, there were also positive reasons for disbanding CIÉ:

> It would provide an opportunity . . . to improve staff and management motivation in the individual public transport businesses.
> 1. Set goals that everyone can understand and pursue [and] replace the broad generalities of present Board policy for CIÉ as a whole.
> 2. Ensure widespread recognition of the positive contribution to the economy made by public transport. As government becomes more closely involved in the management of public transport, it will gain a deeper understanding of the businesses, and hence be able to give greater support and commitment to the goals of public transport than is possible at present. (McKinsey, The Transport Challenge, p. C10)

The last sentence of this extract was a wry comment on existing government attitudes. McKinsey believed that by relocating responsibility for setting service levels and pricing policies with government, the state would be forced into a new appreciation of the value of public transport and begin to treat it more fairly than hitherto. The terms of reference, as we've noted, asked for 'corrective measures' to bring about an improvement in the financial position. Once again the railway was quickly identified as the main cause of the financial problem. In its analysis of possible solutions McKinsey concluded that 'increasing railway volumes could not be justified on economic or financial grounds' while reducing the size of the railway network would 'offer no significant economic advantages'. Like McKinsey's earlier study (1971), the final judgment on the future of the railways was neutral. The issue was a political rather than an economic one.

> The cost to the nation over 25 years either of keeping or of closing the mainline railway would be broadly similar; the choice will depend on the perceived value of the railway to the community as a whole.
> (ibid., p. 5)

Against that background specific recommendations were summarised as follows:

– Discontinuing the sundries business, since no prospect for its recovery now exists
– Closing Road Freight operations, the rationale for which is the sundries business
– Discontinuing individual container services, which are viable on a 'marginal cost' basis when carried on sundries trains
– Closing Freight Division, since its remaining businesses could be managed by other parts of the organisation
– Dismantling the area structure, which will no longer be required once the reason for the 'integrated transport company' concept of CIÉ has disappeared
– Centralising all railway operations . . .
– Strengthening the marketing approach . . . (ibid., p. 4)

With regard to urban bus operations, the recommendations were so obvious that they generated cynical comment about the value of consultants.

1. Improve operational performance, by
   – Introducing one-man-operation . . .
   – Upgrading the bus fleet with new GM stock . . .
2. Improve service performance, by
   – Increasing bus speeds, which will require vigorous pursuit by the Dublin Transportation Authority of traffic management and road improvement measures
   – Adapting bus service levels as a result of a full-scale route and frequency review—but only *after* bus speed improvement measures are under way. (ibid., p. 5)

Concerning rural bus services, the report noted that they were now serving that declining proportion of the rural population which did not have access to private transport. They recommended using the 'standard 54 seat bus only on relatively few high demand routes' and experimenting with smaller buses, including privately owned buses, on thinner routes. McKinsey added its voice to the growing chorus of reports which believed that the state subvention should be paid 'above the line'.

The McKinsey Report presented government with an agenda for those positive decisions which Albert Reynolds said he was eager to make. However, within a few months the burden of making such decisions would slip from his shoulders. In June 1981 Reynolds was replaced by Patrick Cooney in a Fine Gael/Labour coalition, which would last a mere nine months until defeated on a budget resolution in February 1982. Patrick Cooney would be replaced by John Wilson in a minority Fianna Fáil government which would also last for only nine months until December 1982. CIÉ would have to wait until 1983 and 1984, with Jim Mitchell as minister in a new Fine Gael/Labour coalition, before a government decision would be made about its long-term prospects. In the meantime the annual 'aggro' about the subvention would continue. However, before leaving office Albert Reynolds made the long-awaited decision about the building of passenger rolling stock.

CIÉ's reaction to the McKinsey Report ranged between being hostile and dismissive. The government had publicly sought the views of all parties, so CIÉ had an open invitation to express itself. It might have elected to do so privately, but if the debate was going to be in public, the board believed that it should make a public response. At any rate CIÉ's 18,052 staff (average for the year 1980) and their trade unions would expect it to make a public statement. They would see their own future as being critically affected by the proposal to 'disestablish' the organisation.

In the course of a lengthy statement the Board of CIÉ said:

> that it was pleased that the consultants concluded that the main reason for the deterioration in CIÉ's financial situation was due to external factors and that the company's performance in improving its productivity was impressive. (*Nuacht CIÉ*, Márta 1981)

It welcomed the suggestion that government nominate the social services required from public transport at a national level and that this be done by the DTA for the Dublin area—in each case with payments being made 'above the line' for such services. At the same time CIÉ rejected the suggestion that government and the DTA take over responsibility for determining 'service levels and revenue' as being 'unrealistic and unworkable'.

> This was recognised by the joint committee of the Oireachtas as set out in their report on CIÉ. It is also contrary to the EEC policy which recommends that [public transport operators] should have their role clearly defined by the government and then given the authority to fulfil it. (ibid.)

CIÉ was straightforward in its rejection of the suggestions for the break-up of the organisation, commenting as follows:

> The consultants view that 'CIÉ as is now constituted is no longer appropriate to the needs of transport in Ireland in the 1980s' . . . can only be viewed as an opinion. It is unsubstantiated by any facts and there is no case made which would justify the conclusions. The international trends in public transport organisations are towards greater integration and co-ordination. The integrated system which we

have now in Ireland is widely recognised as an advanced approach to the provision of public transport services. The fragmentation of the existing structure would inevitably have the effect of decreasing efficiency and increasing costs. (ibid.)

The argument about the value of an integrated nation-wide transport system was one that CIÉ repeated in subsequent statements. St J. Devlin emphasised it in a *Sunday Tribune* interview. *Modern Transport* played the same theme in a generally favourable article about CIÉ's handling of Ireland's transport problems. In June 1981 a report by a commission of the International Union of Public Transport (UITP) took the same stance. The very prestigious UITP biennial conference, attended by 2,000 transport executives from 65 countries was held in Dublin in May that year. CIÉ's Mícheál Ó Cíosóig was the organising secretary of what was probably the biggest conference held in Ireland up to that date. Fifty five suppliers of transport equipment displayed their products in the RDS as part of the conference, and the first Bombardier double decker was on display.

> The report of the UITP international commission on regional transport . . . highlighted Ireland's unique position in having a single state-owned transport undertaking—Córas Iompair Éireann—charged with the responsibility of providing all forms of public transport throughout the country. Because of this, the problems of co-ordinating rail and bus services, so common throughout the rest of Europe, do not arise in Ireland, they said. (*Nuacht*, Iúil 1981)

CIÉ's statement on McKinsey made several criticisms of its comments on the railways.

> The consultants' understanding of the railway appears to have been limited and lacking in appreciation both of its current value and long term potential. The social contribution was not adequately quantified and the advantages from the viewpoint of energy conservation were dealt with in a dismissive manner.
> The railway's share of inter-urban passenger and freight traffics has been grossly understated. It is estimated by CIÉ that in 1979 the railway, even with a limited network, had 15 per cent of the passenger and 27 per cent of the freight in inter-urban markets.
> (ibid., Márta 1981)

In the *Sunday Tribune* Devlin was quoted as being strongly critical of McKinsey's proposals that carriage of rail sundries and road freight be discontinued. Sundries, he said, were not giving a satisfactory result, but they were being further rationalised, as were rail head services which extensively used private operators. The proposals as they stood raised questions about CIÉ's future existence and its commitment to freight operations. These questions 'emasculated' the company's credibility in the market.

With regard to passenger rolling stock, a year earlier (April 1980), Albert Reynolds met the board and advised that the original proposal that Linke Hoffman Busch (LHB) takeover certain engineering facilities in Inchicore where they would build railway coaches for CIÉ and for export was not acceptable. Accordingly, the board decided to submit a new proposal to build its own coaches at a rate of 35/40 per annum, using their own staff, with LHB as technical consultants. In May the chairman with the general manager met the minister again. Albert Reynolds had noted from early McKinsey briefings that CIÉ was discounting fares to such an extent that '45% of total fares revenue was at a rate of 38% of the standard fare whereas in 1969/70 only 14.1% of the fares were concession fares' (Board Minutes June 1980). The minister observed that if it were not for these concession fares and the traffic which they generated, the pressure for new rolling stock would be much less.

Devlin later reported on that meeting to his own board; he had reviewed factors behind the rail traffic growth of the previous ten years with the minister, but did not reject the logic of the minister's comments; indeed, if the railway priced itself out of the market, no rolling stock would be required. Neither did the minister pursue this argument to any particular conclusion. He was already considering a number of 'hypothetical options' for the railway as a whole, which had been defined for him by McKinsey. Devlin 'assured the Minister that whichever option the government selected would be implemented with the full co-operation of the Board. However, a direction was necessary in regard to the Government's policy for the railway.' (ibid.) In popular parlance Devlin was saying 'Make up your minds' and sometimes plaintively, sometimes angrily, he would repeat this plea each year when writing the chairman's review for the annual report.

The CIÉ Board moved quickly with its new coach-building proposals which were lodged with the Department in June 1980. In the month the revised proposals were submitted, the long-awaited letter was received from the Department granting permission to acquire coaches for the new suburban services. The day that letter arrived, Devlin, answering a question from Mr Haughey at a meeting with heads of state-sponsored bodies, said that he could not give a definite date for opening the electrified suburban line because a decision on rolling stock was still not made. When he reached his office and found the letter waiting for him, he must have called the Taoiseach to correct the record.

The acquisition of new suburban line coaches had now been authorised, but questions remained about mainline rolling stock and about the Inchicore plant. Six months later, on 30 January 1981, the story broke in *The Irish Times* that CIÉ was to acquire 40 two-car EMU sets (electric multiple units) for the suburban rail service from Linke Hoffman Busch. This was about half the total requirement for the new service. Austin Deasy put down Dáil questions which were answered by Albert Reynolds on 10 February 1981. In summary, Reynolds said that it had never been anticipated that the entire rolling stock for the new suburban services would be manufactured at Inchicore and 'provision' for manufacture of further rolling stock for the mainline and suburban lines was being considered. Jim Mitchell was outraged: bus manufacture had already moved to Shannon; the Inchicore workers were being duped and misled. The matter was again discussed at the adjournment of the day's Dáil proceedings, but little extra light was thrown on the question. A number of matters were now coming together in a way which forced a decision out into the open. The McKinsey Report had been published in February, in the aftermath of the Buttevant crash. CIÉ's persistent appeals for new rolling stock had to be addressed; electrification work on the Bray/Howth line was proceeding and its full rolling stock needs had to be met; workers in Inchicore were becoming increasingly restive; and a general election was in the offing. On 24 April 1981 Albert Reynolds visited CIÉ's railway engineering works at Inchicore where he made two important announcements. He announced that government had approved the assembly of 124 mainline coaches at Inchicore.

> This project, which will cost £34 million . . . should allow almost all existing mainline passenger links to be operated by either new coaches or the existing [BR Mark 2] A.C. sets, with Cravens and Park Royals available for the rest of the services. . . . the wood-framed 'laminated' stock which dates from the early 1950s (and was intended for use over a period of about 15 years) will be finally withdrawn.
>
> *(IRRS Journal,* June 1981)

The new mainline coaches were to be based on the British Rail Mark 3 passenger coach, and St J. Devlin said that during the early stages components would be imported in knocked-down condition, but 'as experience is gained an increasing amount of the structural work will be executed at Inchicore' (Annual Report, 1981). Production commenced late in 1983 and the first of the new stock entered service in 1984. The announcement about mainline coach-building had an odd tail to it. During his Inchicore visit Mr Reynolds also announced that 'CIÉ had decided' to institute a new commuter service to Maynooth—on the old MGWR Mullingar line—and that services would begin within three months. This was a surprising announcement. For several years, scarcity of rolling stock was a recurring theme in CIÉ statements. In 1979 it had 344 coaches carrying 17.9 million passengers, which was near enough to twice the passengers carried in 1962 when it had 643 coaches on its books. Regularly CIÉ had warned that it would have to cut services and, as we've seen, the 1980 timetable was so tight that some cuts were introduced in long-established services. Now, a year later, the board had decided to inaugurate a new commuter service to Maynooth, serving Blanchardstown, Clonsilla, Lucan and Leixlip, and no new rolling stock had been acquired in the interim. The *IRRS Journal* commented:

> It will however be patent that to provide the rolling stock for commuter services as suggested by the Minister's remarks must be extremely difficult, especially in the morning period . . . provision of the Friday evening service will be very difficult without cancellation or curtailment of existing mainline or suburban services.
>
> (*IRRS Journal*, October 1981)

The explanation for this decision by the board emerged later: the company 'was required' by government to inaugurate the new service (Annual Report, 1981). The government request may have been prompted by electoral considerations. With a large majority, the Fianna Fáil government still had another year to run, but economic indicators were unfavourable —an 18 per cent increase in the CPI in 1980, with worse projected for 1981. A spring 1981 general election was expected, but the Stardust Ballroom disaster, 14 February 1981, caused the first postponement; the IRA (Bobby Sands) hunger strike caused another, so that the election did not take place until early June. None the less electoral considerations were high in April when government decided that the critical Dublin West constituency deserved the encouragement of a railway commuter service.

An *IRRS Journal* comment in October 1981 indicates the political significance attached to the planned commuter service to Maynooth.

> During the campaign before the General Election timetables were widely circulated in West County Dublin showing trains from Connolly to Maynooth at 6.00, 6.25, 7.20. . . .
>
> (*IRRS Journal*, October 1981)

By the time the service was launched, on 30 November 1981, a Fine Gael/Labour coalition had replaced Fianna Fáil. The *IRRS Journal* recorded that 'public response to the new service has been less than satisfactory . . . and even the existing small allocation of rolling stock to the Maynooth service has had serious consequences elsewhere' (ibid., February 1982). In October the new government confirmed the decision to build mainline coaches at Inchicore. Meanwhile the Park Royal and Craven coaches were being refurbished and the original asbestos insulation was being removed from the Park Royals.

Another feature of railway operations in the early 1980s was an extraordinary level of vandalism, especially in the Dublin area. These attacks had their bus counterparts as a result of which the Finglas route was seriously restricted for an extended period in 1982. Typical railway incidents were reported in the *IRRS Journal*.

> Howth station, only recently refurbished, was broken into in the early morning of Saturday, 25 July, and extensively vandalised by 'politically' motivated intruders. . . . Howth Junction station is simply an adventure playground for the local youths who amuse themselves in placing obstructions on the tracks, interfering with signals, and stoning trains. In the Liffey Junction/Cabra/Glasnevin Junction area, vandalism is a persistent hazard. It is said that on a recent occasion a posse of police, called to the place, refused to tackle a gang . . . Some damage to the railway was suffered on Saturday 18 July when the rioters who fought a battle with police when endeavouring to attack the British Embassy, attempted to use the railway line as a side-approach. (ibid., June 1981)

> Attacks on trains and other railway property reached a new height in September . . . An evening not untypical was 25 September, when the 18.11 ex Drogheda arrived at Connolly with no fewer than seven broken windows, having been attacked at the same place on both its outward and return journey. On the same evening a passenger was removed by ambulance from the 17.35 Dún Laoghaire/Drogheda train at East Wall, after an incident of stoning. (ibid., February 1982)

Bomb scares also happened with tedious regularity causing serious inconvenience to rail passengers.

> Services were badly disrupted on 5 December while Army experts checked Cork trains at various locations . . . Services were again disrupted on Tuesday 8 December, by a bomb scare at Heuston station. (ibid.)

On the Belfast line disruptions were still more frequent and sustained over a much longer period from the early 1970s well into the 1990s. An indication of the difficulties with which CIÉ and NIR had to contend is given by a listing of six separate incidents in the June 1981 issue of the *IRRS Journal*. They occurred on 13 March, 4 April, 28 April, 5 May, 20 July, and 26 July 1981. Conspiracy theorists suspected that road hauliers who benefited from such incidents might have contributed to their frequency. In addition to bomb scares, interference over the years with the Dublin/Belfast line occasionally involved explosions which were generally claimed or attributed to the Provisional IRA. However, on 8 June 1994, six months after the 1993 Downing Street declaration on the future of Northern Ireland, most of the Republic's mainline rail services were disrupted by loyalist bomb scares on the Dublin/Cork line. In the event, no bombs were found in searches which covered the entire line from Dublin to Cork.

To return to the relationship of CIÉ with government: it continued to be dominated by the rising deficit. In 1980 the deficit amounted to £76.5 million and the government subvention after adjustment during the year came to £70 million. In the Annual Estimates for 1981 the same government again set the subvention below the previous year's level at £65 million, i.e. over £10 million less than the actual deficit incurred in 1980. It was but right to set CIÉ a strong challenge, but one must ask whether the targets set in the circumstances of the time were in any way realistic. Inflation at the beginning of 1981 was running at 6 per cent per quarter. From CIÉ's standpoint only a major reduction in services would enable it to live within the £65 million. On 12 March the chairman met Minister Reynolds to discuss the situation. The minister accepted that there was a problem, but he did not want to seek an increase in the subvention from his government colleagues —how could he be confident that CIÉ could live within a larger subvention even if it were authorised? Neither would he agree to the alternative of a substantial reduction in services. However, if CIÉ could give him certain assurances about no unofficial strikes and no wage claims above those provided for in the national understanding, he would see if an increase in subvention could be authorised.

Within days Devlin met the trade unions—ICTU and non-ICTU unions in separate sessions—but by the time he was ready to return to the minister, a general election had been announced. In lieu of the resumed meeting with the minister, Devlin wrote to Noel McMahon, Secretary of the Department, late in May 1981. In addition to inflationary pressures CIÉ 's business was being affected by the depression and a gap of £18.5 million was now expected between the deficit and the subvention. To achieve such a reduction in the remainder of the year meant saving at a rate of £37 million per annum. Jack Higgins told the board that closing down all rail services other than Dublin–Belfast would achieve such a saving, but redundancy payments would absorb a similar amount, leaving CIÉ less than £3 million better off. With a general election in progress government had ceased to function in such matters. It would have to be resolved by the winners of the general election. The year ended with a result even worse than was feared in May. The deficit came to £94.9 million, an increase of £20 million on 1980. The subvention eventually authorised by the new Dáil was £85 million, £20 million higher than the original estimate, but it was still £10 million short of the deficit actually incurred. CIÉ's finances were in total disarray, a description which could also be applied to the public finances as a whole.

The year 1982 would prove to be worse again; inflation was running at 17 per cent and during the year there would be two more general elections. The initial subvention for 1982 had been set at £96 million which was at least sufficient to cover the 1981 deficit if it were contained at that level. However, even this more generous treatment would prove insufficient. In February, after a deal with the Independent TD, Tony Gregory, which *inter alia* promised a freeze on CIÉ fares, Fianna Fáil returned to office. In April CIÉ advised the Department that its revised outlook for the year was a deficit of £105 million or £9 million more than the authorised subvention. Minister John Wilson asked for and received proposals to keep the deficit to the original figure, and there the matter rested.

Government's difficulty in facing up to and accepting the cost of the services which it required from CIÉ cannot have been eased by such confusion and controversy as was caused by the publication during 1982 of *Transport Policy in Ireland* by Dr Sean D. Barrett of Trinity College. Receiving the book for comment from its publisher, the Irish Management Institute, Jack Higgins was dismayed with what appeared to be a sustained assault on CIÉ as part of a review of Irish transport policy. Presented as an academic textbook, Barrett's work was surprising in a number of its comparisons and omissions. A use of statistics which even now, away from the controversy of the day, seems to have been oddly selective, managed to convey an impression of CIÉ which was cruelly at variance with the true record of its performance and of its efficiency relative to other transport companies. CIÉ commissioned the well-established transport planning consultants, Steers, Davies and Gleave Ltd, to review Barrett's book. This firm had worked for British Rail, London Transport, the World Bank and other agencies in all five continents. It also had some familiarity with the Irish scene. Its report confirmed the basis of CIÉ's negative reaction to '*Transport Policy in Ireland*—outdated data, out of date references and . . . apparent errors and omissions [which] are likely to mislead the reader'. CIÉ appended its own detailed observations on the book to the consultants' report and forwarded them to the author and to the publisher. The book was published without amendment, though the Irish Management Institute did provide space in its journal, *Management*, for CIÉ to register its protest. A couple of examples will explain CIÉ's concern. Barrett claimed that 'if the State Company wanted to reach even British Rail's level of productivity it would need to shed almost half its workforce'. The basis for this calculation included taking an incorrect figure for CIÉ's tonne kilometres in 1974 and an incorrect employment figure in British Rail for 1981. Thus there were two errors and one time distortion. The 1974 CIÉ tonne kilometres were understated by 16 per cent while British Rail's 1981 productivity was overstated due to a 30 per cent understatement of its employee numbers. CIÉ asked that its correct data be compared with British Rail's correct data for the same recent year—not 1974, before its rail development plan was published and major improvements in productivity had taken place. If such a comparison were made, 'the calculation shows that CIÉ's productivity . . . is comparable with British Rail' (*Transport Policy in Ireland* by S. D. Barrett, a CIÉ Response'). Barrett's venture into international comparisons was similarly faulted.

> For example, the author claims that 'in the use of factors of production by the railways the Irish output by carriages and wagons is at the lower end of the scale compared to other countries'. This is not correct. In 1973 the CIÉ performance was low but the 1979 statistics, available from the sources used by the author, show the opposite. CIÉ's use of wagons and carriages is one of the best in Europe. Elsewhere in the same Chapter data for other years is also used to support other invalid views. In fact, it is highly significant that over half the tables in the book relate to the period prior to and including 1975 even though the following seven years was a period of major change in Irish transport.
> (ibid.)

St J. Devlin professed to be less concerned than others by criticisms from such commentators as Sean Barrett—one had to keep on with the job. Nevertheless, when a university lecturer is published by a Management Institute and ignores all you have achieved since your appointment, it must be disheartening and can't have eased relationships with one's critics in government and in the media.

In September 1982 the chairman advised the board that the April estimate of a £105 million deficit was likely to be exceeded, noting that there was a continuing fall in rail and road passenger receipts. Freight revenue on the railway was also down. Two important traffics were lost: the Silvermines zinc concentrate traffic had ceased when the mine ran out and dolomite traffic to the Quigley magnesite factory at Ballinacourty, Co. Waterford, also ended when the factory closed down. In addition, as part of the 'Gregory deal' a rates and fares increase budgeted for July had been deferred.

> The outlook for the year now is a loss of £108 m., on the basis that the 5% pay instalment (£3 m.) would be paid out. [Efforts to delay this

payment seemed unlikely to succeed]. While the shortfall in revenue could be attributed to the current recession, the outlook for 1983 is very serious. Budgeting on the same basis as 1982, the deficit for 1983 would be of the order of £120 m.   (Board Minutes, 16 September 1982)

Devlin was not far off in his estimate for the 1982 outcome. The deficit which finally emerged was £109.4 million rather than £108 million; the government subvention was let stand at £96 million. On the other hand, he would prove to be overly pessimistic in his fears for 1983. The 'runaway train' was slowing down. The Fianna Fáil government fell in November. A Fine Gael/Labour government was elected and Jim Mitchell became Minister in December 1982. The new government found that it had to approve a massive fares increase in January 1983 similar to the one which faced the previous Fine Gael/Labour coalition ten years earlier (February 1973). Inflation was about to fall to 10.4 per cent (the lowest figure for eleven years with the exception of 1978) and some political stability seemed in prospect. Jim Mitchell as Minister was about to spend over four years in office—the longest serving Transport minister since Erskine Childers spent ten years in that job (1959–1969). In summary, the tide was turning and the deficit actually fell in 1983 for the first time in almost twenty years. Many issues had to be resolved. The McKinsey Report required action of some sort, but before deciding on its recommendations for a restructured CIÉ, Jim Mitchell would try to impose some order and logic on the exchequer's financial commitment to public transport. Implementation of the long sought and now formally accepted concept of a Dublin Transport Authority was another matter that awaited his attention.

CHAPTER 21

PIT OF THE VALLEY

1983 subvention fixed £21.6 million below 1982 outcome—Jim Mitchell appointed Minister—Additional borrowing authorised—New subvention formula defined —Cherryville accident—Paul Conlon succeeds Liam St J. Devlin—Building on Reality modifies the new subvention formula.

A classic 'square the circle' dilemma faced CIÉ in 1983 and, in several ways, it was a watershed year. The estimates for public expenditure prepared by the outgoing Fianna Fáil government provided for a 1983 subvention of £86 million—£10 million below the 1982 subvention and £21.6 million less than the deficit actually incurred in that year. During the November 1982 General Election campaign Fine Gael maintained a firm 'financial rectitude' stance. Exchequer borrowings for that year were well ahead of what the country could afford at almost £1.7 billion and Fine Gael accepted that the public expenditure estimates for 1983 circulated by the Fianna Fáil government could not be exceeded. In due course the Fine Gael/Labour coalition took office on 15 December 1982; it confirmed that the £86 million subvention would not be increased and on 28 December a near record rise in CIÉ's charges was approved. The *Evening Press* carried the story under a seven-column headline, 'Massive New Year Rise in CIÉ Fares'. The worst news was given to the reader in the first sentence of the report.

> Increases of up to 40 per cent in CIÉ passenger fares come into effect from Monday next. And freight charges are to rise from between 15 to 20 per cent, the company announced today.
>
> The Government—which recently sanctioned increases in bottle

> gas, coal and other items—has given CIÉ the go-ahead to introduce increases in fares and freight costs which will cost the public another £24,100,000. Other plans include the introduction of driver-only double deck buses. (*Evening Press*, 28 December 1982)

The report went on to say that there would be an average increase of 25 per cent on Dublin city and provincial bus fares, and on mainline rail and suburban rail fares. Reaching the sixth paragraph of the *Evening Press* story, the opening 40 per cent figure was explained: it applied to 'multiple journey tickets which would be increased up to' that amount. The observation that the increases would 'cost the public another £24.1 million' was hardly a fair presentation of the facts either. The cost was being incurred already and financed by the public through CIÉ borrowings and government subvention: it was merely being transferred directly to the customers.

The following day, the *Evening Press* gave CIÉ another seven-column heading—'CIÉ: "£7,000 tax bill for every job".'

> Each of the 16,000 jobs in CIÉ is costing the taxpayer £7,000 a year, the Minister for Transport, Mr Jim Mitchell, claimed today. And he described the State public transport service as 'an albatross around the nation's neck'. . . . Mr Mitchell revealed that over the past three years CIÉ had borrowed £21 million to finance deficits above what had been budgeted for by the Government of the day.
>
> 'But that is the limit of their borrowing facility', the Minister declared. 'That soft option is now closed. There are now only chronic and acute options.' (ibid., 29 December 1982)

The minister said that fare increases would reduce CIÉ's expected 1983 deficit from £120 million to £100 million. But as the subvention was to be held at the £86 million set by the outgoing Fianna Fail government, another £14 million would have to be found elsewhere. There was no question of the government allowing the target deficit to be breached, nor would further borrowing be allowed.

Jim Mitchell was just two weeks in office and his remarks provoked great distress in CIÉ. The 'albatross around the nation's neck' description of CIÉ shocked and angered people at every level. Management would say that CIÉ had neither been authorised to cut services nor allowed to increase fares so as to live within its approved subventions. The 'soft option' of borrowing to meet the shortfall in the annual subvention was the option chosen by government and was never CIÉ's preferred course. 'Cutbacks', Mr Mitchell had said, would be 'a matter for the Board', but no one really believed that he would give CIÉ a free hand to balance its books. If Mitchell's outburst was partially intended to frighten its workforce, a front-page story in the next issue of the *Evening Press*—the third in succession—gave him little comfort:

> ## NBU TO PRESS FOR 20 P.C. DESPITE CIÉ LOSSES
> The National Busworkers Union are determined to press ahead with a 20 per cent wage claim no matter what the state of CIÉ finances, Mr Tom Darby, general secretary of the NBU, said today. The Government's 25 per cent hike in passenger fares had 'nothing to do with the workers of CIÉ', he said . . .
>
> The NBU . . . would totally resist any government attempts to have a pay pause.' CIÉ is now being used as a political football . . . We are tired of subsidising low fares with low wages, and we will press ahead with our demands for a decent working wage, no matter what the company's losses are. They are not of our making.
> (ibid., 30 December 1982)

The following April Jim Mitchell fended off Dáil questions from John Wilson and other deputies about the cutbacks that seemed to be unavoidable and from Seamus Brennan about the status of the McKinsey Report.

> The first problem I have to deal with is the decision by the previous Government to limit the subvention this year to CIÉ to £86 million. This means there is a £22 million reduction on last year's [deficit] . . . I must make decisions which will enable CIÉ to operate within the limits of the subvention set by the previous Government. Having made decisions in that regard, I will then turn to consideration of the McKinsey Report. (*Dáil Debates*, Vol. 341, Col. 1643)

Responding to a question about the possible closure of branch lines, he reasserted that 'The decision will not be made by me. These decisions are confined by statute to the board of CIÉ.' (ibid.) A week later Dáil Éireann, for the first time in several years, had a full-scale debate on Vote 41 (Transport). Jim Mitchell addressed the situation comprehensively and with more understanding than had been evident in earlier public remarks.

> As Deputies are aware, the central theme of the recent budget has been the need to come to grips with the gigantic problems of the public finances. In numerous areas of the public sector we can find examples which reflect a philosophy of putting off until tomorrow the measures which should be taken today or, more correctly, should have been taken yesterday. (ibid., Vol. 341, Col. 2262)

He confirmed the government's 'determination' that the subvention should not exceed £86 million, and continued:

> In approaching the matter on this basis the Government realised that major economies within CIÉ were unavoidable . . . Consultations with CIÉ in relation to the strategy to be adopted for 1983 are continuing. . . . The need to innovate, and above all the need to develop a much sharper cost consciousness have, I feel, not been sufficiently to the forefront in recent years. I was criticised outside the House for remarks which I made earlier this year. As I have already explained, they were intended not to hurt or wound but rather to stimulate efforts for change which I believe are called for in the present general difficult economic situation. (ibid.)

The minister was referring to reactions to his 'albatross' remark. He accepted that a substantial portion of CIÉ's services were performed for social reasons and made the important policy statement that this should be recognised by treating the subvention as part of CIÉ's revenue as recommended by at least five separate reports of committees and consultants since 1971.

> We all know that many of the services operated at a loss by CIÉ are clearly not justifiable on commercial grounds because of their social significance. It is unfair, therefore, to castigate CIÉ for incurring deficits as if the board rather than the social obligations placed on the board, are mainly responsible for the losses involved. Recognition of the true position can best be given by the introduction of an above-the-line accounting system. Inherent in such a system is the need to express in the board's accounts the amounts received in respect of uneconomic services as revenue rather than as a deficit. The above-the-line accounting system will make a major contribution to the improvement of morale in CIÉ. (ibid.)

Using the language of previous and subsequent Ministers for Finance and for Transport, Jim Mitchell then referred to 'an exceptionally high *allocation* of £60 million . . . provided in the 1983 budget' for CIÉ's capital programme. The normal citizen would be led by this language to believe that the £60 million was being provided by government. In reality, CIÉ was merely being authorised to borrow this amount. Expenditure on new buses and on new mainline coaches were the main causes of this record capital programme. Much leeway had to be made up and after 1983 capital expenditure fell sharply back.

Speakers on all sides were cautious in their references to the McKinsey Report. No one said that CIÉ should be disbanded, nor did they say that it should be retained. The closest any speaker went to expressing an opinion on this issue was a future Minister for Transport, Seamus Brennan, from whose remarks about 'grasping the nettle of CIÉ once and for all' one can deduce that, at the time he would have voted 'aye' to disbanding CIÉ if that question were put. He conceded that 'broadly CIÉ do their best and are a good company . . . but at what cost? Anybody could do well with £100 million of government money per year—that madness must now stop.' Seamus Brennan argued for the construction of a busway on the old Harcourt Street line from Shankhill to Grand Parade on the Grand Canal. He referred to a study of the project he had 'supervised'. However, nine years later and having been Minister for three years, Brennan, in the run-up to the 1992 General Election, found that he could do no more than announce 'agreement in principle . . . to re-open a section of the former Harcourt Street line as a public transport route, subject to an ongoing feasibility study' (*IRRS Journal*, June 1992). Another future Minister for Transport, Brian Cowen, also contributed to the April 1983 debate. Like others he accepted the £86 million subvention limit and had no practical steps to suggest as to how to achieve the cost reduction which this required of CIÉ. He did not want to be attacked for being too critical of CIÉ and recognised that the 'onus is always being placed on [CIÉ] by this House, from a social point of view, to ensure that rail and road passenger services are available'. Reorganisation would be necessary, but he both hoped that jobs would not be lost and believed that fares had risen too high. The question can be fairly put whether anyone genuinely believed that CIÉ could get by with a subvention £22 million less than the previous year's deficit without much more serious service cutbacks than were politically acceptable.

In contrast to the consensus on reducing the CIÉ subvention, two bitter Dáil debates took place on private members' motions concerning school transport. The outgoing administration had provided for no increase in the cost of school transport, resulting in an under-provision of £5.4 million. The outgoing Minister for Education in the Fianna Fail government, Gerard Brady, had indicated that while free transport to national schools would continue to be provided, a charge would have to be introduced for attendance at second level schools. There would be a higher rate for senior cycle than for lower cycle pupils and some concession would be made available for large families. When the Minister for Education in the new government, Mrs Gemma Hussey, introduced the charge—on a season ticket basis, as proposed by her predecessor—and also provided that medical card holders would be exempt, 'all hell broke loose'. The opposition spokesperson on Education, Mrs Mary O'Rourke (17 May 1983), proposed 'that Dáil Éireann condemns the Government for the present chaos and confusion in the school transport system and for inflicting hardship on many thousands of families'. The reader may ask how the scale of cutbacks necessary to achieve a £22 million improvement in CIÉ's finances could be accepted by a Dáil which appeared to be outraged by the change in the school transport scheme.

The proceedings of the CIÉ Board (14 January 1983) reveal the reality behind this conflict in public attitudes.

> The Chairman reported that he had met the Minister before Christmas and the Minister said that within one week he required a detailed submission of the savings which would enable CIÉ to operate within a subvention of £86 m. for 1983. On December 29th, 1982, the General Manager forwarded to the Department a summary of proposals for further reductions on the [CIÉ] budgeted deficit of £96 m. for 1983. It was pointed out in the documentation that the normal budget of CIÉ could be reduced to £93 m. taking into account further additional savings which would be obtained in the normal course. This would leave a shortfall of £7 m. between CIÉ's figure and the Minister's figure. To bridge this gap it would be necessary to make substantial cuts in City and Provincial bus services.

Devlin explained that with management colleagues he went back to the minister on 5 January 1983 with further proposals for living within the authorised subvention, but the minister said that

> he could not put these proposals before the cabinet because he had insufficient information in regard to the effect of the withdrawal and rationalisation of individual services on local communities. The Chairman endeavoured to explain to the Minister that it was unwise for the Cabinet to become involved in the detailed management of CIÉ services. Problems would arise for CIÉ in so much as Government decisions would be interpreted as political decisions and therefore subject to political pressure if the reorganisation of services was found to be unacceptable. The Minister replied that he required a detailed list of the services which it was proposed should be either withdrawn or rationalised and that furthermore he required an individual costing of each of these changes. The material which the Minister requested was provided on the following morning, January 6, 1983. On Tuesday, 11th January, the Chairman and General Manager again met the Minister at his request. He said that he was not satisfied with the material he received because neither he nor the Cabinet would be in a position to make a decision until they had [still] further information. (ibid.)

On 11 March, by which time no decision had been made about service cuts, the minister met the board and senior management. The minutes record a very inconclusive situation.

A general discussion took place and the Minister outlined the problems of Government at the present time and the difficulty in providing additional funds for CIÉ. He confirmed that the subvention of £86 m. for the year 1983 was an arbitrary amount and was based on what was available rather than on which services should be provided. He expressed the hope that it would be possible to maintain employment and that restrictions on service should be minimised to cause the least inconvenience to the community.

In subsequent discussion between CIÉ and the Department of Transport a solution of sorts was arrived at. The service cuts necessary to restrict the deficit to £86 million should not be implemented. Instead, the deficit for 1983 was to be contained at £99 million—almost £10 million less than the previous year's deficit, but still £13 million more than the available £86 million subvention. The difference of £13 million was to be covered by temporary borrowings. In effect the 'soft option', as it had been called only six months previously, was now being resorted to by the hard-pressed government which balked at the measures necessary to keep CIÉ's deficit to the prescribed limit.

On 30 June 1983 St J. Devlin told his board that he had already told the minister he did not wish to be re-appointed when his second five-year term as Chairman expired at the end of 1983. That afternoon, the entire board attended a meeting at the minister's office where he confirmed the subvention arrangements for 1983 and announced a new policy regarding future subventions. The minister's statement—lengthy, firm and conciliatory in tone—was subsequently distributed to all the staff.

> The Government have been reviewing the financial situation of CIÉ. This review . . . took account of the growth trends in the deficits recorded by CIÉ in recent years . . . and the great difficulty which the Exchequer would have in financing a deficit at the rate of recent trends. . . . the fact is that the Board's deficit rose from £2 m. in 1968/69 to £108 m. in 1982, a rate of increase considerably in excess of the rate of inflation . . . the Government has arrived at a number of decisions which affect the subvention, not just the question of the 1983 level but the general framework for the settlement of the subvention for future years. The Government's package of measures also covers arrangements relating to CIÉ capital expenditure and a clarification of the Board's mandate. (*Nuacht CIÉ*, Iúil 1983)

Devlin had complained a number of times that CIÉ's 25-year-old mandate had never effectively been clarified or interpreted for board.

> It shall be the general duty of the Board to provide reasonable, efficient and economical transport services with due regard to safety of operation, the encouragement of national economic development and the maintenance of reasonable conditions of employment for its employees. (Section 7(1), Transport Act 1958)

The 'clarification' of that mandate which the minister gave on 30 June 1983 did not attempt to specify what was meant by 'reasonable efficient and economical transport services' or indicate what regard had to be given to 'national economic development'. It consisted of a statement of financial directives and exhortations rather than clarification of a mandate. It required the board

> to review in depth all aspects of CIÉ's operations in the interest of reducing the Board's dependence on State subvention;
> to review the effectiveness and organisation of CIÉ management and to undertake any re-structuring found necessary;
> to extend and strengthen the role of the financial control function so as to improve the cost effectiveness of expenditure;
> to regard the improvement of staff morale and motivation throughout CIÉ as a major aim. (*Nuacht CIÉ*, Iúil 1983)

This was not a clarification of the mandate in the sense sought by CIÉ. However, it was much easier to complain about the vagueness of the 1958 mandate than to suggest how it should be amended. Jim Mitchell's statement continued:

> The Government have decided that for the future the CIÉ subvention will be paid above-the-line as income and will be determined in accordance with a formula related to the Board's revenue and expenditure performance. Under the formula the Board's subvention will represent a half of the revenue or a third of the expenditure whichever is the lesser.
> In other words every £2 earned by the Board will in principle bring a subvention of £1 subject to the constraint of one-in-three on the expenditure side.
> The subvention so calculated each year will represent the absolute limit of subvention funds which will be paid to the Board subject only to new situations that may arise and that may warrant special consideration. (ibid.)

The decision that in future the subvention would be equal to the lower of one-third of expenditure or half the revenue seemed to be fair. The formula represented a step forward and promised a happier relationship than previously between the company and government. In practice, the level of expenditure rather than the level of revenue would be the determining factor in the level of subvention, but suggesting that it would be determined by revenue sounded more positive. The stated rationale for the new approach was that the government assessed that one-third of CIÉ services could be regarded as social services, deserving state support.

However, another twist was given to the formula: CIÉ would have to reduce expenditure in real terms by 12 per cent over five years, i.e. at a rate of 2.5 per cent per annum. The requirement to reduce expenditure by 2.5 per cent per annum was arbitrary. It would be helped if oil prices, say, were to fall substantially —which they would. If one-person bus operations became possible, that too would be a help. But in different circumstances the constraint on expenditure could require a reduction in services and might prove politically unacceptable. Within twelve months the formula would be eased in a number of ways but the 2.5 per cent figure annual target cut in real expenditure of CIÉ as a whole would be focused on railway expenditure only and made more severe.

The minister advised the board that legislation was being prepared to establish a Dublin Transport Authority, that he would introduce legislation to increase CIÉ's borrowing limits—extra borrowings would be needed to finance the expected 1983 deficit—and that he was giving consideration to the McKinsey recommendations concerning the future of CIÉ. He was also establishing a permanent capital committee comprised of representatives of his Department, CIÉ and the Department of Finance, to vet all future capital expenditure proposals.

No doubt Jim Mitchell believed that the new formula would genuinely meet the requirements of the situation for the period in office of the government he represented. During the meeting with the minister, the board asked him if 'it would be allowed to take the action necessary to operate within the new financial parameters'. After the meeting the board reassembled at Heuston for its third session of the day, where Devlin reflected on the minister's reply. The minister appreciated that CIÉ would require freedom of action successfully to operate the new formula and 'he did more or less give such a guarantee' (Board Minutes, 30 June 1983).

The board agreed that the formula or a similar formula was inevitable. 1984 would be a very difficult year and it might not be possible to 'operate within the parameters of the formula during the initial years'. The board also agreed that the chairman should participate in radio and TV programmes to establish in the public mind that CIÉ was prepared to co-operate with the government in the new arrangements. The chairman should meet the trade unions at the earliest possible opportunity.

A month later the board heard some chilling comments from General

Manager Jack Higgins about how the new formula would work in 1984 and that it would be necessary to save £20 m. on the railway in that year. He did not think this was possible and illustrated the point by showing that if the railway was closed down and only Belfast/Dublin and Dublin/Cork kept open, £16 m. could be saved, but redundancies could cost £13.5 m. 'Thus the net saving would only be of the order of £2.5 m. Substantial reductions would also be necessary in the Road Passenger services and it may be necessary to introduce compulsory redundancy.' (ibid., 21 July 1983)

Jack Higgins pointed out that the subvention formula of 33 per cent of expenditure for the company as a whole was quite inadequate for the railway where the subvention necessary was 57 per cent—or 84 per cent in the case of the suburban line.

Adroitly reviewing the realities of CIÉ's latest position, St J. Devlin said:

> the Board were not in a position to go to the Minister and say that what he was requesting was impossible and that the formula was impractical. To say that the proposals were unworkable would be mutiny....
>
> The Board must be seen to co-operate with the Minister and ways and means must be devised to work within the formula. This may well require the Board to request a 'clearing of the decks' before full implementation of the formula. For example, the Board may ask to be relieved of the annual interest payments of £12 m. on accumulated deficits or might ask to have the interest charges on the suburban rail allowed for on a phased basis. There were undoubtedly difficulties in 1984 because additional wages, including the current round, could amount to £20 m. and the additional cost on the suburban line would be of the order of £10 m. It would not be possible to bridge the extra expenditure by fares increases.
>
> The general consensus was that the Board had to be seen to act constructively. To do otherwise would not have the support of the Government, the politicians or the community. It would be a mistake to conclude that by proposing stringent reductions in services, politicians might force the Government to retract on the formula.
>
> (ibid.)

The board continued to review the situation for 1984 at successive meetings and in September, it agreed that the chairman should inform the minister that it was not possible to plan the 1984 budget 'within the parameters of his formula'. Devlin proposed that the board request a meeting with the minister and seek the 'clearing of decks' which he had suggested earlier. This would involve

1. The subvention of the Dublin Suburban Rail to be treated separately

from the general formula. The cost of funding the electrification should be carried by the State.
2. The Board should be relieved of the liability of accumulated excess deficits arising from decisions of Governments in recent years.
3. The Government should fund the excess cost of redundancy compensation on the railway for pre-1968 staff.
The Chairman's proposal was agreed and it was also agreed that the management structure should be reviewed and that steps be taken to reduce costs of support staff.　　　　　　　　(ibid., 1 September 1983)

Legislation to increase CIÉ's borrowing powers, from £180 million to £230 million in the case of capital borrowings and from £20 million to £40 million in the case of temporary borrowings, was introduced in the Dáil by Minister Jim Mitchell on 7 December 1983. For the second time in one year, there was a full-scale debate on CIÉ. At this stage Mitchell was prepared to accept credit for having 'put a halt to that gallop [of the CIÉ deficit] and for the year now coming to a close, the deficit should be around £104 million, which will be the first reduction achieved in 15 years'. Mitchell's estimate of £104 million arose from the June 1983 board target of £99 million plus the cost of the national pay agreement—£5 million. The largest single factor in reducing the deficit below the 1982 level was the January fare increase mentioned at the beginning of this chapter. Jim Mitchell restated the new subvention policy and gave no indication that CIÉ would find great difficulties with it in 1984, nor did he show his hand about the McKinsey Report.

It would fall to Devlin's successor as chairman to detail the reasons for a reversal from an ever increasing to a declining deficit when the 1983 Annual Report was issued several months later. The final deficit figure was £102.1 million—down £5.5 million on the previous year. Revenue was up £8.7 million as a result of the increase in fares and rates and, despite inflation of 10.4 per cent, the expenditure increase had been held to a mere 1.5 per cent. All road passenger services, especially Dublin City Services, produced better results than in the previous year, though an increase in the railway deficit eroded some of this advantage.

In addition to financial matters, a number of other developments reported on in the 1983 Annual Report merit comment. Electrification of the Bray/Howth line was proceeding very satisfactorily—in scale, in sophistication and in the manner of execution it was the largest and most complex engineering project ever undertaken by CIÉ; the first of the new rolling stock had arrived on Valentine's Day 1983 and was being tested successfully; new mainline rolling stock was at last under construction; and new buses were in operation. Across the range of public transport services significant investment was under way. On the staff side, while unrest continued and remained damaging to DCS, staff numbers had been reduced by 20 per cent over the ten years since St J. Devlin had become Chairman. Of course, the deficit had soared over the same period, but in 1983 it had been reduced by 5 per cent in current terms and by 15 per cent in real terms.

It was time for Liam St J. Devlin to move on, but he was still Chairman when another fatal rail accident occurred. On 21 August 1983 the 17.15 Tralee/Dublin train stopped near Cherryville Junction, Co. Kildare, and the 18.50 Galway/Dublin ran into its rear. Seven people were killed and fifty-five were injured. The investigation which followed recorded the unfortunate confluence of events which contributed to the accident. Difficulties had arisen with the locomotive on the Tralee train as a result of which another locomotive was substituted at Mallow. The fuel register in the replacement locomotive was faulty and its log card omitted some of the previous day's workings; it carried insufficient fuel to complete the journey to Dublin, and this caused the Tralee train to come to a halt at Cherryville. The Galway/Dublin train which was following came to a danger signal and its driver attempted to call the CTC at Connolly station on the line-side telephone. However, the telephone was out of order and the driver proceeded ahead through the signal. The subsequent public inquiry found that the driver proceeded

> at such speed that allowing for visibility, condition of the rails, and gradients of the line . . . when he became aware of an obstruction on the line ahead, could not stop his train before it was in collision.
> (Government Investigation Report, May 1985)

The recommendations of the investigation were many and various, but a critical one was that if a driver decided to pass a danger signal without specific clearance from a controller or signalman, he should do so at no more than ten miles per hour. Another noted that the driver of the Galway/Dublin train had very brief sight of the tail lamp of the stationary train before the collision and the legendary reliability of the old and customary paraffin lamp was called into question. The investigation recommended that two electric lamps be used on every train, and that these be of 'brilliance and conspicuity' comparable with colour light signals.

Another fall-out of the Cherryville tragedy was renewed discussion about the suitability of much of CIÉ's rolling stock for modern rail operations. By the time the Cherryville investigation was completed, the new Mark 3 BREL coaches were in service. Older, wooden-framed stock was being withdrawn as additional Mark 3 vehicles were being acquired. The first 32 were imported virtually complete, but the balance of the 124 units were assembled at Inchicore works from 'completely knocked down' parts. Speed restrictions were introduced on the older carriage stock, on secondary lines, but the speed of the Dublin to Cork trains, using Mark 3 sets, gave a 2 hours 40 minutes run inclusive of three stops and 2 hours 35 minutes in the opposite Cork to Dublin direction—at last approaching the 2 hour 30 minutes first heralded several years earlier in Devlin's ground breaking presentation of 'The Way Ahead'.

THE APPOINTMENT OF G. T. Paul Conlon as Chairman of CIÉ with effect from 1 January 1984 was announced in December 1983. Born in Belfast, where he trained as a chartered accountant, he had worked for a period of nine years with the major international accounting and consultancy group, Peat Marwick Mitchell and Co., in the UK. Then also in the UK, he held a number of appointments in financial and general management with the publicly quoted Stewart and Lloyds, steel tube and pipe makers, and with GKN. He returned to Ireland to work with Nitrigín Éireann Teoranta (NET) for a period of ten years; joined Cork Marts IMP (International Meat Products) as Deputy Group Chief Executive and returned to NET at the request of government in 1980 as Managing Director, the position he held when Jim Mitchell invited him to assume Executive Chairmanship of CIÉ. The post of full-time Executive Chairman was the same as that taken up by Todd Andrews in 1958. Both Andrews and Conlon moved to CIÉ from a managing director position in another state company.

Paul Conlon recalled being asked why he should take up such a daunting task, but he had been asked a similar question when he became Managing Director of NET. That company was in serious difficulties with accumulated losses of £55 million when he accepted the challenge offered him by a previous government. The year he left NET to join CIÉ, NET had a net profit of over £2.5 million and its prospects seemed reasonably secure. In a keynote speech to the Annual Conference of the Irish Management Institute in April 1985, Paul Conlon reviewed the situation he had found in NET, including 'unrealistic trading and investment projections' particularly in relation to the cost of the Marino Point, Cork, ammonia and urea complex which had been constructed on a 'cost plus' basis and cost several times the initial target. Other NET problems were ambiguous organisation structures, overstaffing, a demoralised workforce and poor industrial relations. NET had lost the confidence of its shareholder, had massive bank borrowings and was short of cash. He described the approach he took to effect the turn-round of NET. His experience in Ireland and abroad touched many fields but, jokingly, he advised his family and friends that he wanted no books as Christmas presents. There was much to be read about CIÉ and one document in particular needed his attention—'The Transport Challenge', McKinsey's Report of December 1980.

There were similarities between what he had found in NET and what he found in CIÉ, but there were many dissimilarities. CIÉ was providing a service which was required of it by government; the challenge was to ensure that this service was provided with maximum cost effectiveness within the resources available. This should not involve taking the axe to the operation. Important guidelines had been set by the new subvention formula. The parameters within which he had to operate were preset.

Some sensed that Conlon was being sent to the transport company as a sort of 'hatchet man'. One Dáil deputy (Ned O'Keefe) said

> I congratulate the new executive chairman. I do not envy him his job. It will be a difficult task. But I should not like to see him use the same guillotine methods he did in Nitrigin Eireann Teoranta bringing hardship on many of the people employed and the public.
> (*Dáil Debates*, Vol. 346, Col. 1413)

But in his address to the IMI Conference, Conlon, while recognising the importance of industrial relations, saw it as only part of a wider problem.

> Many people believe, for example that the major problems of CIÉ are in the industrial relations sector. While undoubtedly we have serious deficiencies in this regard, the problems are more fundamental. They relate to the ability or willingness of the State to pay for services which the public demands. The key issue which faces Government is the recognition of the social role of CIÉ, while at the same time ensuring that internal operating efficiencies are maximised.
> ('Winning Against The Odds', IMI Conference, April 1985)

The subvention formula went part of the way to easing this problem, but at least one major uncertainty hung in the air. In December 1983 Jim Mitchell told the Dáil that he awaited the new chairman's advice on the McKinsey Report before making final decisions about the company's future structure.

Paul Conlon had some strong views about organisation. He told the IMI Conference that

> The winning enterprise will require to be so structured that it has –
> 1. A lean hungry and without frills organisation structure.
> 2. A well defined mission in life.
> 3. Crystal clear policies for achieving that mission.
> 4. Well thought-out strategies for implementing policies.
> 5. A board which understands the business and which contributes and monitors but which does not interfere with the day-to-day running of the operation, and which has the capacity to identify the strengths and weaknesses of the organisation.

6. A professional, innovative, aggressive management which works as a team.

7. A motivated and involved workforce which identifies with the organisation.

8. Sound, accurate and timely information systems that support the business strategies. (ibid.)

These were some of the principles that he brought to his consideration of the McKinsey Report (1980). The cynic might say that much of this was good textbook stuff and that it was part of the received wisdom of business leaders in the 1980s. While that may well be true, the point is how would Conlon apply it in practice. To begin with, he set about developing a new statement of CIÉ's objectives or definition of 'mission in life', as he once called it. This, he said, 'should be succinctly and clearly defined and be compulsory reading for all employees'. The new CIÉ mission statement, prominently promoted inside and outside the organisation, read:

> To provide a safe, reliable, efficient, cost effective and customer oriented transportation service of the highest standard possible, in accordance with market demands and conditions and legislative requirements, within the financial support limits defined by Government and where appropriate, at a competitive return on resources.

In CIÉ's organisational structure he found some ambiguity as to roles. Who exactly was responsible for this and that? The area management structure was now over thirty years old; it had been very effective in improving control of operations at local level and several innovations had resulted from the initiatives of area managers. However, it had never worked particularly satisfactorily with regard to the railway and by the time of the second McKinsey Report, it was believed to have outlived its usefulness.

The proposal to set up separate operating companies for rail, Dublin City Services and provincial bus services commended itself to Paul Conlon and he so advised Minister Mitchell. The formation of three operating subsidiaries would allow a restructuring of management into distinct units with separate and definable tasks. But the concept of an integrated transport system should not be totally abandoned. CIÉ should remain as a holding company. As a holding company, CIÉ itself should be small and tightly organised providing a limited number of support services to the main operating companies. Government accepted this approach as it applied to the three operating companies suggested by McKinsey. However, Conlon believed that road freight should also be reorganised into a fourth operating company. Government would not sanction the creation of a separate road freight operating company. In effect, the Department was pessimistic about the prospects of a road freight subsidiary competing with private hauliers in the liberalised environment required by the European Community's road freight policies. Failure at a later stage of a state-owned haulage company could create problems. Better therefore to allow CIÉ's road freight operations to continue as part of the railway company where they could be kept under observation and terminated without undue embarrassment if they failed to become profitable.

The government decisions on McKinsey were promulgated in *Building on Reality 1985–1987* which was published in October 1984. This constituted the 'National Plan' on which the Fine Gael/Labour coalition government had been working since its election in December 1982. First, in March 1983 a National Planning Board had been established under the chairmanship of Professor Louden Ryan which produced important though much neglected research and recommendations in April 1984. *Building on Reality* then appeared six months later. Its section on transport opened by setting out proposals for radical change in the road haulage industry:

> The carriage of goods for payment has been severely restricted over the years by licensing regulations. These restrictions have led to waste and to high freight costs. The following measures are now being taken:
> – legislation is being introduced in the next session to allow free availability of licenses;
> – standards will be maintained through a vigorous enforcement of regulations, particularly those relating to safety.
> The overall result will be a more flexible, less expensive freight service for the producer, the exporter and the consumer.
> (*Building on Reality*, Part 3, 1939/41)

Such legislation would indeed follow, but not until 1986. It would end the restrictions on road haulage imposed in the Road Transport Act (1932) which over more than half a century had manifestly failed to maintain the railway as the dominant freight transport mode.

Building on Reality then discussed CIÉ. It observed that 'the national transport company provides an important though declining, proportion of transport traffic in the State' and then went on to record the government's decisions:

> – CIÉ will be retained but in a restructured form which will involve the separate administration by subsidiary companies of Dublin City

Services, provincial bus services and the railway. This will be effected by legislation to be introduced within a few months;

– a package of retrenchment measures will be implemented on the passenger rail side; this will not affect the existing carriage replacement programme but will mean that there will be no new substantial investment in railways and there will be strict cash limits on other expenditures;

– the interest on the capital expenditure incurred on the electrification of the Howth–Bray line will be met by the State;

– CIÉ's rail sundries traffic and road freight services will be discontinued from January, 1986, unless they are shown to be profitable in 1984–85;

– there will be a new emphasis on the development of efficient bus services, both in the cities and on rural and express routes, partly through implementation of the recommendations resulting from a review of the operation of the Road Transport Act, 1932, which will be completed within the next few months.

For Dublin, a new Dublin Transportation Authority is being established: the necessary legislation will be introduced by the Minister for Communications in the next session. The new Authority will:

– have a key role in the planning and operation of Dublin's transport resources;

– be responsible for traffic management in the Dublin area;

– become part of the reformed local government structure when proposals for reform are being implemented. (ibid., 1942/45)

Some brief summary comments to show what had and would happen will be helpful to the reader lest he/she get the impression that everything would transpire as intended in the plan.

The CIÉ reorganisation legislation was published in mid-1986 and the new operating companies were formally vested on 2 February 1987, some six years after McKinsey had reported. The massive restructuring provoked some resistance and controversy, but in practice it would prove successful, perhaps more so than envisaged at the time. The 'retrenchment measures on the rail passenger side', involving 'no more significant investment' other than that required for safety reasons, would result in a direction to reduce real rail operating expenditure by 20 per cent by 1989 or 3.7 per cent per annum. The suburban electrification scheme was already accomplished and mainline carriages were being replaced. The intention now was that the railways would survive without further replacement or development. The railways would have to 'patch and make-do'. Contraction by attrition is what these policies amounted to, and in time they would come to be regarded as crude and impractical.

The decision that interest charges on the capital expenditure on the Howth/Bray line would be borne by the state brought this project back to the basis on which it was originally approved by government in May 1979, though the compensation for interest would be added to the subvention. In the original arrangement it would not have fallen to CIÉ's account, but would have been borne directly by the exchequer. In addition to the change with regard to interest on the investment in DART, government also decided to make up the accumulated shortfall in previous subventions. These shifts of policy constituted a major change to the subvention formula announced by Jim Mitchell in June 1983. Government came to realise that the June 1983 subvention formula was not going to work despite the improved financial performance of CIÉ in 1983 which was continuing in 1984.

With regard to the threat to close rail sundries and road freight services, sufficient improvement would be achieved in their results to allow them to continue. The 'new emphasis' on efficient bus services, in practice, meant that development would continue, and after the closure of the GAC bus factory at Shannon in 1987, CIÉ would be enabled to acquire buses on 'best terms' from its choice of suppliers. New road passenger legislation did not follow from the planned review of the Road Transport Act 1932, nor, despite much work in the Department of Transport, has it since been introduced. Finally, a Dublin Transport Authority would be established in 1986, independent of any structural reform of Local Government with which it was supposed to be connected. It would survive for a year and be abolished after a change of government.

The intention of *Building on Reality* was admirable: it aimed to establish a new framework in which transport would operate. For a variety of reasons, not all its decisions and intentions would be implemented, but the board gave it a general welcome. Meanwhile, CIÉ had to get on with the job in hand, including completion of DART, acronym for Dublin Area Rapid Transit scheme, a project which was already well under way.

CHAPTER 22

DART AND GREEN PAPER

Opening of DART—Cost of DART—Halt in rise of CIÉ deficit—Green Paper on transport policy—Establishment of Dublin Transport Authority —Transfer of canals—Proposed reorganisation of CIÉ into three operating companies—OPO saga approaches a resolution.

The first paying passengers on the electrified Howth/Bray line boarded the 06.35 from Pearse to Howth on Monday, 23 July 1984. The transfer to electric operation was total, the last diesel-powered train having been operated the previous Saturday. The plan was to let DART run for three months before an official opening by the Taoiseach, Garret FitzGerald. So neither he nor his Minister, Jim Mitchell, attended the first commercial runs. His rival and leader of the opposition, C. J. Haughey, had no need to wait for such ceremony; in a brilliant piece of one upmanship he travelled in the driver's cab of an early train and was the main benificiary of a wonderful news story, to the chagrin no doubt of the Taoiseach as he opened his papers on Tuesday morning.

A marathon of research, planning and construction, of equipment specification, requisition and testing was over. Announced a month earlier, the 23 July change-over date set a deadline for completing negotiations on pay and conditions for one-person operation of the new trains. The negotiations continued right up to the wire. Driver training had been in hand since the previous year, but on 11 July a group refused to attend 'final training' and were suspended. Without warning pickets were placed by the NBU; some suburban services were cancelled and mainline schedules were disrupted. It was mere sabre-rattling; within twenty-four hours pickets were withdrawn and Labour Court conferences resumed; but the inauguration of DART was in doubt until the last minute, with a final Labour Court hearing being held on Sunday, 22 July. The DART drivers received a 24 per cent pay increase as well as compensation for anticipated loss of overtime earnings.

Throughout the three and a half years since the project started, diesel services had continued, though towards the end of that period much disruption to services caused a severe drop in passenger numbers. Some 39 km of track was renewed largely with continuous welded rail (CWR); over 2,000 supports were erected to carry the overhead lines; more than fifty bridges were reconstructed, mostly overbridges, so as to increase headroom for the overhead line; twenty-three stations were reconstructed; two stations, Salthill and Sandymount, were reopened after being closed for over twenty years; eleven level crossings were equipped to operate with automatic barriers, monitored by closed-circuit television and controlled from Connolly station; the Fairview maintenance depot was adapted for the new system and major work at Connolly station included provision of a special passenger entry/exit for DART.

The signalling system, long described as obsolete, was entirely replaced with hi-tech equipment centrally controlled from Connolly. Safety, reliability and efficiency were the controlling considerations in the decisions, beyond number, which had to be made concerning rolling stock and signalling. A 'fail safe philosophy' determined the approach to all the vital questions so that failure of a power supply or malfunction of a train for whatever cause, e.g. operating at excess speed would be compensated for automatically within the system. Articles by C. D. Waters, leader of the project team, R. P. Grainger and P. Cuffe in the *IRRS Journal* (October 1984 and February 1985) provide fascinating detail on the design and execution of civil engineering, electrical, signalling and communications aspects of DART, sufficient for all but the most exacting transport or engineering enthusiast.

Some problems requiring specially innovative solutions are worth recounting.

> Perhaps the most technically difficult section of the line was that between Dún Laoghaire and Sandycove, where there were seven overbridges with substandard clearances, three of them major road bridges. Two alternatives were considered—(i) to lift and reconstruct the bridges and regrade the adjoining road approaches; or (ii) to lower the track in the rock cutting. Option (ii) was chosen, on economical and environmental grounds. This involved closing one track at a time and excavating the rock to a depth of approximately 500 mm and replacing the track on a continuously paved concrete bed.
> (C. D. Waters, *IRRS Journal*, October 1984)

Subsequently some modifications, partly because of drainage problems, had to be made to this 1.5 km section of 'slab track', as it was called. Another solution was found for a problem at Merrion Gates where there was a heavily used level crossing at the confluence of two major road arteries. With trains in each direction every five minutes during peak traffic, local authorities feared that the more frequent closing of the crossing would cause such enormous road traffic hold-ups that a road 'flyover' costing well over £1 million might be necessary. The feared traffic congestion was avoided by changing the alignment of the crossing and integrating the road traffic lights with the level crossing controls. The arrangements were such a success that they merited a 'Transport Innovator of the Year' award from the Eastern Section of the Chartered Institute of Transport in Ireland. Engineering expertise was also evident when, over a weekend at Bath Avenue, Sandymount, indeed within thirty-six hours flat, a 150-year-old masonry arch bridge was demolished and replaced. Train services resumed with few noticing that there had been an interruption to the line.

A very creditable aspect of the project was that CIÉ could justifiably claim that it was completed on time and on budget. But comment is required to put that claim into context. Inflation, 20 per cent devaluation of the Irish punt, additional VAT charges and change of policy with regard to exchequer financing were exogenous factors which moved the goal posts and had an adverse arithmetical impact on the final figure. That the project performed within the original target before allowing for these factors was freely and formally recognised by Minister Jim Mitchell in the December 1983 debate on the Transport Bill increasing CIÉ's borrowing powers. However, he disheartened many in CIÉ by implying that if he had been minister at an earlier stage, the electrification would not have had his support. His precise words were:

> I can say, however, that I would not today be prepared to seek Government approval for a project of this nature put forward in the same way as the Howth–Bray project. This must not be taken as criticism of CIÉ but rather of the lack of suitable appraisal of such proposals by Governments in the past. Within my own Department I have now a permanent capital committee to monitor and appraise all major capital expenditure proposals in CIÉ in the future.
> (*Dáil Debates*, Vol. 346, Col. 1297)

John Wilson assured him that never had a project been so exhaustively examined and the evidence supports that assertion. But to return to the final cost as it emerged: David Waters summarised the figures in his *IRRS Journal* article.

In 1979 the estimated cost of the scheme was £46.4 million; the

> estimated turnout of cost at 1979 prices is £46.1 million. The projected out-turn of cost is £77 million, plus VAT of £10 million. The increase in costs is due to inflation and devaluation of the Punt (£33 million) plus additional VAT charges of £7 million. There also arise interest charges of about £30 million.
>
> It had been intended to fund the project by Exchequer grants, but the Government later directed that CIÉ should fund the scheme by loans, including loans from the European Investment Bank. The Government received an EEC subsidy of borrowing from the EIB of about £11 million, which was not credited to the electrification project. In addition, the Exchequer received an additional £12 million of infrastructural grants from the European Regional Development Fund, which also has not been credited to the project.
>
> (IRRS Journal, October 1984)

The exchequer itself was under severe pressure in those years of revolving-door administrations and without judging the ethics or fairness of what happened, the idea of obtaining external grants and low interest loans to finance DART and then using them for other purposes indicates the desperate state of the public finances and/or an indifference if not hostility at some level to the DART project itself.

From the beginning it was recognised that to achieve its potential passenger numbers DART would need sophisticated and sustained marketing support. The public had to be educated initially to respect the risks involved in interference with the electrified system. Then it had to be made aware of and sold on the advantages of DART in terms of speed, comfort, convenience and price. Market research findings, extensive public and community consultation, and the many aspects of product design —timing of services, use of colour and architectural design, pricing packages, promotion and advertising were usefully summarised in a marketing case study by Barra Ó Cinnéide of Limerick University.

Every aspect of Dublin's suburban rail system was new or renewed. The response of the public was positive and immense. That indefatigable chronicler of the railway scene, the *IRRS Journal*, reported in October on the

> immediate and sustained enthusiasm from the public and the media, with the result that passenger carryings considerably strained the limited services which operated up to Friday 27 July. Nevertheless traffic increased daily, so that by Sunday 29 July the warm sunny weather, in combination with an unlimited-travel introductory Family Ticket priced at £2.50, produced, according to an *Irish Times* report, what CIÉ described as 'record numbers—busier than any day since the line opened in 1834, with at least 45,000 travelling'. . . . Even with the disappearance of summer, patronage continued extremely healthy,

> with off-peak traffic at levels which even the most optimistic would hardly have predicted within two months of the introduction of the services, while in both morning and evening peak-hour periods . . . services provided are . . . already more overcrowded than is desirable on a system which, despite its success to date required to attract even more passengers to increase daily carryings from the current 43,000 to the 80,000 eventually envisaged. (*IRRS Journal*, October 1984)

How the 80,000 figure came publicly to be accepted as a realistic target for DART is difficult to understand. Using all train sets throughout the day the system certainly had an 80,000 passenger capacity, but allowing for commuter peaking and directional flows the 80,000 target erred towards hyperbole. In later years it would be suggested that the figure was intended to cover not merely DART but the other outer suburban rail services as well. A key question perhaps was not the maximum peak day carryings but the annual total of passengers that would be carried by DART. In 1982, a year when traffic admittedly was disrupted by heavy construction work on the Howth–Bray line, passenger journeys amounted to 5.27 million. In 1985, the first full year of DART operations, carryings amounted to 11.7 million and by the 1990s average annual carryings were over 16 million passengers.

If the deadline of 23 July for converting to the electric system served to concentrate the minds of the negotiators so that the terms available on that date were accepted, a similar deadline was not available for concentrating minds on the introduction of feeder buses. Inevitably the feeder buses became tied up with the long-running debate about wider use of one-person bus operation. DART would run for a full eighteen months before feeder buses in special DART livery would begin regular services. Almost two million additional passengers were carried by DART in the first full year of its dedicated feeder buses.

The feeder buses were the only part of the DART system which was not up and running when the Taoiseach, Dr Garret FitzGerald, officially opened the service on Monday, 22 October 1984. Always a railway 'buff', Garret FitzGerald cut a tape at Connolly, drove a train to Dún Laoghaire, visited the computerised signalling centre, had a conversation from that centre with the cab of a moving train, was delighted to accept a set of the first issue of DART passenger tickets and delivered a speech. He said it was a historic day for CIÉ, for Dublin, for Ireland, and departing from his script he claimed that it was the greatest single transport development in the city of Dublin since the first railway in Ireland was opened one hundred and fifty years earlier on 7 December 1834. However, he had one criticism to make:

> the bus feeder services which are such an essential feature of the whole operation, have yet to be started. May I add that the public are rightly

> impatient about the delay . . . taxpayers' money is not to be dissipated in this way . . .
> (*Nuacht CIÉ*, Samhain 1984)

Dr FitzGerald had some comments to make on the economics of public transport generally. Jim Mitchell, who was also present at the official opening, would occasionally comment wryly on the problem of a Minister for Transport in a Cabinet of which its Taoiseach had once lectured on transport economics.

> Public transport in all major cities in the world today is placed in an invidious and economically untenable position by virtue of the fact that one of the most scarce of all resources—road space on the main axes into and out of major cities at peak hours—is provided free of charge to anyone who wants to drive a motor vehicle along it even for the purpose of carrying no one but him or herself.
> In this way the relative economics of private and public transport are totally distorted—because private transport is made available at far below the real cost to the community, while the cost of public transport is enormously increased by the congestion of the roads by under-utilised private vehicles. (ibid.)

Referring to the decision to create three subsidiary companies within CIÉ, the Taoiseach said that it was

> designed *inter alia*, to create new conditions in which these Dublin City Services can be given the necessary degree of managerial attention that will enable existing inefficiencies to be eliminated, and deficiencies of morale, which are known to us all, to be resolved. (ibid.)

Among other speeches at the 22 October 1984 ceremony, Jack Higgins traced DART's origins back to the Dublin Transportation Study which had a consultative committee of which Garret FitzGerald had been a member. He also drew attention to Irish input to the project which had amounted to 42 per cent of the total cost. David Waters noted that at its peak the project provided employment for approximately 500 people and that the Irish content included masts fabricated in Cork, computers in Galway, transformers in Waterford and signalling equipment from a new factory in Tralee (*IRRS Journal*, October 1984). Besides Jack Higgins as General Manager and David Waters as Project Manager, two other key executives merit mention for their vital role in bringing DART on line—Eoin Gahan, Railways Manager, and Noel Kennedy, who at that time was Area Manager, Dublin.

Almost a year later (1985) when reporting on his first full year as

Chairman, Paul Conlon summarised some developments for CIÉ. Its financial results were improving slowly, its relationship with government was more secure, its major investment requirements were being addressed, labour relations had been good, plans were in hand for a restructuring of the company and the subvention was being paid 'above the line'. The chairman spoke of 1984 as a year in which Ireland's railway system was reborn because in addition to DART

> The new InterCity trains [with Mark 3 carriages] introduced in July 1984, enhanced by the upgrading of the track network and extension of the remote control signalling (CTC) have given us, apart from the increased safety factor, a 90 miles per hour ultra modern system with a capacity to materially reduce journey times.   (Annual Report, 1984)

With regard to above the line payment of the subvention, the Annual Report referred to it as a practice adopted by our European counterparts, and added:

> This change is a recognition by Government that a National Public Transport system, combining rail and road services, is essential in the public interest and that certain infrastructure and social service obligation costs should properly be met by the state.   (ibid.)

Taking account of the new method for treating the state subvention, the deficit before exceptional items was £0.95 million compared to £16.113 million in 1983, when government had underfunded the deficit and required CIÉ to finance the shortfall by short-term borrowings. 'Clearing the decks' as to DART interest and to previous deficiencies in the annual subvention were also addressed before the 1984 accounts were finalised. Government authorised CIÉ to borrow £30 million on a term loan basis to finance most of these deficiencies and undertook to provide funds at a rate of £3 million per annum to liquidate the borrowing. In the meantime, however, CIÉ would have to bear the interest on the term loan.

By the time the 1984 report was issued, the hotels had gone to CERT (see above) and legislation to transfer the canals to the Office of Public Works was before the Oireachtas; the cost of maintaining them had increased to £1.34 million in this, the final year before their going. Legislation to establish the Dublin Transport Authority had also been introduced. The chairman's review referred to the number of stoppages of work being down from 31 in 1983 to 15 in 1984 and 'with one exception—all were unofficial and six lasted for less than one day' (ibid.).

But like his predecessors, Paul Conlon was taken aback at the amount of effort—over fifty meetings per week—which seemed to be necessary to maintain balance in CIÉ's industrial relations affairs.

> The complexity of labour relations can be gauged from the fact that over 2,700 meetings took place throughout the Company during 1984 with Union officials or third parties such as the Labour Court, Rights Commissioners and Employment Tribunals. The number of meetings is a tremendous burden on the staff and is of concern to the Board.
> (ibid.)

The 1984 Annual Report, published in September 1985, also recorded that 'the detail design for the new [subsidiary operating] companies has now been completed'. Arthur Andersen had been engaged to advise on the establishment of Iarnród Éireann and Bus Éireann and Córas Iompair Éireann as a holding company. Craig Gardner had advised on the establishment of Bus Átha Cliath. The new companies had been designed with the objective of giving as much autonomy as possible to the three operating companies, particularly in the planning of 'services, marketing and industrial relations'. Each company would have its own managing director and board of directors. For cost effectiveness and operational efficiency, a limited number of functions would be retained by the holding company. Splitting CIÉ's operations into these units was far from easy. The board minutes reveal many issues of concern, of which the most contentious seemed to be whether the railway could survive at all outside the Dublin suburban line, if the provincial bus company was to fulfil its own mandate and compete aggressively. The broad outline of the functions of CIÉ holding company and of the three operating companies was agreed on 11 October 1984, but a year later, on 16 October 1985, when the board eventually approved the new structures, the issue of competition between the provincial bus company and the railway made a consensus impossible. The minutes record that one board member formally dissented from the package—an extremely rare event in the affairs of the CIÉ Board.

When reporting on how the restructuring was progressing, the Annual Report commented that: 'Regretfully, the drafting of the necessary legislation has not kept pace with the reorganisation planning but it is hoped that this situation will be redressed in the coming months.' (ibid.) In the Dáil, questions were asked whether the split-up was still going ahead in the light of serious trade union objections, but there was no change of mind. The legislation was eventually introduced (in the Senate) in April 1986. The new companies were incorporated in January 1987 and commenced trading on 2 February of that year.

BEFORE DEALING WITH the launch of the new companies in 1987, the intervening years, 1985 and 1986, need further comment. Rail passengers grew by 6,175,000 (40 per cent) over the two years, and while 5,522,000 of the extra rail passengers travelled on DART, mainline rail gained 179,000 passengers and other Dublin suburban rail services gained 475,000 passengers. The additional traffic on the non-electric suburban services amounted to 38 per cent and mainly resulted from improved services made possible by the rolling stock released for other duties by DART and by the new Mark 3 mainline coaches. Commuter services to Drogheda and Dundalk, previously pilloried as being operated by cattle wagons, were improved. On the freight side, volumes were not growing; instead they fell by 8 per cent in 1985–86. The general business recession explained part of this slippage and almost half the decline was in mineral ores. Road freight fell even more severely—by 28 per cent—and here continued rationalisation measures were combined with the recession to explain the decline. On the road passenger side, Dublin City Services gained 6 per cent more passengers, provincial city services grew by 3 per cent while other provincial services (including Expressway) grew by 8 per cent.

The financial outcome of these years was a profit of £15.4 million in 1985 and of £12.7 million in 1986 using the new accounting treatment of state grants as revenue, as authorised by government and first used in the year 1984. Jim Mitchell defended this 'profit' presentation. It meant that CIÉ was beating its targets—an entirely laudable result. However, the debate about the treatment of the annual subvention was not yet dead. Some years later (1990) another Minister, Seamus Brennan, directed that this new treatment be modified. The *Irish Independent* first carried this story on 23 July 1990 and the following day it reported that the minister confirmed that he had 'recently told the Board of CIÉ to show losses without state aid taken into account'. He was 'ruling out further increases' and at the same time wanted to make the company's 'dependence on the customer more transparent'. The CIÉ protest that the treatment it was being told to change 'was in keeping with the practice of many of our European counterparts' (Annual Report, 1989) was very mildly expressed and no reference was made to the many consultants and committees who urged above-the-line treatment of the state's financial support to CIÉ. The mildness of CIÉ's comment is explained by a compromise treatment which was agreed to before its accounts were released.

State grants in accordance with the subvention formula promulgated in 1983 and amended in 1984 came to £115 million in 1985 and £116 million in 1986. The description of 'state grants' rather than 'state subventions' had come to be used by CIÉ, though the temptation to call them 'subsidies' was still yielded to in the media from time to time. In real terms the 1986 figure of £116 million, which included the additional item of £9.6 million compensation for 'interest on the DART investment', was 9 per cent less than the 1982 provision and about equal to the famous £86 million of 1983.

The improvement in CIÉ's finances paralleled a somewhat slower improvement in the state of the public finances. Exchequer borrowings peaked at £2 billion in the years 1984 and 1985 and in 1986 fell to £1.8 billion, an out-turn which for the first time since 1978 was lower than the budget estimate. At last some external factors were moving in CIÉ's favour; the price of oil began to decline and inflation had fallen to 5.4 per cent in 1985 and 3.9 per cent in 1986. On the other hand, CIÉ suffered a severe blow in its tours business in 1986, a year when US tourists to Ireland fell by almost 25 per cent due to fear of fall-out from Chernobyl, terrorism in Europe and a weak dollar. As a result, CIÉ's own numbers from the US fell by 41 per cent and its tour business incurred a loss of £927,000 compared to a profit of £276,000 in 1985. This disappointing setback ate into improving results from other divisions.

Led by Jim Mitchell and supported by Junior Minister, Ted Nealon, the Oireachtas debated and adopted more legislation concerning internal transport matters in the two years, 1985 and 1986, than in any previous period since the foundation of the state, not excluding 1932 and 1933 when the original Acts requiring licences for road passenger and road haulage operators were introduced. In each year the Dáil also found time to debate rather merely than adopt the transport vote (No. 41). Government also managed to publish a Green Paper on Transport Policy (November 1985). The legislation included the Dublin Transport Authority Bill (June 1985); the Transport Bill (July 1985) allowing CIÉ to obtain the 10-year term loan to finance previous shortfalls in the state's subvention; the Canals Bill (February 1986) transferring the canals to the ownership and care of the Office of Public Works; the Road Transport Bill (March 1986) deregulating the road haulage industry; and the Transport (Reorganisation of CIÉ) Bill (December 1986).

Some comments on the relevant Dáil debates and on the Green Paper will highlight issues and attitudes of the period. The big question about the Dublin Transport Authority Bill was whether the proposed DTA was being given sufficient muscle or teeth to tackle the question of Dublin's traffic in an effective way. Albert Reynolds, some years earlier, had challenged whether his successor as minister was really grappling with the departmental rivalry which kept decisions about road-building and financing in the Department of the Environment along with vehicle licensing, while traffic management decisions were split between the same Department, Dublin Corporation and the Garda. Traffic law enforcement lay solely with the Department of Justice and decisions relating to public transport remained in the Department of Transport or Communications or

Tourism and Transport, or Transport, Energy and Communications, or whatever it might be called from time to time. For the reader's ease we use the 'Transport' title throughout. Albert Reynolds gave the impression that he had been striving for a DTA based on a total rearrangement of such responsibilities. Perhaps roads should be transferred to the Department of Transport, or vice versa.

In any event John Wilson criticised Jim Mitchell's Bill for being a weak compromise, granting only limited executive powers to the DTA and requiring it to be consulted by various authorities, but having absolutely no financial clout. 'In our opinion all that woolly area of recommendations, appraisals, monitoring, setting of objectives and so on will not make for an effective Dublin Transport Authority.' John Wilson said that the heads of a Bill which he himself had prepared would have created a much more powerful body, though one may speculate whether his finished Bill would have received the approval of other ministers.

Richard Bruton of Fine Gael, a frequent speaker on transport and generally critical of CIÉ, contrasted the proposed DTA with that recommended by the Transport Consultative Commission in 1980.

> According to the TCC, the authority was to have the following functions; overall responsibility for integrated planning and operation of transportation; channelling to Government all plans and budget proposals in relation to Dublin transportation; the release of all Government funds for transportation and monitoring the expenditure of the various bodies like CIÉ and so on; overall responsibility for traffic management; they were to have responsibilities in relation to licensing road passenger and taxi services and for public education, promotion and research in relation to transportation. . . . this bill is very different from what the TCC envisaged . . . In particular the present proposal does not envisage the Transport Authority channelling to government the plans of other agencies like CIÉ and the road authorities. They will not have that control over the investment proposals of these authorities, nor will they have control over the release of Government funds.
>
> (*Dáil Debates*, Vol. 359, Cols 1185/86)

The Bill was passed, its supporters both within the Dáil and elsewhere believing that even without strong executive powers the DTA would give a focus to the city's transport problems and by concentrating on its simple brief it would so discomfit other bodies involved in transport matters that they would be forced to adopt realistic solutions rather than procrastinate, as had been their wont. As noted earlier the DTA, despite its long gestation and difficult labour, would be killed off in its infancy, with John Wilson again Minister for Transport being rather mute in the final stages of its abolition.

The 1985 Transport Bill, allowing CIÉ to obtain a term loan to finance previous shortages in subvention, provided Jim Mitchell with an opportunity to distance himself from previous practice. The situation he had inherited illustrated

> the lack of reality in Governments' handling of CIÉ for years. They were given unrealistic figures plucked out of the air, to fit in with the Estimates two or three weeks before the financial year. The figures were ridiculous and were ignored. For the 15 years 1968–69 to 1982 the deficit in CIÉ went up by a multiple of the rate of inflation . . . This is not something that could be blamed on CIÉ management and workers, although clearly some blame could go to them. The Government played a huge part in bringing about that disgraceful trend because they failed to face the issues. (ibid., 3 July 1985, Vol. 360, Col. 415)

A popular notion in this debate was that CIÉ should be provided with subsidies for specific socially necessary services, an argument which had been supported in the National Planning Board's comments on commercial state-sponsored bodies and which had earlier been advocated by the National Prices Commission and ventilated in the 1971 McKinsey Report. Hitherto this idea had been greeted by official silence, but Jim Mitchell had some forthright remarks to make. His comments had an importance beyond the debate that was before the House and echoed remarks of Seán Lemass in 1949/50.

> I was somewhat depressed with the notion which seemed to run throughout almost all contributions that I, the Minister, should decide what services should go where, at what level, etc. Politicians have meddled too much over the years in deciding what services should go here or be retained there, no matter what changes have taken place in population and transport matters. . . . Effectively, [deputies] went on to argue that I should be deciding on the subsidy for each service, that I should be deciding the social content of each service. Can one imagine any worse political scenario than that? Imagine what would happen to bus and train services as every local or by-election arose.
> (ibid., Vol. 360, Col. 413)

THE GREEN PAPER on the Transport Policy was released in November 1985. The concept of a 'Green Paper' had only recently been imported from Britain—a discussion document exposing the background to some complex issue so as to provoke a public debate as a result of which government would develop formal proposals and publish them in a White Paper. In his introduction to the Green Paper, Jim Mitchell promised that this procedure would be followed and that a 'White Paper setting out Government transport policy and priorities for the years ahead' would be published in 1986. No White Paper was published and conversations with some of the minister's advisers who laboured on the Green Paper convince the author that no one really had the stomach for the follow through to the White Paper stage. The Green Paper covered the whole transport spectrum: shipping, ports, aviation services, international and regional airports, as well as rail and road transport, public and private. The document set out the background to the present state of each sector and listed options for the future. If a White Paper were published, it would have to choose between various options —which could be politically dangerous. On the other hand, so the political and official minds went, if the status quo was tolerable, at least for the time being, why bother eliminating possible options for the future?

The chapter in the Green Paper on mainline railways can be briefly summarised. It demonstrated the 'dominance of the private car for virtually all types of travel' and estimated that the railway share of the inland passenger transport market had declined to 4 per cent of total passenger kilometres, with 12 per cent travelling by buses and 84 per cent by private car. Mainline rail was also estimated to carry only 11 per cent of total freight tonne kilometres. CIÉ would demonstrate (see page 408) that figures for intercity passengers and long-distance freight showed that the railways had a much higher market share than these figures indicated. The Green Paper went on to describe the railway options offered in McKinsey's 'Transport Challenge', and to summarise the government's revised subvention formula, which however was still described as an 'interim measure'. Decisions announced in the National Plan were restated, including the restructuring of CIÉ and further expanded in relation to railway costs: 'further cost containment measures which will reduce railway renewal and depreciation costs by 5.6 per cent each year [in real terms] up to 1989'. This cut in renewal and depreciation of 5.6 per cent per annum would achieve the 3.7 per cent per annum reduction in total railway expenditure, mentioned in *Building on Reality* (see page 376), adding up to an overall reduction in rail costs of one-fifth over five years.

Government culpability (in part) for the financial problems of the railway was again acknowledged. The Green Paper noted the reliance of railways elsewhere on state support and that of ten EEC railway undertakings, eight of them received a proportionately higher level of state support than CIÉ. Energy conservation arguments for rail versus road were aired inconclusively and reference was made to the need to consider the 6,800 railway employees 'who have been noted for their exemplary tradition of public service and a particularly good industrial relations history'.

The reader may ask: where were these comments leading to? Did the Green Paper make any new pronouncement on the railways? The 'interim' nature of a measure forcing a reduction in renewal and depreciation expenditure was very inconclusive. The following quotation provides the answer:

> By virtue of the investment decisions referred to in the previous paragraph [£56 million for the period 1985–87] the Government has in effect decided to retain the railways in the medium-term. The breathing space provided by this decision allows time to consider whether:
> – the existing railway network should be retained in the long-term,
> – retention should be on the basis of a reduced railway network,
> – the railway network should eventually be closed down.
> Retention of a railway network would, of course, be dependent on continuing support from the Exchequer. The trade-off between the costs and the benefits of these alternative strategies is a matter which it is hoped the publication of this Green Paper will cause to be debated further. The conclusions drawn by the Government from this debate will be reflected in the White Paper to be published next year.
> (Green Paper on Transport Policy, 1986, par. 2, p. 29)

Government was making no statement about the long-term future of the railways; on the contrary, the Green Paper raised doubts about that future. The Green Paper's comments on other aspects of CIÉ's operations similarly reviewed performance and restated recently announced policy. In February 1986 Ted Nealon led for government in the Canals Bill. All sides were delighted that the canals were to be looked after by the Office of Public Works. Existing staff were being transferred and a bright future for the canals seemed assured now that they would be removed from the care of a body which was subject to financial inquisition. John Wilson interpolated references to Xerxes, de Lesseps, Brendan Behan and Patrick Kavanagh into his distinctive contribution. Ted Nealon's final sentence summarised it all:

> I am sure the Commissioners of Public Works will be delighted to get this new area of great potential under their control and will use it to the maximum advantage.
> (*Dáil Debates*, 26 February 1986, Vol. 363, Col. 287)

Only the begrudger would murmur that, despite urgings from CIÉ, successive governments for thirty five years had denied themselves the pleasure which they now relished. The canals slipped away from CIÉ's care on 1 July 1986.

Fast on the heels of the Canals Bill came the Road Transport Bill (1986). In accordance with the recommendations of the second report of the TCC (July 1981), it unravelled the remaining restrictions on road haulage. Ted Nealon also piloted this Bill through its various stages (Minister Mitchell had many other Bills moving at the same time). He reviewed the recommendations of the TCC:

> – A first phase which would permit existing hauliers entitled to operate under the Road Transport Acts to compete on equal terms as regards the area of operation and type of goods to be carried—this restructuring to take place during a two-year transition period . . .
> – In the second phase, at the end of the transition period, haulage licences to be made freely available to all applicants including own-account operators who satisfy the EC requirements for access to the profession of road haulage operation.
> The frequent changes of Government following publication of the report have had the effect of deferring adoption of these measures and prolonging the existing restrictive regime, which is really of benefit to no one, least of all in my view the licensed haulier.
>
> (ibid., Vol. 364, Col. 1876)

The Bill with minor adjustments implemented these suggestions. The battle was over. Reality was no longer denied. The steam generated in earlier debates on road haulage was nowhere in evidence, though deputies were still concerned with the need for stricter enforcement of the law concerning loading and safety so that all hauliers including CIÉ would compete equally with one another. John Wilson paid tribute to the TCC's Chairman, Professor Michael MacCormac, 'for the amount of work he did and for the speed with which he carried out that work. He produced sensible recommendations.' (ibid., Vol. 364, Col. 1885) MacCormac's report on Dublin traffic had helped inject some action into that particular scene, though the eventual fate of the DTA must have depressed him. After his commission's report on road haulage the TCC was disbanded.

THE TRANSPORT (REORGANISATION of CIÉ) Bill was first introduced, debated and amended in Seanad Éireann, reaching the Dáil in November 1986—about twelve months after CIÉ claimed that it had completed its own plans for the restructuring. The collapse of Irish Shipping was but one of the issues which had engaged the attention of the department and of the minister and of the Dáil in the interim. Jim Mitchell set the tone for the debate:

> Córas Iompair Éireann is undergoing an exciting period of change and development ... The changes which I am proposing now in relation to CIÉ amount to an historical step equal in importance to the step taken in 1944 when legislation founding CIÉ was enacted. There are striking differences between the two events. The calendar alone demonstrates that the planning for the establishment of CIÉ was undertaken in a wartime situation where all judgements were uncertain. Prophecies of what might happen in the years following the end of the war were completely speculative. The fact that CIÉ succeeded at all is a tribute to the planners of those far-off days.   (ibid., Vol. 369, Col. 2309)

This tribute to the 'planners' of CIÉ, among whom Seán Lemass was the key figure, would have shocked many of Jim Mitchell's Fine Gael predecessors to whom CIÉ was an arrogant ill-conceived creation of Lemass. John Wilson, leading for the opposition, noted and appreciated the tribute. The relationship between Mitchell and Wilson was respectful, courteous and generous to a degree, though both of them claimed credit (a) for deciding on the mainline coach-building programme, and (b) for payment of the subvention above the line. An analyst basing his judgment on evidence as to who made the effective decision as against the timing of statements of policy would probably credit Reynolds rather than Wilson with the final coach-building go ahead and Mitchell with the decision which enabled CIÉ to treat its state support as above-the-line payments. Wilson as usual interlaced his contribution with literary and historical allusions. Mitchell's scripts read as fitting successors to the thoughtful, problem-grasping scripts of Lemass and Childers. He had been in office for three years and had proved to be a decisive minister. The attitude of the Dáil was positive; CIÉ's affairs were improving for a variety of reasons; the reorganisation of CIÉ had been in the public domain for five years and government had announced its intention for the reorganisation two years previously; CIÉ was known to have agreed; the Bill had already been debated in the Senate. Jim Mitchell's review of CIÉ and of transport developments generally since 1945 was comprehensive and fair.

He contrasted the first twenty years or so of CIÉ struggling towards but failing to reach its breakeven target, and the second twenty years when the principle of state support for public transport came to be accepted in Ireland as abroad. He referred to the 'cross subsidisation' argument for keeping CIÉ as one company and the complexities that followed from that decision:

> The financial arguments based on cross supports for holding CIÉ together were exposed to chill reality 20 years ago. In all respects every major activity started to head for losses. The management of CIÉ became increasingly preoccupied with the financial struggle and their

reputation in the market had to suffer. . . . It amazes me that a relatively small central management team kept the whole unwieldy structure going at all or managed to deal on any rational basis with all the problems of infrastructure, rolling stock, supplies, staffing, industrial relations and service. The thought applies not alone to distinctive major activities on rail and road but out to the fringes of tour management, hotel operation, running Rosslare, keeping the canals passable and running ships to the Aran Islands.
(ibid., Vol. 369, Cols 2311/2316)

In recent years Jim Mitchell had been receiving quarterly activity and financial reports from CIÉ. He had also been meeting the board at regular intervals. He may have started by calling CIÉ an 'albatross', but by now he was speaking about CIÉ with a new respect for its performance and an understanding of the difficulties, some originating with government, under which it laboured.

> This vast agglomeration could have been helped often by clear delineation of what Government expected from it, by some better financial judgements and by less interference with the revenue earning plans of the undertaking. I have no hesitation in complimenting CIÉ for the benefits they did produce during what I think should now be identified as years of struggle. (ibid., Vol. 369, Col. 2311)

By this time also Jim Mitchell showed no reservations about DART, 'technically among the most advanced of its kind in the world'. Indeed, the day after the official opening in 1984, the board meeting had been interrupted for the chairman to take a call from the minister to compliment CIÉ on everything to do with the launch. The main point Mitchell sought to explain, comparing his Bill with the McKinsey reports, was the retention of CIÉ as a holding company. Its retention would help to achieve balance between the operating companies in regard to competition.

> The board of CIÉ will settle, within overall sums provided by the Government and, well in advance, the financial targets and allocations for the subsidiaries . . . The board will guard against reckless or ruinous competition between the subsidiaries. Indeed the proposed structure gets close to the optimum. It maintains the overall framework of the integrated approach which many see as essential to our transport system (ibid., Vol. 369, Col. 2328)

The original text of the Bill provided that inter-company competition would be subject to monitoring by the CIÉ Board. But competition was not being discouraged *per se*—'it would help to keep the operating companies on their toes'. None the less the Minister had agreed in the Seanad to another 'control'.

> Fears were expressed in Seanad Éireann about the risks which had been associated with competition between the rail company and the national bus company. In response, I agreed to introduce an amendment providing . . . for a majority of the directors of these two companies to be common to both companies. This should ensure that the boards of the companies will take full account of the interests of the individual companies in exercising their functions.
> (ibid., Vol. 369, Col. 2323)

The boards of the three subsidiaries would each consist of six members, appointed by the CIÉ chairman with the minister's agreement, and at least two members of each subsidiary board would be worker-directors from the main CIÉ Board. Trade union concerns with the 'doubts and fears' of their members expressed in the Seanad had caused another amendment to the Bill:

> The revised text reflects the assurances I gave to the effect that employees transferred to the subsidiaries will find their conditions of employment unaffected by this Bill.   (ibid., Vol. 369, Col. 2330)

The amendments to the Bill in relation to such employee concerns and to the interlocking membership of the Bus Éireann and the Iarnród Éireann Boards so as to protect against destructive competition, illustrate a 'belt and braces' approach. The original Bill gave protection on such points, but if trade unions professed still to be concerned and their concerns were voiced by senators or deputies, the best legislative minds would be applied to seeing what protection could be applied on top of protection so as to appear to be flexible and statesmanlike and to mollify the complainants.

Another Seanad amendment had the reverse effect of removing a 'belt and braces' clause originally inserted for their own purposes by the civil service. It was well known that government, as the sole owner of CIÉ and as its paymaster, consistently called the shots with regard to pay matters. If it chose to give advice, the board would ignore it as its peril. None the less persons in government departments continued to believe that the solution to escalating pay settlements was to take still more control of CIÉ's pay decisions. As a result, the original Bill contained a specific 'restraint on free collective bargaining', as it was called by its advocates. The clause in question was busily being inserted at the time in any legislation concerning state bodies. In the original Bill, clause 29 read:

> In determining the remuneration or allowances for expenses to be paid to its officers or servants or the terms or conditions subject to which such officers or servants hold or are to hold their employment, the Board and each company shall have regard either to Government or nationally agreed guidelines which are for the time being extant, or to Government policy concerning remuneration and conditions of employment which is so extant, and, in addition to the foregoing, each of them shall comply with any directives with regard to such remuneration, allowances, terms or conditions which the Minister may give from time to time to it with the consent of the Minister for the Public Service. (ibid., Vol. 369, Col. 2349)

Government in the Senate assented to its removal.

The official opposition line in the Dáil was that DCS should become one subsidiary and that provincial buses and the railway should form a second subsidiary, so that the railway would be protected from the risk of excessive bus competition. However, the point was not pressed to a division. Some debate took place both at board and in the Oireachtas about the names of the three subsidiaries:

Iarnród Éireann—Irish Rail
Bus Éireann—Irish Bus
Bus Átha Cliath—Dublin Bus

Speakers, including the minister, were hopeful that the companies would be known by their Irish names, but somehow it was felt that the English forms could not be dispensed with, even though the uncompromising Irish form of Córas Iompair Éireann had not been challenged for forty years. The legislators lacked confidence in the capacity of the public to absorb purely Irish language names for the new companies. In subsequent practice, 'Bus Éireann' would be used almost exclusively rather than 'Irish Bus'. The public, media and CIÉ would be ambivalent about the names of the other two entities. John Wilson believed that more 'euphonic' names could be devised. He told the House of his failure in having an Irish language name applied to DART and of his irritation when finding that it was just a variation on BART (Bay Area Rapid Transit) when he visited San Francisco. The similarity between BART and DART was hardly accidental; the San Francisco scheme was well known to CIÉ when DART was being conceived and built. The DART name, however, was tested for public reaction against a number of other names, e.g. Metra, Greenline, Rapidlink, Cityline, though no Irish language name, as John Wilson desired, was tested in the sample.

The Bill passed its second stage without a division on 19 November 1986. As usual Jim Mitchell, although never considered to be a Gaelgeoir like John Wilson, opened his concluding speech in Irish. It was an uncontroversial debate and the minister thanked John Wilson, the opposition spokesman, for his 'wide ranging contribution . . . it was constructive as always'—a far cry from the Lemass/McGilligan, Childers/McGilligan exchanges of the 1950s and 1960s.

BEFORE COMING TO the restructured CIÉ, a breakthrough can be recorded in the long-running issue of one-person operation (OPO) of double deck buses. OPO of single deck buses had been introduced in 1962 for day-tours and private hire, and in 1963 for rural stage carriage services. The resistance encountered in both cases has been outlined earlier (see page 177). OPO on double deck buses was another issue and was first raised formally with trade unions in 1969. Direct meetings with trade unions were followed by conciliation meetings at the Labour Court and then by a Labour Court investigation, which included visits to Lille and Brussels to observe their single deck operations and to Manchester to study its double deck OPO. The subsequent Labour Court recommendation was in favour of OPO, but it improved the terms on offer from CIÉ to the busmen. The investigation had been exhaustive and every aspect of the OPO arrangements affecting busmen had been dealt with.

The question for CIÉ was: should it accept the recommendation and announce a date for implementation? Should it wait until unions balloted on the Labour Court recommendation almost certainly giving it a 'thumbs down'? CIÉ realised that if it went ahead with OPO a strike was virtually certain, and sensed that media and political reaction to a lengthy dispute could force CIÉ to settle on excessively costly terms or to back down. The unsatisfactory consequence of ministerial intervention on OPO in 1963 had to be borne in mind. The decision was to do nothing until the busmen balloted. In due course the ballots showed a large majority against OPO. No further action was taken by CIÉ at that stage.

In the early 1970s further exploratory meetings with senior union officials and with officials of the Irish Congress of Trade Unions made no progress on the OPO double deck issue. In the mid-1970s responsibility for such negotiations was devolved to local management, and intense negotiations at local level confirmed that short of facing a strike, a settlement on terms acceptable to CIÉ could not be achieved.

When Paul Conlon became Chairman, he sought a briefing on the background and the current state of play in the OPO saga. With a fresh remit based on a determination to resolve the issue of OPO of double deck buses, the central personnel function assisted by DCS management recommenced negotiations in 1985. These culminated in Labour Court hearings fifteen years after the first investigation. The Labour Court again favoured OPO on terms which CIÉ believed were fair to all. In November 1985 the chairman and management reviewed the situation once again. All were aware of the background since one-person operation of buses had become an issue in the time of Todd Andrews. The Employer Labour Conference and the Oireachtas Committee on State Sponsored Bodies had both been involved in trying to progress a solution. It could be said that CIÉ and the trade unions had both lost credibility on this issue. A fresh Labour Court recommendation was to hand. Allied to OPO introduction was the matter of DART feeder buses. Fourteen months had passed since DART trains had begun to operate, but the feeder buses were not yet functioning. Was it time to confront the issue? Was CIÉ prepared to withstand the heat? Weighing the odds of success as against failure, considering likely public attitudes to CIÉ if it forced the issue and taking a view on political risks, the meeting decided: yes, action to implement one-person operation of Dublin's double-deckers should proceed as soon as possible—before the end of 1985. Jack Higgins, General Manager, Paddy Murphy, Assistant General Manager (Personnel), and John Browne, Manager of DCS, were all parties to that decision. The fateful date was to be 8 December 1985—the day of the Church holiday, when traffic to Dublin was traditionally heavy.

The executive feeling in CIÉ was that a new sense of reality was developing among bus workers—a recognition that Dublin's buses were losing traffic and that the operation would be in danger if it did not adapt to the market. Since 1960 there had been simply far too many industrial stoppages, sometimes for a day, a half-day, and frequently at one garage only. A change had occurred since 1984. In that year at Phibsboro garage, workers one morning set out to inspect all buses for service acceptability. Five minutes were spent checking every bus and as a result between 7.00 and 8.00 hrs only twelve buses exited the garage instead of the usual eighty. Management suspended those involved and the outcome was an eight-week strike at Phibsboro, unsupported by other garages. It ended with a return to work involving no gains for those on strike. That particular strike was seen to mark a milestone in DCS industrial relations and 'wildcat' stoppages virtually ceased.

On 8 December 1985 fifteen drivers were rostered for training on OPO buses. None attended and all were suspended. Over the following weeks the toll of suspended drivers grew and grew. Dubliners held their breath. Was there going to be a complete stoppage? On 13 December, when Vote 41 was being debated, everyone in the Dáil was conscious of the delicate situation. John Wilson feared that he detected a certain amount of 'machismo on both sides in relation to this dispute'.

It was the eve of the third anniversary of his appointment as minister, and Jim Mitchell was cautious, warning against pushing either side into a settlement which would not be satisfactory.

For instance, if as a result of changes in the package there were no reductions in bus fares, that would be wrong. If as result of a change in the package there was no saving to CIÉ, that would be wrong. If as a result of a change in the package there were no benefits for the workforce, that too would be wrong. Of the £11.6 million per year reckoned to be saveable after the fourth year, more than £6 million will go to the workers and the rest will be shared by the fare paying public and CIÉ, and in due course the taxpayer. There is no room left for change . . . but that does not diminish the desire, clearly expressed on all sides of this House, for a speedy settlement of the dispute.

(ibid., Vol. 362, Cols 2356, 2357)

Through Christmas and the New Year buses continued to run, though services were suffering. By 10 January 1986, 406 drivers had been suspended out of 1,600. On that date a historic settlement was achieved with the assistance of the Labour Court. On 2 February the DART feeder buses began to operate and the first one-person operated double-decker bus ran on the Mulhuddart route on 9 March 1986. By the end of that year 25 per cent of Dublin's double-deckers had converted to one-person operations. It was too much to hope, though, that the break with the past was entirely clean; further disputes about OPO would occur and be resolved in 1987. The December/January stand-off had been tense, but both sides had held their nerve. John Browne, Manager of DCS, with his management team, had established a new base for the operation of Dublin's buses. Bus workers and bus users could look forward to a better future.

CHAPTER 23

THREE IN ONE: THE RAILWAY

New operating subsidiaries established—Iarnród Éireann—Submission to Oireachtas Committee—Modernisation—Market shares—Negative decision on further electrification—New commuter services planned—Upgrading Dublin/Belfast line—EU funding—New commuter rolling stock—New 3200 h.p. locomotives—Rosslare Harbour development.

On 'Vesting Day', 2 February 1987, the new subsidiaries began trading. Defining the roles of the subsidiaries and announcing top appointments in the new entities, the chairman told staff that the purpose of the reorganisation was to

> – give the whole CIÉ organisation a much stronger customer and market focus;
> – provide a structure which allows clear central direction on major strategic and policy issues while giving . . . maximum local autonomy to managers at every level and location;
> – provide for investment in pursuing new opportunities for revenue and profit growth—so moving away from the situation . . . where pretty well every economic pressure on the organisation has led to a programme of cost and service cuts;
> – provide a working environment which gets the best from our workforce, by improving communications, industrial relations and our people management skills.
>
> In short, the re-organisation of CIÉ provides the means for new, efficient and profitable enterprises to provide top class services to the Irish travelling public. (*Nuacht CIÉ*, Eanáir 1987)

The statement reminded staff that the market for transportation was growing rather than declining and that CIÉ's main competition came from the private car rather than from private bus operators. 'This puts a very different perspective on the whole area of competition and competitiveness.' (ibid.)

Edward O'Connor, who had risen through the ranks and had successively been Area Manager, Limerick, Galway and Dublin, before becoming Assistant General Manager (Operations), was appointed Managing Director of Iarnród Éireann. Rosslare Harbour and road freight were to be operated by Iarnród Éireann in addition to all rail services. Noel Kennedy was appointed Managing Director of Bus Éireann. Like Eddie O'Connor, Kennedy had joined CIÉ as a clerical officer; had served in the Waterford area where he was a key figure in developing the sophisticated beet-loading centre at Wellington Bridge, had been Area Manager, Limerick, and was Area Manager, Dublin, where he had been deeply involved in the development of DART. All road passenger services outside Dublin became the responsibility of Bus Éireann, including provincial city services, Expressway, Supabus and school buses. John Hynes became Managing Director of Bus Átha Cliath. New to CIÉ, Hynes had been in the Guinness Group before joining Dublin Gas, where he was General Manager, Commercial, when appointed to Bus Átha Cliath. John Browne, Manager DCS, was also appointed to the Board of Bus Átha Cliath. The holding company became responsible for the overall direction and development of the Group and for CIÉ Tours International, CIÉ Outdoor Advertising, the newly established CIÉ Consult and management of CIÉ property as ongoing businesses.

Employees were notified individually of assignment to one of the new companies, and the process was described as 'trouble free'. All CIÉ's assets, physical and financial, were similarly assigned. Splitting an undertaking, parts of which were one hundred and fifty years old, but which had been operating as a unit for over forty years and the constituents of which had been variously growing or contracting, may be simple in concept but is difficult in practice. Physical assets had first to be identified and then allocated. Financial assets and liabilities needed study to establish whose they should be in the new set-up. The exercise was completed without coming across any 'black hole' of missing assets—a tribute to the integrity of the company's accounting systems. Under the Act, 'land' including the buildings thereon remained the property of CIÉ (the holding company) and were leased to the appropriate operating company.

Since the 1950 Transport Act, there had been no shareholders' equity in CIÉ, but a creative device put some equity into the balance sheets of the subsidiaries. The 'Asset Replacement Reserve' of £71 million provided the vehicle: in the accounts of the subsidiaries this £71 million was distributed as a £25 million equity in Iarnród Éireann and £23 million each in Bus Éireann and Bus Átha Cliath. Michael Grace, who had been with CIÉ for twenty years, carried the load of financially engineering the reorganisation in consultation, of course, with his fellow chartered accountant, Chairman Paul Conlon. In addition to constructing balance sheets for the new companies, CIÉ simultaneously reorganised its main financial statements to conform with the many changes required by the 1986 Companies Act. Altogether it was no mean feat. Michael Grace became Director, Group Finance. Among other holding company appointments Colm Mac Giolla Rí became Director, Group Human Resources, and Joe Daly became Director, Group Business Development, where responsibilities included monitoring such competition problems as might arise between the subsidiaries.

The new companies quickly set about developing their public personae and flexed their muscles for the attack each would launch on its own market. However some things did not change. On 6 February, the board authorised the chairman to write a detailed letter to the minister concerning grants provided for in the 1987 pre-budget estimates. He argued that the provision was not in accordance with the subvention formula introduced in 1983 and amended in 1984.

> If the subvention of £96.421 m. (a reduction of £8 m. on the subvention for 1986) is not increased to the amount which would be payable by the correct application of the subvention formula, it will be necessary to increase rates and fares immediately by at least 5% to bridge the gap between the subvention as now calculated and the expected deficit for 1987 . . . With regard to the provision of £8 m. in respect of interest on DART, I am very disturbed that no provision has been made for the payment of the balance of the DART interest amounting to some £16 m. in respect of the years 1985 and 1986.
> (Chairman's letter to Minister, 6 February 1987)

CIÉ's auditors had previously agreed to treat these interest arrears as a 'deferred' cost and the chairman continued

> Unless I have a firm commitment regarding the date of payment of the balance of the interest grant I will find it virtually impossible to convince the Auditors to allow us to treat the DART interest net of grants received as a deferred cost with a consequential serious impact on the reported results for 1986. (ibid.)

Predictably, government was holding back whatever it could without directly breaching the subvention formula. The chairman would fight his corner firmly and professionally. Three days later another letter to the minister submitted a case for the construction of 18 railcars, together with modification of the later (24) of the Mark 3 mainline coaches being built in Inchicore so that they could be operated with railcars. Railcars would enable CIÉ to reduce by an equal number the number of locomotives required to replace its ageing fleet of 001 Class locomotives. Optimistically, CIÉ pointed out that if approved, this new railcar construction would mean that staff numbers at Inchicore could be maintained when production of the mainline coaches was completed. The employment argument could always be relied on to attract attention. Approval would also have dented the 'no new investment in the railway' policy to which the government had committed itself.

The project was not approved and CIÉ would wait seven years both for new railcars and for new locomotives. The restructuring of CIÉ was not going to be so spectacular in its effect that such projects as building railcars would get by on first submission. Another general election campaign was under way. On 17 February 1987 the Dáil was dissolved. Problems arising from the still serious state of public finances caused the Fine Gael/Labour coalition to crack after being in office for four years and three months. As a result Jim Mitchell ceased to be Minister a month after CIÉ's reorganisation was implemented. He was succeeded by John Wilson in a short-lived single party Fianna Fáil government.

The state grant for the year 1987 at £87 million was less than the figure CIÉ had argued for but, in addition, £44,458,961 million of 'repayable state advances' were written off. However, it would be a mistake to regard this write-off as a 'free gift'. It was a device used by government to avoid making good its subvention arrears and its commitment to recoup DART interest payments to CIÉ. Realistically the £44 million, while bearing the 'repayable' label, had been used to fund capital expenditures and no one seriously believed that CIÉ could ever repay such a sum. In theory, by writing off those 'repayable' advances, the state could say that it was honouring its commitment to clear the arrears of DART interest. In practical cash terms, these arrears were never made good and CIÉ bore additional interest charges of £2.9 million per annum to finance them. Two simple things were achieved by this transaction: CIÉ's complaint about delays in clearing arrears was removed, as was the absurd claim that the state was owed moneys by CIÉ.

At the end of the reorganisation year, 1987, Jack Higgins, General Manager for thirteen years, retired. As the Group had an executive chairman and three managing directors in its operating subsidiaries the board did not appoint another general manager. In the subsequent annual report, Paul Conlon noted the 'many innovative and technically advanced developments' for which Jack Higgins was responsible. These included 'successfully initiating, planning and implementing the DART programme', in itself a very substantial achievement.

As the story of CIÉ continues, we now deal separately with Iarnród Éireann, Bus Éireann and Bus Átha Cliath, though some overlap is unavoidable, and then deal with the holding company, as it closes its half-century of service in a world so very different from that in which it was born.

IARNROD ÉIREANN

The new Iarnród Éireann must have perceived itself in 1987 as the company with the biggest challenge of the three new subsidiaries. Admittedly it had its spanking new and technologically advanced DART system; Rosslare Harbour was profitable and constantly being upgraded; but it was more dependent than the other subsidiaries on state support—a dependency it shared with other railway companies throughout Europe. It had rich traditions and strong nostalgic ties to the past. These ties and traditions partly supported and partly encumbered the new enterprise. A poignant minute of 16 May 1987 showed how deep some of them ran. Iarnród Éireann asked the CIÉ Board to resolve:

> That Ballingrane Junction/Tralee railway line extending from its junction point with the Limerick/Foynes railway line at Ballingrane Junction in the County of Limerick to Rock Street level crossing in the town of Tralee in the county of Kerry be abandoned and an Order to that effect be made and the necessary notices be published in *Iris Oifigiúil*, in the *Limerick Leader* and the *Kerryman*.
>
> (Board Minutes, 16 May 1987)

Rail passenger services between Limerick and Tralee had been withdrawn in 1963 and the last freight train using the Ballingrane/Tralee section had operated in 1977. At that time CIÉ had decided not to make abandonment orders until ten years after services ceased on a particular stretch of line. The ten years had elapsed and management dutifully studied whether the line could ever be reopened.

At the time of the reorganisation the CIÉ Board had signalled, not for the first time, that the era of closures and cutbacks as the principal response to financial problems was over. Going for business and effectively using existing equipment was to be the mark of the new subsidiaries. Abandonment orders for permanently disused lines did not conflict with this approach. Existing rail services were to continue and station closures were also over. The last significant station closure had occurred prior to the reorganisation, in February 1986, with the closure of Moate, Co. Westmeath. Before that, rationalisation of freight services in 1984 had involved the withdrawal of the seasonal beet traffic from an interesting list: Ballinasloe, Ardrahan, Portlaoise, Drogheda, Cabra, Athlone, Listowel and Lixnaw stations. Of course, the sugar manufacturing industry was itself being rationalised; the Tuam factory finally closed in 1986 and the Thurles factory in 1989.

After the establishment of Iarnród Éireann in 1987, one area still required further rationalisation, i.e. freight sundries which McKinsey said should be closed down, with which government agreed, unless they could be made more successful. Gradually some improvement was achieved, but then a major shake-up occurred in April 1991. The number of 'Transtrack' freight terminals for sundries traffic was reduced by two-thirds from 32 to 10. It was hoped to retain all existing business by providing substitute road services to the centres which were being closed while achieving savings of £2 million per annum. This seemed to be an ambitious target, but a heavily promoted 'Railink' concept and brand name managed to maintain the previous volumes. Total tonnes carried in 1992, at 3.3 million, were marginally up on 1991 and in the fifth successive year of growth they were back up to the 1985 level. 'General freight', the omnibus category after the main contract businesses of beer, cement, beet, mineral ores, oil and fertiliser, also increased in 1992 over 1991 and at 1.48 million tonnes it compared well to an average 1.2 million through the 1980s. Another favourable indicator of rail freight performance was that average wagonload in 1992 was 17.9 tonnes, up 18 per cent on 1987 (a slight drop occurred in 1993).

Road freight had also to be rationalised, but rationalisation in this division caused a reduction in traffic from 1.2 million tonnes in the first year of Iarnród Éireann to 1.0 million tonnes in 1993. Significantly, average receipts per tonne (both road and rail) were less in 1993 than in 1987.

Compared to £32.5 million earned on freight (rail £18.7 m. and road £13.7 m.) in 1987, Iarnród Éireann derived revenues of £41 million from passengers. Here a new marketing emphasis became apparent though investment was still required. Renewal of track and signalling continued where possible but was seriously inhibited by lack of capital and by the specific restrictions on rail expenditure built into the 1983/84 subvention formula. A revised formula was notified by John Wilson on 18 October 1988 for the period until 1991; it received little public notice compared to the 1983 formula. The pressure point in the new formula was that it required an annual reduction of 3.5 per cent in real terms in the grants payable to CIÉ as a whole. The directive annually to ratchet railway maintenance and depreciation costs downwards by 5.7 per cent per annum was removed. That particular restriction, as already noted, was impractical in the long term unless the rail system itself was to be pared back bit by bit. The revised formula lapsed at the end of 1991, again without receiving public notice.

Afterwards an *ad hoc* approach operated while investment in the railway was resumed.

By 1990 signalling on the entire Dublin/Cork line, on Dublin/Galway as far as Ballinasloe and on the DART system was automated and controlled from Connolly CTC, but signalling was still mechanically controlled on the Rosslare line south of Greystones, on the Belfast line north of Malahide, on the Waterford line south of Athy, the Tralee line west of Mallow, the Ballina/Westport line west of Knockcroghery (outside Athlone) and on most of the Sligo line where both track and signalling were such that operations were heavily speed restricted. Despite various improvements to the infrastructure since the 1974 Railway Development Plan, 60 per cent of Iarnród's rails in 1990 were over 50 years old, and over half of them were more than 80 years old.

Track renewal was completed on Dublin/Cork mainly with CWR, but older jointed rail prevailed elsewhere outside Bray to Malahide on the east coast. Construction of new coaches had ceased with completion of the 124 Mark 3's in 1988 and the last 24 off the production line had been adapted, as proposed in February 1987, so that they could operate as push/pull units. These new push/pull units operated with the deteriorating 121 Class (single cab) locomotives on Dublin's outer suburban lines, mainly Dublin/Drogheda and Dublin/Maynooth.

Iarnród Éireann began life in 1987 with an excessive number of timber-framed carriages. About half of them had been built in the 1960s, were speed restricted, expensive to maintain and gave an inferior ride to the passenger. Three railcar sets were leased from Northern Ireland Railways between October 1987 and November 1990, while in 1989 15 early British Rail coaches (Mark 2a) were required from a dealer in Leicester to whom they had been sold by BR. Being the best available at the price it could afford, CIÉ brought them to Inchicore for extensive refurbishment. These carriages were brought into service during 1990, costing £2.7 million, including refurbishment. With its 124 Mark 3's, the refurbished BR carriages and its own earlier stock, Iarnród Éireann managed to 'make do', carrying additional passengers year on year until it would receive 17 DMUs (diesel multiple units) in February 1994 (see below).

Iarnród Éireann's locomotives in 1987 were the eighteen 071's purchased in 1976, the 12 twenty-year-old 181 Class introduced in 1966 and 96 of other classes acquired as far back as the mid-1950s. Gradually some older locomotives had to be scrapped, but Iarnród Éireann managed to operate a fairly constant, even marginally increasing, train schedule though with increasing difficulty until new locomotives eventually arrived in late 1994.

In August 1990 Eddie O'Connor, Iarnród Éireann's Managing Director, retired at the age of 60 and was succeeded by David Waters. In April 1991

G. T. Paul Conlon, Chairman 1984–94

Eamon Walsh, Chairman 1995–

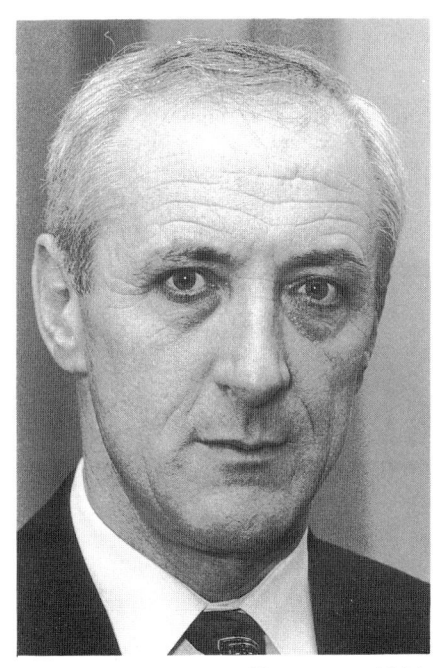

Dermot O'Leary, Chairman 1994
(Robert Allen Photography)

Michael McDonnell, Group Chief Executive 1995–

CIÉ reorganisation, 1987: the Minister with the Group Chairman and the Managing Directors of the newly created operating subsidiaries. From left: Noel Kennedy (Bus Éireann), John Hynes (Bus Átha Cliath), Jim Mitchell TD, Minister for Transport and Communications, G. T. Paul Conlon (Group Chairman), E. A. O'Connor (Iarnród Éireann)

Chairman and Executive Board, March 1995: From left (seated) B. P. Dowling (Group Secretary), N. Kennedy (Acting Group Chief Executive), D. O'Leary (Chairman), J. J. Daly (Director, Group Business Development), M. Grace (Director, Group Finance); (standing): C. Mac Giolla Rí (Director, Group Human Resources), J. Browne (Acting Chief Executive, Bus Átha Cliath), C. D. Waters (Managing Director, Iarnród Éireann), D. Mangan (Managing Director, Bus Éireann)

One of eighteen 071 class locomotives built by General Motors for CIÉ in 1976

The first DART car built by Linke-Hofmann-Busch arrives at North Wall, Dublin, February 1983.

Connolly station (right of centre). Loop line (from top to bottom of picture) straddling Amiens Street, Dublin

Promoting commuter rail travel, St Patrick's Day parade, Dublin, 1989

Rosslare Harbour showing the new terminal building and three ferries at berths, 1990

Rosslare Harbour in 1993 showing extension of the port area in progress (centre right)

City Imp minibus, Mercedes engine, with Eurocoach body built in Gaoth Dobhair, Co. Donegal, 1994

CitySwift single deck, DAF engine, with Plaxton Verde body, 1993

A six-car DART set at Killiney, Co. Dublin, 1994

A four-car Arrow diesel multiple unit train built by the Tokyu Car Corporation, Yokohama, in 1993

First locomotive to travel by air: a 201 class GM locomotive arrives at Dublin airport, 9 June 1994

The 3200 h.p. GM-built 201 series on an inaugural run; thirty-two locomotives were acquired 1994/5

the Oireachtas Committee on State Sponsored Bodies again decided to investigate CIÉ, but the pressure of other events was such that the committee did not issue a report before it lapsed in December 1992 and the reconstituted committee was still 'out' on CIÉ in March 1995. However Iarnród Éireann's 1991 submission to the committee gives a useful picture of how the company was coping with its new identity and challenges. The focus of this submission is on marketing and finance.

Passenger volumes had grown by a spectacular 60 per cent between 1984 and 1987 after which DART traffic stabilised and more normal growth was resumed; freight volumes were being maintained. State grants for the railway, excluding DART interest grant, had been reduced by £3.9 million between 1984 and 1990—a reduction in real terms of 23.3 per cent. Inclusive of the DART interest support, the reduction in real terms was 20 per cent. The two areas of Iarnród Éireann's operations which were ineligible for state grants—road freight and Rosslare Harbour—had performed well. Road freight profit had increased from £41,000 in 1984 to £482,000 in 1990, while the Rosslare Harbour profit increased by 69 per cent from £1.28 million to £2.16 million.

While these trends were favourable, Iarnród Éireann in its submission to the Oireachtas Committee was aware that other questions could be asked. How significant was Iarnród Éireann to the economy? Was the reduced state grant of £76.8 million reasonable in relation to Iarnród Éireann's scale of activity? How did it compare with international practice? Was productivity increasing? Was Iarnród Éireann efficient and imaginative in its marketing? The submission sought to answer such questions.

An imperative in modern management practice is the preparation of a business plan. The Board and management of Iarnród Éireann asked itself the obligatory first question in this process: what business are we in? Honing its responses down from generalities to specifics, Iarnród Éireann focused in on the individual markets for passengers and freight in which it was actually participating. From this followed estimates of Iarnród Éireann's share of these markets. Some interesting figures emerged. 'InterCity', the name now applied to the mainline routes, were carrying more passengers in 1990 than at any time since CIÉ was founded and would grow further in the next few years. *Building on Reality* quoted estimates that only 4 per cent of the state's passenger kilometres were by rail, but Iarnród Éireann's market research gave a different perspective.

Based on interviews with 21,000 people throughout the state the research sought to establish how people made journeys of 30 miles or more. The result confirmed the dominance of the private car but, more specifically, respondents to a survey on seven inter-urban corridors revealed that cars led the field with 68 per cent, but trains were used by 24 per cent, buses by 6 per cent, and one per cent claimed air as their more frequently used mode. On the corridor between Dublin and Cork mainline passenger journeys came to a third of total end-to-end journeys with proportionately more Cork originating passengers using rail travel than those originating in Dublin. This route generated 25.5 per cent of all mainline rail passengers.

In terms of freight movements, Iarnród Éireann's biggest bulk traffic was cement (671,000 tonnes in 1990) followed by lead and zinc ores (379,000 tonnes), fertiliser (208,000 tonnes), ammonia (196,000), shale, gypsum and beet. Significantly, over half of these traffics did not exist in the first twenty years of CIÉ's history. *Building on Reality* and the Green Paper on Transport Policy quoted the CSO's estimate that the rail share of internal freight kilometres was 9 per cent to 10 per cent of the national total. The CSO figures also indicated that the rail share was declining—from 11.6 per cent in 1984, 9.2 per cent in 1989—due, not to a decline in rail traffic, but to a faster growth in total movements. However, the CSO surveys covered all freight movements including milk, bread and local deliveries in which Iarnród Éireann was not involved. Only 26 per cent of tonne movements were 'inter-regional' in nature, i.e. the market in which the railways were seriously active and in which they claimed to have a 17 per cent share.

It might be suggested that segmenting the market in this way is an artificial device deliberately chosen to make the railway seem more significant an operator than it really is. But that would be to discount the legitimate practice and need in modern business to define your actual market and to identify your real competitors. Iarnród Éireann analysed its competitive performance in over twenty inter-regional freight markets. The market shares varied greatly market by market, but in the biggest sector, east to south-west, the responses indicated that 23 per cent of freight movements were by rail. Standing back from possible arguments about definitions and sample sizes the overall finding was that nationwide, 17 per cent was the rail share of tonnes carried on distances exceeding 150 km in 1990—a figure which broadly is being maintained.

Labour productivity was something which Iarnród Éireann could happily explore in its submission to the Oireachtas Committee. Since its formation in 1987, numbers had been reduced by 1,300, making a total reduction of 2,000 since 1984, when staff numbers resumed their descent from a temporary plateau. As a result, Iarnród's 5,762 staff in 1990 was 25 per cent down on the 1984 level, with the reduction achieved through normal wastage, redeployments and voluntary redundancies. Despite the reduction in numbers, relatively low wages compared to other public sector employments, and having staff represented by eighteen trade unions, a similarly satisfactory account could be given of industrial relations. Days lost due to industrial disputes amounted to only 0.14 per cent of total days worked. Despite 24-hour days for seven days a week 'with the concomitant social implications', absenteeism was a low 5 per cent on average.

International comparisons offered to the Oireachtas Committee covered productivity and utilisation factors in which Iarnród Éireann's performance varied from quite reasonable to very good, e.g. utilisation per locomotive, journeys per carriage and tonnes per wagon were high, and low average freight train loading was explained by the smaller size of trains operated. With appropriate caution, Iarnród Éireann noted that care was required in comparing the financial performance of various railway systems because 'each country has different approaches towards financing its railways'. For example, investment in most continental railways was funded by capital grants (80 per cent grants in West Germany), while Iarnród Éireann's investment was funded from bank borrowings.

A good basis for comparison is the amount of state grants attributable to revenue, and the size of these grants relative to total revenue. Iarnród Éireann was below average by this criterion with 38 per cent of its revenue coming from the state, the same figure as Denmark's, while the Italian railways derived 67 per cent of their revenue from state grants, Belgian 53 per cent, Spanish 50 per cent, Dutch 42 per cent, German 32 per cent, with British Rail's figure of 14 per cent being away out of line with all other EC railway companies, as had been noted in the Green Paper. Another question was whether the ratio of state grants to expenditure was rising or falling. Here, too, the company had a good story to relate.

RATIO OF STATE GRANTS TO TOTAL EXPENDITURE
(excl. exceptional items)

	% including DART interest	*% excluding DART interest*
1984	60.2	58.0
1985	61.0	56.9
1986	62.8	58.6
1987	58.7	53.9
1988	57.9	55.7
1989	54.3	51.9
1990	52.5	50.0

To summarise where the railways stood in 1990: no general increase in fares or rates had taken place since 1986, and state grants were falling in money terms—both at current prices and at constant prices, and also as a proportion of expenditure. The improvement was attributed to better market performance and cost savings achieved through increases in labour productivity and in equipment utilisation. Its network, much reduced since the 1960s, still served most major centres of population with a total of 125 passenger stations. Its market research showed that it had a 24 per cent share of inter-urban passenger movements, with larger figures in individual corridors, and a 17 per cent share of long-distance freight (over 150 km). The contribution of rail in containing congestion in the critical Dublin area had been acknowledged by investment in DART, which was generally regarded as a major success. Still, further investment was required if the system as a whole was to be maintained and the Green Paper, the 1986 government statement on railway policy, had held back from making a long-term commitment to the railway.

A consensus developed after the 1987 change of government, that the now ten-year slide in the public finances required resolute action—Fine Gael's 'Tallaght Strategy' promised that it would support such action rather than oppose it for political advantage. Against that background, it was finally announced that the electrified suburban rail system would not be extended. The proposals to extend the system to the new western towns, with a centre city underground link to the Bray/Howth line and a northern spur to Ballymun, had neither been accepted nor rejected by the eight appointees who had occupied the minister's office since they had been submitted by the DRRTS. A decision against these extensions was in accord with the new consensus. Announcing this decision John Wilson asked CIÉ for new proposals for public transport developments to the western towns based on bus-based solutions and diesel services on existing rail lines. The Annual Report revealed in August 1988 that the board's recommendations in response to this request included:

> 1. The opening of four new stations on the Maynooth/Connolly line.
> 2. The introduction of commuter services between Clondalkin and Pearse Station involving the opening of eight stations.
> 3. An expansion of the Localink bus network which was introduced in the Tallaght Area in December, 1987.
> 4. An expansion of bus feeder services to complement the rail extensions.
> 5. The development of a busway along the old Harcourt Street line.
> (Annual Report, 1987)

The four new stations on the Maynooth line—Broombridge, Blanchardstown, Coolmine and Leixlip (Confey)—were opened in 1990. Provision of a commuter service to Clondalkin on the Dublin/Cork line would have to wait until February 1994. The Harcourt St line would still be under consideration in 1994 but as an LRT possibility. Government was told that meaningful commuter services required new commuter rolling stock, i.e. railcars and that existing commuter services to Maynooth, to Drogheda and on the Cork/Cóbh line were not properly serviced by existing equipment. Over three years would elapse before additional rail commuter stock was approved.

Jim Mitchell had said before leaving office that, instead of being his biggest problem as it was when he became Transport Minister, CIÉ was now the area which caused him least worry. However, CIÉ was not as comfortable as that remark would suggest. Two years after its submission concerning new commuter developments, the chairman in the 1990 Annual Report found it necessary to say:

> The level of investment in the rail infrastructure falls short of what the Group's management considers desirable to maintain and develop dependable services. Much of the physical network and our rolling stock is rapidly becoming outdated and requires urgent renewal. The economic and social importance of the rail infrastructure is of such significance that any depletion in its value and usefulness would have a negative downstream effect on localised users of its services.
>
> It has also been noted that under the current EC Regional Development Programme for Ireland, spending on the transport infrastructure is almost entirely directed towards roads to the almost complete exclusion of investment in railways.   (Annual Report, 1990)

The reference to the EC Regional Development Programme was a muted protest at the government sponsored and EC approved Operational Programme on Peripherality 1989–1993. This programme, geared to the establishment of the Single European Market in 1992, sought only £36 million for rail related matters covering such items as a railway extension at Dublin's North Wall, investment in gantries at four main rail heads and development of rail commuter services to Kildare on the Dublin/Cork line. In contrast, £623 million was included for road developments.

In mid-1992 the Annual Report could be much more positive about this subject of EC funding for transport needs. It referred to the previous imbalance in the distribution of EC structural funds between road and rail infrastructure in Ireland.

> Since then there has been increased public awareness of the deteriorating condition of much of our rail infrastructure and the need for major additional investment is now widely recognised. Throughout Europe, governments and national authorities recognise the essential economic, environmental and social value of railways and are now actively pursuing investment in them with the support of substantial EC funding.   (Annual Report, 1991)

The reasons for the change in tone was the decision by the EC to contribute to the development of the Dublin/Belfast line as a major European rail link, supported by both the Irish Government and the Northern Ireland Office of the UK Government. This approval came in between the peripheral development programme 1989–1993 and the later much larger programme of EC supported projects for the period 1994–1999. It may be speculated that the change of approach to the railway was primarily due, initially at least, to thinking in Brussels and Belfast rather than to a rethink in Dublin. In any event, a joint study on the Dublin/Belfast line by Iarnród Éireann and NIR developed proposals which, after consideration in Dublin involving the engagement of consultants, were forwarded to Brussels where they were approved. The chairman continued his mid-1992 comments:

> Government support for this project is regarded as a flagship commitment for railway development. It is confidently expected that similar support will be forthcoming for other radial routes. (ibid.)

This confidence would prove to be well founded. Iarnród Éireann continued to produce financial results which compared very favourably to the results of ten years earlier. A change in government attitude was even more encouraged by the phenomenon of strong support being provided for railways throughout Europe. Railways would help to contain voracious demands for road investment and to ease traffic congestion; they were environmentally more beneficial and more energy efficient. In effect, had the railways not already been in existence, the situation developing in the late twentieth century would have caused them to be invented. The idea that maintenance of the rail infrastructure be separated from railway operating costs was also getting EC support. This concept was first mentioned in Chapter 4 in relation to the 1948 Milne Report. Over forty years on, an EC directive which became effective in January 1991 required that henceforth, in railway accounts, the maintenance of railway infrastructure should be presented separately from the operation of transport services. It also provided that any authorised operator should have access to any member state's rail infrastructure on the grounds that the permanent way was to be regarded as a public asset rather than as the property of the operator. In Ireland the opening of the permanent way to other operators was hardly an issue of significance. For Iarnród Éireann, the significance of the new directive was the spotlight it forced on the cost of maintaining the permanent way which in 1992 and 1993 was reported as being in excess of £45 million per annum.

Between July 1989 and February 1992, during which the plans for development of the Dublin/Belfast line were announced, a new political phenomenon appeared—a coalition in which Fianna Fáil was a participant. Fianna Fáil's partners were the Progressive Democrats; Seamus Brennan,

TD was the Minister responsible for CIÉ. It was this government which approved the purchase of 17 railcars for commuter services at a cost of £18 million; they were ordered in March 1992.

In addition, against the background of EC support a decision was made to lift the almost 20-year-old freeze on the acquisition of new locomotives. The 1991 submission to the Oireachtas Committee had stated that it was 'imperative' that the 001 Class (1250 h.p.) be replaced. These survivors of CIÉ's first substantial diesel acquisition in 1955 were almost forty years old; they had been re-engined; 16 had already been withdrawn and 44 were still in service.

On 5 December 1992 a £60 million contract was signed with General Motors for delivery of ten 3200 h.p. diesel locomotives in 1994. But events were moving rapidly. A further 22 similar locomotives were later ordered for delivery in 1995 and £12.4 million was approved for 10 additional diesel railcars and for related investment for commuter services. It was Máire Geoghegan-Quinn who made that announcement, having succeeded Seamus Brennan as Transport Minister in the reshuffle of the Fianna Fáil/ Progressive Democrat government, when Albert Reynolds succeeded Charles J. Haughey as Taoiseach. Exactly a year later she was followed by Brian Cowen as Transport Minister in a new coalition government of Fianna Fáil and Labour. However, these changes in ministers were less unsettling than the frequent ministerial changes caused by revolving door governments of the early 1980s. Public finances were now in much better shape and EC structural funds were helping public sector investment. Taken together, the acquisition of 32 locomotives and 27 railcars between 1992 and 1995 was the biggest investment in railway motive stock since the decision over forty years earlier, in 1953, to dieselise CIÉ's operations.

A catalyst to these investments was a new programme for Structural (and Cohesion) fund support from the European Community, renamed the European Union (EU) after acceptance of the Maastricht Treaty. This programme, to cover the years 1994 to 1999, included a respectable £275 million for the railway, covering track and signalling renewal as well as motive power. Initially Iarnród Éireann had hoped that its own contribution to this £275 million programme would be limited to £90 million, but this figure increased to £140 million when the plan was finalised. The 1994 outlook for the railways was more positive than at any time since 1945.

In many ways it was a momentous year and the loss in January 1994 of the mail services which Irish railways had been providing for the Post Office since the days of the Dublin/Kingstown railway did nothing to depress the rising hopes. The link between the post and trains with mail being sorted on board TPOs (Travelling Post Offices) simply fell apart with hardly a whimper. The new railcar fleet for the Kildare/Heuston commuter service had much more of a 1990s flavour. The commuter service on the Dublin/Cork line proposed in 1988 was launched by the Taoiseach, Albert Reynolds, on 16 May 1994. Operating as far as Kildare rather than Clondalkin as originally proposed and terminating at Heuston rather than Pearse, it was inaugurated with 10 of the new railcars under the 'Arrow' brand name. Built by the Tokyu Car Corporation of Yokohama, each railcar was powered by an under-floor 350 h.p. Cummins diesel engine with a Niigata hydraulic transmission system. Designed in the same general style as the DART vehicles, each two-car DMU (Diesel Multiple Unit) set with wide automatic doors and facilities for disabled passengers had substantial standing room and could carry up to 329 passengers.

The push for modernisation in Iarnród Éireann's short seven-year life had been pervasive, revealing itself in many ways—some bold, some subtle. However, a spectre of serious industrial strife arose prior to the launch of the Arrow service. Continuous staff reductions in Iarnród Éireann had been achieved against a background of productivity negotiations and internally funded redundancy payments. The issue of more productivity measures came to a head simultaneously with the planned operation of the Japanese railcars on the Kildare commuter service. The situation somewhat resembled what happened with the launch of DART, except that the issues in 1994 were much wider than those attached to the Arrow service itself. The crisis simmered with shifting deadlines for a number of weeks. The media warned of the possibility of 'the first national rail strike' for almost fifty years. However a stoppage was avoided. On 15 April a formula was agreed which enabled a referral to the Labour Court and the eventual outcome was another significant step in the modernisation of the railway system. Some extracts from the Labour Court's recommendations illustrate that perspective.

> The Court recognises that this is the biggest revision of the operation of the Irish Rail system which has ever taken place. That, of itself, implies disruption to the 'way of life' of every employee who will remain and the manner in which work is undertaken.
>
> Change . . . is necessary if the company is to improve its commercial viability, provide an effective and efficient rail service for the community and maintain and develop secure and sustainable employment for its employees into the next century.
>
> Given the intensity and depth of the negotiations which have taken place and which resulted in the 'Blue Book', the Court has not attempted to replace that outcome and is satisfied that generally it should form the basis of the Agreement.
>
> (Labour Court Recommendation, CCR14417, 25 April 1994)

Three in One: the Railway

RAILWAYS IN IRELAND, 1994

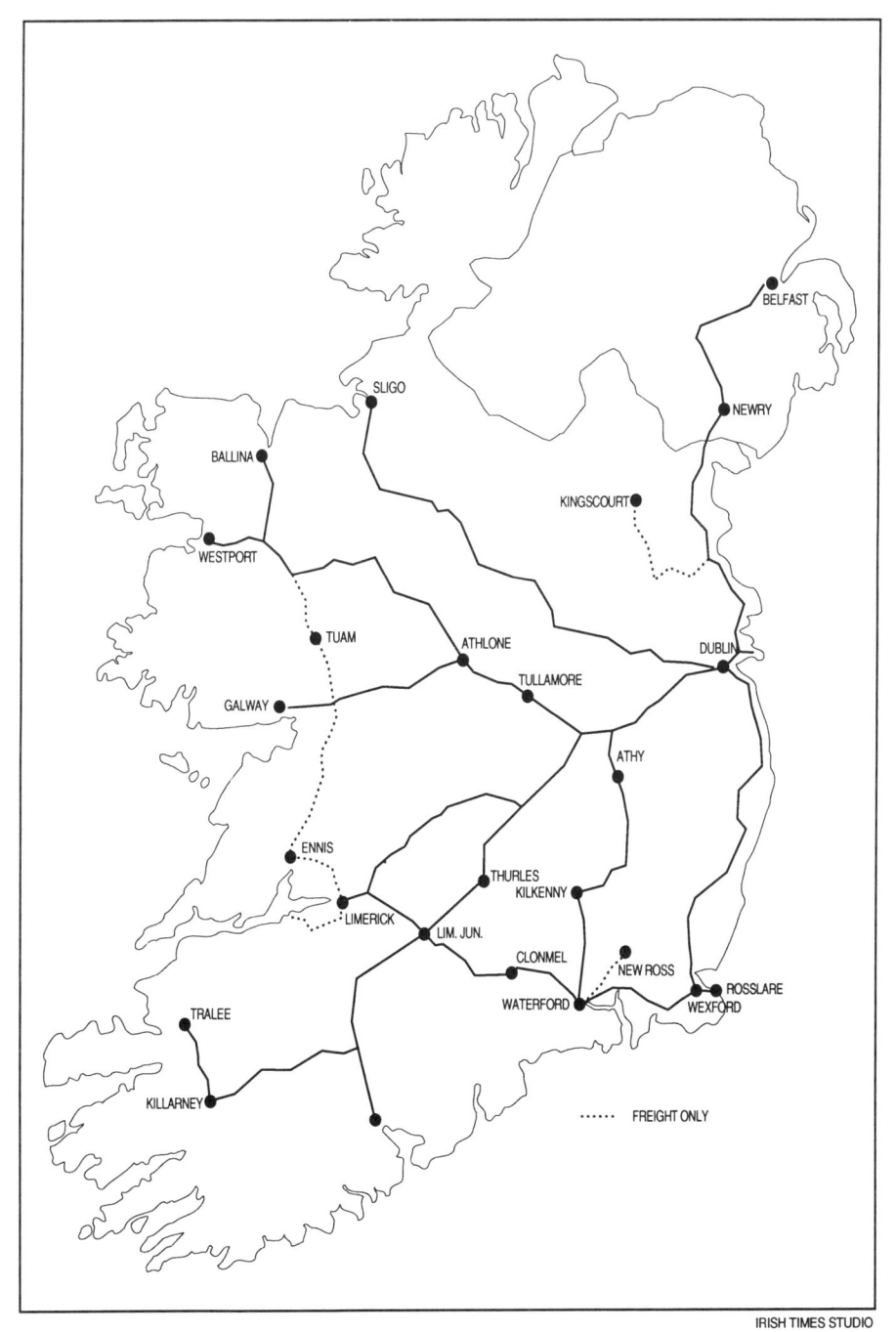

The 'rebirth of the railway' was a phrase used in 1984 at the time of DART's inauguration and the introduction of new mainline coaches, but it was a slow birth. That it was still in progress was dramatically illustrated by an event on Thursday, 9 June 1994.

> The heaviest load ever to land at Dublin Airport . . . having crossed the Atlantic from Ontario, Canada . . . a spectacular operation and an amazing feat of engineering . . . the first of Iarnród Éireann's ten new 3,200 Horse Power General Motors locomotives, the most powerful locomotives ever to operate in this country. The first of the 201 Class locomotive weighed 112 tonnes and was carried by a Ukrainian plane, an Antonov 124, one of the world's largest aircraft . . . The historic flight left Ontario at 18.20 Irish time on 8 June and flew to Montreal, Gander (Newfoundland) and Reykjavik (Iceland). It was transported by air to allow for proving trials, driver and maintenance training and systems performance checks so that the other locomotives can go into service immediately after their arrival in Ireland.
> (*Nuacht CIÉ*, Meitheamh 1994)

The new locomotive was twenty metres long by over four metres high. Train tracks were installed in the aircraft to allow the locomotive to be winched on and off the plane. The balance of the initial order of ten 201's arrived by September 1994. Another twenty were received by April 1995. Two identical locomotives were being acquired by NIR so that the new Dublin/Belfast service would be jointly operated, with a new trade name and logo, by these powerful new 201's. Iarnród Éireann would provide catering for both operators after winning an open competition for NIR's catering. A new Belfast-based subsidiary called Dubel would handle the NIR business. Traffic surged as the peace process took root.

The new investments in the railway had been sought for decades. Somehow, twenty years after the 1974 Rail Development Plan envisaged a modern railway system by the end of the century, it was all happening. However, over those twenty years one non-railway aspect of the company's operations had made steadier progress—Rosslare Harbour. Physically, the change in Rosslare Harbour between 1945 when CIÉ was established and 1995 when it celebrated its half-century, was more dramatic than had occurred at any other location. A single pier harbour serving a British railway company and largely catering for passenger ships had been transmogrified into what arguably is one of Europe's most modern ferryports, catering for four shipping companies serving Fishguard, Pembroke and Liverpool in Britain together with Le Havre and Cherbourg in France. Instead of daily departures in 1945, peak sailings in 1994 came to 66 per week. Volumes were also impressive: 1.3 million passengers, 270,000 passenger cars, 62,000 Ro/Ro freight units, 6,700 coaches and 17,000 cars for the motor trade.

The growth of Rosslare Harbour had been achieved in a number of stages (see page 305). It was a successful operation; capital investment was determined by commercial criteria, ensuring that its profits would not falter but would steadily increase as the port expanded. A second pier had been built in 1979. A much-commended new passenger terminal, designed by CIÉ's own architects, was opened in 1989. Seamus Brennan was Minister on the day of its official opening and was able to announce an £18 million plus development plan. It would fall to Máire Geoghegan-Quinn, as Minister for Transport, to use the executive train for the next ministerial visit to Rosslare on 28 October 1992 when she detonated an underwater blast of 400 kilos of explosives to begin removal of rock to clear access to new berths. The harbour was being deepened to handle the new generation of jumbo ferries. Thirty acres were reclaimed with over 430,000 cubic metres of displaced material. A third berth came into operation and a fourth was being prepared. Sea Lynx, the new high-speed catamaran service, began service in June 1994. Construction of a new harbour wall on the inside of the old pier began in 1994 and the first capital grants ever received for Rosslare Harbour (£5.5 million) were made available by the European Union. Profits had increased from £1.19 million in 1986 before the creation of Iarnród Éireann to £2.2 million in 1993. Even though its contribution to rail traffic was not substantial, Iarnród Éireann and CIÉ could be justifiably proud of its stewardship of Rosslare Harbour.

The story of CIÉ's other maritime concern is very different. Minister Dan Morrisey had caused it to take over the Dún Aengus and provide a Galway/Aran shipping service in 1951. In 1958 the Naomh Éanna went into service and survived until 1988. For the following two years CIÉ chartered vessels to provide a Galway/Kilronan link. Passengers were being lost to air services and to sea services on the shorter Kilronan to Rossaveal route. In April 1991, on CIÉ's advice, the service was put out to public tender and government awarded the contract to local interests. Hardly a tear was shed when CIÉ, through its Iarnród Éireann subsidiary, ceased all its links with the much-storied service across Galway Bay.

CHAPTER 24

THREE IN ONE: BUS COMPANIES AND GROUP

Bus Éireann's performance—Expressway—New buses acquired—Problems with payment for school transport—Bus Átha Cliath's initial near crisis—OPO implemented—Cost of redundancies—Minibuses—Quality bus corridors—Productivity gains—Financial results improve—Dermot O'Leary succeeds Paul Conlon as Chairman.

BUS ÉIREANN

Bus Éireann's first year, 'aggressively competing for business in a highly competitive and unruly market place', was not a good start. Passengers were down, losses were up. The deficit before state grants at £5.1 million was 28 per cent more than in the pre-incorporation year. There were two main reasons. Tumbling air fares resulting from increased competition on cross-channel air routes and a sharp fall in fuel prices ate into the cross-channel carryings of Supabus, as they did into the revenues of all surface operators, triggering B + I's decline into heavy losses. Supabus would survive and recover when stability returned to air fares in the early 1990s.

The second cause of Bus Éireann's slide in 1987 was more resistance to OPO, something which had seemed to be settled in February 1986. The 1987 resistance to OPO in provincial cities largely arose from their operating and staffing arrangements being different from those in Dublin. A very active Labour Court gave a lot of time to the problem, holding investigations in each of the affected provincial cities, which lead to an agreement in September when progress with OPO was resumed. Bus Éireann man-days lost as a result of the OPO issue in provincial cities came to 12,000 in 1987, even more than some 10,000 days lost in the much larger Bus Átha Cliath in the same year. Days lost in CIÉ as a whole never again came near to that year's total of 22,000, which itself was but a fraction of the worst years of the 1960s and 1970s. In Bus Éireann itself, days lost in the next three years averaged only 170 per annum.

Simultaneously with the 1987 fall in revenues, operating expenditure was 'massively pruned'. Despite the 28 per cent increase in the deficit before state grants, these grants were cut by 34 per cent to less than 4 per cent of Bus Éireann's total receipts in 1987—far below the 18 per cent that applied to Bus Átha Cliath. This difference in the level of state support for the two bus companies is partially explained by the profitability of Expressway which cross-subsidised Bus Éireann's loss-making rural stage carriage and provincial city services. Bus Átha Cliath had no similar profit maker to cross-subsidise city services, but it could claim that being able to cover 82 per cent of its expenditure from the 'fare box' was far ahead of what similar undertakings achieved in other countries.

Despite continued growth—legal and illegal—in the number and scale of private bus operators, the growth of Expressway was remarkable. In 1993 Expressway coaches with their logo of a racing Irish setter were carrying 4.5 million passengers, up 125 per cent on the 1987 figure of 2.0 million, while revenues reached £21.1 million compared to £7.1 million in 1987. Including Expressway, Bus Éireann passengers grew by 6 per cent between 1987 and 1993 and tours were another fast-growing segment contributing to this seemingly modest one per cent per annum growth. The tours business of Bus Éireann itself, comprised largely of day tours and bus hire out, increased by 30 per cent over the six years to 1993. Its profit performance was even more impressive, perhaps spectacular is a better word. In 1987 Bus Éireann incurred a loss of £927,000 on tour receipts of £2.7 million. In 1993 a profit of £1.0 million was earned on receipts of £3.6 million. A similarly dramatic transformation occurred in the affairs of CIÉ Tours International, an important and separate subsidiary for which Noel Kennedy, Bus Éireann's Managing Director, was given special responsibility (see page 431).

Bus Éireann decided that it would have to adopt a consciously market-led approach in line with a business plan developed in 1987 and thereafter revised annually. In a paper read to the Chartered Institute of Transport in 1991, Donal Mangan, General Manager of Bus Éireann, said the key issue identified in the planning process was the need 'to move from a position of relative weakness in the inter-urban travel market to a position of strength and domination of the market'; and 'to be cost effective, with elimination of all costs not contributing to revenue generation'. Consumer research in 1987 showed that Bus Éireann's inter-urban network using the Expressway brand name was highly rated for reliability and technical expertise, but had a poor reputation in the critical area of price. A number of daring promotions were launched to create a new awareness of Bus Éireann:

(a) 'Anywhere for £5' for a week in March 1987;
(b) 'Anywhere for £7' for two weeks in May 1987;
(c) Special City and Provincial Fares for one week in September 1987.

The primary purpose of these promotions was to win Bus Éireann a 'more competitive price image', but they produced the 'added bonus' of thousands of new customers, half of whom had rarely or never used bus services before. The perception of being more expensive than the private operators could not be instantly removed. Continued market research showed that the gap was narrowing and tracking research carried out in 1990 showed that it had finally been closed.

The 'market-led' approach required that Bus Éireann have a new customer emphasis in its timetables, fares and vehicle conveniences, if necessary abandoning previous patterns established by tradition and operating convenience. Its staff would have to be professionally competent, friendly, responsive and flexible. A clear corporate identity, good advertising and information, good associated products, and good market research were also needed. Progress was made on all fronts and the 1991 Annual Report boasted that 'Independent market research confirms that customer perception of Bus Éireann's services has improved dramatically.'

The new Bus Éireann was free to select and acquire its own buses. The main reason for this change was Ireland's acceptance of free trade and our joining the EEC in 1973. A condition of the Treaty of Accession was that Ireland would abolish its 1930s controls on the importation of fully assembled motor vehicles. Ireland sought permission to retain its restrictions until 1990. The commission proposed 1980 as the cut-off date, but eventually a compromise date of 1985 was agreed to. Duties against importation of fully assembled vehicles had to be scaled down gradually from the date of accession and the number of vehicles which could be imported fully assembled was to be set at 5 per cent in 1973 and increased by one per cent per annum until 1985 when all restrictions would be removed.

The Van Hool and Bombardier projects had been conceived at a time when the motor assembly industry was politically and socially important. In 1985, the year the restraints on importing fully assembled vehicles finally lapsed, the GAC survivor of Bombardier was in its death throes. In 1987, according to Mangan, only 18 coaches in the Expressway fleet measured up to Bus Éireann's standards for quality long-distance travel. Over the following four years sufficient coaches were acquired to enable it to be said in 1991 that the Expressway fleet 'now consists of 120 modern coaches, all featuring as standard, air conditioning, air suspension, automatic transmission, adjustable seating and stereo sound system'. Bus Éireann was now able to buy from a variety of chassis, engine and body manufacturers and at lower prices than had been possible from the Bombardier/GAC Shannon plant. Acquisition continued and the Expressway fleet in 1993 amounted to 202 long-distance buses—a varied stable, with Cummins the main engine provider, and with chassis from Leyland, DAF and Volvo, and bodies from Van Hool, Plaxton, Duple and Alexander's. A further 20 Volvo/Caetano coaches were acquired in 1994. The rural bus fleet had been renewed over the period 1983–1987 by the GAC integral KR type bus built in Shannon; a total of 226 were built, powered by a DAF engine. The provincial city double-deckers were unchanged except that in 1993, 10 large capacity DAF/Alexander (Belfast) city single-deckers replaced 10 double-deckers.

The school bus story is very different. Part of the plan for the Bombardier plant was that it would build new school buses. With a phased replacement programme, the 750 approx. school buses would provide useful additional demand for the Shannon plant, but that was not to be. In the financially easy early 1970s school buses had been funded by the Department of Education, but in the more difficult 1980s that Department would not supply funds to build new buses or agree to pay the increased charges which would follow from CIÉ finding the capital elsewhere. For CIÉ the problem was that school buses could not continue indefinitely. Bus Éireann eased the fleet question with purchases of second-hand buses—101 from the UK Ministry of Defence and 104 from Ulsterbus—and by converting 95 of its older Expressway vehicles for school use. Then in 1993, 130 used vehicles were found and acquired in Singapore, powered by Volvo engines and manufactured in New Zealand. Some 1,500 privately owned buses were also involved in school transport.

The Bus Éireann business plan recognised the importance of maintaining healthy relationships with key groups—customers, suppliers, local authorities and government. It is ironic that the group with which most difficulty arose was a branch of government—the Department of Education. In Chapter 13, Seán Mac Gearailt was quoted as being extraordinarily appreciative of the CIÉ achievement in bringing the first transport system for second level schools on stream in double quick time. But that was 1968. Twenty years later, 12 January 1988, in an atmosphere of acute and widespread cost cutting by government, CIÉ was advised that £1.5 million was being deducted from the £32 million (including amounts payable to private operators) which was due to CIÉ for providing the service.

The previous September CIÉ had defined certain options for the Department of Education if they wished to curtail expenditure on school transport. It was not now prepared to take the arbitrary £1.5 million cut. If Education was going to pay less they would have to accept a reduction in service. A letter to the Minister for Education on 13 January 1988 suggested

> as a matter of urgency that the options set out in my letter to you dated 1st September 1987, be examined in detail with a view to deciding the action necessary to contain the cost of the Scheme within the financial limits set out in the Government's estimates.
> (Chairman's letter, 13 January 1988)

In reply on 26 February, the minister suggested that the £1.5 million be 'found elsewhere in the CIÉ Group', but no such fudging of the issue would be allowed by CIÉ. Another letter advised the Department of Education that

> No case could be made for cross subsidisation of the School Transport Scheme from the other activities within the CIÉ Group. The School Transport Scheme, as you know, is administered by Bus Éireann, as a separate legal entity, and any shortfall in its revenue would increase the operating loss of that Company and this is not acceptable to the Board.

There the matter seemed to rest. Bus Éireann's monthly invoices were duly paid, but in November the Department of Education advised that £1.5 million would be deducted from the November statement. If anyone thought that this cut would be meekly accepted by CIÉ, they were seriously underestimating the tough commercial ethos which had developed following the reorganisation of CIÉ and the insertion in the subvention formula of a 3.5 per cent per annum reduction in real terms. The chairman wrote at length to the minister (8 December 1988) setting out all the facts, summarising the previous correspondence, referring to the 'support documentation' supplied to Education and ending, 'I respectfully request that as a matter of urgency you issue instructions to authorise the full payment of our account, particularly as this sum is adequately covered by the estimate.'

The letter was copied to John Wilson as Transport Minister who agreed with the stand CIÉ was taking. The issue soon came into the public arena. The 1989 estimates for the Department of Education revealed that government had upped its savings target for school transport from £1.5 million in 1988 to £5.8 million in 1989, almost 18 per cent short of what CIÉ required for the services it was providing. Observers feared that school transport was going to be seriously curtailed and the matter was raised during an adjournment debate in the Seanad of 8 February, and in Dáil questions on 11 February. The government position was that the requisite savings could be made from within the 'existing set up'.

CIÉ understood the need for economies and drew attention to the 'very significant savings we have made . . . in recent years and the fact that the nett cost to the National Exchequer of £31.6 m. for year 1989 represents a betterment of £3 m. in real terms when compared with 1986' (Letter to minister, 24 February 1989). On the grounds presumably that if you have a strong case, you should keep reminding the other party of that case, especially if the other party is a minister who is subject to many other pressures, CIÉ set out its case once more. It was not shifting its ground.

> As you will be aware, the 1975 School Transport Agreement requires your Department to meet all costs (including overhead costs) incurred by Bus Éireann in the operation of the Scheme. There is no profit margin . . . financing of the School Transport Scheme is entirely separate from the general funding to the CIÉ Group.
> There is no case for cross-subsidisation of the Scheme from the other activities within the CIÉ Group and, in fact, such a proposal is unacceptable to the Board of CIÉ and the Minister for Tourism and Transport.
> It must be clear from the foregoing that a reduction of £6 m. is totally unrealistic and it is misleading to say otherwise. I must repeat that if your Department requires the range and standard of service to be maintained at 1988 levels, then the £6 m. is required.   (ibid.)

In January 1990 government introduced a £5 million supplementary estimate to make up parts of the deficiency in its contractual obligations for the School Transport Scheme, but a further £1 million shortfall was planned for 1990 before paying an additional £600,000 to private operators which had been agreed by the Department of Education. Seamus Brennan, TD was Transport Minister at this time and when he met the board on 19 February 1990 he advised that jointly with the Department of Education he had commissioned consultants to study school transport.

> The study which was to be completed over the next few months had been commissioned to look at all possible options which might deliver the same excellent service provided by Bus Éireann but at less cost to the government.   (Board Minutes, 19 February 1990)

The consultants, Deloitte and Touche, concluded that the school transport service carrying 165,000 children on 6,000 routes every day was being operated at or near minimum cost. The 1990 Annual Report calmly and publicly noted that underpayments from the Department of Education amounted to £3.7 million at 31 December 1990.

The dispute continued into 1991. In August, the board learned that a memorandum to government, which was being submitted by the Department of Education with the support of the Department of Transport, was being objected to by the Department of Finance. Bus Éireann had studied its options exhaustively and was recommending to the CIÉ Board that 'if full payment was not made in respect of the current year's contract, then Bus Éireann would suspend the contract for a period of time until the savings achieved matched the shortfall in payments' (ibid., 7 August 1991). The board held off for a couple of months, but in October 'having noted that all avenues of discussion and persuasion had been exhausted and in the light of the Minister's support [Seamus Brennan's], approved the decision to suspend the School Bus Service for a period, possibly two weeks, until the savings matched the shortfall in payments' (ibid., 2 October 1991).

The suspension did not take place but matters were coming to a head. In February 1992 Seamus Brennan moved to Education and more consultants, Bastow Charleton, were engaged to review the scheme, but broadly they came to the same conclusion as Deloitte and Touche. The state was getting value for money for its payments for school transport. CIÉ announced that it would not renew its contracts with private operators unless it was properly paid. That action brought further movement from government and early in 1994 arrangements were finally agreed whereby the total arrears of payments under the School Transport Scheme, amounting to £4.5 million, would be made good. The affair proved that even a government department had to be careful about attempting to ease its own financial problems by shifting them on to the new CIÉ and its commercially minded subsidiaries.

Overall, Bus Éireann in 1993 earned a surplus of £3.4 million after a state grant of £4.0 million which, according to the annual report, was a payment 'towards the cost of the social role of many of the company's services'. A similar surplus was in prospect for 1994, in contrast with a deficit of £4.2 million for Bus Éireann in 1987, the year of its establishment.

Bus Átha Cliath

Bus Átha Cliath in 1987 had much in common with its sister subsidiaries, but there were differences. Iarnród Éireann was a very scaled-down version of the railway of 1945. While criticised for its heavy dependence on state support, it was recognised as having some significant pluses: despite poor mainline equipment, passenger numbers were beating all previous records; its Dublin suburban services, its freight operations and Rosslare Harbour were thoroughly modernised. In the case of Bus Éireann, its provincial city and rural services were similar in range and volumes to those which had always been provided, but it had developed the highly successful and profitable Expressway network. In contrast, Bus Átha Cliath had little to hold up for public applause.

The city had expanded greatly since the DUTC was absorbed into CIÉ. The total population of County Dublin (city included) had increased by 45 per cent over the previous thirty years, but over the same period DCS passengers had fallen by a third from 249 million in 1957 to 167 million in 1987. Once a provider of profits to cross-subsidise the railway, DCS had ceased to be profitable in the early 1970s. The prime reason for the decline was the private car, but a secondary reason was the slowness of public authorities in grappling with traffic problems, thus aggravating the problems of public transport causing further passenger loss, and so on. DCS's labour record was another problem. An observer might say that the trade unions insisted that CIÉ should have a monopoly of public transport in the city, but failed to co-operate with change which could help to maintain that status. The public perception was that bus transport in Dublin was losing passengers, was losing market share at an even faster rate, and was requiring more and more exchequer support to maintain its problem-laden operations. However, there had been some recovery since 1981 and the state subvention was actually falling in percentage and in cash terms.

Through the 1960s and 1970s the battle for better traffic management and bus priority measures had made some progress. CIÉ's own bus control and monitoring systems had been continuously refined including bus priority at traffic lights on a limited scale. However, CIÉ may have been too ready to blame the traffic environment for its difficulties. Periodically it checked its route structure, e.g. fifty-four changes were introduced in 1986, but new service concepts were rare. Of course, it had developed far-reaching rapid transit plans for the city, including busways and electrified commuter lines which also involved a centre city underground and transportation centre. These proposals had lain unaccepted and unrejected. As time passed they lost whatever initial credibility they had possessed, but there were no substitute initiatives. Significantly though, all buses acquired since the 1960s were capable of one-person operation. The stand-off between management and unions in December/January 1985/1986 had achieved a breakthrough on that issue. The challenge to deliver on the promise of that breakthrough dominated much of the period of John Hynes as Managing Director of Bus Átha Cliath from February 1987 to August 1990.

An OPO-related dispute in Clontarf garage disrupted services for a while in 1987, but in September that year further flexibility was achieved. By the end of 1988, 75 per cent of DCS services were operating on a driver-only basis and in that year's accounts the first heavy provision had to be made for voluntary severance settlements, primarily related to OPO. At the end of

1990, staff numbers were 934 lower than in 1987—down almost 25 per cent. The push towards OPO had distorting effects on services: driver shortages occurred while waiting for conductors to elect for driver training; excessive overtime was being worked; schedules were affected and between 1987 and 1989 passengers fell by 4.5 per cent. By the end of 1989, Bus Átha Cliath had got over the hump of this problem and the annual report claimed that a 98 per cent scheduled timetable performance was being achieved.

Marketing support for OPO introduction included appointment of retail agents to sell prepaid tickets, the promotion of such tickets and the installation of electronic ticket cancelling machines on buses. In the first OPO-dominated years of Bus Átha Cliath some other starts were made which would help in later years. Minibuses were acquired to begin internal but low frequency services in the Tallaght, Blanchardstown and Finglas areas; new double-deckers were ordered—Leyland Olympian, with bodies built by Alexander's of Belfast which were described as having 'lower entry steps, comfortable seating, faster acceleration capabilities and greater reliability'. They entered service in 1991. At the bus stop—a useful innovation—information carousels told the customer when the bus should arrive. These carousels, invented in Dublin, were later adopted in Portugal and in some US and UK cities.

Financially, the first years of Bus Átha Cliath were alarming. In its first year (1987) the deficit before state grants increased by 32 per cent to £19.4 million, varying little until it reached £21 million in 1990. These deficits were before taking account of heavy exceptional items. State grants were consistently lower than the deficit, opening at £16.4 million in 1987 and reducing to £14.7 million by 1990. Somewhat out of character with the rest of the Annual Report for 1990, CIÉ's unease with this situation is evident in a defensive explanation of the state grant to Bus Átha Cliath.

> To permit it to provide non-commercial but socially necessary public transport facilities including subsidised travel for school children, services to outlying areas and early morning, evening and Sunday services where demand is often insufficient to cover the cost of providing a service.

In aggregate, state grants to Bus Átha Cliath fell £16 million short of its deficits for the years 1987–1990. Add the exceptional items, particularly £13.5 million for voluntary severance payments to that shortfall, and it will be obvious that Bus Átha Cliath's balance sheet by 31 December 1990 had to be in serious difficulty. The situation was such that with an accumulated deficit of £29.3 million Bus Átha Cliath's net assets had fallen to 22 per cent of its shareholders' funds. Under the Companies Amendment Act 1983, it was necessary to hold an extraordinary general meeting to consider the situation. That meeting, consisting of its own board, its CIÉ owners and its auditors, was held on 20 February 1991. One of those present was a somewhat surprised Mr Robert Montgomery who two days earlier had taken up the position of Managing Director in succession to John Hynes. Bob Montgomery had been involved with different types of bus companies for over twenty years in the UK, large and small, companies owned by the state, by local authorities and privately owned, both before and after bus deregulation.

CIÉ's auditors needed assurances that Bus Átha Cliath could continue to trade and eventually were sufficiently satisfied on that score to be able to provide an acceptable certificate to the accounts. It was not a simple issue. If Bus Átha Cliath were to perform as badly in 1991 as it had in 1990, it would have required a special capital injection or specific guarantee from government, either of which could have undermined the rationale of the 1987 reorganisation. However a turning point had been reached. Revenue grew substantially in 1991 due to the increased passengers, but more importantly due to major fare increases, 7.5 per cent in December 1990 and 12 per cent in September 1991; the deficit before state grants fell by almost 50 per cent and Bus Átha Cliath ended the year with a surplus, after state grants, of £4.7 million compared to the previous year's shortfall of £8.4 million.

The coincidence of Bob Montgomery's arrival and a turning point in Bus Átha Cliath's fortunes was fortuitous. So much trauma had occurred in the previous few years that a period of stability was needed so that traffic could be recovered and revenues increased on the now 85 per cent driver-only operation. In restrained language the 1991 Annual Report reflected on the change.

> Bus Átha Cliath has undergone considerable operational change in recent years with substantial improvement in the cost base as a result of changed work practices.
>
> In 1991, Bus Átha Cliath carried 172.6 million passengers, the highest number recorded for many years. Passenger journeys increased by 3.3% in 1991 and overall passenger journeys are now 4.7% higher than the average of the last five years. This trend in passenger demand reflects the increasing reliability and effectiveness of the service, such that the share of commuter travel into the city centre by bus has increased from 22% in 1990 to 24% last year.
>
> Revenues generated increased by 12.0% to IR£87.0 million in 1991, while costs have been reduced by more than IR£4.0 million due to the further implementation of one-person-operation and reduced accident claims costs.

But no laurels were to be rested on that improvement. It merely fixed the springboard for further improvement and innovation. There were now 211 conductors compared to 1,565 some years earlier. An early decision was to increase driver recruitment, enabling better service performance, reduction in overtime, and allowing management to regain control and flexibility which was not possible with depressed driver numbers, a hangover from the OPO struggles. The assumption that the double-decker was always the best way to serve city routes had to be challenged. The route network had been adjusted through the years, but a more fundamental review was overdue. A major structured network review was launched: 300,000 on-board questionnaires were distributed in October/November 1991. The results were analysed and various solutions tested, adjusted and re-tested on a computer simulation package acquired from Colin Buchanan, the UK transport consultants. The city was divided into nine areas which were to be the basis for future route planning.

As 1991 drew to a close, management looked out for a route on which to experiment—not a major trunk route but a relatively low traffic, perhaps declining, route. The test would be to see how traffic would respond to a new approach and the experiment took place in April 1992. Route 83 (Kimmage/College Street via Rathmines) had long been served by double-deckers at a frequency of about three per hour. The experiment would be to see how the route would perform with eight 25-seat minibuses per hour. But before undertaking the experiment, driver pay would have to be settled for the minibus duties. Bus Átha Cliath proposed that minibus drivers be paid 20 per cent less than regular double deck drivers. Naturally the trade unions could not readily accept such a change. But if there was to be change there had to be action. Advertisement for drivers in early 1992 resulted in 1,200 applications. Bus Átha Cliath said that as these were new jobs for people performing new duties, it was entitled to fix the remuneration. So twenty-five drivers were hired and trained. As the launch deadline approached, agreement was reached on overtime and weekend working allowances within the overall pay envelope proposed by the company.

The experiment using the 'City Imp' brand name dramatically justified the contention that service should be adjusted to the convenience of the customer or potential customer rather than the other way round. Almost immediately the number of people travelling on the 83 route increased from 10,000 to 30,000 per week. Market research established that of the additional 20,000 passengers, about half were new bus passengers and half had diverted from other services. Looking to the other services where traffic should have fallen, it was found that new passengers had arrived to take up the capacity that had been vacated. It all seemed to be too good to be true; but the general conclusion could be summarised thus: passengers will be attracted to a convenient, dependable 7 or 8 minute frequency service on attractive buses and the 83 route experiment had brought 10,000 to 15,000 additional weekly passengers to Bus Átha Cliath. Nite Link services providing late night transport from the city centre to main suburban centres were inaugurated in 1991 and expanded in 1992, meeting a long felt want.

The scene was now set for another and more far-reaching experiment —the Quality Bus Corridor (QBC). The QBC concept was based on a rethink of what the public most wanted from bus services. The evident popularity of light rail systems abroad and developing support for light rail in Ireland suggested some questions. Did light rail services have attributes which bus systems could adopt and thereby enhance their appeal? Bus Átha Cliath systematically studied all aspects of its services and concluded that improvement could be achieved under six headings.

- The Alignment: the word used to denote the fixing of a definite path for each bus route, one which would be popular and well known. The practice of splitting a route into subroutes, labelled A, B, C, or experimenting with alternative routings could cause confusion and involve erosion of frequencies on the main trunk line.
- The Frequency: research and experiments indicated that a 7 or 8 minute frequency best appealed to the public. If the traveller could always be confident that a bus would arrive within that time limit, more customers would travel by bus.
- The Bus: clean, easy to board, minimum noise, aesthetically attractive buses could attract new business.
- The Staff: bus drivers needed more than driving skills which traditionally had been the sole criterion for selection. Ability to relate well to the public, to handle cash, and to work well at irregular times should influence selection and training. Each driver should know who was his or her supervisor and a reorganisation was planned to achieve that arrangement.
- The Infrastructure: a rather pretentious word principally denoting bus stops. An attractive, well-maintained shelter should be there, with lighting, a seat, even a telephone at larger centres.
- Traffic Priority: when everything else was in order and a realistic prospect held out that more passengers would use buses, traffic authorities should be more amenable to granting priority to buses, thus facilitating easier flow through congested sections and making faster journeys possible.

In short, the QBC involved overhauling a route or group of routes. The first QBC was to be launched using new single-deckers with the Cityswift brand name and a bright blue and grey livery on the 39 route to Blanchardstown serving the newly defined Area 7. The nominated date was 24 May 1993, but once again worker resistance caused difficulty and the start-up date was deferred to 6 June. As usual the problem was aggravated by the workforce being split between SIPTU and NBRU (previously the NBU), with each of them manoeuvring carefully so as not to be outflanked by the other. However, Bus Átha Cliath was determined that the bus corridor would be successful; some sixty suspensions took place, causing a two-week stoppage in Area 7. SIPTU members voted for a city-wide stoppage which happily lasted for only twenty-four hours. Three months later the introduction of City Imp minibuses in part of Area 7 caused a forty-eight-hour stoppage. In 1994 more QBCs followed to Ballyfermot, Finglas and Bray, with minibuses being introduced in the Marino/Drimnagh and in the Tallaght/Rathmines/Crumlin areas.

The public face of Bus Átha Cliath was being reshaped with new brand names, new colour schemes and new buses, but bus maintenance also needed changing. With 578 maintenance workers in 1987 and 564 in 1991 numbers were fairly constant. The fleet (over 800 units) stood at about the same level as in 1987, but its composition was constantly changing. By December 1994 over 345 new vehicles were acquired: 195 Leyland/Alexander double-deckers; 80 DAF powered single-deckers; and 70 minibuses powered by Cummins or Mercedes engines, some of which had bodies built in the Donegal Gaeltacht. The Van Hool double-deckers on Leyland AN68 chassis were being retired (they would be almost wholly gone by the end of 1994). The newer vehicles had higher reliability and longer intervals between major maintenance and overhauls; new systems required a different approach from that appropriate to older vehicles. In 1991, with uncompetitive pay scales and craft workers exiting to new employments, it was time for an overhaul of working practices which could justify some pay increases.

Talks about talks on a new productivity agreement began as early as September 1991, but the unions looked for 'up-front' pay increases to which management could not agree. A determined effort at negotiations got under way, but in May 1993 the craft unions decided to withdraw their labour. A new pattern emerged for an industrial dispute in CIÉ. Bus Átha Cliath studied its service needs against its resources and concluded that if necessary it could guarantee, for an extended period, to provide its public with 75 per cent of its normal schedule. Some troubles occurred in the early stages of the dispute as drivers and other staff passed the craftsmen's pickets, but the commitment to a 75 per cent schedule was well judged and was maintained for six weeks until work was resumed on 3 July. It was not an easy period, but it again proved that change requires strong nerves if it is to be successfully introduced.

Bus Átha Cliath's results for 1993 were the best for almost twenty years. The six-week craftsmen's strike had depressed passenger numbers and revenues, but still the deficit before state grants was below the 1992 level. The state grant itself at £8 million was down 50 per cent on the 1987 level. The CIÉ Annual Report revealed a singularly commercial perspective concerning Bus Átha Cliath, referring to future cash flows rather than arguing and explaining problems as in earlier years.

> Overall, the ratio of revenue to total costs before State Grants . . . at 96.8% (1992 – 95.6%) is exceptionally strong when compared with bus operations in other European cities . . . Cash flows of over IR£12 m. generated from operations, were reinvested in the fleet . . . It is essential for the company's future that positive annual cash flows of at least IR£12 m.–IR£15 m. from operations are sustained for continued investment in the business. (Annual Report, 1993)

The Bus Átha Cliath balance sheet showed that the accumulated deficit was almost halved since 1990 when the extraordinary general meeting had been found to be necessary. By 1994 net assets exceeded 90 per cent of shareholders' funds compared with 22 per cent in December 1990. Progress since 1987 is also indicated by a 50 per cent reduction in the interim in the state grant.

THE HOLDING COMPANY

The progressive thrust within the restructured CIÉ was also evident within the 'ancillary business' directly managed by the holding company. One of these was CIÉ Tours International, 'the only significant Irish tour operator involved in packaging and marketing Irish holiday products in overseas markets' (Annual Report, 1992). CIÉ Tours International covered the whole range of accommodation, entertainment and travel services—both to and within Ireland. Its business was subject to fluctuations in international tourist flows and depended on promotion of new products with new brochures being brought to the market every year. It maintained offices in New Jersey (US), Dusseldorf and London, and was also represented in France, Canada, Australia, New Zealand and South Africa. In 1987 CIÉ Tours International incurred a loss of £980,000, largely for reasons which also affected the Irish tourist industry as a whole (see page 387). In 1988 the CIÉ Board gave Noel Kennedy, Managing Director of Bus Éireann, responsibility for the reorganisation of CIÉ Tours International. It was comprehensively restructured and given a new marketing emphasis. A break-even was achieved in 1990 and by 1994 it had recorded a profit of £725,000. While its profit performance for CIÉ is important, its significance as a promoter of Irish tourism can also be noted. Incoming tourists handled by CIÉ Tours International in 1993 came to 60,000 and expenditure in Ireland on goods and services, financed by foreign earnings, amounted to £16 million.

SALE OF ADVERTISING space at transport properties and on buses and trains had always been a practice of transport companies and in CIÉ this activity had long been centralised in a profit centre of its own. Under the name CAN (Commuter Advertising Network) it continued to be centralised in the holding company. Now and again sensitivities would be upset by particular advertisements, and use of the loop line near the Gandon masterpiece of Dublin's Custom House as an advertisement hoarding prompted occasional protest in newspapers. An increasing sharpness became evident in CAN's activities, even if 'colourbuses' caused brief visual shock on quiet suburban roads. Useful revenues of almost £2 million and profits of £1 million, for distribution among the subsidiaries, were expected for 1994.

CIÉ CONSULT WAS the name launched three months after the 1987 restructuring for marketing the then small business of providing engineering and transport management expertise to mostly foreign customers. In its first year projects were undertaken in Botswana, Mozambique, Ethiopia, Liberia, Sudan, Saudi Arabia and Vietnam. Subsequent contracts involved consultancy for the establishment of a bus overhaul facility in Cairo, a privatisation project in Belarus and various work in Hungary, Lithuania, Estonia, Bulgaria , Egypt and Pakistan. Nearer to home, CIÉ Consult provided technical assistance and signalling, training and civil design work in the UK, including work for Eurotunnel, and provided engineering, particularly bridge design, services to Irish local authorities. By 1994 CIÉ Consult was providing profits to the Group of the order of £250,000 per annum.

THE MANAGEMENT OF CIÉ's properties also received new attention after the 1987 restructuring. An undertaking as old and as dispersed as CIÉ had accrued buildings and land which tended to be taken for granted and which were retained on ill-defined assumptions that sometime circumstances could change which would justify their use. It could also be said that many such properties were not particularly desirable or saleable. It is only when an organisation formally decides to challenge such attitudes that radical change will occur. Responsibility for an aggressive programme of rationalising property and maximising income from existing properties became a task for the holding company under Brian Dowling, the Group Secretary. First of all, every property had to be reviewed and whatever was surplus to operating requirements listed for disposal. Disposals took place throughout CIÉ's system and significant among them was the Point Depot, a fine example of nineteenth-century railway architecture beside the new East Link toll bridge on the River Liffey. The Point Depot, which became a prominent entertainment venue, was sold for £950,000. The nearby Wool Store and other property in the Dublin Docks areas realised £458,000. Old railway property in Maynooth realised £245,000 and in Cóbh £225,000. But in addition to properties inherited from the past, a substantial property bank had been built up in central Dublin in the 1970s and 1980s as a site for a transportation centre. The story of this property bank deserves a brief and final loop back into transport policy.

The idea that Dublin needed a central bus station had been advanced by Schaechterle in the 1960s. Up to that time, Nelson Pillar in the city's widest street (O'Connell St) had served as a reasonable focus for the city's buses and trams. Schaechterle, with his experience of continental and UK cities, argued that fast-growing Dublin needed a centre where all important bus routes would meet, passengers could change from one route to another while vehicles could be held out of the way of city traffic awaiting their next assignment. The DTS in 1971 and the DRRTS in 1975 supported this concept. Dublin, because of the history of its rail services, had five rail termini originally—Broadstone, Amiens Street, Kingsbridge, Westland Row and Harcourt Street. Subsequent rationalisation left two main rail termini renamed Connolly and Heuston. The DRRTS proposal for underground links between Connolly and Heuston via the Dublin City Transportation Centre would link the city's buses with the electrified rail system along the east coast and with new commuter systems to the west.

With government agreement CIÉ began to acquire property on which such a centre would be built. The focus of this activity was the area south of the Liffey, behind Aston Quay, which has since become famous as Temple Bar. Between the years 1976 and 1989 a total of 46 buildings and sites covering 1.6 acres were acquired in Temple Bar itself, East Essex St and adjoining areas. The properties, mostly of little architectural merit, comprised various occupied and unoccupied shops, catering outlets, workshops and residences, as well as vacant lots. While awaiting sanction to build, CIÉ let its properties to such tenants as were interested in low-cost, short-term leases. The result was to create an ambience in Temple Bar which caused it occasionally to receive the sobriquet of Dublin's left bank. Across the Liffey, on the northern quays (Bachelor's Walk), CIÉ owned Transport House, a substantial block and marshalling area once used by the GSR as a bus and road freight depot. CIÉ acquired other property in this area. The grand design was to have a Transportation Centre straddling both sides of the river, linked by an underground tunnel.

As Temple Bar gained in atmosphere the proposal to use the area for a transportation centre came under attack and it was scotched by Charles J. Haughey, as Taoiseach in 1982, who avowed that it would happen 'Over my dead body!' The Temple Bar conservation lobby had won a total victory. A special state company was set up to develop the area as a cultural centre with substantial EU grant aid. At the time, the case for a transportation centre was not specifically rejected by government, but if it was to be built, it would have to be somewhere else. The cynic could say that the voiceless bus travellers could endure the discomfort of long walks between bus stops while everyone else, motorists especially, could continue to berate CIÉ for using streets as parking lots, blocking traffic and causing visual and noise pollution.

CIÉ sold its Temple Bar property portfolio in 1991 to the new state company, Temple Bar Properties Ltd, for £3.7 million. Despite this major disposal and other sales realising some £13 million, CIÉ's management of its remaining properties in over 500 locations was such that its total rental income was one-third higher in 1993 than it had been in 1988. In passing, it may be said that without CIÉ's prolonged interest in Temple Bar, it is possible that the area's potential as a social and cultural area might never have been realised. Various unsympathetic developments would probably have excessively altered its character during the 1970s and 1980s. A senior civil servant hinted that the sale could be financed by writing off the appropriate sum from 'repayable state advances' but, as noted already, these had been cleared out in 1987. CIÉ was happy to be paid in cash.

On the other side of the Liffey, the possibility remained of building a bus station on a smaller scale in the general area bounded by Bachelor's Walk, Wellington Quay and Middle Abbey St. CIÉ's ambition here was focused on the idea of a joint development with a commercial property company, Arlington Securities. Arlington were assembling a site adjacent to Transport House which they eventually purchased from CIÉ in 1988 for £700,000. CIÉ did not propose to incur substantial capital expenditure on the project. The concept was that the total available site which reached up to Ormond Quay and Upper Abbey Street would be commercially developed in a way that would offer attractive amenities to bus passengers, while providing on-site or adjacent bus parking facilities. In the exigencies of the property market this project was floated and refloated a number of times, but eventually Arlington withdrew. Some property off the north quays remains in CIÉ's possession and is used for off-street bus parking, awaiting a possible change of the official mind on the merits of the transportation centre argument. No change has occurred, and almost forty years after the idea of a central station for city buses seemed to appeal to everyone, Dublin has no such facility and appears unlikely to get one.

No such backwards look appeared in CIÉ's public statements as its fiftieth birthday approached. Of course, there were problems—an uncommercial debt level; inter and intra-union rivalries continued to 'demonstrate the desirability of streamlining trade union representation within the Group'; efforts to establish a code of practice with trade unions were 'of no avail'; the 1933 Road Passenger Acts remained unchanged, so that the regulatory system was wholly out of sync with practice in the market; and passenger and public liability claims fed by a new litigious surge in Irish society were causing worry.

But there was much to be positive about: increasing traffic and modern standards in equipment and facilities. Staff productivity had increased remarkably; staff numbers stood at 10,289 in 1993 compared to 12,831 in the split-up year of 1987 and 15,374 in 1983. Despite occasional alarms industrial relations had greatly improved and the more focused operations of the new subsidiaries helped in that improvement. Reliance on state grants was gradually diminishing: they had been reduced from £119 million in 1987 to £105 million in 1994, and over the same period they had fallen from 50 per cent to 33 per cent of CIÉ's revenues from all other sources. CIÉ had also managed to reduce its debt from £229 million in 1987 to £152 million in 1993. When Paul Conlon retired on 30 June 1994, he could use language which would have been impossible for his predecessors. His final Chairman's statement spoke of a 'visionary government approach towards the development of public transport'.

> The National Development Plan sets the stage. The levels of funding negotiated at European level will enhance public transport services and ensure that public assets are supported and modernised . . . The recommendations of the Dublin Transport Initiative (DTI) to better the transportation environment in Dublin are additionally welcome and have the full support of the CIÉ Board. £200 million has been earmarked for investment in public transport development in the Dublin area. (Annual Report, 1993)

Among the DTI's recommendations were further development of Quality Bus Corridors, extension of DART, new road development and traffic management measures, new park and ride facilities and the introduction of light rail transit (LRT) routes. It appeared at last that the Harcourt Street line would be restored to a transport use.

In July 1994 Mr Dermot O'Leary, a member of the CIÉ Board since 1989, was appointed to the post of non-executive Chairman. Dermot O'Leary, the founder of Crane Hire Ltd, a major plant supplier to the construction industry, was also a member of the Board of Aer Rianta and Chairman of Great Southern Hotels, an Aer Rianta subsidiary. At the same time, Noel

Kennedy, who was nearing retirement, was appointed on an interim basis, Acting Chief Executive of the CIÉ Group pending the appointment of a new Group Chief Executive. The position of Managing Director of Bus Éireann, vacated by Noel Kennedy, was filled by Donal Mangan, but in a reorganisation in April l995 Mangan became Chief Executive of Bus Átha Cliath and John Browne transferred to a similar post in Bus Éireann.

However much more substantial changes were in the offing. Government decided that the previous full-time executive nature of the Chairmanship of CIÉ should be restored. Michael Lowry, Minister for Transport, Energy and Communications since January 1995 in a new Fine Gael, Labour and Democratic Left coalition, announced that the government had agreed 'in the context of managing necessary change in public transport' to his proposals for a restructuring of CIÉ's top management, including the appointment of a new Executive Chairman of the Group. With effect from 25 April 1995, Eamon Walsh, recently retired from the post of Chief Executive of Hibernian Insurance and an accountant by profession, became Executive Chairman of the CIÉ Group. Dermot O'Leary, Chairman of CIÉ since July 1994, resigned and was thanked by the Minister for 'his efforts in starting the process of necessary change in CIÉ over the last nine months'.

The Government Information Services released a statement from Mr Lowry who said that CIÉ would receive over £1 billion from the exchequer and from the European Union over the next five years. Included in this amount was EU funding of over £600 million for the biggest ever mainline investment programme and the Dublin light rail project. The mandate of the new Executive Chairman would be to 'ensure that CIÉ's customers and the taxpayer would obtain the maximum return on these investments'.

Achievement of this objective required 'a multi-skilled top-quality management team' and the Minister said that 'the government is determined that CIÉ will have such a team. There is a need for new blood and expertise at top management level to be recruited from outside the Group so as to achieve a blending of internal and external skills.'

Accordingly, so the release continued, the first task of the new Executive Chairman would be to strengthen the existing management team by recruiting a 'Group Chief Executive (Operations Officer)' and senior executives in the following areas: project management, marketing and sales, financial and treasury, and human resources.

Mr Lowry put these decisions into context. 'The quality and cost of public transport is a major factor in determining the competitiveness of Irish industry and services. The government's drive for a substantial increase in permanent job creation must be underpinned by an Irish public transport sector, which at least matched, in quality and price terms, those of our competitors. The government's initiative, in providing very substantial financial resources for CIÉ and strengthening its top management, demonstrates its commitment to a strong public transport system.'

The release ended by saying that a 'new deal' was being announced 'for the Irish travelling public and other users of the public transport infrastructure' and that the Minister 'was confident that this would lead to a strong increase in public transport usage'.

Within two weeks on 3 May 1995 a Group Chief Executive was appointed — Michael McDonnell, an economist by training with an extensive transport background in the Department of Transport, Energy and Communications where he had served for several years after earlier being in the Department of Finance.

CIÉ's new Chairman and executive team will have new decisions to make and difficulties to encounter. CIÉ's past suggests that the new team with all their colleagues will overcome these difficulties and that it can carry the company and the Irish public through another fifty years. It is a prospect which would bring pleasure to the generations who served the company in the past, so that it in turn could serve to the best of its abilities an always demanding public.

APPENDIX 1

CIÉ — 50-YEAR OVERVIEW
(Based on data from CIÉ Annual Reports)

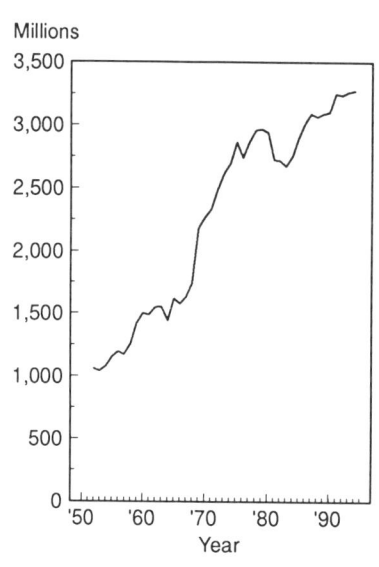

PASSENGER KILOMETRES
(Road and Rail)

FREIGHT TONNE KILOMETRES
(Road and Rail)

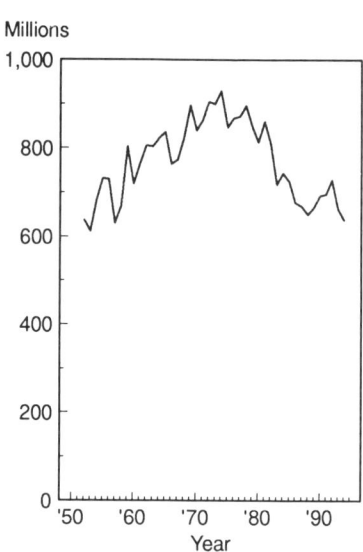

NUMBER OF EMPLOYEES

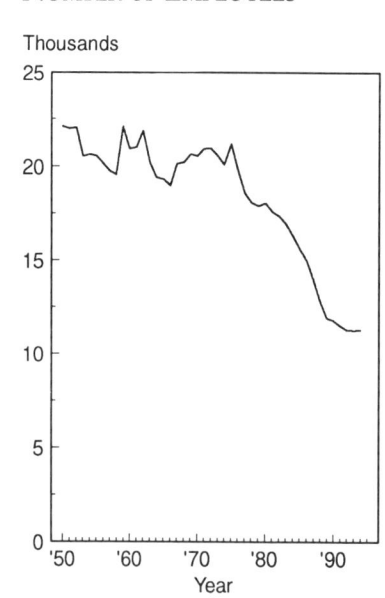

TRAFFIC UNITS PER EMPLOYEE

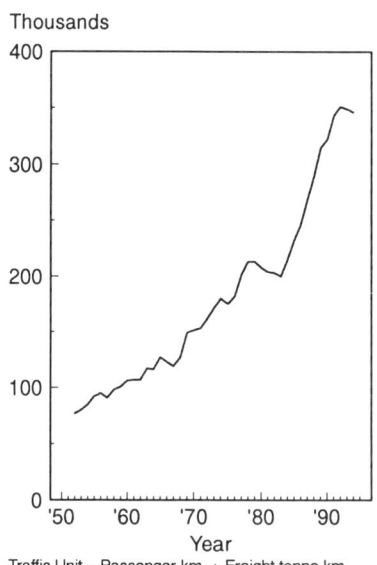

Traffic Unit = Passenger km. + Freight tonne km.

Appendixes

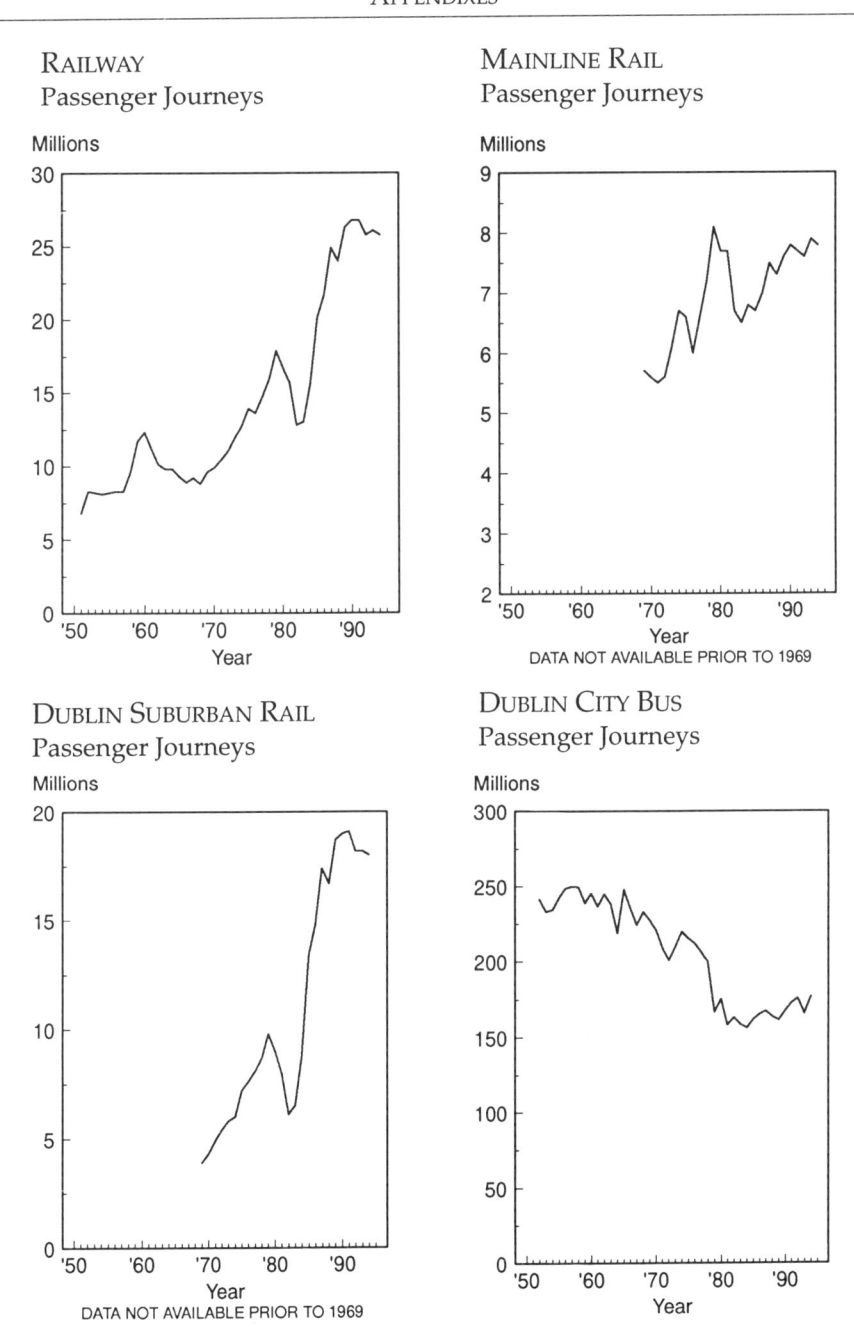

Railway
Passenger Journeys
Millions

Mainline Rail
Passenger Journeys
Millions

DATA NOT AVAILABLE PRIOR TO 1969

Dublin Suburban Rail
Passenger Journeys
Millions

DATA NOT AVAILABLE PRIOR TO 1969

Dublin City Bus
Passenger Journeys
Millions

'Dublin suburban rail' comprises DART, Balbriggan/Kilcoole and Maynooth line services.
'Mainline rail' comprises all other passenger services.

Appendixes

LONG DISTANCE BUS
Passenger Journeys

PROVINCIAL CITY BUS
Passenger Journeys

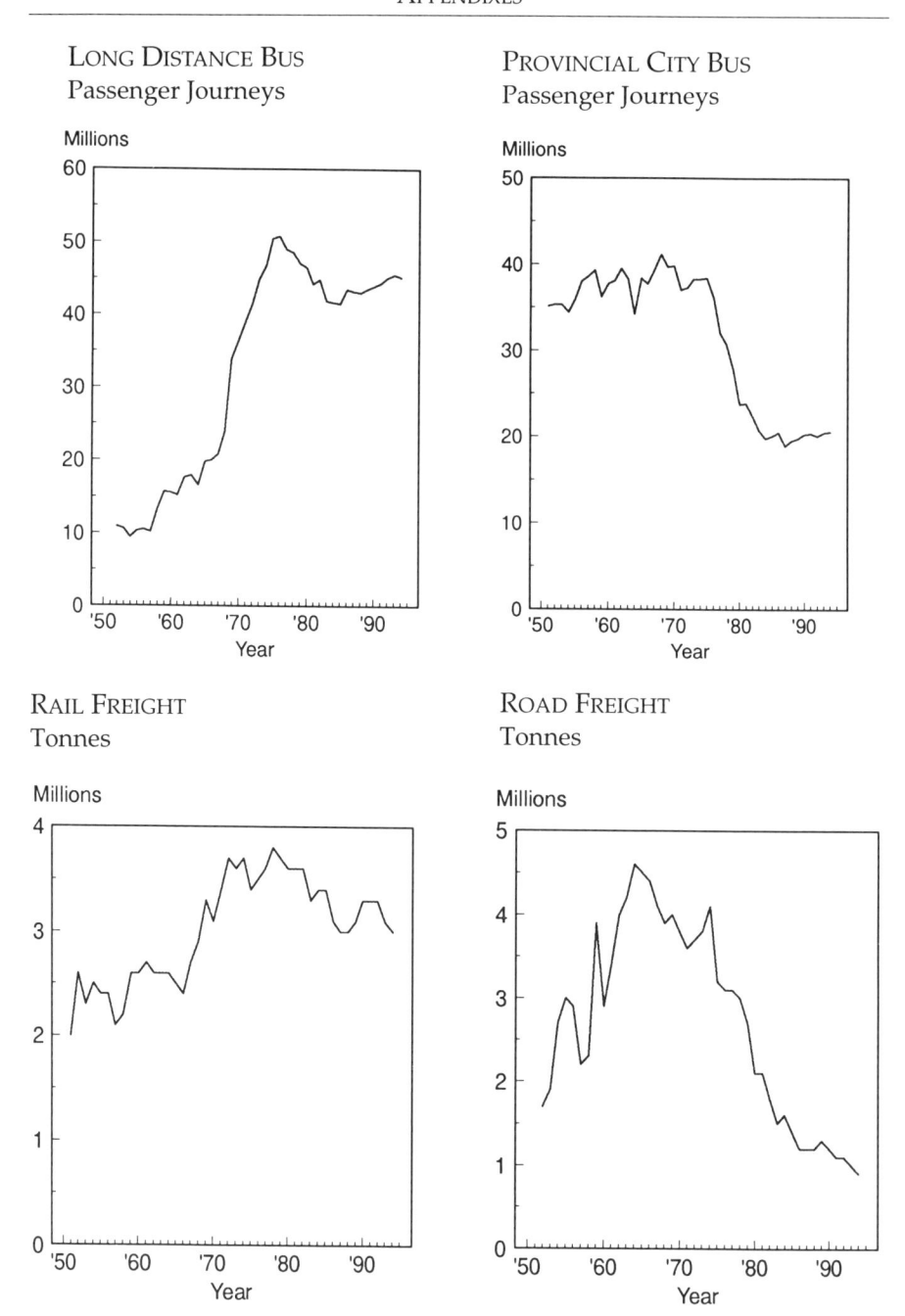

RAIL FREIGHT
Tonnes

ROAD FREIGHT
Tonnes

'Long distance bus' includes expressway and rural stage carriage services.
'Provincial city bus' comprises bus services in Cork, Limerick, Galway and Waterford.

APPENDIX 2

MINISTERS RESPONSIBLE FOR PUBLIC TRANSPORT SINCE FOUNDATION OF STATE

Name	Department	Time in Office
Joe McGrath	Industry and Commerce	Dec. 1922 – Mar. 1924
Paddy McGilligan	Industry and Commerce	Apr. 1924 – Mar. 1932
Seán Lemass	Industry and Commerce	Mar. 1932 – Sept. 1939
Seán MacEntee	Industry and Commerce	Sept. 1939 – Aug. 1941
Seán Lemass	Industry and Commerce	Aug. 1941 – Feb. 1948
Daniel Morrissey	Industry and Commerce	Feb. 1948 – June 1951
Seán Lemass	Industry and Commerce	June 1951 – June 1954
William Norton	Industry and Commerce	June 1954 – Mar. 1957
Seán Lemass	Industry and Commerce	Mar. 1957 – June 1959
Jack Lynch	Industry and Commerce	June 1959 – July 1959
Erskine Childers	Transport and Power	July 1959 – July 1969
Brian Lenihan	Transport and Power	July 1969 – Jan. 1973
Michael O'Kennedy	Transport and Power	Jan. 1973 – Mar. 1973
Peter Barry	Transport and Power	Mar. 1973 – Nov. 1976
Tom Fitzpatrick	Transport and Power	Dec. 1976 – July 1977
Padraig Faulkner	Tourism and Transport	July 1977 – Dec. 1979
George Colley	Tourism and Transport	Dec. 1979 – Jan. 1980
Albert Reynolds	Transport	Jan. 1980 – June 1981
Patrick Cooney	Transport	June 1981 – Mar. 1982
John Wilson	Transport	Mar. 1982 – Dec. 1982
Jim Mitchell	Transport and Communications	Dec. 1982 – Mar. 1987
John Wilson	Communications	Mar. 1987 – July 1989
Seamus Brennan	Tourism and Transport	July 1989 – Feb. 1992
Máire Geoghegan-Quinn	Tourism and Transport	Feb. 1992 – Jan. 1993
Brian Cowen	Transport, Energy and Communications	Jan. 1993 – Dec. 1994
Michael Lowry	Transport, Energy and Communications	Dec. 1994 –

APPENDIX 3

CHAIRMEN

A. P. Reynolds Jan. 1945 – Feb. 1949
T. C. Courtney Feb. 1949 – Aug. 1958
C. S. Andrews Sept. 1958 – Oct. 1966
T. P. Hogan Oct. 1966 – Dec. 1973
L. St J. Devlin Jan. 1974 – Dec. 1983
G. T. P. Conlon Jan. 1984 – June 1994
D. O'Leary July 1994 – Apr. 1995
E. F. Walsh Apr. 1995

APPENDIX 4

MEMBERS OF THE CIÉ BOARD

A. P. Reynolds* Jan. 1945 – Feb. 1949
J. Dwyer Jan. 1945 – Oct. 1947
H. A. Henry Jan. 1945 – Mar. 1945
C. D. Hewat Jan. 1945 – May 1950
J. McCann Jan. 1945 – May 1950
J. McMahon Jan. 1945 – Mar. 1945
W. E. Wylie KC (Vice Chairman) Jan. 1945 – May 1950
H. B. Pollock Mar. 1945 – May 1950
J. F. Costello Apr. 1945 – May 1950
T. C. Courtney* Feb. 1949 – Aug. 1961
J. Bruton June 1950 – Feb. 1955
D. L. Daly June 1950 – June 1957
P. J. Floyd June 1950 – Aug. 1958
E. H. Murphy June 1950 – Aug. 1958
W. Murphy June 1950 – Aug. 1958
J. T. O'Farrell June 1950 – Aug. 1967
L. Ferris June 1955 – Aug. 1972
T. P. Hogan* Aug. 1957 – Dec. 1973
C. S. Andrews* Sept. 1958 – Oct. 1966

W. McMullen Sept. 1958 – Aug. 1968
M. F. Molony Sept. 1958 – Aug. 1973
E. Cassidy Dec. 1961 – Aug. 1973
F. Lemass Oct. 1966 – June 1974
W. J. Fitzpatrick Sept. 1967 – Nov. 1980
J. Dunne Sept. 1968 – Jan. 1969
J. M. Cox Sept. 1969 – Apr. 1972
D. Larkin Sept. 1972 – Nov. 1980
M. Purcell Sept. 1972 – Aug. 1974 and Sept. 1977 – Aug. 1985
L. St J. Devlin* Jan. 1974 – Dec. 1983
E. Markey Mar. 1974 – Aug. 1977
J. A. Bristow May 1974 – Aug. 1978
B. Connaughton Aug. 1974 – Aug. 1979
E. Farrell Feb. 1975 – Aug. 1979
H. L. McKee Sept. 1978 – Aug. 1983
C. Faller Sept. 1979 – Aug. 1984
J. Keenan Sept. 1979 – Aug. 1984
J. A. Flynn† Dec. 1980 – Nov. 1986 and Mar. 1988 – Jan. 1989
J. McLoughlin† Dec. 1980 – Nov. 1989
R. O'Donovan† Dec. 1980 – Nov. 1983
T. A. Tobin† Dec. 1980 – Apr. 1991
J. F. Higgins Dec. 1980 – Nov. 1986
S. Linehan Dec. 1980 – Oct. 1984
L. O'Brien Dec. 1980 – July 1984
G. T. P. Conlon* Jan. 1984 – June 1994
M. Faherty† Dec. 1983 –
J. F. Meagher Feb. 1984 – Dec. 1993
A. Barry Oct. 1984 – May 1989
R. Burrows Oct. 1984 – July 1986
C. J. Collins Oct. 1984 – Aug. 1989
J. A. Mealy Oct. 1984 – Aug. 1989
J. McCullough Oct. 1986 – Oct. 1991
S. O'Connor Oct. 1986 – Oct. 1991
B. Byrne† Dec. 1986 – Dec. 1987

S. Harrington Jan. 1987 – Jan. 1992

J. J. Harrington Oct. 1989 – Oct. 1994

R. Kelleher Oct. 1989 – Oct. 1994

D. O'Leary* Oct. 1989 – Apr. 1995

S. Feely† Dec. 1989 –

F. Kenny† Dec. 1989 –

A. J. O'Brien† June 1991 –

J. M. Maguire Feb. 1992 –

C. Brennan Dec. 1992 –

K. Mulrooney Dec. 1992 –

T. Honan Nov. 1994 –

A. Coffey Nov. 1994 –

A. Rooney Dec. 1994 –

N. O'Callaghan Dec. 1994 –

E. F. Walsh* Apr. 1995 –

* Chairmen (see Appendix 3)
† Worker Director

APPENDIX 5

Directors of Bus Éireann
(up to 1 May 1995)

G. T. P. Conlon, Chairman Jan. 1987 – June 1994

J. J. Daly Jan. 1987 – Jan. 1993

N. Kennedy Jan. 1987 –

J. McLoughlin* Jan. 1987 – Nov. 1989

S. O'Connor Jan. 1987 – Jan. 1990

T. A. Tobin* Jan. 1987 – Apr. 1991

S. Feely* Dec. 1989 –

J. J. Harrington Jan. 1990 –

A. J. O'Brien* July 1991 –

D. O'Leary Jan. 1993 – Chairman July 1994 – Apr. 1995

D. Mangan July 1994 –

* Worker Director

APPENDIX 6

DIRECTORS OF BUS ÁTHA CLIATH
(up to 1 May 1995)

G. T. P. Conlon, Chairman Jan. 1987 – June 1994
J. Browne Jan. 1987 – Jan. 1993
M. Faherty* Jan. 1987 –
J. A. Flynn* Jan. 1987 – Nov. 1989
S. Harrington Jan. 1987 – Jan. 1993
J. Hynes Jan. 1987 – Aug. 1990
R. Kelleher Jan. 1993 –
F. Kenny* Dec. 1989 –
J. M. Maguire Jan. 1993 –
R. Montgomery Feb. 1991 – Oct. 1994
D. O'Leary, Chairman July 1994 – Apr. 1995

* Worker Director

APPENDIX 7

DIRECTORS OF IARNROD ÉIREANN
(up to 1 May 1995)

G. T. P. Conlon, Chairman Jan. 1987 – June 1994
E. J. O'Connor Jan. 1987 – July 1990
J. J. Daly Jan. 1987 – Jan. 1993
J. McCullough Jan. 1987 –
J. McLoughlin* Jan. 1987 – Nov. 1989
T. A. Tobin* Jan. 1987 – Apr. 1991
S. Feely* Dec. 1989 –
C. D. Waters Sept. 1990 –
A. J. O'Brien* July 1991 –
J. J. Harrington Jan. 1993 –
D. O'Leary, Chairman July 1994 – Apr. 1995

* Worker Director

APPENDIX 8

MEMBERS OF GROUP EXECUTIVE BOARD
(up to 1 May 1995)

G. T. P. Conlon, Chief Executive Feb. 1987 – June 1994
J. J. Daly Feb. 1987 –
B. P. Dowling Feb. 1987 –
C. Finegan Feb. 1987 – July 1989
M. Grace Feb. 1987 –
J. Hynes Feb. 1987 – Aug. 1990
N. Kennedy Feb. 1987 – Apr. 1995
C. Mac Giolla Rí Feb. 1987 –
E. J. O'Connor Feb. 1987 – July 1990
J. Browne Sept. 1990 – Feb. 1991; Oct. 1994 –
C. D. Waters Sept. 1990 –
R. Montgomery Feb. 1991 – Oct. 1994

Select Bibliography

REPORTS CONCERNING CIÉ AND VARIOUS TRANSPORT ISSUES
1922: Railway Commission
1939: Committee of Inquiry into Internal Transport (Ingram Report)
1944: Committee of Inquiry into dealings in GSR stocks
1945: Annual Reports of Córas Iompair Éireann
1948: Transport in Ireland (Milne Report)
1956: Submission of the Board of CIÉ to Beddy Committee
1957: Committee of Inquiry into Internal Transport (Beddy Report)
1963: Pacemaker: CIÉ report on internal public transport
1964: The Morale of Dublin Busmen: Tavistock Institute
1966: The Dublin Region—An Advisory Regional Plan and Final Report (Myles Wright)
1967: A Plan for Dublin Bus Services (Schaechterle)
1970: Dublin Transportation Study: An Foras Forbartha
1971: Defining the Role of Public Transport in a Changing Environment: McKinsey International
1971: Dublin Suburban Rail Study: De Leuw Chadwick Ó hEocha
1972: Railplan 80—a plan to modernise the rail system by 1980: CIÉ taskforce
1973: Dublin Rapid Rail Transport Study: CIÉ Consultants
1972/3: National Prices Commission Occasional Papers, Nos 4, 8 and 10
1975: Road Freight Transport Study 1973–74: Confederation of Irish Industry
1977: National Development Plan 1977–1980: Government of Ireland
1979: Joint Oireachtas Committee on State Sponsored Bodies, Fourth Report, Córas Iompair Éireann
1979: Transport Policy: NESC No. 48: (Foster Report)
1980: Passenger Transport Services in the Dublin Area: Transport Consultative Commission
1980: The Transport Challenge—the opportunities in the 1980s: McKinsey International
1981: Road Haulage in Ireland: Transport Consultative Commission
1984: Building on Reality 1985–1987: Government of Ireland
1985: Green Paper on Transport Policy: Government of Ireland
1988: Programme for National Recovery: Government of Ireland
1990: Operational Programme on Peripherality: Government of Ireland
1993: National Development Plan 1994–1999: Government of Ireland

PUBLISHED BOOKS
C. S. Andrews, *Man of No Property*, Dublin 1982.

Select Bibliography

Michael H. C. Baker, *Irish Railways since 1916*, London 1972.
Sean D. Barrett, *Transport Policy in Ireland*, Dublin 1982.
Peter Clarke, *Royal Canal—The Full Story*, Dublin 1992.
J. C. Conroy, *History of Irish Railways*, Dublin 1928.
Colm Creedon, *The Cork, Bandon and South Coast Railway: The Final Farewell*, Cork 1991.
Gerard D'Arcy, *Portrait of the Grand Canal*, Dublin 1969.
Oliver Doyle and Stephen Hirsch, *Railways in Ireland 1834–1984*, Dublin 1984.
Tony Farmar, *A History of Craig Gardner*, Dublin 1988.
Tom Ferris, *Irish Railways in Colour*, Dublin 1992.
J. Ingram, Transport and Communications, in *Saorstát Éireann—Official Handbook*, Dublin 1932.
Institute of Public Administration, *Ireland—The past twenty years 1967–1986*, Dublin 1987.
J. J. Lee, *Ireland 1912–1985*, Cambridge 1987.
C. Mac an tSaoir and P. J. Flanagan, *Dublin Buses*, Dublin 1968.
Jack McQuillan, *The Railway Town—The Story of the Great Northern Railway Works and Dundalk*, Dundalk 1993.
James F. Meenan, *The Irish Economy since 1922*, Liverpool 1970.
Fergus Mulligan, *150 Years of Irish Railways*, Belfast 1983.
J. W. P. Rowledge, *The Turf Burner*, Dublin 1972.
Patrick Taylor, *The West Clare Railway*, Brighton 1994.

Published Directories
O. Doyle and S. Hirsch, *Locomotives and Rolling Stock of Córas Iompair Éireann and Northern Ireland Railways*, Dublin 1979.
Peter Jones, *Irish Railways Traction and Travel*, Baildon 1987.
H. Richards and B. Pender, *Irish Railways Today*, Dublin 1967.

Pamphlets etc. published by CIÉ
1947: Can we Afford Branchlines?
1970: Córas Iompair Éireann 1964–1969 (statistical review)
1975: The Dublin Transport System
1975: Devlin, Liam St J., CIÉ and the Future
1977: Devlin, Liam St J., CIÉ The Way Ahead—a review of progress
1978: Higgins, John F., The Railway—progress and objectives
1979: Higgins, John F., Railways in Ireland
1980: Higgins, John F., Transport in Ireland—past, present and future
1981: Facts about CIÉ
1982: CIÉ response to Transport Policy in Ireland by Sean D. Barrett
1984: Higgins, John F., Public transport in the Dublin Conurbation
1985: Conlon, G. T. Paul, Winning Against the Odds

1986: Higgins, John F., Railway Policy—on the right rails?
1986: C. Finegan and B. Ó Cinnéide, DART—A Case Study in Transport Marketing

NEWSPAPERS AND JOURNALS
Files of *The Irish Times, Irish Press, Irish Independent, Cork Examiner* and occasional other newspapers as mentioned in text
Journal of The Irish Railway Record Society
Administration, special issue on Córas Iompair Éireann, Winter 1968
Forum, October 1964
Nuacht CIÉ, 1960–
Irish Times Supplements on Bus Éireann (January 1993) and Iarnród Éireann (June 1993)
Engineering in CIÉ, supplement to *The Engineers Journal*, January 1984
Various issues of *Modern Transport* as identified in text
Scrapbooks of newspaper and magazine cuttings lent by Donal V. Stephens

OTHER SOURCES
Dáil Éireann: *Parliamentary Debates, Official Reports*; 1924–
CIÉ Board Minutes, 1944–
National Archives, e.g. 1955/56 papers about CIÉ cash shortage and attempt to postpone payment to suppliers of diesel locos at request of the Department of Finance
Various papers from files of the Chartered Institute of Transport in Ireland, e.g. by Paul Conlon (CIÉ—a new beginning, 1984), David Waters and Donal Mangan
International Railway Congress papers, 1964
The Irish International Road Haulage Industry, CITI 1987

STATISTICS
Inflation statistics (CPI) obtained from the Central Bank of Ireland
Motor registrations statistics obtained from statistical abstracts
Bus and rail fare price indices obtained from the CSO

Index

Administration, 216
advertising, 432
AEC, 40, 73, 74
Aer Lingus, 82, 157, 172, 232
Aer Rianta, 157, 303
Aerlód, 200, 262, 303–4
Agricultural Credit Corporation, 153
Agriculture, Department of, 84
Alexander's of Belfast, 421, 426, 430
Algeo, Sir Arthur, 171–2
Allison transmission, 326, 328, 329
Allport Commission, 9
Amalgamated Society of Locomotive Engineers and Firemen (ASLEF), 111
American Motors General Corporation, 328
Amiens Street station, 25, 141
  extensions, 233
  level crossing monitoring, 379
  parcel post, 254
  refurbishment, 143–4
  renamed 'Connolly', 205
Andersen, Arthur, 385
Andrews, C. S. (Todd), 60, 165, 182, 200, 216, 231, 260, 268, 372, 436
  becomes Chairman, 137–40, 141–2
  branch closures, 150–54, 158–9
  canals, 169–70
  on Childers, 197–8
  criticised in Dáil, 189–90
  five-year plan, 146–50
  hotels, 170–72
  industrial relations, 172–81, 203
  IPA speech, 184–5
  management, 144–6
  OPO, 398
  retires from CIÉ, 206–7
  staff amenities, 232
  staff friction, 267
  stations renamed, 205
Andrews, Eamonn, 206
Andrews, Mary, 172
Antrim, County, 43
Aran Islands, 85–6, 149, 217, 417
Áras Éanna, Dublin, 146
Archdale, Mr, 10
Arigna colliery, 16
Arlington Securities, 434
Arrow service, 414
Arts Council, 170–71
Asahi factory, 306
Atlantean double-deckers, 210–11
Automatic Vehicle Monitoring (AVM), 321–2

B + I, 157, 418
Babington, Sir Anthony, 98
Baker, Michael H. C., 43–4, 157
Ballinacourty, Co. Waterford, 358
Bank of Ireland, 93
bank strike, 203
Banteer–Newmarket line, 81
baronial guarantees, 16, 19
Barrett, Dr Seán, 192, 230–31, 233, 238, 357–8
Barrett, Sylvester, 260, 278–9, 280
Barrow navigation, 83, 110, 124, 139, 168
Barrow viaduct, 277, 279
Barry, Peter, 256, 278, 279, 281, 303
  appoints Devlin, 250
  becomes minister, 240
  canals, 170
  investment programme, 252–3
  road haulage bill, 308–9
  Transport (No. 2) Bill 1974, 259–60
BART, San Francisco, 396
Bastow Charleton, 424
Bayside station, 249

INDEX

Beddy, Dr J. P., 21, 80, 98, 101–2, 121. *see also* Beddy Report
Beddy Report, 73, 77, 80, 81, 88, 101–25, 159, 163, 192, 225
  assessment of, 118–25
  canals in, 138–9
  CIÉ submission, 92, 102–10
  committee established, 95, 182
  cuts recommended, 162, 186, 226
  on finances, 115–16, 122–5
  geographic aspects, 110–11
  railways in, 113–18
  responses to, 126–30
  road freight in, 85, 135
  Rosslare Harbour, 304
Bedford Company, 325
Beeching, Dr, 183
Beere, Thekla, 90–91, 197
Belfast, 172, 212, 251, 298–9, 416
Belfast & Ballymena Railway, 2
Belfast & County Down Railway, 2
Belfast & Northern Counties Railway, 77
Belfast–Cork service, 69
Belfast–Dublin line, 245
  disruption, 355–6
  number of trains, 247
Bentinck, Lord George, 6
Birdhill–Killaloe line, 80
Birmingham Railway Carriage and Wagon Company, 75
Blanchardstown, 319, 426
Blennerhasset, Mr, 8–9
Board, 45–7, 206, 294, 295, 394
  in 1944 Bill, 30
  under Andrews, 138–9
  and Beddy Committee, 102–10, 128
  concordat proposed, 339
  Corporate Aims, 262–3
  and deficit, 337–9
  duties of, 68–9
  early concerns of, 38–41
  five-year plan, 146–50

  government-appointed, 64
  industrial relations, 112–13, 201–2
  locomotives, 271–2
  in Milne Report, 54–5
  new Executive Board, 259, 260–66
  new subvention formula, 1983, 368–70
  and OIÉ, 299–300
  restructuring, 385
  'Resuscitation' report, 74–5
  school transport charges, 365–6
  and Transport department, 289–94
  worker directors, 316, 345
Board of Trade, 6
Board of Works, 1, 40, 170, 290
bomb scares, 249, 355–6
Bombardier, 328–31, 351, 420–21
Booterstown station, 249
Booth, Lionel, 164
Bórd Fáilte, 141
Bord na Móna, 30, 137–9, 144, 157, 172, 174
Brady, Gerard, 364
Brady, Kerry, 179
branch lines, 41–3, 64, 73, 118, 149, 190, 191, 217, 404
  abandonment orders, 152–4
  in Beddy Report, 119–22
  closures, 20–22, 35
  closures, 1963, 161–2
  closures, 1970s, 269, 276–80
  Cork controversy, 155–61
  'Exemption Orders', 80–81, 121
  GNR closures, 98–9
  Harcourt Street closure, 150–54
  Limerick–Claremorris, 276
  in Milne Report, 48, 51–2, 56–7, 61
  pamphlet on, 50–51
  and Transport Tribunal, 79–81
Bray, Co. Wicklow, 4, 6, 205
Bredin, C. E., 38
BREL, 204, 245, 371–2, 406
Brennan, Seamus, 362, 363–4, 386, 412, 413, 417, 423–4

Bretland, Arthur W., 281
British Rail, 183, 204, 245, 304, 305, 358, 406, 409
Broadstone station, 141, 245, 433
Broadstone works, 24, 53–4, 62, 67
Browne, John, 398, 399, 401
Browne, Noel, 128, 178–9, 189–90
Bruton, Richard, 388
Buchanan, Colin, 428
Buchanan Report, 319
Buckley, Lily, 214, 215
Building on Reality, 375–7, 407, 408
Bulleid, O. V. S., 62, 75, 77, 162
Bus Átha Cliath, 401, 402, 419, 424–31
  established, 385
  finances, 426–7
  maintenance, 430
  market research, 428–9
  name, 396
  types of bus, 430
bus-building, 268, 285, 324–32, 370, 420–21
Bus Éireann, 83, 318, 401, 402, 418–24, 431, 436
  Board, 395
  established, 385
  finances, 418, 419
  market research, 419–20
  name, 396
  school transport, 421–4
  types of bus, 421
bus lanes, 232–3, 323–4, 429–30
Bus Scoile, 214
bus services, 18–20, 23, 81–3, 106, 112–13, 128–9, 317–18, 363, 374. *see also* Bus Éireann; Dublin City Services; one-person operation
  driver/conductor relationships, 210–11
  heating, 83
  improvements, 167–8
  industrial relations, 174–81
  investment in, 70
  management of, 145–6
  in McKinsey 2, 349
  mobile radios, 320–21
  'musak', 322
  in Pacemaker report, 193
  passenger numbers, 168, 311
  police protection, 249
  private, 261, 263, 318, 420, 421
  radio control, 209
  strike, 1962, 185
  types of bus, 210–11, 325–6
bus shelters, 322
bus stops, 426, 429
Busáras, 44, 63, 66, 72, 97, 141, 179
  in Milne Report, 53, 61
  opened, 82
Business and Finance, 237, 280
busways, 364
Buttevant accident, 344–5, 353
Byrne, Alfie, 63
Byrne, Hugh, 279
Byrne, John, 233, 242, 249, 251, 257, 271, 327
  resignation, 267–8
Byrne, Patrick, 129

canals, 25, 38–9, 49–50, 80, 83–4, 222, 262, 290, 303, 384
  in Beddy Report, 138–9
  CIÉ responsibility ends, 168–70
  CIÉ submission on, 110
  list of depots, 168
Canals Act 1986, 387, 391–2
Cape Clear Island, Co. Cork, 86
Carndonagh Extension Railway, 7
Carroll, John, 230
Carse, B., 247–8
Casey, Seán, 157, 197
Castlecomer colliery, 16
catamaran, 417
Cavan, County, 7, 97, 153, 317
Central Bus Station, 53, 61, 63, 66, 72, 97, 141, 179
  opened, 82

Central Highways Authority
  proposed, 48–9, 60, 107
  rejected, 64–5
Central Sorting Office, 254
Central Statistics Office, 308
CERT, 302, 384
Channel Tunnel, 249, 432
Chartered Institute of Transport, 306, 342, 380, 419
Cherryville Junction accident, 371
Childers, Erskine, 163–4, 190, 203, 233, 240, 267, 281, 310, 359, 393, 397
  becomes minister, 157–8
  canals, 170
  cross-border electricity, 299
  debate on finances, 1969, 219–21
  five-year plan, 183–4
  hotels, 171
  minister of P & T, 207
  traffic problems, 210
  Transport Act 1963, 186–7
  Transport Act 1964, 196–8, 199
  transport policy, 188, 194–5
Chubb, Basil, 178
CIÉ Consult, 401, 432
CIÉ Group, 374–7, 385, 402, 426–7, 431–6
CIÉ Outdoor Advertising, 401
CIÉ Tours International, 401, 419, 431–2
City Imp, 428–9, 430
City of Dublin Junction Railways Company, 8
Cityswift, 429–30
Civil War, 14
Clancy, Basil, 83
Clann na Poblachta, 44–5, 56
Clann na Talmhan, 28, 36, 45
Clara–Banagher line, 81
Clare, County, 161
Clarke, Peter, 169
clearways, 209, 324
Clondalkin, 319
Clontarf garage, 425
Clough Bridge accident, 274–5

Cóbh, 70, 410, 433
Colley, George, 212, 334, 342
Colley, Harry, 63
colour schemes, 167
Comhlucht Siúicre Éireann, 168, 277–9, 405
Committee of Inquiry into Public Transport. *see* Beddy Report
Commuter Advertising Network (CAN), 432
Companies Act 1986, 402
Companies (Amendment) Act 1983, 426
Confederation of Irish Industries, 235, 295, 308
Conlon, G. T. Paul, 372–5, 384, 402, 403, 435
  industrial relations, 384–5
  OPO, 397
Connolly, James, 205
Connolly station, 205, 233, 245, 433. *see also* Amiens Street station
  level crossing monitoring, 379
  parcel post, 254
Conroy, John, 175
consultants, 145
Consumer Price Index, 218, 234, 266, 333, 334
Consumers' Association, 241
containerisation, 147, 148
Containerway, 148
Continental Freight Services, 262
continuous welded rail (CWR), 281–2, 379
Coogan, Tim Pat, 89
Cooney, Patrick, 330, 349
Córas Iompair Éireann (CIÉ), 24, 41–2, 157. *see also* Board; CIÉ Group
  Administration special issue, 216
  area management, 145–6, 258–9
  assets of, 38–9
  Beddy Report, 101–28
  capital structure, 122–3
  'common carrier' obligations, 115, 124–5

Córas Iompair Éireann *contd*
  Corporate Aims, 262–3, 280
  criticisms of, 294–5
  cross subsidisation, 393–4
  debate on establishment of, 27, 28–37
  finances. *see* Finances
  holding company. *see* CIÉ Group
  'image' of, 149–50
  management structure, 258–9, 264–5
  McKinsey Report, 224–9
  McKinsey Report 2, 346–52
  Milne Report, 47–63
  mission statement, 373–4
  nationalisation, 64–7
  NPC fares study, 235–41
  Pacemaker study, 187–98
  papal visit, 340–41
  policies, 1975, 263–4
  property, 154, 262, 401, 432–5
  railway study, 288–9
  reorganisation bill, 392–7
  shareholders, 41–2
  social role, 227, 295, 363, 364, 366–7, 373
Cork, 145, 163, 177, 205, 247, 309, 410
  bus terminal, 168
  buses, 317
  commuter service, 414
  Cork–Belfast service, 69
  Cork–Macroom line, 80
Cork, Bandon & South Coast Railway, 16, 60
Cork, County, 7, 43, 161, 190, 191, 221
  Bandon line closure, 155–61
  Skibbereen–Schull line, 80
Cork Dockyard Company, 86
Cork Examiner, 127, 128, 159, 191
Corry, Martin, 190
Cosgrave, Liam, 80, 97, 163–4, 309
Cosgrave, W. T., 15, 16, 31
Costello, John A., 63
Counterpart Fund, 146
County Donegal Railways Joint Committee, 7, 39, 102
Courtney, T. C., 60, 62, 68, 111, 206
  and Department of Finance, 91–3
  first report, 72–3
  resignation, 137, 138
Cowan, Peadar, 66
Cowen, Brian, 364, 413
Craig, William, 171–2
Craig Gardner, 41–2, 385
Cravens Ltd, 204
Crawford, Leo, 176
Creedon, Colm, 159–61
cross-channel transport, 303, 318
Crossley Bros Ltd, 76, 203–4
Cú Uladh, 179
Cuffe, P., 379
Cumann na nGaedheal, 19
Cummins engines, 325, 326, 329, 414

Dáil Éireann, 183–4, 269, 373, 380
  branch closures, 156–8
  canals, 391
  CIÉ finances, 189–90, 219–21, 362–4, 370
  CIÉ reorganisation, 392–7
  DART system, 295–6, 343–4
  DTA bill, 387–9
  Dublin transport, 323–4
  industrial relations, 178–9
  NESC report, 342–3
  road haulage, 308–9, 392
  rolling stock, 286–7
  school transport, 364–6, 422–3
  Transport Act 1950, 64–7
  Transport Act 1963, 186–7
  Transport Act 1964, 195–8
  Transport Bill 1944, 28–36
  Transport Bill 1958, 132, 134–6
  Transport (No. 2) Bill 1974, 259–60
Dalkey accident, 342
Dalkey tram, 63
Daly, Joe, 402
Darby, Tom, 362

Dargan, William, 1–3
Darmody, P. J., 255–6
DART, 205, 285, 288, 341, 387, 394, 403, 410, 414, 435
  approval, 290, 292, 296–7, 337
  costs, 343–4, 402, 403
  Dáil questions, 295–6, 343–4
  feeder buses, 382–3, 398, 399
  name, 396
  opened, 378–83
  passenger numbers, 382, 386
  preparatory studies, 243, 248–9, 268, 281, 332
  subvention, 369–70, 376–7
De Leuw, Chadwick and Ó hEocha, 248, 249
de Valera, Éamon, 28, 35, 36, 44–5, 157, 160
de Valera, Major Vivion, 183–4
Deasy, Austin, 286–7, 343, 353
decimalisation, 239
Defence, Department of, 341
Defence, Ministry of, 421
Deloitte, William, 41
Deloitte and Touche, 423, 424
Dempsey, J. F., 102
Derry, 317
Desmond, Barry, 286–7
Desmond, Daniel, 136
Deutz locomotives, 81
Devereux, Matt, 264
Devlin, Liam St J., 250–51, 269–70, 278
  bus fleet, 326, 328–9
  coach-building, 284–5, 352–3
  deficits, 334–5, 337–40, 356–7, 358–9
  hotels, 299, 300–302
  industrial relations, 312, 313, 316
  management reorganisation, 264–5
  management style, 267
  McKinsey 2, 350–51
  new locomotives, 272–3
  new subvention formula, 366–8
  'peanuts speech', 266
  Railway Development Plan, 254–6, 258–9, 260–62, 280–84
  retirement, 372
  road freight, 306, 308
  Rosslare Harbour, 304–5
  school transport charges, 365–6
  staff reductions, 371
  and Transport department, 289–94
Dictaphones, 143–4
Dillon, James, 36, 45
Dockrell, Maurice, 30
Donegal, County, 4, 7, 43, 97, 99
Donegal Railway, 7
Donegan, Paddy, 309
Donnybrook garage, 83, 313
Dowling, Brian, 433
Downing Street declaration, 356
Drogheda, Co. Louth, 205, 340, 386, 410
Drumm, Professor James, 24
Drumm battery trains, 24, 43, 70
Drummond, Thomas, 1, 3–6
Dubel, 416
Dublin
  car bombs, 313
  CIÉ properties, 432–5
  GNR services, 97
  growth, 83–4
  Harcourt St closure, 150–54
  papal visit, 340
  population, 209, 320, 425
  traffic problems, 195, 207, 208–11, 232–3, 295–6, 318–22, 323–4, 425
  trams, 23, 63
Dublin & Blessington Steam Tramways, 16
Dublin & Bray Railway, 150
Dublin, Dundrum & Rathfarnham Railway Company, 150
Dublin & Kingstown Railway Company, 2
Dublin & Lucan Railway, 16
Dublin & South Eastern Railway, 15–16
Dublin & Wicklow Railway, 2, 150

Dublin Airport, 82, 220, 416
Dublin–Belfast line, 100, 162
  sabotage, 206
  upgrading, 411–12
Dublin Bus. *see* Bus Átha Cliath
Dublin Chamber of Commerce, 146, 150
Dublin City Services, 32, 129, 216, 232–3, 254, 311–16, 318–24, 370, 374. *see also* Dublin Bus
  central terminal proposed, 209–10
  cross-subsidies, 238
  growth, 386
  losses, 222–3
  OPO strike, 177
  in Pacemaker report, 193
  working conditions, 217
Dublin City Transportation Centre, 433–5
Dublin/Cork line commuter service, 414
Dublin Corporation, 169–70, 210, 232–3, 249, 318–19, 323–4, 387
  wayleaves, 34
Dublin County Council, 151
Dublin–Greystones line, 163
Dublin International Exhibition, 1853, 2
Dublin–Kingstown railway, 1–2
Dublin Opinion, 36
Dublin Port, 74, 148, 271–2
Dublin Rapid Rail Transit Study (DRRTS), 285, 332, 344, 410, 433
Dublin suburban railways, 105–6, 163, 194–5, 219, 272, 406. *see also* DART
  losses, 226, 227–8
  in McKinsey Report, 238
  pressure on, 233
  rolling stock, 410–11
Dublin Transport Authority, 323–4, 337, 343, 359, 368, 376, 377, 384, 392
  legislation for, 387–9
  in McKinsey 2, 346
Dublin Transportation Centre, 332
Dublin Transportation Study, 233, 248, 285, 320, 323–4, 332, 383, 433

Dublin United Tramways Company (DUTC), 18, 20, 176
Dublin United Tramways (Omnibus Services) Act 1927, 18
Dublin United Transport Company (DUTC), 23–4, 29, 38, 40–41, 133, 285, 425
  GSR merger, 29–33, 123
Dún Aengus, 85–6, 87, 417
Dún Laoghaire, 2, 205, 272, 298, 303
Dundalk, Co. Louth, 205, 386
Dundalk, Newry & Greenore Railway, 39
Dundalk Engineering Company, 99–100, 133
Dundalk works, 96, 99–100
Dunne, Seán, 190
Dyer, Dr, 39

Eagle Lodge, 39
Eason's, 40
Easter Rising commemoration, 204–6
Economic Planning and Development, Department of, 336, 337
economic policy, 292–3, 331, 359, 360–61, 387, 413
  Economic Development, 171
  First Programme for Economic Expansion, 130
  inflation, 73, 163, 185–6, 211, 221–2, 232, 266–7, 333, 345, 357
  recession, 1950s, 89–90
Economic War, 20
Economists' Advisory Group (EAG), 236, 238
Education, Department of, 212, 213, 215, 224, 278, 364, 421–4
Electrical Trades Union, 174
Electricity Supply Board (ESB), 24, 30, 32, 108, 157, 172, 202, 203, 232
Emergency Powers Act 1976, 309
Emergency Powers Order, 1942, 23
Employer Labour Conference, 235, 322, 398

Energy, Department of, 342
Engineers Journal, 281, 282
English Steel Corporation, 76
Ennis, Co. Clare, 7
Enniskillen, Co. Fermanagh, 317
Enterprise Express, 69
Environment, Department of the, 233, 323, 324, 337, 342, 387
European Community (EEC and EC), 229, 230, 259–60, 261, 268, 375, 411–12, 417, 420, 434
  Structural Funds, 413
European Parliament, 296, 337
European Regional Development Fund, 381
European Union (EU). *see* European Community
Eurotunnel, 432
Evening Press, 152, 360–61
Ewart Biggs, Christopher, 309
Expressway, 179, 317–18, 386, 401, 419–21
External Relations Act, 67

Fairview depot, 379
fares, 18, 128–9, 207, 249–50, 280, 311
  decimalisation, 239
  discounting, 352
  Dublin buses, 291–2
  freeze, 357, 358
  government intervention, 211
  increases, 44, 185, 217–18, 220, 222–3, 224
  increases, 1951, 73; 1974, 254; 1983, 360–61
  in Milne Report, 48
  NPC study, 234–41
  reduced, 42
  reduced, 1975, 266–7
Farmar, Tony, 41–2
Fastrack, 254
Faulkner, Brian, 299
Faulkner, Pádraig, 170, 290–96, 332, 341

CIÉ deficit, 334–5, 337–9, 345
Road Transport bill, 309–10
Federation of Irish Manufacturers, 127
Federation of Trade Associations, 235
Fermanagh, County, 99
ferry services, 148
Fianna Fáil, 44, 61, 71–2, 89, 161, 240, 292–3, 349, 354, 357, 359, 403
  coalition, 412–13
  line closures, 278–9
  subvention shortfall, 360, 361
  Transport Bill, 1944, 28–36
  transport policy, 19, 26, 27, 295, 308–9, 330
Field, William, 9–10
Finance, Department of, 224, 240, 292, 331, 336
  CIÉ accounts, 89–95, 123
  CIÉ finances, 30, 64, 107, 271, 272, 289, 300, 337
  school transport, 424
finances, 69, 107, 114, 130, 163, 409. *see also* subvention
  accounts, 41–2, 386
  in Beddy Report, 115–16, 122–5
  capital, 30
  crisis, 1947, 45–7
  Dáil debates, 188–91
  deficits, 73, 360–61
    1969, 211
    1940s, 42–3
    1970s, 237–8, 289
    1980s, 345, 356, 358–9
  and Department of Finance, 89–95
  effects of 1958 Act, 182–6
  effects of inflation, 333–7
  financial year changed, 259
  grants, 1951, 71–2
  in Milne Report, 49
  railway investment, 70–71, 253–5
  road freight, 307
  sinking fund, 183
  subsidiaries, 401–2

finances *contd*
  Transport Act 1958, 133–5
  Transport Act 1964, 199–200
  Transport Bill 1950, 65–7
Fine Gael, 36, 135, 190, 254, 330, 403
  branch closures, 278–9
  Building on Reality, 375–7
  coalitions, 240, 349–50, 354, 359
  committee on state-sponsored bodies, 315
  financial rectitude, 360–61
  Inter-party Government, 45
  railway safety, 286–7
  Tallaght Strategy, 410
  transport policy, 31, 221, 267, 310, 393
Finglas, 426
Finn Valley Railway, 7
Fishguard & Rosslare Railways & Harbours Company, 16, 38, 304
Fishguard Harbour, 124, 304, 305
FitzGerald, Garret, 188–9, 190, 220, 378, 382–3
Fitzpatrick, P. J., 170
Fitzpatrick, T. J., 278–9, 296
Flanagan, Oliver, 161, 190
foot and mouth disease, 219
Foras Forbartha, An, 233, 248, 249, 285
Forum, 320–21
Foster, Professor Christopher D., 336–7, 343
Frank Sherwin Bridge, 324
free transport (pensioners), 216, 229
Freeman's Journal, 7
freight transport, 70, 84. *see also* rail freight; road freight
  improvements, 1960s, 164–6
French, Percy, 156, 157
Fry, C. L., 141
fuel supplies, 43–4, 70, 76, 81, 94

Gahan, Eoin, 383
Galway, 6, 14–15, 145, 163, 205, 245, 247, 340
  buses, 317

Galway/London bus service, 318
  road haulage, 309
Galway Bay Steamship Company, 85–6
Garda Síochána, 232–3, 314, 323, 324, 340–41, 387
General Automotive Corporation (GAC), 328, 331, 377, 420
General Motors, 162, 204, 271, 325, 326, 328, 329, 413, 416
General Omnibus Company, 23
Geoghegan-Quinn, Máire, 413, 417
Gladstone, William, 7, 8, 10
Glanmire station, Cork, 83
Glentoran, Lord, 99
Gordon Hotels Limited, 87
Gormanston accident, 274
Gortalea–Castleisland line, 81
Government Information Bureau, 58–9, 128
Grace, Michael, 402
Grainger, Richard, 78, 379
Grand Canal, 4, 24, 73, 83–4, 110, 138–9, 153, 273
  CIÉ responsibility ends, 168–70
  in Milne Report, 49–50
Grand Canal Company, 1–2, 39, 47, 64, 83, 123, 133
grants. *see* subventions
Great Famine, 4
Great Northern Hotel, Bundoran, 133
Great Northern Railway, 7, 25, 39, 43, 59, 62, 70, 82
  acquisition of, 72, 95–100
  bridge collapse, 83
  Cork service, 69
  formation of, 16
  losses, 21–3, 73, 112
  in Milne Report, 47, 49–50, 53
  turf-burning experiment, 77
Great Northern Railway Board, 96–100, 102, 104, 132–3, 161, 186, 260
  last train, 139–41
Great Southern & Western Railway, 2,

458

14–16, 39, 77, 285
Great Southern Hotels, 38, 70, 87–8, 170–72, 200, 207, 211–12. *see also* Ostlanna Iompair Éireann
  problems, 298–303
Great Southern Railway, 46, 68, 104, 195, 285, 304
  DUTC merger, 29–33, 123
  finances, 16–17, 21–3, 41, 49
  formation of, 15–16, 95
  government control, 23
  hotels, 65
  insider dealing scandal, 26–7, 37
  logo, 40–41
  and road transport, 18–19
  stock, 20, 24–5, 29–30
Great Western Railway Company, 304
Greene, Dr Juan N., 102
Gregory, Tony, 357, 358
Gresham, Thomas M., 2
Groome, Joe, 151
Guinness, 168–9

H-Block hunger strikes, 354
Hamburg Consult, 328
Hamilton, Lord Claude, 8
Harcourt Street line, 149, 150–54, 410, 435
  reopening proposed, 364
Harcourt Street station, 433
Haughey, Charles, 23, 324, 342, 352, 378, 413, 434
Hayden, Mr, 10
Hayes, M. J., 257–8
Health, Department of, 220
Henderson, Hughes and Busby, 288–9
Herlihy, Daniel, 62, 233–4, 267
Heuston, Seán, 205
Heuston station, 205, 433. *see also* Kingsbridge station
  Fastrack, 254
  improvements, 244
Hibernia, 187–8

Higgins, Jack, 293, 323, 356, 357
  Board member, 345
  bus investment, 329
  DART, 295, 341, 383
  Director of Transportation, 264
  General Manager, 268
  OPO, 398
  rail investment, 369
  railway investment, 283, 286
  retirement, 403–4
  urban bus control, 320–21
Hillery, Patrick, 212
Hilliard, M. J., 143–4
Hogan, T. P., 207, 249, 250, 263
holiday camping coaches, 144
Holland, 146
Hone, Evie, 171
horse boxes, 78
horse carters, 22, 40, 85
Horse Ferries International, 217
horse transport, 200, 206
hotels, 65, 87–8, 146, 251–2, 262, 338, 384. *see also* Ostlanna Iompair Éireann
Howden, G. B., 62, 70, 75, 140
Howth station, 355
Hussey, Gemma, 364
Hyde, Douglas, 36
Hynes, John, 401, 425, 427

Iarnród Éireann, 400–417, 424
  Board, 395
  business plan, 406–7
  established, 385
  EU investment, 412–13
  expenditure, 405–6
  finances, 409, 412
  industrial relations, 408–9, 414
  name, 396
  submission to Oireachtas committee, 406–9
  track renewal, 406
Inchicore works, 24, 62–3, 70, 245, 403, 406

Inchicore works *contd*
  bus-building, 167, 325–32
  carriage assembly, 78–9, 372
  chassis-building, 74
  coach-building, 284–7, 352–4, 355
  construction ends, 204
  improvements, 142–3
  locomotives, 76, 163
  in Milne Report, 53–4
  water supply, 39–40
  work to rule, 270
Industrial Development Authority, 284
Industrial Engineering Company, 133
industrial relations
  and Andrews, 144
  in Beddy Report, 111–13
  Bus Átha Cliath, 430–31
  bus strike, 1947, 44
  DART threat, 378–9
  OPO, 322, 397–9, 418–19, 425–6
  1950s, 71
  1960s, 167, 172–81, 185, 201–3, 207, 231
  1970s, 270, 294–5, 312–16, 335
  1980s, 385, 408–9
  1990s, 414, 435
  'sundries' freight, 288
Industry and Commerce, Department of, 19, 26–7, 64, 72, 84, 107, 109, 178
  and Beddy Report, 128–30
  and CIÉ finances, 90–92
  Keating minister, 240
  price control, 235
  split up, 157
Ingram, John, 17–18, 21, 23
Ingram Report, 25, 28–9, 61, 101–2, 104, 225
Institute of Advanced Studies, 36
Institute of Public Administration, 184–5, 216, 272
Institute of Transport, 194
Institution of Engineers in Ireland, 78
Inter-party Government, 1948, 44–5, 71
Inter-party Government, 1954, 89–90

InterCity, 384, 407
Interdepartmental Steering Committee, 347, 348
Interlink, 318
International Union of Public Transport, 351
'Investment in Education', 212
Irish Congress of Trade Unions (ICTU), 173–4, 176, 202, 235, 313, 316, 356
  OPO, 397
Irish Continental Line, 262, 303, 305
Irish Employers' Confederation, 336
Irish Ferryways, 148, 217, 262, 303, 304
Irish Free State, 14
  Railways Commission, 9, 15–16, 68
Irish Housewives' Association, 235, 241
Irish Independent, 33, 56, 58, 60, 127, 128, 135, 191, 268, 386
  Harcourt Street closure, 150–52
Irish language, 25, 146, 205–6, 396
Irish Management Institute, 357–8, 372–3
Irish North Western Railway, 7
Irish Omnibus Company, 18
Irish Press, 61–2, 66, 126, 147, 252, 253, 272
Irish Railway Record Society, 77
Irish Railways Commission, 1922, 15–16, 68
Irish Railways Executive Committee, 14
Irish Shipping Ltd, 157, 204, 305, 392
Irish Times, The, 11, 126–7, 139, 143, 191, 202–3, 204, 267, 271, 278
  Dalkey crash, 342
  DART, 296
  fare increases, 236–7, 238
  new locomotives, 272
  papal visit, 341
  railway development, 252–3, 254–5
  Transport Act 1964, 194, 195–6
Irish Transport and General Workers' Union (ITGWU), 139, 142, 174–5, 177, 179–80, 203, 230, 313, 315

and NBU, 181
OPO, 322
IRRS Journal, 245–8, 270, 272, 274, 281, 286, 344, 353, 364
  bomb scares, 356
  DART, 379, 380–82, 383
  Maynooth service, 354
  papal visit, 341

Jennings, P. O., 281, 282–3
John Paul II, visit of, 314, 340–41
John XXIII, Pope, 151, 340
Johnston, Thomas, 15
Joyce, James, 9
Jury, Capt. Peter, 151
Justice, Department of, 387

Keating, Justin, 240
Kennedy, Dr Henry, 21–2
Kennedy, Noel, 383, 401, 419, 431, 436
Kenny, Fitzgerald, 31
Kerry, County, 7, 153, 404
  Tralee–Dingle line, 80, 153
Kilbarrack station, 219
Kildare, County, 84, 411, 413–14
Kilkenny, 205
Kilkenny County Council, 279
Killilea, Mark, 286–7
Kimpton, E. A. C., 86
Kingsbridge station, 39, 70, 141
  renamed 'Heuston', 205
Kirkstall axles, 329
Klockner Humboldt Deutz, 163
Knock, Co. Mayo, 106, 276, 340
Kyne, Deputy, 190

Labour, Department of, 178, 291
Labour Court, 180, 385, 414
  bus strikes, 202–3, 313–14
  DART, 378–9
  established, 44
  OPO, 177, 322, 397–8, 418
  pay claims, 175–6, 223, 294, 335

  'special claims', 184
Labour Party, 28, 45, 89, 221, 315, 403
  Building on Reality, 375–7
  coalitions, 240, 349–50, 354, 359, 360, 413
  fare increases, 254, 267
  railway safety, 286
  split, 36
  transport policy, 15, 190
Lalor, P. J., 235, 236, 240
Lambourne Racehorse Transport Limited, 217
Lands, Department of, 86
Larkin, Jim, 31
Larkin, Jim, Jnr, 142, 175
Leitrim, County, 4, 7, 97
Lemass, Frank, 41, 91, 93, 233, 237
  and Andrews, 142
  Assistant General Manager, 38
  Beddy Committee, 103
  canals, 138
  Chief Executive, 207, 216, 231–2
  Chief Officer, 62
  Drumm trains, 70
  fare increases, 223
  General Manager, 75
  industrial relations, 176–7, 201, 202
  Little report, 267
Lemass, Noel, 190
Lemass, Seán, 23, 24–5, 38, 46, 71–2, 102, 171, 190, 289, 310, 389, 393, 397
  1916 commemoration, 205
  and Andrews, 137, 138
  Beddy Report, 128–9
  branch closures, 157, 158, 160
  Busáras, 82
  canals, 139
  establishment of CIÉ, 28–37
  fares increase, 73
  and GNR, 96, 97
  and GSR, 26, 27
  industrial relations, 178, 185
  Milne Report, 48

Lemass, Seán *contd*
  O'Neill meeting, 299
  resigns, 207
  road freight, 107
  Taoiseach, 161
  Transport Act 1944, 50
  Transport Act 1958, 130–36
  transport acts, 1933, 19, 20
  transport bill, 1950, 65–6
  transport policy, 55, 187
  Transport Tribunal, 80
  turf-burning engines, 77
Lenihan, Brian, 220, 222–4, 229, 234–5, 237, 240, 308
Letterkenny & Burtonport Extension Railway, 7
level crossings, 164, 283, 379, 380
Leyland Motors Ltd, 40, 54, 167, 324–5, 426, 430
  chassis, 326
light rail, 429, 435
Light Railway Acts, 6, 7
Limerick, 145, 168–9, 205, 270, 276–9, 340, 404
  buses, 317
  road haulage, 309
  station, 113
  works, 70
Limerick, County, 162, 226
Limerick Junction, 53, 63, 226, 231
Limerick Leader, 277
Linke Hoffman Busch, 284–5, 286–7, 352, 353
Listowel & Ballybunion Railway, 16, 77
Little, A. D., 267, 300
Livestock Exporters Association, 127
livestock transport, 81, 165, 221, 269, 308
Local Government, Department of, 160, 232–3, 249
Localink, 410
locomotives, 207, 228, 244, 406
  800 Class, 24
  dieselisation, 42, 52–3, 60, 65, 162–3

General Motors, 203–4, 272, 406, 416
  from GNRB, 141
  investment in, 270–73, 413, 416
  livestock trains, 81
  in Milne Report, 50, 52–4, 56–7, 61
  number of, 186
  oil conversion, 44
  problems, 24, 264–5
  railcars, 403
  steam engines scrapped, 75–6
  turf-burning, 62, 77, 162
logos, 25, 40–41, 201, 214
Londonderry & Lough Swilly Railway, 7, 39, 102, 114
Longford, County, 43–4
Lough Erne Canal, 1
Louth, County, 97, 99
Lowry, Michael, 436
Lucey, Dr, Bishop of Cork, 160
Lynch, Jack, 29–30, 176, 178–9, 207, 292, 299, 324, 334, 341
Lynch, Patrick, 212
Lynch, Thaddeus, 190

Maastricht Treaty, 413
MacBride, Seán, 44–5, 77
McCarron, E. T., 23
McCarthy, George, 8
McCleery, Mr, 95–6, 98
MacCormac, Professor Michael, 343, 392
McDonnell, Michael, 436
MacEntee, Seán, 61–2
Mac Gearailt, Seán, 213, 215, 421
McGilligan, Paddy, 15–17, 31, 135–6, 183, 196–7, 221
McGilligan, Patrick, 397
Mac Giolla Rí, Colm, 402
Macken, Matthew, 319
McKinsey International Inc., 339–40
McKinsey Report, 224–9, 233, 238–9, 242, 248, 252–3, 336, 389, 394
  criticisms of, 230–31
  road freight in, 306

McKinsey Report 2, 279, 339–42, 344–5, 346–52, 353, 359, 362–3, 368, 370, 394
 in Green Paper, 390
 recommendations implemented, 374–7
McMahon, Noel, 290–91, 337, 356
McMullen, W., 139
McQuillan, Jack, 178–9, 189–90
McVeagh, Mr, 10
Maginness, Mr, 98
mail services, 413
Malahide Castle, Co. Dublin, 141
Malcolm, Archibald, 91
Management, 357
Mangan, Donal, 419, 420, 436
marketing, 163, 200
Markievicz, Countess, 9
Martin, J. B., 329
Martin and Voorhees Associates, 288–9
Matt Talbot Bridge, 324
Maybach Motorenbau, 162–3
Maynooth service, 353–5, 410, 433
Mayo, County, 4, 153
Meath, County, 97
Mediation Board, 201–2
Mendicity Institute, 205
Merrion Gates, 380
Metropolitan Cammell Carriage and Wagon Co. Ltd, 76, 79
Metropolitan Vickers, 53, 63, 75, 76, 93, 203–4, 268, 271
Midland Great Western Railway, 2, 15–16, 24, 38
Midland Railway, 7
Milne, Sir James, 35, 65, 67, 101. *see also* Milne Report
Milne Report, 39, 47–55, 65, 70, 74–5, 80, 95, 102, 104, 107, 127, 225, 231, 325, 412
 on Leyland link, 40
 responses to, 56–63
minibuses, 426, 428–9
Mitchell, Jim, 353, 372, 386, 403, 411
 canals, 170

CIÉ deficit, 361–4, 365–6
CIÉ reorganisation bill, 392–7
DART, 378, 380, 383
DTA bill, 387–9
line closures, 279–80
McKinsey recommendations, 373–7
minister, 302, 349–50, 359
OPO, 398–9
rolling stock, 287
subvention formula, 367–70
Moate, Co. Westmeath, 404
Modern Transport, 62, 351
Monaghan, County, 153, 313, 317
monopoly, 33, 37
monorail system, 16
Montgomery, Robert, 427
Morgan Travers, 319
Morpeth, Lord, 4
Morrison, Herbert, 37
Morrissey, Daniel, 45–7, 49, 58, 72, 95, 97, 135, 417
 Transport Act, 64–7
Moss, Cruse, 328, 331
Mott, Hay & Anderson, Messrs, 249
Mulcahy, General R., 32, 37
Mullingar, Co. Westmeath, 244–5
Munro, Hugh, 187–8
Murphy, Michael Pat, 157–8, 221
Murphy, Paddy, 173, 336, 398
Murphy, William Martin, 176
Murray, D., 247–8, 270

Nally, Tom, 102
Naomh Éanna, 86, 149, 417
narrow gauge railways, 6–7, 16, 20–21, 70, 80, 104
National Association of Transport Employees, 315
National Bus and Railworkers' Union (NBRU), 430
National Bus Company, 318
National Busworkers' Union (NBU), 174, 181, 201–2, 291, 294, 313, 315

National Busworkers' Union *contd*
  DART threat, 378–9
  OPO, 322
  pay claims, 362
National Development, White Paper on, 295
National Economic and Social Council, 336–7, 339, 342
National Farmers' Association, 148
National Gallery of Ireland, 3
National Labour Party, 36, 45
National Planning Board, 375, 389
National Prices Commission, 235–41, 250, 254, 292, 336, 389
National Progressive Democrat Party, 189
National Transport Council, 21, 295–6
National Wage Agreements, 294
nationalisation, 30–32, 48, 58, 62, 64–7
Nealon, Ted, 387, 391
Niigata transmission, 414
Nite Link, 429
Nitrigin Éireann (NET), 165–6, 186, 372–3
Normandy Ferries, 305
North Wall depot, 70, 71, 206, 411
Northern Ireland (NI), 127, 128, 218, 229, 249, 271, 299, 313. *see also* Great Northern Railway
Northern Ireland Office (NIO), 412
Northern Ireland Railways, 355–6, 406, 416
Northern Ireland Road Transport Board, 98
Norton, William, 26, 30–31, 36, 86, 89–90, 98, 130, 135, 310
Nuacht CIÉ, 149–50, 173, 179, 214, 249–50, 268, 272–4, 282, 326, 366–7
  Buttevant crash, 345
  CIÉ reorganisation, 400–401
  DART, 382–3
  locomotives, 416
  McKinsey 2, 350–51

papal visit, 340
Railway Development Plan, 255–7

O'Brien, Fergus, 260
O'Brien, J. F. X., 10
Ó Cinnéide, Barra, 381
Ó Ciosóig, Mícheál, 351
O'Connell, Daniel, 2, 8
O'Connor, Edward, 401, 406
O'Connor, J. A., 277
Ó Dálaigh, Cearbhall, 176, 309
O'Donnell, Tom, 220–21, 223–4, 310
O'Donovan, Dr John, 208, 221
O'Farrell, J. T., 68, 208
Office of Public Works, 169, 384, 387, 391
Official Handbook of Saorstát Éireann, 17–18
O'Flaherty, Ned, 165
O'Higgins, Michael, 135
O'Higgins, Tom, 32, 35–6, 59
Oireachtas Committee on State Sponsored Bodies, 295, 315–16, 322, 324, 335–6, 339, 398, 407–9, 413
O'Kennedy, Michael, 229, 279
O'Leary, Dermot, 436
O'Leary, Michael, 314
O'Mahony, Donal, 221–2
O'Malley, Donogh, 212
O'Mara, Mr, 10
one-person operation, 111, 167, 177–9, 203, 322, 361, 425–6, 428
  breakthrough, 397–9
  disputes, 418–19
O'Neill, Terence, 299
Operational Programme on Peripherality, 411
O'Regan, James P., 160–61
O'Reilly, Fr Luke M., 150
Ó Riordáin, Diarmuid, 92–3, 194, 197–8, 224
O'Rourke, Mary, 364
O'Shaughnessy, Mr, 10
O'Shea, Willie, 8

Ostlanna Iompair Éireann (OIÉ), 171–2, 186, 211–12, 222–3, 234
  problems, 251–2, 298–303
Pacemaker Report, 181, 187–98, 199, 225
parking meters, 209
Parnell, C. S., 8, 78
passenger sales bureau, 168, 171
Paul VI, Pope, 340
Pearse, Patrick and Willie, 205
Pearse station, 205, 233, 433. *see also* Westland Row station
  commuter services, 244–5
pension schemes, 217
pensioners, 216, 228
People, The, 277–8
People's Democracy, 299
Phibsboro garage, 321, 398
Portlaoise, Co. Laois, 161, 281
Portobello Bridge, 168
Post, An, 207
Post Office, 85, 254, 413
Posts and Telegraphs, Department of, 207, 294–5, 342
Power, Dr Con, 236–7
Price Waterhouse, 41
private transport, 102, 106, 118, 192, 225, 317, 401, 425
  car numbers, 72–3, 217, 320
Programme for National Development 1978–1981, 295
Progressive Democrats, 412–13
promotions, 234, 246–7
Provisional IRA, 298, 309, 356
public relations, 146, 149–50
Public Service, Department of the, 294
Public Services Organisation Review Group, 250

Quality Bus Corridors (QBC), 429–30, 435
Quinn, Ruairí, 296, 323–4, 342–3

Radio Trains, 69

rail freight, 48, 105, 106, 115, 164–5, 204, 217, 243, 310, 386
  closures, 255–8, 269–70, 404–5
  losses, 46, 358
  market analysis, 408
  sundries, 288, 351–2, 405
  UTA, 200–201
rail hostesses, 163
railcars, 403, 406, 413–14
Railink, 405
Railplan 80, 226, 234, 241, 242–8, 251–2, 255–6, 261, 271, 288
Railway Acts, 15–16, 18
Railway Clauses Act 1845, 124
Railway Clerks' Association, 68
Railway Commission, 6
Railway Companies (Accounts and Returns) Act 1911, 41
Railway Development Plan, 254–8, 261, 268, 269, 271, 406, 416
  effects of, 287–9
  press conference, 280–84
  tangential lines, 276–7
Railway Protection, Repair & Maintenance Corps, 14
railways, 1–6, 24, 186, 222, 264, 374. *see also* branch lines; Iarnród Éireann; locomotives; rolling stock
  accidents, 39, 274–5, 342, 344–5, 371
  average speeds, 247
  in Beddy Report, 104–6, 113–18
  block trains, 243
  catering, 163
  communications, 144, 283–4
  competition, 17–20
  cutbacks, 369
  and Department of Finance, 94
  dieselisation, 70, 73–5, 104, 110, 115, 130
  Dublin. *see* Dublin suburban railways
  finances, 16–17, 199, 225–8
  gauge, 6–7
  high frequency timetable, 270–71

railways *contd*
  infrastructure grant, 228–9
  investment in, 69, 70–71
  longterm study, 1976, 288–9
  maintenance, 52, 281–2
  map, 1860, 5
  map, 1924, 13
  map, 1957, 117
  map, 1994, 415
  in McKinsey 2, 347–9
  monopoly, 19
  in Pacemaker report, 193
  passenger numbers, 130, 163–4, 249, 287, 311, 317, 386
  Railplan 80, 241, 242–8
  rationalisation plans, 230
  signalling system, 283
  single-track, 24–5
  state ownership, 7–11, 12–27
  station closures, 162, 255–8, 404–5
  stations renamed, 1966, 205–6
  statistics, 216, 217
  track renewal, 281–3
  track total, 1968, 162
  Viceregal Commission, 10–11
Railways Act 1924, 16–17
Railways Act 1933, 30
Railways and Canal Traffic Act 1851, 124
Railways Commission, 3–4, 7, 15–16
Railways (Miscellaneous) Act 1932, 19
Railways (Road Motor Services) Act, 1927, 18
Regional Development Programme, 411
remote control signalling (CTC), 384
Republican Publicity Bureau, 206
research and development, 146
Restaurant na Mara, 298, 302–3
Reynolds, Albert, 170, 286, 387, 414
  CIÉ deficit, 356
  DART, 343–4
  DTA, 324
  Maynooth service, 353–4
  McKinsey 2, 346, 349

  minister, 342
  rolling stock, 352, 353, 393
  Shannon works, 329, 330
  Taoiseach, 413
Reynolds, A. P., 25–6, 30, 62, 65, 96, 99, 105, 151, 206, 324
  chairs CIÉ, 38, 40
  chairs GSR, 23
  and Milne Report, 56, 58–61
  powers of, 54–5
  seeks subvention, 1947, 45–7
Rights Commissioners, 385
Ringsend docks, 304
road freight, 54, 64, 84–5, 115, 165–6, 261, 376, 405
  CIÉ submission on, 106–10
  compared to rail, 225–6
  developments in, 306–10
  'helpers', 180
  losses, 217, 386
  in Pacemaker report, 193
  policy, 1975, 264
  remains with CIÉ, 375
  restrictions, 19–20, 57–8, 115, 307–10
Road Passenger Acts 1933, 435
road transport, 20, 130, 135, 154–5, 199, 386
  competition for railways, 17–20
  Cork, 160–61
  in Pacemaker report, 193–4
Road Transport Act 1932, 19, 375, 376, 377
Road Transport Act 1933, 19, 57, 109, 307
Road Transport Act 1956, 310
Road Transport Act 1972, 269
Road Transport Act 1978, 290, 309–10
Road Transport Act 1986, 387, 392
Road Transport Acts, 135
Rockwell axles, 328
rolling stock, 186, 228, 241, 243, 363, 370
  BREL coaches, 245–7
  coach-building, 77–9, 284–7, 352–4

Cravens, 245, 274, 287, 345, 353, 355
  inadequate, 24, 371–2, 410–11
  investment in, 70, 104, 163
  Mark 3 coaches, 386
  Park Royals, 78–9, 204, 245, 248, 274, 287, 353, 355
  shortages, 344, 354–5
  timber-framed, 406
Rosslare Harbour, 38, 124, 148, 247, 318, 401, 403, 424
  development of, 303, 304–5
  growth, 416–17
  line closure, 270–80
Rowledge, J. W. P., 77
Royal Canal, 4, 38–9, 110, 169
Royal Dublin Society, 39, 46
RTE, 206
Russell Court Hotel, Belfast, 172, 251, 298–300, 303
Ryan, Professor W. J. L., 235, 239, 375
Ryan, Richie, 163–4, 220, 240, 266–7, 296

St James's Street Harbour, 304
St Johns, Islandbridge, 154
Sallins–Tullow line, 150
Salthill station, 379
Sands, Bobby, 354
Sandymount station, 379
Save Our Railway Association, 159
Schaechterle, Professor K., 208, 209–10, 318–19, 433
school tours, 163
school transport, 207, 224, 228, 421–4
  buses, 421
  Dáil debates, 364–6
  free scheme, 212–16
  private operators, 263
Schultz, Otto, 328
Scott, Michael, 82, 151
Sea Lynx, 417
Sealink, 305
Shannon Airport, 109
Shannon factory, 328–31, 353, 377

Shannon navigation, 83, 86–7, 139, 168–9, 262
Shields, Professor B. F., 16, 22–3, 29
Sidney Parade station, 249
signalling system, 24, 379, 406
Silvermines, Co. Tipperary, 166, 358
Single European Market, 411
SIPTU, 322, 430
Sligo, County, 4, 97, 205, 245
Sligo, Leitrim & Northern Counties Railway, 39, 102, 135, 161
Sligo & Leitrim Railway Company, 99
Social Welfare, Department of, 63, 72, 216
Sommerville-Large, P. T., 267
Spencer docks, 304
staff. *see also* industrial relations
  absenteeism, 409
  amenities, 71, 231–2
  bonuses, 39
  clerical grades, 33–4, 195
  driver/conductor relationships, 210–11
  driver recruitment, 428
  increase in, 237
  labour costs, 223
  in Milne Report, 54
  number of, 39, 435
  overmanning, 25, 111, 263
  productivity, 263, 322, 347, 408–9, 430
  and Railway Development Plan, 255, 257, 261
  recruitment embargo, 265–6
  reductions, 243, 251, 269, 288, 361–2, 371, 425–6
  redundancies, 33, 195, 414
  school bus drivers, 214
  and technological change, 321–2
  women drivers, 214
  worker directors, 316
  workers' dwellings, 154
  working conditions, 217
Staff Club, Earl Place, 71
Stafford, J. J., 102

Stardust Ballroom disaster, 354
Statistical and Social Inquiry Society of Ireland, 16, 22, 29
Steers, Davies and Gleave Ltd, 357
Stena Sealink, 304
Stephens, Donal, 50, 187–9
Strabane & Letterkenny Railway, 7
Strabane, Raphoe & Convoy Railway, 7
Straboe collision, 39
strikes, 217
  1947, 44
  1950, 71
  army assistance, 313
  Cork, 177
  craftsmen, 430–31
  electricians, 1952, 74
  one-day strikes, 201–2
  1960s, 176, 177, 185, 203
  1970s, 313–14
subventions, 185, 266–7, 279, 435
  1974, 259–60
  accounting treatment, 386–7
  Bus Átha Cliath, 425
  call for reduction, 360–64
  concordat proposed, 339
  effects of inflation, 219–24
  in Green Paper, 390–91
  Group, 402–3
  international comparisons, 409
  McKinsey proposals, 226–8
  new formula, 1983, 366–70, 377
  principle of subsidy, 199
  railway investment, 252–5
  railways, 10–11
  shortfalls, 211, 216, 293–4, 333–7, 357, 358–9, 366
  sought, 1947, 45–7
  Transport Act 1958, 133–5
  Transport Act 1964, 195, 196–7, 207
  Wilson formula, 405
sugar beet transport, 277–9
Sulzer engines, 53, 63, 75
Sunday Tribune, 351

Sunday World, 271
Supabus, 318, 401, 418
Supertrain, 246–7, 248
Sweden, 48
Sweetman, Gerard, 80, 90, 93–4, 101, 186–7
Switzerland, 53, 146

Tallaght, 319, 410, 426
Tara Street station, 205
Tavistock Institute of Human Relations, 181, 210
Technical Traffic Unit, 323
Telecom Éireann, 207
Telford, Thomas, 1
Temple Bar, 433–4
Theurer EM50 Track Recording Car, 282
Thompson, S. F., 102
Thurles, Co. Tipperary, 277–9, 405
Tighe, Tommy, 141
Tillie Lykes, 272
Times, The, 9
Tipperary, County, 162, 277–9
Tipperary Star, 277
Tokyu Car Corporation, 414
Torc Great Southern, 212
Toronto, 322
tourism, 141, 171, 200, 249–50, 262, 387, 431–2
  recession, 299, 301
Tourism and Transport, Department of, 292, 301–2, 388
  relations with CIÉ, 289–94
  school transport, 423, 424
trade unions, 25, 71, 107, 147, 235, 241, 288, 338, 385, 425. *see also* industrial relations
  and containerisation, 148
  and deficit, 356
  mediation boards, 202–3
  NBU recognised, 201
  and new locomotives, 273
  and NPC study, 237

number of, 173–4, 408
  restrictive practices, 112–13
  rivalries, 312, 313, 430
  'special claims', 184
  Tavistock survey, 180–81
training, 146
Tralee, Co. Kerry, 205
Tramore, Co. Waterford, 155–6
trams, 23, 24, 63, 106, 141
Tramways (Ireland) Act, 1883, 6
Transport, 329
Transport, Department of, 330–31, 337, 347, 359
Transport, Energy and Communications, Department of, 388
Transport Act 1944, 27, 50, 59–60, 63
  debates, 28–37
Transport Act 1950, 22, 64–7, 70, 73, 97, 102, 124, 128, 401
  Beddy Report on, 123
  CIÉ responsibilities, 104
Transport Act 1958, 130–36, 138, 152, 155–6, 163, 182, 187, 231, 340
  breakeven clause, 189–91
Transport Act 1960, 169
Transport Act 1963, 165, 186–7
Transport Act 1964, 195–8, 199, 207
  section 6 repealed, 259–60
Transport Act 1970, 229
Transport Act 1983, 380
Transport Act 1985, 387, 389
Transport and Communications, Department of, 221
Transport and Power, Department of, 157, 180, 183, 207, 210, 229, 235, 259, 332
  Barry minister, 240
  coach-building project, 284–5
  corporate aims of CIÉ, 263
  Fitzpatrick minister, 278
  Lenihan minister, 220
  locomotive purchases, 271
  railway modernisation, 252–5

Transport Consultative Commission, 295–6, 324, 328, 337, 339, 342, 388, 392
Transport Control and Planning office, 146
Transport House, 433
Transport (No. 2) Act 1974, 259–60
transport policy, 72–3, 137, 239, 280, 295–6, 384
  Green Paper, 1985, 229–30, 387, 389–92, 408, 410
  Milne Report, 47–55
  Pacemaker study, 187–98
Transport (Reorganisation of CIE) Act 1986, 387, 392–7
Transport Salaried Staff Association, 295, 340
Transport Tribunal, 16, 64, 84, 102, 121
  abolished, 132
  branch closures, 79–81
  'Exemption Orders', 153
  and GNR, 98–9
Transportation Centre, 268
Transtrack, 405
travel kiosk, 168
Travelling Post Offices, 413
Tribunal of Inquiry on Public Transport, 1939, 17, 21
Tuam, Co. Galway, 276, 405

Ulster Railway, 2
Ulster Transport Authority, 49, 75, 96, 98, 133, 141
  hotels, 171–2
  last GNR train, 140
  rail freight ends, 200–201
Ulsterbus, 213, 421
United Ireland, 7
United Nations, 233

Van Hool McArdle, 268, 285, 326–7, 420, 430
vandalism, 249, 270, 344, 355–6

Viceregal Commission, 10–11, 12, 14, 15, 31
Victoria, Queen, 3
Victoria and South Australian Railways, 104
Viney, Michael, 305
Voith transmission, 326, 329
Voorhees, Alan M. and Associates, 249
Voorhees Report, 343

wages, 94, 195, 334, 362
  DART drivers, 379
  increase, 1947, 44
  labour costs, 217–18
  national agreements, 235, 266–7, 294–5
  pay claims, 15
  wage restraint, 395–6
Walker railcars, 156
Walsh, Dr, Archbishop of Dublin, 10
Walsh, Eamon, 436
War of Independence, 216
Waterford, 145, 177, 205, 278, 279, 305
  buses, 317
  depot, 70
  road haulage, 309
Waterford, County, 161, 162
  Waterford–Tramore line, 155–6
Waters, C. D., 379, 380–81, 383, 406
'Way Ahead, The', 280–85, 292, 300, 306, 312, 372
wayleaves, 34
weighbridges, 70

West Clare Railway, 8, 41, 70, 76
  closure, 155–7
West Donegal Railway, 7
Westland Row station, 2, 8, 233
  renamed 'Pearse', 205
Westmeath, County, 169
Wexford, County, 4, 43, 205, 277–80
Whelan, John, 214
Whitaker, Ken, 93, 171
White Paper, 229
Whitley Councils, 173
Wilson, John, 349, 357, 362, 392, 393, 398
  accounts formula, 405
  canals, 391
  DART, 380, 396–7
  DTA, 388–9
  hotels, 302
  minister, 403
  railway extensions, 410
  school transport, 422
Wolfhill colliery, 16
Worker Directors (State Enterprises) Act 1977, 316
Workers' Union of Ireland (WUI), 175, 203, 313, 322
works councils, 173
World War I, 14
World War II, 22–4, 25, 28, 40, 41, 307
Wright, Professor Myles, 319
Wycherley, Florence, 157
Wylie, Judge W. E., 46, 56–7, 58, 62, 64